W9-AZJ-669

PAGE 52 | **ON THE ROAD**

YOUR COMPLETE DESTINATION GUIDE
In-depth reviews, detailed listings
and insider tips

TOP EXPERIENCES MAP **NEXT PAGE**

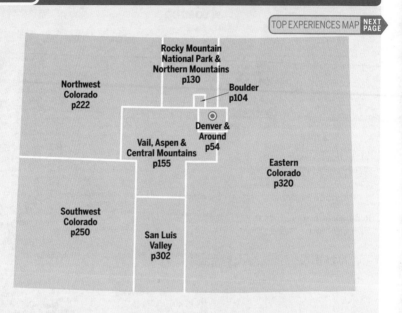

Rocky Mountain
National Park &
Northern Mountains
p130

Northwest
Colorado
p222

Boulder
p104

Denver &
Around
p54

Vail, Aspen &
Central Mountains
p155

Eastern
Colorado
p320

Southwest
Colorado
p250

San Luis
Valley
p302

PAGE 367 | **SURVIVAL GUIDE**

YOUR AT-A-GLANCE REFERENCE
How to get around, get a room,
stay safe, say hello

Directory A–Z 368
Transportation 375
Index 384
Map Legend 391

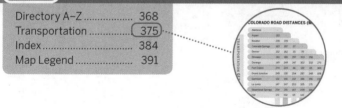

COLORADO ROAD DISTANCES

THIS EDITION WRITTEN AND RESEARCHED BY

Nate Cavalieri, Adam Skolnick,
Rowan McKinnon

❯Colorado

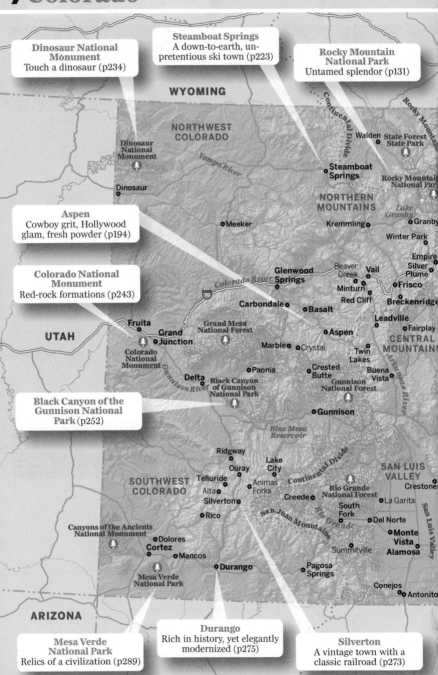

Dinosaur National Monument
Touch a dinosaur (p234)

Steamboat Springs
A down-to-earth, un-pretentious ski town (p223)

Rocky Mountain National Park
Untamed splendor (p131)

Aspen
Cowboy grit, Hollywood glam, fresh powder (p194)

Colorado National Monument
Red-rock formations (p243)

Black Canyon of the Gunnison National Park (p252)

Mesa Verde National Park
Relics of a civilization (p289)

Durango
Rich in history, yet elegantly modernized (p275)

Silverton
A vintage town with a classic railroad (p273)

WYOMING

NORTHWEST COLORADO

Dinosaur National Monument

Dinosaur

Yampa River

Meeker

Walden   State Forest State Park

Steamboat Springs

NORTHERN MOUNTAINS

Continental Divide

Rocky Mountains

Lake Granby

Rocky Mountain National Park

Granby

Kremmling

Winter Park

Glenwood Springs

Colorado River

Carbondale

Basalt

Beaver Creek   Vail

Minturn

Red Cliff

Empire
Silver Plume

Frisco

Breckenridge

Leadville

Fairplay

CENTRAL MOUNTAINS

Fruita

Grand Junction

Colorado National Monument

Grand Mesa National Forest

Marble   Crystal

Aspen

Twin Lakes

Arkansas River

UTAH

Delta

Gunnison River

Black Canyon of the Gunnison National Park

Paonia

Crested Butte

Gunnison National Forest

Buena Vista

Gunnison

Blue Mesa Reservoir

Ridgway

Ouray

Lake City

Continental Divide

SAN LUIS VALLEY

Crestone

Telluride   Animas Forks

Alta

Silverton

Rio Grande National Forest

La Garita

Creede

San Juan Mountains

South Fork

Del Norte

San Luis Valley

Rico

Rio Grande

Monte Vista

Canyons of the Ancients National Monument

Dolores

Cortez

Mancos

Mesa Verde National Park

Durango

Summitville

Pagosa Springs

Alamosa

Conejos

Antonito

ARIZONA

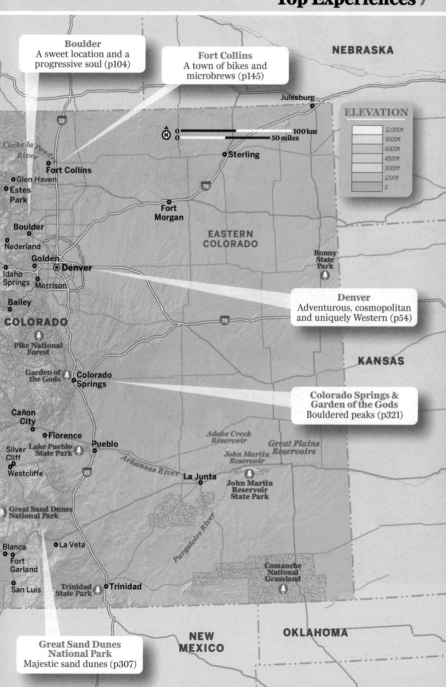

Boulder
A sweet location and a progressive soul (p104)

Fort Collins
A town of bikes and microbrews (p145)

NEBRASKA

Julesburg

ELEVATION

	12,000ft
	9000ft
	6000ft
	4500ft
	3000ft
	1200ft
	0

N 0 ——— 100 km
   0 ——— 50 miles

Cache la Poudre River

Sterling

Fort Collins
Glen Haven
Estes Park

25

76

Fort Morgan

EASTERN COLORADO

Boulder
Nederland

Golden
Denver
Idaho Springs
Morrison

Bonny State Park

Bailey

COLORADO

70

Denver
Adventurous, cosmopolitan and uniquely Western (p54)

KANSAS

Pike National Forest

Garden of the Gods
Colorado Springs

Cañon City
Florence
Silver Cliff
Westcliffe
Lake Pueblo State Park
Pueblo

Adobe Creek Reservoir

Great Plains Reservoirs

John Martin Reservoir

Colorado Springs & Garden of the Gods
Bouldered peaks (p321)

Arkansas River

La Junta

John Martin Reservoir State Park

25

Great Sand Dunes National Park

Blanca
Fort Garland
La Veta

Purgatoire River

Comanche National Grassland

San Luis
Trinidad State Park
Trinidad

NEW MEXICO

OKLAHOMA

Great Sand Dunes National Park
Majestic sand dunes (p307)

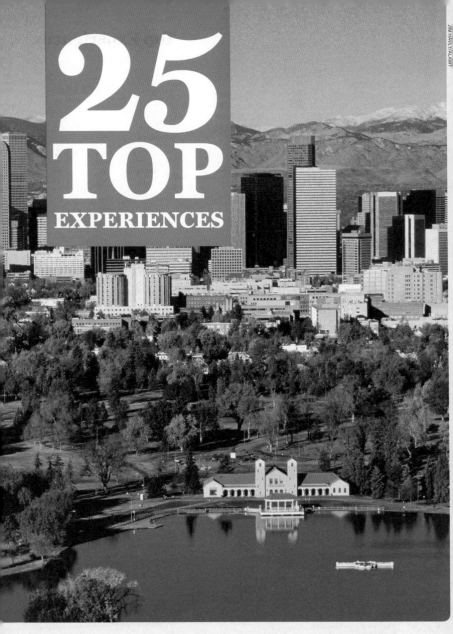

JIM HAVE/ALAMY

25 TOP EXPERIENCES

Denver

1 At last Denver (p54) – adventurous, cosmopolitan and uniquely Western – has found its place among the USA's top cities. With a young population and near-constant blue skies, residents love to show off their neighborhood nightspots, galleries and eateries. It's a dynamic renaissance. Of course, the old Denver – that of thick steaks, mountain sports and plucky frontier spirit – is still alive and well, making this city in the shadow of the Rockies a well-rounded destination for travelers.

Boulder

2 Tucked up against its signature Flatirons, Boulder (p104) has a sweet location and a progressive soul, which has attracted a groovy bag of entrepreneurs, hippies and hardbodies. Packs of cyclists ride the Boulder Creek Bike Path, which links to all abundance of city and county parks purchased through a popular Open Space tax. The pedestrian-only Pearl St Mall is lively, especially at night, when students from the University of Colorado and Naropa University mingle and flirt. In many ways Boulder, not Denver, is the region's tourist hub. Cycling on Boulder Creek

DANITA DELIMONT/ALAMY

Hiking in Rocky Mountain National Park

3 From behind the row of RVs growling along Trail Ridge Rd, Rocky Mountain National Park (p131) can look a bit overexposed. But with hiking boots strapped on, the park's majestic, untamed splendor comes into view. From absolutely epic outings on the Continental Divide National Scenic Trail to family-friendly romps in the Bear Lake area, there's something here for people of every ability and ambition. With a modicum of effort, you'll feel like you have the place all to yourself. Glass Lake, Rocky Mountain National Park

Microbreweries

4 Colorado has more microbreweries per capita than any other US state, and craft brewing has been elevated to a high boutique art throughout. Each September Denver hosts the Great American Beer Festival (p67), which brings 500-odd brewers and countless tasters and afficionados. Best-of-show awards are judged across dozens of categories (best chocolate beer, best coffee-flavored beer...). Small-run handmade commercial brews are produced with passion in long-established and start-up operations. The Colorado Brewers Guild (www.coloradobeer.org) is the peak body, and a font of information. New Belgium Brewery, Fort Collins

Aspen

5 Here's a town (p194), unlike any other place in the US West. A cocktail of cowboy grit, Euro panache, Hollywood glam, Ivy League brains, fresh powder, live music and old money, where you can drop into an extreme vertical double diamond run or stomp to the crest of a Continental Divide pass. There are ice walls to climb, superpipes to ride and profound music to absorb. Oh, and did we mention the fit ski bums, cute ski bunnies, $10 million estates, frothing hot tubs and well-read barflies?

Mesa Verde National Park

6 More than 700 years after the Ancestral Puebloan inhabitants mysteriously abandoned Mesa Verde (p289), it remains unclear why they left and what befell them. Ancestral Puebloan sites are found throughout the park's canyons and mesas. Check out the Chapin Mesa Museum, walk through the Spruce Tree House, take the ranger-led tours of Cliff Palace and Balcony House, and explore quiet Wetherill Mesa. Spruce Tree House, Mesa Verde National Park

Colorado National Monument

7 Witness the setting sun set fire to otherworldly red-rock formations, hike stark and beautiful high desert trails and camp beneath frequent lightning storms as they roll across the distant planes. These canyon walls (p243) rise from the Uncompahgre Uplift of the Colorado Plateau, 2000ft above the Grand Valley of the Colorado River to reveal the twinkling lights of Grand Junction, the green river and tree-lined fields of the Grand Valley – all of it a landscape that was once patrolled by dinosaurs.

STEPHEN SAKS

MCCLATCHY-TRIBUNE/GETTY IMAGES

Denver Restaurants & Nightlife

8 When the sun sets over the Front Range, people pour into Denver's neighborhoods. There's a nightlife scene of every stripe, so pick your poison. Want to knock back microbrews? Make for LoDo. You're into edgy galleries and scrappy independent rock? Hit the South Broadway strip. Delicate cocktails and sustainable fine dining? Direct your attention to the Highlands. It might not always be apparent from the quiet after-hours on the 16th St Mall, but Denver's nightlife scene rewards the adventurous. Falling Rock Tap House, Denver

STEPHEN SAKS

Silverton & Old West Towns

9 Silverton (p273) is Colorado's best rediscovered vintage gem. Launched by rugged pioneer types, (similar to Leadville, Old Colorado City and Cripple Creek), most of its grand buildings were built during the early 1900s. Hollywood shot its share of Westerns here in the 1950s, but when the last mine closed in 1991 it seemed that Silverton was destined to become another charming ghost towns such as St Elmo and Ashcroft (both of which are worth a visit). Then the Durango & Silverton Narrow Gauge Railroad arrived and the town sprang back to life. Silverton

Dinosaur National Monument

10 Tucked into the far northwest corner of the state is one of the few places on Earth that you can reach out and touch a dinosaur skeleton. Paleontologist Earl Douglass of Pittsburgh's Carnegie Museum discovered this dinosaur fossil bed (p234), one of the largest in North America, in 1909. Six years later, President Woodrow Wilson declared it a national monument. The visitor center overlooks thousands of bones in the Dinosaur Quarry.

WITOLD SKRYPCZAK

Old Colorado City & Manitou Springs

11 Yes, Colorado Springs (p321) does have a left wing. Old Colorado City, founded in 1859, wears its history well; a string of art galleries, groovy boutiques and cafes have opened within its 19th century walls. Uphill from here is Manitou Springs, the gateway to Pikes Peak. Discovered as a wellness retreat (there really are cold mineral springs here), it made national news when its famed hippie commune came crashing down beneath a witchcraft scandal in the 1970s. But those green, hippie roots are still alive. Barr Trail, Manitou Springs

PETER PTSCHELINZEW

Hidden Canyons

12 They appear from out of nowhere. One minute you're rocketing through the Central Rockies on I-70 or driving what seems like an endless high-country plateau, when all of a sudden the earth rips open, red rock walls rise, highways diverge of their own accord and you're smack in the middle of Glenwood Canyon (p239) or Rattlesnake Arches (p244), or peering down into Royal Gorge (p334). These gorges are river-carved and so spectacular you'll want to double back, this time by train or, better yet, a raft. Royal Gorge

Mountain Biking in Fruita

13 Although enthusiasm for single-track riding is ubiquitous in Colorado, the trails criss-crossing the red-rock landscape around Fruita (p248) are truly world-class. Sure, it's in the middle of nowhere, but riders here wouldn't have it any other way. The un-crowded trails are maintained by a community of the sport's devotees, who have endowed them with an almost sacred reverence. And for good reason: the spectrum of technical difficulty presents opportunities for every class of rider to ride through a dramatic high desert setting.

Steam Trains

14 You don't have to be a train-spotter to appreciate a good belch of vintage coal-powered steam, the whine of iron on iron and the jilting grind of a narrow-gauge train balancing and rolling slowly through dynamited tunnels and along ridges blessed with some of the most stunning mountain vistas and canyon drop-offs imaginable. The best of the bunch is the impossibly scenic 45-mile Durango & Silverton Narrow Gauge Railroad (p277), but the Georgetown Loop (p100) and Cumbres & Toltec Scenic Railroad (p315) are terrific too. Durango & Silverton Narrow Gauge Railroad

Rafting the Arkansas River

15 Running from Leadville down the eastern flank of Buena Vista and rocketing through the spectacular Royal Gorge at Class V speeds, the Arkansas River is the most diverse, longest and, arguably, the wildest river in the state. White-water outfitters tend to gather south of Buena Vista in Salida, where you'll also find the office for the Arkansas Headwaters Recreation Area (at the northern end of the wildest 99-mile stretch) and down-river near the Royal Gorge Bridge turn-off in Cañon City (p334).

Million Dollar Hwy

16 This is one amazing stretch of road (p270). Driving this asphalt sliver south from Ouray towards Silverton positions drivers on the outside edge, a heartbeat from free-fall. Much of it is cut into the mountains and gains elevation by switching back in tight hairpins and S-bends. The brooding mountains loom large and close, snow clinging to their lofty misty peaks even in high summer. In good weather the road is formidable. In drizzle or rain, fog or snow, it can be downright scary. Million Dollar Hwy in Ouray

STEPHEN SAKS

Hiking Colorado's 14ers

17 Colorado is home to 54 14,000+ft peaks. Let's put that number in perspective. There are 70 14,000+ft peaks in the continental US; 54 of them are in Colorado's Rocky Mountains. One is accessible by road and rail. The rest you'll have to work for. Whether you decide to hike the shortest trail – just 3 miles to Quandary Peak (p173) near Breckenridge – tackle multiday routes to Longs Peak (p133) in Rocky Mountain National Park or make a run at Mt Elbert in Mt Massive Wilderness Area (p213), the tallest of them all, it won't ever be painless. Longs Peak, Rocky Mountain National Park

SALLY DILLON

Rocky Mountain Oysters

18 Munched from Mexico to Spain, from Arizona to Montana, also called prairie oysters, criadillas or huevos del toro, this is a much loved novelty dish. It's most often peeled and pounded thin, coated in flour and spices then deep-fried. Bull testicles, believe it or not, are a Colorado delicacy served in Denver and Colorado Springs restaurants, and at more than a few festivals and fairs throughout the Rockies, including the State Fair in Pueblo.

Fort Collins

19 Here's a perfect day. Check out a free fat-tire cruiser and roll through one of America's most bike-friendly cities. When you get warm, point it towards the shady river path along the Poudre and spend the afternoon tubing along the trickling water. Cap things off by spending the afternoon sampling craft beer from a handful of Colorado's finest breweries. Forget about Fort Collins (p145) as Colorado's underdog college town: this small city on the edge of the Front Range is a delightful destination in its own right.

Durango

20 Durango (p275) – southwest Colorado's cultural capital – is a lovely town, rich in history yet elegantly modernized. The historic central precinct dates back to the 1880s, when the town was founded by the Denver & Rio Grande Railroad, and it remains tastefully authentic. It's a great base for exploring the southwest Rockies and Mesa Verde National Park, and experiencing the nearby outdoors sports opportunities. It's artsy, rootsy and has excellent fine-dining restaurants. The Durango & Silverton Narrow Gauge Railroad toots and puffs up to Silverton several times daily.

Great Sand Dunes National Park

21 Surrounded by rigid mountain peaks on one side and glassy wetlands on the other, this 55 sq miles of sand dunes (p307) seems to appear out of nowhere. Angles of sunlight form shifting shadows on the blond surface. The wind sculpts peaks, dances in ripples and wipes clean your footprints. The most dramatic time is the day's end, when the hills come into high contrast as the sun drops low. Distance is an elusive concept in this monochromatic, misplaced sea of sand.

JOHN ELK III

STEPHEN SAKS

Garden of the Gods

22 Part of a red-rock vein that runs for miles north–south in the Colorado foothills, this compound of 13 bouldered peaks and soaring red rock pinnacles (p321) is accessed by a network of concrete paths and trails. It was originally purchased in 1879 by Charles Elliot Perkins at the behest of his friend and Colorado Springs founder, General William Jackson. Perkins always allowed the public to enjoy his property. It's not a true wilderness experience, but it is darn beautiful.

NEX/IMAGEBROKER

Telluride

23 Let Aspen and Vail grab the headlines; Telluride (p264) is Colorado's most remote ski destination, where tourism has developed at an easygoing pace. Unless you arrive by plane, it's no easy feat to get here, but you're also unlikely to want to leave. Situated in the heart of the rugged San Juan range, the village is snuggled into an isolated box canyon and surrounded by peaks unspoiled by over-development. Out of season, Telluride also throws some of Colorado's best festivals, with banner events celebrating film and bluegrass.

HOLGER LEUE

Steamboat Springs

24 No Colorado ski town is more down-to-earth than Steamboat (p223). It's turned out more Olympians than any other US city, and still greets visitors with a tip of the Stetson and an 'aw, shucks' nonchalance. The area's magnetism knows all seasons: when the weather's warm, visitors rumble down the hills on two wheels, raft rushing white-water and soak off long hikes at the state's most laid-back springs.

STEPHEN SAKS

Black Canyon of the Gunnison National Park

25 This massive cleave in the landscape is especially arresting because the deep, narrow abyss appears among the subdued undulations of the surrounding flat tablelands. The sheer walls of the Black Canyon (p252) – so-called because daylight only briefly illuminates the narrow canyon floor – are dizzying in their height, scored with eerie crevices and pinnacles, and veined with multicolored mineral deposits. It's one of the deepest, narrowest and longest canyons in North America.

welcome to
Colorado

Prepare to lose yourself in spectacular vistas, countless powdery ski runs, extreme terrain parks, steaming hot springs and Old West echoes. Colorado is mysterious, adventurous and all natural.

Summer Playground

The best-known of the Rocky Mountain states, Colorado owes its much-deserved public adoration to that mountainous backbone that rises and rolls from Denver, Boulder and Colorado Springs in the east to Durango and Grand Junction in the west. In between, the Rockies soar to majestic heights and create hiking, biking and climbing terrain unrivaled anywhere in the US West.

This wealth of alpine scenery means that even during the peak summer season, when millions of tourists flood the state, visitors still can find solitude at a remote mountain lake or meadow, or atop a craggy summit. Even Rocky Mountain National Park, the state's premier attraction, offers dozens of backcountry hikes and campgrounds that see few visitors (unless you count that moose, or the fox family that wandered by).

Winter Wonderland

Yet given all that summer sunshine grace, many would argue that summer isn't even the state's best time of year. It's winter when these mountains teem from end to end, from slope to magnificent slope with the best downhill skiing (and some remarkable cross-country and backcountry terrain) on earth. Ski bunnies and hotshot snowboarders arrive in droves to places such as Aspen, Vail and Telluride, and the parties kick into extreme gear. Yes, the long Colorado winters are the stuff of legend. Here you can ski and ride from before Halloween until the beginning of June.

More than Mountains

Don't be fooled: mountains aren't the only attraction. Western Colorado has beautiful desert canyons and mesas, and areas like the sprawling San Luis Valley that open up to reveal a lyrical patchwork of working farms and ranchlands. Rivers, including all-stars the Arkansas, Colorado, and Rio Grande, snake throughout the state, offering outstanding rafting, kayaking and canoeing. Aspen is known almost as much for its summer music festival and think-tank intellect as its adventure opportunities. East of the Rockies the prairie stretches far beyond the horizon and deep into America's expansionist history.

Colorado's urbanity deserves praise, too. Long derided as a glorified cow town, Denver has developed into a lively city with solid entertainment venues, farm-to-table dining and a lively young hipster scene. Nearby, the university town of Boulder draws visitors with its stunning natural setting and progressive intellectual vibe. Fort Collins, which remains under the radar for now, offers a similar vibe.

Diversity is an issue, but south of the Arkansas River, Colorado was once Mexico, and there remain pockets of Hispanic culture here, while some Native Americans still live in the Ute Mountain and Southern Ute Indian reservations in southwest Colorado, near the fascinating ruins of Mesa Verde National Park: just one of Colorado's iconic sights that will leave you wanting more.

need to know

Currency
» US dollars ($)

Language
» English

When to Go

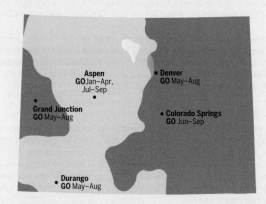

Aspen
GO Jan–Apr, Jul–Sep

• **Denver**
GO May–Aug

• **Grand Junction**
GO May–Aug

• **Colorado Springs**
GO Jun–Sep

• **Durango**
GO May–Aug

Dry climate
Warm to hot summers, mild winters
Warm to hot summers, cold winters
Cold climate

High Season
(late Nov–Apr)

» Ski and ride bums arrive in droves. Vacancies are at a premium and ski resorts capitalize big time, charging three times more than their summer rates, and even more between Christmas and New Year's Day.

Shoulder
(Jun-Sep)

» Summer is a shoulder season because in some spots you can get tremendous room rates while others enjoy a second high season. Crowds can be thick in places.

Low Season
(Oct-Nov & Apr-May)

» Bemoaned locally as 'mud season', many businesses close shop to get ready for the winter crush. Hotels slash room rates and restaurants offer deals, too.

Your Daily Budget

Budget less than
$60

» $10 to $18 for campsites; $20 to $35 for a dorm bed

» Up to $12 for a meal, or self-cater.

» Consider hiking backcountry for free downhill skiing.

Midrange
$60–$200

» Rooms $100 to $150 in the summer.

» Self-cater breakfast and budget $50 per day for meals out in cafés and restaurants.

» Free public transportation is common in resort areas.

Top end over
$200

» Rooms from $200 in summer to over $500 during ski season.

» Dine anywhere and taste plenty of adventure.

Money

» ATMs are widely available in stores and businesses. Most businesses accept credit cards.

Visas

» All foreign visitors will need a visa to enter the USA unless they're Canadian citizens or part of the Visa Waiver Program.

Cell Phones

» Coverage is unreliable in mountain regions. GSM multiband models are the only phones that work in the USA.

Driving

» Colorado is a great road-trip state. Good maps and road atlases are sold everywhere.

Websites

» **Denver Post** (www.denverpost.com) The state's top newspaper.

» **5280** (www.5280.com) Denver's best monthly magazine.

» **Westword** (www.westword.com) Nightlife listings for Denver and Boulder.

» **365 Things to Do in Breckenridge** (www.facebook.com/365breckenridge) At least one suggestion per day.

» **Discount Ski Rental** (www.rentskies.com) Discount rentals at major ski resort retailers.

» **14ers** (www.14ers.com) For anyone interested in climbing Colorado's 14,000+ft summits.

Exchange Rates

Australia	A$1	$0.99
Canada	C$1	$1.01
Euro zone	€1	$1.33
China	Y10	$1.52
Japan	¥100	$1.21
Mexico	MXN10	$0.83
New Zealand	NZ$1	$0.77
UK	£1	$1.59

For current exchange rates see www.xe.com.

Important Numbers

All phone numbers have a three-digit area code followed by a seven-digit local number. For long-distance and toll-free calls, dial 1 plus all 10 digits.

Country code	1
International dialing code	11
Operator	0
Emergency (ambulance, fire, police)	911
Directory assistance (local)	411

Arriving in Colorado

» Denver International Airport (p94)

Taxi – Multiple taxi companies cue outside Ground Transportation. A ride downtown costs about $45.

Bus – RTD operates skyRide buses which leave frequently between 3:30am and 1:10am with routes to downtown Denver ($10, 55 minutes) and Boulder ($12, 90 minutes).

Rent Your Gear

Although mountain adventure often demands gear – which means checking a bag, which raises costs and costs time – you can still be the carefree carry-on person you've always been. The solution: rent your gear. REI (with branches in Denver and Boulder) and dozens of smaller-scale outfitters (they're literally everywhere) rent everything from fishing rods and waders to tents, backpacks and sleeping pads, as well as full-suspension mountain bikes. And www.rentskis.com rents quality skis and boards at steep discounts.

if you like...

Hiking

To try and pin down the 'best hikes' in the Rocky Mountains is kind of like ranking the world's greatest sunsets. But in a mountain range this huge, there are some variations in what you can see.

Rocky Mountain National Park Long's Peak gets all the buzz but there are several loop trails best done in two or three nights; wildlife sightings are the norm here (p136)

San Juan Skyway The hikes here wander between classic alpine country, aspen-edged meadows, red-rock enscarpments and bubbling hot springs (p41)

Maroon Bells Pristine wilderness with epic Continental Divide views from spectacular mountain passes (p209)

Spanish Peaks Stark granite walls rising from mountain meadows, two looming peaks, ample wildlife and thin crowds (p337)

Black Canyon of the Gunnison National Park Outstanding hiking trails with spectacular views around its rim and in the canyon below (p252)

Old West Sites

Everyone from Harvard-educated blue bloods to pioneering entrepreneurs and desperate, Civil War–scorched southern families came west lured by gold, searching for a fresh start and a raw, new America.

Bent's Old Fort This melting pot of Mexican, American and native culture sustained the Santa Fe Trail, the overland lifeline of western expansion (p341)

Old Colorado City The mid-19th century seed of what became Colorado Springs, this was one of the first settlements in the state (p321)

Ashcroft Mining town ruins 10 minutes from Aspen, accessible by cross-country trail in the winter (p209)

St Elmo Snowmobilers and horsemen trek into Collegiate Peaks shadows to see this atmospheric ghost town (p220)

Breckenridge An A-list and historic ski town sprouted in 1859 when the Colorado gold rush first took hold (p169)

Snow Sports

Yes, some prefer the summer, but winter reigns supreme in Colorado's luscious ski towns. Skiers and snowboarders, telemarkers and Nordic skiers: Colorado's resorts have them all.

Vail Known for its spectacular Back bowl terrain, this is Colorado's largest, and one of its glitziest, ski resorts (p180)

Aspen The most high-minded and star-studded of Aspen's ski areas, Aspen's Four Mountains have epic terrain and host the Winter X Games (p194)

Winter Park Linked to Denver by rail, Winter Park is notable for its moguls and tree runs (p158)

Keystone Ski Resort If you want night skiing in Summit County you'll come here (p162)

Arapahoe Basin Ski Area Stripped down, day-use, no frills, big air and big parties (p161)

Telluride An authentic old mining town reinvented as a kick-back ski destination, and the slopes don't disappoint (p264)

Steamboat Ski Area One of the great all-around resorts in the state, with ample runs at every level (p223)

>> Skiing in Telluride

CHRISTIAN ASLUND

Dinosaurs

Humans were not the first living beings to tramp across the Colorado Mountains, deserts and plains. That honor belongs to the dinosaurs. And this state has the bones and fossilized tracks to prove it.

Dinosaur National Monument This is the quintessential stop for dinophiles of all ages; the Visitor Center is set in a quarry with views of over 1500 prehistoric bones embedded in the cliff face (p234)

Picketwire Dinosaur Tracksite The largest documented site of its kind in North America, there are as many as 1300 visible Allosaur and Apatosaur tracks, left behind as they migrated along the muddy shoreline of a large prehistoric lake (p342)

Garden Park Fossil Area One of Colorado's largest Jurassic graveyards, this was the stage of the so-called Bone Wars, an academic battle to discover new dinosaur species (p334)

Dinosaur Ridge Kids love the footprints and fossils; the closest dinosaur option from Denver (p101)

Beer & Microbreweries

Some long-established craft breweries have outgrown their 'micro' status, but each time you turn around another backyard hobbyist has set up a small business.

Aspen Brewing Co At 7822ft, Aspen Brewing Co is lofty about its brews; ales are its specialty (p206)

Wynkoop Brewing Co Denver's perennial favorite has a beer list of a dozen-odd award-winning brews (p84)

Great Divide Brewing Co Produces a delicious array of seasonal brews alongside its perennial list (p83)

Gunnison Brewery Operating out of a main-street shopfront, its brews are sold on tap (p259)

Ska Brewing Co Not the only brewer in town but we reckon it wins by a nose (p280)

Mountain Sun Pub & Brewery Boulder's fave brewpub produces a beer list as eclectic as its clientele (p123)

Odell Brewing Co Arguably the best craft brewer in the state (p149)

Hot Springs

From the hidden, all-natural variety that takes a full day's hike to discover, to day-use private springs in historic downtowns, to splashy resorts in the shadow of Collegiate Peaks, you'd do well to sink into riverside bliss.

Conundrum Hot Springs Aspen locals love to hike high into the mountains above town then slip into all-natural hot springs beneath the stars (p199)

Strawberry Park Hot Springs Absolutely the most laid-back hot spring in the state, Strawberry Hot Springs is a place to check in and chill out (p227)

Hot Sulphur Springs Resort & Spa Set beneath the looming San Juans in historic downtown, the Pagosa Springs namesake is an attractive private concession beloved by locals (p233)

Mt Princeton Hot Springs A splashy, sprawling resort, bubbling with hot springs in an idyllic Collegiate Peaks location (p217)

WITOLD SKRYPCZAK

>> San Juan National Forest

Scenic Railways

Though the popular vintage train to Winter Park is no more, there are still a few narrow-gauge tracks that can provide views, thrills and a bit of oral history.

Durango & Silverton Narrow Gauge Railroad Forty-five miles long and impossibly scenic, this is the longest and best of the bunch; the round-trip takes about 3½ hours and allows about two hours to poke around Silverton (p277)

Georgetown Loop Railroad The closest narrow-gauge steam train to Denver, this steep corkscrew track winds between the old mining towns of Georgetown (still thriving) and Silver Plume (not so much) (p100)

Manitou & Pikes Peak Cog Railway Travels to the summit of Pikes Peak, a journey that helped inspire the song 'America the Beautiful' (p326)

Cumbres & Toltec Scenic Railroad A chance to mount the Cumbres Pass by the power of steam; the depot is in Antonito (p315)

Geology

From hidden 2000ft-deep gorges, to 50ft rock walls rising from the slopes of Spanish Peaks, to god-like rock gardens and mind-bending arches, Colorado is home to some incredible geologic masterworks.

Royal Gorge A deep and spectacular rift in the earth penetrated by the Arkansas River; spanned by a landmark bridge and laced with a scenic railway (p334)

Garden of the Gods This odd formation of boulders and pinnacles is part of a red rock vein that runs through the length of Colorado Springs (p321)

Great Dikes of the Spanish Peaks These 50-to-100ft-high rock walls rise out of nowhere through mountain meadows and run like a primordial fenceline up the shoulders of the Spanish Peaks (p338)

Black Canyon of the Gunnison National Park A deep, narrow abyss with sheer, multicolored walls scored with eerie crevices and pinnacles (p252)

Rattlesnake Arches Getting here is no cake walk, but the concentration of spectacular natural arches is worth every dusty step (p243)

Distilleries

Although microbrew is the state's most lauded tipple, recent years have seen the microdistillery movement emerge with the same bold, independent spirit. Bottles are available across the state, but travelers with a passion for local elixirs should go directly to the source.

Stranahans Colorado Whiskey The most widely celebrated of Colorado's local liquors, this Denver craft whiskey is a staple of high-end cocktail menus around the state (p66)

Peach Street Distillers Though they make a suite of fine spirits, the brightest star on the shelves of this Palisade producer is a vodka infused with local peaches (p243)

Mancos Valley Distillery If only every small town had a visionary like Ian James, who crafts the delicate Ian's Alley Rum and opens his brewing space to live blues and bluegrass (p295)

If You Like...
Mountain Biking
Fruita offers the best mountain biking in the state, and the 128-mile Kokopelli trail leads to Moab, Utah's mountain biking hotspot.

Wildlife

Colorado is home to a wealth of wildlife, from moose, elk, deer and antelope to fox, wolf, black bear and mountain lion to the all-American superstar that is the bald eagle.

Rocky Mountain National Park Despite a few roads snaking through it, this park is the best-preserved slice of the Rocky Mountains; though it's not exactly Yellowstone, wildlife sightings (a moose wading through wetlands, elk herds grazing on high country peaks...) are frequent and satisfying (p131)

Black Canyon of the Gunnison National Park The stomping ground of mule deer, bighorn sheep, black bear and mountain lion (p252)

San Juan Mountains A beautiful and diverse mountain range alive with wildlife; backcountry treks may reveal elk herds, black bears, mountain goats, beavers, river otters, golden eagles and the rare mountain lion; bowhunting season begins in late summer (p302)

Food

Colorado is no longer simply a meat and potatoes palate. With an abundance of creative chefs, and farm to table kitchens blooming across the state, you have some eating to do.

Osaki's For our money, this Vail hole in the wall is as good as sushi gets in Colorado – and it does get so very good here (p187)

Root Down Denver's best new restaurant has an 'eat local' ethos and tremendous high-design elements (p79)

Salt The best and the liveliest of a handful of new Boulder kitchens; the vast majority of its ingredients are local and organic, and the cocktails are tailored, rather than standard issue (p120)

Six89 A destination farm-to-table restaurant in up and coming Carbondale; it means something that when asked where the best restaurant in town lives locals tell you to drive down the mountain and eat here (p242)

Film Locations

Roy Rogers starred in *Colorado,* but it was filmed in California. Kubrick's *The Shining* was set in Colorado but filmed in Montana, Oregon and England. Nonetheless, Colorado has made some star turns.

Silverton Among many film productions shot in and around the town were 1950's *Ticket to Tomahawk,* featuring an uncredited Marilyn Monroe; *Across the Wide Missouri,* starring Clarke Gable; *Viva Zapata,* which garnered an Oscar for Anthony Quinn; the James Stewart and Janet Leigh picture *The Naked Spur;* and 1962's *How the West Was Won,* with Henry Fonda. (p273)

Durango & Silverton Narrow Gauge Railroad Take this historic train across Bakers Bridge where Redford and Newman jumped into the river in 1969's *Butch Cassidy & the Sundance Kid* (p277)

Cañon City The Prospect Heights neighborhood was the United Artists defacto Western backlot; 1969's *True Grit,* with John Wayne and Dennis Hopper, was shot here (p334)

Glenwood Springs The crew of *Mr & Mrs Smith* stayed at the Hotel Colorado while filming part of the flick. (p237)

month by month

Top Events

1 **Aspen Music Festival,** July

2 **Boulder Creek Festival,** May

3 **Telluride Film Festival,** September

4 **Spring Massive,** April

5 **Great American Beer Festival,** September

January

Crowds are at their thickest around New Year, and stay busy through Martin Luther King's birthday. This is also when the snow is as abundant as après-ski parties.

 Winter X Games
ESPN's annual extreme winter sports event takes place at Aspen's Buttermilk Mountain (the summer games are in Los Angeles). The games include day and night events, and feature all sorts of snow sports, including snowmobiling.

 National Western Stock Show
Saddle up for the state's biggest stock show, a Denver tradition since 1906. We're talking rodeos, cattle, cowboys, Wild West shows, hundreds of vendors and more.

February

Still in the height of ski season, powder is luscious and everywhere;
Carnival is celebrated, and resorts get packed for Presidents Day weekend. Advance reservations are crucial, and you'll pay less midweek.

 Carnival
Vail does a high-elevation spin on Mardi Gras, complete with a parade (Bridge St does its best Bourbon St), a king and queen, and plenty of joviality. Breckenridge does its own version with a masquerade ball and, of course, a Fat Tuesday parade.

March

Coloradans swear the sun is always out – and it often is – but March is the beginning of the real sunshine, and spring break attracts families for the start of spring skiing.

 Frozen Dead Guy Days
Irreverent, marginally legal and more than a little creepy, this festival (p144) perfectly suits bizarre little Nederland. Spring is welcomed by rallying around their cryogenically frozen town mascot, 'Grandpa Bredo,' with a snowshoe race, dead guy look-alike contest and copious beer drinking.

April

Spring skiing! Fresh powder is likely. Even as room rates dip slightly, midweek deals aren't hard to find, unless it's Easter week. Colorado Rockies start knocking them out of the park at Coors Field.

Breckenridge Spring Massive
A two-week celebration making the most of the season. It's made up of a range of festivals dedicated to food, microbrews and music. Oh, and there's the longest ski-mountaineering race found in North America.

May

Mud season hits the higher elevations, while the beginning of summer weather graces Boulder and Denver, but this

doesn't mean it won't just snow out of the blue. Summer unofficially begins on Memorial Day weekend – time for paddling.

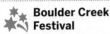 Boulder Creek Festival

One of Colorado's biggest festivals comes to town. Boulder's traditional summer starter is all about food, drink, music and, above all, glorious sunshine. It all comes to a close with Bolder Boulder, a 10km race celebrated by screaming crowds.

Cinco de Mayo

Denver puts its back into this traditional celebration, hosting hundreds of exhibitors and food merchants and a good dose of margaritas. These days it's one of the biggest of its kind in the country.

June

Summer festivals are in high gear, early-season rivers are running high and Arapahoe Basin finally closes for the season. All mountain passes are open, and road-tripping families start to hit the major parks and landmarks.

Telluride Bluegrass Festival

Thousands of fans descend on Telluride for a weekend-long homage to bluegrass. Camping out is a popular option for this well-organized outdoor festival. Along with bluegrass, a fair few straight-up rockers can be found here.

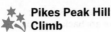 Pikes Peak Hill Climb

When the first road to Pikes Peak was complete, this car race was born. Different classes of vehicle (pro trucks, motorbikes, stock cars...) hammer over 12 miles of road and 4700ft of increased elevation.

July

July ushers in 10 weeks of prime time for backcountry hikes now that the snow has melted and water is beginning to filter through the streams and meadows and down the valley.

Aspen Music Festival

Classical musicians come from around the globe to play, teach and learn at this famous festival (p201). Top-tier performers put on spectacular shows, while students form orchestras led by sought-after conductors or bring street corners to life with smaller groups.

Kayaking the Arkansas River

Early-season rivers have mellowed out by this time, so it's a good time to learn to kayak on the Arkansas River. Buena Vista is as good a place as any to get onto the water and test out your paddling arms.

Cowboys' Roundup Days

The Old West is alive and well in Steamboat Springs. Don your cowboy hat and join the locals in an old-fashioned Fourth of July parade, fireworks, rodeos and cattle drive.

August

A great time of year to get into the backcountry; warm temperatures at high elevations make this prime hiking season. Down the mountain, bulls and bronco busters square off at dozens of rodeos and country fairs.

Racing in Leadville

The highlight of Leadville's racing season is the Leadville Trail 100, held annually since 1983. This race is no picnic: it's not unusual for less than half of the competitors to make it to the finish line before the 30-hour limit is up.

Mountain Biking

This is a great time of year to jump on the bike. Ski resorts are now dedicated to fat tires: there's great deals and terrific terrain to be found in Snowmass, Vail, Breckenridge and Copper Mountain. Winter Park hosts the epic King of the Mountains (p159).

September

The aspens are beginning to turn and there's an unmistakable fall chill in the air. The ski resorts start to empty and businesses to close up. Crowds are thin and prices low.

Great American Beer Festival

Beer – we're talking microbrews – is big business in Colorado, so it should be no surprise that this celebration is so popular it always sells out in advance. How big is it? More than 500 breweries get in on it.

 Telluride Film Festival

Little ol' Telluride can now hold its own against the likes of Utah's Sundance. Plenty of celebrated films make their debut here, and it's helped launched the career of the likes of Michael Moore and Robert Rodriguez.

Jazz Aspen Snowmass

The Labor Day incarnation of this festival leans away from jazz and more towards popular rock. (Jazz aficionados should head for the June version.) Big-name acts take to the outdoor stage in Snowmass Town Park.

October

Mud season redux. Weather has turned completely, but at least

the Denver Broncos **are are back in action. Discounts can be steep – even in Aspen – and you'll likely see snow fall and the beginning of ski season in Arapahoe Basin, Loveland, before Halloween.**

Colorado Springs Coffin Racing

One of the state's kookier events sees custom-built wheeled coffins racing through the town in the build up to Halloween. It's all to 'celebrate' the time a coffin was unearthed by erosion and slid down Red Mountain.

November

Ski season begins throughout the state. Early season ski deals abound, though you won't find any bargains around Thanksgiving weekend, when the families come back.

December

Colorado: the winter wonderland. Some early-season steals might be around the first half of December. Once the schools let out, the airports are jammed, rooms are booked out and you'd better have reservations.

Snow Daze

Historically marking the opening of the mountain, Vail lets loose with one of the biggest early-season celebrations. This week-long festival features all sorts of competitions and activities and plenty of live performances from big-name musical stars.

Lights of December

Boulder's Pearl St Mall gets spruced up for the city's traditional Christmas Parade: floats from local businesses, children in costume and St Nick himself. Not the biggest parade in the world, but a pleasant way to get in the spirit of things.

itineraries

Whether you've got four days or 40, these itineraries provide a starting point for the trip of a lifetime. Want more inspiration? Head online to lonelyplanet. com/thorntree to chat with other travelers.

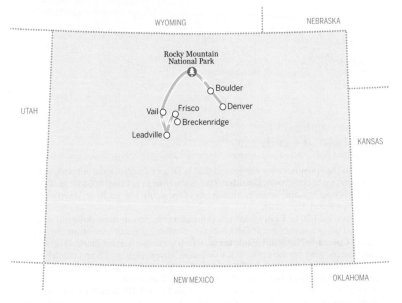

One Week
Denver & the Northern Rockies

❯ A combination of the oh-so urban and the rustic mountain adventure is yours on this unforgettable road trip. Spend a couple of days in **Denver**, riding the bike paths, shopping in Cherry Creek and South Broadway, dining and partying in LoDo and taking in a ball game. Head north through fun and funky **Boulder** to **Rocky Mountain National Park** to spend a few days in the wilderness.

Hit the road south on Hwy 40 through Winter Park then west on I-70 to **Vail**, where there's technical downhill mountain biking and access to a network of bike paths that lead all the way to Breckenridge. Consider a river trip or perhaps a paraglide, and take the gondola up to Eagle's Nest for a taste of the Continental Divide.

Then drive the backroads through Minturn and Red Cliff into **Leadville**, where you can stroll through history before taking Hwy 91 through lonely mountain towns, back to Hwy 6, into **Frisco** and onto **Breckenridge**. Spend your last days here, exploring the quaint historical district in the evenings and biking and hiking in the daylight. Get in a river trip before heading back to Denver.

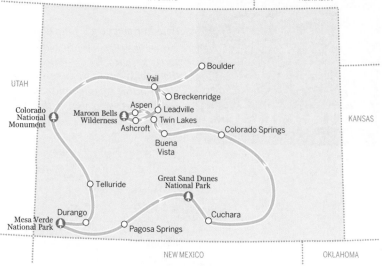

Two Weeks (Spring–Fall)
The State of Colorado

Fly into the bedouin-esque compound that is Denver International Airport, rent a car and head up to eco-groovy **Boulder**. This is the time to get your outdoor gear prepped and stretch your legs and lungs by hitting one of the many bike paths or, if you're in Boulder, hike the Royal Arch Trail.

Head west on I-70 to **Vail**, where you can run a river, get in some downhill mountain biking and enjoy a sushi feast at Osaki's before continuing west to the stunning climbing mecca of **Colorado National Monument**. Camp overnight and hit Black Ridge Canyons Wilderness the next day for a hike in Rattlesnake Canyon. Head south and climb back into the Rockies and into hippie-chic **Telluride** before heading south to **Durango**, where you can hop the **Durango & Silverton Narrow Gauge Railroad**.

Next go deep into the Four Corners to see **Mesa Verde Cliff Dwellings**, then dip into **Pagosa Springs**. If you're here in the middle to late summer, consider a two-day back-packing trip in the nearby San Juan high country. Otherwise take the 160 east to the **Great Sand Dunes National Park** on your way to **Cuchara** in the Spanish Peaks Wilderness – another fine under-the-radar hiking destination. Indulge yourself with a night at the Broadmoor in **Colorado Springs** on your way north to Hwy 285, which you'll take to Hwy 24 and the up-and-coming paddlers' paradise of **Buena Vista**, a great place to get into some white water. There's free camping and some sweet B&Bs here, too. Then head north on Hwy 24 and turn onto Hwy 82 through **Twin Lakes**, over Independence Pass (with epic Continental Divide views), and into tony, musical, adventurous **Aspen**. Hike in the **Maroon Bells Wilderness**, bicycle to **Ashcroft** and eat at the **Pine Creek Cookhouse**. And when you've had your fill, double back over Independence Pass, through **Leadville**, stop for fuel at the Minturn Saloon, before winding your way through **Vail** and into historic **Breckenridge** for one last day and night of cycling, hiking, hot tubbing and star gazing.

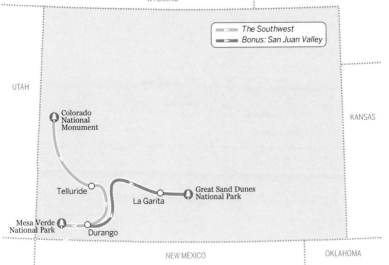

The Southwest
Bonus: San Juan Valley

UTAH

Colorado
National
Monument

KANSAS

Telluride
La Garita   Great Sand Dunes
National Park

Mesa Verde
National Park
Durango

NEW MEXICO   OKLAHOMA

Five Days
The Southwest

❯ Head south from Grand Junction into the stunning **Colorado National Monument** – a climbing paradise. Camp overnight and hit Black Ridge Canyons Wilderness and a hike beneath nine rock arches in Rattlesnake Canyon before nesting in übergroovy **Telluride**. Surrounded on three sides by towering 13,000ft peaks, Telluride is all strong coffee, historic buildings and big nature. You have some hiking to do here, whether it's to the top of Ajax Peak, Bridal Veil Falls (Colorado's highest waterfall; 365ft) or to the summit of 14,246ft Mt Wilson, in the Lizard Head Wilderness Area.

Drive the **Million Dollar Hwy** through Silverton to **Durango**, where you can hop the **Durango & Silverton Narrow Gauge Railroad** (a must). Explore the turquoise jewelry and art galleries of the town before driving deeper into the Four Corners and **Mesa Verde National Park**. These Ancestral Puebloan cliff dwellings are massive and transporting: every breath of whistling wind has more meaning here. Spend the night beneath the stars here and you might feel your mind wander deep into dreamtime.

Three More Days
Bonus: San Juan Valley

❯ If you're lucky enough to have the time, the southwest does deserve a full week. This way you can spend more time in Telluride, ensure you don't miss **Durango's** train ride and take your time on the **Million Dollar Hwy**. Then you can hike backcountry trails through luscious **San Luis Valley**, where the terrain includes out-of-nowhere volcanic rock formations, and Hispanic adobe churches sprout in otherwise classic high-country alpine zones.

We love the hikes into Penitente Canyon; trails are best accessed from **La Garita**. From here you can head east to the **Great Sand Dunes National Park**, or if you're a cyclist you might disregard Pagosa Springs and the San Juans entirely, and instead head from Mesa Verde back to **Fruita**, outside of Grand Junction, where you have the best single-track mountain biking in the US at your doorstep.

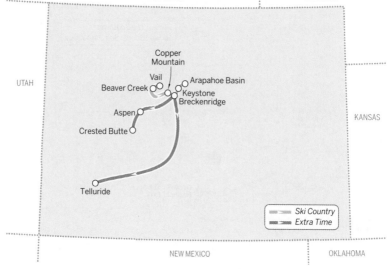

Five Days
Ski Country

> Begin the experience in **Vail** (just three hours from Denver and a shorter hop from Eagle County Airport), where you'll have access to the most acreage (5289 to be exact) of any ski area in the state. What makes Vail so special is the back bowl terrain (over 3000 acres). That's where you'll find the experts, unless they happen to be at the three terrain parks. Lift tickets in Vail can also be used at **Beaver Creek**, which fancies itself even more exclusive than Vail. It was built to attract the 1976 Olympics (it didn't), but still boasts a World Cup downhill course.

Spend your next three days in Summit County. Base yourself out of **Breckenridge**, which has a nice percentage of beginner runs, and some killer chutes and tree runs, and a ski resort spread over four mountains. Summit County is also well connected by free public transport, which means you can get from here to the night slopes at **Keystone** and over to **Copper Mountain**, too. And your lift ticket is also good at **Arapahoe Basin** if you fancy a whiff of 'the Beach.'

Four More Days
Extra Time

> Those with more time up their sleeves will be able to hit more classic Colorado ski areas. In that case, we'd advise you to make **Breckenridge** your first stop. It's closer to Denver than Vail, and you get more free public transit access to neighboring resorts than in Vail (although, to be fair, the free public transit within Vail and Beaver Creek is great, too).

From Breckenridge you should head further west to **Aspen**, where you can ski on four mountains: Aspen, Aspen Highlands, Snowmass and Buttermilk, home to the Winter X Games. Also, Aspen has the best parties. Spend two nights here then, when you get your fill of fluff and nose-upwardness, venture to nearby but remote **Crested Butte**, on the other side of the Maroon Bells, with over 1000 skiable acres, a healthy chunk of intermediate runs and a massive superpipe. Or ditch the Aspen idea entirely and go from Breck to **Telluride** in one long day. Catering to the expert skier, Telluride, locals like to say, is what Aspen used to be.

Outdoors

Top 10 14ers

There are 54 mountains topping 14,000ft in the state of Colorado. Locals call them '14ers', and many try to bag 'em all.

Northern Mountains
Longs Peak

Central Mountains
Mt Elbert
Quandary Peak
Mount of the Holy Cross
Mt Princeton
Mt Massive
Uncompahgre Peak
Maroon Peak
Snowmass Mountain

Eastern Colorado
Pikes Peak

Other destinations may offer a different mix of mountains, rivers, rock-climbing routes, hiking and cycling terrain, but no other place offers more or better outdoor adventure than Colorado. Winter or summer, snow, rain or shining sun, there is always somewhere to go or something to do that will crack open your mind and buckle your knees with wonder, pump your bloodstream with adrenaline – or all three at the same time. Here are 54 peaks above 14000ft, hundreds of river miles and thousands of miles of single track and networked bike paths that link towns more than 40 miles a part. Of course, all of this joy is happening in the state's robust national, state and county parklands, forests and wilderness areas, which hold almost unspeakable natural beauty. There are knife-edge ridges overlapped against rounded granite domes, high mountain meadows, red-rock canyons and stark cliffs that drop into narrow gorges.

Hiking & Backpacking

Trails across the state beckon for day hikers and overnight backpackers between late May and early October. Many of these trails are accessible by county and forest service roads that are subject to closure. Contact the local ranger district if you plan on hiking early or late in the season. Trails are accessible year-round in lower elevation destinations, such as Boulder and Colorado National Monument.

Where to Hike

The Colorado Trail

The state's signature trail, also known as USFS Trail 1776, starts at Chatfield Reservoir near Denver, before winding 500 miles to Durango through eight mountain ranges, seven national forests, six wilderness areas and five river systems. The Colorado Trail Foundation (p103) offers maps and books that describe the trail in detail.

Boulder

Boulder, a visionary small city, is surrounded by parkland paid for by a self-assessed tax that has been used to purchase vast swaths of city and county-owned open space, including Chautauqua Park (p106), which is precisely where you'll find the best hiking in the area. In the mountains above the city, past the town of Nederland (only a 30-minute drive from downtown) is the Indian Peaks Wilderness Area, where you'll find miles of hiking trails and backcountry campsites. The hike up to 12,000ft Arapaho Pass, accessed from the Fourth of July campground, is an especially nice day hike.

Rocky Mountain National Park

The star attraction of the northern Rockies, and one of the top draws in all of Colorado, the Rocky Mountain National Park is interesected by the Continental Divide, which offers some of the best wildlife viewing in the state, and its excellent hiking trails cross alpine meadows, skirt lakes and bring travellers into the wild and deeply beautiful backcountry. Our Rocky Mountain National Park chapter offers over two dozen campsites and hiking trails to consider. Just know that in the peak season (July and August) you will have to make reservations for backcountry campsites. This is especially true if you plan on climbing Longs Peak and staying overnight on the mountain.

Central Mountains

Breckenridge, Vail and Aspen are all tremendous resort areas with more hiking trails nearby than can be explored in an entire season. Most ski areas have a summer lift to a ski lodge with trail access. Views can be excellent, particularly in Vail and Snowmass, and the groomed trails give you a taste of the high altitude with relatively smooth footing, but it ain't the wilderness.

Our favorite hiking destination in the region is the Maroon Bells (p208). It's no secret, but if you start early and plan to hike all day, you can avoid the bussed-in crowds and head up and over Buckskin Pass where solitude can be yours and the views are breathtaking. But there are other options in the Aspen area, including a hike to the famous Grottos and a trail to Conundrum Hot Springs. The Collegiate Peaks Wilderness is a close second. Best accessed from sweet Buena Vista on Hwy 24, here are eight peaks above 14,000ft. Vail and Minturn are the best departure points for the famous trail to Mount of the Holy Cross, while Quandary Peak holds the distinction of being the most accessible 14,000ft peak in the state. It's just outside Breckenridge.

And if you want to sample the backcountry without having to rough it (it's OK, you can admit it), look into the 10th Mountain Division Hut Association (p199). They manage 29 backcountry huts between Vail and Aspen, connected by 350 miles of trails.

Northwest Colorado

Dominated by the Routt National Forest, there are three wilderness areas in this region: Flattops Wilderness, Sarvis Creek Wilderness and Mt Zirkel Wilderness, which is one of the state's five original wilderness areas. All are laced with excellent hiking trails, but the Mt Zirkel Wilderness is especially magical. Untamed and roadless, it's dotted with icy glacial lakes and

SAFE HIKING

Hikers should always have their own maps. Adequate trail maps can be found at park headquarters, ranger district offices or outdoor clothing and supply stores such as REI. Weather conditions can change in a blink, so bring layers and rain gear. Summer afternoon monsoons are frequent, and lightning is a real concern above timberline. The catch-all rule is to stay off mountain peaks and passes after noon. And always carry more than enough food and water (and water purification equipment). Dehydration will sap your energy and can provoke altitude sickness.

FIVE WAYS TO BE A GOOD BACKPACKER

» Leave only footprints, take only pictures. There's no garbage collection in the backcountry. Make sure that whatever you pack in, you pack out.

» Water. Water. Water. You should have water sanitation or a water filtration system to enjoy the backcountry. The best way to eliminate potential bacteria is to boil the lake, creek or river water, but filters work well, too.

» Have the essentials: a map, extra layers of clothing, rain gear, extra food and water, flashlight, fire starter kit (with waterproof matches and/or a lighter), camp stove, first aid kit (with blister care items), sunglasses, sun screen, sleeping bag, tent and a pocket knife.

» Only build fires where permitted, and only use dead and down wood, rather than breaking dead limbs from standing trees. Make sure you put out your fire completely before breaking camp.

» Due to high density backcountry traffic, Colorado authorities are now suggesting that campers actually pack out their own personal solid waste, and are even offering free bags with which to do the trick. No joke. Human waste does impact the environment and the new guidelines are a response to that. At the very least, bury yours at least six inches below the surface at least 50ft from any watercourses, and pack out your toilet tissue.

granite faces, and is intersected by the Continental Divide and two major rivers, the Elk and the Encampment, both of which are being considered for protection under the Wild & Scenic Rivers Act. In the center of it all is the 12,180ft Mt Zirkel.

Fans of canyon country will want to check out Colorado National Monument (p243). There are no real backpacking opportunities here, and most of the trails are relatively short, but there's the rewarding 6-mile Monument Canyon Trail that skirts many of the park's most interesting natural features, including the Coke Ovens, the Kissing Couple and Independence Monument.

Southwest Colorado

Colorado's most diverse region features red rock canyons, Great Sand Dunes National Park (p307) and spectacular high country – you may just want to head here directly. The Black Canyon of the Gunnison National Park (p252) is a good place to stretch your legs. The easy 1.5-mile Oak Flat Trail offers good views of Black Canyon. At sunset take the 1.5-mile Warner Point Nature Trail to either High Point or Sunset View overlooks.

Telluride (p264) is a day-hiker's dream town, with many trails accessible from downtown, including the 2.7-mile Jud Wiebe Trail. The Bear Creek Trail is slightly shorter, just over 2 miles, but includes a 1040ft climb to a waterfall. This trail also intersects the 12-mile Wasatch Trail. Backpackers should seek their solitude surrounded by the 14,000ft summits in the nearby Lizard Head and Mt Sneffels Wilderness Areas.

The region's jewel is the epic, craggy San Juan Range. There are more than 25 peaks over 11,000ft here, including 14 of Colorado's 54 14ers. Over the years, skiers have tried to tame them, mountaineers have tried to summit them and miners have tried to burrow into them, but one look is enough to see that it's still untamed.

Eastern Colorado

Pikes Peak (p321) gets all the press, and with good reason. After all, it is the most famous, but not nearly the tallest, of the 14ers. Some drive to the top, others take the train, but the 13-mile Barr Trail leads from the Cog Railway station through Barr Camp at the halfway point and finally through the scree fields to the summit. You can make it a very doable day hike by taking the train halfway up to a spur that leads into Barr Camp, where you can join the Barr Trail to the summit, then ride the rails back down.

While there is certainly something to be said for taking down a big-name mountain, backpackers seeking pristine nature, dramatic views and solitude will love the Spanish Peaks Wilderness (p337). Extinct volcanoes that aren't part of the Continental

Divide cordillera include East Spanish Peak at 12,683ft and West Spanish Peak at 13,625ft. There are trails to both summits and spectacular dikes that seem to erupt from the earth. All told there are three campgrounds and 65 miles of trails to explore.

Skiing & Snowboarding

Colorado's wealth of ski and snowboarding terrain is well known. There are bunny slopes and moguls, tree runs and back bowls, terrain parks and superpipes. Winter recreation built this state's tourism industry, transforming places like Aspen and Vail, and putting towns like Crested Butte and Telluride on the map. And powder is why those adrenaline-addled slackers are manning the reception desk, working the espresso machine, parking the cars and mixing your drinks. Colorado's resort area service sector has a second life where all they see and feel is powder and take orders only from the mountain. These people live to carve and ride, rocket downhill and perch on the edge of dramatic chutes. In Colorado, winter is bliss.

Where to Ski
Northern Mountains

Although this section of the state does have tremendous hiking and mountain biking – normally indicators of a nearby ski resort – much of the best mountain terrain is protected in the Rocky Mountain National Park (p131). However, there is one day-use resort just up the road from Boulder. More convenient than epic (although the 1400ft vertical drop in Corona Bowl will get your attention), Eldora Mountain Resort (p144), 4 miles west of Nederland, has around 500 skiable acres and 25-plus miles of well-groomed Nordic trails.

Central Mountains

There are more skiable acres in this part of Colorado than anywhere else. The resorts, it seems, are strung out like snow-white pearls off I-70 or the parallel Hwy 6. All are covered extensively in the Central Mountains chapter (where we also include tips and advice on the best runs for all levels), but if you're trying to decide where to base your winter vacation here are the basics.

Vail & Beaver Creek

Vail (p180) is the largest ski resort in the US, with 5289 skiable acres, 193 trails and three terrain parks. It lacks the downtown cohesion of an Aspen or Telluride, as this is classic plaza-style resort development, but for sheer variety and thrills Vail is top-notch. And what makes it really special are the back bowls – more than 4000 of their acres are on the back side of Vail Mountain with postcard views. The drawback has always been expense. Historically, Vail has angled to be the most expensive lift ticket in Colorado (often outpricing Aspen by $1), and lodging doesn't come cheap here either, but at least your ticket is also good at nearby Beaver Creek.

Beginners love it at Beaver Creek because the mountain is upside down, with easier runs at the top of the mountain plus great views. But there's plenty of expert terrain, including a World Cup Downhill course. Plus, this was the first Colorado resort to incorporate European-style village-to-village skiing.

Aspen & Around

With celebrity glitter, a historic downtown core and some of the best skiing in the state, Aspen (p194) is a terrific choice. One lift ticket grants access to the Four Mountains. Aspen and Aspen Highlands (the locals' under-the-radar choice) don't offer much for beginners, but there is plenty of green terrain here. Snowmass is the biggest, and some say the best, of the bunch, with over 3000 acres, three terrain parks and 60 miles of groomed Nordic trails. Buttermilk is the host to the Winter X Games. Cross-country skiers should also make their way to historic Ashcroft and the Pine Creek Cookhouse.

Breckenridge

Closer to Denver, with a jewel-box historic downtown and a ski resort spanning four luscious mountains covering 2358 acres laced with 155 acres trails, Breckenridge (p169) is a terrific choice. Beginner and intermediate skiers have some of the best runs in Colorado. Advanced skiers have plenty to rave about, too, and there's a state-of-the-art superpipe built for the 2010–11 ski season.

Plus, a lift ticket here is good at Keystone and Copper Mountain, connected to Breck by a free Summit County–wide public transportation system.

NATIONAL PARKS & MONUMENTS

Bent's Old Fort National Historic Site	In southeastern Colorado, on the north bank of the Arkansas River, this small site was an early prairie trading post for settlers.
Black Canyon of the Gunnison National Park	The Gunnison River cut this deep, narrow and scenic western Colorado gorge nearly 2500ft below the adjacent plateau. It also features forests of ancient piñon pines.
Colorado National Monument	Once dinosaur country, this 18,000-acre reserve near Grand Junction, in western Colorado, displays the most colorful, distinctive forms that only erosion can create.
Dinosaur National Monument	The Green and Yampa Rivers flow through this 298-sq-mile reserve in northeastern Utah and northwestern Colorado, where dinosaur fossils lie in impressive quarries. Native American petroglyphs embellish nearby scenic canyons.
Florissant Fossil Beds National Monument	Volcanic ash covered this former lake bed in the mountains west of Colorado Springs, preserving 6000 acres of fossil flora and fauna, including petrified sequoias.
Great Sand Dunes National Park	This spectacular dune field spreads for approximately 55 sq miles in the San Luis Valley, with the tallest rising, staggeringly, to almost 700ft.
Hovenweep National Monument	In southwestern Colorado and southeastern Utah, this 300-acre monument preserves the ruins of defensive fortifications that once protected a vital water supply for pre-Columbian inhabitants.
Mesa Verde National Park	In southwestern Colorado, covering 80 sq miles, this park is primarily an archaeological preserve. Its elaborate cliffside dwellings are relics of Ancestral Puebloans.
Rocky Mountain National Park	Only a short hop from Denver, this park straddles the Continental Divide, offering 395 sq miles of alpine forests, lakes and tundra covered by summer wildflowers and grazed by bighorn sheep and elk.

Keystone

Also in Summit County, the Keystone ski area (p162) encompasses three mountains of 3148 skiable acres laced with 135 trails, about half of which are expert runs. Almost 20% of the trails are beginner runs. The A51 Terrain Park is decked out with an array of jumps, jibs, rails and a superpipe. There's a fun and easy tubing area – perfect for young kids – on Dercum Mountain, and a CAT system that will take the daring above the lifts to the lips of a string of Black Diamond bowl runs at the top of the park.

They're also the only Summit County resort to offer night skiing.

Copper Mountain

A self-contained resort area that's ideal for families, Copper Mountain (p167) has 2450 acres of skiable terrain accessed by 22 lifts and carved by 126 trails that are almost equally divided among beginners, intermediate, advanced and expert. There are 15-plus miles of groomed Nordic tracks, a tubing hill and free transport to Keystone and Breckenridge.

Arapahoe Basin

One of two day-use ski areas in the Central Mountains, locals dig Arapahoe Basin (p161) because the lack of lodging and dining options keeps package tourists to a minimum. Put together by veterans of the 10th Mountain Division (you'll be hearing a lot about them), this was the second resort launched in Colorado. The top lift gets you to the summit (13,059ft) where you can drop into Montezuma Bowl on the back side. A-Basin, as it's affectionately known, is also famous for the Beach, which rages on Gaper Day. Summit County lift tickets are generally accepted here, too. A-Basin and Loveland (see below) have the longest ski seasons, and are usually open from October to June.

Loveland Ski Area

The oldest ski area in Colorado, Loveland Ski Area (p161) opened in 1943, and is set against the Continental Divide, above the Eisenhower Tunnel on I-70. It's only 56 miles from Denver, lift tickets are reasonably priced and they have plenty of intermediate and advanced terrain, with limited variety for newbies.

Winter Park

Connected to Denver by rail, Denver and Colorado Springs locals flock to Winter Park for down-to-earth weekend powder. The 3000 acres of skiable terrain occupy five mountains, with terrific mogul runs and hair-raising off-piste action. There are also six terrain parks serving all levels, from beginners to X Games–caliber talent.

Northwest Colorado

One of the great all-around resorts in the state, Steamboat Springs (p223) has 165 trails (3668ft vertical) and nearly 3000 acres with ample runs at every level. It's particularly renowned for tree skiing, and even intermediate skiers can weave through trees without the typical hazards. Serious skiers will also gravitate to a number of mogul runs on the hill. More than a few Olympic-caliber skiers and riders make their winter home here.

Southwest Colorado

Crested Butte

Tucked behind the Maroon Bells, Crested Butte (p259) isn't the biggest resort in the state, but few, if any, have this kind of scenery. Surrounded by forests, rugged mountain peaks in the West Elk and Maroon Bells Wilderness Areas, the scenery is mind-boggling.

The mountain's 1167 acres are mostly geared toward intermediate and advanced skiers, and they unveiled a new terrain park and superpipe for the 2010–11 ski season.

Telluride

Believe the stellar reviews – the quality of skiing at Telluride (p264) is truly world-class. The steep, fast, north-facing runs are the main reason it has an experts-only reputation, but there are some moderate trails, too, particularly in the Goronno Basin. The best runs for non-experts are the aptly named See Forever and Lookout runs, both of which are graceful gliders with panoramic views. For a bit more adrenaline, try the West Drain run. The Telluride Nordic Center (p264) can set up experienced cross-country skiers on a multiday backcountry trip between Telluride and Ouray along the San Juan Hut System (p264).

Wolf Creek

Located 25 miles north of Pagosa Springs on US 160, this (really rich) family-owned ski area (p283) is one of Colorado's last and best-kept secrets – at least for now. In recent years major development has been proposed by Red McCombs, a founding father of Clear Channel Communications whose name often pops up on Forbes list of richest Americans. But for now it's still mostly a locals' place that isn't overrun with the out-of-state crowd and covered with high-end boutiques, and it can be an awesome place to ride with waist-high powder after a big storm. Seven lifts service 70 trails, from wide-open bowls to steep tree glades.

Slope Grades

Colorado ski and snowboard terrain is graded and signed with shapes and colors. Pay attention so you do not get in over your head.

» Green (circle): Beginner runs can be called 'greenies' or 'bunny slopes'. This is where you learn and build your skills.

» Blue (square): Intermediate runs.

» Blue/Black (blue square with a black diamond): Intermediate to advanced. Must be confident and experienced.

» Black Diamond: Advanced terrain.

» Double Black Diamond: Expert skiers and riders only. Don't be a hero unless you are one.

» Yellow (oval): Freestyle. Used to designate terrain parks.

Cycling & Mountain Biking

There's a reason US cycling is based here and Lance Armstrong purportedly lives here. The cycling and mountain-biking terrain isn't endless, but it sure feels that way. It would take a lifetime to ride every mile of paved path, fire road and single track in a state that has made thin-air mountain passes a badge of honor. And it would take a decade of summer seasons to bomb down every downhill, skid through every hairpin and launch off all the jumps at Colorado ski resorts.

The cycling is so epic that you can ride on dedicated bike paths from Glenwood Springs to Aspen, and from Vail to Breckenridge. Gondolas, buses and even Lake Dillon ferries are all outfitted to tote bikes. These mountains have inspired gruelling 100-mile bike races in Leadville and summer racing seasons throughout the state. They've also prompted more than one eco-minded hipster to ditch the car, and way more than one Aspen millionaire to shave their legs and go full-body spandex on our asses. The point is, in Colorado cycling isn't just a hobby and it's more than exercise. It's all part of the lifestyle.

Where to Cycle

It would take too long to list every worthy path and route in this bike-friendly state. Summer sees many ski resorts wave goodbye to the snow set and say hello to the two-wheelers. To get you oriented:

» **Central Mountains** This whole region is home to one of the state's best network of bike paths. Everything you could want is here: road, tracks and gravel.

» **Denver** A bike-lover's city, complete with bike-share program, bike-friendly public transportation and plenty of paths.

» **Boulder** Possibly more bike-crazed than Denver; paths and bike lanes lead to virtually everywhere in town and beyond.

» **Fort Collins** A bike museum is spread across the whole town; jumping on a fixie is *the* way to get around here.

» **Around Grand Junction** The mix of flat roads and wineries is a tempting combination; some of the USA's best single-track trails are near Fruita.

» **Telluride** Single-track routes and amazing scenery? Check and check.

Rock Climbing & Mountaineering

Rock climbing is so popular in Colorado that along with a wealth of granite, sandstone and even limestone cliffs and outcroppings, there are also many rock-climbing gyms, walls and outdoor bouldering parks – all the better to hone the skills for when you're ready to get serious. All the gyms offer instruction, and plenty of outfitters offer intensive multiday clinics for newbies and those wishing to refine their skills.

Where to Rock Climb

Around Boulder

Boulder's sticky Flatirons offer scores of classic routes. In fact, there are 1145 rock-climbing routes in the Boulder area, with the majority found in the Flatirons (with walls up to 900ft tall), Boulder Canyon and Eldorado Canyon (a spectacular site with dozens of 700ft climbs).

Northern Mountains

There are approximately 44 climbing routes in Rocky Mountain National Park (p131). Buena Vista (p217) has great climbing at Elephant Rock and Bob's Rock off Tunnels Rd, and they have foam-core bouldering in their riverside park.

Central Mountains

Camp Hale (p212) offers 22 climbing routes graded from 5.9 to 5.11c, and Independence Pass has 60 routes, including the intense bulge that is Bulldog Balcony.

Southwest Colorado

Durango (p275) and Ouray are the stars of southwestern Colorado. Ouray Ice Park is a narrow slot canyon with 200ft walls and waterfalls frozen in thick sheets – perfect for ice climbing. Colorado National Monument (p243) near Grand Junction has superb climbing in Unaweep Canyon and Monument Canyon, and you can climb in Black Canyon of the Gunnison National Park (p252).

Southeast Colorado

All the best climbing in southern Colorado can be found on the limestone cliffs and pinnacles along Shelf Rd, near where the state's best early dinosaur finds were discovered. The Gallery, the Bank and the

North End are the best sites. Colorado Springs has a strict permit process for its top climbing destinations: Garden of the Gods (p321) and Red Rock Canyon (p326).

There are dozens of high-country routes here, too, if you would rather scale than hike up a 14er. Longs Peak, Quandary Peak, Pikes Peak, Mount of the Holy Cross, the Maroon Bells, Castle Peak and Snowmass Mountain are among the 14,000ft peaks with known climbing routes. And if you're in Telluride, consider the 13,113ft Lizard Head, a popular climb in its own right.

Mountaineering

Unless you plan on tackling one of the estimated 161 technical high-altitude rock-climbing routes, mountaineering isn't necessary to bag peaks in Colorado. However, intrepid mountaineers may wish to summit the 14ers in the winter, a highly technical pursuit that requires training and proper gear (usually ice axe, crampons, snowshoes and trekking poles), not to mention cold-weather clothing. Cold climes can exacerbate the effects of altitude sickness, and avalanches are a serious concern here.

But if you're hell-bent on bagging icy peaks, you may as well go for Mt Elbert (p213) – Colorado's highest peak is one of the least technical and avalanche prone in winter. Longs Peak and Pikes Peak (p321) are also popular and reasonably low-risk (though that can change in a blink) winter climbs. The Maroon Bells (p208), on the other hand, are as risky and technical as Colorado mountaineering gets. **Summit Post** (www.summitpost.org) is a solid online resource with basic climbing route information, but proper maps and consultation with local ranger districts are a must, and guide services are always a good idea. It's recommended to climb with a beacon, and to never go out alone.

Paddling & Tubing

Colorado is one of the great paddling destinations, with a long white-water season lasting from late May until September. Everything from class II float trips to a raging class V can be yours on five rivers. The Arkansas River is the most paddled body of water, with 150 miles of open water running from Leadville to the Royal Gorge. The best Arkansas paddling happens in June and July. July is also a terrific time to move from group rafting trips into your own kayak.

You can take lessons in the urban Denver climes, but the Rocky Mountain Outdoor Center in Salida has better scenery. The class III Blue River runs through Breckenridge in the heart of Summit County in the early season. Vail's Eagle River is a nice high-country early-season run, while the class V Gore Canyon is so big it's not even open to paddlers until late season. The Dolores River in southwest Colorado threads through the San Juan mountains past Anasazi ruins and petroglyphs.

White-water parks are *de rigueur* for municipalities throughout the state, including relatively new parks in Boulder, Denver, Fort Collins, Buena Vista and Cañon City. But you don't have to slip into a hull to get wet. Tubing is a popular summer pastime on Boulder Creek, on the Poudre River in Fort Collins, on the Yampa in Steamboat and in Pagosa Springs, and you can run the Arkansas River in Cañon City in a tube or boogie board.

Rocky Mountain Road Trips

Driving Distances

Cottonwood Pass
60 miles

Top of the Rockies
115 miles

Independence Pass
27.2 miles

Collegiate Peaks
57 miles

Trail Ridge Rd
47 miles

San Juan Skyway
236 miles

Gold Belt Tour
131 miles

Pikes Peak Hwy
38 miles

West Elk Loop
205 miles

Peak to Peak Hwy
55 miles

Highway of Legends
110 miles

Trail of the Ancients
480 miles

Santa Fe Trail
188 miles

Colorado has 25 nationally designated Scenic & Historic Byways, and a number of mind-blowing drives that didn't make the official list, but should definitely make yours. Some will take all day and have you discussing the blows of history and time; others are short hops to lonely mountain passes that are sure to leave you speechless and smiling.

Cottonwood Pass

60 MILES

Cottonwood Pass Rd (p218) alternates between asphalt and graded gravel (those sections are few and far between) as it winds its way for 60 miles from the quaint and, dare we say, damn cute prison town (and paddler paradise) of Buena Vista to the fly-fishing mecca of Almont.

In Buena Vista (p217), W Main St becomes Cottonwood Pass Rd. It swerves past beaver ponds along Cottonwood Creek, and skirts Cottonwood Hot Springs (p218) in the San Isabel National Forest. On the east side of the road is a turnoff to the Avalanche Trailhead, a spur of the Colorado Trail with access to spectacular Collegiate Peaks Wilderness (p217). Indeed, there is no shortage of hiking options here, as the road goes from moderately sinuous to downright jagged as you approach the edge of the timber line. To the east the Collegiate Peaks lay out against the blue sky as you drive through boulder field moonscape. It's just spectacular country.

Bring a picnic and take a long lunch at the pass before dropping into the Gunnison National Forest and down through the Taylor River Canyon to Almont, where the Taylor and East Rivers form the mighty Gunnison. And if you've forgotten your rod and reel, check into the Almont Resort. They'll sort you out.

Worth a Stop

Before leaving Buena Vista, make sure you check out Tunnels Rd (p218) and Bob's Rock.

Top of the Rockies

115 MILES

You'll cross three mountain passes, drop into four watersheds and glimpse Colorado's tallest peaks, as well as the headwaters of the Arkansas River. Not bad for a day's drive.

Historic Leadville (p212), the highest incorporated city in the US, which made its name and plenty of cash in the silver boom, is the hub of this drive, which can be done in two phases. After a wander through the National Historic District (check out the Delaware Hotel) and a stop at the Burrito Bus, where you can find authentic Mexican food for a change, head north from town on Hwy 91 over Fremont Pass before meeting up with I-70 west of Frisco.

Take the Interstate past Vail to Hwy 24, where if you time it right you can have a stroll through a terrific farmers market in downtown Minturn (p210), drive through tiny Red Cliff, pay homage to the 10th Mountain Division, and perhaps get some stellar rock climbing in at Camp Hale (p212), before swerving up and over Tennessee Pass where Mt Massive looms supreme as you drive south through Leadville.

Further south, Mt Elbert dominates the horizon. Hang a right on Hwy 82 and head up to Twin Lakes, a historic mining town with some ruins on the lake shore, three inns, spectacular mountain and lake views and countless stars. Bed down here or drive up and over Independence Pass and into Aspen.

Detour

If you've had 14ers on the brain, why not climb one of the the state's two tallest peaks? Trailheads for both Mt Elbert (p213) and Mt Massive (p213) are easily accessible from this route.

Independence Pass

27.2 MILES

If you don't have time to drive the entire Top of the Rockies route, this stretch of Hwy 82 from Twin Lakes through Aspen's back gate will do just fine. Twin Lakes (p215) is a worthy destination in its own right. This 'town' (and to call it a town is a bit of a stretch) started life as a mining camp fed by steady stage-coach lines plying the trail between Leadville and Aspen. You'll see plenty of old mining ruins.

Although the pass is closed in the winter time, you should be able to get up to the vast Twin Lakes, where the cross-country skiing, snowshoeing and ice-skating (yes, you can skate on the lakes) is magnificent. And if the pass is open, drive up a narrow ribbon of road above tree line where the views are cinematic and spectacular – swatches of glacier are visible along the ridges of Twin Peaks. And tundra blooms at the top of the pass, where at 12,095ft you'll be on the edge of the Continental Divide. This, friends, is your own IMAX film.

If you're here late in the season, you'll see camo-clad hunters, last-gasp family vacationers, Harley men and women and their hogs with bedrolls on the tailgate, and million-dollar road cyclists with shaved legs and iPhones in their saddle bags. As Hwy 82 continues over the pass the views are just as marvelous, and multimillion-dollar properties begin to dot the landscape as you edge toward Aspen. One of them belongs to Kevin Costner.

Detour

If you have time, there's a terrific trail to the Interlaken (p215), an old abandoned hotel fashionable in the 1890s. The trail leaves from the lower of the Twin Lakes.

Collegiate Peaks

57 MILES

The Collegiate Peaks Byway begins where the Top of the Rockies route ends, at Twin Lakes on Hwy 82, just below Independence Pass. Expect stark and soaring granite cliffs, multiple 14,000ft peaks, geothermal hot springs, the powerful Arkansas River and a bit of ghost town history, too.

If you haven't yet explored the mining camp ruins at Twin Lakes (p215), they're worth a look before you get on the road and head east on Hwy 82 to Hwy 24 South. Mt Yale will be the first of the Collegiate

Peaks, part of the Sawatch Range, to reveal itself as you head into Buena Vista (p217), a town that is absolutely worth your time. Ostensibly it's a prison town, but it's also recently become a magnet for groovy entrepreneurs who have opened restaurants, cafés, coffee roasters and even a yoga studio. There's rock climbing and plenty of paddling accessible from Main St, and even some spectacular free campsites on Tunnels Rd.

From here the official byway advises you to stay on Hwy 24 out of town. We beg to differ: instead, drive west on Co Rd 306 from the center of town for 0.7 miles. Turn left on Co Rd 321 and continue south for 7.2 miles. Turn right onto Co Rd 322, drive 0.8 miles to a fork in the road. Bear right and you'll be on Mt Princeton Rd, which will take you to the sprawling Mt Princeton Hot Springs (p217), at the base of magnificent Mt Princeton. Whether you choose to dip into the hot water by the river or scramble up to the peak is a question only you can answer.

You could also continue from the gates of the resort up Co Rd 162 to St Elmo (p220), an old abandoned gold-mining town. The road narrows as it runs further up the canyon, with the river flowing by and towering mountains laid out on both sides. The remaining buildings were built in and around 1881.

From St Elmo make your way south again toward Hwy 285, and the historic districts of Poncha Springs and Salida, which is also the gateway to the wild and scenic Arkansas River. From there, there is 99 miles of Arkansas River paddling all the way to the Royal Gorge. Salida is also a great place to slip into a kayak for the first time.

Worth a Stop

On the way back to the Mt Princeton resort from St Elmo, you'll see the Love Meadow on your right. Once a pioneer homestead belonging to an impressive woman widowed in her youth, it's now a small and dramatically beautiful wildlife sanctuary.

Trail Ridge Rd

47 MILES

The signature drive in Rocky Mountain National Park, Trail Ridge Rd (US 34) over the Continental Divide was once a highway of a different sort – a trade route used by generations of Ute, Arapaho and Apache

people to traverse Milner Pass. Of course, even the 19th century seems modern when you consider that archaeological evidence collected here suggests that humans have been traversing this pass for 6000 years. Which begs the questions, how old is this Milner guy and how many languages does he speak?

Originally surveyed in 1927 and not completed until 1932, Trail Ridge Rd opens in late May and is closed at Many Parks Curve on the east side by mid-October. This is the highest continuously paved through road in North America, so expect outrageous views. On the drive from Estes Park to Grand Lake, you'll see snowcapped peaks, meandering streams, high-country meadows dotted with wildflowers in midsummer, and, with luck, some wildlife too.

It's a well-traveled route, so consider including a backcountry hike along the way. You're more likely to see dramatic snowy scenery in May, when the pass first opens.

Worth a Stop

Before driving into the park, stop by the Stanley Hotel (p140) in Estes Park, the inspiration for Stephen King's *The Shining*.

Detour

Consider a 9-mile detour up the original Fall River Road, where you're likely to spot elk outside the Alpine Visitor Center (p136).

San Juan Skyway

236 MILES

Cruise along the San Juan Skyway in late September or early October, when the aspen trees glow and there's a hint of snow and pine in the crisp air, and you'll feel your stress drift right out the window. The tension of the daily grind gets lost somewhere among the towering peaks, picturesque towns and old mines around each bend, or evaporates in the bright sun in an intensely blue Colorado sky.

Driving the 236 miles of the San Juan Skyway is the best way to experience the drama of the San Juan range without strapping on your boots. The route is circular, including the so-called Million Dollar Hwy, a handful of the region's coolest mountain towns and Mesa Verde National Park (p289).

The climb on Hwys 62 and 145 skirts the biggest of the San Juans before you enter Telluride (p264), preferably in time

ROAD MUSIC

Music has never been more personal, accessible and transportable. Almost everyone has the perfect song for the perfect moment, and can have it cued up and ready to go. But given the unique mix of asphalt and gravel, mountain, grassland and desert canyon that you're likely to greet on the Colorado highways, we offer the following suggestions...

» **Aspen-inspired** Bounce between violinist Sarah Chang, African banjo legend Béla Fleck, and fusion bands Pink Martini and Calexico, all recent performers at the Aspen Music Festival and Jazz Aspen Snowmass.

» **Wille Nelson** The country legend wrote the songs on *Red Headed Stranger*, arguably his greatest record, while on a road trip through Colorado in 1975. It's as indigenous to this rugged country as the aspens themselves.

» **Bluegrass** With multiple bluegrass festivals in the state, including the biggie in Telluride, you must have fiddler and singer-songwriter Alison Krauss, and guitarist and singer-songwriter Gillian Welch on the shortlist.

» **Hippie spillover** With hippie, earthy roots running deep in Colorado (think: Boulder, Telluride, Manitou Springs), you must have hippie band of the moment, Edward Sharpe & the Magnetic Zeroes, ready to roll. They played triumphant and sold-out shows in Denver, Boulder and the Telluride Bluegrass Festival in 2010.

for some morning thrills on the slopes of the ski resort. If you're traveling in summer, just climb on a mountain bike instead of the skis – just as fun and *way* cheaper. Grab lunch at The Butcher & The Baker and enjoy a bit more of the hills before pointing the car south for Cortez (p296), where you should follow dinner at Peppercorn with a rowdy session of cheap beer and live rock at Blondie's.

Take a ranger-guided tour of the Cliff Palace in Mesa Verde National Park, before you hit the road for Durango (p275). Depart on the Durango & Silverton Narrow Gauge Railroad for a fascinating trip into the mineral-rich heart of the mountains.

Now you choose your own adventure: either continue north along the Million Dollar Hwy to Ouray to end the San Juan Skyway loop, or head east to catch a surreal sunset over at Great Sand Dunes National Park (p307).

Gold Belt Tour

131 MILES

This wasn't the state's first golden vein, but between 1891 and 2005 (yes, the golden days did last that long) more than 23.5 million ounces of gold were pulled from this mountain corridor. That's more gold than was ever found during the California and Alaska gold rushes combined! So, yes, this route takes in some of the old mining

haunts, but it also includes quirkier sights, such as petrified tree stumps (they're cooler than you think), a Royal Gorge, dinosaur footprints and an up-and-coming gallery district. In between you'll glimpse a long and wide mountain plateau that has all the country romance of a Willie Nelson tune on a sunny day with the windows down.

This drive is best accessed from Colorado Springs, where you'll take Hwy 24 past Pikes Peak (p321) and Manitou Springs into the high country, where you'll find Florissant Fossil Beds National Monument (p331). The entire area was once buried beneath ancient volcanic ash. The nature trail leads past sequoia-sized petrified stumps, and the surrounding countryside is special, too. While you're here consider stopping by the 1878 homestead, the Hornbeck House.

Most of the gold was mined in the twin cities of Cripple Creek and Victor. Both have seen better days. Cripple Creek is now a low-rent gambling destination with a strip mine still active above town, but the Cripple Creek & Victor Narrow Gauge Railroad is a treat. This 45-minute tour leads to Victor and back and includes many an old mining yarn. The views are marvelous. Cripple Creek also offers tours through an actual underground mine and a unique jailhouse museum.

From here you can travel south through the high-country meadows ringed with mountains along High Park Rd, which leads to Hwy 50, and the incredible Royal Gorge. The Royal Gorge Bridge & Park (p334) has historic kitsch and incredibly impressive views from the aerial tram, incline railway and that adrenaline-addled Skycoaster. Or you could take the slow journey along the graded Shelf Rd, a one-time stagecoach route. There is some fantastic rock climbing in the area, and it's also where you'll find the Garden Park Fossil Area (p334), which once gave the world five new dinosaur species. Cañon City has some charm in its own right, along with easily arranged raft and train tours of the the gorge.

Detour

Not far from Cañon City, Florence should not be missed. It's blossoming with vintage, antique and found-art galleries, and there's a fabulous Florence Rose here, too. You can take the scenic Phantom Canyon Rd directly from Victor to Florence.

Pikes Peak Hwy

38 MILES

You can thank eccentric tycoon Spencer Penrose for this luscious ribbon of surprisingly sound asphalt that winds up and up and up to the tippy (flat) top of Pikes Peak (p321). On clear days you can look down on four states.

First you'll skirt knife-edge drops into the valley below as Manitou Springs and Old Colorado City become scattered specks in the distance, then you'll roll through thick stands of pine and cedar and finally scree fields. The road is open most of the year, though it's sometimes closed during the winter. After Penrose built the road, he christened it with the first ever Pikes Peak International Hill Climb (p327). The race still runs.

Before you embark on your journey make sure your brakes and tires are sound, and remember that at altitude your car will have about half the horsepower it usually does. When driving back down, do so in a low gear. Access to the Pikes Peak Hwy, also known as Pikes Peak Toll Rd, is off Hwy 24 in Manitou Springs, which is a fine place to have lunch, stroll and shop afterwards. This is one of two toll roads (Trail Ridge Rd is

the other) and costs $40 per car (up to five people).

Detour

After you get back into the flats, stop for a drink at the Broadmoor, where you can experience Penrose's game-changing resort and one of the earliest tourist draws to Colorado.

West Elk Loop

205 MILES

This gorgeous six- to eight-hour lasso is pinned down by the twin summits of Mount Sopris on one end and the spectacular Black Canyon of the Gunnison on the other. And in between are historic gold-mining towns, two mountain passes, a top-shelf ski area and (if you drive to the end of the rope) a destination farm-to-table restaurant in up and coming Carbondale.

Redstone is famous for its coke ovens used to process coal, and its historic downtown is a pleasant stroll, too. From here you'll navigate McClure Pass through 35 miles of stunning mountain scenery before descending along the North Fork River into Paonia (p262), a quirky town with the Grand Mesa on one side, Mount Lamborn on the other, a coal mine and a green streak. The Victorian buildings in downtown's 10-block historic district are as cool as the locals.

Head south from here and you'll see the stark, spectacular Black Canyon of the Gunnison National Park (p252), a 2000ft-deep gorge with outstanding hiking trails and rock climbing. From here the route follows Hwy 50 east to Gunnison from where you'll loop around on Hwy 135 into Crested Butte (p259), a town surrounded by wildflowers in springtime (it's been dubbed the wildflower capital of Colorado) with a restored Victorian core and that looming Crested Butte Mountain, a special ski destination. Next, wind through Kebler Pass and back to Carbondale (p242), where you're table at Six89 will be waiting.

Detour

If Crested Butte sucks you in, overnight at Inn at Crested Butte (p261) and wake up early the next day for a hike into the nearby Maroon Bells-Snowmass Wilderness Area, one of the most dramatically beautiful wilderness areas in all of Colorado.

Peak to Peak Hwy

55 MILES

The particular magic of driving the Peak to Peak Hwy – one of Colorado's most scenic drives and an excellent option for the trip between Rocky Mountain National Park and Denver – depends largely on the time of year you hit the road. In summer wind the windows down and watch big cumulus clouds rolling lazily over the green and granite peaks. In fall, the aspens set the hills afire with a show of gold, orange and red, while winter brings a stark landscape and pristine white-snow plains.

Stretching some 40 miles between Nederland and Estes Park, this north–south route takes you past a series of breathtaking mountains, including the 14,255ft Longs Peak, alpine valleys and open meadows, passing a number of one-horse towns along the way. These include Ward, a former boom town and bohemian magnet that has settled into an artfully ramshackle state of disrepair; Peaceful Valley, notable for its little onion-domed church perched on a hillside; and several other tiny towns with expansive mountain vistas.

There are national forest campgrounds near Peaceful Valley and Allenspark, as well as the Longs Peak Campground (p135), part of Rocky Mountain National Park. There are also places to stay in Peaceful Valley, Ferncliff, Allenspark and south of Estes Park, mostly in the form of lodges, cabins and B&Bs; prices range from $60 to $100.

At the southern end of the trip, the Peak to Peak Hwy starts from Nederland (p144), which has a couple of great dining options. Although most of the route – everything north of Allenspark – follows Hwy 7, at Nederland it follows Hwy 72.

Detour

To stretch your legs along the way, take the road opposite the turnoff for Ward that leads up to Brainard Lake. The lake itself is small but enjoys a gorgeous setting and several great trails. If hiking around here works up your appetite, stop in at the Millsite Inn, just north of the turnoff to Ward. The food is nothing special, but it's an interesting place for a bite to eat or a beer, with plenty of local color – some of it in the form of a local rock band who appear to have just arrived in a time machine from 1971.

Highway of Legends

110 MILES

This brief but epic detour liberates you from the Interstate and escorts you through some of Colorado's most glorious countryside as you head north toward Pueblo, Colorado Springs or Denver on I-25. Or maybe you're already privy to the majesty of the Spanish Peaks Wilderness (p337), in which case: welcome home.

Your trip begins in Trinidad (p338), where present-day Main St was once an important limb of the Santa Fe Trail. The Trinidad History Museum offers a primer, and while you're in town drop into Danielson Dry Goods for some road sustenance. Coal mining was also an important part of Trinidad's history. You'll see a 'canary in the coal mine' statue on Main St, which is where Mother Jones once marched with miners during the strike that led to the Ludlow Massacre, a turning point in US labor relations.

From Trinidad take Hwy 12 through Cokedale, where you'll see 350 coal ovens on the roadside (they look almost Roman), then head up and over majestic Cucharas Pass and into Cuchara (p337).

You'll need to take a deep breath, because this place is magic. It's dominated by extinct volcanoes, the Spanish Peaks, and defined by the Great Dikes that jut and sprawl across meadows and onto the shoulders of the great mountains. The rambling Cucharas River has terrific fishing, the Dog Bar & Grill serves tasty pizza and occasional live music, and the hiking in the Spanish Peaks Wilderness is some of the best in the state. You can extend the nature bliss by veering east on a recently added extension to the byway.

Co Rd 46 weaves through the San Isabel National Forest for 35 miles to Aguilar on the I-25, but we suggest staying on Hwy 12, which continues down the valley and into exceptionally cute La Veta, where there are more churches than paved roads, and the Spanish Peaks make for a spectacular backdrop as you check into historic 1899 Inn.

Worth a Stop

On your way down Hwy 12 from La Veta toward the I-25, stop at the excellent mining museum (p337) in Walsenberg before heading north.

Trail of the Ancients

480 MILES

A homage to the indigenous people who once walked gently through the canyons, mountains and plains of Colorado, and who developed complex and highly evolved cultures that understood the interconnectivity of all things, our longest road trip connects Mesa Verde with Canyon of the Ancients and Hovenweep National Monuments, and also wanders down to the Four Corners state boundaries.

Mesa Verde National Park (p289) is not only the starting point for the drive, but in many ways it's also the deepest sight on the itinerary. There are more than 5000 archaelogical sites within the 52,073-acre national park, of which 600 are Ancestral Pueblano cliff dwellings. The Ancestral Pueblano are believed to have lived here for 750 years.

Access to the park is possible only with the accompaniment of a Ute guide. Half-and full-day tours can include visits to their adjacent reservation. In addition to the cliff dwellings, original pottery is prevalent; you may even see shards along the trails. Take Hwy 491 north from Mesa Verde and you'll drive through a windswept high desert landscape of cracked red earth, coyotes and sage brush to Dolores.

Stop at the Anasazi Heritage Center (p298), where you can peruse more ancient artifacts, including pottery from AD 400, before visiting Canyon of the Ancients and Hovenweep National Monument, both of which are Ancestral Pueblano treasures that have been largely left alone for hundreds of years. You can almost hear spirit guide whispers on the wind.

Another branch of the byway leads southwest from Mesa Verde on Hwy 491 and then Hwy 160 to the actual Four Corners state boundaries.

Detour

From the state line you can continue your journey on Utah's Trail of the Ancients Byway or head to other Ancestral Pueblano treasures such Chaco Canyon in New Mexico or Canyon De Chelly in Arizona.

Santa Fe Trail

188 MILES (EACH WAY)

History buffs will love this day-long spin through southeastern Colorado. Although the official byway follows the original trail for 188 miles from the Kansas border into Trinidad, you can cut the route down to its best bits and make it a fun four-hour journey.

An endless prairie unfurls on both sides of the open two-lane highway as you take Hwy 350 northeast of Trinidad to La Junta. The scenery is all grasslands and wheat fields, sugar-beet farms, horse corrals and railroad yards. One of the best parts of driving the Santa Fe trail is this countryside.

The signature sight is Bent's Old Fort National Historic Site (p341). Set just north of the Arkansas River – the natural and official border between the US and Old Mexico until 1846 – it was once a cultural crossroads. From 1833 to 1849 Native Americans, Mexicans and Americans with gold-rush dreams met, mingled, traded, danced and clashed here. The well-restored adobe fort has a blacksmith's shop, wood shop and fully stocked general store. The knowledgeable staff in period clothing lead tours, and a roughly 1-mile trail runs around the fort to the edge of the Arkansas River and back to the parking lot.

Kit Carson is probably the most famous of the Old West characters who frequented the fort, but his last base of operations and final resting place is about 16 miles east of here in Boggsville (p341). If time is short, you could ignore Boggsville, turn back at the fort, and head west again into more history.

You'll want to stop at Iron Spring (p342), where you can see authentic Santa Fe Trail wagon ruts and, if daylight is on your side and you've made an advance reservation, you can drive to the famed Picketwire Dinosaur Tracksite (p342), where dinosaur footprints are frozen in time. Both sites are in the Comanche National Grassland.

When the Santa Fe Trail brings you back to Main St in Trinidad, don't forget to stop at the fabulous Trinidad History Museum (p339) to round out the journey.

Detour

If you have time there are two sites further east of Bent's Old Fort that shed light on America's dark side. Westward expansion made America, but it meant misery for many. The Sand Creek Massacre National Historic Site (p342), just off the Santa Fe Trail north of Lamar, was a pivotal point in US–Native American relations – an estimated 163 of Chief Black Kettle's Cheyenne people were massacred here by Colorado Volunteers, in compliance with the then recently indoctrinated American law. The event ended the Indian Wars and paved the way for further white settlement in Colorado and beyond.

South of Lamar are the ruins of Camp Amache, a World War II Japanese internment camp.

Travel with Children

Best Regions for Kids

Denver
Museums, family attractions and plenty of parks and wide open spaces.

Boulder
Outdoor exploration is the big-ticket option.

Central Mountains
Every ski resort offers lessons catering to the next generation of snow lovers.

Northern Mountains
Why not start the outdoor adventure at Rocky Mountain National Park? Avoid the crowds if you can.

Northwest Colorado
Kids can become junior rangers and paleontologists at Dinosaur National Monument – and they can touch fossils!

Southwest Colorado
Family-friendly rafting and hiking abound, plus there's an incredibly scenic train ride and low-key skiing.

San Luis Valley
Great Sand Dunes National Park is unlike any other Colorado park. The Monteville Nature Trail is a good family-friendly hike.

Eastern Colorado
The Garden of the Gods is the main attraction, and Colorado Springs and its surrounds have plenty of kid-friendly activities.

Amazing vistas and mountainsides, ghost towns, hands-on museum exhibits and interactive art spaces, river-rafting, and some of the best family-friendly skiing and biking facilities in the US: all this makes traveling families spoilt for options in Colorado. Add to that the endless blue skies and fresh air, archaeological ruins, long hikes and horseback-riding trails, and you'll find that kids seem somehow less interested in their gaming consoles, cell phones and iPods.

Colorado for Kids

In Colorado's main cities junior travelers should head for the many hands-on science museums, playgrounds, theme parks and family fun centers, not to mention the main attraction of wide open spaces.

Denver, despite being the state capital, sets the tone as a truly outdoorsy city, with miles of cycling and walking trails, riverside parks and gardens, and outdoor events and theme parks. Indoors, the kids can roam the excellent museums and galleries. The rest of the state offers much more of the same as well as historic railroads to ride, canyons and peaks to climb, and old Western towns to explore.

Most national and state parks aim at least some exhibits, trails and programs toward families with kids. Kids and families can join organized wildlife-spotting tours in the parks and reserves, or hook a trout in a tumbling mountain river. Tubing and rafting on some of these rivers is as exhilarating for kids as it is for parents, and camping and hiking in the wilderness areas are always popular.

Children's Highlights
Festivals & Events

» Boulder Creek Hometown Fair – A more manageable version of the Boulder Creek Fair

» Cherry Creek Arts Festival – Three days of food, fun and arts

» Great Fruitcake Toss – The cake that flies the furthest wins!

» Lights of December – A classic Christmas parade

» Strawberry Days – Glenwood Springs' civic festival is one of the longest-running in the state.

Indoor Options

» Buell Children's Museum – Classic cars, bridges, jellyfish, fairy lands...

» Buffalo Bill Museum & Grave – For the young cowboys and cowgirls

» CU Wizards – Monthly science shows at Boulder's university

» Denver Children's Museum – Engaging exhibits and activities

» Denver Firefighters Museum – Interactive displays that make fire safety fun

» Denver Museum of Nature & Science – The IMAX Theater and Planetarium are always a hit

» Manitou Penny Arcade – Introduce the next generation to the last generation's games

» Rocky Mountain Dinosaur Museum – Watch lab techs assemble casts and clean fossils.

Dude Ranches

» Harmel's Dude Ranch – On the banks of the Gunnison River; fly-fishing, white-water rafting and horseback riding

» Drowsy Water Ranch – Horseback riding and home cooking with accommodations in western-themed cabins

» Blue Lake Ranch – An angling-family's paradise

» Echo Basin Ranch – Basic, affordable and offers the whole gamut of ranch experiences

» Beaver Meadows Resort Ranch – Horseback riding, rafting, fishing and hiking activities

» Vista Verde Guest Ranch – The most luxurious experience

» Yellow Pine Guest Ranch – Terrific accommodations in deluxe log cabins

Planning

Perhaps the most difficult part of a family trip to this region will be deciding where to go, and avoiding the temptation to squeeze in too much. Distances are deceptive, and any single corner of Colorado could easily fill a two-week family vacation.

Choose a handful of primary destinations to serve as the backbone of your trip. Connect these dots with a flexible driving plan that includes potential stops. Book rooms at the major destinations and make advance reservations for horseback rides, rafting trips, scenic train rides and educational programs or camps (particularly if you're traveling in peak season), but allow a couple of days between each to follow your fancy.

A few days in the small mountain towns can rejuvenate the bodies and spirits of even the most time-poor family. Small-town festivals, rodeos and state fairs can be an excellent umbrella under which to plan your trip.

Outdoors

For more outdoor advice, read *Kids in the Wild: A Family Guide to Outdoor Recreation* by Cindy Ross and Todd Gladfelter, and Alice Cary's *Parents' Guide to Hiking & Camping*. For all-around information and advice, check out *Lonely Planet's Travel with Children*.

Websites

» Family Travel Colorado (www.familytravelcolorado.com)

» Family Travel Files (www.thefamilytravelfiles.com)

» Go City Kids (www.gocitykids.parentsconnect.com)

» Kids Can Travel (www.kidscantravel.com)

» Kids Go Too (www.kidsgotootravel.com)

» Kids.gov (www.kids.gov)

regions at a glance

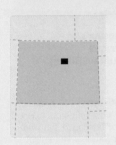

Denver

Outdoors ✓✓✓
Local Food & Beer ✓✓
Seeing a Game ✓✓

Rocky Mountains
There's a certain irony to the fact that so many Denver residents take such pride in how easy it is to get *out* of their city; for all the vibrant urban culture, Denver's most winning feature is as a staging area for the majestic Rockies. In an afternoon's drive you can fly fish streams in Front Range, mount a 14,000ft peak or ski a double black diamond run. Welcome to Denver – now get out!

Food & Beer
Sure, go ahead and order the Rocky Mountain Oysters, but bull balls are only the beginning of the culinary thrills. Those who leave the fancy-burger bore of the 16th Street Mall for adventuresome dining districts like the Highlands and South Broadway will be deliciously rewarded. And beer? Forget about watery Coors; Denver's inspired brewers have made the city a beer drinker's nirvana.

Museums
Though heavy hitters like the Denver Art Museum (p59), the Museum of Nature & Science (p62) and the US Mint (p61) get the monstrous crowds, they're only the beginning of the city's clutch of wildly varied, family-friendly exhibits. From the Black American West Museum (p61) to the Molly Brown House (p60), if you can't find something of interest, check your pulse. They are, by far, the best in the West.

Boulder

Hiking ✓✓
Cycling ✓✓
Nightlife ✓✓

Hiking
Of the hundreds of miles of hiking trails within an hour's drive of Boulder, most folks start with the Chautauqua Park trails. However, you can access stunning high alpine country from trails in nearby Nederland. Long's Peak, the closest 14er, is just a (long) day trip away.

Cycling
Pedals are pushed by the shaved and unshaven on the flat creekside path, up and over lung-crushing passes and onto burly single-track trails built for full-suspension mountain bikes.

Live Music
It never hurts the nightlife when more than 30,000 students call a place home. Promoters continue to bring the bands and DJs to Boulder. Whether it's big-time jazz, up-and-coming progressive rock or world-music greats, Boulder don't skimp on live music.

p104

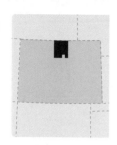

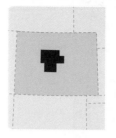

Northern Mountains

National Parks ✓✓✓
Camping ✓✓
Mountain Drives ✓✓

Vail, Aspen & Central Mountains

Snow ✓✓✓
Hiking ✓✓✓
Paddling ✓✓✓

Northwest Colorado

Dinosaurs ✓✓
Canyons ✓✓✓
Mountain Biking ✓✓

Rocky Mountain National Park
During busy summers, the Rocky Mountain National Park can seem like an amusement park without the rollercoasters. But even when it's jammed, the jaw-dropping beauty is still worth the trouble. With a dollop of effort you can blaze your own trail and find solitude in this vast and stunning alpine wilderness.

Camping
From RV parks with wi-fi to the remote and rustic backcountry, this piece of the state has an amazing variety of camping. The four-star experience can't hold a candle to the smell of woodsmoke, the bite of fresh mountain air and the ceiling of stars.

Mountain Drives
Navigate the winding pavement through the region for stunning views: red canyons, snow capped peaks and elk and mountain sheep.

p130

Skiing & Snowboarding
From the glamour of Aspen and Vail to historic Breckenridge and the stripped-down clarity of Arapahoe Basin and Loveland, you'll find more powdery tree runs, extreme terrain parks, back bowls, cross-country paths and *après-ski* parties within a couple of hours' drive than seems reasonable.

Hiking
Over a thousand miles of trails lead to secluded grottos and waterfalls, swimming holes and hot springs, wind over high-mountain passes with epic, if lonely, Continental Divide views, or hike to the summit of one of Colorado's 53 14,000ft-plus peaks.

Paddling
While the most rugged stretches of river accessible here have their equals elsewhere, there isn't a single other place that you can access four rivers offering epic paddling from the early season (late May) until early September.

p155

Dinosaurs
The whole of Colorado is a big ol' bone yard, but Dinosaur National Monument allows armchair palaeontologists to walk among nearly whole skeletons of the largest animals ever to walk on earth – eerily frozen in rock.

Canyons
Elegant formations of red rock are lovely from the rim, but hiking in and around Colorado National Monument or, better yet, sleeping at the bottom of one of the canyons gives visitors a chance to commune with magnificent geology.

Mountain Biking
If you like to rumble down a tight single track, you can hardly go wrong – with excellent biking in the desert and the Rockies, this part of the state has some of the best, and most wildly diverse, riding in the state.

p222

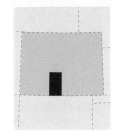

Southwest Colorado

National Parks ✓✓✓
Historic Towns ✓✓✓
Skiing ✓✓

National Parks

It's difficult to decide which of the two wildly different national parks is more stunning. The cliff dwellings of Mesa Verde offer a walk through the region's mysterious ancient residents. Black Canyon of the Gunnison is menacingly steep, and a gash in the crust of the earth that rewards those brave enough to descend to the bottom.

Historic Towns

Silver mining left this region dotted with charming historic villages, where you can get a whiff of the history by strolling past bullet-pocked storefronts of the Wild West or chugging through scenic mountain passes on a narrow-gauge rail.

Pristine Skiing

Telluride may be Colorado's most remote ski destination, but it's the least overdeveloped, allowing visitors to carve down the steep slopes with huge views of the western San Juan Mountains.

p250

San Luis Valley

National Parks ✓✓
Hiking ✓✓
Rock Climbing ✓✓

Great Sand Dunes National Park

Sand dunes and snow-capped peaks, shimmering wetlands and expansive ranch land – the nation's newest national park is like looking at nature's jigsaw puzzle all scrambled up. It's startling, bizarre and the best reason to visit the San Luis Valley.

Hiking

Somehow the sights from the high trails of the rugged Sangre de Christo Range are even more dramatic than the name (Blood of Christ). Untrodden by the crowds who trample Colorado's northern Rockies, this is a place with all the beauty and twice the solitude.

Rock Climbing

With climbing that suits every skill level, and red-rock formations with a history of housing religious cults, this area has the potential to forever ruin the rock gym.

p302

Eastern Colorado

History ✓✓✓
Hiking ✓✓✓
Paddling ✓✓

History

Everywhere you look American history glints its migratory, gold mining, war-dancing, mountain-conquering eye at you. Colorado Springs is home to the state's first settlement, the Overland Trail brought some 350,000 folk from eastern and southern states, and the Santa Fe Trail passes many a historic site.

Hiking

It's true there aren't as many options in the east, but what is here must not be ignored. The big options include hiking to Pikes Peak, exploring the red-rock vein from the Garden of the Gods to Red Rock Canyon, and the solitude of the Spanish Peaks Wilderness.

Paddling

The Arkansas River barrels between the majestic rock walls of the Royal Gorge. This is the signature, set-piece trip on the most paddled river in Colorado.

p320

Look out for these icons:

 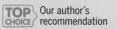 Our author's recommendation

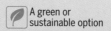 A green or sustainable option

 No payment required

DENVER & AROUND 54
DENVER. 56
AROUND DENVER. 95
Golden 95
Mt Evans 98
Idaho Springs & Georgetown. 99
St Mary's Glacier 100
Empire 101
Denver Mountain Parks & Platte River 101

BOULDER. 104

ROCKY MOUNTAIN NATIONAL PARK & NORTHERN MOUNTAINS 130
ROCKY MOUNTAIN NATIONAL PARK 131
ESTES PARK 137
AROUND ESTES PARK . . . 143
Glen Haven 143
NEDERLAND. 144
ELDORA SKI AREA 144
INDIAN PEAKS WILDERNESS AREA 145
FORT COLLINS. 145
RED FEATHER LAKES. . . . 150
CACHE LA POUDRE RIVER 151

GRAND LAKE 151
GRANBY 154

VAIL, ASPEN & CENTRAL MOUNTAINS 155
DENVER TO VAIL 158
Winter Park & Fraser 158
The Moffat Rd & Rollins Pass. 160
Arapahoe Basin Ski Area. 161
Keystone Ski Resort. 162
Montezuma 162
Dillon 163
Frisco 164
Copper Mountain Ski Resort 167
BRECKENRIDGE 169
VAIL 180
BEAVER CREEK 191
ASPEN 194
AROUND ASPEN 208
Maroon Bells. 208
Basalt 209
ALONG HWYS 24 & 85 . . . 210
Minturn 210
Red Cliff 211
Leadville. 212
Fairplay. 215
Twin Lakes. 215

Buena Vista. 217
Bailey 220

NORTHWEST COLORADO 222
STEAMBOAT SPRINGS. 223
AROUND STEAMBOAT SPRINGS. 231
Stagecoach State Park . . . 231
Mt Zirkel Wilderness 231
Hahns Peak 231
WALDEN 232
KREMMLING. 232
HOT SULPHUR SPRINGS. 233
CRAIG 234
DINOSAUR NATIONAL MONUMENT. 234
SOUTH OF DINOSAUR NATIONAL MONUMENT. 236
Dinosaur 236
Rangely 236
Cañon Pintado National Historic District 236
MEEKER. 237
ALONG I-70. 237
Glenwood Springs 237
Carbondale 242
Marble 242
Crystal 242

On the Road

Colorado National Monument............. 243

Grand Junction......... 244

Fruita 248

Grand Mesa............ 249

SOUTHWEST COLORADO....... 250

GRAND JUNCTION TO CORTEZ................252

CRESTED BUTTE & GUNNISON.............252

Black Canyon of the Gunnison National Park 252

Montrose.............. 254

Curecanti National Recreation Area 257

Gunnison 257

Crested Butte 259

Paonia 262

Delta.................. 262

TELLURIDE.............264

SAN JUAN MOUNTAINS............269

Ridgway 269

Ouray & the Million Dollar Hwy............. 270

Silverton 273

Durango................275

Chimney Rock Archaeological Area......281

Pagosa Springs.........281

South Fork............. 283

Around South Fork...... 284

Creede & Around 284

Lake City & Around 287

MESA VERDE & THE FOUR CORNERS 289

Mesa Verde National Park 289

Mancos................ 294

Cortez................. 296

Dolores............... 298

Rico................... 299

Hovenweep National Monument............. 300

Four Corners Navajo Tribal Park 300

Ute Mountain Indian Reservation.............301

SAN LUIS VALLEY...302

WESTCLIFFE & SILVER CLIFF 304

CRESTONE 306

GREAT SAND DUNES NATIONAL PARK 307

SAN LUIS STATE PARK... 310

BLANCA................ 310

FORT GARLAND......... 310

ALAMOSA & AROUND ... 311

SAN LUIS............... 313

ANTONITO 314

CONEJOS RIVER 315

MONTE VISTA........... 316

LA GARITA.............. 317

DEL NORTE............. 318

EASTERN COLORADO....... 320

COLORADO SPRINGS ... 321

SOUTHERN FRONT RANGE................. 331

Florissant Fossil Beds National Monument......331

Pueblo 332

Cañon City & Royal Gorge............. 334

Florence............... 336

La Veta & Around 337

Trinidad 338

SANTA FE TRAIL 341

Bent's Old Fort National Historic Site 341

Boggsville Historic Site...341

Fort Lyon 342

Timpas & the Comanche National Grassland 342

NORTHEAST COLORADO.............342

Pawnee National Grassland.............. 342

Fort Morgan............ 343

Sterling 343

Julesberg.............. 344

Denver & Around

Includes »

DENVER 56
GOLDEN 95
MT EVANS 98
IDAHO SPRINGS &
GEORGETOWN 99
ST MARY'S
GLACIER 100
EMPIRE 101
DENVER MOUNTAIN
PARKS & PLATTE
RIVER 101

Best Places to Eat

» Biker Jim's Dogs (p73)

» Rioja (p73)

» Stueben's Food Service (p77)

» Root Down (p79)

» SAME Café (p77)

Best Places to Stay

» Jet Hotel (p70)

» Queen Anne Bed & Breakfast Inn (p71)

» Hotel Monaco (p70)

» Hotel Teatro (p70)

» Brown Palace Hotel (p67)

Why Go?

Spirited, urbane and self-aware, Denver is the West's cosmopolitan capital. Blessed with tons of sunshine, cyclists cruise miles of trails before hitting town or heading for the Rockies on the horizon.

Head to Commons Park (p63), do a 360-degree turn and try to process the ridiculous abundance of adventures within your gaze. There's the gleaming skyscrapers of Denver's Downtown and historic LoDo districts, packed with breweries and the most exciting culinary scene between Chicago and California; the hulking forms of two of America's most famous sports arenas, Mile High Stadium (p89) and Coors Field (p89), where home runs, high fives and mobs of the city's rabid sports fans are nearly a nightly spectacle; and way off in the distance, rising though the high-altitude haze and all that clean, thin air, is the jagged purple line of the Front Range, a gateway to some of the most spectacular wilderness on the continent. There's a whole lot to do in Denver.

When to Go

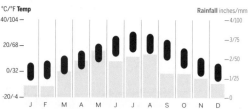

Denver

May–August Crowds and costs are high. Hot days, balmy evenings, extended daylight.

September–November Cooler temperatures see parklands and mountainsides at their prettiest.

December–March Short days and cold weather sends Denver indoors. Crowds and prices drop.

Springing into the Great Outdoors

Denver is smack in the middle of some of the most stunning nature in the Lower 48 and, frankly, you'd be a fool to miss it. If you're flying, don't bring gear from home. The airlines' baggage fees will destroy your budget and there's tons of affordable, world-class gear to rent. REI Flagship Store (p91) is a top option for camping and mountaineering supplies, kayaks, snowshoes and skis (*way* cheaper than renting at the slopes).

If you're only camping, call Outdoors Geek (p64), a mom-and-pop operation that packages kits (tents, packs, stoves and all the trimmings) for solo campers and groups. The B Cycle (p95) program doesn't cut it for serious cyclists, so rent road or mountain bikes at Bicycle Doctor (p64). Its sister store, Edgeworks (p64), rents snowboards.

BEST DAY TRIPS

This city has more than enough to do within its borders, but for those who have the itch to rent a car and explore a bit, here are a couple options all within two hours' drive:

» Campy history buffs: hit the Buffalo Bill Museum & Grave (p96).

» Those who love rock (or rocks): catch a show or wander through Red Rocks Park & Amphitheatre (p102).

» People who want to get high: put that rental car to the test on Mt Evans (p98), America's highest highway.

» College junket: spend the day hanging out in Boulder, and hike the Royal Arch Trail (p111) through the Flatirons.

Farmers Markets

See www.denverfarmersmarket.com for complete details of Denver's fresh, open-air markets.

» Wednesday: Tiri's Garden Farmers Market

» Wednesday and Saturday: Cherry Creek Fresh Market

» Sunday: Old South Pearl Farmers Market

» Sunday: City Park Esplanade Market

WHEN COLD WINDS BLOW

» Get tropical in the conservatory at the Denver Botanic Gardens (p61)

» Booze by the crackling fire at Lost Lake Lounge (p85)

» Commiserate with polar bears at the Denver Zoo (p61)

» Steam in the baths at Pura Vida Fitness & Spa (p64)

Denver's Enormous Art

» *I See What You Mean* (p56), Lawrence Argent

» *Mesteño* (p64), Luis Jimenz

» *The Yearling* (p61), Donald Lipinski

» *The Big Sweep* (p61), Claes .Oldenburg and Coosje van Bruggen

» *Dancers* (p56), Jonathan Borofsky

Resources

» Visit Denver (www.denver.org)

» Denver International Airport website (www.flydenver.com)

» Denver.com (www.denver.com)

» Downtown Denver (www.downtowndenver.com)

» City of Denver (www.denvergov.org)

» Regional Transport District (www.rtd-denver.com)

» eat.shop Denver (www.eatshopguides.com)

DENVER

History

Between hell-raisin' gold rushers, US Army generals, waring Native American tribes and 'unsinkable' frontier women, Denver's past is colorful and chaotic, and people here relish and romanticize the Wild West history. It was rumors of gold that brought the human tide to the Front Range in the middle of the 19th century and established Denver as a major supply point at foot of the Rocky Mountains, but Arapaho and Cheyenne buffalo hunters already occupied hundreds of camps in the area.

General William H Larimer was the city's white founder; in late 1859 he established a township at the confluence of Cherry Creek and the South Platte River and named it after the person who appointed the area under his control, Kansas Territorial Governor James W Denver. However, without water or rail transportation, Denver's overnight rise soon stagnated, ending the first of many boom-and-bust cycles that have defined the city's growth.

Supplying these gold- and silver-miners fostered the city's boom, until 1893 when the Silver Panic destroyed the economy and sent the state into depression. The following year discovery of gold deposits in Cripple Creek rejuvenated Denver's stature as a center of finance and commerce. When this dried up it was coupled with the Great Depression.

In 1952 Denver's 12-story height limit was repealed and the skyline sprouted high-rises, but many of these suffered during the mid-1980s when an office construction boom went – you guessed it – bust. The cycle reversed yet again in the 1990s, and by the millennium Denver was a hub for computer, telecommunication and tech firms, many which are now struggling to recover from the global financial crisis.

◉ Sights

Most of Denver's sights are in the Downtown district. The 16th St Mall is the focus of most retail activity, while Lower Downtown (LoDo), which includes historic Larimer Sq, is the heart of Denver's nightlife scene.

DOWNTOWN & LODO

FREE **I See What You Mean**   PUBLIC ART
(Big Blue Bear; Map p68; 700 14th St; ♿; ☒D Line) Lawrence Argent's *I See What You*

Mean is better known around town as the Big Blue Bear, who peers into the mammoth convention center as if wondering 'What are those little pink conventioneers prattling on about?' Standing at the feet of the 40ft tall beast and taking in the blue sky above is among the city's most provocative vistas.

Dancers   PUBLIC ART
(Map p68; cnr Champa St & N Speer Blvd; ♿; ☒1, 30, 31, 36L, 48 RTD) Frozen in joyful two-step, Jonathan Borofsky's whimsical *Dancers* invite rushing traffic to stop and play. The centerpiece of Sculpture Park, they supervise live music and lounging picnickers in summer and rise eerily from the snow in winter. Initially a controversial buy for conservative citizens, they're a symbol on scale with Denver's ambition to be the cultural capital of the West.

Colorado History Museum   MUSEUM
(Map p78; ☎303-866-3682; www.colorado history.org; 1300 Broadway; ℗) The excellent Colorado History Museum was closed at the time of research in preparation for its move to the corner of 12th and Broadway, due to to be completed in 2011. The museum provides excellent interactive displays on the state's development.

Denver Firefighters Museum   MUSEUM
(Map p68; ☎303-892-1436; www.denverfire fightersmuseum.org; 1326 Tremont Pl; adult/child $6/4; ☉10am-4pm Mon-Sat; ♿; ☒7, 8, 16, 16L RTD) Fire Station No 1 was built in 1909 and in 1978 was turned into a museum that explores the history of firefighting in Denver. See the old steam equipment, slide down a pole and get kitted out in some firefighting gear. The upstairs section is the old quarters where the firefighters slept.

The galleries include a dedicated children's section with interactive displays based on fire-safety education. Great for kids and fascinating for adults.

FREE **Robischon Gallery**   GALLERY
(Map p68; ☎303-298-7788; www.rob ischongallery.com; 1740 Wazee St; ☉11am-6pm Tue-Fri, noon-5pm Sat; ℗; ☒1, 2, 12 RTD) Robischon operates with a focus on emerging dialogues in art, often bringing in notable, progressive foreign artists from around the world. You'll find work here by internationally renowned artists, too, including Robert Motherwell, Christo and Jeanne Claude, Jessica Stockholder and Li Wei.

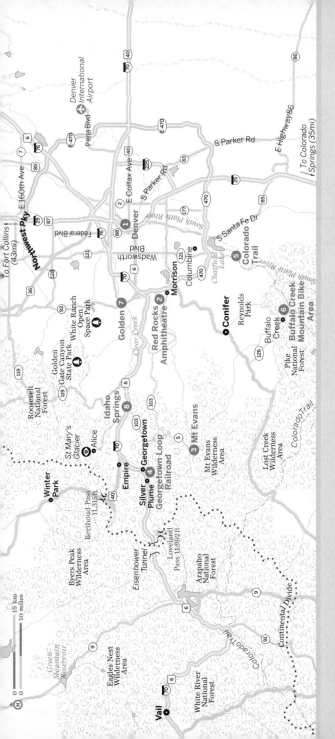

Denver & Around Highlights

1 Mix outdoor spaces with cosmopolitan modernism in the **state capital**

2 After hiking through spectacular rock formations, take in a show at **Red Rocks Amphitheatre** (p102)

3 Point the rental car up a 14er at **Mt Evans** (p98) – North America's highest paved road

4 Chug through mountains on the historic narrow gauge track of the **Georgetown Loop Railroad** (p100)

5 Stetch your legs on the **Colorado Trail** (p103)

6 Bomb down a single track trail at the **Buffalo Creek Mountain Bike Area** (p103)

7 Pay your respects to an icon of the American West at the **Buffalo Bill Museum & Grave** (p96) in Golden

8 Venture into boom-town **Idaho Springs** (p99) and visit one of the area's best breweries

To Lumber Baron Inn Gardens (0.2mi)

To Forney Transportation Museum (1.2mi)

Zuni St
Wyandot St
23
17
W 33rd Ave
Osage St
30
Tejon St
W 32nd Ave 22
W 30th Ave
8
W 29th Ave
19th St
40 32
Larimer St
Lawrence St
4
W 27th Ave
Commons Park
Coors Field
26
24th St
W 23rd Ave
Amtrak-Union Station
Larimer St
Lawrence St
22nd St
1
21st St
Welton St
See Platte River Valley Map (p82)
Wynkoop St
Blake St
Market St
19th St
Children's Museum
Auraria Pky
14th St
15th St
16th St Mall
17th St
Champa St
California St
Glenarm Pl
Court Pl
Broadway St
E 20th Ave
E 19th Ave
E 18th Ave
Mile High Stadium Cir
37
W Colfax Ave
40
W Colfax Ave
Delaware St
See Downtown Area Map (p68)
16
W 13th Ave
Osage St
See Capitol Hill & Five Points Area Map (p78)
15
34
E 10th Ave
14
W 10th Ave
38
6
E 9th Ave
13
W 8th Ave
E 8th Ave
18
21
W 6th Ave
Denver Health Medical Center
E Speer Blvd
W 7th Ave
Cherry Creek
0   200 m
5
Kalamath St
Santa Fe Dr
W 4th Ave
7
W 2nd Ave
E 2nd Ave
Yuma St
Broadway St
39
Acoma St
W 1st Ave
25
27
W 1st Ave
Broadway St
Lincoln St
Logan St
36
28
See Enlargement
42
31
S Lincoln St
Sherman St
3
W Archer Pl
W Bayaud Ave
W Bayaud Ave
9
To Divino Wine & Spirits (1.3mi)

Museum of Contemporary Art   GALLERY
(Map p82; ☎303-298-7554; www.mcadenver.org; 1485 Delgany St; adults $10, students & seniors $5; ⊙10am-6pm Tue-Thu, Sat & Sun, 10am-10pm Fri; ℗; ☐6 RTD) This space was built with interaction and engagement in mind – there's no front door – and Denver's home for contemporary art can be provocative, delightful or a bit disappointing, depending on the show. The focus is on contemporary mixed-media works from American and international artists.

David B Smith Gallery   GALLERY
(Map p68; ☎303-893-4234; www.davidbsmith gallery.com; 1543 Wazee St; ⊙10am-6pm Tue-Sat; ☐20, 28, 32, 44 RTD) David B Smith's taste for progressive American and international artists has made this space one of the most engaging small galleries in Denver. Artists featured here include Dutch painter Bas Zoontjens, American hyper-realist painter Christina Empedocles and portrait artist Kris Lewis.

FREE **Millennium Bridge**   CABLE BRIDGE
(Map p82; extension of 16th St Mall) Allow us to be geeky for a second: this is the world's first cable-stayed bridge using a post-tensioned structural construction. If the technical jargon goes over your head, you'll be impressed by just looking up – the sweeping forms of the cables and white mast are a dramatic sight against Denver's consistently blue sky.

CAPITOL HILL & GOLDEN TRIANGLE

TOP CHOICE **Denver Art Museum**   GALLERY
(DAM; Map p78; ☎ticket sales 720-865-5000; www.denverartmuseum.org; 13th Ave; adult/child/student $13/5/10, 1st Sat of each month free; ⊙10am-5pm Tue & Wed, 10am-7pm Thu, 10am-10pm Fri, 10am-5pm Sat & Sun; ℗⊡♿; ☐9, 16, 52, 83L RTD) The DAM is home to one of the largest Native American art collections in the USA, and puts on special avant-garde multimedia exhibits. The Western American Art section of the permanent collection is justifiably famous.

The $110-million Frederic C Hamilton wing, designed by Daniel Libeskind, is a strange, angular, fanlike edifice. It's inspired and mesmerizing. If you think the place looks weird from the outside, look inside: shapes shift with each turn thanks to a combination of design and uncanny natural-light tricks.

◎ Top Sights

Black American West Museum &
Heritage Center E1
Children's Museum A3

◎ Sights

1 Blair-Caldwell African American
Research Library................................. D2
Colorado Sports Hall of Fame ......(see 37)
2 Denver Botanic Gardens......................... F5
3 Illiterate Media B7
4 Plus Gallery D1
5 Rule Gallery B6

Activities, Courses & Tours

6 Bicycle Doctor D5
7 Denver Bouldering Club A6
8 Denver Skate Park B1
Edgeworks ....(see 6)
9 Stranahans Colorado Whiskey C7

◎ Sleeping

10 Castle Marne Bed & Breakfast............... F4
11 Holiday Chalet F4
12 Hostel of the Rockies F3

◎ Eating

13 Arada Restaurant & Bar.......................... C5
14 Buckhorn Exchange Restaurant B5
15 Cuba Cuba Café & Bar C4
16 Domo Restaurant B4
17 Duo... A1
18 El Taco De Mexico................................... C5
19 Fruition Restaurant E6

20 Gypsy House Café E4
Hornet ....(see 25)
21 Mizuna D5
22 Root Down B1
23 Rosa Linda's Mexican Cafe B1
24 SAME Café F4
25 Señor Burrito B6
26 Snooze.. D2
Squeaky Bean ....(see 23)
27 Sweet Action Ice Cream B7
28 Walnut Room Pizzeria B7
29 WaterCourse Foods E3
30 Z Cuisine A1

◎◎ Drinking

31 Beatrice & Woodsley B7
32 Crema Coffee House D1
Sputnik..(see 42)
33 Thin Man Tavern F3

◎ Entertainment

34 Bar Standard D5
35 Charlie's E4
36 Hi-Dive B7
37 INVESCO Field at Mile High A3
38 La Rumba D5
39 Landmark Mayan Theater..................... B6
40 Larimer Lounge D1
41 Ogden Theatre E4

◎ Shopping

42 Fancy Tiger.. B7
43 Peppermint Boutique E3

FREE **Colorado State Capitol**

PUBLIC BUILDING

(Map p78; ☑303-866-2604; 200 E Colfax Ave; ☺9am-5:30pm Mon-Fri; ⬚0, 0L, 2, 3L, 6, 7, 10, 12, 15, 16, 16L, 83L) Sitting commandingly atop Capitol Hill, this stately neoclassical government building looks out across the grand Civic Center Park region. The ornate interior befits such a grand building; visitors can join free tours that depart every 45 minutes.

Construction began in the 1890s from locally quarried rose onyx (Beulah red marble) and in 1908, to celebrate the Colorado gold rush, the superb dome was covered in 200 ounces of gold leaf. In 1909 the 15th step on the western entrance was designated one mile above sea level. Subsequent measures inscribed this marker at the 17th step in 1969 and the 13th in 2003.

 Molly Brown House Museum

HISTORIC BUILDING

(Map p78; ☑303-832-4092; www.mollybrown. org; 1340 Pennsylvania St; adult/child/senior $8/4/6; ☺tours 10am-3:30pm Tue-Sat, noon-3:30pm Sun; ℗♿; ⬚2, 10, 15, 15L RTD) This outstandingly preserved house, designed by the well-known architect William Lang, was built in 1889 and belonged to the most famous survivor of the *Titanic* disaster. Having survived the ill-fated voyage of 1912, Molly Brown became active in progressive politics and women's organizations, and was also a keen theater performer. She died in 1922, a woman ahead of her time.

Molly Brown House offers educational workshops, residencies and scholarships.

FREE **Yearling** PUBLIC ART
(Horse on the Chair; Map p78; 10 W 14th Ave; ☐16, 83L RTD) This wonderful sculpture by Donald Lipski sits outside the Denver Public Library, where it was installed in 1998 after spending a year in New York City's Central Park. The Horse on the Chair, as it's known, stands 21ft high and has a whimsy, humor and magic to it that has helped it become one of the city's favorite landmarks.

FREE **Bronco Buster** PUBLIC ART
(Map p78; Civic Center Park; ♿; ☐9, 16, 52, 83L RTD) Denver sculptor A Phimister Proctor became nationally famous with this 1920 bronze of the Bronco Buster, a symbol of the city. Fun fact: Proctor's model for the cowboy was arrested for murder before the statue was done. At Proctor's insistence, the accused was allowed to continue posing until the sculpture was finished.

Denver Botanic Gardens GARDENS
(Map p58; www.botanicgardens.org; 1005 York St; prices vary; ☺9am-9pm; ☐2, 3, 6, 24 RTD) If you're hankering for greenery, this 23-acre expanse of Rocky Mountains shrubbery is the perfect place in which to hide from the hustle and bustle of the city. Local flora mixes it up with relatives from faraway continents such as Australia and Africa. Exhibitions and events are staged.

FREE **Denver Public Library** LIBRARY
(Map p78; ☏720-865-1111; www.denver library.org; 10 W 14th Ave; ☺10am-8pm Mon & Tue, 10am-6pm Wed-Fri, 9am-5pm Sat, 1-5pm Sun; P@☂♿; ☐16, 83L RTD) Hardly a dusty bibliotheca, the Denver Public Library is an active and hip place. In addition to its voluminous stacks, the library lends CDs and DVDs from its extensive archive, and it streams music from its website. There's a schedule of lectures, and self-help and skills courses. Shifting exhibits feature local historical and contemporary photography.

Book a meeting room or join one of the community learning sessions. On the 5th floor is the Western History & Genealogy Department, and affiliate campuses include the Blair-Caldwell African American Research Library.

Civic Center Park PARK
(Map p78; btwn Bannock St & Broadway; ♿; ☐6, 7, 9, 10, 16, 16L, 52 RTD) In the shadow of the State Capitol's golden dome, this centrally located park hosts lounging drifters waiting for their bus connections, politicos yammering into Bluetooth headsets and some of the most iconic public sculptures in the city.

Byers-Evans House Museum
HISTORIC HOUSE
(Map p78; ☏303-620-4933; www.colorado history.org; 1310 Bannock St; adult/child $6/4; ☺10am-4pm Mon-Sat; P♿; ☐9, 52 RTD) It's an amazing experience walking through this period house, painstakingly restored to the 1920s era; the rooms aren't roped off so you can wander into them. Guided tours run every half-hour from 10.30am to 2.30pm.

William Byers was the publisher of the *Rocky Mountains News* when he commissioned this grand house in 1883. He soon sold it to William Gray Evans, who was with the Denver Tramway Company.

Big Sweep PUBLIC ART
(Map p78; 100 W 14th Ave) Large enough to whisk away a Volkswagen, this giant dustpan's color was chosen by Claes Oldenburg and Coosje van Bruggen to complement Denver's clear skies.

FREE **United States Mint** PUBLIC BUILDING
(Map p68; ☏303-405-4761; www.usmint. gov; 320 W Colfax Ave; ☺8am-2pm Mon-Fri; ♿; ☐7, 16, 16L RTD) The Denver Mint produces about 7.5 billion coins each year and offers free guided tours each weekday. A limited number of standby tickets are available at the door, but it's best to book through the website. You're not allowed to take purses, handbags or strollers into the facility, and guns, knives, fireworks and martial arts weapons are expressively forbidden. You've been warned!

FIVE POINTS, UPTOWN & CITY PARK

Denver Zoo ZOO
(☏303-376-4800; www.denverzoo.org; 23rd Ave; adult/child/senior $12/8/10; ☺9am-6pm, last admission 5pm; P♿; ☐24, 32 RTD) Denver's world-class zoo has more than 650 animal species represented in naturalistic settings in considerate enclosures. There are native and exotic animals including rhinos, gorillas and giant Komodo dragons. An active breeding program is helping arrest the loss of endangered species. A schedule of monthly free-admission days is published on the zoo's website.

Black American West Museum & Heritage Center MUSEUM
(Map p58; ☏303-482-2242; www.blackamerican westmuseum.com; 3091 California St; adult/

Two Days

Start at rejuvenated LoDo and see its historic stables and warehouses converted into restaurants and boutiques. Visit the glorious **Union Station** and **Oxford Hotel** before brunching at **Snooze** or **Stueben's**. Check out glamorous Larimer Sq and the **Big Blue Bear**, then head to **Civic Center Park** with its Greek amphitheater and stately buildings flanking three sides. Spend the afternoon touring the **Mint** and **State Capitol Building** before decided between **Rioja**, **Barolo Grill** and **Mizuna** for dinner.

On day two, head to Golden Sq and visit the **Denver Art Museum**, **Byers-Evans Museum** and **Firefighters Museum**, and poke around the **Denver Public Library**. Walk through the Golden Sq residential area down to the Cherry Creek walking track and head south towards the ritzy **Cherry Creek Shopping Center** or north back to Downtown for respite at **Appaloosa Bar**. See what's happening that night at the **Denver Performing Arts Complex**.

Four Days

On day three, get yourself to the **Denver Zoo** or the **Denver Museum of Natural History & Science**, then stroll through the huge City Park to stock up at the weekend farmers markets. Make you way over to **Confluence Park** to cool off in the river. Grab a **B Cycle** and pedal down the river to the fun park at **Elitch Gardens** to ride the 'Mind Eraser' roller coaster. Check out **Cuba Cuba Café & Bar** for dinner and **Church** for aprè-dinner dancing.

If it's summer, find some wheels and make for the mountains. Head north on Rte 36 through Estes Park about an hour from Denver, and up the stunning Old Fall River Rd to the Rocky Mountain National Park's **Alpine Visitor Center**. The views are breathtaking. Or take a drive out to **Red Rocks Park & Amphitheater**, 15 miles southwest of Denver in Morrison. The setting, between 400ft-high red sandstone rocks, is spectacular.

child/senior $8/6/7; ☺10am-2pm Mon-Fri, 10am-5pm Sat & Sun, closed Mon & Tue winter; ⚑101 D-Line) This excellent museum is dedicated to 'telling history how it was'. It provides an intriguing look at the contributions of African Americans (from cowboys to rodeo riders) during the pioneer era – according to museum statistics, one in three Colorado cowboys were African American.

**Blair-Caldwell African American
Research Library**　　　　　　　　　　LIBRARY
(Map p58; ☑720-865-2401; www.aarl.denver library.org; 2401 Welton St; ☺noon-8pm Mon, 10am-6pm Wed & Fri, 9am-5pm Sat; ⚑38) Dedicated to the history and culture of the African American people of Denver, Colorado and the Rocky Mountains region, this institution provides fabulous resources on a rich cultural heritage. Art, music, literature, religion and oral histories are documented, and an active research program continues with the help of visitor donations and philanthropists. The Blair-Caldwell Library is affiliated with the Denver Public Library.

Plus Gallery　　　　　　　　　　GALLERY
(Map p58; ☑303-296-0927; www.plusgallery. com; 2501 Larimer St; ☺noon-6pm Wed-Sat; ℗; ⚑44, 48 RTD) When Ivar and Karen Zeile opened Plus Gallery in 2001 it was quickly established as one of the leading contemporary art galleries in the Western US. It often hosts events on Friday evenings.

Denver Museum of Nature & Science
　　　　　　　　　　　　　　　　　　MUSEUM
(☑303-322-7009; www.dmns.org; 2001 Colorado Blvd; museum adult/child $11/6, museum & IMAX or Planitarium $16/10, museum & IMAX & Planitarium $21/14; ☺9am-5pm; ℗ ♿; ⚑20, 32, 40 RTD) The Denver Museum of Nature & Science, 3.5 miles east of Downtown, has an IMAX theater, the Gates Planetarium and absorbing exhibits for all ages.

HIGHLANDS & PLATTE RIVER VALLEY

TOP CHOICE / 🚲 / FREE **Confluence Park**　　PARK
(Map p82; 2200 15th St; ♿; ⚑10 RTD) This wonderful place of healthy outdoors activity is a magnet for families with picnic blankets and prepared lunches, smooching young lovers and singles buried

in a book or newspaper. Cool off on a hot summer's day by swimming or wading over the rocks.

Confluence Park is where Cherry Creek and Platte River meet, and bike/jogging trails connect it to all the other waterfront parks. It's a wonderfully egalitarian place where all types from all backgrounds come to celebrate their city.

Children's Museum
MUSEUM

(Map p58; ☑303-433-7444; www.mychilds museum.org; 2121 Children's Museum Dr; adult/ child/seniors $8/6/6; ⊙9am-4pm Mon & Tue, to 7:30pm Wed, to-4pm Thu & Fri, 10am-5pm Sat & Sun; ⚐) If you've got kids, check out the Children's Museum, full of excellent interactive exhibits. A particularly well-regarded section is the kid-sized grocery store, where your little consumerists can push a shopping cart of their very own while learning about food and health. In the ARTS a la Carte section kids can get creative with crafts that they can take home – all use recycled materials.

FREE Commons Park
PARK

(Map p82; www.denvergov.org/parksand recreation/; cnr 15th & Little Raven Sts; ⚐; 🚌10 RTD) Affording views of the city and a bit of fresh air, this spacious, hilly patch of green is the best place to take yourself out of the Downtown bustle. There are bike paths, benches and plenty of people sprawling with take-out lunch. You can also access Denver's best stroll, along the Platte River Parkway.

Elitch Gardens
AMUSEMENT PARK

(Map p82; ☑303-595-4386; www.elitchgardens. com; 2000 Elitch Circle; adult/child $41/30; P⚐; 🚌1, 20 RTD) If you're finding all the museums a bit too serious, loosen up here – your kids will love you for it. This amusement park is packed with nearly 50 rides, with varying levels of fright-inducement. Opening times vary, so call for the season's schedule. Tickets purchased online receive a $2 discount.

Forney Transportation Museum
MUSEUM

(☑303-297-1113; www.forneymuseum.org; 4303 Brighton Blvd; adult/child/senior $8/4/6; ⊙10am-4pm Mon-Sat; P⚐; 🚌8, 38, 52 RTD) This fascinating museum exhibits antique vehicles of all types – cars, motorbikes, bicycles, tricycles, railway engines and rolling stock, fire engines, airplanes and more. Even if you're not an automotive aficionado, the shifting industrial design over the years is interest-

ing. Among many highlights is Amelia Earhart's 1923 Kissel Speedstar in stunning canary yellow.

Downtown Aquarium
AQUARIUM

(Map p82; ☑303-561-4450; www.aquarium restaurants.com; 700 Water St; adult/child/ senior $16/10/15; ⊙10am-9pm Sun-Thu, 10am-9:30pm Fri & Sat; P⚐; 🚌10 RTD) Denver's old Ocean Journey Aquarium was sold in 2003 to a business that specializes in aquarium-themed restaurants. So it is that Downtown Aquarium is both a novelty restaurant and a public aquarium (and tiger den). It's a great place to take the kids...and a novel place to have a meal. Try the fish burger.

FREE Colorado Sports Hall of Fame
MUSEUM

(Map p58; ☑720-258-3888; www.coloradosports. org; 1701 Bryant St; ⊙10am-3pm Thu-Sun Sep-May, 10am-3pm Tue-Sat Jun-Aug; P⚐; 🚌16, 16L, 28, 30, 30L, 31, 36L RTD) This temple to Colorado's sporting prowess is in the INVESCO Field at Mile High Stadium (p89). It has exhibits on the Broncos and themes grouped under such purple headings as 'endurance' and 'sacrifice.' It's nothing to go out of your way for, but a good way to kill time before an event at the stadium.

SOUTH CENTRAL DENVER

FREE Washington Park
PARK

(WashPark; www.washpark.com; cnr S Downing St & E Virginia Ave; P⚐; 🚌12 RTD) Denver's best local park, this great little strip of green is where moms zip by on in-line skates, Frisbees float around all afternoon and clusters of friends lounge beneath the proud Denver skyline. A bike path around the park makes for an excellent ride.

SOUTH BROADWAY

FREE Illiterate Media
GALLERY

(Map p58; ☑303-993-4474; www.illiterate magazine.com; 82 S Broadway; ⊙11am-7pm Tue-Sat; @☎; 🚌0 RTD) This gallery grew out of Illiterate Magazine, a locally published art publication, and its thrust maintains a multidisciplinary edge, hosting events and hanging shows of regional artists such as Denver painter Ravi Zupa. Progressive and hip, it fits perfectly in the South Broadway neighborhood.

Rule Gallery
GALLERY

(Map p58; ☑303-777-9473; www.rulegallery. com; Suite 101, 227 Broadway; P; 🚌0 RTD) Robin Rule, whose name is lent to this clean space, has been a matron of Denver's experimental and contemporary art scene since the late 1980s. Usually hosting works by only one or two artists at a time, the Rule Gallery is a magnet for the city's artistic vanguard.

BEYOND CENTRAL DENVER

Mesteño PUBLIC ART
(Mustang; Peña Blvd) Nicknamed 'Bluecifer,' this 32-ft blue stallion with hellish, gleaming red eyes greets visitors to and from DIA (p94), and is the subject of much controversy in Denver. Morbid factoid: during its creation, one of the stallion's legs fell on creator Luis Jiménez, severing an artery in his leg and leading to his death.

Lakeside Amusement Park
AMUSEMENT PARK
(☑303-477-1621; www.lakesideamusementpark.com; 4601 Sheridan Blvd; rides $0.50-3, unlimited rides Mon-Fri/Sat & Sun $14/20; ☉hrs vary; P ♿; 🚌44, 44L, 51) This old-school fun park has rides for adrenaline junkies as well as tots and toddlers. It's in a great lakeside location with views west over the mountains... although you might not notice as you freefall from the 140ft-drop tower!

🏃 Activities

There's a lot of talk about how the people of Denver are, on average, the slimmest in the USA, and it's easy to understand why. The city is checkered with lovely parks and green spaces; it has smooth bike lanes and an increasingly popular community bikeshare program; and the siren call of the rugged Front Range is ever-present. Plus, the sun is *always* shining here. City elders and wags at the Chamber of Commerce are wont to brag about the 300 annual days of sunshine with which Denver is blessed, and the residents seem determined to soak up every minute of it.

The South Platte River is lined on both sides with lanes for cycling, jogging and strolling. Pick up a bike at one of the B Cycle Stations (p95) that are littered around the Downtown area – there are more than 40 in all. When things get hot, roll up your pants and escape into the cool currents near Confluence Park (p62); take a kayaking lesson from Confluence Kayaks (p66); or rent some gear at the impressive REI Flagship Store (p91) and head for the mountains.

 **Outdoors Geek**
OUTDOORS RENTAL
(☑303-699-6944; www.outdoorsgeek.com; 3140 S Pioria Ct; ☉8am-8pm Mon-Sat; ♿) This mom-and-pop gear outfitter is a lot friendlier to deal with than fighting through the mobs at REI. It works like this: you call and talk to Will, who puts together a package of top gear for hiking and camping and either ships it to you or arranges a time for you to pick it up at his Aurora distribution center.

This personalized service, along with high-quality goods, is the reason we love the Outdoors Geek. Also, the website is perfect for novice campers, with tips that will help dispel the anxiety of getting out into nature for the first time.

FREE Denver Skate Park SKATING
(Map p58; ☑720-913-0786; 2205 19th St; ☉5am-11pm Mon-Sun; ♿; 🚌6, 10, 52 RTD) Possibly the best free skate park in the US, this large outdoor area has various bowls and surfaces to suit all abilities. It's best for young skaters early on the weekends. For advice and a snack between shredding, look for Sharon, the 'skate park mom,' who keeps a watchful eye on the scene.

Pura Vida Fitness & Spa SPA
(☑303-321-7872; www.puravidaclub.com; 2955 E 1st Ave; $30 for guest day pass; ☉5am-9pm Mon-Thu, to 8pm Fri, 6am-7pm Sat, from 7am Sun) Sleek as the Starship *Enterprise,* this modern spa is Denver's best. It isn't cheap, but it's a sure bet for modern workout facilities, yoga classes, group fitness sessions and a chance to sweat alongside Denver's business class.

Bicycle Doctor BIKE RENTAL
(Map p58; ☑303-831-7228, toll-free 877-245-362; www.bicycledr.com; 860 Broadway; ☉10am-7pm Mon-Fri, to 5pm Sat, varies Sun; 🚌0, 6, 83L RTD) The guys behind the counter at this small shop might be the friendliest bike mechanics in the area, and their rental gear is top-notch.

Edgeworks OUTDOORS RENTAL
(Map p58; ☑303-831-7228, toll-free 877-245-362; www.bicycledr.com/edgeworks; 860 Broadway; ☉10am-7pm Mon-Fri, 10am-5pm Sat, varies Sun; 🚌0, 6, 83L RTD) For snowboard rentals and superior service (hand edging and waxing, stone grinding and repair) this is Denver's best shop. The staff is extremely friendly as well, and can point boarders to the best rides in the area.

START: MILLENNIUM BRIDGE
FINISH: DENVER STATE CAPITOL STEPS
DISTANCE: 3 MILES
DURATION: 4 HOURS

Walking Tour
Denver Walk

❯ Strap on some comfortable shoes; this afternoon tour brings you past a clutch of highlights, out of the tourist turkey shoot on the 16th St Mall and into the heart of the Mile High City.

Begin by leaving the pedestrian mall and strolling across ① **Millennium Bridge**. This modernist footbridge is a bold symbol of contemporary Denver and the perfect place to reflect on its past. Look ahead to the river: the city was born when gold was discovered in the currents below. Pass the rolling hills of ② **Commons Park**, where you can soak up the Denver skyline before crossing another footbridge over the South Platte River. Descend to the far bank and take the paved path upstream. In a few minutes you'll see kids across the river splashing in ③ **Confluence Park**, swimmable rapids where Platte River meets Cherry Creek, and the perfect place to cool off.

If you're planning to head to the mountains, wander up to the enormous ④ **REI Flagship Store**, where you can stock up on awesome gadgets. Done shopping? Cross back over the water and take the foot path upstream along the banks of Cherry Creek before taking the stairs up to Wynkoop St. At the corner you can hit ⑤ **Tattered Cover Bookstore**, our favorite bookstore in Denver. But you're getting hungry, right? Choose your own adventure: a burger and microbrew at the ⑥ **Wynkoop Brewing Co** or a bison sausage at ⑦ **Biker Jim's Dogs**.

Walk your meal off by heading a few blocks over to the ⑧ **Denver Performing Arts Complex**, where you can stand agape under ⑨ **Dancers** and give a hug to ⑩ **I See What You Mean**. It's a straight shot up 14th St to ⑪ **Civic Center Park**, where you can pose by ⑫ **Bronco Buster** and climb to the 13th stair of the ⑬ **Colorado State Capitol** – exactly one mile above sea level.

DENVER FOR FREE

For cheapie fun you can tour the Colorado State Capitol (p60) for free on weekdays, and almost all of the city's museums have free admission days at least once a month. The city's lovely public parks and clear skies provide tons of fresh entertainment and, if you're clever, you can use the B Cycle (p95) program for *almost* free. After you pay the $5 daily membership, break your ride into 30-minute segments. If you check in the bike at one of the ubiquitous stations every half-hour you won't have to pay a usage fee.

 Courses

Confluence Kayaks KAYAKING
(Map p82; ☏303-433-3676; www.confluence kayaks.com; Unit B, 2373 15th St; 2hr class $129; ⊙10am-6pm Mon-Thu & Sat, 10am-7pm Fri, noon-5pm Sun; ☻; ☐28, 32, 44 RTD) Situated under a health-food store, this centrally located kayak shop offers gear rental and lots of advice about the area's white water from laid-back, amiable staff. If you're a beginner, it offers lessons at nearby Confluence Park, but the classes fill fast so it's best to sign up several days in advance.

Seasoned Chef COOKING
(☏303-377-3222; www.theseasonedchef.com; Suite 100, 999 Jasmine St; classes $70-135) This well-established cooking school offers three-hour classes on everything from knife skills and cooking basics to menu building and end-to-end sessions such as 'Tapas of the Southwest.'

Cook Street School of Fine Cooking
COOKING
(Map p68; ☏303-308-9300; www.cookstreet.com; 1937 Market St; classes $79) Classes here are sharply focused, taking on ethnic flavors and cooking techniques from distant regions (such as North Africa, India or Spain) or an intense look at our favorite foods ('Scotch and Steak' class, anyone?). The instructors are well pedigreed and you'll leave stuffed.

Denver Bouldering Club ROCK CLIMBING
(Map p58; ☏303-709-8657; www.denverboul deringclub.com; 2485 W 2nd Ave) The instruction for serious climbers is better at the

Colorado Mountain School (p139) in Estes Park, but this climbing gym in the heart of the city is a good way to get psyched for a trip into the mountains. It's also huge: a 1500-sq-ft facility that stays open 24 hours a day.

 Tours

Stranahans Colorado Whiskey DISTILLERY
(Map p58; ☏303-296-7440; www.stranahans.com; 200 S Kalamath St; ⊙tours 11am, 1pm, 3pm, 5pm Mon, Wed, Fri & Sat) Only a dozen barrels of whiskey are produced from this family distillery each week...and they're damn good. Using water from the Rockies, Colorado barley and white-oak barrels, it's a rare taste of quality over quantity. Short tours of the facility are available, though limited space means it's best to sign up online.

Denver Microbrew Tours MICROBREWERIES
(☏303-578-9548; www.denvermicrobrewtour.com; per person $23) This popular tour samples local craft beers from the boutique makers in the LoDo district. It takes a couple of hours in the afternoon on Friday, Saturday or Sunday. The tour kicks off from the Great Divide Brewing Company (p83).

Culinary Connectors FOOD
(☏303-495-5487; www.culinaryconnectors.com; tours $39-99) Foodies will want to try the varied list of guided tours that visit Denver's best restaurants on foot or by chauffeured vehicle.

Denver Inside & Out HISTORY
(☏303-330-9871; www.denverinsideandout.com; adult/under 5yr/child $40/free/35) This outfit offers interesting historical walking tours based on the 1922 daylight robbery of the Denver Mint. They're cleverly done, with some of the robbers coming to life along the way, and mysteries and clues acted out in situ.

Platte Valley Trolley HISTORY
(Map p82; ☏303-458-6255; www.denvertrolley.org; Platte St; adult/child $4/2; ⊙departures noon-3:30pm Fri-Sun; ☻; ☐6, 10, 28, 32, 44) Ride the historic Platte Valley Trolley that trundles along its tracks from the REI store south to the downtown Denver area. To be honest the sights aren't much – mostly the same stuff you see in a short walk around the area – but the staff of history buffs is enlightening.

✿ Festivals & Events

FREE Cinco de Mayo   CULTURE
(☑303-534-8342; www.cincodemayoden
ver.com; Civic Center Park; 🚻; 🚌2, 7, 15, 15L, 16,
16L RTD) Enjoy salsa music and margaritas
at one of the country's biggest Cinco de
Mayo celebrations, held over two days on
the first weekend in May. With three stages
and more than 350 exhibitors and food vendors, it's huge fun.

Taste of Colorado   FOOD
(☑303-295-6330; www.atasteofcolorado.com;
Civic Center Park; ☉Labor Day weekend; 🚻; 🚌0,
15, 40, 44 RTD) More than 50 restaurants
cook up their specialties at food stalls;
there's also booze, live music, and arts-and-
crafts vendors at this Labor Day festival.

Cherry Creek Arts Festival   ARTS
(www.cherryarts.org; cnr Clayton St & E 3rd Ave;
🚻) During this sprawling celebration of vi-
sual, culinary and performing arts, Cherry
Creek's streets are closed off and over a
quarter million visitors browse the giant
block party. The three-day event takes place
around July 4.

Great American Beer Festival   BEER
(☑303-447-0816, 1888-822-627; www.
greatamericanbeerfestival.com; 700 14th St; 🚻;
🚈101 D-Line, 101 H-Line, 🚌1, 8, 30, 30L, 31, 48
RTD) Colorado has more microbreweries
than any other US state, and this hugely
popular event in early September sells out
in advance. More than 500 breweries are
represented, from the big players to the
home-brew enthusiasts. Only the Colorado
Convention Center is big enough for these
big brewers and their fat brews.

🛏 Sleeping

Denver is an enormous hub for big conven-
tions and, as such, it's dense with hotel rooms
– there are more than 5000 places to stay in
the city center alone. The majority of these
are in high-rise buildings with lovely views
of the skyline and prices starting at around
$150 for a standard double room. But don't
count on finding something for this price –

the rates are painfully capricious and things
skyrocket when the conventioneers flood the
streets. Your chances of finding a good-value
stay in a major chain get quite a bit better
if you're willing stay in the Denver 'burbs,
which isn't as bad as it sounds thanks to the
city's solid network of public transportation.

If you're looking for accommodation that
falls outside these mainstream options –
something unique, cheap or without comi-
cally bad paintings on the wall – things can
be a bit trickier. Denver is downright brutal
on budget-conscious backpackers; consider
one of the (fairly dreary) single-story motels
on E Colfax Ave. The options widen if you
want a stay to remember and price is of no
concern.

DOWNTOWN & LODO

TOP CHOICE Brown Palace Hotel
                          BOUTIQUE HOTEL **$$$**
(Map p78; ☑800-321-2599, 303-297-3111; www.
brownpalace.com; 321 17th St; r $149-1400;
🅿❄@🛜; 🚌20 RTD) Standing agape under the stained-glass crowned atrium, it's
clear why this palace is shortlisted among
the country's elite historic hotels. There's
deco artwork, a four-star spa, imported
marble, and staff who discretely float down
the halls. The rooms, which have been hosting presidents since Teddy Roosevelt's days,
have the unique elegance of a distant era.

Guests and diplomats mingle around
the piano as melodies float up to the rooms
above (according to the piano man rooms
on the 4th and 5th floors have an acousti-
cally perfect perch).

If it's out of budget ask a concierge for a
free self-guided tour or hang out for a while
in the lobby and just pretend. The martini is
predictably perfect and served with a sterling bowl of warm pecans.

Oxford Hotel   BOUTIQUE HOTEL **$$$**
(Map p68; ☑303-628-5400, toll-free 800-228-
5838; www.theoxfordhotel.com; 1600 17th St; d
from $180; ❄❋🛜; 🚌6, 20, 28, 32, 44 RTD) Mar-
ble walls, stained-glass windows, frescoes
and sparkling chandeliers adorn the public

ONLINE BOOKINGS

Given the huge inventory of rooms, the best way to save money on a hotel is to book
using a third-party booking website such as Priceline.com or Expedia.com. If there
aren't a lot of conventions in town, these sites can magically reduce a $200 rack rate
on a four-star hotel to $70.

0 — 200 m
0 — 0.1 miles

See Platte River Valley Map p82

22nd St

40

39
48

Wazee St
47

4
35
Blake St

6
52

20th St

13

Amtrak-
Union Station
33

21st St

Wynkoop St
12

57

18
10

17th St

Market St

18th St

Larimer St

19th St

Denver Bus
Center

2
24

22

Lawrence St

Arapahoe St

Curtis St

20th St

27

37

Market St
Bus Station

30

Champa St

19th St

Stout St

Tabor
Center
28

Curtis St

18th St

Rtd-18th
and Stout
Station

43
56
15th St

58
45

15

44
46

17th St

8

Rtd-18th and
California
Station

California St

42
32

38
49

16th St Mall

11

16

55

25
26

Rtd-16th
and Stout
Station

Lawrence St

29
36

9
7

15th St

Champa St

Rtd-16th and
California
Station

59

53

51

14th St

13th St

Stout St

California St

14

34
54
19

17

Welton St

50

Rtd-Theatre
Dist/Conv
Center

I See
What You
Mean

23

21
31

16th St Mall

1

Champa St

Stout St

Colorado
Convention
Center

Glenarm Pl

Tremont Pl

Court Pl

41

Cleveland Pl

Welton St

14th St

13th St

3

W Colfax Ave

Cherry Creek

Speer Blvd

Speer Blvd

5

Civic
Center Park

See Capitol Hill &
Five Points Area
Map p78

W 14th Ave

Kalamath St

Santa Fe Dr

Speer Blvd

Fox St

Elati St

Delaware St

Cherokee St

Bannock St

W 13th Ave

W 13th Ave

◎ **Top Sights**
 I See What You Mean B5

◎ **Sights**
 1 Dancers A5
 2 David B Smith Gallery A2
 3 Denver Firefighters Museum............... C6
 4 Robischon Gallery B1
 5 United States Mint................................ C6

➕ **Activities, Courses & Tours**
 6 Cook Street School of Fine
  Cooking C1

🛏 **Sleeping**
 7 Curtis B4
 8 Hotel Monaco... C3
 9 Hotel Teatro A4
 10 Jet Hotel A2
 11 Magnolia Hotel....................................... C3
 12 Oxford Hotel... A1

🍴 **Eating**
 13 9th Door B1
 14 Anthony's Pizza C4
 15 Biker Jim's Dogs B3
 16 Bistro Vendôme...................................... A3
 17 Cooks Fresh Market D5
 18 Dixon's Downtown Grill A2
 19 Earls Restaurant & Bar D4
 20 Elway's C2
 21 Food Court at Republic Plaza.............. D5
 22 H BurgerCo A2
 23 Hard Rock Café...................................... D5
 24 Illegal Pete's A2
 25 Laguna's Mexican Bar & Grill.............. B4
  Little India...................................(see 25)
 26 Los Cabos II.. B4
 27 Marrakesh Restaurant A2
 28 Mellow Mushroom Pizza Bakers B3
 29 Oceanaire Seafood Room..................... B4
 30 Organixx A2
 31 Pizza Colore Express............................. D5
 32 Rioja A3
  Thunderbird Burgers & BBQ .... (see 27)
 33 Trios Enoteca... A1
  Vesta Dipping Grill...................... (see 13)

🍷 **Drinking**
 34 Appaloosa Bar & Grill............................ D4
 35 Celtic Tavern B1
 36 Corner Office B4
 37 Croc's Mexican Bar & Grill................... B2
 38 Crú A3
 39 Falling Rock Tap House B1
 40 Great Divide Brewing Company........... D1
  Jet Lounge ....(see 10)
 41 Katie Mullen's Irish Pub &
  Restaurant D5
 42 Mynt Lounge... A3
 43 Nallen's A3
 44 Prime Bar.. B3
 45 Red Square Euro Bistro........................ B3
 46 Rock Bottom Restaurant &
  Brewery.. B3
  TAG... (see 32)
 47 Wynkoop Brewing Co A1

🎭 **Entertainment**
 48 Beta Nightclub....................................... B1
  Bovine Metropolis Theater.......... (see 26)
  Colorado Ballet..............................(see 51)
  Colorado Symphony Orchestra... (see 51)
 49 Comedy Works.. A3
 50 Denver Center for the
  Performing Arts.................................. A4
 51 Denver Performing Arts
  Complex... A4
 52 El Chapultepec C1
 53 Ellie Caulkins Opera House A4
  Lannie's Clocktower Cabaret....... (see 15)
  Opera Colorado..............................(see 51)
 54 Paramount Theatre............................... D4

🛍 **Shopping**
 55 Champa Fine Wine & Liquor................. C4
  Colorado Rockies Dugout Store . (see 34)
  Cry Baby Ranch.............................(see 16)
 56 EVOO Marketplace................................ A3
  Goorin Brothers............................ (see 16)
 57 Tattered Cover Bookstore.................... A2
 58 Tewksbury & Co B3
 59 Wild West Denver Store....................... C4

spaces of this classy hotel built in 1891 in red sandstone. Denver's first hotel has large rooms decked out with imported English and French antiques. The extensive art collection on display includes several notable works and the art-deco Cruise Room Bar is one of Denver's swankiest cocktail lounges.

Rates vary dramatically based on season and demand; check the website for the best rates and packages.

Hotel Monaco
BOUTIQUE HOTEL **$$$**

(Map p68; ☏800-990-1303, 303-296-1717; www.
monaco-denver.com; 1717 Champa St; r from
$179; P🐾🌀❄🅟; 🚇0, 6, 30, 30L, 31, 36, 48, 52
RTD) This ultrastylish boutique is a favorite
with the celebrity set. Modern rooms blend
French and art-deco styles – think bold
colors and fabulous European-style feather
beds. Don't miss the evening 'Altitude Ad-
justment Hour,' when guests enjoy free
wine and five-minute massages. The place
is 100% pet-friendly; staff will even deliver a
named goldfish to your room upon request.
Discounts are routinely offered online.

Hotel Teatro
BOUTIQUE HOTEL **$$$**

(Map p68; ☏303-228-1102; www.hotelteatro.com;
1100 14th St; d $239; 🌀❄🅟; 🚇10, 15 RTD) Ele-
gant surroundings and impeccable service
make this luxurious boutique hotel one of
Denver's best. The 112 rooms and suites are
gorgeous, done up with Indonesian sandstone foyers, art-deco and cherry-wood furnishings, and thick damask curtains.

Just across the street from the Denver
Performing Arts Center, it's not surprising
that the Hotel Teatro would incorporate
the theater into its decorating scheme. Old
costumes and photos from shows at the
center decorate the glamorous lobby and
posh rooms. The rooms are done up in either lush gold or soft sage color schemes,
and have glorious baths. Pour some of the
hotel's high end bubble bath into the Indonesian marble tub and have a soak while
staring at the sprig of fresh orchids on the
sandstone countertop across the room. Afterwards you can relax on the plump white
comforters, snuggled into one of the hotel's monogrammed bathrobes. Now that's
luxury.

Curtis
BOUTIQUE HOTEL **$$**

(Map p68; ☏303-571-0300; www.thecurtis.com;
1405 Curtis St; d $129-239; 🌀❄@🅟; 🚇15 RTD)
Pop culture is worshiped at this boutique
joint that also sells happy relaxation. Atten-
tion to detail – be it through the service or
the decor in the rooms – is paramount at
the Curtis, a one of a kind hotel in Denver.

There are 13 themed floors and each is
devoted to a different genre of American
pop culture. Rooms are spacious and very
mod without being too out there to sleep –
fluffy white comforters and muted colors
on the walls help induce easy slumber. Still
they offer the Curtis' signature flair – yel-
low 'peace' car alarm clocks, lamps made
to resemble a twisted gold telephone wire.

The hotel's refreshingly different take on
sleeping may seem too kitschy for some –
you can get a wake up call from Elvis – but
if you're tired of the same old international
brands and looking for something different,
this joint in the heart of Downtown might
be your tonic.

Magnolia Hotel
BOUTIQUE HOTEL **$$$**

(Map p68; ☏888-915-1110; www.magnolia
hoteldenver.com; 818 17th St; d $161-200; 🌀❄@
🅟🐾) Housed in an old bank building, this
13-story European-style hotel offers old-
world charm, modern amenities and good
value in the heart of Downtown. Its super-
central location, good deals and bedtime
milk and cookies are three major selling
points.

Tasteful, stylish rooms and suites come
in a variety of shapes (and prices), although
some are a bit small, with a Western meets
Euro flavor. Beds are decked out with loads
of crimson-, copper- and chocolate-colored
pillows, and covered with bright, patterned
spreads. Walls are painted a soothing cream;
well-placed paintings and floor-to-ceiling
windows offer breathtaking city views. This
place has super-friendly service, and gym
junkies will dig the on-site fitness center.

Denver International Youth Hostel
HOSTEL **$**

(Map p78; ☏303-832-9996; 630-638 16th Ave;
dorm $19; P@❄; 🚇15, 15L, 20 RTD) If cheap
really matters then the Denver International Youth Hostel might be the place for
you. It's basic and vaguely chaotic, but has a
ramshackle charm and a great Downtown
location. All dorms have attached bathroom facilities and the common area in
the basement has a large-screen TV, library
and computers for guests to use. The three-
bunk dorms have been hosting guests for
more than 25 years.

Jet Hotel
BOUTIQUE HOTEL **$$**

(Map p68; ☏303-572-3300; www.thejethotel.
com; 1612 Wazee St; d $99-169; P🐾❄@❄;
🚇16th St Shuttle) Priced for partying, this
slick (if slightly pretentious) boutique in the
heart of LoDo is all about fun, especially on
weekends. That's when Denver's beautiful
people come for the slumber-party-with-
bottle-service experience. You can dance
all night in the swank 1st-floor lounge, then
stumble up to your Zen quarters, burrow
under the thick white comforters and sleep
until brunch.

Stay on a weekday if you want a posh central hotel room without the boozy party scene and accompanying noise. The healthy Asian fusion menu of the Swing Thai is perfect for kicking last night's hangover.

CAPITOL HILL & GOLDEN TRIANGLE

Capitol Hill Mansion B&B
B&B $$$

(Map p78; ☑303-839-5221, 800-839-9329; www.capitolhillmansion.com; 1207 Pennsylvania St; r incl breakfast $130-200; P☺✿☎⬛; ⬚2, 10 RTD) Stained-glass windows, original 1890s woodwork and turrets make this delightful, gay- and family-friendly Romanesque mansion a special place to stay. Rooms are elegant, uniquely decorated and come with different special features (one has a solarium, another boasts Jacuzzi tubs).

11th Avenue Hotel
HOTEL $

(Map p78; ☑303-894-0529; www.11thavenuehotel.com; 1112 Broadway; dm $20, s/d without bathroom $37/48, with bathroom $43/54; ☺✿☎; ⬚0, 6 RTD) This is a budget hotel with a good location in the Golden Triangle district. The lobby looks vaguely like something from a Jim Jarmusch movie. The upstairs rooms, some with attached bathrooms, are bare but clean. The hotel is actively involved in assisting people recovering from drug and alcohol problems (staff and residents) by providing affordable accommodations. It's safe, secure and a decent place for budget travelers.

FIVE POINTS, UPTOWN & CITY PARK

TOP CHOICE Queen Anne Bed & Breakfast Inn
B&B $$$

(Map p78; ☑303-296-6666; www.queenannebnb.com; 2147 Tremont Pl; r incl breakfast $165-215; P☺✿☎; ⬚28, 32 RTD) Soft chamber music wafting through public areas, fresh flowers, manicured gardens and evening wine tastings create a romantic ambience at this ecoconscious B&B in two late-1800s Victorian homes. Featuring period antiques, private hot tubs and exquisite hand-painted murals, each room has its own personality, but all are ecofriendly. Check online for special rates.

Green features include mattresses made from recycled coils and green-tea insulation, organic fabrics (just like the delicious full breakfast), and products and produce purchased from local merchants when possible. It even encourages you to take the house bikes out rather than your car.

Castle Marne Bed & Breakfast
B&B $$$

(Map p58; ☑303-331-0621; www.castlemarne.com; 1572 Race St; r incl breakfast $120-270; P☺✿☎; ⬚15, 15L, 20 RTD) Fall under the spell of Castle Marne, one of Denver's grandest old mansions. Located in the Wyman Historic District, it dates from 1889 and is on the National Register of Landmarks. The feel is pre-1900 old-world elegance with modern-day convenience and comfort. Furnishings are authentic period antiques and family heirlooms, and offer a mood of quiet charm and romance.

Each of the nine rooms is a unique experience of taste and style – the turret room has a solarium and Jacuzzi for two. Castle Marne is popular with bridal parties and honeymooners, and perfect for a romantic weekend getaway. Afternoon tea is served in the parlour at check-in.

Holiday Chalet
B&B $$

(Map p58; ☑303-437-8245; www.denver-bed-breakfast.com; 1820 E Colfax Ave; d incl breakfast $95-145; P☺✿☎; ⬚15 RTD) Big breakfasts and cozy ambience are standard at this beautifully restored Victorian mansion in Denver's historic Wyman District just outside central Downtown. Swathed in lace, floral carpets and rich woodwork, this revamped brownstone mansion features rooms with high ceilings, hardwood floors and period decor. Breakfast includes everything from crepes to lox and strong coffee.

Warwick
HOTEL $$$

(Map p78; ☑303-861-2000; www.warwickdenver.com; 1776 Grant St; d $130-375; ☺✿☎⬛; ⬚20, 28, 32 RTD) Affordable luxury just east of downtown Denver is how the Warwick bills itself and, with some very cheap online specials, this can be true. Rooms here are larger than average and done up with an American country-classic decor. Quality varies, so check out a few before deciding. The deluxe rooms here are absolutely enormous, and the rooftop pool is a summertime perk.

Melbourne International Hotel & Hostel
HOSTEL $

(Map p78; ☑303-292-6386; www.denverhostel.com; 607 22nd St; dorm/s/d/f $20/34/45/52; @☎⬛; ⬚8, 48 RTD) The Melbourne is clean, comfortable and secure, sitting above a dry-cleaner shop on the corner of Welton St. It's basic but offers decent dorms, singles and doubles in a great location just minutes from the 16th St Mall. There's a common kitchen and bathrooms are shared. One family room offers sleeping for six.

Hostel of the Rockies   HOSTEL **$**
(Map p58; ☑303-861-7777; www.innkeeperrockies.com; 1717 Race St; dm $24; ▣@⑦; ☐20 RTD) This hostel can be a fun place to stay. On the city's lower-income east side, the original apartment building has been standing for more than a century, and has been converted into a basic 50-bed backpackers. The congenial hosts are a bonus and throw regular BBQs where guests mingle. Dorms on the upper floor have private balconies.

HIGHLANDS & PLATTE RIVER VALLEY

⬛ **Lumber Baron Inn Gardens**   B&B **$$$**
(☑303-477-8205; www.lumberbaron.com; 2555 W 37th Ave; d from $150; ▣☺✳⑦❖; ☐38 RTD) Murder mystery dinners and romance -inducing suites make this elegantly quirky B&B stand out from the pack – even the locals choose to stay here for a weekend mystery getaway! The five suites are all different, although all feature Jacuzzis and giant plasma TVs.

Lumber Barons is popular with honeymooners and wedding parties – check out the Indonesian wedding bed in the Persian-themed Valentine Suite. The Greco-Roman Anniversary Suite comes with a real 1865 carved Victorian bed and huge marble columns. Check online for cheap package deals. Booking ahead is advised at any time.

SOUTH CENTRAL DENVER

┌────┐ **JW Marriott Denver at Cherry**
│TOP │ **Creek**   HOTEL **$$$**
│CHOICE│
└────┘
(☑303-316-2700; www.jwmarriottdenver.com; 150 Clayton Ln; d from $245; ▣☺✳⑦❖; ☐1, 2, 3, 46 RTD) This luxury hotel wears its accolades effortlessly having had both Conde Nast and Zagat confirming it as Denver's best hotel. Spacious digs come with high-thread count sheets, plump beds and marble bathrooms featuring top class soaps and shampoos.

The outside of the building looks a little tacky, but inside it feels like an old-world European hotel. Local artwork and colorful blown glass grace lobbies and rooms, and your dog can dig the digs in a special sheepskin bed.

BEYOND CENTRAL DENVER
Omni Interlocken Resort & Golf Club
                                 HOTEL **$$$**
(☑303-438-6600; www.omniinterlocken.com; 500 Interlocken Blvd; d $300; ▣☺⑦✳❖) Have a glass of champagne while checking into this impressive four-diamond Omni. Although the location isn't so hot – it's about 20 minutes from downtown Denver – the hotel is. Rooms are spacious and well-appointed. The service is top-notch, with helpful and friendly staff.

It's almost as if the Omni is trying extra hard to make up for that out-of-the way location with its fabulous staff, a gorgeously maintained building and very comfortable rooms. Many rooms feature Rocky Mountain views, and all come with high-thread count linens, fluffy comforters, flat-screen TVs and oversized king beds. And if you want to split your time between Denver and Boulder, the location halfway between the two might actually work in your favour (its suburban locale also allows it to feel more like a resort than a hotel). For a four-star property, the price is also very pleasing, and there are usually cheap deals to be found online. Have an afternoon read in the comfortable lobby in the impressive entrance hall.

✗ Eating

Though Denver's culinary scene has grown a damn sight more adventurous than Rocky Mountain oysters in the last decade, most menus around town are firmly rooted in the conservatism of conventional American comfort food: burgers, mac and cheese, steaks and meat loaf. It might seem pretty humdrum at first glance, but a visionary approach to mom's Monday-night standards has led to a clutch of fantastic upscale diners. And then there's brunch, a meal which inspires endless debate among Denver locals and endless one-up-manship among Denver chefs. That humble little meal between breakfast and lunch is nothing short of an art form here, and the luckiest eater would spend a dozen late-rising Sundays joining the country's most discerning brunch audiences.

Although most hungry conventioneers flooding the 16th St Mall are likely satiated by the lounges and chains serving upscale (if unimaginative) pub food, the city's best eats are outside the tourist district. The Highlands neighborhood, just to the north of LoDo, is where to find the cutting-edge action. If you're chained to the Convention Center, make your way to the twinkling lights of Larimer St, home to wide-ranging options.

DOWNTOWN & LODO

TOP CHOICE Rioja CONTEMPORARY AMERICAN **$$$**
(Map p68; ☎303-820-2282; www.rioja denver.com; 1431 Larimer St; mains $22-29; ◷11:30am-2:30pm Fri-Wed, 10am-2:30pm Sat & Sun, 5-10pm Sun-Thu, 5-11pm Fri & Sat; ☑; ☐2, 12, 15, 16th St Shuttle) This is one of Denver's best restaurants, lauded in foodie media and patronized by the city's glitterati. Smart, busy and upscale, yet relaxed and casual, Rioja features select regional wines and an interesting menu of cocktails. Starters include a superb fresh bacon and a flight of artisan goat cheese. For mains, try the plump, juicy, seared nori-wrapped scallops or the sublime handmade artichoke tortellini.

Snooze BRUNCH **$**
(Map p58; ☎303-297-0700; www.snooze eatery.com; 2262 Larimer St; mains $4-12; ◷6:30am-2:30pm Mon-Fri, 7am-12:30pm Sat & Sun; ☻; ☐8, 38 RTD) This bright, cheery cafe is a specialty breakfast-and-brunch spot dishing up eggs, breakfast burritos and even a smokin' salmon benedict. The coffee's always good, but you have the option of an early-morning Bloody Mary. Snooze has a strong sustainability focus, buying carbon offsets for its energy consumption, recycling and composting, and sourcing local organic produce.

Cooks Fresh Market PASTRIES, SANDWICHES **$**
(Map p68; ☎303-893-2277; www.cooksfresh market.com; 1600 Glenarm Pl; $6-10; ◷7:30am-8pm Mon-Fri, 9am-6pm Sat; ☑; ☐Glenarm) Far and away the best deli in Downtown, the attention to quality is obvious in the take-out salads and sandwiches, selection of cheeses and expert pastries. Some gourmet cooking staples and bulk selection complete the picture, making this an ideal stop for supplies if you're picnicking in the park or heading out of town.

Though mostly for take-out, there are a few tables to eat at inside and a small sidewalk patio. The partner team running the place, Ed and Kristi Janos, are two of Denver's most highly credentialed chefs.

Palace Arms EUROPEAN **$$$**
(Map p78; ☎303-297-3111; www.brownpalace. com; 321 17th St; mains from $20; ◷dinner served 5:30-9pm; ☻☜☑☑; ☐16th St Shuttle) The

patriotic pioneer decor inside the award-winning restaurant of the Brown Palace Hotel (p67) dates back to the 1700s – check out the silver centerpiece the British royal family commissioned. The food is as impressive as the old-world ambience, and the wine list features 900 bottles. Signature dishes include Kobe rib-eye steak and seared bison tenderloin.

Marrakesh Restaurant MOROCCAN **$$$**
(Map p68; ☎303-623-3133; www.houseofmar rakeshdenver.com; 1530 Blake St; $13-19; ◷11am-2:30pm Mon-Fri, 5-10pm Mon-Thu & Sun, 5-11pm Fri & Sat; ☻; ☐Blake St) Berber rugs and belly dancers complete the atmosphere of this cherished Moroccan den where patrons recline at low tables set around a courtyard to evoke the North African feel. The menu is strong across the board but the lamb is the house specialty, perfectly paired with steaming cups of mint tea.

Illegal Pete's MEXICAN **$**
(Map p68; ☎303-623-2169; www.illegalpetes. com; 101, 1530 16th St; mains $5-7; ◷11am-10pm Sun-Wed, 11am-2:30am Thu-Sat; ☐Wazee St) Around lunch, you'll queue to the door at Pete's, the best option for quick Mexican on the 16th St Mall. With rock posters

plastering the window, a worn plank floor underfoot and an inked-up staff behind the counter, the place has charm galore. Margarita specials, beer-battered fish tacos and shredded beef tacos keep 'em coming back.

Little India   INDIAN $$

(Map p68; www.littleindiadenver.com; 1533 Champa St; mains $9-19; ⊘11am-2:30pm & 5-10pm; ➔; ⌨15 RTD) The lunch buffet ($9) attracts a load of office workers. After dark the atmosphere gets a bit more upscale, with couples snuggling into booths for a selection of curries and generously spiced rice dishes. One of three Denver locations, this place also has a full bar in back.

Anthony's Pizza   PIZZA $

(Map p68; ☑303-573-6236; www.anthonyspizza andpasta.com; 1550 California St; mains $3-7; ⊘11am-7:30pm Mon-Fri, 11am-6pm Sat; ⌨38 RTD) There's nothing fancy about this hole-in-the-wall pizza counter, but for a Downtown lunch less than $3, you'd be hard pressed to do better. New York–style thin crust is available by the slice and perfect for ultra-low-budget shoestringers.

9th Door   SPANISH $

(Map p68; ☑303-292-2229; www.theninthdoor. com; 1808 Blake St; tapas $5-9; ⊘4:30pm-2am Mon-Fri, 5:30pm-2am Sat; ➔🖉🚻; ⌨1, 2, 12 RTD) The decor is as juicy as the Spanish tapas at this hot Denver restaurant. The ambience is intimate, with low lights, beaded glass chandeliers and booths you can disappear into – great for groups, as they easily fit six. After dinner it becomes a popular lounge with live music.

Bistro Vendôme   FRENCH $$$

(Map p68; ☑303-825-3232; www.bistrovendome. com; 1420 Larimer Sq; mains $16-23; ⊘5-10pm Mon-Thu, 5-11pm Fri, 10am-2pm & 5-11pm Sat, 10am-2pm Sun; ➔; ⌨12, 15 RTD) When you discover Vendôme, tucked behind the storefronts of Larimer, it feels like your own little secret. Brunch is more casual than dinner, but both are done with scrupulous French technique: mussels in white wine and herb-roasted chicken are well-executed standards, while things get more adventurous with the avocado and scallion omelets and blackberry glazed pork loin.

Earls Restaurant & Bar   BURGERS, PIZZA $$$

(Earls Glenarm; Map p68; ☑303-595-3275; www.earls.ca; 1600 Glenarm Pl; $10-24; ⊘11am-11:30pm Sun-Thu, 11am-midnight Fri-Sat; ➔; ⌨Glenarm) This upscale bistro is lit by a bank of golden wine cabinets and the soft glow of a horseshoe bar – too bad the bank of flat-screen TVs adds a harsh flicker. Even so, the atmosphere is romantic enough to please couples, while the menu of fancy burgers and pizza is straightforward enough to please everyone else.

Oceanaire Seafood Room   SEAFOOD $$$

(Map p68; ☑303-991-2277; www.theoceanaire. com; 1400 Arapahoe St; mains $17-35; ⊘5-10pm Mon-Thu, 5-11pm Fri & Sat, 5-9pm Sun; ➔; ⌨10, 15, 20 RTD) Flying in seafood daily, this dinner spot has the city's freshest produce and a menu that changes nightly. The space, styled like the dining room in a 1930s ocean liner, is large and impressive. A roost at the oyster bar offers a slightly more casual option.

Mellow Mushroom Pizza Bakers

                                          BURGERS, PIZZA $$

(Map p68; ☑720-328-9114; www.mellowmush room.com; Suite 108, 1201 16th St; mains $6-12; ⊘11am-1am; ➔; ⌨16th St Shuttle) The strut of funky organ jazz and a space-age interior set the mood for this gently psychedelic choice on the 16th St Mall, where a selection of 30 beers on tap washes down a menu of creatively built pizza and hoagie sandwiches.

H BurgerCo   BURGERS $

(Map p68; ☑720-524-4345; www.hburgerco. com; 1555 Blake St; mains $6-13; ⊘11am-10pm Mon-Thu, to 10pm Fri to midnight Sat, noon-8pm Sun; ➔) Sure, the formidable burgers at this futuristic diner get rave reviews – especially the Angus beef, chili-infused, cheddar-crowned H Burger – but the visionary milkshake menu might be worthy of skipping the main course altogether. The Nutella marshmallow variety, topped with roasted marshmallows and infused with liquid nitrogen(!) is an icy, creamy wonder. If you're into something with a bit more kick than a milkshake, fear not; there's a full bar.

Trios Enoteca   PIZZA, TAPAS $$

(Map p68; ☑303-293-2887; www.triosenoteca. com; 1730 Wynkoop St; tapas $4-6, pizzas $11; ⊘5pm-midnight Tue & Wed, 5pm-1am Thu, 5pm-2am Fri & Sat; ➔🚻; ⌨16th St Shuttle, 🚉Union Station) Art-glass lampshades, bare brick walls and old pinups from the 1920s create a speakeasy atmosphere in this sleek LoDo wine bar. There's excellent live jazz, blues and R&B Tuesday to Saturday with no cover charge. Order a wood-oven pizza or tapas from the varied bar menu. The kitchen stays open late.

Vesta Dipping Grill
BARBECUE **$$**

(Map p68; ☎303-296-1970; www.vestagrill.com; 1822 Blake St; mains $15-25; ⊙5-10pm Sun-Thu, 5-11pm Fri & Sat; ☺☗; ⬚0, 1, 2, 12 RTD) Pick a type of meat, then choose from 30 different sauces to dip it into. It's a simple concept that works exceedingly well. The melt-in-your mouth quality of the creative dishes – many Asian inspired – makes Vesta one of Denver's favorite restaurants. The atmosphere is relaxed and funky.

Wazee Supper Club
BURGERS, PIZZA **$**

(Map p82; ☎303-623-9518; www.wazeesupperclub.com; 1600 15th St; mains $6-9, pizzas $10-18; ⊙11am-2am Mon-Sat, noon-midnight Sun; ☺☗; ⬚6, 10, 28, 32 RTD) Once you step into Wazee, on Denver's most historic street, there's little chance you'll turn around – it smells so delicious. Known for some of the best pizza and *stromboli* in the city, this long-time local favorite is a buzzing place day and night.

Dixon's Downtown Grill
GRILL **$$**

(Map p68; ☎303-573-6100; www.dixonsrestaurant.com; 1610 16th St; mains $9-16; ⊙7am-2am Mon-Fri, 8am-2am Sat & Sun; ☺; ⬚Wazee) Lots of LoDo travelers, pregame Rockies fans and business folks meet here at all times of the day. Depending on what's going down in the neighborhood it can be calm or chaotic, but the most reliable food is dished out at the lauded brunch (expect a wait).

Elway's
STEAK **$$$**

(Map p68; ☎303-312-3107; www.elways.com; 1881 Curtis St; steaks $30-50; ⊙6:30am-10pm; ☺; ⬚0, 1, 2, 12 RTD) One candid Denver sports fan explained John Elway's significance this way: 'It's like everyone goes to bed hoping to wake up and find him miraculously 22 years old and winning Super Bowls again.' Since that's unlikely, our consolation prize is to carve into a pricey medium-rare porterhouse at Denver's top steakhouse, located inside the Ritz Carlton.

Thunderbird Burgers & BBQ
BURGERS **$**

(Map p68; ☎303-534-3330; www.thunderbirdburgers.com; 1530 Blake St; burgers $5-13; ⊙10:30am-10pm; ☺☗; ⬚16th St Shuttle) Thunderbird cooks up fresh burgers with beef, lettuce, tomato, onions, pickles and a special secret seasoning. Choose from a dozen varieties or you can customize your own. There's a full-service bar and ribs are available as well.

Organixx
SALADS, SANDWICHES **$**

(Map p68; ☎303-825-1550; www.organixxrestaurant.com; 1520 Blake St; breakfast $6-9; ⊙8am-3pm; ☑☗; ⬚1, 2, 12 RTD) This breezy cafe is geared towards healthy eating, serving breakfasts – eggs, sandwiches, granola, yogurt etc. Lunchtime sandwiches have some innovative fillings. Organixx maintains a sustainability and fair-trade philosophy.

Hard Rock Café
PUB FOOD **$$$**

(Map p68; ☎303-623-3191; www.hardrock.com; 500 16th St; mains $14-19; ⊙11am-11pm Sun-Thu, 11am-midnight Fri & Sat; ☺; ⬚Glenarm) The food isn't the focus at these ubiquitous rock pubs; Denver's branch stands out for the caliber of memorabilia cluttering the place. Hanging the walls is a blouse worn by Jimi, a voided check of young Linda Ronstadt (for $10!) and guitars from Willie, Clapton and the Clash. The real treasure is upstairs: a pair of patent leather shoes Johnny Cash wore at the venue in 1965.

Laguna's Mexican Bar & Grill
MEXICAN **$**

(Map p68; ☎303-623-5321; www.lagunasmexicanbarandgrill.com; 1543 Champa St; mains $7-13; ⊙11am-9pm Mon-Sat; ⬚6, 10, 32 RTD) The basement space can feel a bit like a distant uncle's dim basement until you make your way out to the seating under the sunlit four-story atrium. The food leans toward cheese-laden Tex Mex platters with sides of free chips and pleasantly *picante* salsa.

Pizza Colore Express
ITALIAN **$**

(Map p68; ☎303-534-2111; www.pizzeriacolore.com; 1647 Court Pl; pizzas $7-16; ⊙11:30am-10pm; ☗; ⬚12, 20, 16th St Shuttle) Big portions of inexpensive pasta and wood-oven pizzas are served at this casual Italian restaurant. The food is delicious (especially considering the price) and there's ample outdoor seating if the weather cooperates.

Los Cabos II
PERUVIAN **$$**

(Map p68; ☎303-595-3232; www.loscabosii.com; 1525 Champa St; mains $8-15; ⊙11am-9pm Mon-Thu, 11am-10pm Fri & Sat, 11am-5pm Sun; ☺☗; ⬚Champa) Start things off at this popular Peruvian lunch spot with an excellent pisco sour before getting into the perfectly seasoned *lomo saltado* (grilled strips of steak with peppers, onions and veggies over fries) or a distinctly Peruvian take on chow mien. And before you leave, be sure to pet that giant stuffed llama.

Food Court at Republic Plaza   FAST FOOD **$**
(Map p68; 303-534-5128; 370 17th St; mains $5-12; 10am-3pm Mon-Sat; ; Court Pl) With chains big and small and fast-food prices, the last remaining food court on the 16th St Mall is easy for families and rushed office jockeys. The nosh isn't limited to the frightening thrill of Chik-fil-A patties, either; there are a few healthy options. Chinja has the long lines and fresh Americanized Chinese dishes.

CAPITOL HILL & GOLDEN TRIANGLE

Mizuna   CONTEMPORARY AMERICAN **$$$**
(Map p58; 303-832-4778; www.mizunadenver.com; 225 E 7th Ave; mains $32-45; 6-11pm Tue-Sat; ; 6 RTD) Mizuna is exclusive, expensive and exquisite. The small dining room only adds to the rarefied atmosphere and there's a certain pride knowing you're eating at one of the country's most renowned restaurants. The menu is eclectic and ever-changing, with an emphasis on fresh seafood and locally sourced seasonal produce. Try the pan-roasted ostrich loin with glazed beets or the signature softshell crab.

Wholefoods Market   SELF-CATERING **$**
(303-832-7701; www.wholefoodsmarket.com; 900 E 11th Ave; 7:30am-10pm; ; 10, 12 RTD) Part of a national chain, Wholefoods sells organic and natural foods, products and ingredients. There are juices, organic produce and meats, vitamins and all manner of healthy edibles. It's a perfect picnic pick-up stop, plus there's a cafe and a good deli counter. The commitment to sustainability on a large corporate scale is laudable. Local and independent suppliers are supported.

Cuba Cuba Café & Bar   SPANISH **$$**
(Map p58; 303-605-2822; www.cubacubacafe.com; 1173 Delaware St; mains $10-22; 5-11pm; ; 9, 52 RTD) Try the mango mojito (rum-based cocktail) at this swanky Cuban joint serving finger-lickin' BBQ spareribs, flavor-packed fried yucca and a sumptuous coconut-crusted tuna. The back patio offers fantastic sunset city views; the bright blue-walled environs emit an island vibe. There's sometimes music on Thursday nights. Bookings not accepted.

Gypsy House Café   MEDITERRANEAN **$**
(Map p58; 303-830-1112; 1279 Marion St; mains $6-12; 6:30am-11pm; @ ; 12 RTD) This is an unusual place. A family-run operation that dishes up fine Middle-Eastern mains, desserts and snacks, Turkish coffee as well as espresso, and house-blended loose-leaf tea. The chaotic decor is true to theme, and there's live music, poetry, belly dancing and dub-reggae DJs performing on an erratic schedule. Internet terminals and free wi-fi make it popular with locals.

City O' City   VEGETARIAN, VEGAN **$**
(Map p78; 303-831-6443; www.cityocitydenver.com; 206 E 13th Ave; mains $8-21; 7am-2am Mon-Fri, 8am-2am Sat, 8am-midnight Sun; ; 2, 9, 52 RTD) This popular vegan/vegetarian restaurant mixes stylish decor with an innovative spin on greens, grains and granola. The menu offers tortillas and burritos, salads, soups and pizzas, and the bar has drinks for accompaniment. The comfy dining room also features shifting artworks by local artists.

WaterCourse Foods   VEGETARIAN **$**
(Map p58; www.watercoursefoods.com; 837 E 17th Ave; mains $8-10; 7am-9pm Mon-Thu, 7am-10pm Fri, 8am-10pm Sat, 8am-9pm Sun; ; 12, 20 RTD) The unrelentingly meaty menus of Denver can be a chore to navigate for vegetarians, so the smart, straightforward fare at WaterCourse is a welcome reprieve. The breakfasts are cherished by locals (people go off about the banana-bread french toast) and dinner options – many of them with an Asian or Mexican influence – are uniformly well done.

Great Wall   CHINESE **$**
(Map p78; 303-832-6611; www.greatwalldenver.net; 440 E Colfax Ave; mains $5-11; 11am-11pm Mon-Thu, 11am-midnight Fri & Sat, 11:30am-11pm Sun; ; 2, 7, 15 RTD) Great Wall bills itself as a New York–style Chinese restaurant. You can eat in, take out or enjoy free home delivery within a 3-mile radius (minimum order $10). The numbered menu goes to 192 (we tried a delicious shrimp and snow peas). No MSG, and only 100% vegetable oil is used.

TOP CHOICE Steuben's Food Service

AMERICANA $$

(Map p78; ☑303-803-1001; www.steubens.com; 523 E 17th Ave; mains $8-21; ◎11am-11pm Sun-Thu, 11am-midnight Fri & Sat; ⊕; ☐0 RTD) Although styled as a midcentury drive-in, the upscale treatment of comfort food (mac and cheese, fried chicken, lobster rolls) and the solar-powered kitchen demonstrate Steuben's contemporary smarts. In summer, open garage doors lining the street create a breezy atmosphere and after 10pm they have the most unbeatable deal around: a burger, hand-cut fries and beer for $5.

Look around town for Steuben's mobile truck, powered by recycled veggie oil and often seen dishing out portable versions of the restaurant's staples to thankful politicos at Civic Park. Follow the restaurant on Facebook or Twitter to get details about where the mobile unit will park.

SAME Café

AMERICANA $

(So All May Eat Café; Map p58; ☑720-530-6853; www.soallmayeat.org; 2023 E Colfax Ave; by donation; ◎11am-2pm Mon-Sat; ⊕⊕; ☐15 RTD) This nonprofit cafe was founded by two former food-bank workers, who wanted to provide healthy, by-donation lunches for those who were struggling to make ends meet. The standard American cafeteria fare is delicious. Walk-in volunteers are welcome, though you can reserve a spot in advance online.

Volunteering here or dropping in for lunch is one of the most unique and heartwarming experiences in Denver, and demonstrates the most progressive thinking in the city's sustainable, local, community-oriented food movement.

Jonesy's EatBar

PUB FOOD $

(Map p78; ☑303-863-7473; www.jeatbar.com; 400 E 20th Ave; mains $12-15; ◎5-11pm Sun-Thu, 5pm-midnight Fri & Sat, 10am-3pm Sat & Sun; ⊕⊕☑⊕; ☐28, 32 RTD) This is a great place for a simple pub-style meal and a beer. This former high-end restaurant has been

reborn as a gastropub with an excellent, select wine list. There's live music several nights a week, a pool table and a lovely outdoors seating area. The crowd is eclectic and the wait staff is friendly.

Horseshoe Lounge

PIZZA $

(Map p78; ☑303-832-1180; www.thehorseshoe lounge.com; 414 E 20th Ave; mains $8-10; ◎4pm-2am Mon-Wed, 2pm-2am Thu, noon-2am Fri-Sun; ⊕⊕; ☐28, 32 RTD) This neighborhood lounge-bar has a wonderfully laid-back atmosphere, with a pool table and sports on a large TV screen. The bar counter is composed of about 23,000 dice (they say). Pizza, subs and salad are the items du jour, and they're all pretty good. Beer is the beverage, and there are a couple dozen to choose from.

Wahoo's Fish Taco

MEXICAN $

(Map p78; ☑303-292-0850; www.wahoos.com; 225 E 20th Ave; mains $5-8; ◎10:30am-9pm Mon-Sat, to 8pm Sun; ⊕⊕☑⊕; ☐28, 32 RTD) A converted corner gas station done out with skater-surfer-snowboarder decor, TVs showing video loops of rad maneuvers and stickers adorning every surface. And then there's the food. Tex-Mex, yes, but fish tacos? And in landlocked Denver? Go on: try one. We did and they were brilliant.

Wahoo's has two other locations in Denver.

La Pasadita

MEXICAN $

(Map p78; ☑303-832-1785; 1959 Park Ave; mains $6-9; ◎11am-9:30pm Mon-Sat; ⊕⊕☑⊕; ☐28, 32 RTD) This tiny family-run Mexican joint is a favorite among locals. The food is authentic and cheap, and it's all handmade from whole ingredients. The restaurant sits on a small triangular allotment surrounded by streets on all sides.

Avenue Grill

CONTEMPORARY AMERICAN $$$

(Map p78; ☑303-861-2820; www.avenuegrill. com; 630 E 17th Ave; mains $14-22; ◎11am-11pm Mon-Thu, 11am-midnight Fri, 4pm-midnight Sat, 10am-4pm Sun; ⊕⊕; ☐2 RTD) On a quiet street corner a short walk from Downtown, the Avenue Grill has been dishing up interesting

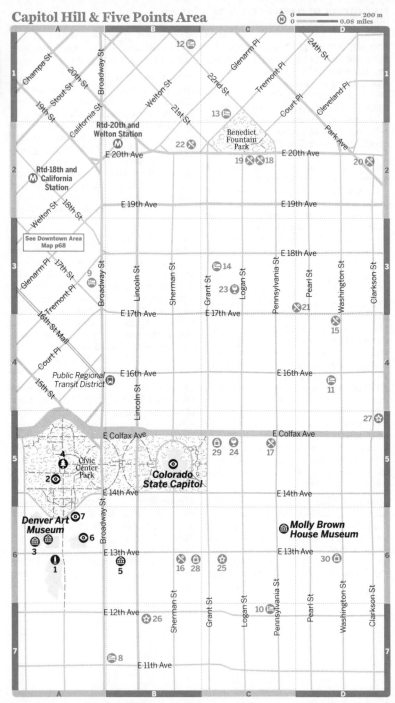

⊙ Top Sights
Colorado State Capitol.........................B5
Denver Art Museum.............................A6
Molly Brown House Museum...............C6

⊙ Sights
1 Big Sweep A6
2 Bronco Buster...................................A5
3 Byers-Evans House Museum A6
4 Civic Center Park...............................A5
5 Colorado History Museum...................B6
6 Denver Public Library.........................A6
7 Yearling A6

🛏 Sleeping
8 11th Avenue Hotel..............................B7
9 Brown Palace Hotel............................A3
10 Capitol Hill Mansion B&B....................C7
11 Denver International Youth
   Hostel D4
12 Melbourne International Hotel
   & Hostel...B1
13 Queen Anne Bed & Breakfast
   Inn C1
14 Warwick..C3

✗ Eating
15 Avenue Grill D4
16 City O' City......................................B6
17 Great Wall C5
18 Horseshoe Lounge............................C2
19 Jonesy's EatBar................................C2
20 La Pasadita......................................D2
   Palace Arms ....(see 9)
21 Stueben's Food Service.....................D3
22 Wahoo's Fish Taco B2

🍷 Drinking
23 Denver Wrangler C3
24 Uptown Brothers Brewery...................C5

☆ Entertainment
25 Benders Tavern.................................C6
26 Church B7
27 Fillmore Auditorium...........................D5

🛍 Shopping
28 Buffalo Exchange...............................B6
29 Capitol Hill Books..............................C5
   Jerry's Record Exchange............(see 29)
   Pandora Jewelry.........................(see 28)
30 Wax Trax Records D6

fusion creations for more than 20 years. Clam chowder, baby spinach and octopus salad, and tempura prawns are some of the offerings given special treatment. The bright space is surrounded by windows with pleasant lunchtime views of passing pedestrians.

HIGHLANDS & PLATTE RIVER VALLEY

TOP CHOICE 🍴 **Root Down**
CONTEMPORARY AMERICAN $$$
(Map p58; ☎303-993-4200; www.rootdown denver.com; 1600 W 33rd Ave; small plates $6-15; ☺5-10pm Sun-Thu, 5-11pm Fri & Sat, brunch 10am-2:30pm Sat-Sun; ⊜; 🚌6, 52 RTD) In a converted gas station, chef Justin Cucci has undertaken one of the city's most ambitious culinary concepts, marrying sustainable 'field-to-fork' practices, high-concept culinary fusions and a low-impact, energy efficient ethos. The menu changes seasonally, but consider yourself lucky if it includes the sweet-potato falafel or hoisin-duck confit sliders.

Unlike the troupe of restaurants jumping on the sustainable bandwagon, Root Down is largely wind powered, decorated with reused and reclaimed materials, and recycles *everything*. It's conceptually brilliant and one of Denver's most thrilling dining experiences.

🍴 **Z Cuisine**
FRENCH $$$
(Map p58; ☎303-477-1111; www.zcuisine online.com; 2239 & 2245 W 30th Ave; mains $19-29; ☺5-10pm Wed-Sat; ⊜☎; 🚌32, 44 RTD) It'd be better if you could look at the bill before you ate at this self-styled neighborhood bistro, because when your mouth is overwhelmed by any variety of braised lamb dishes or a simple, perfect steak and fries combination, you'll forget it. There's no better place around for (fancy) casual French fare, a fact well noted by national critics.

Rosa Linda's Mexican Cafe
MEXICAN $
(Map p58; ☎303-455-0608; www.rosalindas mexicancafe.com; 2005 W 33rd Ave; mains $6-12; ☺10am-9pm Mon-Sat; ⊜🍴👶; 🚌44) For more than 20 years the Aguirre family has been serving reasonably priced, authentic Mexican comfort fare with a side of old-fashioned hospitality. Winner of numerous awards – including Top 15 nachos in the

SETTING YOUR DENVER BUDGET

Budget travelers can eat well in Denver: cheap restaurant meals cost $7 or $8 and there are good options for self-caterers. Inexpensive lodgings are harder to find, but the city has a handful of well-located backpacker options where a dorm bed will cost around $20 and a double costs from about $50.

Midpriced restaurant meals cost $10 to $15. Midrange travelers will be torn between cheaper $80-a-night motel rooms in the 'burbs and digs nearer Downtown, where the average room costs $100 to $200 a night.

Top-end travelers can choose among the many boutique hotels and B&Bs in the $180+ bracket, often in quiet leafy streets just outside Downtown. Fine-dining options are plentiful.

nation by the *Wall Street Journal* – Rosa Linda's also does excellent chiles rellenos and mole, and plenty of vegetarian and health-conscious choices (check out the wholewheat grilled-cactus burrito).

Duo
CONTEMPORARY AMERICAN **$$$**

(Map p58; ☑303-477-4141; www.duodenver.com; 2413 W 32nd Ave; brunch $8-12, mains $17-23; ☺5-10pm Mon-Fri, 10am-2pm & 5-10pm Sat, 10am-2pm Sun; ☻; ☐32 RTD) All the lip service about the city's best brunch can be a little overwhelming, but Duo's cider-glazed pork 'Benedict' – poached eggs and a savory pile of slow-roasted pork, sourdough and wholegrain mustard – is the city's best brunch dish. With some french-press coffee, the bright corner cafe makes a perfect start to the weekend.

Squeaky Bean
CONTEMPORARY AMERICAN **$$$**

(Map p58; ☑303-284-0053; www.thesqueaky bean.net; 3301 Tejon St; mains $9-19; ☺7:30am-2:30pm Mon, 7:30am-10pm Tue-Thu, 7:30am-11pm Fri, 9:30am-11pm Sat, 9:30am-2:30pm Sun; ☻; ☐32, 44 RTD) 'Shake N Bake Veal Sweatbreads' gives you a sense of the bipolar approach to high dining here – this is contemporary American cuisine with good humor and technique. Somehow, the drinks list is even better. Try the 'Drinkable Molly Brown' – Stranahan's Colorado whiskey, Rothman Orchard apricot liqueur, tawny port, cinnamon extract, and a drunken apricot.

Fruition Restaurant
CONTEMPORARY AMERICAN **$$$**

(Map p58; ☑303-831-1962; www.fruitionrestau rant.com; 1313 E 6th Ave; mains $22-26; ☺5-10pm Mon-Sat, 5-8pm Sun; ☐2, 6, 12 RTD) Alex Seidel and Blake Edmunds are heavy hitters in Denver's fine-dining scene, pulling off their contemporary American plates (potato-wrapped oysters Rockefeller, duck with red-onion marmalade) with understated panache. The food is simply conceived, carefully executed and elegantly presented. Many of the greens, the chickens and the eggs come from Seidel's farm.

SOUTH CENTRAL DENVER

TOP CHOICE Barolo Grill
ITALIAN **$$$**

(☑303-393-1040; www.barologrilldenver.com; 3030 E 6th Ave; mains $19-35; ☺6-11pm Tue-Sat; ☻☑; ☐6 RTD) This deluxe Italian restaurant is one of Denver's best. It offers a shifting à la carte menu as well as a five-course degustation menu featuring the flavors of Italy's Piedmont, Tuscany and Veneto districts. The signature dish is a braised duck with olives. There's a select wine list and an outstanding dessert menu. Bookings essential.

Arada Restaurant & Bar
ETHIOPIAN **$$**

(Map p58; ☑303-329-3344; www.aradarestau rant.com; 750 Santa Fe Dr; mains $10-15; ☺5-10pm Wed-Sat, 5-8pm Tue & Sun; ☻☻; ☐1 RTD) You'll use soft, slightly sour *injera* bread as the vehicle to shovel down tomato *fit-fit* (diced tomato, onion and jalapeños in vinegar-based sauce) and combination platters such as Arada Six (which includes delicious *siga wot*, a spicy beef stew). The tile floor means no frills, but for those keen to share, this place is loads of fun.

Devil's Food
AMERICANA **$$**

(☑303-733-7448; www.devilsfoodbakery.com; 1020 S Gaylord St; pastries $4; ☺7am-3pm Sun-Wed, 7am-10pm Thu-Sat; ☐11 RTD) It does supper and sandwiches, but the decadent pastries are reason enough to visit this lovely Washington Park cafe. The hardest to resist is the red velvet hedgehog – a moist red cake covered in cream cheese icing and shaped like a little monster. The brunch menu, crowned by an excellent salmon Benedict, is a neighborhood favorite.

bang!
AMERICANA **$$$**

(☑303-455-1117; www.bangdenver.com; 3472 W 32nd Ave; mains $15-19; ☺11am-9pm Tue-Fri, 10am-9pm Sat, 10am-2pm Sun; ☻; ☐32, 28 RTD)

One of Denver's reigning kings of comfort food, bang! goes full-on for cuteness. The place is tiny and colorful, the wait staff are winsome and chatty, and the menu has tater tots, which are dished out on bright, mismatched Fiesta dinnerware.

El Taco De Mexico
MEXICAN $

(Map p58; ☑303-623-3926; 714 Santa Fe Dr; mains $5-9; ⊙7am-10pm Sun-Thu, 7am-11pm Fri-Sat; ☐1 RTD) Forget about ambience – it's a big yellow counter, florescent lights and a couple of slouching figures shoveling down tacos – but it's all too easy to forgive when you rip into the chili relleno burrito – a glorious disaster of peppers, cheese, refried pinto beans and salsa verde.

Remember when you're asked: yes, you want it smothered and yes, you want salsa and onions. This is *the* best place to get cheap eats in the Santa Fe Arts district, to the west of Capitol Hill.

Buckhorn Exchange Restaurant
STEAK $$$

(Map p58; ☑303-534-9505; www.buckhorn. com; 1000 Osage St; mains $22-38; ⊙11am-2pm & 5:30-9pm Mon-Thu, 5:30-10pm Fri-Sat, 5-9pm Sun; ⊜) If you've been waiting to try the Rocky Mountain oysters, you're in the right place; founded by a scout of Buffalo Bill Cody, this out-of-the-way steakhouse has bull nuts, rattlesnake, elk and all sorts of (relatively edible) game dishes. Good luck enjoying them with a clear conscience as the hundreds of stuffed heads gaze down on your table.

Domo Restaurant
JAPANESE $$$

(Map p58; ☑303-595-3666; www.domorestau rant.com; 1365 Osage St; mains $10-22; ☐30 RTD) 'Japanese country food' doesn't really capture the refinement of dishes at Domo, Denver's best Japanese restaurant. The spicy *maguro* and *hamachi* combination *donburi* is an explosively flavorful combination of fresh fish, seaweed and chili-soy dressing. Each main is served with seven traditional Japanese side dishes.

⌐TOP⌐ Sweet Action Ice Cream
CHOICE
ICE CREAM $

(Map p58; ☑303-282-4645; www.sweetaction icecream.com; 52 Broadway; cones $3-6; ⊙1-10pm Sun-Thu, 1-11pm Fri-Sat; ☐0 RTD) Don't wander past this neighborhood ice-cream parlor expecting the same old chocolate chip; the seasonal, house-made flavors include baklava, salted butterscotch and five

spice. In the summer there are tons of fruit-based varieties such as ginger peach and blackberry lavender. Bonus: they also do vegan varieties.

Señor Burrito
MEXICAN $

(Map p58; ☑303-733-0747; 12 E 1st Ave; mains $4-10; ⊙8am-9pm Mon-Sat; ☐0 RTD) If you need a quick bite to fortify you before drinking down the South Broadway strip, Señor Burrito is adequately quick and cheap. Authentic? Not so much. Morning options include an egg- and ham-loaded, Denver-style breakfast burrito, while the crunchy tacos – filled with ground beef, cheddar, lettuce and tomato – are just like mom used to make... back in Michigan.

Walnut Room Pizzeria
PIZZA $$

(Map p58; ☑303-736-6750; www.thewalnut room.com; 2 Broadway; pizzas $11-20; ⊙11am-10pm Mon-Tue, 11am-midnight Thu, 11am-3am Fri, noon-3am Sat, noon-10pm Sun; ☐0 RTD) Good, chewy thin crust and several inventive house specialties (such as the meaty, pineapple- and jalapeño-dressed Mile High Club Pie and pesto-covered Walnut Special) make this Broadway newcomer impressive. Framed photos of jam bands and local rockers playing at the associate Walnut Room venue line the tall walls of the booths.

Hornet
FUSION $

(Map p58; ☑303-777-7676; www.hornetrestau rant.com; 76 Broadway; mains $6-13; ⊙11am-2am Mon-Fri, 10am-2am Sat, 10am-midnight Sun; ☎; ☐0 RTD) At first glance it might seem uninspiring – standard sandwiches, grilled meats and pasta plates dominate – but this elegant corner diner punches things up with wide-ranging Southern, Latin American and Asian influences. It's atmospheric too, with tall windows, classic black-and-white tiles and fans that spin lazily overhead the brunch crowd.

BEYOND CENTRAL DENVER

Pho 95
VIETNAMESE $

(☑303-936-3322; 1002 S Federal Blvd; mains $8; ⊙9am-9pm; ♿; ☐30 RTD) The best place for *pho* (noodle soup) in Denver is a bit out there, parked in the middle of a strip mall on a bleak stretch of Federal, but slurping your way through a big, cheap bowl of noodles is worth the hike.

Drinking

If you consider yourself a beer snob, you might mistake Denver for a foamy, malty

Platte River Valley

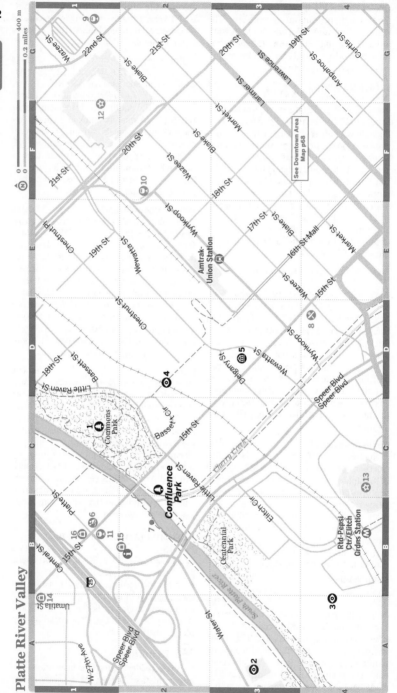

◉ **Top Sights**
Confluence Park C2

◉ **Sights**
1 Commons Park C1
2 Downtown Aquarium A3
3 Elitch Gardens... A4
4 Millennium Bridge D2
5 Museum of Contemporary Art D3

Activities, Courses & Tours
6 Confluence Kayaks B1
7 Platte Valley Trolley B2

⊗ **Eating**
8 Wazee Supper Club D4

◉ **Drinking**
9 Breckenridge Blake St Pub G1
10 Denver Chophouse & Brewery F2
11 My Brother's Bar B1

◉ **Entertainment**
12 Coors Field F1
13 Pepsi Center...C4
Sing Sing.. (see 10)

◉ **Shopping**
Metroboom ....(see 16)
14 Mona Lucero A1
15 REI B2
16 Wilderness Exchange Unlimited B1

corner of heaven. Forget about that watery stuff made in Golden, the brewing culture around these parts is truly world class – with craft and seasonal brews by the gallon, restaurants that sideline as microbreweries and kegs that arrive from the beer regions as near as Boulder and as far as Munich. Simply put, Denver adores beer.

If beer isn't your tipple, though, there are abundant options for spirits – try touring Stranahans Colorado Whiskey (p66), an excellent family operated distillery. Colorado's underdog wine producers turn out capable reds but are more celebrated for their whites, and don't forget Denver's small but excellent coffee houses.

DOWNTOWN & LODO

TOP CHOICE **Appaloosa Bar & Grill** BAR
(Map p68; ☎720-932-1700; www.appaloosagrill.com; 535 16th St; ⊙11am-2am Mon-Sun; ☐Welton) It's tricky to find a place on the Mall with a local feel, but plank floors, nightly local bands and kindly bartenders give the employee-owned Appaloosa a unique environment. There's not a whiff of the plastic corporate venture of other nearby bar-and-grill joints. With a killer hummus plate and two daily happy hours (2pm to 6pm and 10pm to midnight), you'll wobble out satisfied.

Red Square Euro Bistro VODKA BAR
(Map p68; ☎303-595-8600; www.redsquarebistro.com; 1512 Larimer St; vodka shots $4.50; ⊙5-9pm Sun-Thu, 5-11pm Fri & Sat; ☐10, 15, 20 RTD) Even if the vodka list is morea than 80 bottles deep – including staples from Russian origin, and also surprise sources such

as El Salvador – the most creative tipple on offer is house-infused. Horseraddish vodka? Dill? Anise? Garlic? The menu, of meaty bistro fare with an Eastern European influence, includes fancy stroganoff, veal and wild boar chop.

Located back from the street within Writer Sq.

Great Divide Brewing Company BREWPUB
(Map p68; ☎303-296-9460; www.greatdivide.com; 2201 Arapahoe St; ⊙2-8pm Mon-Tue, 2-10pm Wed-Sat; ☐48 RTD) This excellent local brewery does well to skip the same old burger menu and the fancy digs to keep its focus on what it does best: crafting exquisite beer. Bellying up to the bar, looking onto the copper kettles and sipping Great Divide's spectrum of seasonal brews is an experience that will make a beer drinker's eyes light up.

Corner Office LOUNGE
(Map p68; ☎303-825-6500; www.thecornerofficedenver.com; 1401 Curtis St; ⊙6:30am-11pm Sun-Thu, 6:30am-midnight Fri & Sat; ☎; ☐10, 15 RTD) The cheery sensibility of this excellent retro-style lounge is demonstrated in the wall of clocks frozen at 5pm and waggish menu of cocktails ('The Secretary' comes with a rim of grape Kool-Aid powder). It's perfect for a quick, sophisticated bite before the theater, and the chicken and waffles are highlights of a killer brunch menu.

Falling Rock Tap House BAR
(Map p68; ☎303-293-8338; www.fallingrocktaphouse.com; 1919 Blake St; ⊙11am-2am; ☐52, 55X, 58X, 72X RTD) High-fives and hollers

punctuate the scene when the Rockies triumph and beer drinkers file in to forget an afternoon of drinking Coors at the ball park. There are – count 'em – 75 beers on tap and the bottle list has almost 150. With all the local favorites, this is *the* place to drink beer Downtown.

Wynkoop Brewing Co   BREWPUB
(Map p68; ☎303-297-2700; www.wynkoop. com; 1634 18th St; mains $9-13; ☺11am-2am Mon-Sat, 11am-midnight Sun; ☝; ☐44, 48 RTD) Wynkoop's Rail Yard Ale is the city's most celebrated red ale, and beer fans file into to this spacious brewpub to knock them back while tossing darts, shooting pool or taking in the breeze on the wide porch. The taps change with the season and the menu offers passable pub standards. Call ahead for Saturday brewery tours.

The basement of the brewery hosts a long-running sketch comedy show on the weekends, and the jokes are appropriate for all ages.

Crú   WINE BAR
(Map p68; ☎303-893-9463; www.cruawinebar. com; 1442 Larimer St; glass of wine $9-26; ☺4-10pm Sun-Wed, 5-10pm Thu, 3pm-2am Fri & Sat; ☐6, 9, 10, 12, 15, 15L, 20, 28, 32, 44, 44L RTD, 16th St Mall Shuttle) This classy Larimer Sq wine bar is decked out in wine labels and posters, with dim lighting and gentle music. It looks so bespoke it's surprising to learn it's a chain (Dallas, Houston); there's another Denver branch at Park Meadows. Wine flights are the perfect way to sample some of the world's best plonk. The kitchen serves dishes designed for sharing.

Denver Chophouse & Brewery   BREWPUB
(Map p82; ☎303-269-0800; www.chophouse. com; 100/1735 19th St; ☺11am-11pm Mon-Thu, 11am-midnight Fri & Sat, 11am-10pm Sun; ☝) Chophouse brews are mostly European in style – pilsner, ales and lagers – and there's a good American pale ale. The Chophouse Brewery has sites in Boulder, Cleveland and Washington DC.

Breckenridge Blake St Pub   BREWPUB
(Map p82; ☎303-297-3644; www.breckbrew.com; 2220 Blake St; ☺11am-11pm; ☝; ☐8, 38 RTD) Blake St is home to the, ah, Breckenridge Blake St Pub, also known as the Breckenridge Ball Park Brewpub. Breckenridge's portfolio of beers is long and includes an unusual vanilla porter. The Trademark American pale ale is the signature brew and probably a good place to start.

TAG   COCKTAIL BAR
(Map p68; ☎303-996-9985; www.tag-restaurant. com; 1441 Larimer St; cocktails $9-12; ☐2, 12, 15 RTD) TAG's dinner menu, with it's bold and bizarre concoctions, might make more sense after a hit of acid; we still can't decided if hiramasa kingfish dressed in Pop Rocks candy is revolutionary or revolting. Apply this same mad scientist meddling to the drinks menu, however, and it's amazing. Jalapeño kumquat mojito? Yes, please.

Prime Bar   LOUNGE
(Map p68; ☎303-586-8888; www.primebar america.com; 1515 Arapahoe St; ☺11am-2am Mon-Thu, 4pm-2am Sat & Sun; ☐Arapahoe) Among all the area lounges with identical pedigrees – patio seats, creative cocktails, fancy french fries, tons of see-and-be-seens – the Prime Bar is a classy standout. Maybe it's the carved deer heads and wood paneling, lending it the feel of a postmodern hunting lodge, or a playlist mixing electronic patter with the Velvet Underground, but it simply works.

Jet Lounge   BAR
(Map p68; ☎303-572-3300; www.thejethotel. com; 1612 Wazee St; ☐16th St Shuttle) Designed to blend into the Jet Hotel's lobby, this lounge is the place to see and be seen in Denver. There is a bedroom-meets-house-party vibe: candles, cozy couches, a weekend DJ and lots and lots of beautiful people. Jet Lounge was a favorite with the *Real World Denver* housemates. Order bottle service, sit back and melt into the party.

Mynt Lounge   BAR
(Map p68; ☎303-825-6968; www.myntmojito lounge.com; 1424 Market St; ☐16th St Mall Shuttle) This place offers one of the best happy hours in town – from 3pm to 9pm the martinis cost around $3 and there is a massive list to choose from. Mynt is a white-themed minimalist lounge with a very sexy vibe.

Nallen's   IRISH PUB
(Map p68; ☎303-572-0667; www.nallensdenver. com; 1429 Market St; ☺2pm-2am; ☐6, 9, 10, 15L, 20, 28, 32, 44, 44L RTD) Nallen's is Denver's oldest Irish pub, and since opening in 1992 it seems to have started a craze. Happy hour is from 2pm to 7pm.

Celtic Tavern   IRISH PUB
(Map p68; ☎303-308-1576; www.celtictavern. com; 1801 Blake St; mains $6-15; ☺11am-2am Mon-Fri, 5pm-2am Sat; ☝; ☐1, 2, 12 RTD) The Celtic Tavern is a warm and convivial

place with 50 beers on tap and a selection of top-shelf Scotch, Irish and American whiskeys to sample. The bar menu features traditional Irish stew, potato and leek soup, welsh rarebit and the like, as well as classic American favorites.

Rock Bottom Restaurant & Brewery
BREWPUB

(Map p68; ☎303-534-7616; www.rockbottom. com; 1001 16th St; ☺11am-2am; ☻; ☐Arapahoe) Drinkers are met with the gleaming stainless sheen of brew kettles as they enter this chain brewpub, perched on the prime real estate of the 16th St Mall. It's outgrown 'micro' status and is not so hot compared to smaller craft brewers in the region, but the award-winning Red Rock Red and people-watching from the patio make for a pleasant afternoon.

Katie Mullen's Irish Pub & Restaurant
IRISH PUB

(Map p68; ☎303-573-0336; www.katiemullens. com; 1550 Court Pl; ☺11am-1:30am; ☐15 RTD) Denver's largest Irish Bar – an enormous 11,000 sq ft – maintains a surprisingly snuggled-down feel through dark wood, polished brass, book shelves and fireside seating (the faux embers glow even when the heat outside rages). If the environs are a bit mannish, it seems to suit the guys who loosen their ties and talk business over a Guinness.

There's also an extensive menu on hand. Don't mess around with the traditional Irish comfort food; go straight for the halibut.

Croc's Mexican Bar & Grill
BAR

(Map p68; ☎303-436-1144; www.crocsmexi cangrill.com; 1630 Market St; ☺11am-2am Mon-Fri, noon-2am Sat & Sun; ☻; ☐Market St) This bar and grill is central to the Market St stumble, a cavernous space that turns out passable Mexican food in brawny portions and pipes in big-screened sports from every corner of the world. When the party goes off, winsome waitresses stomp along the bar pouring tequila down patron's throats under the glassy gaze of Hal, a giant stuffed alligator.

CAPITOL HILL & GOLDEN TRIANGLE

Uptown Brothers Brewery BREWPUB

(Map p78; ☎303-263-3164; www.uptownbroth ers.com; 320 E Colfax Ave; ☺10am-2am Mon-Sat, 10am-midnight Sun; ☻; ☐15 RTD) When we checked in, the Brothers were just getting their brewing operation off the ground, but

looking at their selection of taps and bottles gives us high hopes. The menu? More of the typical bar-food standards. Come here to drink and wander around Colfax to work up an appetite.

FIVE POINTS, UPTOWN & CITY PARK

TOP CHOICE **Crema Coffee House** CAFE

(Map p58; ☎720-235-2995; www. cremacoffeehouse.net; 2862 Larimer St; ☺7am-7pm Mon-Fri, 9am-5pm Sat & Sun; ☎; ☐44 RTD) Noah Price, a clothing-designer-turned-coffee impresario, takes his job seriously, selecting, brewing and pouring Denver's absolute best coffee. The espresso and french-pressed are complete perfection, but it's the oatmeal latte, delicately infused ice teas and the toast bar – with a mess of jams and toppings – that puts this place over the top.

Thin Man Tavern
BAR

(Map p58; ☎303-320-7814; www.thinmantavern. com; 2015 E 17th Ave; ☺1pm-2am; ☐20 RTD) The Thin Man is a damn sight more stylish than most neighborhood taverns; it's decked out in all kinds of old Catholic paintings, and vintage lampshades cast the place in a warm, sentimental glow. Since a local magazine named it among the best low-key singles' spots in the city, the crowd is looking a bit more stylish, too.

In addition to a good beer selection and stiff drinks, it also hosts free art films in the basement-level Ubisububi Room and, in the summer, showS classics flicks outside in the parking lot.

Lost Lake Lounge
BAR

(☎303-333-4345; 3602 E Colfax Ave; ☺7pm-2am) According to the guys behind the bar, the photobooth in the back has 'seen more action than the Whitesnake tour bus.' This is one of the million reasons we love Denver's newest hipster magnet. Cheap drinks, a crackling fire and prowling 20-some-things in vintage tees are a few more.

Mezcal
BAR

(☎303-322-5219; www.mezcal-restaurant.com; 3230 E Colfax Ave; ☺11am-2am; ☻; ☐15 RTD) Sure they serve food, but we won't lie – we come here to drink. They have a bundle of tequilas (though, strangely, not much mezcal) and the margaritas pack a punch. After a few you will inhale the $1 tacos, which are available after 10pm. It's a great place to warm up before a show at the Blue Bird Theater.

Denver Wrangler
GAY BAR

(Map p78; ☎303-837-1075; www.denverwrangler.
com; 1700 Logan St; ☺11am-2am; 🚇101 RTD)
Though it attracts an amiable crowd of gay
male professionals after work, the central
location endows Denver's premiere bear bar
with a flirty pick-up scene on the weekend.
The sidewalk seating is a plus.

HIGHLANDS & PLATTE RIVER VALLEY

My Brother's Bar
BAR

(Map p82; ☎303-445-9991; 2376 15th St; ☺11am-
2am; 🚇28, 32, 44 RTD) Classic rock and roll,
lacquered booths and tables made from old
wood barrels greet you inside Denver's oldest bar. Grab a seat on the leafy patio if it's
nice outside. The bar is on a popular cycle
path, and has been a local institution since
it opened.

SOUTH CENTRAL DENVER

Divino Wine & Spirits
LIQUOR

(☎303-778-1800; www.divinowine.com; 1240 S
Broadway; ☺10am-10pm Mon-Thu, 10am-11pm
Sat, 10am-6pm Sun; 🚇0 RTD) Bottles are
stacked from floor to ceiling in this southwest shop – a little out of the way, but worth
it for serious wine drinkers. It hosts events
and does tastings on the weekend, and the
staff know their stuff. The budget conscious
want to keep an eye on the rotating selection on the '10 under 10 rack.'

SOUTH BROADWAY

TOP CHOICE Beatrice & Woodsley
BAR

(Map p58; ☎303-777-3505; www.beatrice
andwoodsley.com; 38 S Broadway; cocktails $8-
12; ☺5-10pm Sun-Wed, 5-11pm Thu & Fri, 10am-
4pm & 5-11pm-Sat & Sun; 🚇0 RTD) The menu of
small plates is whimsical (such as the corn-
fed scallop – a scallop served with toasted
cornbread and spicy slaw) and brunch here
is the fanciest on S Broadway, but it's the
cocktails that kill us. The Europa '51 exem-
plifies this bar's artistry, combining gin,
cynar, apple juice, citrus-pepper tincture
(whatever that is) and orange.

Beatrice and Woodsley is also the most
artfully designed dining room in Denver. Chainsaws are buried into the wall to
support shelves, there's an aspen growing
through the back of the dining room and
the feel is that of a mountain cabin being
elegantly reclaimed by nature.

Sputnik
BAR

(Map p58; ☎720-570-4503; www.sputnikdenver.
com; 3 S Broadway; ☺10:30am-2am Mon-Fri,

10am-2am Sat & Sun; 🕾; 🚇0 RTD) The Sputnik
does it all – it's simultaneously a plucky
brunch spot, a neighborhood dive bar and
an excellent place for espresso. Still, it's
never more fun than when there's a show
next door at the Hi-Dive and the indie rockers spill over for strong pours and a seat in
the old-school photo booth.

If spending a long night of drinks, snacks,
and rock and roll still isn't enough for you,
the long-running 'Hangover Brunch' does it
right, with spicy Bloody Marys and lots of
ragged morning-after style.

BEYOND CENTRAL DENVER

Del Norte Brewing Company
BREWPUB

(☎303-935-3223; www.delnortebrewing.com;
2-0/1390 W Evans Ave; ☺3:30-6:30pm Fri)
Makes a range of lightly hopped Mexican-
style beers as well as the stunning 7.8%
Luminaria Bock. All have won awards. You
can buy direct from the sales room on Friday afternoons only.

★ Entertainment

Nightclubs

TOP CHOICE Bar Standard
NIGHTCLUB

(Map p58; ☎303-534-0222; www.co
clubs.com; 1037 Broadway; ☺8pm-2am Fri & Sat;
🚇0 RTD) From the sleek deco interior to the
DJ roster that spins *way* outside the typically mindless thump, Bar Standard is an
inimitable gem in Denver's nightclub scene.
It's ice cold without the attitude, and when
the right DJ is on the tables it can be some
of the best dancing in town.

Tracks
GAY CLUB

(☎303-863-7326; www.tracksdenver.com; 3500
Walnut St; ☺9pm-2am Fri & Sat, hrs vary Sun-
Thu) Events in Denver's biggest and wildest
gay-orientated nightclub are a blast and
many of them are huge; the monthly Babes-
ArounDenver event is the largest women's
dance party in the country. There's a mix of
musical tastes and crowds, so consult local
listings.

Beta Nightclub
NIGHTCLUB

(Map p68; ☎303-383-1909; www.betanightclub.
com; 1909 Blake St; ☺9am-2am Thu & Fri; 🚇52
RTD) This huge club swaps musical flavors
like fashionable boutique sneakers. The
best parties go off in the interior Beatport
lounge, sending *au courant* bass, hip-hop
and electro through a sound system that
will rattle your fillings loose.

Charlie's
GAY CLUB

(Map p58; ☎303-839-8890; www.charliesdiner.com; 900 E Colfax Ave; ☺11am-2am; ☐15 RTD) Who says Colorado is a straight state? There are masses – predominantly male – at this friendly place who would happily contest that. Shoot some pool, croon a tune in the karaoke lounge, jabber around one of the bars or get down to some music on the roomy dance floor.

Church
NIGHTCLUB

(Map p78; ☎303-832-3538; 1160 Lincoln St; cover $10; ☺Thu-Sun; ☐0, 6, 10, 16 RTD) There's nothing like ordering a stiff drink inside an old 1865 cathedral. Yes, this club, which draws a large and diverse crowd, is in a former house of the Lord. Lit by hundreds of altar candles and flashing blue strobe lights, the Church has three dance floors, a couple of lounges and even a sushi bar! Arrive before 10pm Friday through Sunday to avoid the cover charge.

La Rumba
NIGHTCLUB

(Map p58; ☎303-572-8006; www.larumba-denver.com; 99 W 9th Ave; ☺9pm-2am Fri-Sun; ☐0, 3L, 6, 83L RTD) Though this place wobbles along as a salsa club the rest of the weekend, the Club Lip Gloss on Friday nights is a great party. Indie rock, garage and British pop bring an ultra-hip, gay-friendly vibe to the dance floor.

Live Music

TOP CHOICE Hi-Dive
LIVE MUSIC

(Map p58; ☎720-570-4500; www.hi-dive.com; 7 S Broadway; ☐0 RTD) Local rock heroes and touring indie bands light up the stage at the Hi-Dive, a venue at the heart of Denver's local music scene. During big shows it gets deafeningly loud, cheek-to-jowl with hipsters and humid as an armpit. In other words, it's perfect.

El Chapultepec
LIVE MUSIC

(Map p68; ☎303-295-9126; 1962 Market St; ☺7am-2am, music from 9pm; ☐38, 52 RTD) This smoky little old-school joint attracts a diverse mix of people. It's a dedicated jazz venue where the music is the main focus. Since it opened in 1951 Frank Sinatra, Tony Bennett and Ella Fitzgerald have played here, as have Jagger and Richards. Local jazz bands take the tiny stage nightly, but you never know who might drop by.

Grizzly Rose
LIVE MUSIC

(☎303-295-1330; www.grizzlyrose.com; 5450 N Valley Hwy; cover $5-10; ☺from 6pm Tue-Sun; ☒)

This is one kick-ass honky-tonk – 40,000 sq ft of hot live music – attracting real cowboys from as far as Cheyenne. The Country Music Association called it the best country bar in America. If you've never experienced line dancing, then put on the boots, grab the Stetson and let loose.

Just north of the city limits off I-25 (you'll have to drive or cab it), the Grizzly is famous for bringing in huge industry stars – Willie Nelson, Lee Ann Rimes – and only charging $10 per ticket.

Bluebird Theater
LIVE MUSIC

(☎303-322-2308; www.bluebirdtheater.net; 3317 E Colfax Ave; ☒; ☐15, 15L RTD) This medium-sized theater is general admission standing-room, and has terrific sound and clear sight lines from the balcony. This venue often offers the last chance to catch bands on their way up to the big time.

Ogden Theatre
LIVE MUSIC

(Map p58; ☎303-832-1874; www.ogdentheatre.net; 935 E Colfax Ave; ☒; ☐15 RTD) One of Denver's best live-music venues, the Ogden Theatre has a checkered past. Built in 1917, it was derelict for many years and might have been dozed in the early 1990s, but it's now listed on the National Register of Historic Places. Bands such as Edward Sharpe & the Magnetic Zeros and Lady Gaga have played here.

Harry Houdini performed at this theater in 1919 and it appeared in the movie *The Rocky Horror Picture Show*. Jack Nicholson drove his Winnebago past the Ogden pulling into Denver in *About Schmidt*.

If the house is packed, make for the upstairs level, where the catwalk extends on the wings and you'll have a beautiful bird's-eye view and plenty of room to move.

Larimer Lounge
PIANO BAR

(Map p58; ☎303-291-1007; www.larimerlounge.com; 2721 Larimer St; ☺noon-2am; ☐38, 48 RTD) This dive is a proving ground for acts from across the indie rock spectrum – last time we checked in metal heads in clown makeup were sound checking. With shows seven nights a week, it's a reliable bet for upcoming locals and good touring indie acts. There's also a patio to escape from the noise.

Sing Sing
PIANO BAR

(Map p82; ☎303-291-0880; www.singsing.com; 1735 19th St; cover $7; ☺7pm-late Wed & Thu, 6pm-late Fri & Sat; ☒; ☐31X, 40X, 52, 80X, 86X, 120X RTD, ☒Union Station) This lively dueling piano bar is very popular with bachelorette parties. Sing Sing fills quickly; arrive around 6:30pm to score a table near the pianos. It's pretty noisy (don't expect much talking) but the atmosphere is fun. Song requests are taken (usually accompanied by $5), but many folks request the same songs.

Fillmore Auditorium
LIVE MUSIC
(Map p78; ☎303-837-0360; www.livenation.com; 1510 Clarkson St; ☐15 RTD) One of the major music venues in town, this big open space has hosted classic acts such as Parliament Funkadelic, big indies such as Feist, and even roller derby. The acoustics are far from perfect, but it's certainly one of Denver's essential venues.

Benders Tavern
LIVE MUSIC
(Map p78; ☎303-861-7070; www.benderstavern. com; 314 E 13th Ave; occasional cover charge; ⊙7pm-2am Mon-Wed, 4pm-2am Fri & Sat; ☐2, 10 RTD) Benders is one of the premier music venues for smaller punk and local bands in Denver. It's a great space kitted out with a quality PA system and a good bar. Most nights it's free, but sometimes there'll be a modest cover charge. There's a weekly karaoke night and an open-mic night.

Comedy & Cabaret

Comedy Works
COMEDY
(Map p68; ☎303-595-3637; www.comedyworks. com; 1226 15th St; ☐6, 9, 10, 15L, 20, 28, 32, 44, 44L RTD) Denver's best comedy club occupies a basement space in Larimer Sq (enter down a set of stairs at the corner of Larimer and 15th) and routinely brings in up-and-coming yucksters from around the country. It can be a bit cramped if you're claustrophobic, but the seats are comfortable and the quality of acts is top-shelf.

Performances also take place at the slightly bigger Comedy Works South location across town.

Lannie's Clocktower Cabaret
CABARET
(Map p68; ☎303-293-0075; www.lannies.com; 1601 Arapahoe St; tickets $25-40; ⊙1-5pm Tue, to 11pm Wed-Thu, 1pm-1:30am Fri & Sat; ☐Arapahoe) Bawdy, naughty and strangely romantic, Lannie's Clocktower Cabaret is a wild child standout among LoDo's rather straight-laced (or at least straight) night spots. A table right up near the front will get you in the sparkling heart of the action, and if you parse the schedule, you might get a glance at the sexiest drag queens in Denver.

Bovine Metropolis Theater
COMEDY
(Map p68; ☎303-758-4722; www.bovinemetro polis.com; 1527 Champa St; ☐15 RTD) This long-standing black box theater hosts a clutch of fresh-faced improv comedy performers and shows most days of the week for under $20. It also offers afternoon workshops for tour groups.

Performing Arts

TOP CHOICE / Denver Performing Arts Complex
THEATER
(Map p68; ☎720-865-4220; www.artscomplex. com; cnr 14th & Champa Sts; ☐1, 30, 30L, 31, 36L, 48 RTD) This massive complex – one of the largest of its kind – occupies four city blocks and houses several major theaters, the historic Ellie Caulkins Opera House and the Seawell Grand Ballroom. It's also home to the Colorado Ballet, Denver Center for the Performing Arts, Opera Colorado and the Colorado Symphony Orchestra.

Paramount Theatre
THEATER
(Map p68; ☎303-623-0106; www.denverpara mount.com; 1621 Glenarm Pl; ☐10 RTD) Lots of red velvet and gold trimming deck out the Paramount, one of the premiere midsized theaters in the West. Listed on the National Register of Historic Places, its recent acts include Rufus Wainwright, Margaret Cho and 'Weird Al' Yankovic.

GAY & LESBIAN DENVER

Even though Colorado has some very socially conservative areas, Denver is a very progressive and broad-minded place, and gay and lesbian travelers should expect no particular trouble. Overt displays of affection in public might cause some raised eyebrows, but this is probably true for heterosexual couples as well. The bohemian Capitol Hill district is the center of the gay and lesbian scene. Some of the city's gay and lesbian clubs include La Rumba (p87), where Friday night is a dedicated hipster night called Lip Gloss, and Tracks (p86). The centrally located Denver Wrangler (p86) is a neighborhood watering hole that attracts middle-aged gay men.

Opera Colorado
OPERA

(Map p68; ☑303-468-2030; www.operacolorado. org; 950 13th St; ⊙box office 10am-5pm Mon-Thu, 10am-noon Fri; ⬛; ☑1, 8, 15L, 30, 31, 48 RTD) Founded in 1983, Opera Colorado is based in the Denver Performing Arts Complex.

Colorado Symphony Orchestra
LIVE MUSIC

(CSO; Map p68; ☑303-623-7876; www.colorado symphony.org; 1000 14th St; ⬛; ☑1, 8, 15L, 30, 31, 48 RTD) The Boettcher Concert Hall in the Denver Performing Arts Complex is home to this renowned symphony orchestra. The orchestra performs an annual 21-week Masterworks season, as well as concerts aimed at a broader audience.

Denver Center for the Performing Arts
THEATER

(Map p68; ☑303-893-4100; www.denvercenter. org; 1101 13th St; ⬛; ☑1, 8, 15L, 30, 31, 48 RTD) The Denver Center for the Performing Arts is the theater wing of the huge Denver Performing Arts Complex. Productions have included *Shrek the Musical, Billy Elliott, Les Miserables, The Lion King* and *West Side Story*.

Colorado Ballet
DANCE

(Map p68; ☑303-837-8888; www.coloradoballet. org; cnr 14th & Curtis Sts; ⊙box office 9am-5pm Mon-Fri; ⬛; ☑1, 30, 30L, 31, 36L, 48 RTD) The Colorado Ballet company has 30 professional dancers who come from all over the world. Most performances are staged at the Ellie Caulkins Opera House within the Denver Performing Arts Complex.

Ellie Caulkins Opera House
THEATER

(Map p68; ☑303-468-2030; www.operacolorado. org; 1101 13th St; ☑1, 30, 30L, 31, 36L, 48 RTD) A major overhaul of this historic performance house has endowed it with luxurious acoustics, excellent sight lines and a very modern feel. It's also huge - more than 2000 seats - so if you buy cheap seats be sure to bring opera glasses.

Sports
INVESCO Field at Mile High
SPORTS ARENA

(Mile High Stadium; Map p58; ☑720-258-3000; www.invescofieldatmilehigh.com; 1805 S Bryant St; ⬛; ☑16, 16L, 28, 30, 30L, 31, 36L RTD) The much-lauded Denver Broncos football team and the Colorado Rapids soccer team play at Mile High Stadium, 1 mile west of Downtown. This stadium is also home to the Denver Outlaws lacrosse team and has an eclectic schedule of events including major rock

concerts for superstars such as U2. Stadium tours are organized through the Colorado Sports Hall of Fame.

Coors Field
SPORTS ARENA

(Map p82; ☑800-388-7625; www.mlb.com/col/ ballpark/; 2001 Blake St; prices vary; ⊙hrs vary; ⬛; ☑Union Station, ☑16th St Shuttle) Denver is a city known for manic sports fans, and boasts five pro teams. The Colorado Rockies play baseball at the highly rated Coors Field.

Pepsi Center
SPORTS ARENA

(Map p82; ☑303-405-1111; www.pepsicenter. com; 1000 Chopper Circle; ☑C line, D line Union Station) The mammoth Pepsi Center hosts the Denver Nuggets basketball team, the Colorado Mammoth of the National Lacrosse League and the Colorado Avalanche hockey team. In off season it's a mega concert venue.

Cinemas
Landmark Mayan Theater
CINEMA

(Map p58; ☑303-744-6799; www.landmark theatres.com; 110 Broadway; ☑0 RTD) Even without the fancy sound system and enormous screen, this is the best place in Denver to take in a film. The 1930s movie palace is a romantic, historic gem and - bonus! - it serves beer.

🛍 Shopping

Despite the same old American chain stores that dominate Denver's shopping scene, the city has some excellent independent boutiques scattered throughout its neighborhoods, posing a problem for serious shoppers who are in Denver without a car. If you are on foot, the three best districts for browsing are LoDo, Cherry Creek and South Broadway, all of which are walkable areas with lots of appealing shops, some featuring locally designed clothes, art and housewares.

Most visitors will pass through LoDo, where the crowded and bustling pedestrian-only 16th St Mall gets a lot of foot traffic. Unfortunately there's not much unique shopping on the mall beyond the kitschy Western souvenir shops (we're talking dream catchers, buffalo statuettes and suspect 'authentic' Native American wares). Just off of the mall, the Larimer Sq area along Larimer St has a clutch of high-end boutiques suitable for more discerning shoppers. The Cherry Creek neighborhood, about a mile to the south of LoDo is another a good place for shoppers to take a stroll. The massive Cherry Creek Shopping Center (p93) towers above the neighborhood – it's Denver's ritziest indoor mall – but a wander among the blocks to the north will reveal lots of galleries and spendy boutiques. The South Broadway district, where rents are cheaper, has a unique set of stores catering to alternative tastes and younger crowds. The heart of the neighborhood can be explored on foot along S Broadway between 1st and Alameda Aves.

DOWNTOWN & LODO

TOP CHOICE **Tattered Cover Bookstore** BOOKS
(Map p68; ☑303-436-1070; www.tatter edcover.com; 1628 16th St; ⏱6:30am-9pm Mon-Fri, 9am-9pm Sat, 10am-6pm Sun; ⎗Wazee St) There are plenty of places to curl up with a book in Denver's beloved independent bookstore, one of three locations in the Denver area. Bursting with new and used books, it has a good stock of regional travel guides and nonfiction titles dedicated to the Western states and Western folklore. It also has an on-site cafe, and hosts free film and literature events.

Goorin Brothers ACCESSORIES
(Map p68; ☑303-534-4287; www.goorin.com; 1410 Larimer St; ⎗1, 2, 10, 12, 44L RTD) A stylish fedora will put a little bounce in your step while strutting through the ritzy Laimer Sq district. This San Francisco–based source of hip, quality headwear has a great range for men and women.

Champa Fine Wine & Liquor LIQUOR
(Map p68; ☑303-571-5547; 1456 Champa St; ⏱11am-midnight Mon-Sat, 11am-11pm Sun; ⎗Champa) Descending the stairs into this freshly remodeled bottle shop opens up a heavenly find for discerning self-caterers. It offers a top selection of wine (though most is imported from California) and a mix-and-match six-pack option for visitors who want to take a Colorado beer tour on the cheap.

Colorado Rockies Dugout Store CLOTHING
(Map p68; ☑303-832-8326; Suite 150, 535 16th St; ⏱10am-6pm Mon-Fri, 10am-5pm Sat, 11am-2pm Sun) This official shop of the Rockies baseball team is tucked into a mall along 16th St, packed wall-to-wall with official gear, hats, pendants and team-signed baseballs. During the season you can also buy tickets and get information about games.

Wild West Denver Store SOUVENIRS
(Map p68; ☑303-446-8640; 715 16th St; ⏱9am-8:30pm Mon-Sat, 9am-2:30pm Sun; ⎗California) There's a mess of Western trinket stores along the upper Mall with nearly identical stock, but this is the brightest of the bunch. It's full of knickknacks, key chains, kitty sweatshirts and all manner of stuff featuring wolves, buffalo and marginally PC depictions of Native Americans. Higher quality items include some moccasins and gold aspen-leaf pendants.

Cry Baby Ranch WESTERN
(Map p68; ☑303-623-3979; www.crybabyranch. com; 1421 Larimer St; ⏱10am-7pm Mon-Fri, 10am-6pm Sat, noon-5pm Sun; ⎗12, 15 RTD) Peeking at the price tags of boots hand-tooled with skull and crossbones, it's quickly evident that this store is not for your work-a-day cowpoke, but the Western-themed home wares and eclectic, bizarre goods (John Wayne lunchbox, anyone?) are a blast to browse.

Tewksbury & Co WINE
(Map p68; ☑303-825-1880; www.tewksburycom pany.com; 1512 Larimer St; ⎗10, 15, 20 RTD) 'Colorado's Lifestyle Store' is a real 'man cave' selling hand-rolled cigars (which you can smoke inside!), local wine and fly-fishing trips. The staff is a little surly and the bottle selection is limited, but for a glimpse into the local psyche, it's a worthy stop.

EVOO Marketplace GOURMET FOOD
(Map p68; ☑303-974-5784; www.evoomarket place.com; 1338 15th St; 375ml bottles $15-19; ⏱11am-7pm Tue-Sat, 11am-4pm Sun; ⎗6, 9, 10, 15L, 20, 28, 32, 44, 44L RTD) This specialty shop sells extra-virgin olive oils and balsamic vinegars from across the US and around the world.

CAPITOL HILL, GOLDEN TRIANGLE & CITY PARK

TOP CHOICE **Wax Trax Records** MUSIC
(Map p78; ☑303-831-7246; www.wax traxrecords.com; 638 E 13th Ave; ⎗2, 10, 15, 15L RTD) For more than 30 years Wax Trax Records has been trading at this Denver location, stocking a huge quantity of CDs, DVDs, vinyl and music paraphernalia. Indie, alternative, punk, goth, folk, rock, hip-hop, jazz, reggae – anything that's a bit edgy you'll either find in store or they'll order for you. There are two adjacent shopfronts – one selling CDs and DVDs, the other exclusively vinyl.

Mod Livin'

HOMEWARES

(5327 E Colfax Ave; ⊙10am-9pm Mon-Sat, 11am-9pm Sun; 🚍15 RTD) Fans of midcentury modern furniture will be giddy running around this enormous showroom, littered with pristine vintage gear and newly manufactured designer furnishings.

Capitol Hill Books

BOOKS

(Map p78; ✆303-837-0700; www.capitolhill books.com; 300 E Colfax Ave; ⊙10am-6pm Mon-Sat, 11am-5pm Sun; 🚍15 RTD) It doesn't have the selection or elan of the Tattered Cover (right) but over its 30-year life Capitol Hill has retained the rare magic of a *real* bookshop. The rugs are threadbare. The floor creaks. There's a random cardboard cutout of Humphrey Bogart. Best of all, the staff of book lovers is quick with helpful suggestions.

Jerry's Record Exchange

MUSIC

(Map p78; ✆303-830-2336; 312 E Colfax Ave; ⊙10am-7:30pm Mon-Sat, noon-5pm Sun; 🚍15 RTD) Behind an out-of-place Bavarian storefront on a scrappy stretch of Colfax is Jerry's, a den of musty vinyl records that will delight dedicated record hunters. Those willing to thumb through stacks of yesteryear's hair-rock bands, midperiod Streisand and Herb Albert will be rewarded by a smattering of moderately priced gems.

Twist & Shout

MUSIC

(✆303-722-1943; www.twistandshout.com; 2508 E Colfax Ave; ⊙10am-10pm Mon-Sat, 10am-8pm Sun; 🖷; 🚍15, 15L RTD) The selection of used CDs at this brightly lit store is extensive, but head to the little den of used vinyl in the back for rare goodies, original pressings and surprising foreign imports. It also brings a discerning roster of in-store performances that run the gamut of musical taste.

Peppermint Boutique

CLOTHING

(Map p58; www.peppermintdenver.com; 1227 E 17th Ave; ⊙10am-7pm Mon-Sat, 11am-5pm Sun; 🖷; 🚍20 RTD) This boutique has an effortless charm, and stocks accessories, interesting jewelry and dresses that are hip and casually sophisticated. Considering the careful selection and high quality, it's also surprisingly inexpensive.

Plastic Chapel

TOYS

(✆303-722-0715; www.plasticchapel.com; 3109 E Colfax Ave; ⊙noon-6pm Tue-Sat, 11am-4pm Sun; 🚍15 RTD) Rows of clear plastic cubes house all kinds of designer toys, collectible Japanese-made figurines and other limited edition off-the-wall stuff to make this Denver's wickedest toy store. The toys are mostly suited for adult collectors – you're getting high-dollar stuff such as Kid Robot and StrangeCo, not Fischer Price. Also hosts design competitions and graphic arts shows.

Tattered Cover Bookstore

BOOKS

(✆303-322-7727; www.tatteredcover.com; 2526 E Colfax Ave; ⊙9am-9pm Mon-Sat, 10am-6pm Sun; 🚍15 RTD) Massive and bursting with new and used books, Denver's beloved independent bookstore has a particularly good selection of niche travel guides to the surrounding region and western-states nonfiction and folklore. The East Colfax location has a few more titles, if not the atmosphere, of the original location at the foot of the 16th St Mall. All sites host top-drawer literary events.

Buffalo Exchange

CLOTHING

(Map p78; ✆303-866-0165; www.buffaloex change.com; 230 E 13th Ave; ⊙11am-8pm Mon-Sat, noon-7pm Sun; 🖷) Part of a growing nationwide chain, Buffalo Exchange in Capitol Hill is a huge space with new and used clothing: retro, futuristic, trad and garish. You want a hip 1950s shirt or a little something for a costume party? This is the place. Garments, shoes and accessories are bought and sold.

🖉 Pandora Jewelry

ACCESSORIES

(Map p78; ✆303-832-7073; www.pandora jewelrydenver.com; 220 E 13th Ave; ⊙10am-7pm Mon-Sat, 11am-5pm Sun; 🖷; 🚍2 RTD) This is a friendly shop selling tasteful jewelry – ladies and mens – as well as cards, trinkets, gifts and novelties. The shop doesn't stock items that incorporate animal products.

HIGHLANDS & PLATTE RIVER VALLEY

TOP CHOICE REI

SPORTING GOODS

(Recreational Equipment Incorporated; Map p82; ✆303-756-3100; www.rei.com; 1416 Platte St; ⊙10am-9pm Mon-Fri, 10am-7pm Sat, 10am-6pm Sun; 🖷; 🚍10, 28, 32, 44 RTD) The flagship store of this outdoor equipment supplier is an essential stop for those using Denver as a springboard into the great outdoors. In addition to top gear for camping, cycling, climbing and skiing, it has a rental department, maps and the Pinnacle: a 47ft indoor structure of simulated red sandstone for climbing and repelling.

DENVER FOR KIDS

With clear skies, tons of museums and lots of wholesome family attractions, Denver is an excellent destination for families. The centrally located LoDo district is a real magnet for tourists of all ages; for little ones there are great shops, a ubiquity of kids' menus and, if they start to get a little cranky, an ever-present ice-cream stand or a splash in the park to perk them up.

Outside with Kids

With loads of outdoor spaces and parks, there's plenty space for the little ones to burn off their excess energy. Free activities in the fresh air include a drive up to Mt Evans summit (p98), a trip to Red Rocks Amphitheatre (p102) and a swim and splash at Confluence Park (p62). For a few bucks you can paddle a kayak from Confluence Kayaks (p66) or rent the whole family bikes from the city's B Cycle (p95) program. If Johnny or Jenny are keen skaters or rollerbladers, go to Denver's awesome skate park (p64) and watch them, ah, shred…dude.

Best Museums

Though the Children's Museum (p63) is perhaps a little underwhelming for moms and dads, Denver has plenty of museums that are more fun for the *whole* family.

» Denver Art Museum (p59): grown-ups will love the excellent collection and kids can get creative in terrific hands-on workstations.

» Firefighters Museum (p56): great for a few hours of fun, this will help teach the kids how not to burn the house down.

» Denver Zoo (p61): squeals of delight will greet the gross-out kids' program on animal excrement.

» Denver Museum of Nature & Science (p62): Egyptian mummies and dinosaur bones make this a great place to geek out.

There's also a desk of Colorado's Outdoor Recreation Information Center, where you can get information on state and national parks and an on-site Starbucks, in case you need some caffeine to accompany the adrenaline.

Dragonfly ACCESSORIES, CLOTHING
(☑303-433-6331; www.dragonflydenver.com; 3621 W 32 Ave; ☉10am-6pm Tue-Sat, 11am-4pm Sun & Mon; 🚌32 RTD) Cute, casual skirts and sweaters and a small, seasonal selection of accessories make this among the best women's clothing boutiques in Denver. The small label goods from Oliver Sang, Kier + J and Aude are well selected and classically hip.

Wilderness Exchange Unlimited

SPORTING GOODS
(Map p82; ☑303-964-0708; www.wilderness exchangeunlimited.com; Ste 100, 2401 15th St; ☉10am-8pm Mon-Fri, 10am-7pm Sat, 10am-6pm Sun; 🚌10, 32 RTD) Although it's easy to spend some serious cash at the enormous REI just up the street, it's worth looking into Wilderness Exchange Unlimited before you put down the plastic. In addition

to carefully selected outdoor equipment, this shop has an impressive collection of quality used gear (including good deals on hiking boots and down jackets) in the basement.

Metroboom BEAUTY
(Map p82; ☑303-477-9700; www.metroboom. com; 1550 Platte St; ☉10am-7pm Tue-Sat) This place is ideal for the man who wants a little pampering, either with custom menswear, personal grooming products, designer fashion or a shave. The packages range between the basic ('Presley') to downright luxurious ('Cary Grant') including haircuts, hot towels and hand treatments (that's just man-talk for a manicure).

Mona Lucero CLOTHING
(Map p82; ☑303-458-0090; www.monalucero. com; 2544 15th St; ☉2-6:30pm Mon & Tue, 2pm-noon Wed-Sat, noon-3pm Sun) With brick walls and an airy space, the interior of this upscale boutique is fittingly like a gallery. The selected designer clothing is artfully made, and it's an excellent space to browse. It has versatile, fun women's fashion with a

touch of kitsch, and the collection of handbags are one-of-a-kind.

SOUTH CENTRAL DENVER

Cherry Creek Shopping Center MALL
(☑303-388-3900; www.shopcherrycreek.com; 3000 E First Ave; ☺10am-9pm Mon-Sat, 10am-6pm Sun; ☒; ☐3, 83L RTD) A large collection of exclusive international brands (Louis Vuitton, Burberry, Ralph Lauren, Tiffany, Coach) decorate the corridors of Denver's high-end shopping facility, anchored by large department stores of Saks Fifth Avenue and Neiman Marcus. Food choices range from cheap-and-quick mall standards such as Panda Express to the elegant Tuscan fare and linen-draped dining room of Brio.

5 Green Boxes HOMEWARES
(☑303-282-5481; www.5greenboxes.com; 1705 S Pearl St; ☺10am-6pm Mon-Sat, noon-5pm Sun) The sister store down the street sells simple and chic women's clothing and accessories, but this is the place to get a one-of-a-kind piece for your home. From custom remodeled furniture to home items large and small, the aesthetic is classy, vintage and whimsical.

SOUTH BROADWAY

Fancy Tiger CRAFT
(Map p58; ☑303-733-3855; www.fancytiger.com; 1 S Broadway; ☺11am-7pm Mon-Sat, noon-6pm Sun; ☐0 RTD) So you dig crochet and record collecting? You knit a mean sweater and have a few too many tattoos? Welcome to Fancy Tiger, a sophisticated remodel of granny's yarn barn that's ground zero for Denver's crafty hipsters. There are classes in the basement (including ones by Jessica, 'mistress of patchwork') and a rad selection of fabric, yarn and books.

If you are a little bit more hands-off with your homemade clothes, try the Fancy Tiger Boutique across the street, where local designers hock their wares.

BEYOND CENTRAL DENVER

Colorado Mills MALL
(☑303-590-1634; www.coloradomills.com; 14500 W Colfax Ave; ☺10am-11pm Mon-Sat, 11am-6pm Sun; ☒☒) This is a shoppers' paradise: a huge shopping mall west of the Downtown area with more than 200 specialty stores and 1,100,000 sq ft of retail fun. All the big retailers are represented, some with discounted factory outlets, and there are restaurants and food halls. Catch a movie at the United Artists multiplex theater.

ℹ Information

ATMs are widely available and major banks will exchange foreign currency.

Internet Access

If you're traveling with a laptop, you'll have no trouble finding wi-fi: it's nearly ubiquitous in Denver's restaurants, bars and cafes. There is also free wi-fi on the 16th St Mall. If you're not traveling with a computer, things get a bit more tricky, but there are computer terminals available 24 hours a day inside the **FedEx/Kinko's Business Center** (☑303-298-8610; 1750 Welton St; @☎) office in the Denver Grand Hyatt, if you're willing to pay the ridiculously high rate of $0.20 per minute.

Medical Services

Denver Health Medical Center (☑303-436-6000; www.denverhealth.org; 777 Bannock St; ☐52 RTD) Formerly known as 'DG' (Denver General).

Rose Medical Center (☑3030-320-2121; www.rosemed.com; 4567 E 9th Ave)

St Joseph Hospital (☑303-837-7111; www.exempla.org; 1835 Franklin St)

University of Colorado Hospital (☑303-399-1211; 4200 E 9th Ave; ☺24hr) Emergency services.

Post

Central Post Office (☑303-296-4692; www.usps.com; 951 20th St; ☺8am-2:30pm Mon-Fri, 9am-2:30pm Sat; ☐38 RTD) Main branch.

Tourist Information

The Visit Denver website, www.denver.org, has great information about events.

DIA Information Booth (☑303-342-2000; Denver International Airport) Tourist and airport information is available at this booth in the terminal's central hall.

ORIC Desk (Outdoor Recreation Information Center; ☑REI main line 303-756-3100; www.oriconline.org; 1416 Platte St; ☎; ☐10, 28, 32, 44 RTD) Inside REI (p91), this information desk is a must for those looking to get out of town. It has maps and expert information on trip planning and safety information. It also hosts free Discover Colorado classes every Sunday at 3pm. The desk is staffed by volunteers, so hours vary wildly, but arriving on a weekend afternoon is a good bet.

Visitors & Convention Bureau Information Center (☑303-892-1112; www.denver.org; 1600 California St; @☎☒; ☐California) When you get to town, make for the largest and most centrally located information center. Located on the 16th St Mall, you can load up on brochures and get information about local transport. There's also a tourist info desk in the Colorado Convention Center.

Getting There & Away

Served by the largest airport in the US, criss-crossed by major highways and intersected by one of the country's few Amtrak lines, it's easy to get to and from Denver. Flights, tours and rail tickets can be booked online at www.lonely planet.com/travel_services.

Air

Denver International Airport is a major hub for several American carriers, including Frontier Airlines and United Airlines.

Denver International Airport (DIA; ☑information 303-342-2000; www.flydenver.com; 8500 Peña Blvd; ☺24hr; @☏) Twenty-four miles from Downtown, DIA is connected with I-70 exit 238 by the 12-mile-long Peña Blvd. The facility has an automated subway that links the terminal to three concourses and 94 gates. Concourse C is almost a mile from the terminal, hence the need for automated transport of people and baggage, and a little extra time for finding your way around. DIA is a major air hub and one of the country's busiest facilities.

DIA's website is a helpful tool for navigating your way around this massive air hub – flights and airlines, hire cars, public transport and commuter shuttles for getting into town.

Bus

Greyhound and affiliate TNM&O offer frequent buses on routes along the Front Range and on transcontinental routes. All buses stop at the Denver Bus Center.

The **Front Range Express** (☑719-636-3739; www.frontrangeexpress.com; Arapahoe at Village Center Station) offers trips to Colorado Springs ($11, two hours), Castle Rock and Monument. **Powder River Coach USA** (☑800-442-3682), offering services north to Cheyenne, WY, and on to Montana and South Dakota, also runs from the Denver Bus Terminal.

RTD buses to Boulder (route B) carry bicycles in the cargo compartment and offer frequent service from the Market St Station at the corner of 16th and Market Sts. The Denver to Boulder one-way RTD fare is $4.50. To reach Golden, take either the 16 or 16L bus that stops at the corner of 15th and California Sts.

Denver Bus Center (☑303-293-6555; 1055 19th St; ☺6am-midnight; ☐8, 48 RTD) Greyhound buses stop here. Services run to Boise (from $140, 18 hours), Billings (from $105, 14 hours) and Los Angeles (from $150, 20 hours).

Market St Bus Station (cnr 16th & Market Sts) All transportation companies have booths near the baggage-claim area, including the

Front Range Express, with service to Colorado Springs and Denver's Regional Transit District.

Car & Motorcycle

At the intersection of I-70 and I-25, Denver is pretty hard to miss: even the poorest navigators should have no trouble finding this place.

Train

Amtrak (☑800-872-7245; www.amtrak.com; 1701 Wynkoop St; ☐Union Station) Amtrak's *California Zephyr* runs daily between Chicago and San Francisco via Denver's grand and gothic Union Station. For recorded information on arrival and departure times, call ☑303-534-2812. Amtrak can also provide schedule information and train reservations.

Union Station (☑Amtrak 303-534-2812; cnr 17th & Wynkoop Sts; ☐31X, 40X, 80X, 86X, 120X RTD) The red neon atop this stoic 19th-century fortress glowers down and demands you 'travel by train' – and you still can.

Getting Around

To/From the Airport

A complete Ground Transportation Center is centrally located on the 5th level of DIA's terminal, near the baggage claim. All transportation companies have their booths here and passengers can catch vans, shuttles and taxis outside the doors.

Complimentary hotel shuttles represent the cheapest means of getting to or from the airport. Courtesy phones for hotel shuttles are available in the Ground Transportation Center.

RTD buses are available outside door 506 in the West Terminal and door 511 in the East Terminal. Travel time is typically less than an hour to or from the city and fares cost $8, or $12 one-way – exact fare only. Buses (routes AS, AF and AB) run every 15 minutes between DIA and Stapleton Transit Center, providing access to lodging and budget parking. The fare is $8. For DIA-Boulder travelers, fares for the 1½-hour trip cost $12 one-way.

Taxi service to downtown Denver costs a flat fare of $43, excluding tip.

There are a number of airport shuttle van and limousine services.Airport shuttles to the Front Range and mountain/ski areas are also not hard to come by.

Denver Express Shuttle (☑303-342-3424, toll-free 800-448-2782)

Shuttle King Limo (☑303-363-8000; www.shuttlekinglimo.com) Charges $20 to $35 for rides from DIA to destinations in and around Denver.

SuperShuttle (☑303-370-1300, toll-free 800-258-3826) Van services (from $22) between the Denver area and the airport.

Bicycle

Denver has lots of bike lanes on the city streets and an excellent network of trails to get out of town. These include routes along the Platte River Parkway, the Cherry Creek Bike Path and a network that heads out all the way out to Golden (about a two hour ride). You can get all the information you need from a pair of excellent websites, **BikeDenver.org** (www.bike denver.org) or **City of Denver** (www.denvergov. org), which has downloadable bike maps for the city.

B Cycle (☑303-835-3325; www.denver.bcycle. com; 1-day membership $5; ☺5am-11pm Mon & Sun; ♿) The first citywide bicycle-share program in the US was launched in April 2010. The website explains how it works, where you can become a member and where you collect a bike from 42 curb-side B Station kiosks.

Bus

Cultural Connection Trolley (☑303-289-2841; www.coloradograyline.com; adult $16; ☺8:30am-5:30pm) This trolley bus is just a bus dressed up as a trolley. Ticket holders are entitled to 24 hours' unlimited hop-on and hop-off rides. It loops around the city's tourist areas including the Denver Zoo, Museum of Natural History & Science, Cherry Creek Mall and the Denver Botanic Gardens.

Regional Transportation District (RTD; ☑303-299-6000; www.rtd-denver.com; 1500 Broadway; local fares $2, express fares $3.50; @) RTD provides public transportation throughout the Denver and Boulder area. Free shuttle buses operate along the 16th St Mall. RTD also runs a SkyRide service to the airport from downtown Denver hourly ($10, one hour). The website has schedule, routes, fares and a trip planner.

Car & Motorcycle

Street parking can be a pain, but there is a slew of pay garages in Downtown and LoDo. Nearly all the major car-rental agencies have counters at DIA, though only a few have offices in downtown Denver.

Check the ride boards at the hostels or at the north wing of Driscoll University Center at the University of Denver, which is connected to the main campus by the pedestrian walkway over E Evans Ave.

A-Courtesy Rent-A-Car (☑303-733-2218, toll-free 800-441-1816; 270 S Broadway) Accepts cash deposits, but vehicles cannot be driven outside Colorado.

Auto Driveaway (☑303-757-1211, toll-free 800-758-1211; www.autodriveawaydenver. com; Suite 109, 5777 E Evans Ave; ☑21 RTD) If you're 21 or over, Auto Driveaway, south of downtown, may be able to provide free transportation in exchange for vehicle delivery – get

a drive-away just like Jack Kerouac did in *On the Road*. Be prepared to post a substantial deposit that will be forfeited if you damage the car (as Kerouac did).

Light Rail

RTD's light rail line is used mostly by commuters traveling between the city center and suburbs. It serves 16 stations on a 12-mile route that passes through Downtown; NB (northbound) trains run on California St, while SB (southbound) trains follow Stout St. The northern end of the line follows Welton St through the Five Points neighborhood to the Black American West Museum & Heritage Center at the corner of 30th and Downing Sts. The southern end passes the Auraria Campus and terminates at Santa Fe and Mineral Sts. Trains operate between 4:30am and 1:30am and run every five minutes during peak periods. Fares are the same as for local buses. Fares are set up with a zone system and cost $2 to $4.50, depending on how far you ride. Bikes may be taken on the train if there is space.

Taxi

Three taxi companies offer door-to-door service in Denver:

Metro Taxi (☑303-333-3333)

Yellow Cab (☑303-777-7777)

Zone Cab (☑303-444-8888)

AROUND DENVER

Golden

POP 17,500

This might raise the dander of a few residents of Golden, but we would have been in the majority of the 1867 vote that moved the territorial capital down the road to Denver. Apparently Denver bested Golden (then Golden City) by a single vote – one which history wags claim was rigged by then-territorial governor John Evans. Today, Golden isn't much to see. The city has been mostly enveloped in sprawl from its rival neighbor but still pulls in big numbers of tourists to see the home of Coors beer.

The town has a small historic district, a few interesting museums and the highly regarded Colorado School of Mines. Some may find Golden an interesting day trip, but it probably doesn't warrant on overnight stay, particularly since accommodations are fairly expensive.

History

Golden was founded in 1859 at the mouth of Clear Creek Canyon, after prospectors discovered gold in the stream that flows through town. Golden served as the Colorado Territorial capital from 1862 to 1867. You can win plenty of bar bets with visitors who assume Golden is named for the glinting yellow mineral found in them thar hills – the truth is, the seat of Jefferson County was named for Thomas L Golden, who camped near the creek in 1858.

◎ Sights

Golden has a small but attractive historic district with some interesting museums. 'First Friday' events bring a pleasant street carnival with wine and local gallery openings on (you guessed it!) the first Friday of every month. The First Friday hubbub takes place along Washington St, with the epicenter at 12th St.

Buffalo Bill Museum & Grave   MUSEUM

(📞303-526-0744; www.buffalobill.org; 987 1/2 Lookout Mountain Rd; adult/child/senior $5/1/4; ⊙9am-5pm; P) This museum celebrates the life and legend of William F 'Buffalo Bill' Cody, an icon of the American West. At his request he was buried at this site overlooking both the Great Plains and the Rockies, and today it attracts a steady stream of RVs to snap pictures of his statue. The museum and gift shop are pure kitsch and probably not recommended for those with a progressive view on Native American history.

Still, Bill's biography is a fascinating one: when he began his show-business career at 26 in Chicago in 1872, he had already spent more than a decade as a fur trapper, gold prospector, cattle herder, Pony Express rider and army scout, crossing the Great Plains many times in the West's pioneering years. His show became hugely popular and traveled to England in 1887 for Queen Victoria's Golden Jubilee celebrations.

Colorado Railroad Museum   MUSEUM

(📞303-279-4591, toll-free 800-365-6263; www.coloradorailroadmuseum.org; 17155 W 44th Ave; adult/child/family $8/5/18; ⊙9am-5pm; P) With more than 100 railroad engines, cabooses and rolling stock, as well as paraphernalia and regalia, this is a must-stop for train tragics touring the region. There is also a comprehensive library of all things locomotive, the Restoration Roundhouse and a working turntable.

FREE Coors Brewery   BREWERY

(MillerCoors; toll-free 866-812-2337; www.millercoors.com; 13th & Ford Sts; ⊙10am-4pm Mon-Sat, from noon Sun; P) Coors Brewery is now officially called MillerCoors, but try telling the locals that. There's been brewing on this site since 1873. Coors survived the prohibition years by producing malted milk and porcelain products, and went on to produce the world's first beer shipped in aluminum cans. Each year 250,000 people take the brewery's free self-guided tour. A free shuttle takes people from the car park.

American Mountaineering Museum
MUSEUM

(Bradford Washburn American Mountaineering Museum; 303-996-2755; www.mountaineeringmuseum.org; 710 10th St; adult/child/senior $6.50/4.50/5; ⊙10am-5pm Tue-Fri, 10am-6pm Sat, 11am-4pm Sun; P) If you've come to Colorado to climb, this museum will give you tingles of inspiration. There's a pile of stunning photos, historic climbing gear (some of which, like Peter Schoening's ice axe, are from legendary missions) and a display on the 10th Mountain Division, who climbed and fought in WWII.

🏃 Activities

Cycling

Nearby parks offer plenty of opportunity for off-road rides, and road riders will find a number of loops beginning in Golden. Immediately south of I-70 along Hwy 26, Matthews/Winters Park has trail access to the Mt Vernon town site, which in 1859 was the capital of the provisional Territory of Jefferson. East of Matthews/Winters Park and Hwy 26, the Dakota Ridge Trail follows the spine of Hogback Park south for 2 miles before crossing Hwy 26 near Morrison to Red Rocks Trail, which returns to Matthews/Winters Park.

If you're in good shape and don't mind a steep climb, try White Ranch Open Space Park, which has miles of challenging single-track and fire-road rides. There are two trailheads: one just off Hwy 93 on the way to Boulder; the other 15 miles up Golden Gate Canyon Rd en route to Golden Gate Canyon State Park.

Golf

Even if you're not building your Colorado itinerary around golf, it might be worth knocking around a few holes at the Fossil Trace Golf Club (p97).

Golden

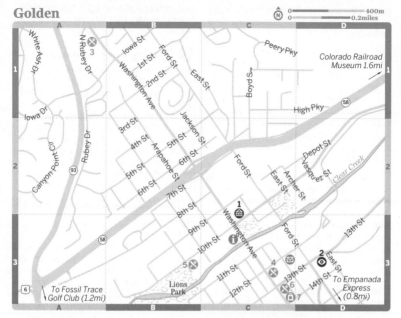

Fossil Trace Golf Club GOLF
(☏303-277-8750; www.fossiltrace.com; 3050 Illinois St; 18 holes nonresident $62) Routinely considered among America's best courses, this unique round of golf offers a glimpse of fossils, challenging play and sweeping views. The course isn't cheap, but it's certainly memorable.

This golf club might be the only place on Earth where you can hit the ball off the fairway and into the shadow of triceratops' tracks. The course is built in the scarred terrain of old mines, giving a fascinating landscape where rock formations jut upwards abruptly from the grass.

✗ Eating

There's no trouble finding a passable meal in Golden, though most of the sit-down eateries are serving up a fairly uninspired roster of burgers, chops, pizzas and big salads. If you're willing to look a bit harder, there are some real gems. On Saturdays between June and September, the city hosts the Golden Farmers Market (p98) at the parking lot just west of the library.

Empanada Express VENEZUELAN $
(☏720-226-4701; www.theempanadaexpress. com; 2600 East St; dishes $4-5; ⏱10:30am-8pm; ⊖⛟) This family-operated hole in the

Golden

◎ Sights
1 American Mountaineering Museum C2
2 Coors Brewery D3

✗ Eating
3 Ali Baba Grill A1
4 D'deli.. C3
5 Golden Farmers Market...................... B3
6 Woody's Woodfired Pizza & Watering Hole.................................... C3

🛍 Shopping
7 Bent Gate Mountaineering C3

wall is worth seeking out for filling, flaky empanadas filled with savory carnitas seasoned chicken and cheese. The chile *arepas* (fried, stuffed corn cakes) are also excellent. The tables are tiny, so it's probably best to get it on the go.

D'deli DELI $
(☏303-279-5308; www.ddelisubs.com; 1207 Washington Ave; sandwiches $6-7; 🛜⛟) Crusty, fresh bread and stacks of ingredients make this cozy deli an excellent place for lunch. The 'Heater' – a massive pile of pastrami, jalapeños, banana peppers and chipotle

ranch – is the choice for spice fiends. A second location on the creek also has excellent ambience.

Woody's Woodfired Pizza & Watering Hole
BURGERS, PIZZA $

(☑303-277-0443; www.woodysgolden.com; 1305 Washington Ave; all-you-can-eat pizza $10; ⊙11am-midnight; ☺) After you make it past the 'watering hole' part of the evening, with its selection of some of the area's best brews, order up a crusty, wood-fired pie. It's hard not to love the laid-back locals and sustainable-business focus.

Ali Baba Grill
LEBANESE, MEDITERRANEAN $$

(☑303-279-2228; www.alibabagrill.com; 109 N Rubey Dr; mains $10-15; ⊙11am-9pm; ☻) Sure, it looks like another drab strip-mall joint from the parking lot, but the Lebanese and Mediterranean cuisine here is *awesome* and every bit as surprising as the elaborate interior, likely Golden's only harem-themed dining room.

Golden Farmers Market
SELF-CATERING

(www.goldencochamber.org; cnr 10th & Illinois Sts; ⊙8am-1pm Sat Jun-Sep; ☻) On Saturdays during the summer Golden's small farmers market hosts local food producers from throughout the region.

🛍 Shopping

Bent Gate Mountaineering
OUTDOOR GEAR

(☑303-271-9382; www.bentgate.com; 1313 Washington Ave; ⊙10am-8pm Sun-Thu, 10am-5pm Fri) This outdoor equipment shop focuses on skiing and mountaineering and has a good selection of high-quality gear for sale. It also hosts occasional events.

❶ Information

You won't have trouble finding an ATM machine as the tourist areas are loaded with them.

Golden Chamber of Commerce/Visitor Center (☑303-279-3113; www.goldencochamber.org; 1010 Washington Ave; ⊙8am-5pm Mon-Fri, 10am-4pm Sat) This is the tourism nerve center for Golden, and you can stock up on brochures, maps, hotel and local info here. You can also pick up a walking-tour guide to the 12th St historic district.

Jefferson County Open Space Office (☑303-271-5925; www.co.jefferson.co.us; 700 Jefferson County Pkwy; ⊙7:30am-5:30pm Mon-Fri) This office has information and permits for camping in the county's park system. Camping permits for Reynolds Park can be obtained here or arranged through a phone call.

Post Office (☑303-216-0320; 619 12th St; ⊙9am-5pm Mon-Fri, 10am-1pm Sat) Centrally located.

❶ Getting There & Away

BICYCLE Riding from Denver takes about an hour and a half: the Clear Creek Bike Trail will get you most of the way along a clearly marked route.

BUS RTD (p95) connects Golden with downtown Denver (at the corner of 15th and California Sts).

CAR & MOTORCYCLE The easiest route from Denver is I-25 north to I-70, then I-70 to exit 265, from where you can catch Hwy 58 west into town. From downtown Denver, Golden is about 16 miles.

Mt Evans

ELEV 14,264FT

The pinnacle of many visitors' trips to Colorado is a drive to the alpine summit of **Mt Evans** (☑303-567-3000; www.mountevans.com; Mount Evans Rd; ⊙late May-early Sep; ℗☻), less than an hour west of Denver's skyscrapers. It was opened in 1930 and remains the highest paved road in North America. (The highest paved road in the world? Ticlio Pass in the Andes, which tops it by about 1500ft.) From I-70 exit 240 at Idaho Springs, Mt Evans Hwy takes you through dramatic scenery and a 6725ft elevation change. Near the exit in Idaho Springs, the USFS Clear Creek Ranger Station (p100) offers information and a good selection of books and topographical maps of the area.

The lower portion of the road travels through a montane ecosystem for 13 miles to Echo Lake, where the University of Denver's High Altitude Lab is situated in the subalpine ecosystem at 10,700ft. USFS campsites at Echo Lake Campground (p99) can be reserved online or over the phone from **Reserve America** (☑California State Park Reservations 800-444-7275, Colorado State Park Reservations 800-678-2267, NRRS Federal Campground Reservations 877-444-6777; www.reserveamerica.com; 40 South St). They get plenty of use and cost $15, plus the $10 reservation fee. Freezing temperatures can be experienced here throughout the year – the lab once recorded a low of -52°F.

The last vestiges of forest before ascending to the alpine tundra, the gnarly bristlecone pine, can be visited on foot at the Mt Goliath Natural Area. Four miles above Echo Lake, take the Alpine Gardens

Trail for just over a mile downhill and back. Continuing on the road past Summit Lake, which freezes solid in winter, you are likely to encounter Rocky Mountain goats and bighorn sheep. From the end of the highway it's then a 200ft scramble to the summit.

The area is typically open from Memorial Day to Labor Day. The onset of cold temperatures returns Mt Evans' slopes to their rightful inhabitants.

Idaho Springs & Georgetown

IDAHO SPRINGS
POP 2000 / ELEV 7526FT

Most people who parachute into Denver for a convention or who have limited time in the area can barrel down the road to Idaho Springs for a quick taste of Colorado's rough-and-tumble gold-rush history. The rowdy gaggle of prospectors, gunslingers and rapscallions who rushed here to get rich in 1859 have been mostly replaced by a notably more genteel crowd of day-tripping Denver baby boomers and retirees on blindingly chromed-up Harleys, but the historic buildings along Miner St retain the creaking floors and antique character of the city's colorful past.

Activities

You can't go wrong by wandering Miner St (plenty of signs around town will point you in the right direction) but if you want to stock up on brochures and chat up a rosy-cheeked staff of volunteers, make for the Idaho Springs Visitors Center & Museum (p100).

Clear Creek Outdoors   WATER SPORTS
(303-567-1500;   www.clearcreekflyfishing.com; 1524 Miner St; full-day expedition $250; 10am-6pm;) Situated in a small shop selling rods, reels and outdoor gear, Rob Brozovich operates excellent fly-fishing tours to a private high-mountain lake in the area. The lake routinely gives up brown, rainbow and cutthroat trout. You can also call in for a condition report for streams in the area.

A&A Historical Trails   HORSEBACK RIDING
(www.aastables.com; 238 2 Brothers Rd; 1 hr $40, additional hr $30;) Traveling through Virginia Canyon is a beautiful way to soak in the history of the area. There are guided

and unguided options including a visit to the canyon's historic graveyards.

Indian Springs Resort & Spa   HOT SPRINGS
(303-567-1303;   www.indianhotsprings.com; 302 Soda Creek Rd; day pass Mon-Fri $18, weekends $20; 7:30am-10:30pm) You can't argue that this hot springs is the cheapest soak in close proximity to Denver, but lovers of thermal waters might be better off driving further for more up-to-date facilities. The geothermal caves are clothing-optional but given a few of gawkers, we'd suggest you go for the 'on' option.

Tours

Argo Gold Mill & Museum   MINING
(303-567-2421;   www.historicargotours.com; 2350 Riverside Dr; adult/child $15/7.50; 9am-6pm, last tour at 4pm;) This boxy red beast of a building lurks over the highway just east of Idaho Springs, making it a bit hard to miss. It's built into the side of the hill, A tour brings visitors up into the Double Eagle Gold Mine, which was once among the state's most lucrative.

When the tour is over, you're allowed a free gold-panning session – don't expect to get rich, but it's a thrill for the kids. The onsite museum and gift shop are pretty tacky, but the whole experience makes for a fun, informative and intimate look at the states rush for gold.

Sleeping

Staying in Idaho Springs can be cheaper and more interesting than finding a chain hotel in Denver, but the accommodations tend to be dreary midcentury motels, the best of which is the Blair.

Blair Motel   MOTEL $
(303-567-4661; 345 Colorado Blvd; d $72;) The family-run Blair – a humble, single-story roadside motel of the blandest variety – won't win any beauty contests, but the rooms are well maintained and fairly good value. They're fitted out with a microwave and small refrigerator.

Echo Lake Campground   CAMPGROUND $
(303-567-3000; Squaw Lake Rd; campsites $15;) This heavily used campground has tent and RV sites and is the nearest organized campground to Mt Evans Pass. It is a popular staging area for (masochistic) bikers and runners who try to make it to the top of the highest paved road in the US.

✕ Eating & Drinking

Buffalo Restaurant & Bar AMERICAN **$$**
(www.buffalorestaurant.com; 1617 Miner St; mains
$10-24; 😋 🖶) The buffalo burger – all natu-
ral, antibiotic and hormone free – is the way
to go at this popular place on the main drag.
The historic building gets lively at lunch,
when people pack in under the bright sky-
lights for plates of standard American fare
in large portions.

Two Brothers Deli DELI **$**
(✆303-567-2439; www.twobrothersdeli.com;
1424 Miner St; sandwiches $6-8; 😋6am-8pm Mon-
Thu, 6am-9pm Fri-Sun; 🖶) Simple and busy,
this is an excellent option for a quick lunch,
with wraps, fresh sandwiches and baguette
pizzas. The Green Forest is a great vegetar-
ian option with a tangy dill sauce.

TOP
CHOICE **Tommyknockers Brewery & Pub**
BREWPUB
(✆303-567-2688; www.tommyknocker.com; 1401
Miner St; 😋11am-2am Mon-Sat, 11am-11pm Sun;
🛜🖶) You don't even have to like beer to
know these guys are good: scores of medals
from beer competitions hang overhead the
sunlit dining space in a testament to the
expert brews. Excellent pub food (mains $9
to $12) and an amiable staff clinch it. Beer
fans should go out of their way for a visit.

🛍 Shopping

Annie's Gold ANTIQUES
(✆303-567-2676; www.anniesgold.com; 2712
Colorado Blvd; 😋10am-4pm Sun-Fri, 9am-5pm
Sat) Loving displays and moderate prices:
this is our favorite antique shop in Idaho
Springs. Wander through the courtyard to
the cabin in back to find even more goodies
(dishes, tools and collectible housewares).
It's well worth a look before heading to-
wards pricier antique shops in the historic
downtown.

ℹ Information

Idaho Springs Visitors Center & Museum
(✆303-567-4382; www.historicidahosprings.
com; 2060 Miner St; 😋9am-5pm Sep-May,
8am-6pm Jun-Aug; 🖶) This is the place to
get local information about skiing, historical
attractions, area camping, and history and
walking tours.

USFS Clear Creek Ranger Station (✆303-
567-3000; 101 Hwy 103) The rangers at this
district office are helpful resources when
planning trips into the surrounding USFS land,
including dispersed camping near Echo Lake.
There's also a small museum.

GEORGETOWN
Georgetown Loop Railroad
SCENIC RAILROAD
(✆toll-free 888-456-6777; www.georgetown
looprr.com; 507 Taos St; adult/child $22.50/16.50;
😋departures 9:25am-2:55pm summer, seasonal
hrs vary; 🖶) Chugging along this loop is an
entertaining way to leave the I-70 corridor
and enjoy expansive views over Clear Creek
Valley. The ride is short – only 15 minutes
out and 15 minutes back, with a pause to
tour a mine in between – but the scenery
from one of the open passenger cars can
be make for a breathtaking, if chilly, after-
noon.

Once part of a system that snaked
through Clear Creek Canyon to connect
Denver with rich mines in Silver Plume, the
ride's operators have done an admirable job
making it a bit more upscale, with events
themed around wine or beer tastings and
seasonal packages in the fall and winter.
(We've heard mixed reviews about the sit-
down dinner experience.)

You can also add on a tour of the Leba-
non Silver Mine – interesting for adults but
possibly a bit scary for young travelers. It's
smart to call in advance if you're interest-
ed, as tickets sell out during peak season.
Plan on spending about half a day on the
adventure.

St Mary's Glacier

Wildflowers and wind-swept trails, boul-
ders and ice fields – these are the dispropor-
tionately big rewards for the beginner hike
up to St Mary's Glacier area. It's a quick day
escape from Denver, and the modest eleva-
tion gains, short distance and well-marked
trails make it ideal for the littlest hikers.
Although the area gets fairly busy on sum-
mer weekends, the views on a clear day are
remarkable, and a scramble around the
lake will bring you to the ice itself. Get here
while you can – according to the locals, cli-
mate change has visibly shrunk the glacier
in the past decade.

To get here, take I-70 West from Denver,
past Idaho Springs to the Fall River Rd exit.
Turn right on Fall River Rd, though the tiny
community of Alice, to the parking areas.
There is a loosely enforced parking fee of $5
for these lots, and it's best not to park else-
where; the neighbors don't tolerate strang-
ers parking on their turf.

Empire

POP 355 / ELEV 8614FT

Most traffic rushes along I-70 toward the Continental Divide, but dusty little Empire sits astride US 40, the historic route toward scenic 11,315ft Berthoud Pass. When dedicated in 1938, US 40 was the first hard-surfaced transcontinental route. Summer traffic bound for Granby or Winter Park, on the western slope over Berthoud Pass, continues to follow US 40, and in the winter Empire plays host to many skiers returning from Winter Park. Drivers take heed: Empire is a prime hideout for the highway patrol ready to ambush those who flout the town's 35mph speed limit.

The only reason to stop for more than a stretch of the legs is the Peck House (303-569-9870; www.thepeckhouse.com; 83 Sunny Ave; s $135, d $75-105; P☺⊛❄☗). Established in 1862, it's the oldest hotel in Colorado. Without phones or televisions in the room, there's a kind of classic charm down the creaking and crooked halls, even if the frilly Victorian touches can be a bit overwrought. The staff exudes a kind of old-world posture – the kind of thing where the barman tends to start shaking the martini shaker before you've even finished your order. Excellent dinners in a French preparation cost between $17 and $27.

Denver Mountain Parks & Platte River

MORRISON

POP 420 / ELEV 5764FT

Billing itself as 'the nearest faraway place,' little Morrison is a National Historic District 32 miles southwest of Denver on Hwy 8, hidden from the Denver skyline by the Hogback rock formations. It echos the feel of some of Colorado's more remote mountain towns. While the spectacular upturned red rocks on the banks of Bear Creek are an attractive escape from Denver, most people visit Morrison either on the way to, or from, Red Rocks Park & Amphitheater (p102) or to fuel up before climbing the big hills in the surrounding Jefferson County Open Space Parks.

◉ Sights

You'll see plenty of cyclists in the area; the smooth pavement and undulating terrain make for excellent road biking. Excava-

tions of what is called the Morrison Formation began in 1877 and have yielded fossils of more than 70 dinosaur species. You can view dinosaur footprints by taking a self-guided tour of Dinosaur Ridge, about 2 miles north of Morrison along Hwy 26.

FREE **Dinosaur Ridge**
(303-697-3466; www.dinoridge.org; 16831 W Alameda Pkwy; ☺9am-5pm May-Oct, 11am-4pm Nov-Apr; P☗) Unless you are an extremely dedicated dinosaur nut, the drive out to Dinosaur National Monument is a long haul. The footprints and sandstone-encased fossils here are extremely impressive, and worth the detour, and the tours are awesome for the kids.

🛏 Sleeping & Eating

Cliff House Lodge B&B $$$
(303-697-9732; www.cliffhouselodge.net; 121 Stone St; cabins from $175; ☺@⊛❄☗) If you spend the night in Morrison, this historic brick B&B is by far the best choice. The decor might be a little overboard, but some of the cottages have hot tubs and the gardens are a peaceful place to catch up on some reading.

Mill Street Deli GRILL $
(303-697-1700; 401 Bear Creek Ave; mains $7-10; ☺11am-midnight Mon-Sat; ☺☗) Of all the casual eats in Morrison, this place is tops. The grilled sandwiches are crispy and dripping with cheese and the Angus burger is a savory mess. You can sit next door in the bar while you wait for your order and eat late after concerts.

Willy's Wings BBQ $
(303-697-1232; www.willyswings.com; 109 Bear Creek Ave; mains $5-10; ☺11am-8pm Mon-Sat, 11am-7pm Sun; ☗) Frills? Forget about it. Situated in what looks like the mobile home of a displaced Texan auntie, this place has some good wings. Stay away if you're watching your waistline: just about everything on the menu is deep fried, except the potato salad, which is thick with mayo.

Morrison Inn MEXICAN $$
(303-697-6650; 301 Bear Creek Ave; mains $9-18; ☺11am-10pm Sun-Thu, 11am-11pm Fri & Sat; ☗) A former drugstore and soda fountain turned Mexican restaurant-bar pours formidable margaritas and dishes out passable Mex standards and hand-cut fries. The rooftop seating is great when it's warm, and historic photos of early Morrison line the restaurant walls.

RED ROCKS PARK & AMPHITHEATRE

Red Rocks Amphitheatre (☎303-640-2637; www.redrocksonline.com; 18300 W Alameda Pkwy; ⊙5am-11pm; 🚻) is set between 400ft-high red sandstone rocks 15 miles south-west of Denver. Acoustics are so good many artists record live albums here. The 9000-seat theater offers stunning views and draws big-name bands all summer. To see your favorite singer go to work on the stage is to witness a performance in one of the most exceptional music venues in the world. For many, it's reason enough for a trip to Colorado.

When the setting sun brings out a rich, orange glow from the rock formations and the band on stage launches into the right tune, Red Rocks Amphitheatre is a capti-vating experience, wholly befitting the park's 19th-century name, 'Garden of Angels.'

The natural amphitheater, once a Ute camping spot, has been used for perfor-mances for decades, but it wasn't until 1936 that members of the Civilian Conserva-tion Corps built a formal outdoor venue with seats and a stage. They wisely chose a performance area between two 400ft-high red sandstone rocks. Though it originally hosted classical performances and military bands, it debuted as a rock venue with style; the first rock quartet on this stage was John, Paul, George and Ringo. Since then, the gamut of artists who have recorded live albums here – such as U2, Neil Young, Dave Matthews and new-age piano tinkler John Tesh – is a testament to the pristine natural acoustics.

You scored tickets? Great. Now for the nitty gritty: eat in Morrison beforehand as the junk food from the food vendors is predictably expensive and the restaurants are crowded. Alternatively, you can bring a small cooler into the show, as long as there's no booze and it'll fit under your seat. Climbing on the stunning formations is prohib-ited; however, 250-plus steps lead to the top of the theater, offering views of both the park and of Denver, miles off to the east.

Amazingly, Red Rocks park can be almost as entertaining when it's silent. The amphitheater is only a tiny part of the 600-acre space; there are miles of hiking trails, opportunities to lose the crowds and take in lovely rock formations. There's informa-tion about the entire area on the website.

Tommy's Subs　　　　　　　DELI $
(☎303-697-5530; www.tommyssubs.com; Suite J, 14011 W Quincy Ave; subs $7-11; ⊙10am-7pm Mon-Fri, 10am-3pm Sat; 🚻) Seated in a strip mall right at the edge of the park, this local-ly owned sandwich shop gets a lot of lip ser-vice for the Philly cheesesteak and French dip subs. All of them come on locally baked bread rolls.

REYNOLDS PARK
For those on a tight schedule who need a little peace and quiet, Reynolds Park (sometimes called Reynolds Ranch Park) is a perfect escape from Denver. It's the di-versity of landscape that makes the place so desirable. In the park's lower elevation visitors amble along in the gentle mead-ows, picnic by the stream and camp in the secluded Idylease Campground (www.co.jefferson.co.us; Foxton Rd; 🚻). A hike in the area's rugged upper elevations offers panoramic vistas and bigger challenges to

the legs. Among this varied terrain lives a large diversity of wildlife – you're likely to see mule deer, elk, wild turkey and blue grouse. You may even spot a black bear. It is a half-mile hike or horseback ride from the parking lot to the campground, where there are fire rings, grills and bear lockers. You must reserve a spot here, which you can do through the Jefferson County Open Space Office (p98) in Golden.

PIKE NATIONAL FOREST & PLATTE RIVER
Just south and west of Denver's urban area, the green swath of the Pike National For-est feels the pressure from the nearby ur-ban populations looking for a getaway – its trails and camping areas can get discon-certingly crowded. Still, the forest offers good hiking, camping and fly fishing, and the drive from Denver is easy. Start by pick-ing up information available at the USFS South Platte Ranger Station (☎303-275-

5610; 19316 Goddard Ranch Ct; ⏱8am-4:30pm Mon-Fri), about 5 miles from Morrison.

For hikers, the area's trails are among the state's most accessible. Starting at Chatfield Reservoir, the 500-mile-long **Colorado Trail** (USFS Trail 1776) enters the Rocky Mountains along the South Platte River on its way to Durango. It crosses eight mountain ranges, seven national forests, six wilderness areas and five river systems. The lower section of the trail through Platte Canyon to Strontia Springs Reservoir is used heavily during the day. The Colorado Trail Foundation (CTF; ☎303-384-3729; www. coloradotrail.org/; PO Box 260876; ⏱9am-5pm Mon-Fri) offers maps and books that describe the trail.

Another worthy day hike southwest of Denver can be had at **Devil's Head Lookout** (elevation 9748ft), on the highest summit in the forested Rampart Range. Although the area offers USFS campsites ($9), they are typically full and sometimes very noisy. Picnics and day hikes, however, are highly recommended. In just over a mile, you climb almost 1000ft to the fire lookout, which offers a commanding 360-degree view of Spanish Peaks to the south, Mt Evans to the north, South Park to the west and the eastern plains. To get there from Denver, follow US 85 south to Sedalia, then take Hwy 67 west for 10 miles to Rampart Range Rd, which leads 9 miles to the Devils Head National Recreation Trail and picnic grounds.

If you're into single-track mountain biking, the Buffalo Creek Mountain Bike Area (Pine Valley Ranch Park), which also lies within the South Platte District, has about 40 miles of bike trails, including the sections of the Colorado Trail that permit bikes. There are two access points: the busiest is 3.5 miles south of Buffalo Creek where Jefferson County Rd 126 (S Deckers Rd) intersects the Colorado Trail. Another option is the Miller Gulch trailhead, reached from Bailey by taking Park County Rd 68 for 5 miles, then veering left on Park County Rd 70 for another mile before taking a left on USFS Rd 553. Miller Gulch Rd (USFS 554) will be on your right within half a mile. The South Platte Ranger Station can provide you with a free pamphlet outlining some of the rides.

Boulder

POP 293,161

Includes »

SIGHTS 106

ACTIVITIES. 111

FESTIVALS &
EVENTS. 114

SLEEPING. 114

EATING 117

DRINKING. 122

ENTERTAINMENT. . . 124

SHOPPING 125

Best Places to Eat

» Jax (p117)

» Med (p120)

» Lucile's (p120)

» Frasca (p117)

Best Places to Stay

» Chautauqua Lodge (p115)

» St Julien Hotel & Spa
(p116)

» Quality Inn Boulder Creek
(p116)

» The Alps (p115)

» Hotel Boulderado (p116)

Why Go?

Tucked up against its soaring signature Flatirons, this idyllic college town has a sweet location and a palpable eco-sophistication that has attracted entrepreneurs, athletes, hippies and hard-bodies like moths to the moonlight.

Boulder's mad love of the outdoors was officially legislated in 1967, when Boulder became the first US city to tax itself specifically to preserve open space. Thanks to such vision, packs of cyclists whip up and down the Boulder Creek corridor, which links to the city and county parks those taxpayer dollars purchased. The pedestrian-only Pearl St Mall is lively, and perfect for strolling. Especially at night, when students from University of Colorado and Naropa University mingle into the wee smalls. In many ways it is Boulder, not Denver, that is the region's tourist hub. The city is about the same distance from Denver International Airport, and staying in Boulder puts you 45 minutes closer to the ski resorts west on I-70 and the extraordinary Rocky Mountain National Park.

When to Go

Boulder

June–August
Long sunny days, summer showers, farmers markets, hiking, biking and tubing.

September–October Students return, Indian Summer, fall color, warm days, cool nights.

January–February Powder on the slopes, and quirky Arapahoe Basin beckons.

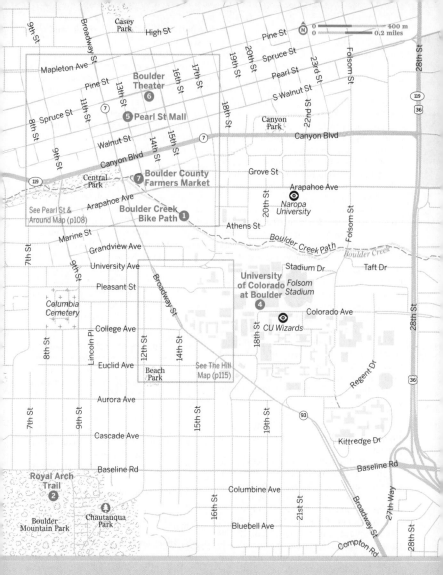

Boulder Highlights

1 Commute and coast with the masses on the **Boulder Creek bike path** (p111)

2 Hike among the Flatirons to **Royal Arch** (p111) in Chautauqua Park

3 Ride the contours of the whitewater park then lay back and enjoy the lower reaches as you tube **Boulder Creek**

4 Explore the museums, gardens and plazas of the **University of Colorado** (p106), one of the States' finest public universities

5 Stroll, sip coffee, grab lunch or simply people watch on **Pearl St Mall**

6 Whether you're basking in the glow of jazz pioneer

Charlie Hunter, post punk globalists Gogol Bordello or yet another screening of *Lebowski*, a show at **Boulder Theater** (p124) is a must

7 Hitting the **farmers market** (p122) on a sunny Saturday morning in Central Park

History

The early 19th-century nomadic Arapahoe nation wintered in the Boulder foothills. Utes, Cheyennes, Comanches, and Sioux are also documented to have spent time in the Boulder valley before Europeans arrived. Later in the 19th century American explorers Zebulon Pike and John Fremont were commissioned to explore the Boulder area. One of Fremont's men, William Gilpin, became the first governor of the Colorado Territory. It was he who reported that there was gold to be found in Boulder, which inspired easterners, mired in a depression, to set out for Colorado.

The first European settlement in Boulder County was established at Red Rocks, on October 17, 1858. One of those early settlers, AA Brookfield, organized the Boulder City Town Company. In February 1859, he divided and sold land on either side of Boulder Creek, giving birth to the present day city.

Boulder has always had strong educational roots. The state's first schoolhouse in Colorado was erected at the southwest corner of Walnut and 15th St in 1860. In 1872 six of Boulder's most prominent citizens donated 44.9 acres of land in an area known as 'The Hill' for the establishment of a university. Two years later the first building, Old Main, was built with a combination of public and private dollars, and it is still standing. The University of Colorado opened its doors in September of 1877, to 44 students, one professor and a president.

In 1898, Texas educators and local leaders conspired to bring a summer-long educational and cultural festival to Boulder. This was part of the famed Chautauqua Movement and drew orators, performers and educators, who traveled a national Chautauqua circuit of more than 12,000 sites bringing lectures, performances, classes and exhibitions to small towns and cities. Theodore Roosevelt called it, 'the most American thing in America.' Boulder's Chautauqua was completed July 4th, 1898, and it had an incredible impact, not least of which was launching Boulder's parks and open space preservation. The day after Chautauqua's grand opening, the city of Boulder purchased the eastern slope of Flagstaff Mountain from the United States Government. Purchasing land for preservation became and remains one of Boulder's top priorities. It now has over 54,000 acres dedicated to parks and open space today.

In the 1950s, '60s and '70s, Boulder went through a major real-estate and business boom, with the arrival of megacompanies like IBM and Ball Aerospace and the meteoric rise of local enterprise Celestial Seasonings. Today, Boulder has over 103,000 residents and nearly 30,000 students, yet its founding themes – nature, education, culture and progress endure.

◉ Sights

Few towns have this combination of nature and culture. Whether you're climbing the Flatirons, cycling up Flagstaff, roaming the two faces of Pearl St or patrolling the campus and surrounds one of America's finest public universities, there are plenty of sights and activities to keep you and the family smiling. Most sites are fairly centrally located, along east Pearl St or on the Hill, where you'll also find the university. Some sights, like Flagstaff and the reservoir, are set further afield north and west of town.

TOP CHOICE **FREE** **Chautauqua Park** PARK
(☑303-442-3282; www.chautauqua.com; 900 Baseline Rd) This historic landmark park is not just the gateway to Boulder's most magnificent slab of open space (we're talking about the Flatirons), it also has a wide, lush lawn that attracts picnicking families, sunbathers, frisbee folk, and – gasp – even studious students from CU down the road. It also gets copious hikers, climbers and trail runners.

This was once an important site for the inspired rural educational organization, the Chautauqua movement. These days, it's a park, a lodge and an auditorium where world-class musicians perform each summer.

FREE **University of Colorado at Boulder**
UNIVERSITY
(CU; Map p115; ☑303-492-6301; www.colorado.edu; Euclid Autopark; parking per day $6.50; ◷tours 9:30am & 1:30pm Mon-Fri, 10:30am Sat; P🅿🛜♿; 🚌203, 204, 209, 225, AB, B, DASH, DD, DM, GS, J, SKIP, STAMPEDE) It is possible for prospective students and curious visitors to tour one of the finest public universities in America, and one of the best schools overall. It's a beautiful campus set above downtown, on what is known as the Hill. Free tours begin with a one-hour informational session followed by a 90-minute walking tour.

As you stroll, remember you are moving in the footsteps of notable alumni such as astronaut Scott Carpenter (one of 17 astronauts with CU diplomas), Apple's Steve Wozniak, Sidney Altman (one of six Nobel Laureates), Robert Redford (didn't graduate), *South Park* creators Trey Parker and Matt Stone (smoked a ton of dope, did graduate), actor Jonah Hill (stopped by for one semester), and the always memorable Lynne Cheney (married Dick).

Boulder Museum of Contemporary Art
MUSEUM

(BMOCA; Map p108; ☑303-443-2122; www.bmoca.org; 1750 13th St; adult/senior & students $5/4, free Sat & 4-8pm Wed; ⊙11am-5pm Tue, Thu & Fri, to 8pm Wed, 9am-4pm Sat, noon-3pm Sun; ⓗ; ▣203, 204, 205, 206, 208, 225, DASH, JUMP, SKIP) A historic brick house divided into three galleries filled with evocative modern art. Mixed-media exhibits can include such whimsy as neon installations and life-sized cards, while strange fashion concepts are displayed in the costume and wardrobe gallery upstairs. All exhibitions are temporary and rotate every three months. Admission is free when the farmers market (p122) blooms out the front on Wednesdays and Saturdays.

FREE Flagstaff Mountain Trailhead VIEW
(www.osmp.org; Flagstaff Summit Rd; P ⓗ) A trailhead and parking area just below the summit (elev 7283ft) and a short drive from downtown Boulder with great Boulder and Denver views to the east and spectacular Continental Divide Views to the west. From here you can access a handful of fun hikes to even better vistas. There's a reason people get married up here.

If Flagstaff Summit Rd is closed for winter, park on Flagstaff Mountain and hike 0.6 miles to the top.

FREE Naropa University UNIVERSITY
(☑303-245-4643; www.naropa.edu; 2130 Arapahoe Ave; ⊙tours 2pm Mon-Fri school year; P ⓗ; ▣JUMP) Founded by Tibetan Buddhist master Chögyam Trungpa Rinpoche who escaped Tibet and climbed over the Himalayas into India as a young man. In 1970, at just 30, he began presenting teachings in the US and founded the Naropa Institute (which became Naropa University) in 1974. It offers a contemplative education in psychology, environmental studies, music, performing arts and more.

Naropa is also home to the Jack Kerouac School of Disembodied Poetics, co-founded by his fellow Beat Allen Ginsberg, and poet Anne Waldman.

Butterfly Pavilion BOTANIC GARDEN
(www.butterflies.org; 6252 West 104th Ave; adult/senior/child $8.5/6.50/5.50; ⊙9am-5pm; P ⓗ) With four indoor exhibit halls and acres of outdoor gardens fluttering with over 1200 butterflies from all the jungles and rainforests of the world – not to mention furry tarantulas, armored scorpions and fuzzy millipedes – this spot is a whirl of color, excitement and joy for the kids, and mom and dad too.

FREE Central Park PARK
(Map p108; Canyon Blvd; P ⓗ; ▣206, JUMP) Spanning from the northern edge of downtown to the Contemporary Art Museum at 13th St, and encompassing the public library, a twice-weekly seasonal farmers market (p122), and a large swatch of the Boulder Creek bike trail, it's hard to avoid this park. And really, why would you want to? It's a nice spot for a picnic and a nap.

Here is a long blade of lush lawn, ample shade and sun and a ramp leading to the Boulder Creek trail and the creek itself.

Boulder Reservoir RESERVOIR
(☑303-441-3461; www.bouldercolorado.gov; 5565 N 51st St; adult/child/teen & senior $6/3/4; ⊙dawn-dusk; P ⓗ) When you're this far from the ocean, the reservoir is where folks come to suntan, swim, boat, and wakeboard. Unfortunately there were no boating or wakeboarding concessions open at research time, so you may have to settle for a dip. And on the right day at the right time, that will be good enough, we assure you.

Dogs are not allowed into the park between May 15 and Labor Day, but are allowed in during the off-season.

FREE CU Wizards KIDS
(☑303-492-5011; www.colorado.edu/phys ics/Web/wizards/cuwizards.html; Duane Physics Building G1B30, Colorado Ave; ⊙program begins at 9:30am; P ⓗ; ▣209, STAMPEDE) Science can be cool, and kids dig the free monthly shows put on by CU's Wizards program. The science-based shows such as 'Physics of Sound' or 'Magic of Chemistry' are free, and held on one Saturday per month. Shows are geared toward fifth- to ninth-graders.

Pearl St & Around

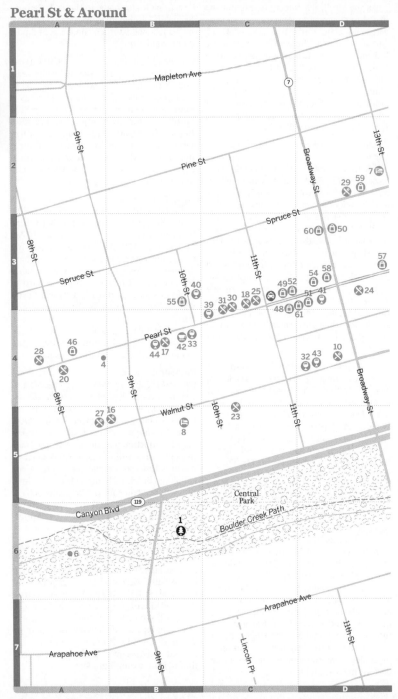

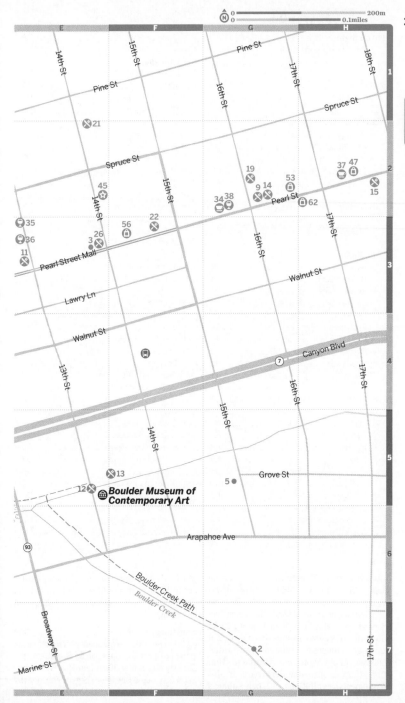

200m
0.1miles

Boulder Museum of Contemporary Art

Boulder Creek Path
Boulder Creek

Pearl St & Around

◎ **Top Sights**
Boulder Museum of
  Contemporary Art E5

◎ **Sights**
1 Central Park...B6

Activities, Courses & Tours
2 Boulder Creek Bike Path......................G7
3 Pop Jet Fountain....................................E3
4 Six Persimmons......................................A4
5 Tube Boulder Creek G5
6 Yoga Rocks the Park A6

🛏 **Sleeping**
7 Hotel Boulderado...................................D2
8 St Julien Hotel & Spa............................B5

🍴 **Eating**
9 Ají G2
10 Boulder BOP..D4
11 Boulder Cafe..E3
12 Boulder County Farmers'
   Market..E5
13 Dushanbe Teahouse F5
14 Foolish Craig's G2
15 Frasca...H2
16 Happy..B5
17 Jax..B4
   Juanita's...(see 18)
18 Kitchen..C3
19 Leaf...G2
20 Lolita's Market & Deli A4
21 Lucile's E2
22 Mai Berry..F3
23 Med..C5
24 Powell's Sweet Shoppe.........................D3
25 Salt...C3
26 Salvaggio's Italian Deli E3
27 Sherpa's Adventurers A5
28 Spruce Confections...............................A4
29 Sushi Zanmai..D2
30 Tahona Tequila Bistro C3

31 Two Spoons C3

🍷 ☕ **Drinking**
32 Absinthe House D4
   Bitter Bar ....(see 16)
33 Blending Cellar.......................................B4
   Catacombs Bar............................. (see 7)
34 Cup...G2
35 Draft House E3
36 Ku Cha House of Tea E3
37 Laughing Goat...H2
38 Mountain Sun Pub & Brewery G2
39 'Round Midnight.....................................C4
40 Saxy's Cafe...B3
41 Sundown Saloon......................................D3
42 Trident Cafe...B4
43 Walnut Brewery......................................D4
44 West End Tavern B4

🎭 **Entertainment**
45 Boulder Theater......................................E2

🛍 **Shopping**
46 Bayleaf On Pearl A4
47 Beat Book Shop.......................................H2
48 Blue Skies Boulder C3
49 Boulder Bookstore C3
50 Chelsea...D3
51 Cypress Beauty & Co D3
52 Goldmine Vintage...................................C3
53 Momentum..G2
   Oliv...(see 60)
54 Outdoor Divas D3
55 Outdoor Outlet..B3
56 Pedestrian Shops F3
57 Peppercorn Gourmet Goods D3
58 Prana...D3
59 Rebecca's Herbal Apothecary D2
60 Savory Spice Shop D3
61 Smith Klein Gallery.................................D3
62 Starr's Clothing Co.................................H2
   Weekends..(see 24)

Boulder History Museum MUSEUM
(Map p115; ☎303-449-3464; www.boulderhis
tory.org; 1206 Euclid Ave; adult/under 5yr/child
& student/senior $6/free/3/4; ⊙10am-5pm Tue-
Fri, noon-4pm Sat & Sun; 🅿🚼) History buffs
will want to breeze through this simple but
informative museum, home to a substantial
collection of old photos and documents that
offer glimpses into Boulder's past. It also
hosts special exhibitions on such subjects

as the 'History of Flight in Colorado,' 'Influ-
ential Women in Boulder's Past' and, gulp,
'Pocketbook Anthropology: The History of
Handbags.'

Sunflower Farm FARM
(☎303-774-8001; www.sunflowerfarminfo.com;
11150 Prospect Rd; admission $5-8; ⊙10am-3pm
Sat May-Aug & Nov, 10am-1pm Mon-Fri, to 3pm
Sat & Sun, Sep & Oct; 🅿🚼) Set in the nearby
suburb of Longmont, this 50-acre working

farm with century-old barns strewn across the land welcomes families to Farmfest (its child-friendly program). Help feed baby animals, collect eggs, ride ponies and climb the giant treehouse.

🏃 Activities

This is a great town to get outdoors. Its much-deserved reputation as an ecotopia (see: King, Stephen; *The Stand*) is rooted in the residents' collective jonesing for outdoors adventure. Boulder's also a place to go inside and tune in with your inner Om. Naropa (p107) is just one petal in the New Age/spiritual/yoga flower that's blossomed here. And aside from the various yoga studios and day spas, most of the activities are nature oriented, with hundreds of miles of hiking and biking trails, and shady Boulder Creek running through town. Yeah, if you get bored here, it really is your own fault.

FREE **Boulder Creek Bike Path** CYCLING
(Map p108; ⊘24 hr; ♿) The most utilized commuter bike path in town, this fabulously smooth and mostly straight creekside concrete path follows Boulder Creek from Foothill Parkway all the way to the spilt of Boulder Canyon and Four Mile Canyon Rd west of downtown – a total distance of over 5 miles one-way. The path also feeds urban bike lanes that lead all over town.

Six Persimmons MASSAGE
(Map p108; ☑303-413-9596; www.sixpersimm ons.com; 840 Pearl St; massage $60-75; ⊘10am-6pm Mon-Sat; 🚌206) West of the Pearl St Mall, this tiny apothecary offers Chinese herbs and organic facials, and has an attached acupuncture clinic. In addition it offers a range of deep tissue, lymphatic, Swedish and sport massages. Your Zen wishes will be fulfilled here. Massage is available by appointment only.

Boulder Ski Deals SKI GEAR, BOOKINGS
(☑303-938-8799; www.boulderskideals.com; 2525 Arapahoe Ave; ⊘10am-7pm Mon-Fri, 10am-6pm Sat, 11am-5pm Sun; 🚌JUMP) Arguably the best deals on skis, snowboards, glasses, goggles and snow gear can be found in this laidback but professional temple to all things extreme and powdery. It sells, it rents and the staff bro out – even with the ladies. And it offers exceptional deals on season passes to Vail, Breckenridge, Beaver Creek and Arapahoe Basin.

Tube Boulder Creek WATER SPORTS
(Map p108; ☑720-379-6056; www.whitewater tubing.com; 1717 15th St; tube rental $13-16; ⊘10:30am-6pm Jun-Aug; ♿; 🚌205, 206, BOLT, JUMP) Boulder's favorite summer ritual is to pick up an inner tube at this tubing and rafting center and float down Boulder Creek from the whitewater park at **Eben G Fine Park** (Boulder Canyon Dr) to 30th St. Speak to the staff about safety.

The park's high water and sculpted ledges can get rocking in early season, and you may even get flipped. But the creek mellows below 9th St, and can get low in late summer, leaving a much more placid whitewater park as the only navigable stretch.

Yoga Rocks the Park YOGA
(Map p108; www.yogarocksthepark.com; Central Park and Carpenter Park; per person $10; ⊘2-4pm Aug & Sep; ♿) An ambitious melding of yoga teachings and world music, Boulder's fit, bronze yogis descend to the green grassy environs of Central Park (in August) or Carpenter Park (in September) for this fun series that includes a sweaty asana session and some soulful live music. After all, they do call the man Damon Zen Drummer for a reason.

Yoga Pod YOGA
(☑303-444-4232; www.theyogapod.com; #2020 1750 29th St; adult/student & senior $17/12; ⊘6:30am-8:45pm Mon, Tue & Thu, to 9pm Wed, to 6:45pm Fri, 9am-5:15pm Sat, to 7:15pm Sun; 🚌BOUND) One of the hippest, if most oddly located, studios in Boulder. But don't let the 29th St Mall location throw you off. There's plenty of free parking, the place isn't corporate and the instruction is first rate. When the Fourmile Canyon Fire hit Boulder, they offered free yoga to those displaced by the Fourmile Fire.

FREE **Pop Jet Fountain** WATER SPORTS
(Map p108; Pearl & 14th Sts; ⊘daylight hours summer; ♿; 🚌205, 206) Bursts of water spring from the ground, sending kids squealing around in circles at this public fountain. It's a great (free) place to bring the kiddies when the temperatures rise, but be aware that the surface underfoot isn't soft.

Hiking & Rock Climbing

TOP CHOICE **FREE** **Royal Arch Trail** HIKING
(www.osmp.org; 900 Baseline Rd; ♿) Challenging but not excruciating, this roughly two-hour, 3.6-mile, well-signed trail leads you up along the Flatirons, through a

START: CHAUTAUQUA PARK
END: BOULDER THEATRE
DISTANCE: 4.8 MILES
TIME: 3-4 HOURS

Walking Tour
Boulder Walk

Boulder isn't a huge town, but it's big enough to have pockets of different personalities, which you'll be able to absorb on this walking tour. It's fitting to begin the tour at **1 Chautauqua Park**, which park marked the city's initial foray into open-space preservation, a notion that now defines the city. From here, walk downhill along Baseline Rd and turn right along 9th St through one of Boulder's oldest residential neighborhoods. Turn right on Euclid Ave to the **2 Boulder History Museum**, set in one of Boulder's historic homes. Continue east on Euclid before turning left on 13th St.

Now you'll be in the Hill, a student district with all the tumbledown, hipster-slacker element that is the grist of any good college town. To sip college life, step into the **3 Sink** before you continue on 13th St. This merges with Broadway – make a right onto Pleasant St, and head onto the **4 University of Colorado** campus. Stroll through academia, skirt Folsom Stadium,

make a left on Folsom and merge onto the **5 Boulder Creek Bike Path**.

Walk along the gurgling creek until you hit **6 Central Park** and the **7 Boulder Museum of Contemporary Art**. Ideally it'll be a Saturday and you can enjoy the Boulder County Farmers Market. Either way, stop in the striking **8 Dushanbe Teahouse** for sustenance.

Continue north on Broadway to Boulder's historic downtown center. Head left on Walnut to find the **9 Med** (great for happy hour), then double back and head up 11th St. In a couple of blocks you'll hit Pearl St, with Pearl St Mall to your right, where you'll find countless shops, cafes, restaurants and bars. Browse the **10 Boulder Bookstore** before strolling Spruce St, sipping from the historic **11 Hotel Boulderado** spring before finishing your tour with a show at the **12 Boulder Theater**.

There aren't many towns like Boulder. Even in Colorado it's an anomaly. We're not just referencing its ability to simultaneously nurture the adventurous and athletic, the intellectual and spiritual, the beer drinking masses and the culinary snob set. We're talking about Boulder, the place. You know, that town so close to Denver it could easily have become a mere suburb or satellite town. Just look at the Hwy 36 corridor. From the I-25 north this highway roars through one suburb after another, but as it approaches Boulder the development stops and all you see are those gorgeous Flatirons looming to the west. Why? Because long ago the city and county of Boulder got into the land acquisition business.

It all started back in 1898 when the city helped purchase and set aside land that was marked for gold exploration and became Chautauqua Park. In 1907 the government floated a public bond to buy Flagstaff Mountain and in 1912, 1200 more pristine mountain acres were purchased and preserved. Then, in 1967, Boulder voters legislated their love of the land by approving a sales tax specifically to buy, manage and maintain open space. This was historic. No other US city had ever voted to tax themselves specifically for open space. The sales tax measure passed with 57% of the vote and Boulder's **Open Space & Mountain Parks** (www.osmp.org) office was launched. In 1989, 76% of voters increased the tax by nearly 100%.

Still, even with an income stream, these days the government usually can't afford to buy whole parcels, and instead purchase 'conservation easements,' a legal agreement between the city and a landowner to protect their land's conservation value. Often they're used to purchase and protect wetlands and streams, keep agricultural land from being developed, and protect forests. While a good deal of Boulder's open space has been developed with trails, mapped and opened to the public, some parcels remain closed to visitors. But residents still feel the benefits: they live in a town buffered on all sides by vast open spaces that give Boulder its natural serenity.

vaguely red-rock canyon, through a keyhole and up to a wonderful natural rock arch where you'll perch on boulders, gaze at the Boulder basin, and, on clear days, glimpse the Denver skyline. Grab a trail map at the park office before hiking.

FREE **Wonderland Lake Trailhead** WALKING (www.osmp.org; 4201 N Broadway St; 🚼; 🚍SKIP) This easily accessed North Boulder trailhead links to 2.4 miles of trails within the City of Boulder's terrific open space mountain parks program. Better for runners or fast walkers than hikers (trails are pretty flat here), the trails skirt a lovely artificial lake, surrounded by knee-high grasses and tucked up against the foothills. Dogs are allowed but must be leashed.

The fields are golden in the summer and green in the spring and during the icy winter, you can ice skate at your own risk.

Boulder Falls Trail HIKING (www.bouldercolorado.gov; Boulder Canyon Dr; 🚼) A quick and relatively easy ramble along the upper reaches of Boulder Creek and into its headwaters. This trail begins approximately 10 miles west of downtown Boulder,

bends into a cozy but dramatic canyon with soaring granite walls and ends at Boulder Falls, which alternates between trickling and gushing depending upon the season. A bit more than a one-mile roundtrip.

Boulder Rock Club ROCK CLIMBING (☎303-447-2804; www.totalclimbing.com; 2829 Mapleton Ave; day pass adult/child $15/8, private lessons $50, three two-hour intro classes with gear rental $130; ⊘8am-10pm Mon, 6am-11pm Tue-Thu, 8am-11pm Fri, 10am-8pm Sat & Sun; 🚼; 🚍205C, 205W, BOLT) Before you head up to the climbs in Eldorado Canyon State Park, get your chops at this indoor climbing gym, popular with Boulder's local rock rats. This massive warehouse is full of artificial rock faces cragged with ledges and routes, and the auto-belay system allows solo climbers an anchor. Staff are a great resource for local climbing routes and tips too.

CLIMBING THE FLATIRONS
The iconic Flatirons, jutting from Chautauqua Park (p106) above Boulder, aren't necessarily the most challenging climbs in the area, but they must be climbed. The most popular route is the Class 5.6, 10-pitch First

Flatiron 'direct climb.' It's a slab crawl up 1000ft to amazing views in all directions, but it gets crowded on weekends.

The classic Third Flatiron route is the standard east face (Class 5.4, eight pitches). It's been climbed naked and in drag, but it isn't for beginners. Most push down in one 200ft 'super-rappel.' The climber's access trail off the second-third Flatirons trail will put you at the base of this route.

ELDORADO STATE CANYON PARK

Eldorado Canyon State Park is one of the country's best rock-climbing areas, offering Class 5.5 to 5.12 climbs. They also have nearly a dozen miles of trails suitable for all levels of visitors – from hardcore athletes to toddlers and seniors.

The park entrance is on Eldorado Springs Dr. Take Hwy 93 south from Boulder, head west on Hwy 170 and continue on the dirt road through town to the park gates. Stop by Boulder Rock Club for climbing tips before hitting these red rock walls.

★ Festivals & Events

FREE Boulder Creek Festival
SUMMER FESTIVAL

(303-449-3137; www.bceproductions.com; Central Park, Canyon Blvd; Memorial Day Weekend; 203, 204, 225, AB, B, DASH, DD, DM, GS, SKIP) Billed as the kick-off to summer and capped with the fabulous Bolder Boulder (p114), this summer festival is massive. There's more than 10 event areas featuring more than 30 live entertainers and 500 vendors. There will be food and drink, music and sunshine. What's not to love?

Bolder Boulder
RUN

(303-444-7223; www.bolderboulder.com; adult $44-48; Memorial Day;) In a self-consciously hyper-athletic town, this is the biggest foot race within the city limits. It doesn't take itself too seriously, even though you have to qualify to enter (running 10km at mile high is much easier written about than done) and top pros circle this date on their race calendar. Spectators scream and celebrate, and there's live music on stages throughout the course.

FREE 29th Street Live
MUSIC

(303-449-3137; www.bceproductions.com; 29th St Mall; various Fri & Sat Jun-Aug; ; 205, 206, BOLT, BOUND) Boulder's corporate mall goes rock '89*n roll on selected summer nights. Crowds can get thick and the surroundings aren't the greatest, but

live bands are like pizza – good, bad...who cares? There's music in the air!

FREE Boulder Creek Hometown Fair
SUMMER FESTIVAL

(303-449-3137; www.bceproductions.com; Central Park, Canyon Blvd; Labor Day Weekend; ; 203, 204, 225, AB, B, DASH, DD, DM, GS, SKIP) As much as the Boulder Creek Festival (p114) marks the beginning of summer, this Labor Day fest marks its coming mortality. This time there are only 100 vendors involved and only one event area, but plenty of laughs, including a pie eating contest, the Great Zucchini Race (yes zucchinis are outfitted with wheels) and plenty of live music.

FREE Boulder Pride Fest
LGBT

(303-499-5777; www.outboulder.org; Pearl St Mall; early Sep; ; 208) Held in early September, this is a diverse, joyful, multiblock party on the Pearl St Mall that pools into a stage in front of the court house lawn. Vendors set up booths to sell food, clothes, jewelry, and there's live music and poetry performances, speeches from community leaders, and a fair amount of wellness and health care information.

Boulder Adventure Film Festival
FILM

(www.adventurefilm.org; 2032 14th St; November; ; 208) Held in late November at the Boulder Theater, this outdoor adventure film fest is one of three sponsored by Patagonia (the other two are in Chamonix and Patagonia). It features films documenting the best climbing, surfing, snowboarding, diving (and more) the world has to offer. If you're in town it is worth seeking out.

FREE Lights of December
CHRISTMAS

(1st Sat in Dec;) Every town deserves a Christmas parade. Floats are created and decorated by local businesses, churches and civic groups. Decorated fire engines and marching bands are featured, while Scouts dressed as snowflakes and candy canes stroll along with them. Even Santa makes an appearance. The parade loops Pearl St Mall heading up Walnut to 11th, and down Spruce to 15th.

🛏 Sleeping

Boulder has dozens more hotels than we have space to list. Most are within spitting distance of Hwy 36 and, unfortunately, most are overpriced. Try to compensate by booking online to score the best discounts and special packages, which can include everything from spa treatments to meal

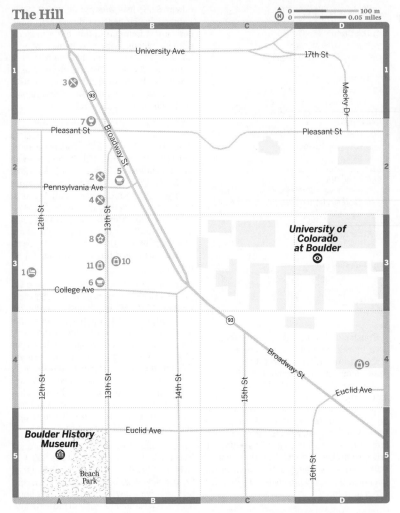

coupons or champagne. Budgeteers may have to pony up a few more bucks for a bit less than they've imagined. Talk about a town in dire need of a boutique midranger!

TOP CHOICE **Chautauqua Lodge**   LODGE **$**
(☎303-442-3282; www.chautauqua. com; 900 Baseline Rd; r from $73, cottages from $157; P ⊝ ❄ 🛜 🐾) Not just the best setting (nestled at the base of the Flatirons, on the lip of a wide green park), but also the best-value sleep in all of Boulder. Choose a clean, canary brushed lodge room or one of the one-, two- or three-bedroom cottages scat-

tered about the leafy streets. All have full kitchens. Perfect for families.

See all the people walking around and smiling? They're wonder drunk. This place does that to you.

The Alps   B&B **$$$**
(☎303-444-5445; www.alpsinn.com; 38619 Boulder Canyon Dr; r $214-279; P ⊝ ❄ @ 🛜) Named Best of Boulder and one of the 'west's most distinctive inns' by local papers, the Alps offers 12 striking guest rooms. Each is genuinely appointed with authentic Mission furnishings, stained glass windows and restored working antique fireplaces.

⊙ **Top Sights**
Boulder History Museum A5
University of Colorado at Boulder...............D3

🛏 **Sleeping**
1 Boulder International Youth
    Hostel A3

🍴 **Eating**
2 Half Fast Subs A2
3 Kim Food to Go A1
4 Sink A2

🍷 **Drinking**
5 Buchanan's Coffee Pub B2
6 Espresso Roma A3
7 Goose A2

🎭 **Entertainment**
8 Fox Theatre...A3

🛍 **Shopping**
9 CU Bookstore.. D4
10 Meow Meow..B3
11 Posterscene..A3

Constructed in the 1870s and originally used by railway workers, the inn was one of Colorado's earliest resorts. Dark woods, stone floors and log beams running overhead reveal the upgraded and re-appointed flair of this luxurious gem. The inn boasts views of beautiful Boulder Canyon and the Boulder Creek below. Many of the rooms feature private whirlpools for two with French doors leading to gardens, patios or private porches. Attached marbled baths, walk-in showers, claw-foot tubs or generous spa amenities appeal to couples looking for a romantic foray.

Quality Inn Boulder Creek   MOTEL **$$**
(☎303-449-7550; www.qualityinnboulder.com; 2020 Arapahoe Ave; r from $139; ☺✳🛜🐾🚻; 🚌JUMP) A forest-green tinted brick and shingled inn a short walk from downtown, this exceptionally well-run chain is anything but bland. Rooms are sizable and have a touch of class (read: cush linens and flat-screen TVs). Staff – including Samantha the ubiquitous Wheaton terrier – are top notch. This is one of the best-value stays in Boulder.

St Julien Hotel & Spa   HOTEL **$$$**
(Map p108; ☎720-406-9696, reservations 877-303-0900; www.stjulien.com; 900 Walnut St; r from $227; 🅿☺✳🛎@🛜🐾🚻; 🚌208, SKIP) Plunked in the heart of downtown, Boulder's finest four-star option has a modern, refined ski-lodge vibe. The loungy lobby is flooded with light, and has a great back patio with fabulous Flatiron views. This is where live bands descend for world music, jazz concerts and wild salsa parties. Rooms are plush, and so are the robes.

Boulder International Youth Hostel
HOSTEL **$**
(Map p115; ☎303-442-0522; www.boulderinternationalhostel.com; 1107 12th St; dm $27, r with shared bath from $55; 🅿🛜; 🚌203, 204, 205, AB, B, DASH, DD, DM, GS, SKIP) Located amid the frat houses on University Hill, this hostel has been meeting the needs of travelers since 1961. Dorms and private rooms are clean and warm, and the facilities are infinitely better than those in Denver's hostels. Bring bedding or rent linen for $7 per stay.

Boulder Marriott   HOTEL **$$$**
(☎303-440-8877; www.marriott.com; 2660 Canyon Blvd; r $230-260; 🅿☺✳@🛜🐾; 🚌205, 206, BOLT) One of the better options in town, this peach-tinted chain opens up to the west, which mean top-floor rooms get beautiful Flatiron views. Rooms are far from fashionable but they are comfortable and spacious with a desk, sofa and queen bed. Well run, it's less a resort and more of a business hotel with free wifi in the lobby and hard line internet in rooms for a fee. If you're into amenities, it's not a bad splurge.

Hotel Boulderado   BOUTIQUE HOTEL **$$$**
(Map p108; ☎303-442-4344, toll-free 800-433-4344; www.boulderado.com; 2115 13th St; r from $224; 🅿✳🛜; 🚌208, SKIP) Celebrating a century of service in 2009, the charming Boulderado is a National Register landmark and a romantic place to spend the night. Full of Victorian elegance and wonderful public spaces, each antique-filled room is uniquely decorated. The stained glass atrium and glacial water fountain accent the jazz washed lobby.

The property itself is surprisingly sprawling. Queen rooms are spacious, and bathrooms are updated, which means they lack the hotel's requisite charm. Rooms in the guesthouse across the street are slightly bigger and cheaper, but lack the historical gravitas.

Millennium Harvest House HOTEL $$$
(🕿303-443-3850; www.millenniumhotels.com; 1345 28th St; r $199-220; [P][🚶][❄][@][🛜][🏊][♿]; [🐕]HX, S) Dated, formerly grand, but still a plush resort, the cylindrical flagstone and stucco Millennium has a large footprint that sprawls nearly to the edge of Boulder Creek. This place has been alive since the 1950s, and they still have the most rooms in town, along with enough panache to make you feel just a little bit like Don Draper.

Rooms are fairly large if garishly decorated, and those in the main building have wide verandas overlooking the Flatirons, the garden including two pools and 15 tennis courts.

Boulder Mountain Lodge HOTEL $$
(🕿303-444-0882; www.bouldermountainlodge.com; 91 Four Mile Canyon Rd; r from $94, cabin $129-189; [P][🚶][❄][🛜][♿]; [🐕]N) Set in shady Four Mile Canyon, west of Boulder off Hwy 119, this family-owned and -operated lodge in the mountains is gorgeously placed amid pines and cottonwood trees. It offers a rather homey cabin, as well as clean, motel-style rooms with kitchenettes. The kids' fishing pond is a plus.

Boulder Outlook HOTEL $$
(🕿303-443-3322, 800-542-0304; www.boulderoutlook.com; 800 28th St; d $159-169, ste $189; [P][❄][🛜][🏊][♿]) The Boulder Outlook – Boulder's first zero-waste hotel – is just off the highway at the south end of Boulder, making it a great location for those escaping from Denver. With funky colors, a sustainability focus and pet-friendly atmosphere, the Outlook typifies the stuff that draw so many people within the 'Boulder Bubble.'

The hotel is amenity-rich (including a suspiciously sustainable figure-eight pool and hot tub) and has an outdoor slant, making it a well-perched base to explore the surrounding area. The rooms are fairly standard: kings, queens and double suites.

Foot of the Mountain MOTEL $
(🕿303-442-5688; www.footofthemountainmotel.com; 200 Arapahoe St; r $65-90; [P][🚶][❄][@][🛜][♿]) Nothing fancy here, but plenty of family-owned, wood panneled charm. The motel itself looks like a cabin has been stretched out and bent around a parking lot, then tucked into a wooded glen literally at the foot of Flagstaff Mountain. Rooms are more quirky than comfy but there-in lies its

charm and, considering the competition, it's good value at this price.

Twin Lakes Inn HOTEL $$
(🕿303-530-2939; www.twinlakesinnboulder.com; 6485 Twin Lakes Rd; r from $99; [P][🚶][❄][🛜][♿]; [🐕]205W) Owned by a former Olympian, this aging midranger set in northeast Boulder is both far from fancy and from the center of town. Still, rooms are large and they accept pets and have laundry facilities. Plus it's within walking distance of the Twin Lakes along a gravel trail. Some rooms have sofa beds and sleep up to six.

🍴 Eating

Historically, Boulder's restaurant scene could be classified as a case of style over substance. The rooms have always looked good, but the food hasn't always lived up to the ambiance. For years locals simply shrugged their shoulders, admitting that you can't live in Boulder and expect to eat like you're in Manhattan or Chicago. Or even Denver for that matter. However, in recent years things have shifted: 'farm to table' has become the buzz phrase, and local food has been popping up in a twice weekly farmers market and landing in stylish and happening new restaurants. Where once there were one or two 'special occasion' restaurants and a ton of middling eateries, now there is a great selection of places where you can eat like the sophisticate you are, all in the gorgeous foothills of those nearby Rocky Mountains.

Jax SEAFOOD $$$
TOP CHOICE (Map p108; 🕿310-444-1811; www.jaxfishhouseboulder.com; 928 Pearl St; mains $16-25; ⏰from 4pm; [🚶]206, SKIP) More than 15 years running and, for our money, this lively seafood shack still has the finest eats downtown. Belly up to the circle bar for oysters and martinis, then feast on fresh seafood flown in daily – think wild salmon and tuna or a chilled lobster.

If you're after something quick and dirty, order the fried oyster po'boy. It's the only one of its kind in Boulder.

Frasca ITALIAN $$$
(Map p108; 🕿303-442-6966; www.frascafoodandwine.com; 1738 Pearl St; mains $28; ⏰5:30-10:30pm) Frasca has been considered Boulder's finest restaurant since it opened. The service is top shelf and the rotating menu features the freshest farm-to-table

BOULDER IN...

Two Days

No matter what time of year you land here, the first stop should always be **Chautaqua Park**. If you think ahead, stop by **Snarf's** or **Dish** and bring your lunch with you. Grind on the rocks or lay out a blanket on the Chautauqua lawn. We suggest the 4-mile round-trip hike up the vaguely red rock ravine to **Royal Arch**. Afterwards, head down to the Pearl St Mall and explore Boulder's historic downtown, then dine on fresh seafood at **Jax**.

Wake up with brunch at the **Dushanbe Teahouse**, head next door to the **Boulder Museum of Contemporary Art**, then, if it's summer, grab an innertube and float down Boulder Creek. Otherwise rent a bike and roll the **Boulder Creek Bike Path** or pedal up **Flagstaff Mountain**, before heading to West Pearl, where you can dine at **Salt** and wander over to the **Bitter Bar** for a prohibition-era cocktail before catching a show at the **Boulder Theater**.

Four days

If you're here for four days you can cover all of the above and will likely overlap with one of Boulder's fabulous **farmers markets**, held in Central Park on Wednesdays and Saturdays. Before you hit the market, work up an appetite at one of Boulder's famed yoga studios, then head to the **Walnut** or **Mountain Sun Pub & Brewery** for an IPA. Hit **Mateo** for dinner then get down and dirty at one of the dive bars, such as **Catacombs** or the **Sundown**.

The following day grab an early breakfast at **Moe's Bagels**, then drive up to **Nederland** (p144) and go for a hike or mountain bike ride amidst high alpine environs. Get back in time for happy hour at the **Med**, where you can munch cheap and tasty tapas, then head to the roof deck of the **West End Tavern**, before strolling down the street to the **Blending Cellar** for live jazz or **Absinthe House** for a taste of the hot, new club scene.

ingredients available. Reservations must be made days or even weeks in advance.

The menu includes dishes like braised pork shoulder canneloni, house made gnocchi and grilled quail served with local peppers, leeks and wilted pea shoots. This restaurant is as fancy and as snooty as Boulder gets.

Spruce Confections BAKED GOODS $
(Map p108; ☎303-449-6773; 767 Pearl St; cookies from $3.25; ☻6:30am-6pm Mon-Fri, 7am-6pm Sat & Sun; ☻🖬; 🖵206) Boulder's go-to bakehouse, where the favorites are the Ol' B Cookie (chocolate, oats, cinnamon and coconut) and the Black Bottom Cupcake (a chocolate cupcake with cheesecake in the middle). Pair either with the Spruce Juice, possibly the world's greatest iced vanilla latte. It has sinful scones and filling salads too.

Dushanbe Teahouse FUSION $$
(Map p108; ☎303-442-4993; www.boulder teahouse.com; 1770 13th St; mains $8-18; ☻8am-10pm; 🖬; 🖵203, 204, 205, 206, 208, 225, DASH,

JUMP, SKIP) No visit to Boulder is complete without a meal at this incredible Tajik work of art, a gift from Boulder's sister city (Dushanbe, Tajikistan) that boasts incredible craftsmanship and meticulous painting. The fare ranges from Amazonian and Mediterranean to, of course, Tajik. Outside is a lovely, shaded patio. It's an intimate place to grab cocktails or dinner on a warm summer day.

Kitchen CONTEMPORARY AMERICAN $$$
(Mapp108;☎303-544-5973;www.thekitchen cafe.com; 1039 Pearl St; mains $11-25; ☻11am-9pm Mon, to 10pm Tue-Fri, 9am-2pm & 5:30-10pm Sat, 9:30am-2pm & 5:30-9pm Sun; ☻🖥) Clean lines, stacks of crusty bread, a daily menu and lots of light: Kitchen is one of the finest kitchens in town. Fresh farmers-market ingredients are crafted into rustic tapas: think roasted root vegetables, shaved prosciutto and mussels steamed in wine and cream. The pulled-pork sandwich rocks, but save room for the sticky toffee pudding. Thirsty grown-ups dig the upstairs bar.

Sink

PUB FOOD $

(Map p115; ☎303-444-7465; www.thesink.com; 1165 13th St; mains $5-10; ⏰11am-2am, kitchen to 10pm; ⊕; 🚌203, 204, 225, AB, B, DASH, SKIP, DD, DM, GS) Waiters bob and weave under the low-slung, graffiti-scrawled ceiling of the Sink, a Hill classic that's been around since 1923. Colorful characters cover the dimly lit, cavernous space – a scene almost worth a visit itself. Almost. Once you've washed back the legendary Sink burger with a slug of a local microbrew, you'll be glad you stuck around.

Aji

LATIN AMERICAN $$

(Map p108; ☎303-442-3464; www.ajirestaurant. com; 1601 Pearl St; mains $16-23; ⏰11:30am-3pm, from 5pm) Start with the lobster and shrimp empanadas, then move on to a pulled-pork torta, the huevos rancheros (touted by some as the best in Boulder), or the sweet and spicy chiles en nogada (think meat picadillo stuffed inside poblano chiles smothered in walnut sauce). This is Latin American food re-imagined, and whatever you order, dash it with some of the house chile sauce

Dagabi Cucina

MEDITERRANEAN $$

(☎303-786-9004; www.dagabicucina.com; 3970 N Broadway St; mains $11-18; ⏰5-10pm; ⊕) Hidden away in a North Boulder minimall off Broadway is this brickhouse of a Mediterranean joint with Italian and Spanish roots, and a popular tapas menu at happy hour (5pm to 6:30pm). That's when you can devour olives, bruschetta, grilled asparagus, steamed clams, and pancetta wrapped shrimp on small plates for just $3 to $6 each. Or there's always paella Mondays ($12).

Dish

SANDWICHES $

(☎720-565-5933; www.dishgourmet.com; 1918 Pearl St; mains $7-10; ⏰9am-6pm Mon-Fri, 11am-4pm Sat; ⊕📶; 🚌204) This simple and tasty market cafe turns out gourmet sandwiches piled with speck, pate and brie, slow cooked brisket, as well as artichokes, marinated eggplant, house roasted tomatoes and fresh mozzarella made in-house. It has some alluring salads too. Most of the goods are stacked in market cases or listed on the blackboard.

Foolish Craig's

AMERICAN $

(Map p108; ☎303-247-9383; www.foolishcraigs. com; 1611 Pearl St; mains $6-14; ⏰8am-10pm Mon-Sat, to 9pm Sun; ⊕; 🚌204) This brick house of a diner has a cool bar, groovy art on the walls and a fun vibe. In its soul it's simply a longtime and much loved breakfast joint famous for its build-your-own omelets and crepes. Lately Craig's has put together a more upscale dinner menu, with options such as pulled pork, pan-seared trout and fried brussel sprout leaves with warm Brie.

Gurkha's

INDIAN, NEPALESE $$

(☎303-530-1551; www.gurkhasrestaurant.com; 6565 Gunpark Dr; mains $11-14; ⏰11am-2:30pm & 5-9pm Mon-Fri, noon-2:30pm & 5-9pm Sat & Sun; ⊕📶; 🚌205, 205C, 205W) Many of Boulder's Indian residents swear this is the best Indian in town. The drawback is it's way out on the northeast edge, in the bowels of the tech parks and warehouses. But, all things considered, for such authentic homestyle fare (buttered and honeyed naan, creamy tikka masala, tender and fresh coconut fish, some special veggie curries...), it's a fairly short trek.

Happy

PAN-ASIAN $$

(Map p108; ☎303-442-3050; www.happynoodle house.com; 835 Walnut St; mains $12-23; ⏰4pm-late; 🚌206) One of Boulder's better restaurants, Happy serves up what it calls 'Asian inspired comfort food,' which means flavors like wok-seared scallops, a *bahn-mi* (short rib) burger, griddled pork buns, tofu udon and fried brussel sprout leaves (surprisingly memorable). And nobody in town does finer cocktails than the men and women behind Happy's Bitter Bar (p122).

Leaf

VEGAN $$

(Map p108; ☎303-442-1485; www.leafvege tarianrestaurant.com; 2010 16th St; mains $11-16; ⏰11:30am-9pm Mon-Thu & Sun, to 10pm Fri & Sat; ⊕🍴; 🚌204) This ethical and elegant kitchen serves meatless gems (Jamaican jerk tempeh, pad thai, pea and mint ravioli, a popular raw ravioli...) amidst exposed brick walls and tiled ceilings dangling with striking wire lanterns. It's the perfect place to take all vegan cuties in your life. Whether they're 10 or 110, they all love it here.

Powell's Sweet Shoppe

SWEETS $

(Map p108; ☎303-413-3060; www.powellsss. com; 1200 Pearl St; ⏰10am-9pm Mon-Sat, to 8pm Sun; ⊕📶; 🚌208, SKIP) The ideal oasis for those with a retro sweet tooth. It not only remembers candy folks used to scarf during those long gone matinees in the 1980s, it has it in stock! Kids of all ages melt into a sugar frenzy just by walking through the door. It serves tasty and locally crafted Boulder Gelato here too.

Proto's Pizza

PIZZA $$

(☎720-565-1050; www.protospizza.com; 4670 N Broadway Ave; pizzas $5-22; ☺11am-9pm Sun-Thu, to 10pm Fri & Sat) Boulder's finest pizza is served in the town's new North Broadway strip. The colorful, well-lit interior is inviting but we like to grind the rich and savory thin-crust pies (yes, folk from abroad, they call them pies) on the patio or at the outdoor bar. Friday night is popular for the fresh clams and garlic pizza. Salads are fresh and well dressed, and there are gluten-free crusts available.

Salt

CONTEMPORARY AMERICAN $$$

(Map p108; ☎303-444-7258; www.saltboulderbistro.com; 1047 Pearl St; mains $10-25; ☺11am-10pm Mon-Wed, to 11pm Thu-Sat, 10am-10pm Sun; ☻☝; 🚌208, SKIP) One of downtown's newest and most happening spots also serves damn fine farm-to-table cuisine. We're talking small plates like crispy pork belly BLT, heirloom tomato salad and local beef carpaccio. Entrees include fresh fettucine and slow-roasted leg of lamb, and several fresh seafood options. Cocktails are creative and personalized.

The house always feels good, whether you dine downstairs in the basement pub or in the bright brick-wall dining room with a glimpse of the open and rocking kitchen.

Two Spoons

GELATO $

(Map p108; ☎303-545-0027; www.twospoonsboulder.com; 1021 Pearl St; lunch $5-10; ☺11am-8pm Mon-Wed, to 11pm Thu & Sun, to midnight Sat, seasonal variations; ☝; 🚌203, 206, 225) The door handle to this Pearl St favorite is a big wooden spoon, and pulling on it sends you into the sugar-scented world of Boulder's best gelato shop. The flavors are all homemade, with cappuccino brownie and fresh mint almond as our favorites. It also serves excellent soups and light lunches.

Med

MEDITERRANEAN $$

(Map p108; ☎303-444-5335; www.themedboulder.com; 1002 Walnut St; mains $11-27; ☺10am-10pm Sun-Thu, to 11pm Fri & Sat; ☻; 🚌206) A Boulder classic, this friendly, festive joint brings all the many flavors of the Mediterranean under one roof (and patio). Think wood-fired pizza, gyros and terrific tapas from gambas to bacon-wrapped dates to bruschetta. There's a full bar and some fantastic deserts. Terrific happy-hour deals and a fun crowd most nights.

✐ Lucile's

CAJUN $

(Map p108; ☎303-442-4743; www.luciles.com; 2142 14th St; mains $7-14; ☺7am-2pm Mon-Fri, from 8am Sat & Sun; ☻☝; 🚌208, SKIP) This New Orleans–style diner has perfected breakfast, and the Creole egg dishes (served over creamy spinach alongside cheesy grits or perfectly blackened trout) are the thing to order. Start with a steaming mug of chai or chicory coffee and an order of beignets. The powder sugar–drenched French Cajun doughnuts are the house specialty.

Lucile's operates in a few towns, including Fort Collins (p148).

Boulder BOP

PIZZA $$

(Map p108; ☎303-999-3833; www.boulderbop.com; 1175 Walnut St; pizzas $15-12; ☺11am-midnight Sun-Thu, 10am-2am Fri & Sat; ☝; 🚌208) The long-distance import of Italian ingredients might not win this brightly painted pizzeria any sustainability awards, but the organic, thin-crust pies are delicately dressed in the faithful Italian tradition. On weekends DJs spin late for a collegiate crowd.

Boulder Cafe

CONTEMPORARY AMERICAN $$

(Map p108; ☎303-444-4884; www.bouldercafeonpearl.com; 1247 Pearl St; mains $11-26; ☺11am-10pm Sun-Thu, to 11pm Fri & Sat; ☝; 🚌208, SKIP) Score a sidewalk table and check out the Pearl St Mall street performers while waiting for your buffalo burger. The perennially popular Boulder Cafe is one of those 'all things to all people' kitchens, which means anything from shrimp enchiladas to penne pasta or skillets of trout and teriyaki steak to a damn fine raw bar can be yours.

From 3pm to 6:30pm, all appetizers and drinks are half-price. That's the time to go raw.

Half Fast Subs

SANWICHES $

(Map p115; ☎303-449-0404; www.halffastsubs.com; 1215 13th St; subs $7-10; ☺10:30am-midnight Mon, Thu & Fri, to 11pm Tue & Wed, 11am-midnight Sat, to 10pm Sun; ☝; 🚌203, 204, 225, DASH, SKIP) Deal with the line at lunch, or come for a happy hour that's 'guaranteed to kick your butt,' (the 32 oz Long Island Ice Tea suggests they're serious). The extensive sandwich board has tons of stuff for vegetarians, including baked tofu. Meat eaters should go for a gooey cheese steak.

Juanita's

MEXICAN $$

(Map p108; ☎303-449-5273; www.juanitas-boulder.com; 1043 Pearl St; mains $8-12; ☻☺☝; 🚌206, 208) Any place with a mantra of 'Praise the Lard' deserves a look, and even if the platters of Tex-Mex aren't spectacular, the homey atmosphere stands out along the genteel

BOULDER FOR CHILDREN

It's easy to keep the kids happy and busy here: most of what makes adults so giddy about a Boulder holiday – nature and adventure – excites kids too. There's a huge amount of outdoors options for all ages. If your kids prefer something a bit more academic, take them to the free monthly shows put on by CU's Wizards Program (p107). The science-based shows, like 'Physics of Sound' or 'Magic of Chemistry' are free, held on one Saturday per month, and are geared toward fifth- to ninth-graders.

Outdoors Options

Families would be happiest booking a bungalow at the Chautauqua Lodge (p115). These rustic but pleasantly updated homes include a kitchen, a screened-in front porch and back yard, and open onto Chautauqua Park (p106). Which means the kids can ramble through the grasses and interact with nature at ground level, while you keep one eye on them, and another on your glass of wine while you relax on the porch. It's also the best place to glimpse the Boulder stars. The Royal Arch (p111) trail can be a long slog for a toddler, but they do fine on the Boulder Falls Trail (p113).

Kids of all ages love to go tubing on Boulder Creek, and bike shops can rent kid-sized wheels. The Boulder Creek Bike Path (p111) is a perfect family ride. The Boulder Farmers Market (p122) is another fun family experience, with plenty of music and color and flavors, as well as ample grass space for picnicking and the nearby Boulder Creek. There's also the nearby Boulder Museum of Contemporary Art (p107), which offers free guided art activities on their front porch, in the thick of the market, on Saturdays (9am to 1pm).

On hot days, toddlers love the Pearl St Mall's Pop Jet Fountain (p111). Prepare for squeals of delight, and bring a towel and a change of clothes.

A Drive Away

About 20 miles (20 minutes by car on the freeway) from Boulder, halfway to Denver in the suburb of Westminster, is the Butterfly Pavilion (p107). Its indoor atrium is alive with tropical gardens and 1200 butterflies from rainforests around the world – not to mention tarantulas, scorpions, giant millipedes and more. The nearby Sunflower Farm (p110) in Longmont also welcomes families on Farm Fest Sundays (May to November) to help feed baby animals, collect eggs, ride ponies and explore the giant tree house.

BOULDER EATING

Pearl St Mall. Make for the dimly lit cantina in back, where Norteño music pumps and the margaritas are freshly squeezed.

Kim Food to Go VIETNAMESE $
(Map p115; ☎303-442-2829; 1325 Broadway St; mains $4-6; ☺11am-10pm Mon-Sat; ☐203, 204, 225, DASH, SKIP) Sure, this place is a bit rough around the edges and the vegetarian noodles may well come with a wayward piece of chicken, but there's no cheaper, better lunch grub within miles. It's also ideal for the morning after a college town bender. There's no seating, save for a couple picnic tables.

Pupusa's MEXICAN, SALVADORIAN $
(☎303-444-1729; 4457 N Broadway St; mains $2.50-8; ☺10am-9pm Mon-Fri, 9am-9pm Sat, 10am-8pm Sun; ☻☝; ☐SKIP) Simple and soulful Salvadorian and Mexican food (pupusas, tacos, tortas and burritos) served in

heaping portions at affordable prices in a sweet, pastel-brushed hole in the wall with patio seating outside. A humble breath of fresh air to be sure.

Salvaggio's Italian Deli SANDWICHES $
(Map p108; ☎303-938-1981; www.salvaggiosdeli. com; 14th & Pearl Sts; sandwiches $3-8; ☺8am-6:30pm Mon-Fri, 8-11am Sat & Sun; ☝; ☐205) We're happy to wait out the lunch crowd for a slow-roasted prime rib sub, served on a fresh, crusty roll and dressed in horseradish with veggies. The kiosk sits squarely in the Pearl St Mall, and though there is no seating, public benches abound nearby for a simple picnic.

Sushi Zanmai SUSHI $$
(Map p108; ☎303-440-0733; www.sushizanmai. com; 1221 Spruce St; mains $6-15; ☺11:30am-2pm & 5-10pm Mon-Fri, 5pm-midnight Sat, to 10pm Sun; ☝; ☐208, SKIP) As fun and fresh as sushi

gets in Boulder. The chefs shout with delight as customers fill the space, which they do early and often. The chefs shout again as they complete platters of cut sushi, grilled and brushed eel, toro hand rolls and specialty house rolls like the Colorado, made with raw filet mingnon. Trout, a common sushi out in the mountains of Japan, is available here. Get it!

Sherpa's Adventurers
NEPALESE $

(Map p108; ☎303-440-7151; 825 Walnut St; mains $7-10; ☺11am-3pm & 5:30-9:30pm Mon-Fri, 11am-3pm & 5:30-10pm Sat & Sun; ☑ 🖈; 🚍206) A friendly Nepalese cafe set in a coverted home at the edge of downtown. Dishes are simple, homestyle choices including Tofu Aloo and a hearty Sherpa Stew. Lunch specials are cheap, and the vine-shaded patio is a great spot for a mango lassi on a summer afternoon. The chef has summitted Mt Everest 10 times!

Mai Berry
FROZEN YOGURT $

(Map p108; ☎303-444-0483; www.maiberry. com; 1433 Pearl St; ☺10am-10pm Tue-Sun, to 9pm Sat; ☺; 🚍Boulder Transport Center) When you're greeted with the patter of techno and the smell of mashed-up fresh fruit, it's clear that you've found the front line of the hipster fro-yo revolution. This is tart Greek-style frozen yogurt, and the infusions are only part of the package – it also has coffee, smoothies and fresh juice.

Self-catering

TOP CHOICE **FREE** **Boulder County Farmers' Market**
SELF-CATERING

(Map p108; ☎303-910-2236; www.boulderfarm ers.org; 13th St; ☺8am-2pm Sat April-Nov, 4-8pm Wed May-Oct; 🖈; 🚍203, 204, 205, 206, 208, 225, DASH, JUMP, SKIP) A massive spring and summer sprawl of colorful, mostly organic local food. Here you can find flowers and herbs, as well as brain-sized mushrooms, delicate squash blossoms, crusty pretzels, vegan dips, grass-fed beef, raw granola and yogurt. The market stretches from Arapahoe to Canyon along Central Park and around the Boulder Museum of Contemporary Art (p107), which offers free admission on market days.

Prepared food booths offer gyros and tamales. Live music is as standard as the family picnics in the park along Boulder Creek.

Vitamin Cottage
SELF-CATERING

(☎303-402-1400; www.vitamincottage.com; 2355 30th St; ☺9am-4pm Mon-Sat, 10am-6pm Sun; ☺🖈; 🚍BOUND) Set in the same mini-mall complex as the Whole Foods flagship, this less corporate and more affordable organic full-service grocer makes a nice alternative supply line for self-caterers.

Lolita's Market & Deli
SELF-CATERING

(Map p108; ☎303-443-8329; 800 Pearl St; ☺24hr; 🖈; 🚍206) Whether you're on a run for late night munchies, on an early morning hunt for trail grinds or, you know, Sunday morning bacon, this joint should be your defacto supply line. Think deli food and wasabi peas juxtaposed against nice bars of dark chocolate. Oh, and it also rents inner tubes ($10) for would-be Boulder Creek sailors during summer.

Whole Foods Market
SELF-CATERING

(☎303-499-7636; www.wildoats.com; 2584 Baseline Rd; ☺7:30am-9pm; ☺🖈; 🚍203, BOUND) It doesn't sit well with Boulderites that this store, once the flagship of an independent natural grocery chain, is now a part of the Whole Foods monolith. Still, for organic self-catering this place has a good selection as well as a fresh food deli.

🍷 Drinking

The drinking here begins before the sun goes down, with almost every restaurant and bar offering absurd happy-hour deals. Must be a student thing.

Speaking of which, about those students, they tend to rule both the Hill (the neighborhood immediately adjacent to CU) and downtown, where Pearl St becomes a pedestrian party scene. Many restaurants double as bars or turn into all-out dance clubs come 10pm. Of course, the best scenes aren't usually those easily glimpsed on the surface (look for basement dives, jazz lounges, prohibition bars...). And we haven't even mentioned the groovy cafes and coffee houses, the microbrews or absinthe. Ah yes, there will always be a clinking of the glasses in sweet Boulderado.

Bitter Bar
COCKTAIL BAR

(Map p108; ☎303-442-3050; www.happynoodle house.com; 835 Walnut St; cocktails $9-15; ☺4pm-late; 🚍206) In places like NYC, LA and San Francisco, prohibition-era cocktails have gone from back alley whispers of the impossibly hip to mainstream in a few short years. Boulder now has its version, and who cares if it's set in modern pan-Asian environs. These cocktails, and the rums, whiskeys, tequilas and gins used to alchemize, are the best sips in town.

It also offers monthly classes at $35 per person, which buys you the knowhow to mix two drinks that would make a Mad Man weep. You'll leave with three recipes and a gift from the barkeeps. Check the website for dates.

Cup
CAFE

(Map p108; 303-449-5173; www.thecupboulder.com; 1521 Pearl St; 7am-10pm; ; 204) This groovy loftlike space opens onto Pearl St, pouring forth a tempting whiff of damn good coffee and handpicked organic loose-leaf teas. It also does fresh quiche, wonderful cakes in cups, burly sandwiches and swift wi-fi. No wonder it's always packed with the comely, the studious and the industrious. Monday is open mic night.

Mountain Sun Pub & Brewery
BREWPUB

(Map p108; 303-546-0886; www.mountainsunpub.com; 1535 Pearl St; 11:30am-1am Mon-Sat, from noon Sun; 204) Boulder's favorite brewery serves a rainbow of brews from chocolaty to fruity, and packs in an eclectic crowd of yuppies, hippies and everyone in between. Walls are lined with tapestries, there are board games to amuse you and the pub grub (especially the burgers and the chili) is delicious. There's often live music of the bluegrass, reggae and jam-band variety on Sunday and Monday nights.

Trident Cafe
CAFE

(Map p108; 303-443-3133; www.tridentcafe.com; 940 Pearl St; 6:30am-11pm Mon-Sat, 7am-11pm Sun; 206, SKIP) Brick walls, worn wood floors and red vinyl booths steeped in the aromatic uplift of damn good espresso. The attached bookstore sells used and collectible titles. Add in the shady back-garden patio and fine tea selection and you'll understand why this is the longtime favorite of Boulder's literary set. A thousand secrets and plot lines have been shared and hatched here.

West End Tavern
PUB

(Map p108; 303-444-3535; www.thewestendtavern.com; 926 Pearl St; 11:30am-close; 206) Top shelf bourbon? Check. Local IPAs? Check. Knotty wood bar? Check. Loungy booths, fantastic roof deck, tasty pub grub? All of the above. Add in the loyal following, flat-screen TVs and fun-loving staff and you can easily see why this spot remains our favorite pub in Boulder.

Augustina's Winery
WINERY

(303-545-2047; www.winechick.biz; 4715 N Broadway; noon-5pm Sat Nov-Mar, by appointment Apr-Nov; ; 204, SKIP) Augustina's is a one-woman show. She drives an old 1979 U-Haul to Palisades and Grand Junction every autumn to fetch her grapes then goes about the happy, messy business of crushing, fermenting and aging the wine all on her own. If you're looking for a bottle with a story for the campfire, grab one here.

Launched in 1997, this was also the first winery in Boulder and among the first of a handful now sprinkled about the state.

Absinthe House
ABSINTHE BAR

(Map p108; 303-443-8600; www.boulderabsinthehouse.com; 1109 Walnut St; 11am-late; 208, SKIP) New, big and ambitious, the old Foundry has been converted into what is Boulder's brashest club. The dance floor has been expanded. House music blares from a top shelf sound system, and any of the 16 varieties of absinthe from Europe and America can be poured from table side fountains.

Blending Cellar
WINE BAR

(Map p108; 303-447-0475; www.blendingcellar.com; 946 Pearl St; 5-11pm Mon, 3-11pm Tue-Sat, 3-10pm Sun) A sparse but inviting wine lounge just west of the Pearl St Mall with all manner of whites, and reds from all over the world. Swiss-run, it serves tasty tapas to balance the palate, and offers live jazz every night except Tuesday.

Catacombs Bar
BAR

(Map p108; 303-442-4344; www.boulderado.com; 2115 13th St; 4pm-1:30am Mon-Fri, from 6:30pm Sat & Sun; 208, SKIP) A cavernous pool and beer joint in the Boulderado Hotel basement, this dark, dank joint really does feel like the catacombs. Expect a young and rowdy crowd with ultracheap drink specials. The dimly lit rooms are perfect for getting tangled up with a becoming stranger or two. Tuesday is trivia night and Wednesdays bring karaoke.

Draft House
BREWPUB

(Map p108; 303-440-5858; www.boulderdrafthouse.com; 2027 13th St; 11am-2am; 208) Another of Boulder's popular microbreweries. This one brews six handcrafted beers, including an IPA and a Big Bella Brown, which owes it's deep tones to honey and Blackstrap molasses. Food here is pedestrian pub grub, but the open interior, with glassed-in brew tanks, exposed rafters and three gleaming HD flat-screens, offers a touch of class.

There's live music most nights: salsa night is Tuesday; Reggae rocks Wednesdays.

Espresso Roma
CAFE

(Map p115; ☎303-442-5011; 1101 13th St; smoothies $4.50; ⊗8am-8pm; ⊕; ☐203, 204, 225, AB, B, DASH, SKIP) The shaded patio, strung with paper lanterns, is our favorite place to hang with studying students. The bulletin board here is a great place to check for offbeat local events. The menu? Well-done coffee shop standards, with a veggie bent. The yummy smoothies are a highlight.

Ku Cha House of Tea
TEA HOUSE

(Map p108; ☎303-443-3612; www.kuchatea.com; 2015 13th St; ⊗10am-9pm Mon-Sat, 11am-6pm Sun; ☐208) Tea crazy newbies just about lose it at the enormous selection of imported loose-leaf tea downstairs, while more discreet locals snuggle into the room upstairs for steaming cups in quiet booths. If you want to go big, there's a rare yellow tea from Sri Lanka that goes for $20 per ounce.

Laughing Goat
CAFE

(Map p108; ☎303-440-4628; www.thelaughing goat.com; 1709 Pearl St; ⊗6am-11pm Mon-Fri, from 7am Sat & Sun; ☏; ☐203, 204, 205, 206, 208, 225, DASH, JUMP) Sure, the ambiance might be diminished a bit by the glow of two dozen laptops, but the coffee is good enough (served in pint glasses too!) and locally roasted. The scene revolves around eyeballing college co-eds and tapping away at the term papers – at least until the singer songwriters start up.

Sundown Saloon
BAR

(Map p108; ☎303-449-4987; 1136 Pearl St; ⊗3pm-2am; ☐208, SKIP) Only come here if you can stomach outhouse chic bathrooms, throwback tunes, an impossible-to-distinguish odor upon descent into the basement, pick-up shouting (it's straight impossible to hear late night), vicious competition on the shuffle board or pool tables (free 'til 10pm) and waking up hungover from the cheap Pabst Blue Ribbon ($6 pitchers). Every town needs an 'end up bar,' and you will end up here.

Walnut Brewery
BREWPUB

(Map p108; ☎303-447-1345; www.walnutbrew ery.com; 1123 Walnut St; ⊗11am-midnight Sun-Wed, to 2am Thu-Sat; ☐208, SKIP) A hangar-sized sports bar and brewery that crafts and serves seven varieties of microbrew, ranging from golden pilsners to midnight stouts. It also serves liquor, has all the ball games on flat screens, and serves decent pub grub.

'Round Midnight
BAR

(Map p108; ☎303-442-2176; 1005 Pearl St; ⊗5pm-2am; ☐208, SKIP) Another divey basement bar just west of Pearl St Mall, this spot's popularity rolls in waves and of late has still been prone to late-night good times thanks to the music it spins (mostly underground dub, dance-hall and hip-hop). There's free pool during happy hour.

Goose
BAR

(Map p115; www.thegoosebar.com; 1301 Broadway St; ⊗3pm-late; ☐225, SKIP) The wheel of fortune behind the bar ticks to a halt on '$3 Jager Bombs' and the howl of beefy frats is punctuated by high fives. Your choice: throw down $3 or regroup at the beer pong table. Then again, maybe you're not in any shape to be making decisions. Though utterly lacking in atmosphere, this binge drinkers' proving ground can be a riot.

Ladies might want to note the 'Friends with Benefits' Tuesday night, when a group of four or more girls get their first shot on the house.

Buchanan's Coffee Pub
CAFE

(Map p115; ☎303-440-0222; 1301 Pennsylvania Ave; ⊗7:30am-10pm school term, to 8pm summer; ⊕; ☐203, 204, 225, AB, B, DASH, SKIP) Buchanan's enjoys a position just at the edge of campus, and with cheap snacks, wireless and power outlets everywhere, its utility as a study space is likely better than the university library.

Saxy's Cafe
CAFE

(Map p108; ☎303-786-8585; www.saxyscafe. com; 2018 10th St; ⊗7am-6pm Mon-Fri, 8am-6pm Sat & Sun; ☏; ☐208, SKIP) Grilled paninis and good coffee make this an easy choice for something quick and simple off the Pearl St Mall. There's limited outdoor seating, which is nice in the summer, and wi-fi for customers.

☆ Entertainment
Live Music

Boulder Theater
CINEMA, LIVE MUSIC

(Map p108; ☎303-786-7030; www.boulderthe atre.com; 2032 14th St; movies $8.50, shows vary; ⊗vary; ☐204) This old movie-theater-turned-historic-venue brings in slightly under-the-radar acts like jazz great Charlie

Boulder is nothing if not tolerant and progressive, yet it does strike one as strange that such a with-it town could wind up with no gay bars. You read that right. Zero. Zilch. Nada. Such an aberration requires an automatic reduction in liberal street cred and overall style points, but all is not bleak. Local activists have cobbled together enough events, including Boulder Pride Fest (p114), and organized the community so effectively that there is a gay scene here even if it lacks a sense of bar 'ownership.'

Resources

Out Boulder (☎303-499-5777; www.outboulder.org)

Proposition Gay (www.propgay.org; ⊘last Fri of the month)

Hunter, the madmen rockers of Gogol Bordello and West African divas, Les Nubians. But they also screen classic films like *The Big Lebowski* and short-film festivals which can and should be enjoyed with a glass of beer.

Fox Theatre LIVE MUSIC
(Map p115; ☑box office 303-443-3399; www.fox theatre.com; 1135 13th St; cover varies; ⊘10am-8pm Mon-Sat, 11am-8pm Sun; ⌑203, 204, 225, AB, B, DASH, SKIP) You'll be elbowing your way through students to get near the stage of this excellent mid-sized venue, so head upstairs for a perch near the sound board for better views and acoustics. Bands on stage here are national touring acts, popular jam bands and indie rock.

Sports

CU Basketball SPORTS
(☑303-492-8337; www.cubuffs.com; Coors Event Center; prices vary; ⊘games Nov-Mar; ⊡; ⌑209, STAMPEDE) Seldom pushovers, rarely great, CU's basketball games are always fun to watch because the competition is usually stiff. And like most great schools it has a transcendent baller from the not-too-distant past. Chanucey 'Mr Big Shot' Billups starred here before he became an NBA champ and finals MVP.

CU Football SPORTS
(☑303-492-8337; www.cubuffs.com; Folsom Stadium; tickets $50-120; ⊘selected Sat; ⊡; ⌑209, STAMPEDE) Boulder sports fans may have allegiances to Denver's pro teams, but they have several teams of their own too, and they are all called the CU Buffaloes. Still, while college volleyball, gymnastics and baseball have their place, it's their football team that rules campus.

 Shopping

Given the hipster student vibe, the yuppie cash flow and Boulder's status as a go-to green hot spot, it's not all that shocking to find a bit of shopping here. Along with some high-end vintage consignment houses are a few boutiques with happening labels, and there's plenty of eco and athletic gear on offer too. Whether you're patrolling Pearl St Mall and its outskirts, (much) hipper East Pearl, or the more corporate 29th St Mall, you're bound to do some boutique and gallery browsing between bouts of mountain marveling.

TOP **Peppercorn Gourmet Goods**
CHOICE FOOD, HOMEWARES
(Map p108; ☑303-449-5847; www.peppercorn. com; 1235 Pearl St; ⊘10am-6pm Mon-Thu & Sat, to 8pm Fri, 11am-5pm Sun; ⌑208, SKIP) One of the coolest stores on Pearl, this kitchen, bed and bath supplier stocks upscale goods, locally produced foods, scores of specialized cook books and enough gizmos to delight a cooking geek. It's a fun place to spend too much time and money. See the website for classes and events.

Absolute Vinyl BOOKS, RECORDS
(☑303-955-1519; fortherecords@cs.com; 4474 N Broadway St; ⊘11am-6:30pm; ⌑SKIP) Every town needs a temple to vinyl. A place where chilled out musical clerks wipe down wax on Sunday afternoons while listening to classic Memphis blues. Bookworms comb the walls of Little Horse, the shared bookstore, for first editions, young men come here when they're hurting for Smiths records, and there is a paradise of jazz, blues and classical gems. Stay awhile.

Blue Skies Boulder GIFTS
(Map p108; ☑303-440-3304; www.blueskiesboul der.com; 1110 Pearl St; ⊘10am-7pm Mon-Wed,

10am-8pm Thu-Sat, 11am-6pm Sun; 🐾) A cute gift shop stocked with handbags and scarves, elegant perfume, fantastic jewelry and aromatherapy products, much of it sourced from local artists and artisans. The Pearl St Mall doesn't get much groovier.

Boulder Bookstore BOOKSTORE
(Map p108; ☑303-447-2074; www.boulderbook store.indiebound.com; 1107 Pearl St; ☉10am-10pm Mon-Sat, to 9pm Sun; 🛜🐾; 🚌208, SKIP) Boulder's favorite indie bookstore has a huge travel section downstairs, along with all the hottest new fiction and nonfiction. The attached Bookend Cafe has plenty of seating indoor and out to make it an appealing hangout at any time of day, night, year.

Boulder Running Company SHOES
(☑303-786-8044; www.boulderrunningcompany .com; 2775 Pearl St; ☉10am-7pm Mon-Fri, to 6pm Sat, to 5pm Sun; 🐾; 🚌205, 205C, BOLT) Boulder's prime center for all the gear and specialty shoes you'll need for running track, street and trails. In fact, there are more trail runners here than we thought possible. They even video analyze your running stride on a treadmill before the fitting, which helps make sure you aren't injury prone in your new shoes (and probably don't hurt the in-sole sales either).

If you want to know when the next foot race or triathlon is on, come here.

Chelsea WOMENS CLOTHING
(Map p108; ☑303-447-3760; www.chelseabella. com; 2088 Broadway St; ☉10am-6pm Mon-Sat, 11am-4pm Sun; 🚌208) A touch of New York style off the Pearl St Mall, this women's high-fashion boutique has been bringing labels like James Perse to Boulder for 10 years, and it still has some of the sweetest, if priciest, threads in town.

Common Threads VINTAGE CLOTHING
(☑303-449-5431; www.commonthreadsboulder .com; 2707 Spruce St; ☉10am-6pm Mon-Sat, noon-5pm Sun; 🚌205, BOLT) Vintage shopping at its most haute couture, this fun place is where to go for secondhand Choos and Prada purses. Prices are higher than your run-of-the-mill vintage shop, but clothes, shoes and bags are always in good condition, and the designer clothing is guaranteed authentic.

The shop is a pleasure to browse, with clothing organized by color and type on visually aesthetic racks, just like a big-city boutique.

✒ Momentum HANDICRAFTS
(Map p108; ☑303-440-7744; www.ourmo mentum.com; 1625 Pearl St; ☉10am-7pm Tue-Sat, 11am-6pm Sun; 🚌204) Owned by Kevin and Jenny Napatow, an enthusiastic young couple committed to socially responsible and environmentally friendly business practices, Momentum is one of those shops that makes you feel good about spending money. It sells the kitchen sink of unique global gifts – Zulu wire baskets, fabulous scarves from India, Nepal and Ecuador – all handcrafted and purchased at fair value from disadvantaged artisans. Every item purchased provides a direct economic lifeline to the artists.

REI OUTDOORS GEAR
(☑303-583-9970; www.rei.com; 1789 28th St; ☉9am-9pm; 🐾; 🚌205, 206, BOLT) The Denver flagship it is not, but the Boulder branch of America's largest and best outdoor outfitter rents sleeping bags, pads and tents, as well as anything else you might need for your stint in the Rocky Mountains.

Bayleaf On Pearl BOUTIQUE HOMEWARES
(Map p108; ☑720-565-2477; 805 Pearl St; ☉10am-6pm Mon-Sat, to 5pm Sun; 🚌206) While the casual observer will quickly note that whoever runs this boutique selling high-end housewares has impeccable taste, the cookbooks and kitchen goods evidence owner Michale Bugermeister's background as a chef. There are cool toys, oversized coffee-table books on German bookbinding and other classy curios.

Goldmine Vintage VINTAGE CLOTHING
(Map p108; ☑303-945-0845; www.goldminevin tage.com; 1123 Pearl St; ☉11am-8pm Mon-Thu, to 9pm Fri & Sat, to 7pm Sun) Hot pink fishnets and a purple wig adorn the mannequin in the window of this upscale vintage shop. There are trucker caps, *Spinal Tap* tees and turquoise cowboy boots. In back, patrons can try on Monroe-worthy gowns under the watchful gaze of a matador painted on black velvet.

Meow Meow BOUTIQUE GIFTS
(Map p115; ☑303-442-8602; 1118 13th St; ☉10am-7pm Mon-Fri, to 8am Sun; 🐾; 🚌203, 204, 225, DASH, SKIP) Pioneering the concept of 'upcycling,' this is the place for unique gifts, art, jewelery and clothes made from reused materials. It has a great local feel and lots of one-of-a-kind accessories for women. The card selection is hilarious.

Outdoor Divas
SPORTING GOODS

(Map p108; ☑303-449-3482; www.outdoordivas. com; 1133 Pearl St; ⊙11am-7pm Mon-Thu, 10am-7pm Fri, 10am-8pm Sat & Sun; ☑; ☐208, SKIP) This specialized outdoor store for women knows their audience – the gear here is top quality, the prices are competitive and the staff's knowledge on women-specific skiing, hiking and running gear is expert.

Outdoor Outlet
SPORTING GOODS

(Map p108; ☑303-517-3066; www.outdooroutlet boulder.com; 2015 10th St; ⊙11am-6am Mon-Sat, noon-5pm Sun; ☐206, 208) A brilliant business plan and an eager staff make it hard not to cheer for this shop of over-stock outdoor gear. The selection of ladies equipment, cycling apparel and casual clothes might be a bit mismatched, but when you find something that fits, the price is right.

Rebecca's Herbal Apothecary
HEALTH & BEAUTY

(Map p108; ☑303-443-8878; www.rebeccas herbs.com; 1227 Spruce St; classes $20-35; ⊙10am-6pm Mon-Fri, 11am-7pm Sat; ☑; ☐208, SKIP) A groovy herbal apothecary where herbs are sold loose, in lotions and in oils. There are aromatherapy cases of tinctures and a library and expert herbalists that can guide you through it all. The western school of herbal thought dominates the thinkspace here. There are also classes available for those who want to learn the basics about herbs, infusions and salves. And, no, this isn't an outlet for medicinal marijuana.

Savory Spice Shop
GOURMET FOOD

(Map p108; ☑303-444-0668; www.savoryspice shop.com; 2041 Broadway St; ⊙10am-6pm Mon-Sat, 11am-5pm Sun; ☑; ☐208, SKIP) Extremely popular in the Denver–Boulder area, this growing local chain is the place to search for a small-batch habanero hot sauce or to alchemize your own spice rub for your self-catering kit. In all there are 140 spices hand blended from mostly organic sources. Plus, it just smells good. The family chef will love it!

Starr's Clothing Co
CLOTHING

(Map p108; ☑303-442-3056; www.starrscloth ingco.com; 1630 Pearl St; ⊙10am-7pm Mon-Sat, to 6pm Sun; ☐204) Established in 1914 and still Boulder's leading denim resource. This store is damn near warehouse-sized, with all manner of stressed, smooth and relaxed denim. It also carries the odd top-end designer label such as Southern California fave Free People.

Weekends
CLOTHING

(Map p108; ☑303-444-4231; www.weekends boulder.com; 1200 Pearl St; ⊙10am-7pm Mon-Wed, to 9pm Thu-Sat, 11am-6pm Sun; ☐208, SKIP) Manhattan fashion is hard to find in Boulder, but Weekends has a better-than-decent selection of Cole Haan leather jackets, Citizens of Humanity denim and some lovely lesser-known styles, including some rather soft fitted tees, alluring beauty products and terrific handbags.

Beat Book Shop
BOOKS

(Map p108; ☑303-444-7111; www.beatbookshop. com; 1717 Pearl St; ⊙varies; ☐204) Tom Peters is the poet proprietor of this funky pile of consistently brainy, soulful books. We're talking more than 30 Kerouac titles, as well as classics from Ginsberg, Burroughs and (beat-esque) Bukowski, among others. His hours vary but Peters claims to be here from afternoon into the night daily. Well worth a browse.

CU Bookstore
BOOKS

(Map p115; ☑303-492-6411; www.cubookstore. com; 1669 Euclid Ave; ⊙8am-9pm Mon-Thu, 8am-5pm Fri, 10am-5pm Sat; ☐203, 204, 209, 225, AB, B, DASH, SKIP, STAMPEDE) There are scads of CU merchandise outlets along the busy stretch of 13th St, but this is the school's official outfitter. In addition to textbooks and supplies it has the largest selection of gold-and-black goods of any store in Boulder. Located in the University Memorial Center.

Cypress Beauty & Co
BEAUTY

(Map p108; ☑303.442.9100; www.cypress beauty.com; 1142 Pearl St; ⊙10am-8pm Mon-Sat 11am-6pm Sun) This Colorado chain offers organic and all-natural botanicals and lotions, soaps and makeups (with a touch of Botox-laced vanity). It sells local eco-brands such as Indigo Wild and the biggies, including Smashbox, and if you need to restock the vanity sack, it's a decent choice.

Oliv
GOURMET FOOD

(Map p108; ☑303-444-1118; www.olivym.com; 2043 Broadway St; ⊙10am-6pm Tue-Sat; ☐208, SKIP) There is no shortage of cafes and gourmet food shops in Boulder, and this one is easy to miss. Which is a pity as it's unique, with quirky old-time decor, specialty foods, fresh baked breads and luscious olive oil, as well as great coffee named in the English-Aussie vernacular. You know, short white, long black...

Pedestrian Shops   SHOES

(Map p108; ☑303-449-5260; www.comfortable
shoes.com; 1425 Pearl St; ☺10am-8pm Mon-Sat,
11am-6pm Sun; ☐203, 204, 205, 206, 208, 225,
DASH, JUMP) Set smack in the midst of the
Pearl St Mall, this is where to head for the
comfortable kind of footwear that are staples in earthy Bouldertown. Think Crocs,
Ecco and less known brands like Dansko,
Keen and Born. Find the last-pair rack for
the best deals, and if you buy two you'll get
a third pair free.

Posterscene   ART

(Map p115; ☑303-527-2701; www.posterscene.
com; 1138 13th St; ☺10am-9pm Mon-Fri, noon-
8pm Sat, to 5pm Sun; ☐203, 204, 225, AB, B,
DASH, SKIP) Iconic images and original show
posters from Janis Joplin and Dylan and
the Dead make this a rock memorabilia
paradise. But it isn't limited to high-end
collector's items; it has a clutch of cool, inexpensive reproductions too.

🖋 Prana   CLOTHING

(Map p108; ☑303-449-2199; www.prana.
com; 1147 Pearl St; ☺10am-8pm Mon-Sat, 11am-
6pm Sun; ☐208, SKIP) Monks chant to the
patter of beats overhead as shoppers consider organic-dyed yoga outfits. All the clothes
are organized by size – a nice touch – and
the signs encourage an awareness of 'cosmic
order.' Aside from all this new age excite-
ment, Prana is wind-powered and hosts art
events.

Smith Klein Gallery   GALLERY

(Map p108; ☑303-444-7200; www.smithklein.
com; 1116 Pearl St Mall; ☺11am-6pm Mon-Thu,
to 7pm Fri-Sat, noon-5pm Sun) Locally owned
since its inception in 1984, this conserva-
tive-to-quirky gallery is worth a peek for
some interesting paintings and the glass,
bronze and wood sculptures (we like the
ones crafted from vintage car doors).
There's hand blown glass and jewelry too.

ℹ Information

Boulder Convention & Visitors Bureau

(☑303-442-2911, toll-free 800-444-0447;
www.bouldercoloradousa.com; 2440 Pearl
St; ☺8:30am-5pm Mon-Thu, to 4pm Fri; @;
☐204) Set in the Boulder Chamber of Commerce, this visitor center offers basic information, maps and tips on nearby hiking trails and
other activities. There's a more accessible
tourist info kiosk on the Pearl St Mall in front of
the court house.

Boulder Downtown

(www.boulderdowntown.
com) This alliance of downtown businesses
offers comprehensive dining and event listings
in the downtown area – including the Pearl St
Mall.

Get Boulder

(www.getboulder.com) A local
print and on-line magazine with helpful information on stuff to do in Boulder.

ℹ Getting There & Away

Less than an hour from downtown Denver and
just over an hour from the airport, Boulder is
easily accessible by public transport. However,
with plenty of (paid) public parking around and
the mountains beckoning, you may want to rent
a car after all. Flights, tours and rail tickets can
be booked online at www.lonelyplanet.com/
travel_services.

Bus

Buses are run **RTD** (☑303-299-6000; www.
rtd-denver.com; per ride $2-4.50; ♿). Route B
buses travel between Boulder Transit Center
(aka Boulder Station) and Denver Market Street
Station ($3.50; 55 minutes). Route AB runs
between the Table Mesa Park-N-Ride on Hwy 36
in Boulder and the Denver International Airport
($12, one hour), with easy connections to down-
town Boulder and the Hill.

Car & Motorcycle

Boulder sits about 30 miles northwest of Denver off Highway 36, accessible from the I-25N
from downtown Denver. Hwy 36 runs through
Boulder on the way to Estes Park and the Rocky
Mountain National Park. Most of the major car
rental brands (Herz, Avis, Enterprise) have
shingles in Boulder, and if you rent here you can
avoid some of the hefty taxes airport branches
charge.

ℹ Getting Around

To & From the Airport

SuperShuttle (☑303-444-0808; www.
supershuttle.com; per person $33; ☺6am-
midnight) Far pricier than the public bus, but
still cheaper than a cab, the Super Shuttle is
America's favorite midrange airport ride. But
with two or more people in the mix, you'll be
better served by a taxi.

Bicycling

Owning a bicycle is almost a Boulder prerequi-
site. Most streets have dedicated bike lanes and
the Boulder Creek Bike Path (p111) is a must-ride
commuter corridor. There are plenty of places to
get your hands on a rental.

Full Cycle (☑303-440-7771; www.fullcycle
bikes.com; 1211 13th St; rentals $15-75;
☺10am-7pm Mon-Fri, to 6pm Sat, 11am-5pm
Sun; ♿; ☐203, 204, 225, AB, B, DASH, DD,
GS, SKIP) This terrific bike shop rents cruisers
on the cheap and higher-end road and full-

On September 6, 2010 a fire flamed up in 40mph winds on the slopes of Fourmile Canyon, a stunning mountain canyon northwest of downtown. It shot down the parched, overgrown hillside and slammed into a propane tank, exploding into what became known as the Fourmile Fire.

The winds got worse, and the fire spread out of control. For the next week Boulder's wildfire was in the international news as sheets of smoke billowed above the city and ash rained down, as 1000 families were evacuated from their homes, 163 structures (mostly homes) destroyed and 6427 acres charred. Thankfully there were only seven minor casualties and no deaths, as 1100 fire fighters swarmed into the foothills to contain and conquer the blaze at a cost of nearly $7 million.

After initial confusion regarding the cause of the fire, investigators identified embers from an outdoor fire pit, owned by a long-time volunteer firefighter, who was the first to raise the alarm and one of the many to lose his home, as the likely cause. No charges were filed in the case.

suspension mountain bikes by the day for a bit more. Staff will also spare a few words about the best cycling routes (read: Boulder Creek Trail and the Tour de France–level of pain that is the 4-mile ride up Flagstaff Rd to the top of Flagstaff Mountain). There's another branch on East Pearl.

Pete's E Bikes (⏹303-586-1544; www.petesebikes.com; 2232 Pearl St; half-/full-day $40/70; ⊙10am-6pm Mon-Sat; ▣204) One of two locations in town, this small electric bike showroom has cruisers outfitted with a small engine powered by a rechargeable battery that gives you an extra speed boost and can plug into a wall socket. The cheapest hovers around $1800 new, but it does rent them out which is why its noted here.

University Bicycles (www.ubikes.com; 839 Pearl St; ⊙10am-6pm Mon-Sat, 10am-5pm Sun; ▣; ▣206, JUMP, N) There are plenty of places to rent bicycles to cruise around town, but this has the widest range of rides and the most helpful staff. For $15 you can get a townie bike for four hours – enough time to make a loop around central Boulder.

Car & Motorcycle

If you're staying downtown you won't need a vehicle, as countless diversions are all just steps away. But if you are anchored to a car, and you're here on a weekend, consider the free parking lots on 11th & Spruce and at the Boulder Transit Center (p129) and a touch further afield on Arapahoe near the **Boulder Public Library**

(⏹303-441-3100; www.boulderlibrary.org; 1001 Arapahoe Ave; ⊙10am-9pm Mon-Thu, to 6pm Fri & Sat, noon-6pm Sun; @⑀▣; ▣JUMP). Otherwise prepare to pay.

And a word of warning to all drivers: Boulder has recently been equipped with traffic cameras that levy fines to those who speed upon her streets. They aren't moving violations, per se. They're more like parking violations – speeding costs from $40 – but it is a bit of a post-trip downer when one of these beauties lands in your mail box.

Public Transportation

Boulder has superb public transportation, with several RTD (p128) bus routes lacing the city and connecting the Hill with downtown and North Boulder. Almost any area landmark can be accessed by public bus, which are all equipped with bike racks.

Boulder Transit Center (⏹303-299-6000; 1800 14th St) The city's public transportation hub is a good place to pick up maps of the transportation network. Offers free public parking on weekends; not so easy to come by elsewhere in the city.

Taxi

Boulder Yellow Cab (⏹303-777-7777; www.boulderyellowcab.com; 11th St and Pearl St; ⊙24hr) Boulder's biggest and best cab company – actually a subsidiary of Colorado's largest taxi conglomerate. There's a taxi stand on 11th St at the Pearl St Mall.

Rocky Mountain National Park & Northern Mountains

Includes »

ROCKY MOUNTAIN
NATIONAL PARK.... 131

ESTES PARK........ 137

NEDERLAND 144

ELDORA SKI AREA .. 144

INDIAN PEAKS
WILDERNESS AREA...145

FORT COLLINS 145

RED FEATHER
LAKES............. 150

CACHE LA POUDRE
RIVER 151

GRAND LAKE....... 151

GRANBY 154

Why Go?

With one foot on either side of the continental divide and be-hemoths of granite in every direction, Colorado's Northern Mountains allow visitors a glimpse of the top of the world.

With some of the state's most dramatic alpine environ-ments, the northern Rockies make an irresistible call to mountain-lovers, regardless of whether the season calls for mounting them in hiking boots or shushing down on a pair of skis. This is where you come to ski if you'd rather skip the Aspen attitude, go backcountry skiing or just get out on a pair of snowshoes.

In the spring, summer and autumn, hiking and biking in state and national parks and forests continue to draw visitors. Many of the ski resorts transform into groomed mountain-biking areas, and campers make for high-altitude lakes. There's also top-notch fishing, rafting and kayaking, weathered ghost towns, horseback riding, camp-ing and touring the mountains until well after autumn turns the aspens to gold.

Best Places to Eat

» Wild Mountain Smoke-house & Brewery (p144)

» Backcountry Provisions (p148)

» Big Horn Restaurant (p141)

» Tasty Harmony (p148)

Best Places to Stay

» YMCA of the Rockies (p140)

» Armstrong Hotel (p147)

» Longs Peak Campground (p135)

» Stanley Hotel (p140)

When to Go?

Estes Park

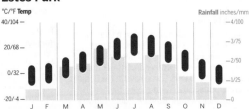

June–September Sunshine, perfect hiking and monstrous thunderheads attract visitors.

September–October Temper-atures drop and the tourists va-cate. The aspens turn golden.

November–May Crisp air and tons of snowfall bring skiers to low-key resort areas.

ROCKY MOUNTAIN NATIONAL PARK

Though Rocky Mountain National Park doesn't rank among the largest national parks in the USA (it's *only* 265,000 acres), it's rightly among one of the most popular, hosting 3 million visitors every year.

This is a place of natural spectacle on every scale: from hulking granite formations – many taller than 12,000ft, some over 130 million years old – to the delicate yellow burst of the glacier lily, one of the dozen alpine wildflowers that explode in a short, colorful life at the edge of receding snowfields for a few days every spring.

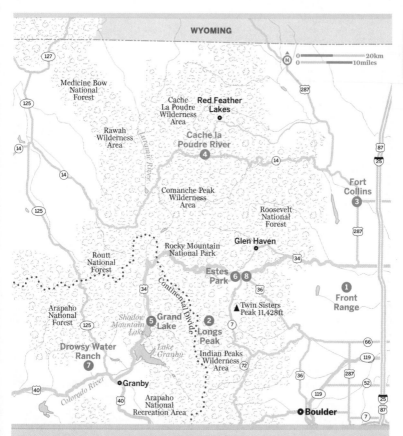

Northern Mountains Highlights

❶ Watch a thunderhead roll over the rugged peaks of the **Front Range**

❷ Scramble to the top of **Longs Peak** (p133), one of Colorado's proud 14ers

❸ Ride a cruiser to **New Belgium Brewery** (p147) for a tour and tasting of Colorado microbrew

❹ Cast a fly for wild trout in the rushing waters of the **Cache la Poudre River** (p151)

❺ Hike all day before curing up by the fire at Grand Lake's **Shadowcliff Lodge & Retreat Center** (p153)

❻ Climb the Rockies after some classes from **Colorado Mountain School** (p139)

❼ Live out the cowboy fantasy ride the range at **Drowsy Water Ranch** (p154)

❽ Creep yourself out at the **Stanley Hotel** (p140), inspiration for Stephen King's thriller *The Shining*

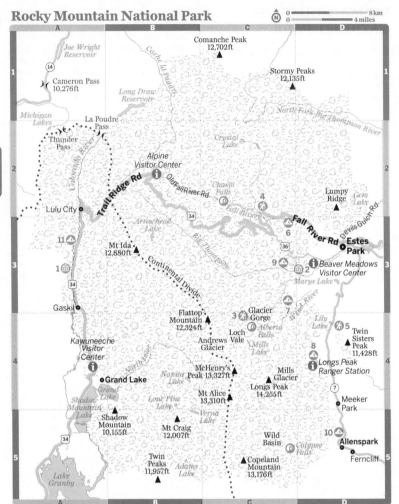

And though it tops many travelers itineraries and can get maddeningly crowded, the park has miles of less-beaten paths, and the backcountry is a little-explored treasure. It's surrounded by some of the most pristine wild area in the west: Comanche Peak and Neota Wilderness Areas in the Roosevelt National Forest to the north and Indian Peaks Wilderness on the south. The jagged spine of the Continental Divide intersects the park through its middle. Excellent hiking trails crisscross alpine fields, skirt the edge of isolated high-altitude lakes and bring travelers to the wild, untamed heart of the place.

⊙ Sights

Wonders of the natural world are the main attractions here: huge herds of elk and scattered mountain sheep, pine-dotted granite slopes and blindingly white alpine tundra. However, there are a few museums and historic sites within the park's borders which are worthy of a glance and good for families.

Moraine Park Museum MUSEUM
(☎970-586-1206; Bear Lake Rd; ⊙9am-4:30pm Jun-Oct) Built by the Civilian Conservation Corps in 1923 and once the park's proud visitors lodge, this building has been

Rocky Mountain National Park

◎ Sights
1 Holzwarth Historic Site A3
2 Moraine Park Museum D3

Activities, Courses & Tours
3 Bear Lake Trailhead C4
4 Lawn Lake Trailhead C2
Longs Peak Trailhead .... (see 8)
5 Twin Sisters Trailhead D4

▲ Sleeping
6 Aspenglen Campground C3
7 Glacier Basin Campground C3
8 Longs Peak Campground D4
9 Moraine Park Campground C3
10 Olive Ridge Campground D5
11 Timber Creek Campground A3

renovated in recent years to host exhibits on geology, glaciers and wildlife.

Holzwarth Historic Site HISTORIC VILLAGE
(Never Summer Ranch; ⬀Park Headquarters 970-586-1206; Trail Ridge Rd/US 34; ⊙10am-4pm Jun-Oct; P♿) When prohibition was enacted in 1916, John Holzwarth Sr, a Denver saloon-keeper, started a new life as a subsistence rancher. This site houses several buildings kept in their original condition, and hosts historical reenactments and ranger-led programs. The Heritage Days celebration happens in late July.

The site lies at the end of a graded ½-mile path, easily accessible with strollers.

🏃 Activities
Hiking & Backpacking
With over 300 miles of trail, traversing all aspects of its diverse terrain, the park is suited to every hiking ability. Those with the kids in tow might consider the easy hikes in the Wild Basin to Calypso Falls or to Gem Lakes in the Lumpy Ridge area, while those with unlimited ambition, strong legs and enough trail mix will be lured by the challenge of conquering Longs Peak. Regardless, it's best to spend at least one night at 7000ft to 8000ft prior to setting out to allow your body to adjust to the elevation. Before July, many trails are snow-bound and high water runoff makes passage difficult. Dogs and other pets are not allowed on the trails. All overnight stays in the backcountry require permits.

LONGS PEAK
As the centerpiece of many hikers' itinerary, you need not worry about getting lonesome on the 15-mile round-trip to the summit of Longs Peak (14,259ft). During the summer peak you're likely to find a line of more than 100 parked cars snaking down the road from the **Longs Peak trailhead**. After the initial 6 miles of moderate trail to

the Boulder Field (12,760ft) the path steepens at the start of the Keyhole Route to the summit, which is marked with yellow and red bulls-eyes painted on the rock.

Even superhuman athletes who are used to the thin air will be slowed by the route's ledge system, which resembles a narrow cliffside stairway without a handrail. After this, hikers scramble the final homestretch to the summit boulders. The view from the top – snow-kissed granite stretching out to the curved horizon – is incredible. The round-trip hike takes anywhere from 10 to 15 hours.

Many climbers make the trail approach in early predawn hours after overnighting at Longs Peak Campground (p135). The Keyhole Route is generally free of snow mid-July to October – otherwise you will need technical climbing skills and equipment to reach the summit. When you dial park headquarters at the Beaver Meadows Visitor Center (p137), the prerecorded message will have information about the conditions on this popular route.

Note that there are no park entrance fees for this hike, as the trailhead is outside park boundaries.

TWIN SISTERS PEAK
This up-and-back hike provides an excellent warm-up to climbing Longs Peak. In addition, the 11,428ft summit of Twin Sisters Peak offers unequaled views of Longs Peak. It's an arduous walk, gaining 2300ft in just 3.7 miles. Erosion-resistant quartz rock caps the oddly deformed rock at the summit and delicate alpine flowers (plenty of mountain harebell) fill the rock spaces near the stone hut. The **trailhead** is near Mills Cabin, 10 miles south of Estes Park on Hwy 7. No fees are required for this hike.

GLACIER GORGE JUNCTION
Accessed from the **Bear Lake trailhead**, this busy network of trails threads through

MAPS

Even though you'll get a driving map when you enter the park and some basic, non-technical photocopied maps are available at some of the most popular trail heads, it's surprising that none of the visitors center stocks high quality topographic maps for hikers. You'll want to pick them up before hand in Estes Park at **Mac-Donald Book Shop** (☑970-586-3450; www.macdonaldbookshop.com; 152 E Elkhorn Ave; ⊙8am-8pm Mon-Sun, shorter hours in winter; 🐾) or in Boulder, at the **Boulder Map Gallery** (☑303-444-1406; www.bouldermapgallery.com; 1708 13th St; ⊙10am-6pm Mon-Fri, to 3pm Sat).

pine forest and over rushing streams, offering a spectrum of difficulty. The easy stroll to Alberta Falls is good for families. Far more strenuous 5-mile options would be to hike up Glacier Gorge, past Mills Lake and many glacial erratics to Black Lake, or via Loch Vale to Andrews Glacier on the Continental Divide. The trailhead is served by the Glacier Basin–Bear Lake shuttle.

Rock Climbing

Many of the park's alpine climbs are long one-day climbs or require an overnight stay on the rock face. Often the only way to accomplish a long climb and avoid afternoon thundershowers is to begin climbing at dawn – this can mean an approach hike beginning at midnight! An alternative is to bivouac (temporary open-air encampment – no tents) at the base of the climb. Free bivouac permits are issued only to technical climbers and are mandatory for all overnight stays in the backcountry.

To minimize the environmental impact of backcountry use, the Rocky Mountain National Park Backcountry Office (p136) allows only a limited number of people to bivouac at four popular climbing areas. Phone reservations may be made March to May 20 for the following restricted zones: Longs Peak area, including Broadway below Diamond, Chasm View, Mills Glacier and Meeker Cirque; Black Lake area (Glacier Gorge), encompassing McHenry Peak, Arrowhead, Spearhead and Chiefshead/Pagoda; the base of Notchtop Peak; and the Skypond/Andrews Glacier Area, including

the Taylor/Powell Peaks and Sharkstooth Peak. Reservations are not needed nor accepted for other bivouacs.

EQUIPMENT RENTAL

For climbing gear try Estes Park Mountain Shop (p140). A small stock of climbing gear also is available from Colorado Mountain School (p139), where you can also find dormitory accommodation in the company of other climbers, shower after a climb for a few dollars or enroll in a climbing course.

Cycling & Mountain Biking

Mountain biking and cycling has continued to gain popularity despite the park's heavy traffic and lack of shoulder. It's a splendid way to see the park and wildlife, though bicycle travel is restricted to paved roads and to one dirt road, Fall River Rd. Those looking to ride technical routes on a mountain bike should go to Roosevelt National Forest.

On either type of bike, climbing the paved Trail Ridge Rd has one big advantage over Fall River Rd (a 9-mile one-way climb of more than 3000ft): you can turn around should problems arise.

Less daunting climbs and climes are available on the park's lower paved roads. A popular 16-mile circuit is the Horseshoe Park/Estes Park Loop. For a bit more of a climbing challenge you can continue to Bear Lake Rd, an 8-mile long route that rises 1500 feet to the high mountain basin.

If you are not up to climbing either Trail Ridge or Fall River Rds, Colorado Bicycling Adventures (p139), offers tours of Rocky Mountain National Park. It also rents bikes.

SAFETY

The pleasant summer weather at lower elevations can suddenly become unmercifully cold at higher altitudes – especially when descending from the park's alpine peaks. Hypothermia is an emergency experienced by many unprepared bicyclists each month: change into a dry shirt, full gloves and a warm, water-repellent outer shell before you get above treeline and into the wind. The only shelter from lightning is at the Alpine Visitor Center (p136). Yet another unpleasantness is the altitude sickness and subsequent dehydration that strikes many people unaccustomed to the 12,000ft elevation reached on Trail Ridge Rd.

Snowshoeing & Cross-country Skiing

From December into May, the high valleys and alpine tundra offer cross-country skiers unique opportunities to view wild-life and the winter scenery undisturbed by crowds. January and February are the best months for dry, powdery snowpack; spring snows tend to be heavy and wet. Most routes follow summer hiking trails, but valley bottoms and frozen streambeds typically have more snow cover and are less challenging. In fact, most of the park should be considered 'backcountry skiing' rather than 'cross-country.' Avalanche hazards are greatest on steep, open slopes in mountainous terrain. Overnight trips require permits, and the USFS NPS will have a list of closed trails.

RANGER-LED EXPEDITIONS

Rangers lead weekend snowshoe hikes in the east side of the park from January to April, depending on snow conditions. Trailhead locations and times are available from the park headquarters (p137).

EQUIPMENT RENTAL

Snowshoe and ski rentals are available at the Estes Park Mountain Shop (p140).

🛌 Sleeping

The only overnight accommodations in the park are at campgrounds; the majority of motel or hotel accommodations are around Estes Park or Grand Lake. The closest thing the park has to the typical CCC-era lodges

of parks like Yellowstone or Yosemite is the YMCA of the Rockies (p140), which is on the park's border.

The park's formal campgrounds provide campfire programs, have public telephones and a seven-day limit during summer months; all except Longs Peak take RVs (no hookups). The water supply is turned off during winter.

You will need a backcountry permit to stay outside developed park campgrounds. None of the campgrounds have showers, but they do have flush toilets in summer and outhouse facilities in winter. Sites include a fire ring, picnic table and one parking spot.

Longs Peak Campground CAMPGROUND $
(970-586-1206; Mile marker 9, State Hwy 7; campsites $20; P) This is the base camp of choice for the early morning ascent of Longs Peak, one of Colorado's most easily accessible 14ers. The scenery is striking and its 26 spaces are for tents only, but don't expect much solitude in the peak of the summer.

There are no reservations, but if you're planning to bag Longs Peak after sleeping here, get here *early* one day before the climb – according to rangers the only way to ensure a site during peak season is to show up before noon.

SAFETY

If you're in easily accessible areas during high season, the biggest annoyance in Rocky Mountain National Park will likely be the other visitors. Roads clog with RVs, garbage fills every can to the brim and screaming children seem to multiply endlessly. Brace yourself, camper: it can be annoying. But it might be more than fellow travelers giving you a headache: it could be the altitude. High elevation can play all kinds of nasty tricks here, from relatively mild problems like a pounding head and winded breathing, to fairly serious symptoms of nausea, dehydration and fatigue.

If you intend to get off the heavily beaten trail, take precautions in the spring and summer to avoid bites from wood ticks, which can transmit Colorado tick fever. Also be mindful of your food, which can attract wildlife. The park is home to black bears and mountain lions, but neither poses a serious threat to visitors.

Weather

Weather in the park, as in all mountainous areas, is highly variable. Summer days often reach 70°F to 80°F, yet a sudden shift in the weather can bring snow to the peaks in July. Nevertheless, the climate follows broad predictable patterns based on season, elevation, exposure and location east or west of the Continental Divide. Strong winds are common above the treeline. July thundershowers typically dump 2in of rain on the park, while January is the driest month. Bear Lake (9400ft) normally has a January snow base of 25in. The Continental Divide causes a pronounced rain-shadow effect: Grand Lake (west of the Divide) annually averages 20in of moisture, while Estes Park receives only about 13in.

FEE & PERMITS

For private vehicles, the park entrance fee is $20, valid for seven days. Individuals entering the park on foot, bicycle, motorcycle or bus pay $10 each. All visitors receive a free copy of the park's information brochure, which contains a good orientation map and is available in English, German, French, Spanish and Japanese. A good option if you plan to visit any of Colorado's other national parks is to buy an annual National Parks and Federal Recreational Lands Annual Pass for $80.

Backcounty permits ($20) are required for overnight stays (May through October) outside of developed campgrounds. Reservations can be made by phone, mail or in person. Phone reservations can be made only from November to April. Reservations by mail or phone are accepted via the **Backcountry Office** (☎970-586-1242; www.nps.gov/romo)

Permits can be obtained in person at Beaver Meadows Visitor Center (p137), Kawuneeche Visitor Center (p137), and (in summer only) at the Longs Peak (p136) and Wild Basin (p136) ranger stations.

Olive Ridge Campground   CAMPGROUND $
(☎303-541-2500; campsites $14; ⊙mid-May–Nov) This well-kept USFS campground has access to four trailheads: St Vrain Mountain, Wild Basin, Longs Peak and Twin Sisters. In the summer it can get full, though sites are mostly first come, first serve.

Moraine Park Campground   CAMPGROUND $
(☎877-444-6777; www.recreation.gov; off Bear Lake Road; campsites summer $20; ▦) In the middle of a stand of ponderosa pine forest off Bear Lake Road, this is the biggest of the park's campgrounds, approximately 2.5 miles south of the Beaver Meadows Visitor Center, and with 245 sites. The walk-in, tent-only sites in the D Loop are recommended if you want quiet. Make reservations through the website.

Reservations are accepted and recommended from the end of May through to the end of September; other times of the year the campground is first-come, first-served. At night in the summer, there are numerous ranger-led programs in the ampitheater.

The campground is served by the shuttle buses on Bear Lake Rd through the summer.

Aspenglen Campground   CAMPGROUND $
(☎877-444-6777; www.recreation.gov; State Hwy 34; campsites summer $20) With only 54 sites, this is the smallest of the park's reservable camping. There are many tent-only sites, including some walk-ins, and a limited number of trailers are allowed. This is the quietest park that's highly accessible (5 miles west of Estes Park on US 34). Make reservations through the website.

Timber Creek Campground   CAMPGROUND $
(Trail Ridge Rd, US Hwy 34) This campground has 100 sites and remains open through the winter. No reservations accepted. The only established campground on the west side of the park, it's 7 miles north of Grand Lake.

Glacier Basin Campground   CAMPGROUND $
(☎877-444-6777; www.recreation.gov; off Bear Lake Road; campsites summer $20; ▦) This developed campground has a large area for group camping and accommodates RVs. It is served by the shuttle buses on Bear Lake Rd throughout the summer. Make reservations through the website.

ℹ Information

MEDICAL SERVICES There are no care facilities in the park, but most rangers are trained to give emergency treatment. Emergency telephones are at Longs Peak (p136) and Wild Basin (p136) ranger stations, as well certain trailheads, including Bear Lake (p133) and Lawn Lake.

MONEY The park has no banking services; for these you'll need to head to either Estes Park or Grand Lake.

RANGER STATIONS Longs Peak Ranger Station (⊙8:30am-4:30pm summer) Eleven miles south of Estes Park on Hwy 7.

Wild Basin Ranger Station (Off State Hwy 115)

TELEPHONE Cell phone coverage? Forget it. The only place calls can be made are from public phones at visitors centers and large, established campgrounds.

VISITOR CENTERS The park has three full-service visitors centers – one on the east side, one on the west, and one in the middle. Though they all have different displays and programs, this is where you can study maps and speak with rangers about permits and weather conditions.

Alpine Visitor Center (www.nps.gov/romo; Fall River Pass; ⊙10:30am-4:30pm late May–mid-Jun, 9am-5pm late Jun–early Sep, 10:30am-4:30pm early Sep–mid-Oct; ▦) The views from this popular visitors center and souvenir store at 11,796ft, and right in the middle of the park, are extraordinary. You can see elk, deer and sometimes moose grazing on the hillside on the drive up Old Fall River Rd.

Much of the traffic that clogs Trail Ridge Road all summer pulls into Alpine Visitors Center, so the place is a zoo. Rangers here give programs and advice about trails. You can also shop for knick-knacks or eat in the cafeteria-style dining room.

Beaver Meadows Visitor Center (970-586-1206; www.nps.gov/romo; US Hwy 36; 8am-9pm late Jun–late Aug, to 4:30pm or 5pm rest of year;) The primary visitors center and best stop for park information if you're approaching from Estes Park. You can see a film about the park, browse a small gift shop and reserve backcountry camping sites.

Kawuneeche Visitor Center (970-627-3471; 16018 US Hwy 34; 8am-6pm last week May–Labor Day, 8am-5pm Labor Day–end of Sept , 8am-4:30pm Oct–end of May;) This is the main visitors center on the west side of the park, offering a film about the park, ranger-led walks and discussions, backcountry permits and family activities.

ℹ Getting There & Away

Trail Ridge Rd (US 34) is the only east–west route through the park; the US 34 eastern approach from I-25 and Loveland follows the Big Thompson River Canyon. The most direct route from Boulder follows US 36 through Lyons to the east entrances. Another approach from the south, mountainous Hwy 7, passes by Enos Mills' Cabin and provides access to campsites and trailheads on the east side of the divide. Winter closure of US 34 through the park makes access to the park's west side dependent on US 40 at Granby.

There are two entrance stations on the east side, Fall River (US 34) and Beaver Meadows (US 36). The Grand Lake Station (also US 34) is the only entry on the west side. Year-round access is available through Kawuneeche Valley along the Colorado River headwaters to Timber Creek Campground (p136). The main centers of visitor activity on the park's east side are the Alpine Visitor Center (p136) high on Trail Ridge Rd and Bear Lake Rd, which leads to campgrounds, trailheads and the Moraine Park Museum.

North of Estes Park, Devils Gulch Rd leads to several hiking trails. Farther out on Devils Gulch Rd, you pass through the village of Glen Haven to reach the trailhead entry to the park along the North Fork of the Big Thompson River.

ℹ Getting Around

A majority of visitors enter the park in their own cars, using the long and winding Trail Ridge Rd (US 34) to cross the Continental Divide. There are options for those without wheels, however. In summer a free shuttle bus operates from the Estes Park Visitor Center (p142) multiple times daily, bringing hikers to a park-and-ride location where you can pick up other shuttles. The year-round option leaves the Glacier Basin parking area toward Bear Lake, in the parks lower elevations. During the summer peak, a second shuttle operates between Moraine Park campground and the Glacier Basin parking area. Shuttles run on weekends only from mid-August through September.

ESTES PARK

POP 6402 / ELEV 7522FT

T-shirt shops and ice-cream parlors, sidewalks jammed with tourists and streets plugged with RVs: welcome to Estes Park, the chaotic outpost at the edge of Rocky Mountain National Park.

There's no small irony in the fact that the proximity to one of the most pristine outdoor escapes in the USA has made Estes Park the kind of place you'll need to escape from. Those expecting immediate views of the pristine beauty of Rocky Mountain National Park may be disappointed to find themselves watching brake lights on E Elkhorn Ave, the town's artery to both park entrances. But it's not all bad. Although the strip malls and low-rise motels can be unsightly, Estes Park promises every convenience for the traveler, and during the off-season the place has a certain charm, as the streets quiet down and the prices of creekside cabins drop.

◉ Sights & Activities

On the doorstep of Rocky Mountain National Park and surrounded by national forest, Estes Park is one of the state's premier supply points for the mountains. With the exception of white-water rafting and skiing (better in other parts of the state), the area has top-notch outdoor activities of every stripe, and a stroll down Elkhorn will take you past a number of operators heading into the park via horse, jeep or hiking boots. Many of Estes Park's sights are a bit out of town and only accessible if you have a car.

FREE **Estes Park Museum** MUSEUM (970-586-6256; www.estesnet.com/museum; 200 4th St; 10am-5pm Mon-Sat, 1-5pm Sun;) This ambitious community museum has a commendable rotation of exhibits on local culture. It's not only corny

Estes Park

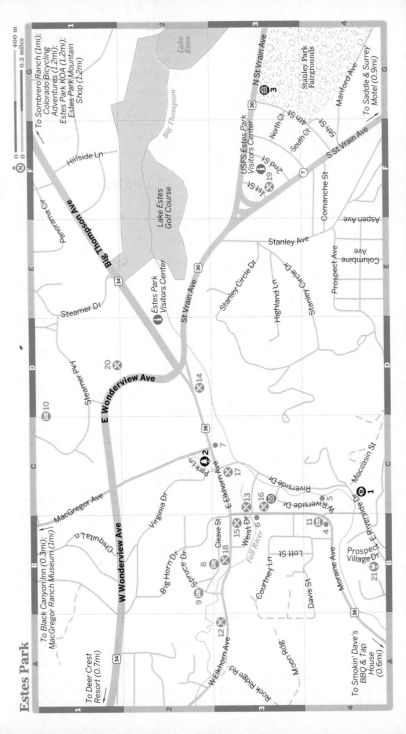

To Sombrero Ranch (1mi);
Colorado Bicycling
Adventures (1.2mi);
Estes Park KOA (1.2mi);
Estes Park Mountain
Shop (1.2mi)

To Saddle & Surrey
Motel (0.9mi)

Lake Estes

Big Thompson

Stanley Park
Fairgrounds

Hillside Ln

N St Vrain Ave

USFS Estes Park
Visitors Center

Lake Estes
Golf Course

Manford Ave

North Ct

4th St

5th St

South Ct

S St Vrain Ave

2nd St

1st St

Comanche St

Aspen Ave

Stanley Ave

Columbine Ave

Prospect Ave

Panorama Cir

Big Thompson Ave

Steamer Dr

Estes Park
Visitors Center

St Vrain Ave

Stanley Circle Dr

Stanley Circle Dr

Highland Ln

E Wonderview Ave

Steamer PKWY

W Wonderview Ave

MacGregor Ave

Chiquita Ln

Virginia Dr

Park Ln

E Elkhorn Ave

Riverside Dr

W Riverside Dr

Moccasin St

E Riverside Dr

Prospect
Village Dr

To Black Canyon Inn (0.3mi);
MacGregor Ranch Museum (1mi)

Big Horn Dr

Cleave St

Weist Dr

Fall River

Spruce St

Courtney Ln

Toft St

Davis St

Moraine Ave

Prospect
Village Dr

To Deer Crest
Resort (0.7mi)

W Elkhorn Ave

Rock Ridge Rd

Moon Rdg

To Smokin' Dave's
BBQ & Tap
House (0.6mi)

Estes Park

⊙ **Sights**

1 Ariel Tramway C4
2 Bond Park C2
3 Estes Park Museum........................... G3

Activities, Courses & Tours

4 Colorado Mountain School B4
5 Estes Angler C4
6 Green Jeep Tours B3
7 Kirks Flyshop C3

⊖ **Sleeping**

8 Estes Park Hostel................................ B3
9 Silver Moon Inn B2
10 Stanley Hotel D1
11 Total Climbing Lodge B4

⊗ **Eating**

12 Big Horn Restaurant............................ A3
13 DeLeo's Park Theatre Cafe &
   Deli C3
14 Ed's Cantina & Grill D2
15 Lonigans.. B3
16 Molly B Restaurant C3
17 Nepal's Cafe C3
18 Penelope's Burgers & Fries B3
19 Pura Vida... F3
20 Safeway.. D1

⊙ **Drinking**

21 Estes Park Brewery B4

Ice Age mannequins either – during our last visit the main attraction was a glimpse into Estes Park's wild days in the 1960s.

Ariel Tramway   CABLE CAR
(970-586-3675; www.estestram.com; 420 E Riverside Dr; adult/child/senior $10/5/9; 9am-6pm Memorial Day–Labor Day; P) In the time you wait to be herded aboard a tram to the top of Prospect Mountain, you could have climbed Lily Mountain on your own two feet, but the tram is a good option for those with modest ambitions who still want the view.

TOP CHOICE **Colorado Mountain School**
     MOUNTAINEERING
(800-836-4008, 303-447-2804; www.total climbing.com; 341 Moraine Ave; half-day guided climbs per person from $125) Simply put, there's no better resource for climbers in Colorado – this outfit is the largest climbing operator in the region, has the most expert guides and is the only organization allowed to operate within Rocky Mountain Nation-al Park. It has a clutch of classes taught by world-class instructors.

Basic courses, such as Intro to Rock Climbing, are a great way for novices to deeply experience the Rockies. There are multiday training expeditions for those with some experience. Courses are taught in an ideal setting – whether it be a towering granite peak in the park or the 10,000 sq ft indoor climbing facility. You can also stay on-site in dorm lodging (p140).

Colorado Bicycling Adventures   CYCLING
(970-586-4241, New Venture Cycling 970-231-273; 2050 Big Thompson Ave; ½-day tour $60) For years this was *the* bike shop in town, so the staff know the surrounding hills like the backs of their contoured, oversized calf muscles. Now the shop has moved to a central location across, from where it leads tours.

Sombrero Ranch   HORSEBACK RIDING
(970-586-4577; www.sombrero.com; 1895 Big Thompson Ave; horse rides from $35) With affordable guided trips into the national park or through a huge private ranch in the foothills, this quality outfitter has a variety of options. The evening 'steak fry' is a popular ride. Sombrero Ranch operates stables throughout the region.

Kirks Flyshop   FISHING
(877-669-1859; www.kirksflyshop.com; 230 E Elkhorn Ave; tours from $150; 7am-7pm) This full-service fly-fishing shop offers a number of guided packages in Rocky Mountain National Park and the surrounding waterways of the Front Range. It also rents equipment, guides overnight hikes, offers kayaking and fishing combos, and group excursions.

Green Jeep Tours   4WD
(970-577-0034; www.epgjt.com; 157 Moraine Ave; tours from $35;) Offerings start with 3½-hour guided tours to waterfalls in Rocky Mountain National Park and move up to all-day affairs. Note that green is the color of the car, and is not representative of an environmentally friendly ethos.

⊨ Sleeping

Be warned: lodgings fill up very fast during the peak July and August period, when the prices are sky high. You're likely to be out of luck if you travel west of Greeley without a reservation during summer. Off-season rates may be down to half that of summer prices, and many accommodations simply close for the winter. Most of the cheaper midcentury motels (which still aren't that cheap) are located east of town along US 34 or Hwy 7. Most of these low-slung motels are remarkably similar: musty carpet and fairly small rooms with television and refrigerator, though some places also boast pools, hot tubs and saunas. There are plenty of cabins to rent here too, with a concentration of them along US 66.

There are some passable budget options for those trying to save money, but the best-value accommodations, hands down, are in area campgrounds which are plentiful, easily accessible and stunning. If you didn't bring your own tent and sleeping bag, you can rent one from **Estes Park Mountain Shop** (☑970-586-6548; www.estesparkmountainshop.com; 2050 Big Thompson Ave; 2-person camping set-up $32; ⊗8am-9pm).

TOP CHOICE **YMCA of the Rockies – Estes Park Center** RESORT $$
(☑970-586-3341; www.ymcarockies.org; 2515 Tunnel Rd; r/d from $99, cabins from $124; P⊕⊗🐾📶♿) Estes Park Center is not your typical YMCA boarding house. Instead it's a favorite vacation spot with families; upmarket motel-style accommodation and cabins set on hundreds of acres of high alpine terrain. Choose from roomy cabins that sleep up to 10 or motel-style rooms for singles or doubles. Both are simple and practical.

This very kid-friendly resort sits in a serene and ultrapristine location in the mountains just outside town. The 860-acre plot is home to cabins and motel rooms along with lots of wide open spaces dotted with forests and fields of wildflowers. Just a few minutes outside of Estes Park (but definitely away from the hustle of town), it offers a range of activities for adults, kids or the whole family, throughout the year. It also runs special themed weekends and longer summer camps where environmental education is taught in a fun and engaging manner. This YMCA is unapologetically outdoorsy, and most guests come to participate in the activities.

Mary's Lake Lodge LODGE $$$
(☑970-577-9495; www.maryslakelodge.com; 2625 Marys Lake Rd; r /cabins from $140; P⊕❄📶♿) This atmospheric old wooden lodge, perched on a ridge looking over its namesake lake, is an utterly romantic place to slumber. Built from polished pine logs, it reeks of Wild West ambience and has an amazing covered front porch with panoramic Rocky Mountain views.

The rooms and cabins are a blend of modern and historic, and many of the latter have private hot tubs. Both the saloon-style Tavern (mains $7 to $20; open 11am to 11pm) and fine-dining Chalet Room (mains $12 to $20; open 5pm to 10pm) serve delicious fresh lake fish (and flown-in seafood), and have seating on the heated porch. A big hot tub under the stars, fire pit and live music five nights per week round out amenities, while an on-site spa takes care of gritty hiking feet and sore muscles. Mary's is 3 miles south of Estes Park off Hwy 7.

Stanley Hotel HOTEL $$$
(☑970-586-3371; www.stanleyhotel.com; 333 Wonderview Ave; r from $159; P📶❄♿) The white Georgian Colonial Revival hotel stands in brilliant contrast to the towering peaks of Rocky Mountain National Park that surround it. A favorite local retreat, the nearly-a-century-old hotel served as the inspiration for Stephen King's famous cult novel *The Shining*. Rooms are cosy and decorated to evoke the Old West, with period and replica antiques.

The grand dame of northern Colorado historic resort hotels, the Stanley boasts great mountain views, splendid dining and even ghost tours of the building on weekend nights! And if it's ghosts you're after, you should book room 401 to increase your chances of ghost-spotting – staff consider it the 'most haunted'. The public areas encompass vast open spaces warmed with stone fireplaces and plump leather couches. If you're looking for old-world charm with a bit of a supernatural twist, the Stanley is the hotel to visit.

Total Climbing Lodge HOSTEL $
(☑303-447-2804; www.totalclimbing.com; 341 Moraine Ave; dm $25; P⊕@📶) A bustling hub of climbers, lodging here is the best dorm option in town. Expect simple pine bunks, a ping-pong table and a laid-back vibe.

Black Canyon Inn CABIN $$$
(☑970-586-8113, 800-897-5123; www.blackcanyoninn.com; 800 MacGregor Ave; 1-/2-/3-bed r from $195/260/399; P⊕❄📶♿) A fine place to splurge is this lovely, secluded 14-acre property offering luxury suites and a 'rustic' log cabin (which comes with a Jacuzzi). The rooms are dressed out with stone fireplaces, dark wood and woven tapestries in rich dark colors.

Deer Crest Resort HOTEL $$
(☏800-331-2324, 970-586-2324; www.deercrest resort.com; 1200 Fall River Rd; d $119-129, ste from $149; P☕❄🛜♿👍) There is a ton of options along the road out to Rocky Mountain National Park, but Deer Creek bests its neighbors with gas grills, lots of green space for the kids to run around and the sound of the creek shushing guests to sleep. The on-site restaurant is also excellent.

Silver Moon Inn HOTEL $$
(☏970-586-6006; www.silvermooninn.com; 175 Spruce Dr; d $139-159; P☕❄@🛜♿👍) The rooms here aren't loaded with personality, but there are plenty of thoughtful touches – a white board where guests leave each other dinner recommendations, a quality continental breakfast, and creekside fire pits. Its central location makes strolling to Estes Park's main drag easy.

Estes Park KOA CAMPGROUND, RV SITE $
(☏800-562-1887, 970-586-2888; www.estes parkkoa.com; 2051 Big Thompson Ave; campsites $31, cabins from $75; 🛜👍) With so much excellent camping just up the road in Rocky Mountain National Park, its hard to see the allure in this roadside RV-oriented camping spot. But for those in need of a staging day before for a big adventure, the proximity to town is appealing.

Estes Park Hostel HOSTEL $
(☏970-586-3149; www.estesparkhostel.com; 211 Cleave St; dm/s/d $26/38/52) This hostel, with a handful of shared rooms and simple privates, isn't going into history books as the plushest digs ever, but there's a kitchen on site, and Terri, the owner, is helpful. The price is right too.

✖ Eating & Drinking

Like lodgings, restaurants here often shift to shorter hours, close for several days of the week or shut down altogether in the snowy off-season. Another unfortunate similarity is poor value for your money. Most menus here are meaty American standards and humdrum pub grub, which too often come at white tablecloth prices. If you're visiting between September and May it's wise to call ahead for reservations. Self-caterers will make out best by stocking up at the local Safeway supermarket (p142) on the way into town to picnic at **Bond Park** (E Elkhorn Ave) or in one of the national park picnic spots up the road.

DeLeo's Park Theatre Cafe & Deli DELI $
(☏970-577-1134; www.deleosdeli.com; 132 Moraine Ave; mains $6-10; ⊙11am-4pm daily; ♿👍) Situated within one of the nation's oldest movie houses, chatty Tom DeLeo serves Estes Park's best sandwich (and according to the Food Network, one of the best in the country). Adapting their names after classic flicks (like the turkey stacked, um, 'Gobblefather') this place has loads of character.

Big Horn Restaurant BREAKFAST $
(☏970-586-2792; www.estesparkbighorn.com; 401 W Elkhorn; mains $6-17; ⊙6am-9pm daily, hours vary seasonally; ♿👍) Here's the local breakfast institution – a place where you can get a side of grits and the local gossip, the best *huevos rancheros* (ranch eggs) and some face time with flannel-clad locals. If you get here on the way into the park, order a packed lunch with your breakfast.

Pura Vida LATIN AMERICAN $$
(160 1st St; mains $10-22; ⊙11am-9pm Mon-Sat, to 8pm Sun; ♿👍) This place is *just* off the beaten path enough to feel like a discovery, situated away from the tourist traffic. The vibe is casual but the Latin American fare is classy – *Casado* (a plate of typical Costa Rican fare), fried yucca and a lunch buffet of fresh, inventive flavors.

Lonigans PUB FOOD $$
(☏970-586-4346; www.lonigans.com; 110 W Elkhorn Ave; ⊙kitchen closes 10pm; ♿👍) This pub and grill is a place to soak up Estes Park local flavor, mostly through the sidelong glances of the good ol' boys at the bar and boozy karaoke crooners. The menu – mostly burgers and American pub basics – includes Rocky Mountain Oysters, otherwise known as bull balls.

Ed's Cantina & Grill MEXICAN $$
(☏970-586-2919; www.edscantina.com; 390 E Elkhorn Ave; mains $10-25; ⊙11am-2am Mon-Fri, from 8am Sat & Sun; 👍) With an outdoor patio right on the river, Ed's is a great place to kick back with a margarita and one of the daily $3 blue-plate specials (think flautas with shredded pork and guacamole). Serving Mexican and American staples, the restaurant is in a retro mod space with leather booth seating and a bold primary-color scheme.

The bar is in a separate room with lightwood stools featuring comfortable high backs.

Rock Inn Mountain Tavern

STEAKHOUSE $$$

(☑970-586-4116; www.rockinnestes.com; 1675 Hwy 66; mains $14-29; ⊘11am-2am; 🛜🐾) After a few days in the wilds of Rocky Mountain National Park, the rare porterhouse here seems heaven-sent (even if the country band on stage can't pass as the accompanying choir of angels). Excellent stick-to-the-ribs fare and a crackling fire make it ideal for hikers looking to indulge.

Nepal's Cafe

NEPALESE $

(☑970-577-7035; 184 E Elkhorn Ave, Unit H; buffet $9; ⊘10am-8pm; 🐾) Lamp-heated lunch buffets are usually a no-no, but it's worth reconsidering dropping by here. The curries are spiced just right and the *momo* (dumplings) are a filling option before or after a big hike. Come early for dinner, as the tiny place gets packed.

Smokin' Dave's BBQ & Tap House

BBQ $$

(☑866-674-2793; www.smokindavesbbqandtap house.com; 820 Moraine Ave; mains $8-20; ⊘11am-9pm Sun-Thu, to 10pm Fri & Sat; ⊜🐾) Half-assed BBQ joints are all too common in Colorado's mountain towns, but Dave's, situated in a spare dining room, fully delivers. The buffalo ribs and pulled pork come dressed in a slightly sweet, smoky, tangy sauce and the sweet potato fries are crisply fried. Also excellent? The long, well-selected beer list.

Penelope's Burgers & Fries

BURGERS $

(☑970-586-2277; 229 W Elkhorn Ave; mains $6-9; ⊘lunch & dinner; 🐾) This burger barn on the main drag is decorated with old clutter – frying pans and spoons and old timey bric-a-brac – but if the place was dressed-up to honor the real workhorse from its kitchen they would have just decorated the place with a deep fryer.

Molly B Restaurant

AMERICAN $

(☑970-586-2766; www.estesparkmollyb.com; 200 Moraine Ave; breakfast $5-8; ⊘6:30am-4pm Thu-Tue; 🐾) This classic American breakfast place in town is easy to find and has a burly omelet and other greasy-spoon delights served among wood paneling and vinyl seats. Even the healthy food is delivered jumbo size, making the 'outrageous granola' no joke.

Safeway

SELF-CATERING

(☑970-586-4447; 451 E Wonderview Ave; ⊘9am-7pm Mon-Fri, to 6pm Sat, 10am-4pm Sun) This large outpost of a Western States grocery chain is the place to stock up in Estes Park. It also has a full pharmacy.

Estes Park Brewery

BREWPUB

(☑970-586-6409; www.epbrewery.com; 470 Prospect Village Dr; ⊘11am-2am Mon-Sun) Ain't nothing fancy about this brewpub – it dishes out pizza, wings and house beer in a big, boxy room that resembles a cross between a classroom and a country kitchen. Nothing gourmet, but cool tables and outdoor seating keep the place popping until late.

Those who are a bit indecisive can head downstairs to the tasting room before taking home a growler. Our favorites are the refreshing bright lager and the Stinger.

ℹ Information

Estes Park Visitors Center (☑970-577-9900, 800-443-7837; www.estesparkcvb.com; 500 Big Thompson Ave; ⊘9am-8pm daily Jun-Aug, 8am-5pm Mon-Fri, 9am-5pm Sat, 10am-4pm Sun Sep-May; 🐾) Try the Estes Park Visitor Center, just east of the US 36 junction, for help with lodging; note that many places close in winter.

Estes Valley Library (☑970-586-8116; www.estesvalleylibrary.org; 335 E Elkhorn Ave; ⊘9am-9pm Mon-Thu, to 5pm Fri-Sat, 1-5pm Sun; 🛜) With free wi-fi, large open spaces and tons of literature on the local area, Estes Park's central library is a good resource for travelers researching on the go.

Police Station (☑970-586-4000; 170 Mac-Gregor Ave)

Post Office (☑970-586-0170; 215 W Riverside Dr; ⊘8:30am-4:30pm Mon-Fri, 10am-1pm Sat) Centrally located post office with a fully staffed service desk.

USFS Estes Park Visitors Center (☑970-586-3440; 161 2nd St) The USFS Estes Park Visitors Center sells books and maps for the Arapaho and Roosevelt National Forests and has camping and trail information for hikers and off-road bicyclists. Camping permits for the heavily used Indian Peaks Wilderness Area, south of Rocky Mountain National Park, are required from June to September 15 and cost $5 per person.

ℹ Getting There & Away

Estes Park is 34 miles west of Loveland via US 34, which you can access from I-25 exit 257. Many visitors can come up by way of Boulder along US 36, passing through Lyons. Both are spectacular drives through rugged foothills, red rock formations and lush forest. A slower but more scenic route is the spectacular Peak to Peak Hwy.

ℹ Getting Around

Considering the traffic, getting around Estes Park's compact downtown is easiest on foot.

Estes Park has started a free shuttle service in the summer along the town's main arteries. The routes seem to change every year, but the service operates daily from about July to August, and then weekends only through September. If you're traveling into Rocky Mountain National Park, there is a free 'Hiker Shuttle' which leaves from the Estes Park Visitors Center (p142), making stops at Beaver Meadows Visitor Center (p137) and the park's Park & Ride lot, where you can transfer to other national park shuttles.

TO/FROM THE AIRPORT **Estes Park Shuttle** (☑970-586-5151, toll-free 800-950-3274; www.estesparkshuttle.com; 1-way/round-trip $45/85) This shuttle service connects Denver's airport to Estes Park about four times a day. The trip takes two hours.

BICYCLE Bicycling is a great way to get around the area, though few visitors seem to use this mode of transport (of course the altitude does make for some huffing and puffing). In summer, bike rentals spring up in the tourist area along E Elkhorn Ave, or you can get some wheels from Colorado Bicycling Adventures (p139).

TAXI **Peak to Peak Taxi** (☑970-586-6111) This minivan taxi service makes runs throughout Rocky Mountain National Park and the Front Range.

AROUND ESTES PARK

Enos Mills Cabin Museum & Gallery
MUSEUM
(☑970-586-4706; www.enosmills.com; 6760 Hwy 7; adult/child under 12yr $5/3; ☺11am-4pm Tue & Wed summer; ♿) Naturalist Enos Mills (1870–1922) led the struggle to establish Rocky Mountain National Park. His infectious enthusiasm and passion for nature lived on with his daughter Enda Mills Kiley (who sadly passed away in 2009). Her father's incredible history is documented in his tiny cabin, built in 1885.

The Mills family maintains an interpretive nature trail leading from the parking lot to the cabin, where news clippings and photographs recount Enos Mills' advocacy to protect the wild. Reprints and vintage

PEAK TO PEAK HWY

The Peak to Peak Hwy is one of the state's most scenic drives. If you're driving between Denver and Rocky Mountain National Park, definitely consider this route.

copies of many of Mills' 16 books are available for sale at the cabin, in addition to an outstanding collection of his writings edited by Enda, *Adventures of a Nature Guide* (New Past Press, 1990).

FREE **MacGregor Ranch Museum**
MUSEUM
(☑970-586-3749; www.macgregorranch.org; 180 MacGregor Ln; ☺10am-4pm Tue-Sat Jun-Aug) In 1872 Alexander and Clara MacGregor arrived in Estes Park and settled beside Black Canyon Creek near Lumpy Ridge. Their granddaughter Muriel MacGregor bequeathed the ranch as an educational trust upon her death. It's a living museum featuring original living and working quarters; the ranch still raises Black Angus cattle. The ranch is one mile north of Estes Park on Devils Gulch Rd.

An NPS scenic and conservation easement helps fund the operation, and provides trail access to Lumpy Ridge.

Glen Haven

Blink and you might just miss Glen Haven, a tiny outpost on the North Fork of the Big Thompson River, 7 miles east of Estes Park on Devils Gulch Rd. There isn't much here except a post office and general store, but the scenic approach makes it a worthwhile afternoon. Follow the narrow canyon road for 8 miles northwest from US 34 at Drake, site of the North Fork's confluence with the main channel in Big Thompson Canyon. Along the way there are handsome picnic spots; our favorite is right in Glen Haven on the narrow banks of the tumbling North Fork. If you forgot to pack a lunch, drop in at the **Glen Haven General Store** (☑970-586-2560; www.glenhavengeneralstore.com; 7499 Country Rd 43; ☺9am-6pm May-Oct, shorter hr in winter) for gooey cinnamon rolls, cherry cobbler and deli items. In winter it's open 'from 9am to whenever we feel like it!'

The prime attraction of town, aside from those passing through on fishing and hiking trips, is the **Inn of Glen Haven** (☑970-586-3897; www.innofglenhaven.com; 7468 Country Rd 43; d w shared bathroom from $95; ☺❋☎), an effete lair of the English gentry, offering delightful B&B rooms (with names such as Lord Dunraven's Room!) and fine dining. It's almost comically stuffy but fun in a kind of Renaissance-fair kind of way.

NEDERLAND

POP 1100 / ELEV 8236FT

From Boulder, the devastatingly scenic 17-mile route through Boulder Canyon emerges in the lively, ramshackle little berg of Nederland, a mountain-town magnet for hippies looking to get off the grid.

These days, Nederland has a sagging, happenstantial quality to its weather-beaten buildings, which are not without a certain rugged charm. There are several worthwhile restaurants and bars which feed the hungry skiers and hikers heading to or from Eldora Ski Area, Indian Peaks Wilderness Area or coming down the Peak to Peak Hwy.

✯ Festivals & Events

Frozen Dead Guy Days   PARADE
(Nederland Chamber of Commerce 303-258-3936; ⊙early March;) This bizarre and wonderful little festival brings life to Nederland in the early spring. Basically an excuse to parade through town and drink beer, the festival celebrates Grandpa Bredo Morstoel, a Norwegian transplant who is cryogenically frozen and held locally in dry ice awaiting reanimation. Seriously.

NedFest   MUSIC
(www.nedfest.com; 151 E St; day ticket $55; ⊙late August) An annual gathering of area folkies and jam bands, perfectly suited to the ex-hippie vibe of this ramshackle mountain town.

🛏 Sleeping

Nederland has a handful of small motels, but you'll find better value and more variety in nearby Boulder, or a bit out of town toward Estes Park. In the summer, camping is by far the best option around here if you have the gear.

There is a variety of sites and back country options in the Roosevelt National Forest (including many free options) and the folks at the visitors center can point you in the right direction. Our favorite camping spot nearby is the **Rainbow Lakes Campground** (off County Rd 116; campsite $6; P), which is at 10,000ft and has access to brilliant hikes in eastern side of Rocky Mountain National Park. Skiers may also consider a stay at the Eldora Mountain Resort (p144).

✕ Eating

Wild Mountain Smokehouse & Brewery
BBQ $$
(303-258-9453; www.wildmountainsb.com; 70 E 1st St; mains $8-12; ⊙11am-9pm Sun-Thu, to 10pm Fri & Sat;) The spectrum of slightly sweet, smoky or brightly spiced BBQ sauces – themed after great classic BBQ regions like Memphis, Texas and Thailand – is a perfect complement to hoppy house brews, making this one of the best dining options in the area.

Back Country Pizza   PIZZA $
(303-258-0176;   www.backcountrypizza.com; 20 Lakeview Dr; pizzas $12-18; ⊙11am-10pm Sun-Thu, 11am-11pm Fri & Sat;) Located in the Caribou Shopping Center, this pizzeria offers delicious, crusty pizza and hearty plates at good value. The place is an easy option for families with its casual atmosphere and video games.

New Moon Bakery   CAFE FOOD
(303-258-3569;   www.newmoonbakery.com; 1 W 1st St; ⊙7am-3pm Mon-Fri, 7:30am-5pm Sat & Sun;) With its rough edges, Nederland needs a cozy and sophisticated place like New Moon, where you can get your latte made with rice milk and your chocolate cookie without gluten.

☆ Entertainment

Things can get pretty quiet overnight, but in recent years Nederland has become a small center for live music, mostly of the acoustic variety. If you're in town at the end of August, you might also run into NedFest (p144), a jam band and folk music blow out. For more of Nederland's festival flavor, try Frozen Dead Guys Days (p144).

ⓘ Information

Nederland Visitors Center (303-258-3936; www.nederlandchamber.org; 4 W 1st St; ⊙10am-4pm daily) Has local information about where to eat and sleep in the area, and information on lots of local activities; located downtown, diagonally opposite the Village shopping mall.

ELDORA SKI AREA

Aside from the Corona Bowl, which boasts a thrilling 1400ft vertical drop, this little ski area is mostly famous for its convenience, its proximity to Boulder and the relatively inexpensive lift tickets. Four miles west of Nederland, **Eldora Mountain Resort** (☑303-440-8700; www.eldora.com; 2861 Eldora Ski Road #140; lift ticket adult/child $65/39; ◷9am-4pm Mon-Fri, from 8:30am Sat & Sun; 🖟; 🖳N, B) primarily gets day visitors who zip around a fairly small facility with around 500 ski-able acres. It's no Telluride, but there is some interesting terrain, and a few expert trails. There are also 40-plus kilometers of well-groomed Nordic trails.

During winter, buses leave for Eldora Mountain Resort from the corner of Boulder's 14th St and Walnut St (round-trip $8).

INDIAN PEAKS WILDERNESS AREA

Forming the impressive backdrop to Nederland, the Indian Peaks area offers many fine hiking and camping opportunities. Especially nice is the hike up to 12,000ft Arapaho Pass, accessed from the Fourth of July campground. It's a gentle ascent but be prepared to spend the entire day – if the altitude doesn't slow you down, the scenery should.

For more information on Indian Peaks check at the Nederland Visitors Center (p144), which has maps and guidebooks. In the mall, the **Ace Hardware** (☑303-258-3132; 74 Hwy 119 S; ◷8am-7pm Mon-Sat, 09-5pm Sun) also sells topographic and USGS maps for the Indian Peaks area and issues camping permits (required June to September 15) as well as hunting and fishing licenses.

FORT COLLINS

POP 138,736 / ELEV 5003FT

Sixty five miles northwest of Denver, Fort Collins straddles Colorado's topographical divide. Look east and the plains stretch endlessly; turn around and the foothills of the Rockies begin their rise.

Though Fort Collins serves as the foil to Colorado's other Front Range college town, Boulder, the town's status as the underdog is a bit unjust. Sure, the landscape isn't as dramatic, the university isn't quite as prestigious and it doesn't have the granola-crunching socialist cultural cache, but the bicycle-packed streets of Fort Collins exude an unpretentious magnetism. This former farming community has developed into

a city with lovely little pockets, especially near the Colorado State University (CSU) campus and refurbished historical buildings of Old Town.

While the rivalry between the towns continues, there's one indisputable fact: the beer here is *way* better. People who love hoppy, handcrafted microbrews might need to pinch themselves to make sure they're not dreaming.

◉ Sights & Activities

Like many Front Range bergs, Fort Collins' activities demand working up a sweat. Proximity to Horsetooth Mountain Park and Reservoir attracts mountain bikers, campers, hikers and cross-country skiers, while the stone's-throw distance to the Poudre River and Rocky Mountains make it a good jumping-off point for white-water and wilderness excursions. If you're staying in town, there are two only absolute musts: the free tour of the New Belgium Brewery (which requires advance reservations) and a cruise around town one of the ubiquitous bicycles – free to check out from the Bike Library (p147) and many of the hotels. The city's extensive network of bicycling paths ranks among the best in the US and provides a pleasant way to see the town.

Swetsville Zoo   ZOO
(☑970-484-9509; 4801 E Harmony Rd; entry by donation; ◷daylight hours; 🖟) Bill Swets, a former farmer, volunteer firefighter and insomniac, created a scrap-metal menagerie during his restless nights, a whimsical roadside curiosity. Swets' creations are a coy lesson in creative recycling – everything from the grinning spider made from a VW bug, to the heavy metal caricature of Monica Lewinsky.

Colorado State Parks   CAMPING PERMITS
(☑970-491-1168; www.parks.state.co.us; 3745 E Prospect Rd; ◷8am-6pm Memorial Day–Labor Day, to 5pm winter) Sharing a building with the Colorado Welcome Center, this office can arrange permits and reservations for camping in Colorado's state parks.

FREE **Avery House Museum**
                                HISTORIC HOME
(www.poudrelandmarks.com; 328 W Mountain Ave; ◷1-4pm Sat & Sun; 🖟) This 1879 home belonged to Franklin Avery, the city planner of Fort Collins. Avery's foresight is

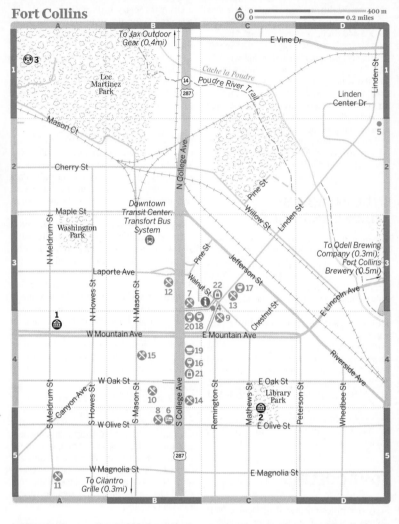

evident in the tree-lined, wide boulevards that grace the city centre. The Avery House is a stop along the self-guided historic walking tour available from the Fort Collins Convention and Visitors Bureau.

Fort Collins Museum & Discovery Science Center   MUSEUM
(☎970-221-6738; www.fcmdsc.org; 200 Mathews St; adult/senior over 60yr & child 3-12yr $4/3; ☺10am-5pm Tue-Sat, noon-5pm Sun; ☐☒) The hands-on science exhibits focusing on electricity, physics and dinosaurs are designed for children, leaving adults

some space to soak up the historical artifacts. The coolest thing on the grounds is an 1860s log cabin from the founding days of Fort Collins.

The Farm @ Lee Martinez Park
                                      PETTING ZOO
(☎970-221-6665; www.fcgov.com; 600 N Sherwood Ave; admission $2.50; ☺10am-5pm Tue-Sat, from noon Sun, to 4pm Nov-May; ☒) Pony rides and a barnyard of cows, turkeys and chickens make this shady riverside park a draw for families. In the summer there are storytellers and special events.

Fort Collins

Sights

1 Avery House Museum ... A4
2 Fort Collins Museum & Discovery Science Center ... C5
3 The Farm @ Lee Martinez Park ... A1

Activities, Courses & Tours

4 Fort Collins Bike Library ... C3
5 New Belgium Brewery ... D2

Sleeping

6 Armstrong Hotel ... B5

Eating

7 Backcountry Provisions ... B3
8 Choice City Butcher & Deli ... B5
9 CooperSmith's Pub & Brewing ... C4
10 Jay's Bistro & Jazz Lounge ... B4
11 Lucile's Restaurant ... A5
12 Pueblo Viejo ... B3
13 Red Table Cafe ... C3
14 Stuft ... B4
15 Tasty Harmony ... B4

Drinking

16 Crown Pub ... B4
17 Elliot's Martini Bar ... C3
18 Lucky Joe's ... B4
Mug's Coffee Lounge ... (see 6)
19 Starry Night ... B4
20 Town Pump ... B4

Shopping

21 Cupboard ... B4
White Balcony ... (see 21)
22 Wright Life ... C3

TOP CHOICE FREE New Belgium Brewery BREWERY

(☎970-221-0524; www.newbelgium.com; 500 Linden St; ⊙tasting room 10am-6pm Tue-Sat, tours daily on the half-hour; @) With the tripartite passion for beer, bicycles and sustainability, a tour of New Belgium's brewery brings you into the freewheeling essence of Fort Collins' character and it's an unforgettable few hours. The tour guides are knowledgeable, smart and playful, the special selection of beers is expertly brewed.

Tours begin with a pint of your choice before meandering through the sprawling, bicycle-cluttered brewing facility. By the time you get to the end, a colorful tasting room with long communal tables, you've probably had enough to consider getting dolled up in one of the costumes that are on hand. All told, the place is a riot. Those without the foresight to book long in advance can still enjoy a selection of brews and good-humored bartenders in the public tasting room.

FREE Fort Collins Bike Library BIKE HIRE

(☎970-221-2453, Café Bicyclette in Old Town Square 970-419-1050; www.fcgov.com/bicycling/library.php; Old Town Sq; ⊙10am-6pm Thu-Sun with seasonal variations;) Yes, it *really* is free. Really. You just hand over a credit-card number as a guarantee and roll out of the kiosk on Old Town Square. Most of the well-maintained bikes are simple, sturdy cruisers for getting around town, but they have a limited number of tandems and kids' bikes.

Sleeping

TOP CHOICE Armstrong Hotel BOUTIQUE HOTEL $$

(☎970-484-3883, toll-free 866-384-3883; www.thearmstronghotel.com; 259 S College Ave; d $99; P @) You'll want to extend your stay at this elegantly renovated boutique hotel in the heart of Old Town. The amenities make it: a fleet of free loaner bikes, large showers, feather duvets and gratis wi-fi. The unique rooms have vintage prints, muted colors and little luxuries such as iPod-ready stereos, art deco reading lamps and flat-screen TVs.

The distinct feel and stacks of charm make it one of the best places to stay in the region and a perfect perch from which to explore Fort Collins in style. It's simply lovely.

Hilton Fort Collins HOTEL $$

(☎970-482-2626; www.hiltonfortcollins.com; 425 W Prospect Ave; d $145-200; P) Right at the edge of the university campus, this is a pleasant and centrally located option. The rooms are comfortably furnished, though bland.

Eating

The best eats are mostly along N College, north of W Mulberry St. The walkable stretch of Old Town, just off the corner of S College and E Mountain, has a plethora of restaurants and bars as well.

Lucile's Restaurant
TOP CHOICE CAJUN $

(970-224-5464; www.luciles.com; 400 S Meldrum St; mains $7-12;) Snuggled in an old house, the restaurant is a cozy dream – replete with creaking floors, winsome waitresses and fluffy, made-from-scratch buttermilk biscuits. The Cajun home cookin' is fantastic; try the eggs Pontchartrain, with pan-fried local trout, or the eggs New Orleans, which comes smothered in spicy sauce.

As if the flavors and atmosphere weren't enough to fall in love with, the restaurant also makes efforts to use organic, locally grown food. Simply put: it's Fort Collins' best breakfast.

CooperSmith's Pub & Brewing
PUB FOOD $$

(970-498-0483; www.coopersmithspub.com; 5 Old Town Sq; mains $9-20; 11am-11pm Mon-Wed, to 11:30am Thu, Fri & Sat to midnight;) Of all Fort Collins' excellent brew pubs, this is the only one with a good menu. It's all about the thick-cut steak fries, chunky burgers and yards of fresh beer. The best thing on tap is also the most inventive: Sigda's Green Chili Golden Ale.

When the weather is warm, sit by the fountain outside and order the summer salad with candied walnuts, dried cherries, gorgonzola and mandarin oranges.

Backcountry Provisions
SANDWICHES $

(970-482-6913; www.backcountryprovisions .com; 140 N College Ave; sandwiches $7-9; 7am-5pm;) This brilliant little deli opens early so that outdoors-bound patrons can get out and on the trail with box lunches in their pack. The Pilgrim – a pile of turkey with cranberry sauce – was named one of the best sandwiches in America by *Esquire* magazine.

Stuft
BURGERS $

(970-484-6377; www.stuftburgerbar.com; 210 S College Ave; burgers $7-10; 11am-10pm Sun-Thu, to 2am Fri & Sat;) Grab a pencil and start scribbling your dream order: the build-your-own burger concept succeeds through a list of high-grade options like chipotle ketchup, apple-cider bacon and fire-roasted chiles. Add fresh-cut, skin-on french fries and a good list of beer specials and lunch takes on unlimited possibilities.

Choice City Butcher & Deli
SANDWICHES $

(970-490-2489; www.choicecitybutcher.com; 104 W Olive St; sandwiches $6-10; 7am-6pm Sun-Wed, to 9pm Thu-Sat;) The butchers here are straight from central casting – all forearms and white aprons – and all of the five varieties of Reuben sandwiches win raves. They serve dinner on the weekend, a predictably meaty selection of American mains.

Tasty Harmony
VEGETARIAN $$

(970-689-3234; www.tastyharmony.com; 130 S Mason St; mains $10-14; 11am-9pm Tue-Thu & Sun, to 10pm Fri & Sat;) Organic, vegetarian dishes at this bright lunch spot are delicious, with a menu focused on hearty sandwiches, baked tofu dishes and soups. Tacos, with tempeh and Mexican jackfruit, are the highlight of the mix-and-match daily plate. End things right with the raw key lime pie.

Jay's Bistro & Jazz Lounge
CONTEMPORARY AMERICAN $$$

(970-482-1876; www.jaysbistro.net; 135 W Oak St; mains $19-33; 11:30am-8:30pm Sun-Wed, 11:30am-10:30pm Thu-Sat) Though the soft light, Frenchie paintings and jazz quartet gives off a whiff of pretension, Jay's is the most sophisticated dining room in town. The menu is straight as an arrow (calamari, lamb shank, duck breast) but well executed and paired with a big wine list.

Red Table Cafe
SANDWICHES $

(970-490-2233; 224 Linden St; sandwiches $6-9; 8am-4pm;) Clean white tables and bright local art give this extraordinarily cute lunch spot a fresh ambience, even if the menu is relatively simple sandwiches. In the morning, go for an egg-and-avocado burrito; for lunch, a bowl of vegetarian chile.

Pueblo Viejo
MEXICAN $$

(970-221-1170; 185 N College Ave; mains $9-18; 10am-10pm Sun-Thu, to 11pm Fri & Sat;) Something of a Fort Collins institution, Pueblo Viejo serves a sizable chile relleno that's better-than-average Colorado Mexican, but the place goes one step better with rich mole dishes, big margaritas and bottomless chips and salsa. It's a bit uneven, but the place is always full. In the summer, there's a breezy patio out back.

Drinking

Crown Pub
PUB

(970-484-5929; www.crownpub.net; 134 S College Ave; 11am-late;) All the dark-wood paneling, friendly barkeeps and a dead-center location make this no-nonsense watering hole a good place to cool your heels after walking around downtown. If you're too pressed for time to hit all the local breweries, this pub has a lot of local beer on tap.

Odell Brewing Company   BREWPUB
(☑970-482-2881; www.odellbrewing.com; 800 E Lincoln Ave; ⊘11am-6pm Mon, Tue & Thu, 11am-7pm Wed, Fri & Sat) New Belgium has the best tour, but Odell makes the best brew – in not only Fort Collins but all of Colorado. The bar is small and comfortable with brewers who take pride in their work. If you taste but one Colorado beer, make it the hoppy, heady Odell IPA (India Pale Ale).

Starry Night   CAFE
(☑970-493-3039; 112 South College Ave; ⊘7am-10pm Mon-Thu, to 11pm Fri & Sat, 7:30am-9pm Sun) Free wi-fi and comfortable seats make this an ideal spot near downtown to take a load off, caffeinate and catch up on email. The baked goods hit the mark as well, especially the delightfully messy whipped-cream layered chocolate-almond cake. For a bit more sustenance, order simple pasta salads or toast and jam.

Elliot's Martini Bar   COCKTAIL BAR
(☑970-472-9802; www.elliotsmartinibar.com; 234 Linden St; ⊘4:30pm-2am Mon-Sat, from 8pm Sun) When you tire of all the beer, hit Elliot's for an exhaustive list of high-octane cocktails. The 'Elliot's' martini is for classicists, but they also entertain with way-out drinks – all served up in a martini glass, of course – including a tequila-based Smoke Monster and Death in the Afternoon, an homage to Hemingway.

Lucky Joe's   IRISH PUB
(☑970-493-2213; www.luckyjoes.com; 25 Old Town Sq; ⊘noon-2am) Lots of wood and brick and a nightly singer-songwriter make this a warm and welcoming Irish pub in the heart of Old Town. When it snows, warm up with an Irish coffee and enjoy the tunes; in summer, hit the big patio and take in foot traffic on the square.

Mug's Coffee Lounge   CAFE
(☑970-472-6847; www.mugscoffeelounge.com; 261 S College Ave; ⊘6am-9pm) Free wi-fi, strong coffee and good sandwiches keep this central, classy little place bustling throughout the day. Flat-bread sandwiches and other savory snacks are housemade.

Town Pump   DIVE BAR
(☑970-493-4404; 124 N College Ave; ⊘11am-2am) A bona fide dive bar with a century of boozing under its belt, this is a comfortable

place to knock back a couple of cold ones while rubbing elbows with the locals. If you go for the Cherry Bombs, beware: they're soaked in Everclear.

🔒 Shopping

If you're on foot, Old Town Sq has lots of cute little shops for browsing, as does the nearby stretch on N College.

Cupboard   HOMEWARES, GOURMET FOOD
(☑970-493-8585; www.thecupboard.net; 152 S College Ave; ⊘9:30am-8pm Mon-Fri, to 6pm Sat, noon-5pm Sun) This is the biggest kitchen supply store in Northern Colorado and as such is filled with every cooking thingamajig under the sun, plus lots of local sauces and jams. The selection of knives and cookbooks is impressive. They have demos on Saturdays and cooking classes on Wednesday evenings.

Jax Outdoor Gear   SPORTING GOODS
(☑970-221-0544; www.jaxmercantile.com; 1200 N College Ave; ⊘8am-9pm Mon-Fri, to 6pm Sat, 9am-6pm Sun) Half camping outfitter, half army-surplus store, Jax is Fort Collins' most well-rounded outdoor supplier – a place where you can buy a fishing rod, a Patagonia jacket and a gas mask. Its rental department has kayaks, snowshoes, sleds and skis.

White Balcony   HOUSEWARES
(☑970-493-3310; www.whitebalcony.com; 146 S College Ave; ⊘10am-6pm Mon-Wed, to 8pm Thu-Sat, 11am-6pm Sun; 🖶) Knickknacks and offbeat collectibles are given artful attention at this unique downtown shop. It's a great place to get a one-of-a-kind gift; there are purses and housewares, kids' gifts, ladies' accessories and cards with an edgy sensibility.

Wright Life   SPORTING GOODS
(☑970-484-6932; www.wrightlife.com; 200 Linden St; ⊘10am-5pm) All the Frisbees – er... sorry, dude: 'discs' – snowboarding gear, hackie sacks and longboards make this local shop seem like the set of an early Keanu Reeves movie. For those not looking to toss or shred, it has some cool Colorado apparel.

🛈 Information

Fort Collins Convention & Visitors Bureau
(☑970-232-3840; www.visitftcollins.com; 19 Old Town Sq; ⊘8:30am-5pm Mon-Sat; 🖶) Under the green awning in Old Town Sq, this brochure-packed information center has a helpful staff who take plenty of time with their guests. History buffs will want to get a copy of

FORT COLLINS SHOPPING

the center's walking tour, which passes buildings of historical import downtown.

USFS Canyon Lakes District Office & Visitor Center (☎970-295-6710; 2150 Centre Ave Building E; ⊙9am-5pm Mon-Fri) The Canyon Lakes Ranger District offers year-round information, and permits for firewood gathering and grazing. It is the hub for information on four wilderness areas, three national recreation trails, two historic districts and the Cache La Poudre, Colorado's only Wild and Scenic River.

Colorado Welcome Center (☎970-491-4775; www.colorado.com; 3745 E Prospect Rd; ⊙8am-6pm Memorial Day-Labor Day, to 5pm winter; ☎⊛) Just off the highway, this office provides information about the Colorado Front Range.

ℹ Getting There & Away

Fort Collins is 65 miles north of Denver, to the west of the I-25 corridor. Those arriving by car should take the Prospect Rd exit to reach downtown. From Boulder, take US 36 east and follow signs for the Northwest Highway. Fort Collins/Loveland Airport is serviced by **Allegiant Airlines** (☎702-505-8888; www.allegiantair.com) by connections through Denver, Las Vegas and Phoenix. This is the closest airport to Rocky Mountain National Park. You can also get here via Greyhound (p376), which has an unmanned stop at the Downtown Transit Center (p150).

ℹ Getting Around

To & From the Airport

Green Ride Colorado (☎888-472-6656; www.greenrideco.com; 1712 Hastings Dr; DIA to Fort Collins one-way $30, 1½ hours) This van shares services from DIA to Fort Collins, the Front Range and southern Wyoming.

SuperShuttle (☎970-482-0505; www.supershuttle.com; $34 one-way Fort Collins-DIA) From DIA, it's 1½ hours to Fort Collins.

Bicycling

This town ranks among America's most bicycle-friendly cities. There are bike lanes (and bikers!) everywhere. To leave Fort Collins' without cruising between breweries or along the Poudre River Trail would be a shame. Bikes to rent and borrow are everywhere.

Public Transportation

Downtown Transit Center (☎970-221-6620; 250 N Mason St; ⊙7:30am-5:30pm Mon-Fri) With a customer information counter, lockers and bicycle racks, this central bus terminal also serves as Fort Collins' Greyhound stop.

Transfort Bus System (☎970-221-6620; www.fcgov.com/transfort) This is the town's public transportation network.

RED FEATHER LAKES

Red Feather Lakes is a remote, scrappy little town in the pine-dotted hills around the Lone Pine Creek drainage, about 50 miles northwest of Fort Collins. This place doesn't have the stunning beauty of Colorado's other mountain areas and the tourist services seem a bit like something out of a homesteader sequel to *Deliverance*, but secluded fishing lakes, good hiking and a Nordic recreation area are worthy charms, and it's an excellent place to simply get lost for a while. Take US 287 north for 21 miles, turn left (west) at Livermore on Larimer County Rd 74E for 24 miles to **Red Feather Lakes Ranger Station** (☎970-881-2937; 274 Dowdy Lake Rd; ⊙9am-5pm Mon-Fri Memorial Day–Labor Day), operated by the Roosevelt National Forest. In winter contact the USFS in Fort Collins for off-season information. Both offices provide trail maps and information on hiking, biking, cross-country skiing and camping.

About 8 miles from the junction of US 287 and County Rd 74E, on the north side, is the Lone Pine Cherokee Park unit trailhead, offering good single-track mountain biking and equestrian opportunities. It's a pretty trail and mostly moderate, though there are some steep sections and technical areas for bikers.

Pleasant, ambling hikes can be had along the Lone Pine Trail, which passes by North Bald Mountain and ascends Middle Bald Mountain. From the latter you can loop back along a jeep road to come out just west of the trailhead. Maps are available from the USFS. To get to the Lone Pine trailhead, follow 74E west for 6 miles. On the way 74E turns into Red Feather Lakes Rd, then Deadman Rd. If you finish your hike early, you'll catch an even more scenic panorama of the Front Range and the Never Summer Range at Deadman Tower (10,710ft), another 10 miles past the Lone Pine trailhead. Just continue on Deadman Rd to USFS Rd 170, then turn right. The tower is open 8:30am to 4pm.

Nordic ski trails for all abilities offer one-hour to full-day loops at **Beaver Meadows Resort Ranch** (☎970-881-2450; www.beavermeadows.com; 100 Marmot Dr 1; d $79-89, condos $139-169, cabins $109-149; ℗⊛), which is open daily year-round. A ski pass costs $20/25 half-day/full-day for adults and includes use of the ice rink and a snow tubing hill (inner tube provided; other equipment is available for rental). Stables supplement the range of activities available here. This can be an unpretentious place for the family to get away in winter, and the cabins can be very good value. Beaver Meadows Resort Ranch also has lodge rooms, condos and cabins for reasonable rates. Package deals including skiing and meals are also available. To get there from the Red Feather Lakes Ranger Station, take 74E west for about 2 miles and turn right (north) on County Rd 73C (gravel) for 5 miles to Beaver Meadows.

Fishing and lakeside USFS campsites are available for $15 at **Dowdy Lake Campground** (🖱reservation through Reserve America 877-444-6777; www.recreation.gov; Dowdy Lake Rd; campsites $15; ⊘May-Sep; 🐾) and **West Lake Campground** (🖱reservation through Reserve America 877-444-6777; www.recreation .gov; off Co Rd 74E; campsites $15; ⊘May-Sep; 🐾). Both campgrounds are overseen by the Canyon Lakes Ranger District (p150). About 9 miles west along 74E/Deadman Rd, there are sites at the **North Fork Poudre Campground** (🖱970-295-6700; 74E/Deadman Rd; sites $11; ⊘Jun-Nov).

CACHE LA POUDRE RIVER

To cruise along Hwy 15 – from the mouth of the Cache la Poudre (rhymes with 'neuter') River Canyon at Laporte to Walden 92 miles west – is a stunning venture. The ribbon of pavement winds through the foothills along aspen- and pine-edged river in some of Colorado's most scenic country. For those who want to camp without the intense backcountry commitment, the sites along the Cache la Poudre are the best highly accessible camping in the west. It offers stunning wilderness at a low barrier of entry, a place where mule deer, elk and wild trout often outnumber human visitors.

The area is largely designated as a National Heritage Area and the Wild & Scenic Rivers Act protects 75 miles of the Cache la Poudre River from new dams or diversions. Thirty miles of the river meet the highest standards and are designated as 'wild' for being free of dams and diversions and having undisturbed shorelines; the remaining 45-mile protected section is designated 'recreational' – meaning it can be accessed by roads. White-water enthusiasts should check with experienced guide services or the USFS before putting into the river and

finding unrunnable rapids, like the frothing Narrows, or a dam looming up ahead.

The tiny little burg of Rustic, 32 miles west of the US 287–Hwy 14 junction, offers services and decent cabin lodging, but the USFS camping along Hwy 14 is the best lodging in the area by far. You can get information at the **USFS Visitor Center** (🖱970-881-2152; 34500 Poudre Canyon Hwy (Hwy 14); ⊘9am-5pm Mon-Fri May-Sep) just west of Idylwilde, which occupies the handsome Arrowhead Lodge, built in 1935 and listed on the National Register of Historic Places. Of the campgrounds under their jurisdiction, **Big Bend Campground** (🖱office 970-498-2770; Poudre Canyon Hwy; tent sites $12; 🅿🐾) is a favorite, with shady sites within earshot of the rushing water. Another excellent reason to head this way is the **Mishawaka Amphitheatre** (🖱970-316-2001; www.mishawakaconcerts. com; 13714 Poudre Canyon Hwy (Hwy 14); ⊘summer only), a cozy 900-seat venue in the heart of the canyon. It's way out there, but the acts who are drawn to the place – everything from hip-hop acts such as Blackalicious to barefoot jam bands – are usually top notch. The food is pretty damn good too.

Stop at the self-service Cache la Poudre Visitors Information Center, 3 miles west of US 287 on Hwy 14, for information on wildlife viewing and fishing regulations. The Picnic Rock River Access opposite the visitors center offers riverside tables, but there is a $5 parking fee from April 15 to September 15 on account of its popularity as a raft take-out point. Watch for bighorn sheep on the steep slopes along a 35-mile section of the north bank from Mishawaka to Poudre Falls, a series of picturesque roaring cascades. The USFS recently developed a particularly good bighorn sheep viewing site equipped with telescopes and explanatory plaques at Big Bend, 41 miles west of the US 287–Hwy 14 junction.

After Hwy 14 branches away from the river it ascends Cameron Pass (10,276ft), where the stunning 12,485ft Nohku Crags form the northernmost peaks of the Never Summer Range.

GRAND LAKE

POP 450 / ELEV 8437FT

As the western gateway to Rocky Mountain National Park, Grand Lake is a foil to the bustling hub of Estes Park. Sure, both are fairly inglorious tourist traps compared to

TIMBER! BLACK BEETLES, BLUE FUNGI & DEAD BROWN HILLS

Sure, the family of nine camped next door with the barking Labrador is a nuisance, but nothing compared to *Dendroctonus ponderosae*, the seemingly unstoppable mountain pine beetle. About the size of a grain of rice, these little cooties have changed great swaths of the Rocky Mountain's verdant hills into a lifeless expanse of dead timber.

The females lay eggs under the bark of ponderosa, limber and lodgepole pines, which the trees resist with increased resin production. No problem, unless the beetles are dusted with blue stain fungi – a kind of pine tree Kryptonite – which halts the flow of resin and eventually suffocates the tree.

Climate change has only hastened the problem, as beetle larvae thrive during warm wintering conditions. The outlook isn't rosy: without a massive dose of chemicals or a wicked winter cold snap, some experts predict all of Colorado's mature lodgepole pine could be killed within five years.

the magnificent park in their shared backyard, but Grand Lake is more remote, suffers less traffic and exploits its history as an old mining town for the feel of an 'intimate' tourist trap. The namesake lake – with a yacht club founded in 1901 – is handsome, and offers a different suite of recreational thrills in the summer. An amble along the boardwalk lining Grand Ave is pleasant, with a hodgepodge of corny souvenir shops, decent restaurants, T-shirt stores and a few character-filled bars. Unless you're staying for a few days at the sublime Shadowcliff Lodge (p153), Grand Lake is no destination unto itself – it's more of a lunch-and-supplies stop on the way in and out of the west side of the park.

◉ Sights &Activities

Regardless of season, there's no problem keeping busy in Grand Lake; the town's bike and boat rentals give way to sleds and skis as the season changes. Because of its location abutting multiuse federal and state land, Grand Lake is a popular destination for snowmobiles – you can even ride in Rocky Mountain National Park. Get information about rentals and trails at the visitor center.

Several Rocky Mountain National Park trailheads are just outside the town limits, including those to the Tonahutu Creek Trail and the Cascade Falls/North Inlet Trail, both near Shadowcliff Lodge. Entering the park from these trailheads is an excellent way to dodge many of the crowds which plug up the park's eastern side.

The town is 35 miles north of Winter Park, a popular ski destination.

Kauffman House Museum   MUSEUM

(☑Grand Lake Historical Society 970-627-3351; www.kauffmanhouse.org; 407 Pitkin St; entry by donation; ⏱1-5pm Jun-Aug; ⏸) The Ezra Kauffman House is an 1892 log building that operated as a hotel until 1946. Now on the National Register of Historic Places, it contains period furniture, old skis, quilts and other dusty artifacts. Hardly hair-raising, but a nice stop for history buffs.

Grand Lake Metro Recreation District
CYCLING, HIKING

(☑970-627-8328; www.grandlakerecreation.com; 928 Grand Ave, Suite 204; ⏱8am-5pm Mon-Fri; ⏸) With good maps and information about biking and hiking in the Arapaho National Forest, Nordic skiing and golf, this government office serves all-season outdoor recreation information. It can also offer dog owners guidance about getting Fido on the trail.

Beacon Landing Marina   BOAT RENTAL

(☑970-627-3671; www.beaconlanding.us; 1026 County Rd 64; 2hr pontoon rental $75; ⏱10am-6pm Mon-Sat, from noon Sun) This marina on Granby Lake, just south of Grand Lake, can arrange pontoons, speedboats, jet skis and other waterborne machines for rent, and hosts guided fishing expeditions on the lakes.

Grand Lake Nordic Center & Grand Lake Golf Course   NORDIC SKIING, GOLF

(☑970-627-8328; www.grandlakerecreation.com; County Rd 48; skiing per day $12, 9-hole golf $20; ⏸) This facility, just west of town, hosts golf in the summer and a network of trails for skiing when the snow falls. The ski trails cover a range of difficulty, though it's not incredibly scenic – most of the trails are open, along the golf course fairways.

In winter you can also rent gear and go snowtubing. Those who travel with their dog might want to try skiing here too – there's a dedicated dog loop.

Sombrero Ranch HORSEBACK RIDING
(📞970-627-3514; 304 W Portal Rd; rides $50; ⏲rides depart on the hour 8am-4pm Jun-Aug; 🐾) The best ride with this branch of Sombrero Ranch is simply named 'The Ride.' It takes two hours and traverses some lovely Rocky Mountain vistas, fields of wildflowers in the spring and rushing streams.

🛏 Sleeping

[TOP CHOICE] 🌿 **Shadowcliff Lodge & Retreat Center** LODGE $
(📞970-627-9220; www.shadowcliff.org; 405 Summerland Park Rd; dm/d/cabins $23/60/125; ⏲May 25-Sep 30; 🚭@🛜🐾) Overlooking Grand Lake, this ecofriendly mountain resort, in a beautiful setting perched with a view of the lake and mountains, is among the best-value accommodation in Colorado. Rooms and dorms are simple and clean, and guests gather around the fire or grand piano in the book-lined common room downstairs.

Families and larger groups may also want to look into the Shadowcliff cabins, which are along the river. They also host a number of sustainability workshops, and the property abuts hiking trails into Rocky Mountain National Park. Reservations are essential. A two-night minimum stay is required for rooms.

Lemmon Lodge CABINS $$
(📞970-627-3314; www.lemmonlodge.com; 1224 Lake Ave; cabins $90-460; 🏊🐾) Right on the water, these are a collection of privately owned cabins managed by one company. There's a range of prices, but quality varies widely too. This is good for a family or large group; for the best all-around stays rent either cabin 17 or 23.

🍴 Eating & Drinking

[TOP CHOICE] **O-A Bistro** CONTEMPORARY AMERICAN $$
(📞970-627-5080; 928 Grand Ave; prix fixe $25-30; 🍴) Less than 10 tables fit inside this little jewel box, a favorite of Grand Lake's dining scene for made-from-scratch soups and a long, thoughtful wine list. A five- or six-course *prix fixe* is the best dining experience in the area; for lunch they have light snacks and crepes.

Fat Cat Cafe BREAKFAST $
(📞970-627-0900; 916 Grand Ave; mains $5-10; ⏲7am-1pm; 🚭🐾) Consider yourself lucky if you find yourself rolling into Grand Junction half-starving on a Sunday morning. The Fat Cat does its breakfast buffet ($12) and brunch with hearty expertise: biscuits and gravy, bottomless drinks, scrambled 'Scotch eggs' and omelets that come drooping off the plate.

Sagebrush BBQ & Grill BBQ $$
(📞970-627-1404; www.sagebrushbbq.com; 1101 Grand Ave; mains $9-20; ⏲7am-9pm Mon-Thu, to 10pm Fri & Sat; 🐾) Peanut shells litter the floor and bric-a-brac covers the walls of this BBQ joint, a place keenly balancing casual atmosphere with a slightly upscale menu of steak and local game dishes such as wild boar sausage. It's best when simplest though, so go for the burger.

Mountain Food Market SELF-CATERING
(📞970-627-3470; 400 Grand Ave; ⏲9am-7pm Mon-Sat, to 5pm Sun; 🐾) This grocer, right at the entrance to town, is a good place to pick up supplies when heading into the park and the best grocery store in Grand Lake. They have a deli counter for to-go meals and a small supply of basic camping equipment.

Grand Lake Brewing Co BREWPUB
(📞970-627-1711; www.grandlakebrewing.com; 915 Grand Ave; ⏲noon-8pm Sun-Thu, to 9pm Fri & Sat; 🐾) Patrons look over the brewing tanks in this narrow pub, sipping pints of Super Chicken, an ass-kicking barley wine that's a heady 11%. The bar burgers are well built, but the Ruben is a brilliant disaster – stacked tall, loaded with sauerkraut, and served on thick slices of rye (mains $8 to $12).

ℹ Information

The **Grand Lake Visitor Center** (📞800-531-1019, 970-627-3402; www.grandlakechamber.com; cnr West Portal Rd & Hwy 34; ⏲9am-5pm Mon-Sat, 10am-4pm Sun Jun-Aug) is at the junction of US 34 and W Portal Rd but they have another office downtown at 928 Grand Ave (enter from the Garfield Ave side). For information and permits for Rocky Mountain National Park, visit the Kawuneeche Visitor Center (p137), a bit north of town on US 34.

ℹ Getting There & Away

By car, Grand Lake is 102 miles northwest of Denver. Take I-70 west to I-40 exit and continue west over the Berthound Pass, which can be a white-knuckle experience in inclement weather. If you don't have your own wheels, Home James Transportation Services (p160) runs door-to-door shuttles to Denver International Airport ($90, 2½ hours). Reservations are required.

GRANBY

POP 1200 / ELEV 7939

At the junction of US 40 and US 34, Granby isn't so easy on the eyes, but the crossroads service center is a convenient stop for those heading into Rocky Mountain National Park or several other nearby recreation and ski areas. The USFS Sulphur District Ranger Office (☑970-887-4100; 62429 US 40; ⊙8am-5pm Mon-Fri, plus 8am-5pm Sat & Sun summer) for the Arapaho National Forest is at the east end of town and has useful hiking brochures for the Continental Divide National Scenic Trail, the Never Summer Wilderness Area and the Winter Park–Fraser–Tabernash area. It is also the place to get permits for backcountry camping in the Indian Peaks Wilderness.

If the open skies and mountain terrain inspire a yearning for a home on the range, Granby's Drowsy Water Ranch (☑970-725-3456, 800-845-2292; www.drowsywater .com; 1454 County Hwy 219; weekly rates from $1820; ℗🐎) should be on the shortlist. As an all-exclusive experience home cookin', daily guided horseback rides and evening programs are included in the weekly price. Even though it ain't fancy, the Fosha family offer the most genuine dude ranch experience in Colorado. The cabin accommodations are decked out in Western-themed style coziness and it's an ideal space for families looking to escape the urban grind. Hitting the trail on horseback is the main focus; even those with no horse sense will leave with basic riding skills.

If you're just here for a bite, the best place is Ian's Mountain Bakery (☑970-887-1176; www.iansmountainbakery.com; 358 E Agate Ave; mains $5-9; ⊙6:30am-7pm Mon-Fri, to 2pm Sat), where Ian covers the breakfast burrito in a tangy sauce, turns out killer biscuits and gravy and chats up patrons over strong coffee.

Vail, Aspen & Central Mountains

Includes »

WINTER PARK &
FRASER............ 158

ARAPAHOE BASIN
SKI AREA 161

KEYSTONE SKI
RESORT............ 162

COPPER MOUNTAIN
SKI RESORT........ 167

BRECKENRIDGE 169

VAIL............... 180

BEAVER CREEK..... 191

ASPEN............. 194

ALONG HWYS 24
& 85 210

Why Go?

If you ask us where you can find the most trillion-dollar sights, where you can run the gnarliest rivers and charge the sickest runs, and to choose one hike that is sure to save your citified soul within a single afternoon, we would take out the map of Colorado, trim the edges and zoom into the center. Because here's where you'll find more magic per square mile than anywhere else in Colorado (the US, the world, the universe).

It's the stomping ground of war heroes and X Games warriors, and the hideaway of billionaires, ski bums and gonzo fugitives. Celebrified, intellectualized and musical, it's patrolled by bear, fox, elk and eagle, laced by trail, rail and river, and linked by free transport, epic bike paths and more friendly smiles than seems reasonable. But then again, of course these people are smiling. They freaking live here!

Best Places to Eat

» Osaki's (p187)
» Mothers (p219)
» Westside Cafe (p187)
» Pine Creek Cookhouse (p204)
» Syzygy (p204)

Best Places to Stay

» Viceroy (p201)
» Hotel Lenado (p201)
» Barn on the River (p176)
» Vail Plaza Hotel (p185)

When to Go?

Vail

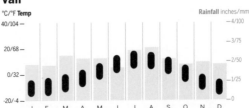

June–August
Long sunny days means biking, hiking, climbing and paddling. And Aspen Music Fest.

September & October The last gasp of high-country camping and terrific lodging deals.

January & February Snow dusted peaks, powdery slopes, *après-ski* parties deluxe.

Vail, Aspen & Central Mountains Highlights

1 Ski or ride the Back Bowls of **Vail Mountain** (p181)

2 Hike to Buckskin Pass in the spectacular **Maroon Bells Wilderness** (p208)

3 Backcountry hike or snowshoe between **10th Mountain Division Huts** (p199)

4 Cross-country ski to the **Pine Creek Cookhouse** (p204)

5 Relax on the Listening Lawn at the **Aspen Music Festival** (p201)

6 Experience the up-and-coming paddler's paradise that is **Buena Vista** (p217)

7 Explore historic **Breckenridge** (p169)

8 Have a drink at Hunter S Thompson's favorite tavern, the **Woody Creek** (p206)

9 Ski the Four Mountains in **Aspen** (p194)

10 Visit the Beach at **Arapahoe Basin** (p161)

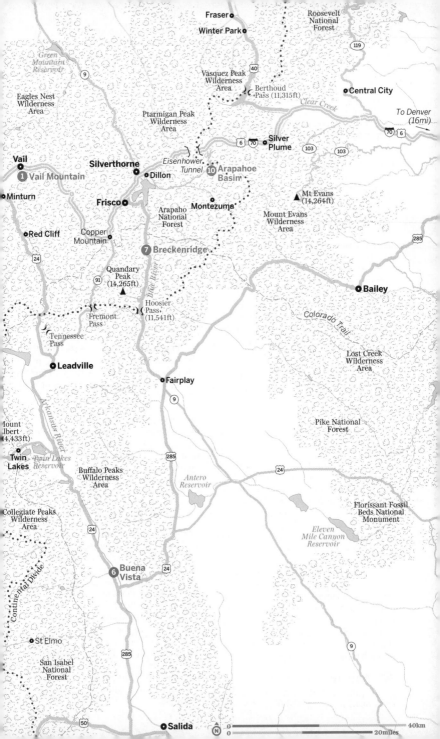

If you've had visions of powder or been eye-balling that luscious snow-dusted Front Range that looms magnificently and just out of reach from the Denver streets, then don't be surprised if you subconsciously swerve onto I-70 west and hit the gas, winding your way to the doorstep of some of the best skiing in the world. For here are seven ski resorts, some sprawling over five mountains and leaking over the top into epic back bowls.

All told there are over a thousand skiable miles, more than a dozen terrain parks, hundreds of ski instructors, infinite *après-ski* cocktails, a sprinkling of gold-mining gravitas, and a few hairy dudes barreling down the slopes in skimpy Onesies. But forget about that for a second, because you are about to embark on the epic winter adventure of your dreams. And by the time you are through skiing, snowboarding, skating, snowmobiling, drinking and dancing your way through this spectacular Front Range, it may well be June. And by then you can ditch the skis for a full-suspension mountain bike. Park the snowmobile and drop into world-class white water. Kick off the snowshoes and lace up the hiking boots. Or you could just keep fly-fishing the trout-heavy rivers and creeks. Sun or snow or both (and there's often both), the fish will be biting.

Winter Park & Fraser

Located less than two hours from Denver, unpretentious Winter Park Resort (p158) is a favorite with Front Rangers who flock here from as far as Colorado Springs to ski fresh tracks each weekend. Beginners can frolic on miles of powdery groomers while experts test their skills on Mary Jane's world-class bumps. The congenial town is a wonderful base for year-round romping. Most services are found either in the ski village, which is actually south of Winter Park proper, or strung along US 40 (the main drag), including the visitor center (p160). Follow Hwy 40 and you'll get to Fraser, then Tabernash and finally Granby. All of these towns are ostensibly part of the Winter Park swirl.

🏃 Activities

It all begins and ends with those five mountains offering epic downhill in the winter,

and sensational mountain biking in the winter. But cross-country (p158) enthusiasts, hikers and equestrians will be kept happy here too.

Winter Park Resort   SKIING/SNOWBOARDING
(☑970-726-5514; www.winterparkresort.com; Hwy 40 & Colorado 81; 2-day lift ticket adult $120-172, child $66-86, rental packages $25.99-49.99, full-day lessons adult/child from $95/135; ⊘lifts 9am-4pm Mon-Fri, from 8:30am Sat & Sun Nov 18-Apr 18; 🖷) South of town, Winter Park Resort covers five mountains and has a maximum vertical drop of more than 2600ft. Experts love it here because more than half of the runs are geared solely for highly skilled skiers. The most hair-raising rides are available off-piste at Vasquez Cirque, but there is plenty of spine-tingling action on Vasquez Ridge and Mary Jane, too.

Good thing roughly one third of the main Winter Park mountain is groomed for greenies. Twenty-five lifts service the more than 3000 skiable acres, which doesn't include the 1212 acres (490 hectares) of backcountry skiing. Winter Park also has six terrain parks geared for all levels. You can learn to ride rails and pipes at Starter and Bouncer, kick it up a notch at Ash Cat, or catch big air in the Rail Yard. The resort-owned ski school offers group lessons and clinics for the little ones and their parents (separately, of course). During the summer there are more than 45 miles of lift-accessible mountain-biking trails connecting to a 600-mile trail system running through the valley. Other fine rides in the area include the Moffat Rd up to Rollins Pass.

Devil's Thumb Ranch
CROSS-COUNTRY SKIING/HORSEBACK RIDING
(☑800-933-4339; www.devilsthumbranch.com; 3530 County Hwy 83; trail passes adult/child & senior $18/8, rental packages $20/10, ice skating $10, horseback riding per person $90-170; 🖷) Located north of Fraser, this ranch offers an abundance of outdoor adventure. In the winter Nordic fiends descend for a scenic 65-mile network of groomed cross-country trails. Lessons and rentals are available, and the ranch offers ice skating, too. In the summer it's all about the horseback riding on 5000 acres of Colorado high country. If you just can't leave, spend a night in one of the cabins (from $165) or the Bunkhouse (from $93).

Grand Adventures

SNOWMOBILING/HORSEBACK RIDING

(☑970-726-9247; www.grandadventures.com; 81699 US Hwy 40; tours $70-210; 🚗) This ubiquitous Winter Park outfitter takes the masses on tours through the nearby Arapaho National Forest on horseback in the summertime and snowmobiles in the winter. Guided tours depart from Winter Park Mountain Lodge.

★ Festivals & Events

FREE **Alpine Art Affair**　ART SHOW
(www.alpineartaffair.com; US Hwy 40 & Fraser Valley Parkway E; ☉late Jul; 🚗) Still rocking after 37 years, this two-day art walk is held in a park in downtown Winter Park, right off the highway. Booths overflow with people, paintings, sculpture, handicrafts and jewelry. You won't be able to miss it.

FREE **King of the Mountains**　CYCLING
(☑970-726-1590; www.epicsingletrack. com; Fraser River Trail; ☉late Aug; 🚗) The finale of the Epic Singletrack Race Series, this was the first and remains the best of a long summer of mountain-bike races.

Fat Tire Classic　CYCLING, HIKING
(www.events.nscd.org; Winter Park Resort; adult/ child $200/25; ☉late Jun; 🚗) Winter Park's first major summer event is the Fat Tire Classic, a pledge-based mountain-biking and hiking event held in late June and benefiting the National Sports Center for the Disabled.

Winter Park Jazz Festival　MUSIC
(☑800-903-7275; www.playwinterpark.com; Hideaway Park; ☉late Jul; 🚗) A two-day jazz festival held in Hideaway Park in downtown Winter Park, which has been known to attract the occasional big name.

🛏 Sleeping

TOP CHOICE **Rocky Mountain Inn & Hostel**
HOSTEL $
(☑970-726-8256, 866-467-8351; www.therocky mountaininn.com; 15 Co Rd 72; dm $25, r $99-119; P🚗❄🛜🚗) Proof that if you are reasonably priced and reasonably cute, you will be popular among the budget traveling set. Add in the warm and welcoming staff, outstanding service and international crowd and handily you have a winner in all categories. Highly recommended.

Outpost Bed & Breakfast Inn　B&B $$
(☑970-726-5346; www.winter-park-colorado -lodging.com; 687 Co Rd 517; r $115-245; P🚗❄🛜🚗) Set on a lovely meadow sur-

rounded by conifers, this is a nice choice for those who appppreciate a simple, cute and quiet B&B. There are seven rooms in all, each with private bathrooms and TV and DVD player. The wide verandah out back has magical views and ample seating, or you can lay back in a hammock and let the stream sing you to sleep. Ski packages are available in the winter.

Zephyr Mountain Lodge　LODGE $$$
(☑866-239-3994; www.winter-park-colorado -lodging.com/hotels/zephyr; 201 Zephyr Way; condos $229-594; P🚗❄@🛜🚗) Privately owned and resort managed, the Zephyr is arguably as luxurious as it gets in Winter Park. This is true ski-in, ski-out lodging with one- to four-bedroom condos perched about 100 steps from the Zephyr Express lift. Each condo has its own full kitchen, and there's also a fitness center and four frothing hot tubs on the property.

Mountainside units overlook the village, while the Divide-side units overlook the looming Continental Divide. Not bad at all.

TimberHouse Ski Lodge　LODGE, HOSTEL $
(☑970-726-5477; www.timberhouseskilodge. com; Winter Park Ski Area; dm $65-73, r $88-121; P🚗❄@🛜) A ski-in, ski-out hostel? Yes, this groovy wooden mountain lodge is set at the base of the ski resort on the Billy Woods Trail. Sleep in a four- or six-person dorm, or grab a private room with shared or private bathroom. Rates include breakfast, dinner, tea and shuttles to the village.

There's always a roaring fire, a frothing hot tub, and something from the Warren Miller collection – including his early work – is usually cued up in the DVD player.

Vintage Resort & Conference Center
HOTEL $$
(☑800-472-7017; www.vintagehotel.com; 100 Winter Park Dr; r & condos $159-396; P🚗❄🛜🚗) The Vintage Resort & Conference Center is right at the base of the mountain and less than a half-mile from the village. Standard rooms are smallish, but have high ceilings, big windows and comfortable decor. The on-site restaurant and bar serves decent food. Service is efficient and very friendly.

✗ Eating & Drinking

There are plenty of options in the village and downtown Winter Park, but some of the best eats can be found as far away as Tabernash and Granby.

TOP CHOICE Tavern at Tabernash

CONTEMPORARY AMERICAN **$$$**

(📞970-726-4430; www.facebook.com/pages/Tabernash-Tavern; 72287 US Hwy 40; mains $17-32; ⏱5-9pm Tue-Sat; 🚫🅿) Arguably the best restaurant in the Winter Park orbit. Set in Tabernash, just north of Fraser, this place is loved for its creativity and use of fresh local ingredients. The menu includes inspired offerings such as barbecued pork chops glazed with house-made peach barbecue sauce and served with grilled Palisades peaches. Tabernash also does a Korean-style rib eye served with house-cured kimchi, and usually there's a special on the menu to keep vegetarian diners happy. Reservations recommended.

Fontenot's Seafood & Grill SEAFOOD **$$$**

(📞970-726-4021; www.fontenotswp.com; 78336 US Hwy 40; mains $19-24; ⏱11am-9pm; 🅿) This place has been bringing New Orleans' tasty brand of seafood love to the Winter Park people for more than 20 years now. It has everything from fried okra and steamed mussels to crawfish and crab cakes – and that's just the starters. Main courses include catfish and shrimp (fried, of course), crawfish etoufee and gumbo – there'll always be gumbo.

Rise & Shine Bakery CAFE FOOD **$**

(📞970-726-5530; 78437 Hwy 40; mains $5-12; ⏱7am-2pm; 🚫🅿) Locals park their dogs out front of this funky cafe, formerly the Base Camp Bakery, then head for delicious breakfast sandwiches, rich, creamy lattes, and healthy bison burgers or veggie sandwiches on home-baked bread. Paintings by resident artists grace the cozy stonewashed interior.

Brickhouse 40 GREEK AMERICAN **$$**

(📞970-887-3505; 318 E Agate Ave; mains $9-23; ⏱11am-2pm & 4-8:30pm Mon-Thu, to 9pm Fri & Sat, from 9am Sun; 🚫🅿) A stylish bistro with a Greek leaning in nearby Granby. It serves pizza, much-loved gyros, rack of lamb, and greek yogurt and donuts for dessert. It's not your typical laid-back Colorado mountain restaurant and you won't find any microbrews on tap, but there's an air of elegance, and some damn good wine in the cellar.

ℹ Information

Winter Park Visitor Center (📞970-726-4118, 800-903-7275; www.winterpark-info.com; 78841 Hwy 40; ⏱8am-5pm Mon-Fri, 9am-5pm Sat & Sun; 🅿) The resort town's terrific visitor center offers useful tips and can arrange room reservations at resorts throughout the Winter Park area, both in town and in the ski village. It's located along Hwy 40.

ℹ Getting There & Around

Greyhound (📞800-231-2222; www.greyhound.com; 78841 US Hwy 40; 🅿) services stop at the visitors center on US 40 in Winter Park.

Home James Transportation Services (📞970-726-5060; www.homejamestransportation.com; adult $60-65/child 12yr & under $52-57; 🅿) offers door-to-door service between Winter Park and Denver International Airport.

The famed Ski Train between Winter Park and Denver no longer operates. After 69 years the Anschutz Co decided to dismantle the rail line and sell the cars to a Canadian line in 2009. And we thought America needed more trains, not less.

But Amtrak (p94) is still rocking. It stops regularly in Fraser at the unmanned depot on the corner of Fraser and Railroad Avenues. Check online for detailed scheduling information.

Free Town Shuttle (The Lift; 📞970-726-4163; www.allwinterpark.com; US Hwy 40; ⏱7:30am-10pm; 🅿) Winter Park's frequent free shuttle carries skiers around Winter Park and Fraser; it runs every 10 to 15 minutes in winter, hourly in summer, and stops completely for a few weeks during spring and fall.

The Moffat Rd & Rollins Pass

In the mid-1860s, JA Rollins established a toll wagon-road over this 11,660ft pass from Nederland and Rollinsville, and early in the 20th century David H Moffat's Denver, Northwestern & Pacific Railway crossed the Continental Divide here. First known as Boulder Pass, then Rollins Pass, it also earned the appellation 'Corona' because railroad workers considered it the crown at the 'top of the world.' Until 1928, when the Moffat Tunnel made the route superfluous, there was a railroad station, hotel, restaurant and workers' quarters on the summit.

At the south end of Winter Park, just beyond the USFS Idlewild Campground, **Moffat Rd** (www.moffatroad.org; ⏱Jun-Oct; 🅿) (also known as Corona Rd, Rollins Rd and USFS Rd 149) to Rollins Pass is a good dirt road usually open by late June. The upper stretches before Rollins Pass are poorly maintained and a high clearance

LOVELAND SKI AREA

Open since 1943 and set against the Continental Divide above the I-70 Eisenhower Tunnel, Colorado's oldest ski resort (☏800-736-3754; www.skiloveland.com; Hwy 6 & Hwy 70; lift tickets adult/child $47/17; ☺lifts 9am-4pm Mon-Fri, from 8:30am Sat, Sun & holidays) is only 56 miles west of Denver. Convenient access to Denver and reasonable lift tickets make Loveland a popular day trip.

Its base elevation is 10,600ft and the summit is 12,280ft. Of the 1570 skiable acres, 41% are intermediate, 46% are advanced (including Patrol Bowl accessible from Lift 9), and the remaining 13% are for beginners.

Loveland has a cozy, unassuming atmosphere that makes for a nice change from some of Colorado's snobbier resorts. The Ski and Ride school serves parents and children.

Access from Denver is via I-70 (exit 216).

vehicle is advisable, though 4WD is not necessary. Before driving it, try to find the self-guided auto tour pamphlet *The Moffat Road*, available for $1 from the chambers of commerce in Winter Park or Fraser. The most interesting roadside attraction is the Loop Trestle and Tunnel 33 at the 11-mile point, where the train, emerging from a tunnel, circled 1.5 miles to gain just 150ft in elevation.

From the parking lot at the summit of the pass, the **High Lonesome Trail II**, a segment of the Continental Divide National Scenic Trail, enters the Indian Peaks Wilderness to the north. Offering superb views of the Divide, the trail drops 2000ft to intersect the 20-mile long High Lonesome Trail in Devil's Thumb Park, which continues north to Junco Lake, Monarch Lake and beyond to Rocky Mountain National Park.

Another hiking possibility is the **Rogers Pass Trail**, which leaves Rollins Pass Rd near the Loop Trestle; its continuation, the James Peak Trail, climbs to 13,294ft and is named for Dr Edwin James, who made the first recorded ascent of Pikes Peak. The total length is 3.5 miles one-way, with the last half-mile largely unmarked.

For maps and guides, go to the USFS Sulphur Ranger District Office in Granby.

Arapahoe Basin Ski Area

Near the Continental Divide where US 6 crosses 11,992ft Loveland Pass, 6 miles east of Keystone Resort and 90 miles west of Denver, Arapahoe Basin (☏970-468-0718, 888-272-7246; www.arapahoebasin.com; lift adult/child/15-19yr/senior $54/29/49/51; ☺9am-4pm Mon-Fri, from 8:30am Sat & Sun),

aka A-Basin, is Colorado's second oldest, and North America's highest, ski area.

☀ Activities

Simple and rugged, this downbeat, stucco ski resort has charm in its 'don't bother me with the glam and glitz, just get me onto the mountain' character. Locals dig it because the lack of lodging and dining options (it's a day-use ski area only) keeps the package tourists away. You come here for powder, and powder alone, as well as Summit County's most extreme skiing.

A-Basin's original lift was a tow rope put together by vets of the Tenth Mountain Division who launched this resort out of spare parts left over from WWII gear, but now you can hop on the high-speed quad, the Black Mountain Express. It will take you up halfway, then take the top lift up to the summit at 13,059ft, where you can ski down front side or carve Montezuma Bowl, its luscious back bowl. In all there are 105 ski trails (accessible from seven lifts) to choose from.

The foot of the mountain, aka the **Beach**, is a major tailgate spot where people come at 6am to stake out their space. Common sights include: men skiing in prom dresses, pole dancing, barbecues heavy with burgers, sausages and ribs, and portable hot tubs. It's a free-for-all and it's almost all first come first serve, except for the first five spots closest to lift. Those are available by reservation.

Two-hour private lessons are just $110. Full-day group lessons for kids are $119 including rental gear and lunch.

✖ Eating & Drinking

Black Mountain Lodge, the complex with all of A-Basin's dining options, runs a Full

VAIL, ASPEN & CENTRAL MOUNTAINS ARAPAHOE BASIN SKI AREA

Moon Snowshoe Dinner Series ($65 to $89), where you can hike beneath the full moon and dine from lavish buffets inspired by the great mountain ranges of the world.

The resort is dormant in the summer, but during the ski season, the Sixt Alley Bar at Black Mountain Lodge is an *après-ski* favorite. The Bloody Marys are legendary.

ℹ Getting There & Around

A-Basin is served by the Summit Stage (p179), Summit County's diesel powered new-world stage coach.

Keystone Ski Resort

In operation since 1970, Keystone is a family-oriented resort on the Snake River 5 miles east of Dillon on US Hwy 6. It attracts downhill and cross-country skiers as early as mid-to-late October, while other ski areas are still waiting for snow. Keystone is definitely a resort in that almost all accommodations, restaurants and services are owned and operated by a single company (um, that would be the eerily ubiquitous Vail Resorts). As a result, while the base area lacks the character and variety of real ski towns such as Breckenridge and Aspen, Keystone has been well planned and it is easy to book reservations and get information. The nicer west village is known as River Run, and though you can access about 100 miles of spectacular bike trails from here, it is a ghost town in late summer. But it is quite picturesque, tucked up against steep pine-draped slopes accessible summer and winter. The east village, Keystone Village, is where you'll find more winter lifts, two golf courses, a medical clinic and plenty of condos for rent.

🎿 Activities

The big draw is the **Keystone Ski Area** (www.keystoneresort.com; lift per adult 13-64yr $63-94, senior 65 & over $53-84, child 5-12yr $44-54, Ski & Ride School adult per day from $109, child from $140; ☺8:30am-4pm Nov 5-Apr 10, to 8pm most days Dec-Mar; ♿) , which climbs from 9280ft to 12,408ft in elevation, and encompasses three mountains or 3148 skiable acres laced with 135 trails, about half of which are expert runs. Beginner runs make up 19% of the trails. The Ski and Ride School is geared for adults and children, and the A51 Terrain Park is decked out with an array of jumps, jibs, rails and a Superpipe.

There's a fun and easy tubing area – perfect for young kids – on Dercum Mountain, and a CAT system that will take the daring above the lifts to the lips of a string of black-diamond bowl runs at the top of the park. It's also the only Summit County resort to offer **night skiing**, which often attracts folk from Breck. The night-skiing schedule varies year to year, but it's on until 8pm most days between December and March.

🛏 Sleeping

At research time Keystone Lodge & Spa was the most happening choice. Technically part of Keystone Village, it's actually set between the two villages, offers hotel-style (rather than privately owned condos) accommodation and makes for a convenient and rather luxe base. Across the river at the foot of the mountain, **Lone Eagle Lodge** (☎970-627-3310; www.loneeaglelodge.com; 712 Grand Ave; d $80-180; P☺✳♿) is a true ski-in, ski-out lodge, with an outdoor fire pit perfect for marshmallow roasting, a downstairs piano bar and exquisite slope-side views. And there are literally dozens more condo options. Check the website or call the main reservations number for details.

🍴 Eating & Drinking

There are more than 30 restaurants sprinkled throughout the two resorts. **Wolf Rock Steakhouse** (☎970-262-2202; www.keystone resort.com; 91 River Run Rd; mains $11-35; ☺4-9pm Mon-Fri, from noon Sat & Sun) has built its reputation on tender grilled meats and in-house microbrews. **Kickapoo Tavern** (☎970-468-0922; www.kickapootavern.com; River Run Village; mains $8.99-19.99; ☺11am-10pm) is your basic, friendly Colorado tavern with veggie, buffalo and beef burgers, brisket sandwiches, rib baskets, wraps and burritos, and it does steaks and chops too. The patio has special mountain views. **Inxpot** (☎970-262-3707; www.inxpot.com; 195 River Run Rd; ☺7am-5pm), a groovy, hippie-run, rock-and-roll coffeehouse, does righteous breakfast sandwiches, jet-fueled coffee, soups and sandwiches for lunch, and beer, wine and bloodies, and it has a booknook too.

Montezuma

POP 70 / ELEV 10,400FT

The old silver mining town of Montezuma, 7 miles east of Keystone on Montezuma Rd, has a few second homes on the slopes and ridgelines but otherwise has little in common with the moneyed neighboring resorts. Folks here post homemade signs asking motorists to slow down, but even at 10mph a visit to Montezuma doesn't take long. Cross-country skiers and mountain bikers will want to explore the nearby trails, especially to the ghost town of Saints John (also a former silver mining village), or up Peru Creek to the huge Pennsylvania Mine, or on to Argentine Pass on the Continental Divide.

South of town, near the Snake River crossing, is the secluded **Western Skies Lodge** (970-468-9445; www.westernskies -keystone-cabins.com; 5040 Montezuma Rd; r from $190; P☺🐾). You can stay in one of three cabins with a kitchen, or one of four doubles in the main lodge. Rates range from $190 to $245 and include breakfast. The Hideaway Cabin – perfect for anniversaries or honeymoons – has an outdoor hot tub on its deck. For lunch and dinner out, most head to Keystone.

Dillon

Similar in nature to Silverthorne, Dillon is essentially a mini-mall town. Where everything, including the town hall is one kind of a drive-in mall or another. Still, the developments here are slightly more upscale and the fact that it lies south of Hwy 70, is shadowed by Buffalo and Red Mountains to the northwest, and is nestled on the shores of Lake Dillon, which itself is backed by jagged, picturesque Peak One, gives the area a bit more grace. One of Summit County's fabulous paved bike paths wraps most of the way around Lake Dillon on its way to Frisco and Breckenridge. You can also take the same trail to Keystone in one direction or all the way to Vail if you're willing.

✻ Activities

It's possible to rent a sail- or powerboat from Dillon's terrific **marina** (970-468-5100; www.dillonmarina.com; 150 Marina Dr; 2-hr rental runabouts $105, 22-25ft pontoons $135-210, 22ft sailboats $110; ☺8:30am-6pm Memorial Day to Sep 27; 🐾; ☐Summit Stage, Lake Dillon Water Taxi). If taking a sailboat, you should plan on shoving off after 11am when aid generally picks up. Pontoons and runabout powerboats are best in the morning before the cold winds blow. There's no kayak rental here as, unlike Frisco, there are no channel islands nearby, but it is possible to

simply hop on a water taxi to Frisco and paddle there.

🛏 Sleeping & Eating

Ptarmigan Lodge   MOTEL $
(970-468-2341, 800-842-5939; www.ptarmi ganlodge.com; 652 Lake Dillon Dr; r from $68; P☺❄🐾; ☐Summit Stage) The only place to stay in Dillon with views of the lake, rooms at the Ptarmigan Lodge all have unbroken views from their doorway. Otherwise it's a fairly plain motel disguised meekly as a lodge. But nondescript can be comforting and the location and price are outstanding.

Dillon Inn   MOTEL $
(970-262-0801; www.dilloninn.com; 708 E Anemone Trail; r $55-125; P☺❄@🐾; ☐Summit Stage) Were it not for it's tremendous orientation to those massive Buffalo and Red Mountains to the west, this stuccoed and boxy inn might not be worth considering. But it does have nice touches such as old wagons on the lawn and plenty of flowers, as well as an indoor pool and deck. Rooms are simple, clean and decent value.

TOP CHOICE **Arapahoe Cafe & Pub**   CAFE FOOD $
(970-468-0873; www.arapahoecafe. com; 626 Lake Dillon Dr; mains $7.95-15.75; ☺7am-2pm & 4-9:30pm, pub open to late; 🐾; ☐Summit Stage) The joint began life in the 1940s as a roadside cafe and motel, and it's still the grooviest place to eat breakfast in Dillon. The breakfasts are filling and original with offerings such as pork tamales and eggs, best enjoyed on the lakeview patio (weather permitting). There's a dark, funky basement pub with ample seating that is a fun diversion after sundown.

Red Mountain Grill   AMERICANA $$
(970-468-1010; www.redmountaingrill.com; 703 E Anemone Trail; mains $9-24; ☺11:30am-11:30pm, kitchen closes 10pm; 🐾; ☐Summit Stage) Another of Colorado's endless line up of grill houses. This one serves Mexican food, po' boys and chicken parma. Steaks and brisket are available after 5pm, and there's a popular Sunday brunch. The interior, with dangling wrought iron chandeliers and massive mountain views through floor-to-ceiling windows, makes for an attractive place to burn some hours. Does a brisk business on football Sundays.

Dillon Dam Brewery   BREWPUB $$
(970-262-7777; www.dambrewery.com; 100 Little Dam Rd; mains $7.95-19.95; ☺11:30am-

VAIL, ASPEN & CENTRAL MOUNTAINS DILLON

11:30pm, kitchen closes 10pm; ☺🕾; 🖵Summit Stage) This brewpub seems to draw the biggest crowds in town. The menu augments typical pub fare with dishes like ruby red trout finished with lemon butter sauce, and ginger glazed and seared 'sashimi grade' ahi. It does weekly live music in the summer and winter, and, of course, beer is the favorite thing.

There's nine kinds of suds, from wheat to a double black to an IPA, and the creators have earned several gold medals from various festivals and associations.

The place is especially busy on game days, when the circle bar, in view of the vats and several flat screens, is packed and patrolled by attentive staff.

☆ Entertainment

Skyline Cinema   CINEMA
(📞970-468-6315; www.storytellertheatres.com; 312 US Hwy 6, Dillon Ridge Rd; adult/child & senior $13.25/10, matinee $7.50/7; ⊘screenings 1-9:30pm; 🕾; 🖵Summit Stage) The only movie house in the area attracts moviegoers from Breck, Frisco, Keystone and Silverthorne for current, first-run Hollywood fare.

❶ Getting There & Away

Dillon is 85 miles west of Denver via I-70 to exit 205, then 1 mile south on US 6. The nearest Greyhound bus stop is in Silverthorne. Summit Stage offers free public transport to and from Dillon to stops throughout Summit County.

Frisco

POP 2790 / ELEV 9097FT

It's almost startling to find such a cute turn-of-the-20th-century mining town, set high in the Rockies, ringed by peaks wooded and bald, and with another vast sculpted range flexing all the way to Breckenridge. It startles not because it's strange to find such a soothing, tempting setting in the central Rockies, but rather because Frisco stands alone, flaunting her 19th-century history, rather than kneeling at the foot of some recently developed ski resort. Yet it's still within 30 minutes of Vail and 10 to 20 minutes of Loveland, Arapahoe Basin, Copper Mountain, Keystone and Breckenridge, and the distance means that lodging and rental gear is cheaper here.

Historic Main St is a six-block stretch where you'll find almost everything you could need. There are cute inns and tasty

dining, and it dead-ends at stunning Lake Dillon where you'll find a small marina (p165). Romantic and welcoming, with ample free parking year round, there are a lot of reasons to fall for Frisco.

◎ Sights & Activities

Frisco is lousy with options in winter or summer. This town is within spitting distance of five top-shelf ski resorts and world-class white water, and it's at the hub of one of Colorado's best bike-path networks. And we haven't even mentioned the sailing. Yes, you can sail here.

FREE Frisco Historic Park & Museum
MUSEUM, PARK
(📞970-668-3428; www.townoffrisco.com/activities/historic-park-museum; cnr 2nd Ave & Main St; ⊘10am-4pm Tue-Sat, 10am-2pm Sun Oct-Apr, 9am-5pm Tue-Sat, 9am-3pm Sun May-Sep; 🅿🕾) Set on the site of the original town saloon in 1889, and later converted into the town's second school in 1901, this museum features a number of historical displays, including one on the Ute nation, a diorama of the original Ten Mile Canyon railroad that fed and connected the mining camps of Leadville and Frisco, and a historic map of Colorado (c 1873). The adjacent leafy park is also worth a wander.

You'll see half a dozen old mining cabins scattered over a rolling lawn. Aficionados of log-construction techniques will appreciate the double-dovetail joints at the Dills Ranch House (c 1890) and the Bailey House (c 1895). Inside the Trappers Cabin, visitors will find the kind of pelts that once sustained the area's meager economy prior to mining. Our favorite was the Frisco Jail, now decked out with local minerals and pottery in glass cases, and vintage mining equipment mounted on the walls.

TOP CHOICE **FREE** Lake Dillon Bike Path
CYCLING
(www.summitcolorado.com/summit-county/ biking; Main St & Summit Blvd; ⊘best May-Oct; 🕾) Frisco is the hub for Summit County's fabulous paved bike paths. From the Frisco Marina you can wrap most of the way around Lake Dillon on its way to Copper Mountain (8 miles) and Keystone (12 miles), pedal around the other side to Breckenridge (10 miles), or branch off, climb the Vail Pass and roll all the way down to Vail Village (14 miles) and beyond. Simply outstanding work. Take a bow, Summit County.

Frisco Nordic Center   CROSS-COUNTRY SKIING

(☑970-668-0866; www.breckenridgenordic.com; 18454 Hwy 9; adult/child $17/12, rental packages $8-17; ⊗9am-4pm Nov-Feb; 🖬) The Frisco Nordic Center offers about 20 miles of set cross-country ski trails on the Dillon Reservoir peninsula east of Frisco. Lessons and rentals are available. The main trailhead and parking is off Hwy 9 about 1 mile east of Frisco, or you can reach the center from the Frisco Marina parking area at the foot of Main St.

Blue River Anglers   FISHING

(☑888-453-9171, 970-668-2583; www.blueriveranglers.com; 281 Main St; day trips $200-355, rods/waders rental per day $25/20; ⊗10am-6pm; 🖬) Set on Main St is Frisco's best fly-fishing guide and rental outfitter, open year round, even when the rivers are ice. It takes anglers to the Blue River for three-hour lessons, five-hour half-day trips and full-day and overnight float trips. It also has evening casting clinics. Take it from the young but wise owner-operator. 'You don't have to cast 80-feet or be chest deep to catch a fish.'

Frisco Marina   WATER SPORTS

(☑970-468-5006; www.windrider.us; Main St W; 2hr rental 1-person kayaks $24, tandem kayaks $32, canoes $32-38, 18-22ft sailboats $95-130, 4-/6-/12-person fishing boats $60/132/142; ⊗8:30am-6pm Memorial Day to Sep 27; 🖬) The small marina at Frisco Bay, a small finger wandering off Lake Dillon, bobs with dozens of sailboats and motorboats available to rent for fishing trips in two- and four-hour intervals. Kayaks and canoes can also be rented, with numerous channel islands looming at the edge of the bay providing much needed shelter for paddlers when winds kick up 2ft swells. It's best to get your paddling in before noon.

Kodi Rafting   WATER SPORTS

(☑970-668-1548; www.whitewatercolorado.com; 503 Main St; day trips $54-160; ⊗summer 7am-8pm, winter 9am-6pm; 🖬) Friendly, honest river talk and vast experience on rafting the local rivers are what you'll find at Kodi Rafting, located in Rivers Clothing Company. Guides will take you down class II, III, and IV runs on the Blue and Arkansas Rivers.

🛏 Sleeping

Although Frisco lacks the selection of other mountain areas, you can often find some incredible deals here, even during the ski season.

TOP CHOICE Hotel Frisco   INN $$

(☑970-668-5009; www.hotelfrisco.com; 308 Main St; r $89-99; 🅿⊖❄@🛜🖬) Very cute, lovingly kept rooms with two-tone paint jobs, moldings and wall-mounted flat-screen TVs. King rooms ($99) are largest and brightest, and some have direct access to the hot tub on the back porch. For $89 you can have a Queen standard, which are slightly smaller but otherwise every bit equal to a King room. It's one of the better value options in this entire ski region.

Frisco Lodge   B&B $

(☑800-279-6000; www.friscolodge.com; 321 Main St; r summer $59-84, winter $118-168; 🅿⊖❄@🛜🖬) Right on the main drag is Frisco's oldest, longest-running hotel. It's been receiving guests since it first opened in 1885 as the area's stagecoach stop. The main lodge is the original log cabin and it also has a 1960s-era shingled annex. All rooms are lovingly detailed with antiques and Victorian-inspired flourishes, such as four-poster beds, moldings and ceiling fans.

The annex rooms are larger and have kitchenettes. It's a B&B so a full breakfast is included. Think waffles, egg casserole, and fresh-baked bread and muffins. Oh, and there's a hot tub too.

🍴 Eating & Drinking

TOP CHOICE Log Cabin   AMERICAN $

(☑970-668-3947; 121 Main St; mains $5.25-12.95; ⊗7am-3pm; ⊖🖬) Every town has one – the unequivocal local champion of all things breakfast. In Frisco, it's Log Cabin. It could be the sassy, no-nonsense servers or the bomb French toast or the gold-medal-worthy huevos rancheros or maybe even the pan-fried Cajun trout and eggs. The point is, joints like this deserve our praise and affection.

Bagali's   ITALIAN $$

(☑970-668-0601; 320 Main St; mains $9-20; ⊗from 11am Mon-Fri, from 9am Sat & Sun; ⊖🖬) This cute main street bistro is one of Frisco's most popular options, serving tasty artisan pizzas and build-your-own pasta dishes where you can have linguini, fettucini or penne smothered with one of eight sauces and paired with one of 10 proteins. You can also order small plates, such as hummus or grilled scallops, as well as salads and subs. On weekends brunch is served from 9am.

Butterhorn Bakery & Cafe
CAFE FOOD **$**

(☎970-668-3997; www.butterhornbakery.com; 408 Main St; mains $6.50-8.95; ⊙7:30am-2:30pm; ☻☗) This fun, bright and funky pastel-brushed diner is always packed for breakfast and lunch. In addition to house-baked breads, bagels and croissants, it does mean breakfasts, salads and a variety of sandwiches, from BLTs to muffalettas to turkey rubens, plus a couple of vegan options.

Himalayan Cuisine
INDIAN, NEPALESE **$$**

(☎970-668-3330; 409 Main St; mains $10.95-15.95; ⊙11am-2:30pm & 5-9:30pm Mon-Sat, 5-9:30pm Sun; ☗) No, the name doesn't leave a lot to the imagination, but so what? Here's a little ray of Himalayan sunshine in the Rockies. The Indian and Nepalese food is authentic and delicious so get your vindaloo, masala or tandoori fix here. Vegetarians will be happy with the selection, too.

Island Grill
BAR

(☎970-668-9999; www.islandgrillfrisco.com; Main St & Summit Blvd; dishes $7-9; ⊙11am-7pm Memorial Day to Labor Day; ☗) Overlooking Frisco Bay, this all-outdoor marina bar has a fantastic rooftop deck and downstairs patio bar. Owners keep it simple here, offering decent grub, but it stakes its reputation on blended island cocktails, New Belgium IPA on tap and reggae on the stereo. It has live music on Friday nights.

Tea Bar
TEA HOUSE

(☎970-668-9291; 409 Main St; ⊙10am-6pm Sun-Tue, to 8:30pm Wed-Sat; ☞☗) This tea bar has a stunning selection of more than 30 varieties of green, black and oolong loose-leaf tea. With wi-fi and plenty of seating – not to mention the adjacent killer bookstore Next Page – you may just want to refill that pot.

🛍 Shopping

Most of the Frisco retail business has an outdoorsy bent, but there is a sensational bookstore that you shouldn't miss.

TOP CHOICE ### Wilderness Sports
SPORTING GOODS

(☎970-668-8804;www.wildernesssports online.com; 400 Main St; ski packages per day from $45, bike rental per day $35-75; ⊙9am-6pm Thu-Tue, to 4pm Wed; ☗) Billed as a wilderness store, this place stocks rental gear such as climbing ropes, backpacks, ice axes and crampons, along with selling some great literature and guidebooks to local mountain trails. But come summertime, it's ostensibly a bike shop with the area's best available mountain-bike rentals. Repairs can be done here too. In the winter it's all about telemark skis and skins.

Next Page Bookstore
BOOKS

(☎970-668-9291; www.nextpagebooks.com; 409 Main St; ⊙10am-6pm Sun-Tue, to 8:30pm Wed-Sat; ☞☗) A terrific bookstore that merges local naturalist literature, hiking guides, maps and childrens books with modern, offbeat and classic fiction. Skinny but deep, it's worth having a good long browse.

Ardent Style
CLOTHING

(☎970-668-0551; www.ardentstyle.com; 416 Main St; ⊙11am-5pm) A surprisingly cute boutique staffed by a sometimes surprisingly surly shopkeeper. It sells everything from Asha sundresses and African dashikis to Sessions snow gear and LIB Tech snowboards, though between October and April the snow gear lives at the upstairs boardshop. You'll find some nice beaded jewelry here, too.

❶ Information

Information Center (☎800-424-1554; www.townoffrrisco.com; 300 Main St; ⊙9am-5pm; @☞☗) Frisco's visitor center is set in the town's original town hall built around 1890 with volunteer labor. It remained the town hall until 1982, but now this is the place to come to stock up on town maps and activities brochures, if that's what you're after. Also offers free internet access on in-house computers, and wi-fi.

❶ Getting There & Around

Frisco has the only **Greyhound** (☎800-231-2222; www.greyhound.com; 1010 Meadow Dr; ☗) bus stop in the area.

Colorado Mountain Express (☎800-525-6363, 970-926-9800; www.ridecme.com; DIA to Frisco $55 one-way; ☗) offers service between Denver International Airport and Summit County.

From Denver, take I-70 west 95 miles to exit 203. Frisco lies just southeast of the interstate on Hwy 9.

Summit Stage operates local buses from 6am to 11pm from the Frisco Transit Center. Free buses leave Copper Mountain, Keystone, Breckenridge and Silverthorne at the top of the hour, and meet in Frisco on the half-hour – give or take five, 10 or 15 minutes.

Lake Dillon Water Taxi (☎970-486-0250; www.dillontaxi.com; Main St & Summit Blvd; adult/child one way $10/8, round trip $18/15, bike surcharge $1; ⊙11am-5pm Mon-Fri, 10am-6pm Sat & Sun) Lake Dillon's ferry service runs between the marinas in Frisco and Dillon. Dogs and bikes welcome.

Copper Mountain Ski Resort

Opened in 1973, this picturesque, self-contained resort town west of Lake Dillon, just off Hwy 70 at exit 195, was the last addition to Summit County ski country. Set high on the eastern slope of Vail Pass and tucked into a bowl, it's surrounded by mountains with long runs carved between evergreen and copious powder in the winter. In summer there's everything from golf to go-karts to cycling, and you can almost always hear that ever-present rush of Copper Creek over the roar of the nearby highway. Almost.

 Activities

Like most of the Summit County resorts, Copper Mountain is all about the outdoors. Activities here range from down-hill skiing and snowboarding to cross-country skiing and snowshoeing in the winter, and hiking and biking in the summer.

Copper Mountain

CYCLING, SNOW SPORTS

(☎Central Reservations 866-841-2481, Copper Ski & Ride School 866-416-9865; www.coppercolorado.com; 209 Ten Mile Cir; 2-day lift tickets $114-164, adult lessons per day from $119, youth lessons from $139, summer lift $10/free with $10 resort purchase, climbing wall $10, mini golf $10; ☺lower lifts 9am-4pm, upper lifts 9am-3:30pm; ♿) It may be too isolated and overly planned for some, but even the staunchest critics wouldn't thumb their noses at the mountain itself. Rising from a base elevation of 9712ft to 12,441ft at the summit, Copper Mountain has 2450 acres of skiable terrain accessed by 22 ski lifts and carved with 126 trails almost equally divided among beginners, intermediate, advanced and expert skiers.

Which means this is the kind of place families would love. The resort's ski and ride school can get adults and kids up to speed and feeling comfortable on the mountain, and Nordic fiends will enjoy the 15 miles of groomed trails snaking through the picturesque White River National Forest. There's also a tubing hill in the East Village. You'd be wise to buy your lift tickets online where you can save up to 20%. During the summer the usual activities are on offer in the village. There's a climbing wall, miniature golf,

and even a go-cart race track (Copper Kart). The American Eagle lift (the only summer lift) leaves you at Solitude Station, where you can have a BBQ lunch and take one of the two nature or hiking trails available The Hallelujah Loop is a short nature trail, or take Andy's Encore to the alpine overlook then continue cross-country through some loose scree fields to Copper Peak (12,441ft), before hiking back down. You can also take the mountain bike up and ride down all day long for $10, or it's free if you've spent $10 or more at the resort that same day. Guest Services will provide the voucher for proof of purchase.

Woodward at Copper

SNOWBOARDING

(☎888-350-1544; www.woodwardatcopper.com; 505 Copper Rd; multiday camps from $949, Drop-In/One Hit Wonder sessions $30/60; ☺hours vary; ♿) If your grommet wants to learn his or her way around a snowboard park – including those gnarly half-pipes and super pipes – you'll send them here, a year-round ski and snowboard training camp. It serves all levels of athlete – beginners to the young and sponsored. Choose from daylong and weeklong camps, One Hit Wonder intro classes or Drop-In sessions.

During the summer it opens the indoor wing to skateboarders, BMXers and inline skaters.

Copper Creek Golf Course

GOLF

(☎reservations 866-286-1663; www.coppercolorado.com; 509 Copper Rd; prices vary; ☺8am-5pm Jun-Oct; ♿) An affordable and scenic 18-holes are yours to play here. Check in at the Athletic Club between the two villages as you enter the resort.

Paddle Boats

WATER SPORTS

(www.coppercolorado.com; Ten Mile Cir; 15-min bumper boat rental $10, 30-min paddle boat rental $10; ☺10am-5pm; ♿) A nice diversion for the little ones on the small manmade lake in Copper's West Village. It has standard plastic paddle boats, as well as more burly bumper boat variations wrapped with an outer tube.

FREE **Burning Stones Outdoor Theater**

CINEMA , LIVE MUSIC

(☎866-841-2481; www.copperchamber.com; Ten Mile Cir; ☺concerts 6-8pm Fri; ♿) The theater would be that Stonehenge-looking building steps from the American Eagle lift, notable because it's the site of free summer concerts on Friday evenings, followed by movies projected onto a big screen. Families love it.

Peak Sports OUTDOORS RENTAL
(☎970-968-2372; www.coppersports.com; 214 Ten Mile Cir; ski & snowboard packages $21-47, 4-hr road-/mountain-bike rental $19/25; ☺8am-6pm winter, 9am-5pm summer; ♠) This highly professional Copper Mountain outfitter is located just steps from the American Eagle lift. Ski and snowboard prices quoted here are walk-in rates; you'll do better if you rent online at www.rentskis.com.

✸ Festivals & Events

FREE Copper Country Arts Festival
MUSIC FESTIVAL
(www.villageatcopper.com/coppercountry; Ten Mile Cir; ☺Labor Day Weekend; ♠) Copper Mountain's much loved country music and arts festival hosts a range of events around the Labor Day weekend, with arts and crafts exhibitions, pony rides for the kids, and lots of country music acts on the line-up, although bluesy interlopers, such as Dr John, have been known to drift in.

🛏 Sleeping

All Copper Mountain lodging comes in condo form and there are three management companies that manage the condo properties: **Copper Mountain Lodging** (☎970-968-2882; www.coppercolorado.com; condos from $115; P⊖✳@⊚✻♠), **Copper Vacations** (☎800-525-3887, 970-968-6840; www.coppervacations.com; condos from $114; P⊖✳@⊚✻) and **Carbonate Lodging** (☎800-526-7737, 970-968-6854; www.carbonate-real-estate.com; condos from $115; P⊖✳@⊚✻♠), and all of the properties are given a Bronze, Silver, Gold or Platinum rating.

The rating system corresponds to price, but also to property management. Bronze and Silvers are the cheapest, and their owners can decorate these condos any way they want, which may be why you're waking up next to a picture of someone's Aunt Edna on the nightstand. A Gold rating means the condos are almost always more standardized with features such as granite counters and wash basins, and flat screens. Gold buildings also have their own pool, hot tub and fitness center. The nicest are the Platinum properties. There are no studios available among them and they can get downright lavish.

If you book through Copper Mountain Lodging, all check-in is at the Athletic Club, which you'll be able to use. It has an indoor lap pool, spa and a larger gym than what you'll find in the Gold buildings.

🍴 Eating & Drinking

Incline Bar & Grill CONTEMPORARY AMERICAN $$$
(☎970-968-0200; www.inclinegrill.com; Copper Mountain Village; mains $17-29; ☺11am-8pm summer, 11am-2:30pm & 5pm-close winter; ♠) Set strategically at the base of Copper Mountain, steps from the American Eagle lift, this bar and grill has a roomy interior, a patio with tables overlooking the slopes, an open-minded and ambitious menu (try the goat cheese and roasted vegetable lasagna or the seared salmon dusted with Indian spices served with a smoked gouda potato cake) and more than a few earthy microbrews on tap.

Endo's Adrenaline Cafe CAFE FOOD $$
(☎970-968-3070; 209 Ten Mile Cir; mains $8-18; ☺10:30am-11pm Mon-Thu, to midnight Fri & Sat; ♠) A laid-back but still hard-rocking place on the main village plaza. It has kayaks dangling from the ceiling, and snowboarding stills and flat-screen TVs decorate the walls. The menu is mostly sandwiches and wraps, but it does have a few departures from the usual fare, such as beef samosas and green bean fries served with mango salsa.

Chubs SANDWICHES $
(☎970-262-2482; www.chubsatcopper.com; 239 Ten Mile Cir; mains $4.50-7; ☺11am-6pm; ⊖♠) Chubs will stuff crepes or baguettes with steak and swiss, chicken and artichoke, BBQ brisket or meatballs. Sweet tooths needn't stress. It blesses crepes with caramel and apple, the almighty chocolate, and lemon and powdered sugar.

McCoy's Mountain Market SELF-CATERING
(☎970-968-2182; Ten Mile Cir; ☺8:30am-8pm Sun-Thu, to 9pm Fri & Sat; ♠) This is the one-stop grocer in the village and an essential resource for self-caterers.

Green Fairy Bar ABSINTHE BAR
(☎970-968-2222; www.greenfairybar.com; Ten Mile Cir; ☺hrs ary) Part absinthe bar, serving the once forbidden anise-flavored spirit that was the tipple of choice in *Moulin Rouge*, part nightclub with guest international DJs, this is where the nocturnal fun takes place in the village.

❶ Getting There & Around

Copper Mountain is 77 miles west of Denver at I-70 exit 195. It's most convenient to drive, but Colorado Mountain Express (p166) offers shuttle service to Summit County's Frisco Transfer

Center, and from there you can hop on the free Summit Stage to Copper Mountain.

Summit Stage (www.summitstage.com; ⊗6-11pm; 🚌) Provides free services throughout Summit County, via the Frisco Transfer Center.

BRECKENRIDGE

POP 3420 / ELEV 9600FT

Set at 9600ft, at the foot of a marvelous range of timberless peaks that dominates the western horizon, is this sweetly surviving gold-mining town and national historic district. Breckenridge exudes down-to-earth grace, and boasts family friendly ski runs that don't disappoint, and always draw a giddy crowd.

Breckenridge's vast, hulking mountains (numbered, not named) rise and fall, and crowd and merge into one another. Smooth and sculpted, they lack the majesty of Aspen's granite knife edge – until you get on top of Peak 8 and find enormous mountains on all sides. Laced with ski runs and stitched together with pine groves, they blaze bright gold in the morning, pink at dusk and fade into a deep shadowy blue as the sky pales then darkens, revealing endless stars best viewed from a frothing hot tub next to the roaring Blue River.

The town of Breckenridge is on the Blue River south of Frisco and the Dillon Reservoir. Farther south, Hwy 9 and the narrow river valley rise to 11,541ft Hoosier Pass, leading to the South Park Basin and its surrounding five 14,000ft peaks. The ski resort is centered around the Breckenridge Village and Beaver Run complexes on Peak 9 south of S Park Ave, and Peak 8, accessed by the gondola off N Park. In total, the ski resort sprawls onto four mountains (Peaks 7 through 10).

History

Like other Central Rockies towns, Breckenridge was blessed twice with sought after natural resources. The first time, the masses came searching for gold buried in the peaks surrounding town. The second time it was for the snow-capped mountains themselves.

It all started upon the discovery of gold in the Pike's Peak area and again in nearby Idaho Springs in 1859. Later that same summer, gold was discovered along the Blue River, the river that bisects present-day Breck. Now, where there's miners there

will be whiskey and the first bar, the Gold Pan Saloon opened on Main St in 1859. It still stands, and is the longest tenured business in town. For the next several decades the town grew, acquired the first post office between the Continental Divide and Salt Lake City, saw the Southern Pacific Railroad arrive in town and nurtured its share of historic characters. Folks like Edwin Carter and Barney Ford, an escaped slave turned pioneer, turned entrepreneur, turned politician.

In 1945, the Country Boy Mine, the last of its breed, closed down and without jobs or industry the population of Breckenridge crashed to just over 300 people in 1960. Then in July, 1961 a permit was granted to build and open a ski resort in the mountains behind Breckenridge. The first lift opened on December 16, 1961, and more than 17,000 skiers visited Peak 8 that first season. Peak 9 opened in 1971 and 10 years later the world's first high-speed quad lift opened on Peak 9.

The resort innovated further in 1984 when it became the first ski resort open to snowboarders. (It even hosted the first Snowboarding World Cup on Peak 10 in 1985.) In 1997 Breckenridge and Keystone Ski Resorts merged with Vail and Beaver Creek to form the present day conglomerate, Vail Resorts.

◉ Sights

Breckenridge's intriguing boomtown history – well preserved by the unsung heroes at the Summit County Historical Society – means there's a lot to see here. Although there are a plenty excuses to duck and dodge the museums, you really shouldn't. They're all well looked after, hugely informative and worth even the briefest wander.

TOP CHOICE / FREE **Barney Ford Museum**

MUSEUM

(✆970-453-5761; www.summithistorical.org/barneyfordhouse.htm; 111 E Washington Ave; suggested donation $5; ⊗11am-4pm Tue-Sun; P🚌) Barney Ford was an escaped slave who became a prominent entrepeneur and Colorado civil-rights pioneer, and made two stops in Breckenridge over the course of his incredibly rich, tragic and triumphant life. The museum is set in his old home, which he built behind the boarding house. It's a can't-miss site.

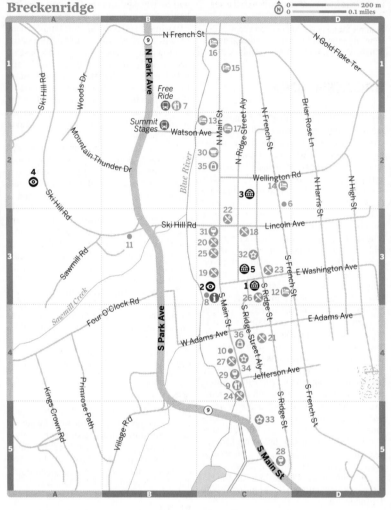

FREE **Edwin Carter Museum** MUSEUM
(☎800-980-1859; www.townofbrecken
ridge.com; 111 N Ridge St; suggested donation
$5; ◷11am-4pm Tue-Sun; Pﬁ) An award-
winning museum that sheds light on a
pioneer lured west by the Pike's Peak Gold
Rush in 1858-9. He reached the Blue River
valley in 1860. An original environmen-
talist he noticed the impact of mining on
wildlife early on, documenting genetic de-
formities (such as two-headed animals) he
suspected were linked to leaching toxins.

He must have seen the handwriting on
the wall because he became a taxidermist
to preserve the wildlife he encountered in
the area. At its height he had a collection
of 3000 pieces, and displayed them in his
house, which is now a museum. The 12ft
ceilings, an anomaly in his day, were there
to display his collection. What you'll see
here is the best of his work. He eventually
became – don't laugh – one of the world's
finest taxidermists and was among the first
to create the facial expression motif. Even
though now it seems strange to kill wildlife
in order to preserve it, at the time it made
sense. This kitschy museum is an interesting browse.

⦿ Sights

1 Barney Ford Museum............................C3
2 Blue River Plaza....................................C3
  Breckenridge Arts District.............(see 5)
3 Edwin Carter Museum.........................C2
4 Lomax Placer Gulch A2
5 Quandary Antiques Cabin &
    Ceramic Studio..................................C3
  Tin Shop ....(see 5)

Activities, Courses & Tours

6 Active Healing.....................................C2
7 Breckenridge Ski Area B1
8 Historic Walking Tours.........................C3
9 Main Street Sports C4
10 Mountain Angler C4
11 Ski Hill Rd B3
  Tibetan Mind & Bodywork ....(see 25)

⦿ Sleeping

12 Abbet Placer Inn C3
13 Barn on the River C2
14 Fireside Inn...C2
15 Great Western Lodging.........................C1
16 Paragon Lodging C1
17 Woodwinds Lodging.............................C2

⦿ Eating

18 Briar Rose..C3

19 Clint's Bakery & Coffee
    House C3
20 Columbine Cafe...................................C3
21 Food Kingdom C4
22 Giampetro..C3
23 Hearthstone...C3
24 Mimi's Fried Pies C4
25 Modis...C3
26 South Ridge Seafood............................C3
27 Wasabi C4

⦿ Drinking

28 Breckenridge Brewery..........................C5
  Downstairs at Eric's ....(see 25)
29 Green Fairy Bar C4
30 Kava Cafe...C2
31 Motherloaded Tavern C3

⦿ Entertainment

32 Backstage Theater...............................C3
33 Cecilia's...C5
34 Three20South C4

⦿ Shopping

  Big Hit..(see 22)
35 Carvers..C2
36 Magical Scraps C4
  Underground ....(see 36)

Quandary Antiques Cabin & Ceramic Studio GALLERY
(☎970-453-2251; www.townofbreckenridge.com; 131 S Ridge St; per person $12; ⊙adults 5-9pm Mon, adults & children 2-6pm Mon & 11am-3pm Sat; P 🛈) Part of the Breckenridge Arts District, this small ceramics studio is set in an old log cabin. It's open to the public three days a week. Out front are a gathering of excellent lodgepole, multi-media totems created by artist Harriet Hoffman and her students.

FREE **Tin Shop** GALLERY
(☎970-453-2251; www.townofbreckenridge.com; 117 E Washington Ave; ⊙studios 2-6pm Thu-Sun; 🛈) Set in a historic home and part of the Breckenridge Arts District, this live-work studio space is offered to working artists to live, work and share their art for a week, two weeks or a month. Resident artists open their studio doors to the public and may sell their work here too.

Breckenridge Arts District GALLERY, STUDIO
(☎970-453-2251; www.townofbreckenridge.com; S Ridge St & E Washington Ave; ⊙hrs ary; 🛈; 🚌Free Ride) A block-long stretch of historic Breckenridge where you'll find the blossoming of a bourgeoning arts scene. There's a live-work art space for visiting artists, a ceramic studio open to the public and a yoga studio. It's not much, but it's a start.

Lomax Placer Gulch MINING
(☎970-453-9022; www.summithistorical.org/Lomax.html; 301 Ski Hill Rd; tours $6; ⊙tours begin 3pm Tue-Sun June 22-Labor Day; P 🛈) Here's a chance to pan for gold, learn how old mining-town chemists assayed the valuable claims and check out the actual sluices and flumes they used, as well as sniff around a miner's cabin, complete with wood-burning stove, musical instruments, snowshoes, pack saddles and anything else they might need to temper boredom and support their survival.

FREE **Blue River Plaza** PLAZA
(201 S Main St; P) A beautifully landscaped riverside plaza with ample seating looking out onto the numbered peaks. There is sculpture, an old 19th century wagon, a small toddler sandbox and a murmuring stretch of the Blue River; the Breckinridge Welcome Center and bike path are just off the plaza. It's a fine place to sip coffee in the sun.

FREE **Rotary Snowplow Park**
HISTORICAL SITE
(www.allsummitcounty.com/attractions/rotary _snowplow_park.php; 189 Boreas Pass Rd; suggested donation $5; noon-4pm Tue-Sun Jun-Sep; P ; Free Ride) Not much of a park but notable for its display of a vintage narrow-gauge rotary plow and the locomotives that powered it up the famed, rugged, gut-wrenching Boreas Pass railroad (that track is one of the last remaining swatches) to keep gold-mining production open. This rail was a lifeline to miners, indie and corporate alike. Kids will dig it here.

🏃 Activities

Thanks to its endless adventure opportunities, Breckenridge is easily the highlight of Summit County. Here's a place where in the late spring you can ski in the morning, paddle white water in the early afternoon and go for a hike or mountain-bike ride at sunset. And if you have one, bring your rod and reel. Even the Blue River, which runs through town, has plenty of trout. Or, maybe you'd rather book a massage while the kids rock the alpine slide.

Snow Sports

When main street is at 9600ft and the peaks are so plentiful the founders went with numbers over names, you know the skiing is going to be absurdly good. In winter, which starts early here, it's all about the snow. **Breckenridge Ski Area** (800-789-7669, 970-453-5000; www.breckenridge. snow.com; 150 Watson Ave; lift ticket adult/child/ senior $63/44/53; lifts 8:30am-4pm, gondola 8am-5pm Nov-April;) spans four mountains (Peaks 7 to 10) serviced by 33 lifts, covers 2358 acres with 155 trails, and features some of the best beginner and intermediate terrain in the state .

The green runs are flatter than most in Colorado, there are killer steeps, chutes and bowls for daredevils, and five terrain parks including two half-pipes. Lift tickets are good at Breckenridge and Keystone, just 13 miles away, and are cheaper than those at Vail and Aspen. You access the mountain from the Breck Connect Gondola, which runs from Breckenridge Station (Watson Ave) to the base of Peak 8. From there you can access the other mountains. Peak 8 is also the only mountain with a lift to the summit at 12,998ft, which also happens to be the highest elevated chairlift in North America. You can also access powder on Peaks 9 and 10, from the Quicksilver lift in the village at the base of Peak 9. During the summer the fun is focused on Peak 8 exclusively.

Main Street Sports SKI RENTAL
(800-228-9136; www.mainstreetsports.com; 401 S Main St; rental packages per day $23-27; 8am-8pm;) A family-owned joint since it opened in 1991, this is a Spyder concept store, which means they rent demo skis, snowboards and sell all the latest Spyder ski apparel too.

Mountain Biking

If you'd rather pedal than ski, take the chairlift to the Vista Haus summit (11,059ft) and cruise (or fly, depending on the run) down one of several designated cycle trails, two of which wander over to Peak 9 where you can access more runs.

Several outfitters in town rent the full-suspension mountain bikes you'll need for this, and they will also be able suggest a few more rides (the kind where you have to work to get downhill), as there are over 200 miles of off-road trails in the Breckenridge area.

The free *Summit County Mountain Bike Guide,* available at bike shops and information offices, offers a decent run-down of the area's more than 200 miles of biking trails, and lists degrees of difficulty.

BRECKENRIDGE TO VAIL

Summit County's tremendous system of paved bike paths connects Breckenridge to the system's hub in Frisco 11 miles away via a smooth rolling trail that parallels the Blue River. From Frisco you can hump the gorgeous Ten-Mile Canyon Trail through auto-free road-bike heaven over Vail Pass to Vail Village and Lionshead, and if you don't want to ride all the way back, hop on the Summit Stage.

Hiking

MOHAWK LAKES TRAIL

The first 1.9 miles from the **trailhead** (Spruce Creek Rd;) is a single track along the creek, then the trail intersects the 4WD fire road at the creek diversion (you'll know it). Follow the road for 300ft and continue on the marked trail into the trees and eventually the high country with amazing views, and a lovely waterfall that's very impressive. Best from June to October.

Deep-green Lower Mohawk is tucked onto a tundra shelf with the ruins of a miner's cabin, and mining works just below. An outstanding, if slightly exposed, campsite is just south of the cabin. Upper Lake views are an even more spectacular moonscape: marbled rocks, stunted trees, inky lake views. That clear buzz is the quiet roar of the cosmos.

QUANDARY PEAK
Known as Colorado's easiest 14-er, Quandary Peak is the state's 15th highest peak at 14,265ft. And calling it the 'easiest' is a bit misleading. The mountain will hurt you, but because the peak is just three painful miles from the trailhead (www.fs.usda.gov; County Rd 851; 🚻), it is the most easily accessed. The best time to hike here is between June and September.

The trail ascends to the west and after about 10 minutes of moderate climbing follow the right fork to a trail junction. Head left, avoiding the road, which looks like a ditch, and almost immediately you'll snatch views of Mt Helen and Quandary peak (though the real summit is still hidden from view).

Just below the timberline you'll meet the trail from Monte Cristo Gulch. Be sure to note which trail is which so you don't take the wrong fork on your way back down. From here it's a steep haul to the top. At one point the trail disappears but keep following the ridgeline, and have no fear: the trail does return. Start early and make sure to come back down from the peak by noon, as lightening is a legitimate threat during the summer. It's a six-mile hike round-trip and will probably take between seven and eight hours. To get here take Colorado 9 to County Rd 850. Make a right and turn right again onto 851. Drive 1.1 miles to the unmarked trailhead. Park parallel on the fire road.

MCCULLOUGH GULCH
Short and only moderately steep (there's only 800ft of elevation gain here), this hike is perfect even for small children. The best time to do it is between June and October. You'll enter the forest from the trailhead almost immediatley and follow meandering streams that turn into thundering falls.

The trail splits below the falls. One branch leads you to a lower falls and the other to a series of about eight cascades, stepping down from a glacial lake, about 1.3 miles from the trailhead (🚻970-878-4039; off County Rd 851; 🚻). You'll notice Quandary Mountain (14,265ft) on the southside of the lake and 13,950ft Pacific Peak to the north. To get here drive 7.5 miles south from Breckenridge on Colorado 9. Turn right onto County Rd 850 and right again on 851. Drive on for two miles and park near the water diversion structures.

Other Activities

TOP CHOICE **Active Healing**   DAY SPA
(🚻970-389-9444; www.activehealing massage.com; 106 N French St, Ste 210-8; massage per hr/90min/2hr $60/90/120; ☺by appointment) The best day spa option in all of Breckenridge, offering Ashiatsu, Swedish and deep tissue massage, as well as neuromuscular therapy. Therapists are top notch, and highly recommended. They are located on the 2nd floor of the Bank of the West building.

Mountain Angler   FISHING
(🚻970-453-4669; www.mountainangler.com; 311 S Main St; guided fishing trips per person from $295; ☺8am-5:30pm; 🚻) Fisherpeople will want to stop into this shop tucked inside a Main St mall. It offers a wide range of outdoor clothing, fishing gear and guided fly-fishing and float trips on the Blue, Eagle, Colorado, Arkansas and Platte Rivers.

Peak 8 Fun Park   AMUSEMENT PARK
(🚻970-453-5000; www.breckenridge.com/peak-8-fun-park.aspx; Peak 8; half-/full-day pass $50/65, maze, climbing wall $8, bungee trampoline $10, mountain-bike park adult/child $30/20, bike rental half-/full day $42/52; ☺8:30am-5pm Jun-Aug; 🚻) Just because the snow melts, it doesn't mean the mountain closes. In summer the Peak 8 Fun Park opens with a laundry list of made-for-thrills activities, including a big-air trampoline, climbing wall, mountain-bike park and the resort's most celebrated warm weather attraction, the SuperSlide. Here you slide down a luge-like course on a sled at exhilarating speeds.

Experienced riders should try the giant slalom track. It has multiple dips built into it, allowing your sled to catch some serious big air and your stomach to seriously drop. The adrenaline rush is well worth the $12 ticket. There's also a mini-golf course and the Mineshift Maze, which is part split-level

BRECKENRIDGE SKI TIPS

Thanks to the easy 'green' runs on Peak 9, the Breckenridge Ski Area has always been known as a great family mountain and a terrific place to learn, but there are adrenaline-addled diversions on the resort's four towering peaks.

To go where the air and the crowds are thin, take the highest elevated chair lift in North America to the top of Peak 8, then hike the rest of the way up to the true summit where, depending upon where you are on the ridge, you'll be looking down onto the mountain's most unforgiving terrain. There's North Bowl, George's Thumb, Whale's Tail and Peak 7 Bowl, and if you're into extreme vertical terrain you can drop into the Lake Chutes. A favorite intermediate or 'blue' run is the Cashier run on Peak 9. Long, mellow and not super-technical it's a place to refine your skills and practice your jib tricks. It's also not a bad spot to make the switch from skis to snowboard. Another great intermediate run on Peak 7 is Wire Patch, featuring a series of 'rollers' – mini-hills, not moguls.

There's a favorite expression around Breck: 'There's no friends on powder days.' You certainly won't catch locals waiting around for their friends when powder blesses the people. They'll be skiing through the forest on the south side of Peak 10 where the tree runs are legendary. Get here by dropping into Trinity, then veer into the trees where the powder is fluffy and abundant.

labyrinth, part jungle gym and is suitable for the kid in all. You can rent mountain bikes at the park too.

FREE **Ski Hill Rd** SCENIC DRIVE
A scenic drive or rewarding ride up a beautiful winding road toward the ski resort. It's lined with condos and cabins for rent through the town's several rental agencies. There's a turnout about halfway up the mountain with outstanding views of Breckenridge and the eastern range. The mountains look pink at dusk.

Tibetan Mind & Bodywork WELLNESS
(☑970-453-2085; www.tibetanbodyworks.com; 2nd fl, 111 S Main St; treatments $65-120, astrology readings $45; ☺by appointment; ⚑) Not your average mountain massage-joint, this healing center was started by Wangkho, a Buddhist monk, born in the Tibetan hamlet of Amdo. In 2000 he walked for 26 days over Himalayan passes out of China, and into exile. He opened his first center in Dharmasala and now offers astrology readings, yoga classes and deep bodywork at his Main St studio.

Arkansas Valley Adventures RAFTING
(AVA, ☑800-370-0581, 877-723-8464; colo-radorafting.net; 40671 Hwy 24; adult $45-209, child $40-189; ☺May-Sep; ⚑) Voted Summit County's best white-water outfitter three straight years, Arkansas Valley Adventures runs the Arkansas, Colorado, Clear Creek and Eagle River, from the first melt into

the late season. They're based out of Buena Vista, a paddler's paradise, but serve all of Summit County.

Stephen C. West Ice Arena ICE SKATING
(☑970-547-9974; 189 Boreas Pass Rd; adult/child $7/5, skate rental $3; ☺hrs vary; ⚑) An attractive lodge-like arena on Boreas Pass houses the town ice rink. It's open for public skating at least four days a week. Hours vary, so it's best to check the website for the latest schedule.

☞ Tours & Courses

Historic Walking Tours HISTORY
(☑970-453-9767; www.breckheritage.com; 203 S Main St; adult/child $10/5; ☺tours 11am Tue-Sun; ⚑) There are 250 historic structures in Breckenridge, an old mining town founded back in 1860, making it one of the oldest surviving cities in the Central Rockies. On the tour, which should be reserved ahead and meets at the Welcome Center (p179) at 11am, you'll visit old mines, miner's cabins, a saloon boarding house and a few museums too.

There's also an eerie Haunted Breck tour on which you'll learn about unexplained stories of bad old Breck.

Breckenridge Ski & Ride School
SNOW SPORTS
(☑888-576-2754; www.breckenridge.com; group lessons half/full day adult $85/120, child per day $150; ☺8am-4:30pm; ⚑) The resort's ski and snowboard school operates out of three

locations. One on Peak 8 and two different locations on Peak 9 (the Village and Beaver Run). Most people learn on Peak 9 because the green runs there are so flat and easy. Group classes are practical and affordable, but you can also book private lessons.

✵ Festivals & Events

Quirky parades, feats of athletic, creative and culinary agility and ingenuity, and plenty of night music, Breckenridge knows how to throw a damn party. And no matter the time of year, there's always something for the whole family.

Ullr Fest   FESTIVAL
(www.gobreck.com; ☉Jan; ⓓ) In early to mid-January, the Ullr Fest celebrates the Norse god of winter, with a wild parade and four-day festival featuring a twisted version of the Dating Game, an ice-skating party and a bonfire.

FREE International Snow Sculpture Championship   SNOW SCULPTURE
(www.gobreck.com; 150 W Adams Ave; ☉mid-Jan–early Feb; ⓓ) The International Snow Sculpture Championship begins in mid-January and lasts for three weeks. It starts with 'Stomping Week,' when the snow blocks are made, proceeds with Sculpting Week, when the sculptures are created and awards are handed out to the winners, and concludes with Viewing Week, when the sculptures decorate the River Walk and are enjoyed and judged by the adoring public.

Sculptors from around the world descend on Breck to work.

Mardi Gras   PARADE
(www.gobreck.com; ball tickets $40) Breck's take on Mardi Gras features a Fat Tuesday parade down Main St, and a Bacchus Ball (New Orleans–style masquerade ball) at the Beaver Run Resort. The celebrations take place in mid-February.

TOP CHOICE FREE Spring Massive   FESTIVAL
(www.breckenridge.com; ⓓ) From 1 to 18 April, Spring Massive offers a range of events. At the Bite of Breckenridge, sample food from the area's restaurants. The Massive Beer Festival includes a free concert and samples from 20 microbrews. The 5 Peaks is the longest ski-mountaineering race in North America. The closing Massive Music Weekend features a free concert by a big-name act.

Breckenridge Music Festival   MUSIC
(☎970-547-3100; www.breckenridgemusicfestival.com; 150 W Adams Ave; ⓓ) Something of a kid sister to the Aspen festival, the Breckenridge Music Institute and National Repertory Orchestra offer both summer and winter seasons of stunning classical music at the Riverwalk Center, a heated amphiteater on the Blue River. There are more than 50 orchestral concerts and chamber recitals each summer, and a half-dozen dates during the shorter winter season.

FREE Fourth of July   CELEBRATION
(www.gobreck.com; ⓓ) Breckenridge throws one hell of a July 4 party. There are free concerts, an art festival, a parade, a reading of George Washington's Declaration of Independence, a 10km trail run and a free concert and fireworks to wrap it all up.

🌿 FREE Breck Bike Week   CYCLING
(www.gobreck.com; ⓓ) Beginning straight after the July 4 weekend with the USA Cycling Mountain Bike Marathon National Championship, this festival on two wheels includes group rides, demo gear displays and mechanic workshops, as well as some bike-in movie nights.

FREE Kingdom Days   HISTORY
(www.gobreck.com; ⓓ) The 'Kingdom of Breckenridge' was declared after it was discovered that the 1300 sq miles surrounding Breckenridge were not yet part of the US. In early August, the No Man's Land Celebration celebrates this 'independence' with gold-panning, woodcarving contests, an outhouse race (someone call Steve-O) and historic walking tours. The festival is held in mid-June.

🛏 Sleeping

One would think that a cute town like this would have an abundance of B&Bs and boutique nests ideal for weekenders, and there are a few (note: we mean that literally). Most of the pillows in Breckenridge are found in condominiums or rental homes, rented by any of the several agencies with offices on Main St. Prices vary throughout the year, peaking during the winter holidays and bottoming out during the October mud season.

But on the whole, Breckenridge is far more affordable than Vail and Aspen, and the best choice for families and budgeteers. And you can often snag some terrific early ski season deals too.

TOP CHOICE Barn on the River
B&B $$

(☎800-795-2975; www.breckenridge-inn.com; 303B N Main St; r $139-159; P♻️❄️📶🐾) This sweet barn has spacious rooms with queen- or king-size beds and antique-style furnishings. Some have soaring beamed-ceilings and private balconies, and all are within earshot of the Blue River, as is the hot tub, which overlooks the river. The owners are special too, with outstanding local trail and restaurant advice, and plenty of reading material in the library.

Abbet Placer Inn
B&B $$

(☎970-453-6489; www.abbettplacer.com; 205 S French St; r Jun-Aug $119-139, Dec-Feb $129-239; P♻️❄️📶🐾) A quiet choice above the main drag, this bright purple B&B offers five large rooms well decked-out with wood furnishings and massive flat-screens. There are big breakfasts in the morning, warm, welcoming hosts, use of a common kitchenette, and a steady stream of happy, though quiet, guests.

The top-floor room has massive views of the peaks from a private terrace, and there's a timber deck and hot tub out back. Well done all round. Check-in is from 4pm to 7pm.

Fireside Inn
B&B, HOSTEL $

(☎970-453-6456; www.firesideinn.com; 114 N French St; dm $28-40, r with shared bath incl breakfast $66, with private bath $88-165; P♻️❄️@📶🐾) One part B&B, one part hostel, this lovely sky-blue home offers three types of room. You can book a bed in a two-bunk-bed dorm (four beds), book out a cozy but private room with one set of bunks and share a bath, or move upstairs and get a large room with lots of light, a queen-size bed and private bath ($88).

All the rooms are charming, comfortable and clean. Your English host is a delight and all but dorm dwellers get breakfast in the morning. With wi-fi, a hot tub and bike storage, this is among the best values within the entire 10 mile loop.

One Ski Hill
LODGE $$$

(☎877-354-6747; www.oneskihillplace.com; 1521 Ski Hill Rd; r $226-382; P♻️❄️@📶♨️🐾) The newest and swankiest lodge on the Breckenridge slopes, this complex of privately owned condos also has a number of luxury guest rooms on offer. All the amenities including a full-service spa are here. It's set right at the base of Peak 8.

Rental Agencies

Great Western Lodging
RENTAL AGENCY $$$

(☎888-333-4535; www.gwlodging.com; 322 N Main St) Arguably the best and most refined of the rental agencies in Breckenridge. It has a portfolio of 150 homes and condos on the west side (read: slope side) of Main St, with an emphasis on ski-in, ski-out and walk-in, walk-out properties.

Woodwinds Lodging
RENTAL AGENCY $$

(☎800-403-6744; www.woodwindsbreck.com; 300 N Main St; P♻️❄️📶♨️🐾) Offers one- to four-bedroom homes and condos in the flats and on the hill (including some ski-in, ski-out spots). Most require a three-night minimum stay. Check in is at the office on N Main St.

Paragon Lodging
RENTAL AGENCY

(☎970-547-2122; www.paragonlodging.com; 319 N Main St) A vacation home and condo rental in the off-season with rates that dip as low as $90 per night. If you have a big group, it's worth checking into.

🍴 Eating

Kitchens here show some ambition, and the choices, although fewer than you'll find in Aspen or Vail, are every bit as compelling – and a touch cheaper, too. Still, not everyone's an Iron Chef, and it was our experience that the more daring the fusion, the less appetizing the dish.

TOP CHOICE Hearthstone
CONTEMPORARY AMERICAN $$$

(☎970-453-1148; www.stormrestaurants.com; 130 S Ridge St; mains $13-38; ⊙4pm-late; 🐾) One of Breck's favorites is set in a restored 1886 Victorian. This beautiful kitchen churns out special dishes such as house-smoked trout, Colorado green beans wrapped in lamb bacon (we didn't even know that existed), baked Brie, and prosciutto wrapped scallops, and those are just the starters. Entrees include ginger scallops, blackberry-glazed, granola-crusted elk steak, and cedar plank salmon.

The three-course tasting menu is a reasonable $25. Dine in the oh-so-burgundy dining room or on the three tiered patios out front if the weather cooperates. Reservations recommended.

Wasabi
JAPANESE $$

(☎970-453-8311; www.wasabi-breckenridge.com; 311 S Main St; dishes $7.50-35.50; ⊙noon-2:30pm Tue-Sat, from 5pm Tue-Sun; ♻️🐾) If you're salivating for something raw on your tongue, this tiny hole-in-the-wall sushi spot will definitely satisfy. The chef keeps it simple and affordable, especially at lunch when he offers teriyaki tofu and chicken bowls for a song ($8); the volcano bowl, piled with spicy tuna or albacore ($11) is the best deal in the house.

South Ridge Seafood   SEAFOOD $$$
(970-547-0063; www.southridgeseafoodgrill.com; 215 S Ridge St; mains $11.95-34.95; 4pm-late;) A Breckenridge version of a classic New England fish house. The goods are flown in daily from Boston. It does New England (of course) clam chowder, peel-and-eat shrimp, a nice house-smoked and grilled red trout, miso-marinated salmon, and steaks and chops. There's a groovy local *après-ski* scene here on powder days. One of the best choices in town.

Clint's Bakery & Coffee House
SANDWICHES $
(970-453-2990; 131 S Main St; sandwiches from $5.95, coffee drinks from $2; 7am-9pm Sun-Thu, to 10pm Fri & Sat;) The coolest coffeeshop in town, where brainy baristas will steam or ice up a chalkboard full of latte and mocha flavors, dozens of loose leaf teas, and the downstairs bagelry stacks burly sandwiches and tasty breakfast bagels with egg and ham, lox, sausage and cheese. And those muffins look damn good too. The bagelry closes up shop at 3pm.

Modis   FUSION $$$
(970-453-4330; www.modisbreck.com; 113 S Main St; mains $17-32; 4-10pm;) A groovy modern mostly-fusion spot on the main drag. It does imaginative dishes (potato chip-crusted halibut) and international ones (pho with shaved rare-beef). It sears Ahi and veal chops too, and cooks up soulful starters such as heirloom tomato salad, and pei mussels with bacon jalapeño, tomato and white wine. Not cheap but loved widely.

Briar Rose   STEAKHOUSE $$$
(970-453-9948; www.briarrosechophouse.com; 109 Lincoln Ave; mains $19-38; 4-9pm Sun-Thu, to 10pm Fri & Sat;) Set in a magnificent saloonlike frame and on the site of Breck's original saloon, it's named after the famed Briar Rose gold mine on Peak 10. And while it's first and foremost a chophouse, small plates (think shishito peppers, chorizo and mussels and escargot) are served in the dining room and saloon. Fine dining doesn't get any more atmospheric in Breckenridge.

Giampetro   ITALIAN, PIZZA $$
(970-453-3838; www.giampetropizza.com; 100 N Main St; mains $9-15; 11am-9:30pm;) Dig into some consistently good, honest and soulful New York–style pizza. It's sold by the slice and pie, along with dishes such as baked ziti with meatballs (among a dozen pasta dishes), submarine sandwiches (good trail grub) and calzones. It's all served in a bright corner room, decorated with those kitschy red-checkered tablecloths.

Columbine Cafe   DINER $
(970-547-4474; 109 S Main St; mains $6-10; 7:30am-2pm;) If you're looking for a more tasteful, flavorful breakfast dive, duck into this cozy stonewall nook. It does eggs Benedict six ways, huevos and Texas-style French toast flavored with vanilla, cinnamon and nutmeg!

Mimi's Fried Pies   PIES $
(970-547-8330; www.mimisfriedpies.com; 411 S Main St; pies $3.95-4.95; 10am-6pm;) These pies are a cross between Aussie meat pies and Southern-style pot pies, but being handheld there's an empanada influence, and they were dreamt up long-ago in Oklahoma by Mimi's grandmother, who most likely had never seen an empanada, so there's that.

Sweet Mimi fills the flakey dough with cherry, apple, chocolate, coconut cream and pecans, but also gets savory with chicken and broccoli, spinach and mushroom, cheese and pepperoni and more.

Food Kingdom   SELF-CATERING
(970-453-2398; 311 S Ridge St; 8am-9pm;) Conveniently set in the center of town, Food Kingdom is the town grocer, and a lifeline for budgeteers and self-caterers. Don't expect miracles, but your staples will be covered.

Drinking
All the Colorado haunts of the moment are well-represented in Breck. Microbrewery? Check. Basement sports bar? Check. Edgy new school pub? Check. Absinthe joint? Check. Kava cafe? Why yes, but that one is an only-in-Breck original.

TOP CHOICE Kava Cafe   CAFE
(970-453-2661; www.kavabreck.com; 209 N Main St; kava $7.50; 8am-5pm;) A hole-in-the-wall and historic log-cabin cafe, the kind of place in which ragged ass miners may have procured dry goods back in the day. These days they make sandwiches

WHAT'S IN A NAME?

Once gold was discovered in the Pike's Peak and Idaho Springs areas in the late 1850s, it didn't take long for prospectors to make their way to the Summit County peaks. The town of Breckenridge was officially founded in November, 1859 by George Spencer as something of a market town and base camp to support and profit off of the efforts of miners in the local mountains.

Spencer originally named the town 'Breckinridge' after the sitting vice president, John C Breckinridge of Kentucky. It was sheer flattery, of course, and, politicians being politicians, he was rewarded with the first post office between the Continental Divide and Salt Lake City, Utah. But when the Civil War broke out in 1861, and the vice president became a brigadier general in the Confederate army, the decidedly pro-Union citizens of Breckinridge decided to change the town's name. An 'i' was changed to an 'e', and became Breckenridge forever after.

and coffee but are notable for their three specialties: fresh-squeezed lemonade, made-to-order miniature donuts and kava. The first two are self-explanatory.

Kava, on the other hand, is a Polynesian root imported from Vanuatu and used ceremonially for centuries among the Polynesian people. Funky, earthy and served to be sipped at room temperature, it offers a euphoric body buzz. Nothing too intense, but absolutely noticeable. Each cup is two servings. Pair it with a riverside hot tub. Niceness!

Motherloaded Tavern   PUB
(☑970-453-2572; 103 S Main St; mains $5.95-15.95; ⊘11:30am-2am) The choice dive in Breckenridge isn't all that divey. Sure it's a bare bones tavern, but it also attracts the local hipsters and anyone else who dreams of a tastier, well-crafted brand of comfort food, best paired with something buzz-inducing: black bean burgers, grilled PB&Js, homemade mac-and-cheese, meatloaf paninis and a menu of martinis, shooters and hot, steaming boozey sips.

Surprisingly, there are no microbrews on tap so it'll have to be a Pabst, Hank. There's live music every Friday and Saturday night, and Trivia Night draws draws a crowd on Tuesday.

Breckenridge Brewery   BREWPUB
(☑970-453-1550; www.breckenridgebrewery.com; 600 S Main St; ⊘11am-1am) With seven malty aromatic brews being cooked up in the kettles directly behind the bar, you know what this is all about. When we visited the flavors included an agave wheat, a vanilla porter and an IPA. Pub grub is served all day and late into the night, but you're here for beer, no?

There are four other Colorado locations, including three in Denver, but this is where their heart is.

Green Fairy Bar   ABSINTHE BAR
(☑970-968-2222; www.greenfairybar.com; 325 S Main St; ⊘7pm-late) A basement bar tucked into the Columbine Square building. It's a simple spot with Spanish tile floors, wood tables and dark-wood bar and it pours absinthe, the once forbidden aperitif. Labels include St George, Leopold Brothers and Kubler.

Downstairs at Eric's   BAR
(☑970-453-1401; www.downstairsaterics.com; 111 S Main St; ⊘11am-midnight; 🖟) Downstairs at Eric's is a Breckenridge institution. Locals flock to this electric basement joint, with a games room full of vintage pinball machines, for the pitchers, juicy burgers and delicious mashed potatos (mains from $6). There are more than 120 beers, including several microbrews, to choose from.

☆ Entertainment

Breck is nobody's nightclub mecca, and most of the carousing happens in the bars and at house parties, but frequent festivals keep the Breckenridge events calendar filled with live music indoors and out, and in between you can get your fix of set piece entertainment – including some terrific theater at these stalwarts.

TOP CHOICE **Three20South**   LIVE MUSIC, NIGHTCLUB
(☑970-547-5320; www.three20south.com; 320 S Main St; cover varies; ⊘most nights 9pm-late) Breckenridge's only 'true' nightclub brings live music to the people most nights. The taste is wide and deep, ranging from blue grass to jazz to funk to rock 'n' roll. It's mostly indie acts here, but some bigger names, like Citizen Cope and Par-

ticle, do drift in from time to time. Check the website for upcoming showtimes and prices.

Cecilia's   NIGHTCLUB

(☑970-453-2243; www.cecilias.tv; 520 S Main St; ☺2pm-2am) Ski bums love to rag on Cecilia's, but that doesn't stop them from flocking to this long-established party spot nightly. There's a large dancefloor with mostly DJ-spun grooves (and occasional live acts), lots of martini choices, pool tables and even a corner couch for some quiet kissing.

Backstage Theater   THEATRE

(☑970-453-0199; www.backstagetheatre.org; 121 S Ridge St; most shows $12-18; ☺hrs vary; ☉) This is a vibrant, long-running theatre bringing edgy and entertaining fare to the people, staging new and classic shows. It has produced over 200 plays over the years and offer acting workshops too. Take a peek at the on-line calendar to see what's on.

🛍 Shopping

TOP CHOICE **Magical Scraps** CLOTHING & ACCESSORIES

(☑970-453-6023; www.magicalscraps. com; 310 S Main St; ☺10am-9pm Nov-Sep, 11am-6pm Oct; ☉) The girliest shop in Breck, and we mean that in the best way possible. Here are printed fabrics, stuffed toys, tot-sized tees, and dresses and hats for mom and baby. Not to mention funky handbags, scarves and skirts, and luscious handmade soap. All of it set in a sweet Victorian.

Carvers   BIKE, SKI RENTAL

(☑970-453-0132; www.carverskishop.com; 203 N Main St; rental packages child $15, adult $22-37, boards $19-37, bikes per day $21-38; ☺9am-6pm; ☉; ☐Free Ride) A terrific indie bike and ski shop. It has a bit of everything including high-end bikes, boards, skis, boots, camelbacks and disc golf sets (not joking). It does overnight repairs, is just a short walk from the gondola, and offers a better selection than the big conglomerates.

Underground   SPORTING GOODS

(☑970-453-7400; www.undergroundsnowboards. com; 320 S Main St; ☺10am-8pm; ☉; ☐Free Ride) The hippest mountain gear in Breck is found at this apparel and board shop. It sells Burton and Volcom clothing, and Analog and Anon googles, as well as some sick boards, but it doesn't do rentals.

Big Hit   SPORTING GOODS

(☑970-453-1109; www.bighitsnowboards.com; 100 N Main St; ☺11am-8pm Jun-Aug, 10am-9pm Dec-Mar; ☉; ☐Free Ride) Laid-back, knowledgeable and owner-operated, Big Hit has all the big names here (Academy, Society, Nitro and Technine boards, Ride boots and bindings, Red helmets) and it sells skateboards too.

ℹ️ Information

365 Things to Do in Breckenridge (www.365breckenridge.com) A new favorite among locals and tourists alike, this Facebook page offers something new to do in and around town every day of the Breck year. Easily the most creative of the pretrip sites listed here.

Breckenridge Medical Center (☑970-453-1010; www.centura.org; 555 Park Plaza ll; ☺24hr; ☉) A ski village-based urgent care clinic.

Breckenridge Welcome Center (☑970-453-9767; www.gobreck.com; 309 S Main St; ☺10am-6pm; ☉) Along with a host of maps and brochures, this center has a fantastic riverside museum that delves into Breck's gold-mining past. There are antique stoves, phones and furnishings, displays on the danger and ecological consequences of the mining years, and rail route displays of the torturous Boreas Pass (11,481ft), as well as a glimpse into the 1960s ski boom.

Town of Breckenridge (www.townofbreckenridge.com; @) The city's main website is pretty wonky but it does publicize local events and inititatives, area recreation and the arts, and has some helpful maps, and easy links to www.gobreck.com, the main tourism website.

ℹ️ Getting There & Away

Breckenridge is 104 miles west of Denver via I-70 exit 203, then Hwy 9 south. **Colorado Mountain Express** (☑800-525-6363, 970-754-7433; www.ridecme.com; per person $79; ☺by reservation; ☉) offers the best shuttle service to Denver International Airport.

ℹ️ Getting Around

Free Ride (Summit County Public Transport; ☑970-547-3140; www.townofbreckenridge. com; ☉) For free transport within the city limits, hop one of the Free Ride buses that patrol the Breckenridge streets, from the Peak 7 terminal to the Ice Arena to the Wellington neighborhood.

Summit Stages (☑970-668-0999; www.summitstage.com; 150 Watson Ave; ☺6:25am-1:45am; ☉) To get between Breckenridge, Keystone and Vail, hop on a free Summit Stages bus, which run all day.

VAIL

POP 4768 / ELEV 8120FT

Blessed with peaks, laced with streets and plazas, touched by summer sun and fresh powder, carved by rivers and groomed with golf courses, ski terrain and bike trails, Vail is the ultimate Colorado playground.

The real draw has always been Vail Mountain, a hulking domed mass of snowy joy that offers 1000 acres of downhill slopes on the north face, and 4000 acres of back-bowl bliss – all of which overlooks a serrated blade of mountains to the south. And it's those endless, naturally sculpted back bowls that have made this resort beloved and famous, and the largest of its kind in the US. Factor in Vail's brick streets, gushing fountains, blue skies, lodge-like rooms, well-coiffed clientele and pretty young powder-fuelled staff and you have an adrenalin-addled, yuppie utopia. Indeed, stress does not cling to the bones long here...until you get the bill. And even then you'll have had such a time hiking, biking, rafting and horseback riding, or skiing, snowboarding, snowshoeing and fishing that the memories will last far longer than the icy splash of buyer remorse. Just remember going in that this is Colorado's most expensive ski resort.

Orientation

Vail Village, on the south side of I-70 at exit 176, and Lionshead, a half-mile west of the village, are the two principal centers of activity. Motorists must leave their cars at the public parking garages before entering the pedestrian-mall areas of lodges, restaurants and shops at the base of the chairlifts. At the extreme ends of the Gore Valley are East Vail, an exclusive residential zone beyond the Vail Golf Course (p183) and I-70 exit 180, and West Vail at I-70 exit 173, where most highway-oriented services are located. Farther west at I-70 exit 171, US 24 climbs south past Minturn toward Leadville.

◎ Sights

FREE **Colorado Ski Museum** MUSEUM
(📞970-476-1876; www.skimuseum.net; 231 S Frontage Rd E; admission free; ☺10am-6pm; 🚻) This humble but surprisingly informative museum takes you from the invention of skiing in the Norwegian military in 1767 to the Colorado ski pioneers who, in 1887, rode 10ft to 14ft wood-skis they made themselves. You can see these vintage skis and boots (and snowboards for that matter) among the well-curated exhibits.

There's a room dedicated to the Tenth Mountain Division, a high alpine WWII unit who trained in these mountains, as well as the fledgling Colorado Ski and Snowboard Hall of Fame.

🏃 Activities

The draw to Vail is no secret. It looms like a benevolent force, leading you in with wide eyes and goofy smiles as you approach from the east or west. It's the mountain, stupid. And this mountain is the biggest resort in North America, with over 5000 total acres of terrain and four base areas running from east to west. What that means for you is epic skiing and boarding, and terrific snowshoeing and cross-country skiing too. There are also three ice rinks in the area – if you count Beaver Creek (p192), and tremendous year-round fishing. When the snow melts and the sun shines there's more adventure on tap. Hiking, mountain- and road-biking and paddling are all top-shelf in Vail. And at any time of year there are plenty of family-oriented activities on Eagles Nest. In other words, if you get bored here, it's your own damn fault.

BACKCOUNTRY WILDERNESS

If it's wilderness you crave, check with the **USFS Holy Cross Ranger Station** (📞970-827-5715; www.fs.usda.gov; 24747 US Hwy 24; ☺9am-5pm; 🚻), I-70 exit 171 at US 24, for information on nearby backcountry trails including Shrine Pass, but be aware that many of the non-wilderness routes are infested with noisy snowmobiles. The 10th Mountain Division Hut System (p199) offers a system of trails almost 300 miles long connecting 14 overnight cabins, with reservations available through a lottery system and best organized well in advance. Paragon Guides (p182) uses these huts between Vail and Aspen for guided three- to six-day trips for all abilities. Guides provide instruction in telemark, backcountry skiing and winter-mountaineering skills.

The central point of all mountain adventure is Eagle's Nest (Adventure Ridge; ☑970-476-9090; www.vail.com; Lionshead Pl; gondola per day, per person $22; ☺10am-4pm Sun-Wed, 10am to 9pm Thu-Sat; ♿; ☐Vail Transit). Obviously it's all about powder in the peak season, but that can mean snowshoeing, snow-biking, snowmobiling and tubing, as well as skiing and boarding. In summer there are dozens of hikes and mountain-bike trails (bikes ride on the gondola for a small fee), as well as a bungee trampoline, climbing wall and Frisbee golf.

It's the gateway to 5000 acres of winter terrain and 1000 acres of summer mountain-bike madness. But in every season it's a wonderful, family-friendly scene.

Vail Mountain   SNOW SPORTS
(☑970-476-9090; www.vail.com; lift ticket adult/child $99/46; ☺9am-4pm, extended hrs in season; ♿) Vail Mountain is our favorite in the state, with 5289 skiable acres, 193 trails, three terrain parks and the highest lift-ticket prices in the country (OK, so they only out-price Aspen by $1, but still...). If you're a Colorado ski virgin, it's worth paying the extra buck to pop your cherry here. Especially on a sunny, blue, fresh-powder day.

If you're low on coin check the parking lots to see if anyone needs a buddy to split their 2-for-1 lift ticket coupon before paying top dollar at the ticket window. You can also try City Market grocery stores, which often sell reduced-price tickets. Experts will go gaga over Vail's shoots, tree glades and four wide-open, powdery fresh back bowls. The mountaintop Adventure Ridge has child-friendly winter and summer sports including the coming, if absurdist, sport of Frisbee golf, an increasingly common summer pastime. Must have something to do with that new medical marijuana law. Yeah, that's gotta be it.

Alpine Quest Sports   KAYAKING
(☑970-926-3867; www.alpinequestsports.com; 34510 US Hwy 6; kayak classes $169-275; ☺9am-6pm; ♿) This is Vail's top backcountry adventure kayaking resource with gear, rentals and a full kayak school with beginner, intermediate and advanced classes. It also outfits rock and ice climbers with gear and tips, and is the top telemark-skiing outfitter in the area. If you're a hardcore outdoors person, you will feel a certain kinship here.

TOP CHOICE ▸ FREE **Vail to Breckenridge Bike Path**   CYCLING
(www.vail.com; ☺24hr; ♿) From the West Vail Market you can ride along N Frontage Rd, crossing I-70 at the pedestrian overpass to Lionshead. On the south side of the freeway, a paved bike route extends from W Gore Creek Dr through Cascade Village, Lionshead and Vail Village and continues east on the 10-Mile Canyon Trail through auto-free road-bike heaven over Vail Pass to Frisco.

From the road closure at the east end of Bighorn Rd, 6 miles from Vail Village, it's an 8-mile climb to Vail Pass; there you can turn back or continue 11 miles to Frisco, the hub of Summit County bike trails and the gateway to Breckenridge.

Eagle Bahn Gondola   GONDOLA
(☑970-476-9090; www.vail.com; Lionshead Plaza; per person $22; ☺8am-5pm winter, 9am-6pm summer; ♿) A stunning gondola ride from Lionshead Plaza to Eagle's Nest (aka Adventure Ridge) on the rim of Vail Mountain is an attraction in itself. From here you can access Vail's famed back bowls and enjoy massive mountain and valley views in all directions.

Bearcat Stables   HORSEBACK RIDING
(☑970-926-1578; www.bearcatstables.com; 2701 Squaw Creek Rd; horse rides $50-200; ☺by reservation; ♿) One of the best horseback operations in the Vail Valley, it does one- and two-hour rides, as well as six-hour back-country rides, overnight rides to Aspen and horsedrawn sleigh rides in winter. Trips are always fairly intimate with an eight-person maximum.

Zip Adventures   ZIPLINING
(☑970-926-9470; www.zipadventures.com; 4098 Hwy 131; per person $125; ♿) Here's your chance to fly over a rugged canyon at well over 30mph, 200ft above a gushing creek. With six ziplines set up over Alkali Canyon and distances ranging from 150ft to 1000ft long, you'll get plenty of time to work on your primal scream. Easy and exhilarating, the two-hour romp is worth the splurge.

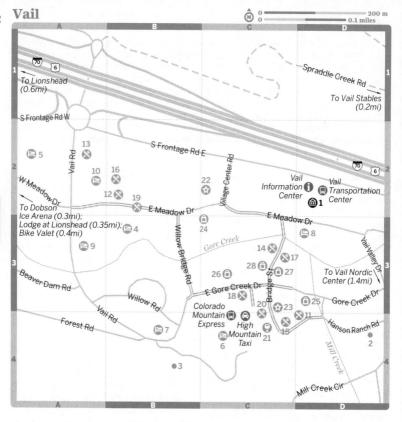

Paragon Guides SNOW SPORTS
(970-926-5299; www.paragonguides.com; Cresta Rd; trips per person from $998;) Guides provide instruction in telemark, backcountry skiing and winter-mountaineering skills.

Cordillera Club SKIING, OUTDOORS ACTIVITIES
(970-569-6480; www.cordillera-vail.com; 2205 Cordillera Way; trail access $5, ski rentals per day $20; 9am-4pm) This club and Nordic center, attached to the lodge of the same name, is set at the western mouth of the Vail Valley near Edwards. It offers 11 miles of terrific cross-country skiing terrain in the winter, and mountain biking, hiking and fly-fishing in the summer.

FREE **Booth Falls & Booth Lake Trail**
HIKING
(www.trails.com; Booth Falls Rd;) A two-mile hike to the 60ft Booth Falls follows USFS Trail 1885 into the Eagles Nest Wilderness Area. The trailhead is off N Frontage Rd west of I-70 exit 180. Continue beyond the falls to encounter meadows filled with wildflowers and views of the Gore Range. The trail continues to Booth Lake, 6 miles from the trailhead, and climbs about 3000ft. Best between June and October.

Vail Valley Paragliding PARAGLIDING
(970-390-8130; www.vailvalleyparagliding. com; per person cash/credit card $150/175;) Here's your chance to fly high above the Rocky Mountain. Join one of these tandem flights – launch in the morning and occasionally in the afternoon. You'll lift off at 8700ft and if the winds are cooperative, you might fly as high as 14,000ft. Duration varies, but an hour is common. Flights depart from diferent locations: check the website for details. Dress warmly. It gets cold in heaven.

◉ Sights
1 Colorado Ski Museum..........................D2

Activities, Courses & Tours
Christy Sports..............................(see 20)
2 Troy's Ski Shop.....................................D4
3 Vail Sports...B4

◎ Sleeping
4 Austria Haus B3
5 Four Seasons A2
6 Lodge at Vail C4
7 Lodge Tower...B4
8 Mountain Haus.....................................D3
9 Sonnenalp Resort A3
10 Vail Plaza Hotel...................................A2

◉ Eating
11 Big Bear Bistro.....................................D4
12 Campo de Fiori.....................................B2
13 Kelly Liken A2
14 Loaded Joe's C3

15 Los Amigos C4
16 Osaki's..B2
17 Russell's...C3
18 Sweet Basil C3
19 Vail Farmers Market B2
20 Vendetta's...C4

◉ Drinking
21 Tap Room C4

◉ Entertainment
22 Böl C2
Cinebistro ....(see 22)
Samana Lounge ....(see 17)
23 The Club..C3

◉ Shopping
24 Bag and Pack..C3
25 Buzz's Ski Shop....................................D3
26 Gore Creek Fly Fishermen....................C3
27 Kemo Sabe C3
28 Pepi Sports C3

VAIL ACTIVITIES

Vail Golf Club   GOLF
(☏970-479-2260; www.vailrec.com/golf.cfm; 1778 Vail Valley Dr; 9-/18-holes $40/75 Jun-Sep; ⌖; ⌂Vail Transit) Hemmed in by Gore Creek and tucked up against the White River National Forest, this 18-hole par 71 course nestled in at 8200ft elevation is a fine place to hit a small white ball, then go hunting for it. Reservations are vital in summer and can be made 60 days in advance. It's partly or fully closed for rehabilitation in the fall.

The pro shop can set you up with rentals, lessons and a cart.

Vail Stables   HORSEBACK RIDING
(☏970-476-6941; www.vailstables.com; Spraddle Creek Rd; horse rides $60-120; ⊙May-Sep; ⌖) A family-run stable highly recommended by Vail locals. It offers horse-riding classes and camps for kids, and one- to three-hour rides in the Gore Range. Kids as young as six can ride their own horse.

Dobson Ice Arena   ICE SKATING
(☏970-479-2271; www.vailrec.com/icearena.cfm; 321 E Lionshead Circle; adult/toddler/child $6/2/5, skates rental $3; ⊙6am-midnight; ⌖; ⌂Vail Transit) Located at the entrance to the Lionshead ski resort, this aging yet more than adequate rink is where local freestylers, aspiring competitive ice dancers, and bruising pick-up hockey jocks come for a good skate. The rink is available for time-block rental and hours are set aside for public skating, along with classes and organized activities and events for all ages.

Visit the website, grab a schedule at the door, or call for details.

Vail Nature Center   HIKING
(☏970-479-2291; www.vailrec.com/hikingprogram.cfm; 841 Vail Valley Dr; half-/full-day hikes $30/40, overnight hikes $180-200; ⊙Jun-Sep; ⌖; ⌂Vail Transit) Register ahead for guided naturalist hikes that run on Tuesday and Thursday at the Vail Nature Center. The hikes are led at a moderate pace and open to all. For a short stroll, the four trails at the Nature Center offer excellent interpretive displays on the plants and wildlife along Gore Creek and can be done in under an hour.

Lakota Guides   RAFTING
(☏970-845-7238; www.lakotaguides.com; 429 Edwards Access Rd, Edwards; river trips $79.50-168; ⊙May-Sep; ⌖) Lakota Guides is another river outfitter with a good reputation serving Vail and Beaver Creek. Lakota can get you on all the nearby rivers – the Eagle, Arkansas and Colorado – and it offers off-road trips in high-alpine country too. It's based just outside of Vail proper in Avon.

Lessons & Equipment Rental

Along with the places set up specifically for gear hire, many of the retailers in town also have hire options.

Troy's Ski Shop
BIKE & OUTDOORS RENTAL

(☑970-476-8769; www.troysskishop.com; 392 Hanson Ranch Rd; ski hire/bike hire per day from $28/$50; ☺9am-5pm; 🚻; ☐Vail Transit) Troy's specializes in two things. It rents high-end, full-suspension mountain bikes in summer, and hires out the best skis on the mountain in winter, both of which can be used to explore the 5000 acres of frontside and back-bowl country that makes the Vail resort great. This shop is independently owned, has friendly staff, and it's been around awhile.

With tips from Troy's you can ski at Vail for a week and never hit the same trail twice. Note: Troy's doesn't rent snowboards.

Christy Sports
BIKE & OUTDOORS RENTAL

(☑970-476-2244; www.christysports.com; 293 Bridge St; front suspension bikes half-day $40, ski & snowboard gear packages per day from $28.76; ☺10am-5pm summer, 8am-6pm Nov-Dec 10, 8am-8pm Dec 11-Apr; 🚻) Another Colorado ski-mountain staple. You'll see Christy at almost every resort in the state, and with good reason – it's been at the gear game since 1958. Prices vary with quality (though it does offer demo packages for gear heads). The best deals are always found online and booked in advance, but they take their share of walk-ins too.

Vail Nordic Center
SNOW SPORTS

(☑970-476-8366; www.vailnordiccenter.com; 1778 Vail Valley Dr; lessons per hour $35-55, rental packages per day $8-22; ☺9am-5pm; 🚻) Vail's top cross-country skiing resource offers lessons and gear rental for aspiring nordic skiers. You can also rent snow shoes. Lessons and ski packages do not include the $8 day-use fee compulsory for cross-country trails. Ask about backcountry trails too.

Bike Valet
BIKE & OUTDOORS RENTAL

(Ski Valet; ☑970-476-5385; www.bikevalet.net; 520 E Lionshead Cir; bike hire per day from $29-65, tours $30-75; ☺10am-5pm; 🚻; ☐Vail Transit) Based in Lionshead. In winter it's run as Ski Valet and offers some of the best discount ski rentals on the mountain, and an overnight repair service. But in the summer, it's known as Bike Valet, one of two independently owned bike shops in Lionshead. Rent path bikes, road bikes, electric bikes, as well as full-suspension mountain bikes for the hardcore.

Owner-operated, Bike Valet will gladly offer riding tips, repair your bike, and it does tours for all levels as well. The Shrine Pass tour includes a vicious two-mile ascent and a 12-mile coast down the backside of Vail Mountain into Red Cliff. The Vail Pass downhill tour on the bike path is also popular, especially with families.

Vail Sports
OUTDOORS RENTAL

(☑970-479-0600; www.vailsports.com; Mountain Plaza, 151 Vail Lane; ski/snowboarding $27-61;

VAIL SKI TIPS

True, with 5289 acres of ski terrain available it's tough to play favorites, but here are a few things to keep in mind as you explore the mountain. Beginners should stay on the front side and work their way up to the back bowls. The Gopher Hill Lift (#12) and Little Eagle Lift (#15) areas are best for never-evers. Beginners will also enjoy Lost Boy in Game Creek Bowl and the terrains in the Sourdough Express Lift (#14) area such as Tin Pants and Sourdough.

Some good intermediate runs are Expresso, Cappuccino and Christmas in the Mountaintop Express Lift (#4) area. Northwoods, in the Northwoods Express Lift (#11) area, Avanti, Lodgepole and Columbine in the Avanti Express Lift (#2) area and Dealer's Choice in Game Creek Bowl are also great. Intermediate skiers also love Blue Sky Basin and runs such as Big Rock Park, Grand Review and the Star.

Advanced skiers flock to Riva Ridge at four miles long on the front side. On the back, hit Forever in Sun Down Bowl (where they've just installed the new high-speed quad lift, #5 – the High Noon Express). Lover's Leap in Blue Sky Basin is another home run. The options here are seemingly infinite and you can ski a week here without ever covering your tracks.

Trickster snowboarders should find their three terrain parks between extreme back-bowl runs.

⊙8am-8pm winter, 10am-7pm summer, to 5pm spring & fall; 🚹) Resort-owned and operated, and one of the closest rental shops to the lifts, you can usually get good deals and solid gear here. It rents bikes in the summer too. Affiliated with discount rental service Rentskis.com (you have to book online to get the 20% discount).

Double Diamond Ski Shop
SNOW GEAR, BIKE RENTAL

(☑970-476-5500; www.doublediamondvail. com; 520 E Lionshead Cir; packages per person $27-57; ⊙10am-5pm summer, 8am-8pm winter; 🚹; 🚐Vail Transit) A top-shelf ski and snowboard outfitter with over 20 years of operation on the mountain, and set just a short stroll from the Lionshead gondola. Packages are tailored for kids, beginners, high-performance skiers and those interested in trying out the latest demo gear. During the summer it rents full-suspension mountain bikes.

★☆ Festivals & Events

CarniVail
CARNIVAL

(www.vail.com/events/carnivail.aspx; Bridge St; crawfish boil $3.50-8.95; ⊙March) Bridge St turns into a somewhat tamer version of Bourbon St as Vail helps celebrate Carnival week. It starts with a high-altitude crawfish boil then gathers steam with a Fat Tuesday parade streaming from Bridge to Selbert Circle – expect a crowning of the King and Queen. There's a concert held after the parade and another the following Friday.

Vail Film Festival
FILM

(☑970-476-1092; www.vailfilmfestival.org; ⊙early Apr; 🚹) It's not the biggest indie film fest on the block, but it brings plenty of star power. Past attendees and honorees include Kevin Smith, Paul Rudd, Olivia Wilde, Hayden Panettiere and Harold Ramis. Screenings take place at the Vail Plaza Hotel in Vail Village, and at the Park Hyatt and the Vilar Performing Arts Center, both in Beaver Creek.

Being Vail, there will be plenty of Hollywood types to schmooze with and parties to attend. The 2010 festival attracted 90 films, 250 filmmakers and 14,000 attendees. It hosts a screenwriting competition too.

Taste of Vail
FOOD

(☑970-926-5665; www.tasteofvail.com; $75-350; ⊙early Apr; 🚹) For more than 20 years this gourmet food festival has offered some of the best mountain food you can imagine. The main event is the grand tasting and auction, with every Vail restaurant included, but the lamb cook-off and *après-ski* wine tasting run a close second.

Spring Back to Vail
FESTIVAL

(www.vail.com/events/spring-back-to-vail.aspx; ⊙mid-April; 🚹; 🚐Vail Transit) The mid-April weekend party that officially closes the ski season with a series of free concerts and barbecues. There's always a big hitter for the Friday night concert – Wyclef Jean was the headliner in 2010. The actual closing ceremony happens on Sunday at the top of Chair 5.

Vail Jazz Festival
MUSIC

(☑970-479-6146, 888-824-5526; www.vailjazz. org; Vail Village, Lionshead; Labor Day concert $45-55; ⊙Jul-Sep; 🚹) This acclaimed international jazz festival features a series of free outdoor concerts in Vail Square, Lionshead, and at the Vail Farmers Market. The festival is anchored by the Labor Day Weekend Party, which is when the big hitters come to town.

FREE Snow Daze
FESTIVAL

(www.vailsnowdaze.com; ⊙early Dec; 🚹) Held annually in early December, this early season party once marked the official opening of Vail Mountain. Now it's just one of the biggest early season ski-town parties on the continent. In 2010, the program featured a photo contest, a demolition derby under the lights (the centerpiece event) and three concerts in Vail Village.

🛏 Sleeping

Aside from camping, don't expect to find any budget lodging near Vail. Ski-season rates reach their peak during the Christmas and New Year holidays, when most innkeepers quote rates double to triple the amount charged after the snow melts. Ask at the Vail Visitor Center (p191) about nightly specials, especially during the off-season. As for the rooms themselves, almost all the lodges included here are actually privately owned condo units, although if all you need is a bed the vast majority of lodges rent one-room studio units which are locked off from the rest of the condo. Just know that one-bedroom condos are a significant upgrade from the studios.

TOP CHOICE Vail Plaza Hotel
LODGE $$$

(☑970-477-8000; www.vailplazahotel. com; 16 Vail Rd; r & condos from $519; 🅿❂❄ 🛜♨🚹) A fantastic Vail Village habitat and one of the area's better-value summer options, but that doesn't exactly make it cheap. After all, the elegant carpeting, lush linens and marble baths cost money. Though room rates dip to affordable in the summer, consider upgrading to a one-bedroom condo instead.

Yes, it's pricey, but the bedroom has north mountain views, while the living area and kitchen open onto a terrace with marvelous Vail mountain vistas. The granite counters in the kitchen aren't bad either. Nor are the two flat-screen TVs, the fireplace, the beautifully beamed ceiling, and the spectacular pool area with a half-dozen hot tubs frothing and spilling over like champagne. Not bad at all.

Austria Haus
LODGE $$
(☑970-754-7850; www.austriahaushotel.com; 242 E Meadow Dr; r $106-559; P🐾❄@🎧🛄♿) Easily the best value hotel rooms in Vail, the service at Austria Haus is outstanding. It offers a selection of rooms, along with one- and two-bedroom condos, and guests can book in their preferred tee-off times at the prestigious Red Sky Ranch golf course located nearby.

Charming details such as wood-framed doorways, Berber carpet and marble baths, as well as armchairs by the fireplace and flower boxes on the window sills make for a very pleasant stay.

Sonnenalp Resort
RESORT $$$
(☑970-476-5656, 800-654-8312; www.sonnen alp.com; 20 Vail Rd; r from $410; P🐾❄@🎧🛄♿) One of the many upscale chalet-style properties in Vail Village. Rooms have beamed ceilings and heated marble floors in the bathrooms. An upgrade to a junior suite gets you stone doorways, a fireplace and sitting area, and a timber accent wall and soaker tub. Parking is $20 per day and bike rental is available for $25 per half-day.

The breakfast buffet is popular here. If you're leaning toward a suite, we suggest the larger Blue Spruce over the Lodgepole variety. Staff will explain.

Arrabelle
RESORT $$$
(☑970-754-7777, reservations 970-754-7894; www.arrabelle.rockresorts.com; 675 Lionshead Pl; r from $675; P🐾❄@🎧🛄♿) The grand dame of Lionshead, the Arrabelle is a massive chalet-style resort with a stone and marble lobby, top-shelf service and a variety of accommodations, from hotel rooms to four-bedroom luxury condos. All have

wi-fi, flat-screen TVs, Bose sound systems, plush linens and marble baths. Call the reservations line for the best available rates and last-minute deals not available online.

Antlers
CONDOS $$$
(☑888-268-5377, 970-476-2471; www.antlers vail.com; 680 W Lionshead Pl; studios from $240; P🐾❄🎧🛄♿) For Vail, this is a good value Lionshead choice. The large studios have fireplaces and private balconies equipped with a BBQ. Decor varies from rustic-cabin cool to 'Grandma's house' chic, and most rooms overlook the creek and the mountain. Multibedroom condos also available.

Mountain Haus
LODGE $$$
(☑800-237-0922; www.mountainhaus.com; 292 E Meadow Dr; r from $220, condos $370-955; P🐾❄🎧🛄♿) A laid-back spot in central Vail. Rooms aren't huge but they do have fireplaces, king-size beds and a view from the upper reaches, and get points for ambience for those vintage skis leaning by the fireplace. Sure, it's not cheap, but it represents good value for ritzy Vail.

Lodge at Lionshead
LODGE $$$
(☑970-476-2700; www.lodgeatlionshead.com; 380 E Lionshead Circle; studios from $210, 1-bedroom condos $316; P🐾❄🎧🛄♿) Friendly and unprentention, this lodge offers a wide variety of private condos from studios (with Murphy bed) to four-bedroom luxury units. It's not the fanciest choice, but is good value in the summertime.

Gore Creek Campground
CAMPING $
(☑970-945-2521; Bighorn Rd; campsites $13; ☺Memorial Day-Labor Day; P♿) This primitive campground at the end of Bighorn Rd has 25 first-come, first-served tent sites with picnic tables and fire grates nestled in the woods by Gore Creek. There is excellent fishing near here. Try the Slate Creek or Deluge Lake trails; the latter leads to a fish-packed lake. The campground is 6 miles east of Vail Village via the East Vail exit off I-70.

Holiday Inn
HOTEL $$
(☑970-476-2739; www.apexvail.com; 2211 N Frontage Rd; r from $189; P🐾❄@🎧🛄♿) As budget conscious as Vail gets at any time of year. So, yes, this is low-rent Vail, but there are still a few perks, such as the sauna and hot tub, and there's even a concrete pond of a pool. Rooms are bland but super clean, service is friendly and there's a fabulous diner next door. Don't go out of your way to land here, but it'll do in a pinch.

Lodge Tower
LODGE $$$

(☎800-654-2517, 970-476-9530; www.lodge tower.com; 200 Vail Rd; r from $350; P ❄ @ 🌐 ♨ 👪) This tower is packed with privately owned one-, two- and three-bedroom condos, but you can rent hotel rooms here too (they're just locked-off bedrooms within a condo). Each is decorated in a different style and most are stodgy, though the Berber rugs and king-size beds are a nice touch, as are the views from upper reaches. Breakfast is included and the location is central.

It ain't hip, but it's not a bad choice either.

Eagle Point Resort
LODGE $$

(☎970-476-6905; www.eaglepointresort.net; 1500 Matterhorn Cir; condos $140-328, 3-night minimum; P ❄ 🌐 ♨ 👪) Set almost halfway between West Vail and Cascade Village, these basic but homey one- and two-bedroom condos are in a picturesque corner of Vail with lovely wooded mountain views, even if you can hear the interstate roar nearby. Still good value, however.

✖ Eating

Prices are generally high, and restaurants are typically busy and blessed with good service, but the food...well, it doesn't often live up to the ambience – which is par for the course for most resort towns. But take heart, there are a few real gems in the vicinity and, if nothing else, there's a kitchen in your condo.

Osaki's
TOP CHOICE
JAPANESE $$$

(☎970-476-0977; 100 E Meadow Dr; sushi $7-15, rolls $5.50-28; ⏱6:30pm-late Tue-Sun; ➗; 🚌Vail Transit) There is no finer sushi in all of Vail, and possibly the state of Colorado, than here. Osaki is a star disciple of Nobu Matsuhisa (yes, *that* Nobu). He worked in the LA restaurant, when Nobu only had one shop, and eventually opened this hole-in-the-wall temple devoted to all that is sweet, tender, raw and holy (we're talking about fish!).

It's not cheap, but what Vail haunt is? Plus, if you go with one of the combo dinners you'll get out for under $50. And whatever you do, do not leave without tasting the salmon. It's simply spectacular. Osaki offers 30% off rolls in the summer, and reservations are advised in peak season. You'll find it hiding behind Campo de Fiori.

Westside Cafe
BREAKFAST $

(☎970-476-7890; www.westsidecafe.net; 2211 N Frontage Rd; mains $6-14; ⏱7am-10pm; ➗ 👪) Set

in a West Vail minimall right off the freeway, this is the most popular breakfast spot in the area among locals, and for good reason. It does terrific breakfast skillets, like the 'My Big Fat Greek Skillet' with scrambled eggs, gyro, red onion, tomato and feta served with warm pita. The 'Southwestern' comes with scrambled eggs, black beans, peppers, onions and tomatoes.

Staff will pour you freshly squeezed orange juice or a steaming large mug of coffee. The Bloody Marys get good word of mouth, and the always satisfying 'Local Special' never fails to bring a smile to the face of weary menu readers (and writers) everywhere.

Game Creek Restaurant
CONTEMPORARY AMERICAN $$$

(☎970-754-4275; www.gamecreekclub.com; Game Creek Bowl; 3 courses $59-99; ⏱5:30-8:20pm Thu-Sat, 11am-2pm Sun, late-Jun–early Sep & Dec-Apr; ➗ 👪) One of Vail's best kitchens isn't in Vail at all, it's on the mountain, nestled in spectacular Game Creek Bowl. Take the Eagle Bahn Gondola to Eagle's Nest and staff will shuttle you to their lodge-style restaurant, which serves an American-French fusion menu with stars like foie gras, elk steak and a succulent leg of lamb.

Or perhaps you'd prefer to snowshoe or ski your way in? Either choice will be unforgettable. It serves a mean brunch on Sundays.

Big Bear Bistro
SANDWICHES $

(☎970-300-1394; www.bigbearbistro.com; Hanson Ranch Rd; sandwiches from $7.99; ⏱7am-7pm; 👪; 🚌Vail Transit) Unless you hit the Sonnenalp Resort's buffet, this is where you come for breakfast. It serves gourmet coffee, tasty breakfast burritos and some damn decent sandwiches at lunch. We suggest 'the Masterpiece.' It comes with prosciutto, capicola, salami, maple-glazed ham, balsamic-tinged arugula, banana peppers and cracked-pepper aioli.

Campo de Fiori
ITALIAN $$$

(☎970-476-8994; www.campodefiori.net; 100 E Meadow Dr; mains $18-34; ⏱5:30pm-late; ➗; 🚌Vail Transit) It's a splurge, but then all of Vail is a splurge – and this is a worthy one. Where else in town can you slurp black mussels and follow it up with a proper spinach and ricotta *agnolotti* (half-moon ravioli), and then follow that with a grilled ruby trout, NY strip or a Colorado lamb rack? The risotto dello chef ain't bad either.

THE VAIL DREAM

Long before two WWII vets who were hooked on powder hiked Vail Mountain (p181) to scout the possibility of a new ski resort halfway between Denver and Aspen – the only resort of its kind at the time – the Gore Range was home to Colorado's nomadic Ute Indians who used to trek from the arid rangeland into the alpine country to beat the summer heat. However, white settlers thirsty for gold arrived and the Utes didn't last.

During WWII the army founded Camp Hale, a training center off the present day Hwy 24. This is where the famous 10th Mountain Division – America's only battalion on skis – lived and trained. These troops fought hard in the Italian Alps and when they came home many became big players in the burgeoning ski industry.

Peter Seibert was one of them. He hooked onto the Aspen Ski Patrol then became the manager of the Loveland Basin Ski Area – Colorado's oldest ski mountain. Together with his friend Earl Eaton, who was a lifelong skier and ski-industry veteran, Siebert climbed Vail Mountain in the winter of 1957, and after one long look at those luscious back bowls, these men knew they'd struck gold.

At the time Vail Mountain was owned by the forest service and local ranchers. Seibert and Eaton recruited a series of investors and lawyers and eventually got a permit from the forest service and convinced nearly all of the local ranchers to sell. Much of the construction budget was raised by convincing investors to chip in $10,000 for a condo unit and a lifetime season pass.

Opening day was on December 15, 1962 (today the resort opens the weekend before Thanksgiving). Conditions were marginal, but the dream was alive. And if you'd skied there that day you would have paid $5 for a day pass and explored nine runs, accessed by two chairs and one gondola.

It's all served in a romanitc Mediterranean villa interior. And the vibe is almost always wine-drenched and alive.

Sweet Basil   AMERICAN $$$
(☑970-476-0125; www.sweetbasil-vail.com; 193 Gore Creek Dr; lunch mains $13-18, dinner mains $27-32; ☺11:30am-2:30pm & 6pm-late; ☻; ⊟Vail Transit) Sweet Basil is still churning out what many critics argue is some of the best food in Vail. The menu changes seasonally, but the eclectic American fare, which usually includes favorites such as Colorado leg of lamb with white-bean ratatouille, is consistently good. The ambience is also fantastic.

Kelly Liken   CONTEMPORARY AMERICAN $$$
(☑970-479-0175; www.kellyliken.com; Suite 100, 12 Vail Rd; meals from $45; ☺6-10pm; ☻; ⊟Vail Transit) Young chef and cable-TV personality Kelly Liken shows off her skills in the lower lobby of the Vail Gateway building. Cooking with seasonal, and mostly local, foods (elk carpaccio anyone?) she blends exquisite ingredients into tasty dishes such as shrimp and grits, pan-roasted duck served with Colorado plums and wild rice salad, and honey and rosemary–glazed local lamb loin.

Sunday's harvest menu features whatever caught her eye at the Vail Farmers Market in Vail Village that morning. Be warned: serving size is small and prices are high, but flavor, presentation and celeb-chef panache should make up for it.

Loaded Joe's   CAFE FOOD $
(☑970-479-2883; www.loadedjoes.com; 227 Bridge St; coffee drinks from $3, breakfast sandwiches from $6; ☺7am-2am; ☻; ⊟Vail Transit) Come to this creekside coffee bar for breakfast. It serves croissants and bagel sandwiches as well as gourmet coffee and espresso drinks. You can sip and munch beneath the cedars as the creek wakes you up with its gentle hum. Oh, and it does cocktails too. Why not make it an Irish breakfast? You'll find it just off the covered bridge in Vail Village.

Vendetta's   ITALIAN $$
(☑970-476-5070; www.vendettasvail.com; 291 Bridge St; pizzas $13-23, mains $18-30; ☺11am-late; ☻☻; ⊟Vail Transit) In overpriced and borderline snooty Vail, this throwback pizza joint wins for aroma, ambience and, well, pizza. It does steaks and chops as well as pasta dishes too, but the pizza is what satisfies.

Russell's
STEAK $$$

(📞970-476-6700; www.russellvail.com; 228 Bridge St; mains $28-64; ◷6pm-late summer, 5:30-10pm winter) If you're looking for center-cut Angus, beef ribs or surf-and-turf in pressed-tablecloth environs, this intimate steakhouse is a decent choice. But leave your cell phone and your vegan friends at home. They aren't tolerated here.

Los Amigos
MEXICAN $$

(📞970-476-5847; 400 Bridge St; mains $8-15; ◷11:30am-late; 🚻 🅿; 🚌Vail Transit) If you want views, tequila, and rock and roll with your *après-ski* cocktail ritual, come to Los Amigos. The Mexican is only decent, but the Happy Hour margaritas ($3.50) and drafts ($3) more than make up for it.

Self-Catering

Vail Farmers Market
SELF-CATERING $

(www.meadowdrivevail.com; E Meadow Dr; ◷10am-3:30pm Sun Jun-Sep; 🅿; 🚌Vail Transit) This farmers market and art show, located on Meadow Dr in the heart of the Vail Village, was established in 2001. You can grab any number of items for your condo kitchen, including fresh picked produce (including organic), fresh baked breads, German pastries, local meats, fresh halibut, mountain honey, and art from dozens of local artists and artisans.

There are more than 120 vendors in all, as well as live jazz curated by the Vail Jazz Festival.

City Market
SELF-CATERING

(📞970-476-1017-; www.citymarket.com; 2109 N Frontage Rd; ◷6am-11pm; 🚻 🅿; 🚌Vail Transit) City Market, along with nearby Safeway – both within 100m of one another off the N Frontage Rd in West Vail, is where you stock up your condo kitchen. Aside from a few minimarkets there are no grocery stores in Vail Village, Cascade Village or Lionshead, so you will wind up here eventually.

🍸 Drinking

Garfinkels
PUB

(📞970-476-3789; www.garfsvail.com; 536 E Lionshead Cir; ◷10am-midnight Sun-Thu, 10am-1:30am Fri & Sat; 🚌Vail Transit) In Lionshead, this wooden lodge–style pub has a wide deck overlooking Vail Mountain. There's a pool table, a killer circle bar with Colorado Native on tap and a dozen flat-screens showing all the sports you could want. Saturday night karaoke starts at 9pm, and before you perform, check out the wall of fame. Frank Sinatra has tossed a couple back here.

Tap Room
SPORTS BAR

(📞970-479-0500; www.taproomvail.com; 333 Bridge St; ◷11am-late Mon-Fri, 10am-late Sat & Sun; 🚌Vail Transit) A favorite stop on the Vail bar-hopping circuit, this laid-back sports bar shows ballgames all day and has a giant selection of beers and day-long drink specials. The kitchen churns out middling pub grub, but the chipped-wood bar is a fine place to sip a Native Z draft. Plus, it has views of the mountain from the back patio. Wi-fi too.

☆ Entertainment

TOP CHOICE Bōl
BOWLING

(📞970-476-9300; www.bolvail.com; 141 E Meadow Dr; plates $12-24, lanes per hour $45, shoe rental $5; ◷3pm-1:30am Mon-Fri, from 11:30am Sat & Sun; 🅿; 🚌Vail Transit) Set in the striking, new Solaris condo complex, there has never ever been a sleeker more upscale bowling alley. Ever! This is damn near space age and at research time was by far the dopest hang in Vail.

With high energy, progressive rock pumping, balls decorated like billiard balls (finger print sized large and central), big-screen TVs strobing at the end of the lanes, and a sleek bar in the neon lobby, Vail's young and pretty hang here. And it serves food too. Think pork buns with ponzu sauce, honey-glazed ribs, balsamic-tossed arugula and pan-roasted baby artichokes.

Cinebistro
CINEMA

(📞970-476-3344; www.cobbcinebistro.com; 141 E Meadow Dr; adult/child/matinees $14/7.50/10; ◷3-9:30pm Mon-Thu, noon-9:30pm Fri-Sun; 🅿; 🚌Vail Transit) Located in the Solaris complex is Vail's slick new cinema, with three premium theaters outfitted with cush seats and a flash bar and restaurant serving serious cuisine in the lobby. On the big screens they play first-rate Hollywood fare.

Samana Lounge
NIGHTCLUB

(📞970-476-3433; www.samanalounge.com; 228 Bridge St; cover varies; ◷9pm-late Tue & Thu-Sat; 🚌Vail Transit) A basement nightclub in central Vail with frequent live music. It's sax-driven funk to classic-rock cover bands, as well as resident and visiting DJs. The calendar gets especially packed in summer and winter, but it brings live tunes to the Vail people in mud season too.

The Club
NIGHTCLUB

(📞970-479-0556; www.theclubvail.com; 304 Bridge St; cover varies; ◷hours vary) It bills itself as 'The World's Greatest Ski Bar,' and while we wouldn't go that far, this is the place to catch Steve Meyer's *Après-ski* show, which is best paired with tequila shots. The club hosts live music seven nights a week in high season and offers good-value drink specials.

Shopping

Snow and adventure trumps style in Vail, which is why most of the shops make their living catering for adventure sports. When it comes to ski and snowboard gear, Vail has few equals.

Bag and Pack   OUTDOOR EQUIPMENT
(☏970-476-1027; 122 E Meadow Dr; ☺9am-7pm Mon-Sat, 10am-6pm Sun; ⊕; 🚌Vail Transit) A small mountaineering shop in Vail Village. It stocks everything you need for a hike or multiple-day trek. Backpacks, stoves, water purifiers, clothing, knives, maps and backcountry guide books. Staff will happily suggest some of the best hikes in the area. There's a branch in Beaver Creek too. Check out the Facebook page for more information.

Burton   SNOWBOARDS
(☏970-476-4532; http://www.facebook.com/pages/Vail-CO/Burton-at-Arrabelle-Vail/102749694413; 675 Lionshead Pl; ☺10am-7pm; ⊕; 🚌Vail Transit) Burton, arguably America's top snowboard brand, has a flagship store in Lionshead where you can get all the gear and boards you'd ever want. Our advice? Consider raiding the summer factory clearance sale in the late summer when you'll get at least 50% off last year's boards and gear.

Kemo Sabe   BOOTS, HATS
(☏970-479-7474; www.kemosabe.com; 230 Bridge St; ☺10am-8pm spring, summer & winter, 10am-6pm fall; ⊕) It would be tough to find a more distinctly Western store in all of resort-land Colorado. It specializes in two things: Stetson hats and Lucchese boots. All are handmade. The boots are crafted from hide and leather, and the hats from rabbit, steer and beaver fur.

Staff will shape your hat and even distress it to make it look like you rode hard and worked hard with it. Listen for the country music and enjoy the hospitality.

Buzz's Ski Shop   SPORTING GOODS
(☏970-476-3320; 302 Gore Creek Dr; ⊕) In tiny, corporate Vail, a laid-back place like Buzz's feels like a breath of fresh powder. Techs are knowledgable, prices are among the cheapest on the mountain, the equipment is solid,

and it's just a few minutes walk to the Eagle Bahn Gondola (p181) in Vail Village. It is only open during the winter season.

Gore Creek Fly Fishermen   SPORTING GOODS
(☏970-476-3296; www.gorecreekflyfisherman.com; 193 Gore Creek Dr; half-day/full-day trips per person $275-375; ☺8am-6pm; ⊕; 🚌Vail Transit) This Vail Village fly-fishing shop and outfitter will set you up with new and used gear for rent or purchase. You can also get Gore Creek fishing tips and sign up for half-day and full-day fishing trips on gold-medal waters. Per person guide price drops when you have a group of three or more anglers.

Information

First Bank of Vail (☏970-476-5686; www.efirstbank.com; 17 Vail Rd; ☺9am-5pm Mon-Fri) ATM.

Plum TV (www.plumtv.com) Because everyone loves tourist TV. Part of a resort network with outlets in Aspen, Sun Valley, Telluride and as far east as the Hamptons and Martha's Vineyard, this local cable channel and website also features daily snow reports in ski season and offers local insights and tips year round.

Vail Information Center (☏970-476-4790; www.vail.com; 241 S Frontage Rd; ☺9am-6pm; ⊕) A slightly informative depot with plenty of maps and informational booklets to get you started. But no real deals or hot tips to speak of here. You're better off quizzing local staff in hotels, restaurants and ski shops for the up-to-the-minute local knowhow.

Vail Post Office (☏970-476-1494; 1300 N Frontage Rd; ☺8:30am-5pm Mon-Fri, 8:30am-noon Sat)

Vail Town Library (☏970-479-2185; www.vaillibrary.com; 292 W Meadow Dr; ☺10am-6pm Mon-Thu, 11am-6pm Fri-Sun; 🛜; 🚌Vail Transit) Free public internet! This small but useful riverside library with a sweet back patio has magazines, music and movies (you can check out two DVDs at a time). And did we mention free public internet? To use the facility, just sign up for a free membership with any valid drivers license. Oh yeah, it has books too.

Vail Valley Information Network (web.vail.net) Tourist information and planning information.

Vail Valley Medical Center (☏970-476-2451; www.vvmc.com; 181 W Meadow Dr; ☺24hr; 🛜) Vail Valley's top hospital. It's also one of the best in the state for orthopedic injuries. It has an emergency room and is centrally located between Lionshead and Vail Village on W Meadow Dr. Provides 24-hour emergency care.

Vail Visitor Center (970-479-1394; www.visitvailvalley.com; Vail Transportation Center; ⊙9am-5pm; 🖶) Provides maps, lodging and activities information and schedules for Vail's outstanding transit system. The visitors center also has a Lionshead office located in the parking garage.

❶ Getting There & Away

Most visitors fly into Denver International Airport (p94) and continue to Vail in a rental car or by shuttle via Colorado Mountain Express. However, during the December to early April ski season, the **Eagle County Airport** (970-524-9490; www.eaglecounty.us/airport; 219 Eldon Wilson Drive; ⊙Dec-early April), 35 miles west of Vail, offers a surprising number of jet services on such carriers as American Airlines, Continental and Skywest.

Greyhound buses stop at the Vail Transportation Center, just off the middle I-70 exit for Vail, on their way between Denver and Glenwood Springs.

❶ Getting Around
To/From the Airport
Colorado Mountain Express (970-926-9800; www.cmex.com; to/from DIA per person $89, to/from Eagle County Airport per person $49; 🖶) Colorado Mountain Express shuttles passengers to/from Denver International Airport year-round. High-season prices are listed but services are discounted in the summer. The trip takes three hours. The trip from Eagle County Airport takes about 40 minutes.

Bicycle
Bike routes connect the outlying free parking areas with Vail Village. From West Vail you can ride along N Frontage Rd, crossing I-70 at the pedestrian overpass to Lionshead. On the south side of the freeway, a paved bike route extends from W Gore Creek Dr through Cascade Village, Lionshead and Vail Village.

Car & Motorcycle
Compact Vail Village, filled with upscale restaurants, bars and boutiques, is traffic free. Motorists must park at the Vail Transportation Center & Public Parking garage before entering the pedestrian mall area near the chairlifts. Lionshead is a secondary parking lot about half a mile to the west. It has direct lift access and is usually less crowded.

Dollar (800-800-3665; www.dollarvail.com; Eagle County Airport; car rental per day $36-124; 🖶) and Enterprise (p194) are among the car rental companies serving Vail and the surrounding areas. Dollar is located at the Eagle County Airport. Enterprise is in Beaver Creek.

Public Transportation
Vail has fine public transportation – it's free, it goes where you need to go and it operates at short intervals. Traveling by bus is thus faster and more convenient than most car trips. The in-town shuttle runs between the base of Golden Peak and Vail Village and Lionshead from 6:15am to 2:15am at intervals of less than 10 minutes.

Eagle County Regional Transportation Authority (970-328-3520; www.eaglecounty.us; per ride $4, per day $8) While the Vail transit system offers free rides between resorts within the wider Vail circuit, the ECO bus offers affordable transport to Avon, Beaver Creek, Edwards and beyond. Buses begin running at 4:30am, and the last coach departs from the Vail Transportation Center for Gypsum at midnight.

Vail Buses (970-328-8143) Serves the local golf course and loops through all the Vail resort areas – West Vail (both North and South), Vail Village, Lionshead and East Vail, as well as Ford Park and Sandstone. These buses run on natural gas, most have bike racks and all are free. In fact, this system is among the largest free public-transport systems in the country. Buses stop only at designated stops.

Vail Transportation Center (970-476-5137; 241 S Frontage Rd) Greyhound buses stop at the Vail Transportation Center en route to Denver ($24 to $34.50, 2½ hours) or Grand Junction ($20 to $29.50, three hours).

Taxi
High Mountain Taxi (970-524-5555; www.hmtaxi.com; airport-Vail $130-140, West Vail–Vail Village $15; ⊙24hr; 🖶) Vail's signature taxi service serves the entire valley from Vail to Eagle, and is equipped for pets and kids, as well as skis and snowboards. Book online or call.

BEAVER CREEK

Breach the regal gates in Avon, 8 miles west of Vail just off the I-70, and you'll emerge onto a private mountain road skirting a picturesque golf course as it climbs to the foot of a truly spectacular ski mountain. Yeah, Beaver Creek feels like one of those delicious secrets shared among the rich kids, and it is indeed a privilege to ski here.

Today the perfectly maintained grounds and neo-Tyrolean buildings lend a certain looming grandeur, as do names like Park Hyatt (p193), set in the main village, and Ritz Carlton (p193), in nearby Bachelor Gulch. And it's certainly fair to say that when the Vail corporation expanded here they envisioned something more exclusive than Vail, but thanks to Vail's own well-funded regulars, high prices and recent additions, that's not entirely accurate. Beaver Creek is a mellower, more conservative place, and typically an older scene. It's the kind of destination where grandparents bring the whole family to enjoy a slew of all-natural adventures.

✦ Activities

In the summer you can climb 14-ers, run rivers and go off-roading. In the winter this mountain has everything from cross-country skiing and telemarking to harrowing downhill runs and pro-grade terrain parks.

Beaver Creek Summer Adventure Center   OUTDOORS

TOP CHOICE

(☑970-754-5373; www.beavercreek.com; Starbucks Plaza; guided hikes per person $65, 3-person min; ⊙9am-4pm, mid-Jun–early Sep; 🖝; 🚐Avon-Beaver Creek Shuttle) Set on Starbucks Plaza in the village, this resort-owned concession arranges 4WD tours, bike rental, and horseback rides, but it's best known for guided hikes to some of the area's most historic mountains and 14,000 ft peaks.

This is a quintessential and lung-crushing Colorado activity and highly recommended. Shorter complimentary hikes and guided mountain-bike rides are also on offer.

Beaver Creek Mountain   SNOW SPORTS

(☑970-496-4900; www.beavercreek.com; Beaver Creek; lift tickets adult $76-94, child under 13yr $5-64, senior $66-84; ⊙9am-4:30pm daily; 🖝; 🚐Avon–Beaver Creek Shuttle, Beaver Creek Shuttle) Beaver Creek isn't exactly a ghost town in the summer, but it's no secret that the winter rules. The mountain boasts a 4040 ft vertical rise serviced by 17 lifts, including 10 high-speed quad chairs. There are 149 trails and a wide variety of ski terrain for all abilities.

Experts will head to the double black diamonds at Royal Elk Glades and Talon's Challenge off the Grouse Mountain Express lift – runs are every bit as challenging as anything at Vail. Golden Eagle (the site of the Birds of Prey Men's World Cup Downhill course) and Stone Creek Chutes also spike the adrenaline. Beginners like it in Beaver Creek because the mountain is literally turned upside down, with beginner runs at the top so they can enjoy the same spectacular mountain views. Red Buffalo is also a winner for beginners. Intermediate skiers enjoy Centennial and Harrier on the

main mountain and Gunder's in Bachelor Gulch. The three terrain parks – 101 (beginners), Lumber Yard (intermediate) and The Rodeo (prograde with massive jumps and a half-pipe) keep extremists happy, and Beaver Creek is also the first US resort to offer European-style village-to-village skiing from the main village over to Bachelor Gulch and then to Arrowhead Mountain Village several miles west.

Red Sky Golf Club   GOLF

(☑866-873-3759; www.redskyranch.com; 376 Red Sky Rd; greens fees $195-250; ⊙8am-6pm May 14-Jun 3 & Sep 20-Oct 10, 6:45am-7:30pm Jun 4-Sep 19) Thirty-six holes of award winning, Tom Fazio and Greg Norman–designed fairway nirvana is available to guests of all Beaver Creek resorts and a handful of Vail lodges too. The courses are separated by a massive ridge, which, according to the Red Sky folks, serves as a wildlife corridor for deer and elk.

Golf being typically an eco-unfriendly pursuit – it's nice to know that the club transplanted or revegetated more than 25,000 native plants during the construction of the Tom Fazio golf course alone. It also applied more than the usual amount of sod to reduce, but not eliminate reliance, on fertilizers. Golf doesn't get much greener and the views are seldom finer from the tee. But it ain't cheap.

Nova Guides   4WD, RAFTING

(☑888-949-6682; www.novaguides.com; Camp Hale; rafting $50-170, jeep tours $60-70; ⊙year-round; 🖝) Officially this outfitter with over 20 years of guiding experience is based in Leadville, but in actuality they live and work out of Camp Hale – the very place where the 10th Mountain Division trained. It offers white-water rafting and jeep trips in the summer and epic snowmobiling adventure in the winter. It serves Beaver Creek, Vail and beyond.

Beaver Creek Ice Rink   ICE SKATING

(☑970-845-0438; www.beavercreek.com; 60 Avondale Ln; adult $14, child under 13yr $8 including skate rental, bring your own skates $5; ⊙noon-9pm Nov 20-Apr 12; 🖝; 🚐ECO) This wide oval of smooth ice is open to the moon and stars and snowflakes and flash-bulbs popping from the cameras of adoring parents and grandparents. It oozes winter charm in this tiny ski village. Of course, on Monday nights from 7pm to 9pm it's one big disco skate party. Which, you know, is also quite charming in a different, more afro-spandex way.

McCoy Park Nordic Center SNOW SPORTS
(☑970-754-5313; www.beavercreek.com; Beaver Creek Village; lift tickets children 12 and under $5-64, adult $76-94, senior $66-84; ⊙9am-4pm Dec 11-Apr 3; ⛷; Strawberry Park Express Lift) Set at the top of the Strawberry Park express lift, McCoy Park is a 20-mile playground for classic and skate skiers, and snowshoers. Groomed and rustic trails cross pine forests, aspen groves and open glades. Nestled between Beaver Creek and Bachelor Gulch, it has terrific views of three mountain ranges. If you need to rent gear head to the **Nordic Sports Center** (☑970-754-5313; www.beavercreek.com; Strawberry Park Ct; lessons & tours $65-147; ⊙9am-4pm; ⛷).

Beaver Creek Tennis Center TENNIS
(☑970-754-5781; www.beavercreek.com; 310 Offerson Rd; per hour $15-25, lessons per hour $65; ⊙8am-5pm Jun 18-Oct 3; ⛷) You can see them beckoning from below your chairlift. Here are five clay and two hard courts for your ball-smacking pleasure. So hit the pro shop next to Highlands Lodge, and make like Nadal. Be sure to drink plenty of water and play with patience, because at this altitude you may be gasping for air. Private lessons available at the pro shop.

Bungee Trampoline TRAMPOLINE
(☑970-845-7531; www.beavercreek.com; Beaver Creek Promenade; per person $10; ⊙9am-6pm Memorial Day-Labor Day; ⛷; ▯ECO) One of three kid-friendly activities set at the base of the Centennial Express chairlift. You've seen this kind of thing before. Kid on trampoline, tethered to bungees to spring them high and tempt them into any manner of twists and flips. But for guest safety there is a double-flip limit on this trampoline.

Beaver Creek Ski and Snowboard School SNOW SPORTS
(☑800-953-0844; lessons per day child $140-295, adult $140-227; ⊙8am-4pm; ⛷) Novice grommets are rounded up at Gerald Ford Hall, and loaded onto the Buckaroo Express which takes them to the Ranch, a state-of-the-art children's ski and snowboard school. Parents can spy through picture windows as their progeny navigate customized slopes designed to facilitate the correct body movements. Adult classes are customized to meet the clients' needs. The adult school is located at 1 Beaver Creek Pl.

🍴 Sleeping & Eating

Food options are limited and, sure, there's a certain artificiality that comes with almost all ski complexes, one that can make the populists among us feel like they've landed in a surrealist's preppy dream. But the thing to do here is to enjoy the dream, and pray that you don't wake up until mud season. Just make sure you have a high credit limit, because you can't sleep cheap here. For last minute reservations, call **Beaver Creek Reservations** (☑970-496-4900, toll-free 800-608-4849).

Ritz Carlton RESORT $$$
(☑970-748-6200; www.ritzcarlton.com; 130 Daybreak Ridge; r $299-1299; ▣⊖❄🛜🏊⛷) Listed as 2010's top Colorado resort by *Travel and Leisure,* included on Conde Nast's gold list, lauded for family and pet friendliness and a prized wedding destination, it's fair to say you won't be disappointed. Grand and as secluded as a 220-room hotel can be. It's all about skiing in and out of luxury here. Located in Bachelor Gulch which is a touch removed from, but still a part of the Beaver Creek area.

⬆TOP Westin Riverfront Resort & Spa
CHOICE RESORT $$$
(☑970-790-2000, 866-949-1616; www.starwoodhotels.com; 126 Riverfront Ln; r from $139-429; ▣⊖❄🛜🏊⛷; ▯ECO) Perched on the Eagle River, this Avon-based resort connected by free public shuttle to nearby Beaver Creek is a steal in the summer, and even in the early part of the ski season. There's a lovely modern mountain lodge motif in the lobby accentuated by soaring ceilings and floor to ceiling windows with epic mountain views. Look for those John Denver black and whites.

Rooms, aka studios, are likewise tastefully indulgent with wood floors in the foyer, a sitting area, a flat screen above the fireplace, a kitchenette, king beds and fabulous views. It rents multi-room condos too. Beware the $20 resort fee. Parking is $25.

Park Hyatt RESORT
(☑970-949-1234; www.beavercreek.hyatt.com; 136 East Thomas Pl; r $499-769; ▣⊖❄@🛜🏊⛷) Definitely the star of Beaver Creek Village, this splashy hotel spills out to the foot of the mountain, practically kissing the Buckaroo Express gondola. Rooms aren't huge but they are plush with French windows and a private terrace. The outdoor

pool and firepits are tucked into a little gulch at the top of the village and the lobby bar and back patio demand a beverage.

One can imagine a poor man's James Bond skiing into the lobby dressed in velvet looking for someone beautiful and dangerous (the actual Bond would probably be staying at the Ritz). Rooms are half price or less in the summer.

Saint James Place   LODGE **$$**
(☎970-845-9300; www.stjamesplace.net; 210 Offerson Rd; r $255-355 winter, $135-175 summer; P⊛❋@✿✖♿; 💻ECO) Frilly, homey condos in Beaver Creek village with flatscreens, antique furnishings tubs and showers in the hotel rooms and more of the same in the one- to four-bedroom condominiums. The ceilings did seem a fraction low for our taste, but that's nitpicking.

TOP CHOICE **Beano's Cabin**
    CONTEMPORARY AMERICAN **$$$**
(☎970-754-3463; 42 Avondale Ln; five course per person $105; ⊙5-10pm Dec-Apr; ⊕♿; 💻ECO) Beaver Creek's can't-miss destination restaurant involves a 20-minute open-air sleigh ride through the snowy night to a glowing cabin on the slopes, warm from a crackling fire and a kitchen turning out Colorado classics such as Colorado rack of lamb and almond-crusted trout. The restaurant is open nightly for the winter season. Reservations – a must – are accepted starting November.

Dusty Boot   PUB FOOD **$$**
(☎970-748-1146; www.dustyboot.com; #304 210 Offerson Rd; sandwiches $8, burgers $12.95, steaks from $19; ⊙11am-11pm; ♿; 💻ECO) This friendly saloon keeps it real. This food may not be for health nuts, but it's damn tasty. The burgers (including veggie burgers), handcut steaks and shaved prime-run sandwiches are all recommended. And the regulars here? All locals.

There is rusted vintage ranching gear in the rafters and the bar is resplendent with terrific tequila including Corzo, Corralejo, and Don Julio 1942, which stands to reason since the freshly mixed margs are a point of pride.

❶ Getting There & Around

The transport options in Beaver Creek mirror those in Vail. Most folks fly to Denver International Airport (p94) and either rent a car or hop on a Colorado Mountain Express (p179) shuttle to Beaver Creek. Major carriers also fly into Eagle County Airport, where Dollar Rent-A-Car (p191) has a shingle.

Enterprise Rent-A-Car (☎970-845-8393; www.enterprise.com; 47 E Beaver Creek Blvd; cars per day $33-105; ⊙8am-5:30pm Mon-Fri, 9am-noon Sun; ♿) is based in Beaver Creek, but you don't necessarily need a vehicle. The Beaver Creek Resort operates a useful and free private shuttle, and Avon's transit department operates a free Gondola Express shuttle for those coming up to ski for the day. Eagle County Regional Transportation Authority (p191) operates ECO buses that link Avon with Vail and Eagle. If you need a cab, High Mountain Taxi (p191) serves Beaver Creek and the Vail Valley.

ASPEN

POP 5914 / ELEV 1890FT

Here's a unique town, unlike any place else in the American West. It's a cocktail of cowboy grit, Euro panache, Hollywood glam, Ivy League brains, fresh powder, live music and old money. It's the kind of place where no matter the season you can bring on a head rush in countless ways. Perhaps you dropped into an extreme vertical run, or stomped to the crest of Buckskin Pass in under three hours? It can come while relaxing at the local music festival, peering down into the bowl of a superpipe or climbing an ice wall. It's possible the horse-drawn sleigh took off too fast for you while you were peering over at yet another $10 million estate, or that cycling to the top of Independence Pass has left you exhausted but smiling. Then again it may have been that way-brainy conversation with a slurring but extraordinarily literate barfly.

Whatever and whomever you've seen, heard or done, there is a common Aspen cure-all. One that has served every Olympic champion, Gonzo journalist, world-class musician, thinker, artist or actor that has ever arrived in this athletic, cultural, intellectual, artistic, absurd ski town. Simply take your body to the frothing hot tub under the stars and leave the head behind. But do bring the bottle. After all, Aspen is nothing if not a place of excellence, extravagance, and, most of all, indulgence. Just remember, whatever you do, don't stand up too fast.

◉ Sights

Aspen, like most Rocky Mountain towns, is less about seeing and more about doing and experiencing. But all that activity does get exhausting, and with a handful of outstanding galleries and some interesting museums downtown, a cutting edge environmental center, and two nearby ghost towns, there are plenty of places to occupy the eyes and calm the mind and body. And don't rule out those park benches – pick one with a good view of those spectacular mountains and the parade of motley Aspen humanity, which, truth be told, is often the most compelling and mind-boggling sight around.

TOP CHOICE FREE **Aspen Center for Environmental Studies**

WILDLIFE SANCTUARY

(☑970-925-5756; www.aspennature.org; 100 Puppy Smith St; ⊙9am-5pm Mon-Sat summer; ℗ ♿) The Aspen Center for Environmental Studies (ACES) is a 22-acre (10-hectare) wildlife sanctuary that hugs the Roaring Fork River. With a mission to advance 'the ethic that the earth must be respected and nurtured,' the center's naturalists provide summertime guided walks, eagle demonstrations and special programs for youngsters at the top of Aspen Mountain and mid-mountain on Snowmass.

Guided walks on Snowmass depart daily at 10am. In the winter, snowshoe and ski tours are available in various locations, and its weekly slide shows may give you some respite from the frigid outdoors. You can take a self-guided tour of the preserve (with snowshoes in winter, if you prefer) surrounding Hallam Lake. The native indoor trout stream may be of interest to anglers and others.

212 Gallery   GALLERY

(☑970-925-7117; www.212gallery.com; 525 E Cooper Ave; ⊙10am-9pm) An amazing, forward-thinking art gallery. When we came through it had an exhibit featuring Daniel Beltra's aerial photos of the BP oil spill, which lent the event an ominous beauty, thanks to the polarized filter on his lens. Ten percent of proceeds of the limited-edition large-format photos went to help the clean up. The large-scale bronze sculptures were striking and the Aurora Robson sculptures were stunning and original.

FREE **Aspen Art Museum**   MUSEUM

(☑970-925-8050; www.aspenartmuseum .org; 590 N Mill St; ⊙10am-6pm Tue-Wed, Fri-Sat, to 7pm Thu, noon-6pm Sun; ℗ ♿) No permanent collection here, just edgy, innovative contemporary exhibitions featuring paint-

ings, mixed media, sculpture, video installations and photography by artists such as Mamma Anderssen, Mark Manders and Susan Phiipszmark. Art lovers will not leave disappointed. Visit in August and you can experience its annual artCRUSH event, an art auction and wine-tasting extravaganza.

FREE **Rio Grande Park**   PARK

(☑reservations 970-920-5140; www.aspen pitkin.com; Rio Grande Pl; ⊙skate park 8am-sunset; ℗ ♿) Aspen's biggest public park runs along the river, and is bisected by the Rio Grande Trail for 2.1 miles. The park is home to an enticing skate park, outdoor basketball courts, a huge athletic field perfect for football or frisbee, an art museum and sculpture garden, and the John Denver Sanctuary.

Set in a grassy riverside meadow and punctuated by boulders that form a natural amphitheater, the sanctuary is a popular sunbathing spot. Some of the stones are engraved with Denver's lyrics including 'Rocky Mountain High.' This peaceful place, with the mountains looming beyond, may even tempt your snarky, protopunk brain to reevaluate the late artist's musical impact. Or not.

🏃 **Activities**

Aspen, for all it's diversity, taste and eccentricity, owes its current status and its cathartic post-war renaissance to its surrounding slopes. Above all else, this is a ski town, and one of the best in America, with four mountains accessible from a single lift ticket – each offering a different flavor and an adventurous twist. But downhill is not the town's only gift. Aspen is surrounded by wilderness areas offering plenty of trails that are typically open from July through early fall, when golden foliage spins in the wind. There are Nordic trails and backcountry huts.

In the summer the same roads, trails and slopes are taken over by cyclists, hikers and climbers. Fisherfolk and paddlers take to the wild-trout water of the Roaring Fork River, although given class V rapids and the short season most paddlers venture down the mountain to get their white-water fix. Many of the beautiful tributary streams to the Roaring Fork – including Lincoln Creek, Hunter Creek, Castle Creek, Maroon Creek and Snowmass Creek – also offer good fishing. And in nearly every season, you can harness into a paraglider and fly high above it all. Arrive with an open mind

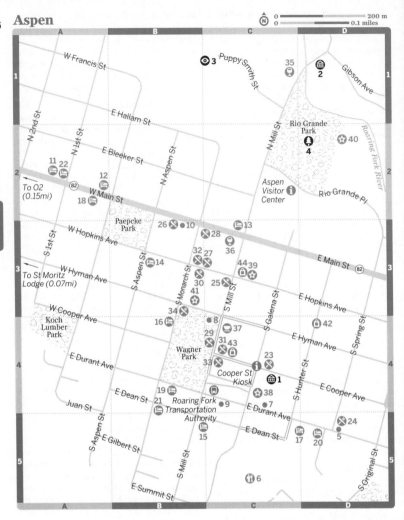

and forget what you've always thought you could and couldn't do. You're in Aspen. There are no rules.

Snow Sports

Aspen Cross Country Center

CROSS-COUNTRY SKIING

(☏970-925-2145; www.utemountaineer.com/aspenxc.html; 39551 Hwy 82; snowshoe rentals adult/child $17.50/9, ski rentals adult/child $21.95/9.95, lessons per hr group/private $35/60; ◷9am-5pm Nov-Mar; ♠) Local outdoor outfitter Ute Mountaineer has operated the Aspen Cross Country Center, set

on Aspen's public golf course, for more than 25 years. Located near the Aspen Snowmass Nordic Trail System (a 60-mile web of Nordic bliss linking Aspen with Snowmass, Ashcroft and Basalt), the center is a convenient spot to demo gear, take a lesson or head out on a guided tour.

Ashcroft Ski Touring

CROSS-COUNTRY SKIING

(☏970-925-1971; www.pinecreekcookhouse.com/ashcroft.html; 11399 Castle Creek Rd; half-/full-day pass $10/15, children & seniors $10, rental packages $20, lessons $75; ♠) This local Nordic outfitter serves 20 miles of groomed trails through 600 acres of subalpine coun-

Aspen

◉ Sights
1 212 Gallery...C4
2 Aspen Art Museum...............................D1
3 Aspen Center for Environmental
　Studies C1
4 Rio Grande Park...................................D2

Activities, Courses & Tours
　Aspen Adventure Collection.........(see 7)
5 Aspen Bike Tours & Rentals.................D5
6 Aspen Mountain.....................................C5
　Aspen Paragliding ....(see 5)
7 Aspen Trout Guides & Outfitters..........C4
8 Hub...C4
9 Silver Circle Ice Rink............................C4
10 Ute City Cycles B3

⊜ Sleeping
11 Annabelle Inn A2
12 Hotel Aspen...A2
13 Hotel Jerome C3
14 Hotel Lenado...B3
15 Hyatt Grand Aspen...............................B5
16 Limelight Lodge.....................................B4
17 Little Nell C5
18 Molly Gibson Lodge..............................A2
19 Mountain Chalet Aspen........................B4
20 Sky Hotel D5
21 St Regis Resort Aspen B4
22 Tyrolean Lodge......................................A2

◉ Eating
23 520 Grill...C4

24 Butchers Block......................................D5
25 Campo de Fiori C3
　Elevation ....(see 32)
26 Escape...B3
　Jimmy's...(see 25)
27 Lulu Wilson C3
28 Matsuhisa C3
29 Pacifica Seafood & Raw Bar................C4
30 Pitkin County Steakhouse....................B3
31 Red Onion C4
32 Syzygy..B3
33 Takah Sushi C4
34 Wild Fig..B3

◉◉ Drinking
35 Aspen Brewing Co................................C1
　Eric's Bar...(see 34)
36 J-Bar..C3
37 Victoria's Espresso & Wine
　Bar C4

◉ Entertainment
38 Belly Up...C4
39 Isis Theatre C3
40 Theatre Aspen.......................................D2
41 Wheeler Opera House...........................B3

◉ Shopping
42 Aspen Saturday Market........................D4
　Explore Booksellers ....(see 26)
43 Kemosabe...C4
　Little Bird ....(see 1)
44 Radio Boardshop C3

try. The mountain backdrop is spectacular, the Ashcroft ghost town eerie. Rent classic cross-country ski equipment, ski gear or snowshoes. Individual and group lessons, as well as snowshoe and ski tours, are available daily. Shuttles ($35) to and from Aspen are available.

Snowmass Club Cross Country Touring Center CROSS-COUNTRY SKIING
(☎970-923-5700; www.utemountaineer.com/snowmassxc.html; 239 Snowmass Club Cir; snowshoe rentals adult/child $17.50/9, ski rentals adult/child $21.95/9.95, per hr lessons group/private $35/60; ◷9am-5pm Nov-Mar; ♠) Set at the Snowmass Club golf course, and operated by Ute Mountaineer for over 10 years, this is your gateway to the 60 miles of free, groomed Nordic trails that connect Aspen, Snowmass, Ashcroft and Basalt.

Treehouse SKI LESSONS, DAYCARE
(☎970-923-8733; www.treehousekidsclub.com; 120 Carriage Way; ◷8am-4pm; ♠) A solid, resort-run ski and snowboard school based in Snowmass. During the summer it shifts into day-care summer-camp mode.

Cycling & Mountain Biking

Hub BIKE RENTAL
(☎970-925-7970; www.hubofaspen.com; 315 E Hyman Ave; bike rental per day $59-99; ◷9am-6pm; ♠) Arguably the best of the Aspen bike shops. This place offers a cycling school, sponsors a weekly road race and bike club, and acts as a booster for local talent, pointing out that Aspen is home to some of the best cyclists in the US, including two top-five time trialists and a dude named Lance. It rents cruisers, full-suspension mountain bikes and carbon fiber road bikes, and will

With four sublime mountains to choose from there's no way you can ski all the terrain on offer in a few days, but if you follow our lead, you can find your bliss on any mountain at (almost) any level.

Snowmass (☎866-352-1763; www.aspensnowmass.com; Aspen Mountain day pass summer $24, Aspen & Snowmass summer $29, Four Mountain two-day pass $158-192; ☺lift 8am-3:30pm; 🚡) The best beginner run is Assay Hill. It's short, typically free of the crowds and sloped perfectly for beginners. Access it via the Assay Hill lift or the Elk Camp Gondola. The top intermediate choice is Sneaky's. Offering sweeping views of the Roaring Fork Valley this wide-open cruiser is the perfect blue 'groomer,' and those looking for a challenge can ski into powder and trees on either side of the run at anytime. Access it with the Sheer Bliss or Big Burn lifts. Any run in the Hanging Valley Headwall will suit the adrenaline set. Make the 10 minute hike to the top of Headwall and head down Roberto's to Strawberry Patch where you can almost always find fresh powder. Accessed via the High Alpine lift.

Aspen Mountain (☎800-525-6200; www.aspensnowmass.com; E Durant Ave; Aspen Mountain day pass summer $24, Aspen & Snowmass summer $29, Four Mountain 2-day pass $158-192, 1-day pass adult/teens & seniors/children $96/87/62; ☺lift 9am-3:30pm Nov 25-Apr 10; 🚡) This is the only one of the four mountains with no beginner terrain. Intermediate skiers and riders will dig Ruthie's, a wide-open groomed run with sweeping views. This is the same terrain skied by Women's World Cup racers each late November/early December when the FIS Women's World Cup comes to Aspen. Local tip: stay skier's right at the top of Ruthie's and you'll head into the Jerry Garcia Shrine. Accessed from the FIS and Ruthie's lifts. Walsh's, on the other hand is for experts. It is steep, deep and breathtaking (visually and physically), with jaw-dropping views of Independence Pass.

Aspen Highlands (☎970-925-1220; www.aspensnowmas.com; Prospector Rd; Aspen Mountain day pass summer $24, Aspen & Snowmass Mountain $29, Four Mountain two-day pass $158-192; ☺9am-3:30pm; 🚡) Beginners head for Apple Strudle, accessed by the Exhibition lift, while intermediate skiers rip the groomed Golden Horn run to Thunderbowl where you'll find wide-open groomed runs with views of Aspen Mountain and the Roaring Fork Valley. Access from Thunderbowl and Exhibition lifts. All the Highland Bowl runs work for advanced skiers and riders. Try G-4 for a steep, deep, tree run and the fairly new cut run, Hyde Park, for one of the longest bump and tree runs you've ever taken. Accessed by Loge Peak and Deep Temerity lifts then hop a free snowcat ride to the top, or just hike it.

Buttermilk (☎800-525-6200, 970-925-1220; www.aspensnowmass.com; Buttermilk Rd & Hwy 82; Aspen Mountain day pass summer $24, Aspen & Snowmass summer $29, Four Mountain two-day pass $158-192; ☺8am-3:30pm; 🚡) Buttermilk beginners head to Westward Ho via the Summit Express and West Buttermilk Express. The Summit Express and Upper Tiehack lifts take intermediate skiers to the blue runs at Buckskin, and the best advanced terrain is Buttermilk Park, starting on Jacob's Ladder. This is where you can ski/ride the same hits and 22ft superpipe as Shawn White, Peter Olenick and all your favorite X Games athletes. You read that right. The X Games happen here.

offer advice on the best road routes and single tracks plying Aspen and Smuggler Mountains, the Montezuma Basin, and Pearl and Independence Pass, but staff aren't always sweet about it. Their motto? 'It's not rude. It's the Hub.'

Ute City Cycles   BIKE RENTAL
(☎970-920-3325; www.utecitycycles.com; 231 E Main St; bike rental per 24hr $75; ☺9am-6pm;

🚡) A high-end road and mountain bike retailer, this place also offers limited rentals from its demo fleet – there's nowhere else in town that you can rent $6500 Orbea road bikes or $2700 Yeti mountain bikes. Rentals are $75 per day with a 2-day maximum; no reservations. Staff can also point you in the direction of Aspen's best cycling.

Aspen Bike Tours & Rentals CYCLING

(☎970-925-9169; www.aspenbikerentals.com; 430 S Spring St; half day $32-40, full day $65-75, 3hr tour per person $100, 2-person minimum; ◷9am-6pm; 🚲) Easily the most laid-back bike shop in town – shaved legs and lycra bravado are nowhere to be found here. Along with premium road and mountain bikes for rent, it also has a network of private guides who can set you up on terrific mountain-biking tours onto trails seldom glimpsed by tourists. Allow 24-hours' notice for staff to set it up.

Hiking

TOP CHOICE / FREE Conundrum Hot Springs

HIKING, HOT SPRINGS

(www.trails.com; Conundrum Creek Rd; 🚲) The steaming, healing Conundrum Hot Springs, west of Castle Peak (14,265ft), are the reward for about 9 miles of tough climbing on the Conundrum Creek Trail (USFS Trail 1981). The trailhead is 5 miles south of the Hwy 82 turnoff for USFS Rd 102, west of town.

There are several pools hewn from craters and fed by plastic pipe, some larger than others and varying in temperature from 102°F to 105°F.

No matter which you sink into, you'll have outrageous alpine views, including glimpses of steep avalanche chutes and waterfalls. For obvious reasons, most folks spend the night at the nearby campsite, unofficially called 'The Bluffs.' From here you can either retrace your steps, or continue over Triangle Pass and return on East Maroon Creek Trail to catch a bus from Maroon Lake back to Aspen.

10th Mountain Division Hut Association

HIKING

(☎970-925-5775; www.huts.org; per person from $25; 🚲) This organization manages a system of 29 backcountry huts – a few with wood-burning saunas – between Vail and Aspen, and connected by 350 miles of suggested routes ideal for cross-country skiing and snow-shoeing in the winter, and hiking in the summer. It's perfect for couples and families. Reservations are by lottery system only and cannot be made online.

FREE Hunter-Fryingpan Wilderness Area

HIKING

(☎970-925-3445; www.fs.usda.gov; 🚲) From Lone Pine Rd in Aspen, the Hunter Valley Trail (USFS Trail 1992) follows Hunter Creek northeast about 3 miles through wildflower meadows to the Sunnyside and Hunter Creek Trails, which lead into the 82,026 acre Hunter-Fryingpan Wilderness Area.

Less visited than other slices of Central Rockies wilderness, you can find some stunning campsites and rugged peaks here, as well as the headwaters to both Hunter Creek and the Fryingpan River.

FREE American Lake Trail HIKING

(www.trails.com; Castle Creek Rd; 🚲) Easily paired with a peek into the ghost town of Ashcroft and/or a meal at the epic Pine Creek Cookhouse, this trail climbs steadily from Ashcroft through aspen and spruce groves to American Lake, in the subalpine Devaney Creek Valley. Views are limited, but the trail meets several more primitive paths to a panoramic overlook. It's a 6.4-mile hike round-trip. Best time to visit is June to October.

Other Activities

T-Lazy-7 Ranch

HORSEBACK RIDING, SNOWMOBILING

(☎970-925-4614; www.tlazy7.com; 3129 Maroon Creek Rd; horseback rides $65-450, sleigh rides per person 4-person minimum $30, snowmobile tours single $200-220, double $300-330; ◷hrs vary; 🚲) Saddle up onto a snowmobile in the winter, or onto a fine steed in the summer at this working ranch down the slope from the Maroon Bells Wilderness Area. It calls itself the oldest working ranch in Aspen. Rides will take you into the spectacular Maroon Bells Wilderness and are highly recommended for families.

Overnight rides ($450) take you all the way to Crested Butte. Snowmobile tours run up to Klondike Cabin in the White River National Forest or Maroon Lake in the Maroon Bells Wilderness. It does sleigh rides in the winter too.

CYCLING TO MAROON BELLS

According to the Aspen cycling gurus, the most iconic road-bike ride in Aspen is the ride to Maroon Bells (p208), mainly because it climbs a lung-wrenching 11 miles to the foot of one of the most picturesque wilderness areas in the Rockies. Most folks drive it or take the bus – the Maroon Bells road is actually closed to incoming car traffic after 9am – but if you crave sweet, beautiful pain, let your quads sing.

Aspen Paragliding
PARAGLIDING

(✆970-925-6975; www.aspenparagliding.com; 426 S Spring St; tandem flights $225; ☺flights 6:45am, 8:30am & 10:30am) Feel like fliying? This paragliding outfitter runs tandem flights year round. During the summer, flights take off from the Silver Queen Gondola on Aspen Mountain. In winter, lift off is from Sam's Knob on the top of Snowmass. Private instruction and group courses are also available.

O2
MASSAGE, YOGA

(✆970-925-4002; www.O2aspen.com; 500 W Main St; yoga class $18, Pilates session $50, massage $120-165; ☺8:15am-7:20pm Mon & Wed, 8:30am-6:50pm Tue & Thu, 8:15am-5:50pm Fri, 9am-5pm Sat, 9am-noon Sun) One of two yoga spots in Aspen, get your yoga, Pilates and massage at this cute Victorian-style-house-turned-studio just off of the main downtown swirl. Highly recommended by locals. Note: the studio sometimes closes between classes if no further appointments are scheduled.

Blazing Adventures
OUTDOORS ACTIVITIES

(✆970-923-4544; www.blazingadventures. com; 48 Upper Village Mall; ⚑) A popular Snowmass-based outfitter that will get you in white water, in the back of a jeep, on a high-altitude ridge at sunset, in a balloon basket at dawn and waist deep in a trout stream anytime you want. It's based in the upper mall (main mall), and consistently gets rave reviews, most notably for the white-water rafting trips on the nearby Arkansas River.

Aspen Expeditions
OUTDOORS ACTIVITIES

(✆970-925-7625; www.aspenexpeditions.com; 115 Boomerang Rd; bike rental adults $40-50, children $21-29; ⚑) Based in the Aspen Highlands ski area, this place does bike tours and rentals, but is most notable for its adventurous itineraries, including some stellar mountain-climbing and rock-climbing trips in the spring and summer, and hut to hut cross-country and backcountry downhill ski trips, as well as ice climbing in the winter. It also runs level one and two avalanche courses. A unique Aspen outfitter, to be sure.

Silver Circle Ice Rink
ICE SKATING

(✆970-925-1710; www.facebook.com/pages/ Aspen-CO/Silver-Circle-Ice-Rink/222463169026; 433 E Durant Ave; adult/child $7/5.50, skate rental $3; ☺noon-9pm Nov-Mar; ⚑) Set at the front of the Hyatt Grand Aspen, across from Rubey Park and at the foot of Aspen Mountain,

HIKING TO THE GROTTOS

One of the most popular summer playgrounds in Aspen, the Grottos area is accessed via a complex web of short trails (most about half a mile in length) that sprout from old Weller Station on the original Independence Pass wagon road, leading to waterfalls and sculpted gorges. The shortest, wheelchair-accessible trail visits a series of thundering falls and swimming holes on the Roaring Fork River.

On the opposite bank, the Old Stage Rd leads upstream to Lincoln Creek, and an offshoot heads to unique water-carved slots known locally as the **Ice Caves**. These are worth hunting for. Head up Independence Pass east of town for 9 miles on Hwy 82 and look for a 'Trailhead' sign on the right-hand side of the road, nearly a mile after passing Weller Campground. Leave your car or bike in the small parking area and start exploring. Be warned: the rocks are slippery and the water icy. Deaths are not frequent, but have been known to happen.

---

this small but ample, centrally located ice rink is ideal for an alfresco family skate.

Aspen Trout Guides & Outfitters
FISHING

(✆970-379-7963; www.aspentroutguides.com; 520 E Durant Ave; half/full-day trips from $245/345; ☺9am-5pm; ⚑) Based out of Hamilton Sports Pro Shop, this has been Aspen's top fly-fishing outfitter since 1981. Trips to the Frying Pan and Roaring Fork Rivers, Maroon, Castle and Hunter Creeks or nearby lakes, including Thomas, Blue and Little Gem, are customized to clients' wishes and include casting instruction. Prices listed are for one angler only; trips are more cost-effective for two or three anglers. Family trips also available.

★ Festivals & Events

Jazz Aspen Snowmass
MUSIC

(✆970-920-4996; www.jazzaspen.org; ☺Jun & Labor Day; ⚑) Aspen's June festival (one of two summer fests) is true to its jazz roots, with horn players such as Christian McBride and Nicholas Payton, crooners such as Harry Connick Jr and Natalie Cole and fusionists such as Pink Martini gracing the Benedict Music Tent or the downstairs venue at the Little Nell in the week leading up to the Fourth of July.

The Labor Day fest, much like the New Orleans Jazz Festival, leans more toward pop-rock these days, attracting superstar acts such as Wilco and The Black Crowes to its outdoor stage in Snowmass Town Park.

Aspen Music Festival   MUSIC
(☑970-925-3254; www.aspenmusicfestival.com; 2 Music School Rd; prices vary; ⊙July & August; ♠) Every summer for the past 60 or so years, some of the best classical musicians from around the world have come to play, perform and learn from the masters of their craft. Students form orchestras led by world-famous conductors and perform at the Wheeler Opera House (p206) or the Benedict Music Tent, or in smaller duets, trios, quartets and quintets on Aspen street corners.

The event schedule is also peppered with classical music stars, many of whom are themselves alumni. All told there are more than 350 classical music events taking place over eight weeks. You can't escape, nor would you want to. And if you're hungry to hear the best music in the sweetest venue, the Benedict is a must. And you don't even have to pay – just unfurl a blanket on the grass just outside the tent and let the music wash over you.

🛏 Sleeping

Aspen is a cute town to nest in, and there are more than a few charming inns to consider. The problem? None of them are cheap. Even in the summer it's tough to find a great room for under $200, and with so many festivals and events scheduled during the summer months rooms can be scarce, so it's best to reserve ahead any time of year. The best summer deal, the Viceory, is a short drive away in Snowmass Village. If you plan a late summer (read: post–Labor Day) mountain getaway you'll get the best value for money in town, while the weather is still sparkling. Rates soar to peak altitude during the winter holiday season. Rates and vacancies are lowest in fall and spring (late April and May).

TOP CHOICE Viceroy   HOTEL $$$
(☑970-923-8000; www.viceroysnowmass.com; 130 Wood Rd; studios summer from $95, winter from $635; ◫◕❀⏱≋♠) By far the best choice in Snowmass and with incredible $95 summer rates, it's the best deal

in all of Aspen (it's the local rate, but just tell them you're a local – staff want you to have it). Here you'll find stylish studios, and condos steeped in glamour, with high ceilings, full kitchens, deep soaker tubs, mosaic showers, seagrass wallpaper, fireplaces and flat-screen TVs.

The lobby bar is all kinds of sleek with a glass bar and floor-to-ceiling wine rack.

Hotel Lenado   BOUTIQUE HOTEL $$$
(☑970-926-6246; www.hotellenado.com; 200 S Aspen St; r $185-385; ◫◕❀⏱♠) There's a certain B&B-style intimacy at this very cute boutique hotel set in what feels like a modern farmhouse. Rooms have old-school woodburning stoves, flat-screen TVs, high ceilings, and large stylish wardrobes decked out with vanities. There's also a wood-barrel hot tub on the roof deck, and a chef shows up every morning to create a gourmet breakfast.

Hotel Aspen   HOTEL $$$
(☑970-925-3441; www.hotelaspen.com; 110 W Main St; r $249-349; ◫◕❀@⏱≋♠) Newer and slicker than its sister property, Molly Gibson, across the street, Hotel Aspen offers modern decor featuring rust-hued accent walls and a wet bar just like Molly. But the pool and poolside lounge here is sleek and the vibe is a touch more hip, with four frothing hot tubs. Rooms are quite large and each has a private patio. One of the best-value options in Aspen.

Hyatt Grand Aspen   HOTEL $$$
(☑970-429-9100; www.hyatt.com; 415 E Dean St; r $200-450, condos $300-1800; ◫◕❀@⏱≋♠) Soak in your private hot tub on your private deck and take in the gorgeous mountain views at sunset. It's the perfect way to end a perfect Aspen day. Specialising in pampering, everything here is pure luxury, and the service and location spot on. Right next to the Silver Queen Gondola, you couldn't ask for a better slope-side location.

Just a few years old, this swank hotel has already made the *Conde Nast Traveller* Gold List for the world's best. Rooms feel more like apartments than hotel abodes, with wide oak floors, kitchens made from granite and marble, and grand stone entranceways. The outdoor pool is heated year-round. Service is fabulous, with staff paying attention to the smallest personalised details. Of course all this pseudo Victorian-meets-King-Louis elegance comes with a hefty price tag, but you can look online to score cheaper deals in the low season – October is a beautiful month, November has even better deals.

Little Nell
HOTEL $$$

(☎970-920-4600; www.thelittlenell.com; 675 E Durant Ave; r from $560; P🐾❄@🛜🏊👷) A long-time Aspen institution offering understated, updated elegance and class at the foot of Aspen Mountain. Gas-burning fireplaces, high-thread-count linens and rich color schemes make up the recently remodeled modernist decor. There are fabulous Balinese pieces in the lobby and hallways decorated with wonderful ski photography. The Greenhouse Bar is perfect for some *après-ski* unwinding.

Redstone Inn
HOTEL $$$

(☎970-963-2526; www.redstoneinn.com; 82 Redstone Blvd; r from $250; P🐾❄@🛜🏊👷) Tucked away behind massive red cliffs, this hotel – and the tiny village of Redstone that surrounds it – occupies a little slice of Rocky Mountain heaven. This is an intimate getaway, perfect for those looking to disappear for few days.

Opened in 1902 as bachelor housing for miners, the historic inn occupies 22 acres (9 hectares) of pristine secluded land surrounded by national forest. The Redstone Inn isn't really near anywhere, which is exactly what makes it so appealing. Paying homage to the American arts-and-crafts movement, the red-roofed lodge features more than 60 pieces of authentic Gustav Stickley furniture. Also look out for locally quarried and hand-cut marble, and gorgeous handcrafted wrought-iron light fixtures in the rooms and lobby. The onsite restaurant and pea-shaped pool mean you needn't go far for food or exercise. It can feel dated, but if you're here for historical charm and natural beauty, rather than up-to-the-minute luxury, you'll leave smiling. It's a one-hour drive from Aspen and 18 miles (29km) south of Carbondale on Hwy 133.

Hotel Jerome
HOTEL $$$

(☎800-331-7213; www.hoteljerome.com; 330 E Main St; r $350-950; P🐾❄@🛜🏊👷) Superb service and relaxed elegance are the trademarks at the historic Hotel Jerome. A long-time favorite with Aspen's old-money crowd, the Jerome occupies an 1889 landmark brick building constructed during Colorado's silver heyday. Rooms are indi-

vidually decorated with period antiques, double-marble vanities and baths with oversized tubs at this intimate and romantic option.

Beds feature lots of pillows and fluffy, feather-down comforters for cold winter nights. If you just want to chill, sink into one of the armchairs facing Aspen Mountain. The hotel also has a great restaurant and lobby, where a hand-carved fireplace is the centerpiece and guests dine on fish and game served by friendly waiters. The Hotel Jerome offers Aspen's most coveted luxury amenity: the ski concierge. This hotel employee takes care of warming your boots before the first run of the morning, and even arranges access up the mountain before lifts open to the general public.

St Regis Resort Aspen
HOTEL $$$

(☎970-925-3300; www.starwood.com; 315 E Dean St; r from $549; P🐾❄@🛜🏊👷) The exterior may be simple Colorado red brick, but the interior of this stylish property is all Victorian excess. Rooms feature old-world European alpine design, with ivory Frette linens and lush red bedskirts. An awardwining luxury hotel, the St Regis Aspen is top notch in the service department; the ski valets here don't just warm your ski boots up, they actually take them off your feet at the end of the day.

Rooms are also posh, in a very grownup and seductively modern fashion. White bedspreads are covered with bright red runners, and carpets and chairs are are beautifully color matched with shades of chocolate and red. Rooms in the old wing are a bit snug, but those marble bathrooms and mountain views will make up for any size shortfall. In warmer weather, check out the outdoor splash pool and landscaped courtyards. If you're looking for sheer lavishness on the slopes, you can't go much better than the St Regis.

Sky Hotel
BOUTIQUE HOTEL $$$

(☎970-925-6760; www.theskyhotel.com; 709 E Durant Ave; r summer from $169, winter $360-505; P🐾❄@🛜🏊👷) At the base of the Aspen ski area, this contemporary resort is an elegant affair with a funky twist. Rooms are minimalist, but playful – yellow walls meet Southwestern wooden beams, white Frette linens and down duvets along with faux-fur throws.

Be sure to check out the huge lobby with its oversized leather chairs, rock wall, lit Aspen trees, and table strewn with board games for guests to borrow. Outside, the hot tub and splash pool are further pluses. Best of all, the Sky is a Kimpton Hotel, which means an eco-conscious and pet-friendly ethos. Fido is not only welcome, he gets his own pet bed! The funky 39 Bar was a hot spot when we came through.

Molly Gibson Lodge LODGE **$$$**
(✆970-925-3434; www.mollygibson.com; 101 W Main St; r $239-349; P✚❄@🖝🔊🖝) One of two good value, tasteful motel-style lodges across from each other on Hwy 82 on the edge of downtown. The owners re-do the rooms every spring, which means clean and tasteful carpeting, fresh paint (including an accent wall) and lush linens. It's all very mod and Ikea-ish but with an upscale slant. Some rooms are huge with massive hot tubs.

Limelight Lodge LODGE **$$$**
(✆800-433-0832, 970-925-3025; www.limelight lodge.com; 355 S Monarch St; r from $325; P✚❄@🖝🔊🖝) A sleek, executive mountain lodge – think brick-and-glass modernism. There's a huge glass lobby with elk and buffalo heads above the massive hearth. Rooms are spacious and have their perks: granite washbasins, leather headboards, desks, sofas and wi-fi. There's a fitness center, pool and two hot tubs on the property too. Low-season and walk-in discounts of up to 50% are common.

Annabelle Inn HOTEL **$$$**
(✆877-266-2466; www.annabelleinn.com; 232 W Main St; r incl breakfast $159-229; P✚❄@🔊🖝) Personable and unpretentious, the cute and quirky Annabelle Inn resembles an old-school European-style ski lodge in a central location. Rooms are cozy without being too cute, and come with flat-screen TVs and warm duvets. We enjoyed the after-dark ski video screenings from the upper-deck hot tub (one of two on the property).

Tyrolean Lodge LODGE **$$**
(✆970-925-4595, reservations 800-220-3809; www.tyroleanlodge.com; 200 W Main St; r $75-210; P✚❄@🔊🖝) One of Aspen's few centrally located and affordable lodges, the Tyrolean is a popular, family-owned option, located within walking distance of downtown. The white condo-style building is adorned with a giant bronze eagle and crossed skis mounted on the outside walls. It's built to resemble a Native American version of an Austrian ski lodge, and is hard to miss.

The rooms here are spacious, and even though they resemble your garden-variety American motel chain, with pine furniture and colored, fire-retardant bedspreads, the Tyrolean goes above and beyond with some nifty decorating features. Each room is slightly different, featuring accents such as fire-engine-red kitchenettes, stone fireplaces and dark-wood paneling behind the two queen beds.

St Moritz Lodge HOSTEL **$**
(✆970-925-3220; www.stmoritzlodge.com; 334 W Hyman Ave; dm $39-54, r incl breakfast $99-239; P✚❄@🔊🖝🖝) Yes, it's a lot of cash to pay for a dorm room, but then again, this is Aspen, and everything is slightly inflated here. That understood, St Moritz is the best no-frills deal in town. The European-style lodge offers a wide variety of options, from quiet dorms to two-bedroom condos. A continental breakfast is included, and the pool and steam room are open to all guests. The cheapest options share bathrooms.

Mountain Chalet Aspen HOTEL **$**
(✆970-925-7797; www.mca.travel.com; 333 E Durant Ave; r $70-460; ✚❄🔊🖝) Just two short blocks from the gondola in the heart of downtown, the Mountain Chalet is in a great location. It's also about as close to budget – although still pricey, sorry backpackers, this is a pricey town – as Aspen gets. Try the internet to score major discounts when the place isn't full.

Rooms at this family-run hotel are a bit outdated and bland, but clean and comfortable nevertheless. Some even have mountain views. Many folks find the lounge a relaxed place to mingle, and the service is friendly. Overall, this casual ski lodge has a homely charm that attracts plenty of repeat customers. The hot tub and sauna are perfect after a long day on the slopes. You can grab free buses to all the Aspen resorts from outside the front door.

✗ Eating

From old-money haunts to hipster steakhouses to top-shelf sushi and some of the finest breakfast burritos we've ever sunk our teeth into (and that's a long list), you won't go hungry here – but you may want to watch your wallet. Costs are often high here, even when the food tends toward the mediocre. Chalk it up to resort pricing and either accept it and move on, or gear your internal clock to Happy Hour (several bars offer late-night Happy Hour menus too) and grind at a discount.

TOP CHOICE Pine Creek Cookhouse

AMERICANA $$$

(☑970-925-1044; www.pinecreekcookhouse.com; 12700 Castle Creek Rd; mains $16-24; ⊘noon-8pm Jun-Sep, seatings at noon, 1:30pm and 6pm Nov-Apr; ☻⌨) Now here's your set piece dining. Think gorgeous log-cabin restaurant serving outstanding, fresh fusion fare, set 11 miles up Castle Creek Canyon past the old mining town of Ashcroft. It does an outstanding shrimp tikka masala, a gorgeous grilled quail served over greens, a terrific house-smoked trout, and tasty buffalo tenderloin. The peaks of Taylor, Star and Cooper loom from the patio.

It's closed in October and May, but stays open all summer and winter, when you can get here from Ashcroft on your cross-country skis or aboard the cookhouse's horse-drawn sleigh! The road is closed at Ashcroft when snow falls.

Syzygy

EUROPEAN $$$

(☑970-925-3700; www.syzygyrestaurant.com; 308 E Hopkins Ave; mains $28-45; ⊘from 6pm; ☻) Tucked into a basement on Aspen's restaurant row, this elegant dining room showcases the considerable talents of a local chef who's been feeding Aspen Jazz Festival VIPs for years (through his catering company). Think truffle-and-potato-crusted turbot, elk tenderloin, veal cheek with sweetbreads, and buffalo carpaccio.

Yes, this fine-dining muse is for the carnivorous gourmand. Translation: beloved by the AARP set, but still a find.

Lulu Wilson

ITALIAN $$$

(☑970-920-1893; www.luluwilsonaspen.com; 316 E Hopkins Ave; mains $23-37; ⊘from 5:30pm) This one's for the casual gourmet. You'll love the shabby-chic chandeliers, gold-washed chairs and exposed-brick interior, and the marble tables outside. You'll also love the branzino stuffed with lobster and roasted whole, the braised rabbit over pappardelle, the housemade gnocchi and the Colorado-grown lamb. The raw bar offers lobster ceviche, tuna crudo and oysters on the half-shell. Groovy all around.

Fuel

SANDWICHES $

(☑970-923-0091; www.snowmassvillage.com/fuel; 45 Village Sq; mains $5.20-8.90; ⊘7am-5:30pm; ☻⌨) This hard-rocking coffeehouse does two things exceptionally well:

jet-fueled espresso and world-class breakfast burritos (it has three kinds – Californian, Mediterranean and southwest). It also has protein bars and energy food to keep you going on the slopes and ridgelines, no matter the season, as well as bagels, paninis, wraps and smoothies.

Staff will pack lunches for the slopes if you ask nicely. It's located just off lot 6 in the lower (main) mall.

Butchers Block

SELF-CATERING $

(☑970-925-7554; 424 S Spring St; sandwiches $8.50-11.95; ⊘8am-6pm; ☻⌨) The depth and breadth of the gourmet spirit of this ski-town deli is striking. Here you'll find gouda, stilton and goats cheese, wild salmon and sashimi-grade ahi, caviar and gourmet olive oil, maple-glazed walnuts, dried mango, incredible deli sandwiches, and terrific roast chicken and salads. It's fair to say that this is the place to get your trail food. It's open until 6pm, but stops making sandwiches at 5pm.

Pitkin County Steakhouse

STEAK $$$

(☑970-544-6328; www.pitkincountysteakhouse.com; 305 E Hopkins Ave; mains $26-58; ⊘from 6pm; ☻) The most popular and down-to-earth steakhouse in town. It does prime dry-aged steaks, prime rib and, to quote one satisfied customer, 'the best fucking crab legs in the world!' Set in the basement of a Hopkins Ave complex, it has an open kitchen with tables scattered about the just-dark-enough environs and an iced-down fish selection for you to check out as you glide to your table.

During the low season the dining room is only open Thursday to Saturday, but its adjacent tavern is always open for business.

Escape

CAFE FOOD $$

(☑970-925-5338; 221 E Main St; mains $12-14; ⊘11am-3pm; ☻⌨⌨) Set on the top floor of Explore Booksellers, this gourmet (mostly) veggie cafe serves up tofu stir-fries, veggie sandwiches and flatbreads. It also has a toe or two in the sea: po'boy, shrimp et al. Also makes tasty omelets.

Elevation

FUSION $$$

(☑970-544-5166; www.elevationaspen.com; 304 E Hopkins Ave; mains $23-34; ⊘5:30-11:30pm; ☻) Another new favorite among Aspenites, Elevation fuses continental and Asian cuisine. Think ahi pizza, slow-roasted rum-and-coke tacos, pork belly and papaya salad, sea scallops and Brie glazed in truffle honey, and hand-cut pappardelle with lobster bolognese. The bar glows, the chipotle-infused olive oil on the tables is striking, and the flashy, funky art on the walls lends a certain edge.

Wild Fig
CONTEMPORARY AMERICAN $$$

(☏970-925-5160; www.thewildfig.com; 315 E Hyman Ave; mains $14-32; ☺11:30am-3pm summer, 5:30pm-close year-round; ☻🖑) This bright, tiled dining room and patio edged with flower boxes packs plenty of gourmet cheer. It does a nightly risotto, a tender grilled-octopus salad and an enticing fig-glazed pork chop. Its small plates are also worth considering – we loved the marinated figs with pancetta, the pan-seared scallops and the fire-roasted clams with chorizo.

Campo de Fiori
ITALIAN $$$

(☏970-920-7717; www.campodefiori.net; 205 S Mill St; mains $36-39; ☺from 5:30pm; ☻) Authentic Italian cooking and festive Mediterranean flair have been the mainstay of this mini-mall kitchen off Aspen's restaurant row for more than a decade. The menu mimics its Vail sister. It's seasonal, the gnocchi is house made, and the seafood – especially the calamari – is excellent.

Matsuhisa
JAPANESE $$$

(☏970-544-6628; www.matsuhisaaspen.com; 303 E Main St; dishes $5-38; ☺from 6pm; ☻) The fifth link in Matsuhisa Nobu's iconic global chain that now wraps around the world. This converted house still turns out spectacular dishes such as miso black cod, Chilean sea bass with truffle, and flavorful uni (sea urchin) shooters. You'll want to keep ordering until you can eat no more.

Takah Sushi
JAPANESE $$$

(☏970-925-8588; www.takahsushi.com; 320 Mill St; rolls $7-24, mains $24-39; ☺5:30pm-late; ☻🖑) It's not as celebrated as Matsuhisa, but it's not quite as expensive either and this fun basement and patio sushi bar has tasty cooked small plates too. Think sirloin wrapped asparagus, Kobe beef sliders, atomic lobster (yeah, it's spicy), the usual sushi and some more creative rolls, such as the ninja (tempura avocado and crab salad wrapped in tuna).

Red Onion
PUB FOOD $$$

(☏970-925-9955; www.redonionaspen.com; 420 E Cooper Ave; mains $15-35; ☺11am-2am) Open since 1892, this saloon has been recently renovated with a certain mountain bistro flair. The fusion menu has a brainy side, starring mango and brie quesadillas, and grilled lamb chops in a habanero preserve, plus you've gotta love a joint that serves chicken and waffles for (late) breakfast. The kitchen stays open well into the night.

520 Grill
SANDWICHES $

(☏970-925-9788; 520 E Cooper Ave; sandwiches $8.95, salads $7.45; ☺11am-6pm Mon-Thu, 11am-4pm Fri & Sat; 🖑) A (mostly) healthy (kinda) fast-food grill, if there is such a thing. Sandwiches are creative, spicy concoctions. The achiote chicken is grilled and piled on the pita with roasted red peppers, avocado and cheese. The Veg Head is an alchemy of roasted portobello mushrooms and garlic, with a pepper medley dressed in balsamic.

It also serves a good-looking, much loved kale and quinoa salad along with epic traditional and sweet potato fries. Locals are devoted to it. The best part? It's affordable!

Pacifica Seafood & Raw Bar
SEAFOOD $$$

(☏970-920-9775; www.pacificaaspen.com; 307 S Mill St; appetizers $13-23, mains $33-39; ☺11:30am-2:30pm & 5:30pm-late; ☻🖑) The newish fish house in town is right on Wagner Park. It has a raw bar and serves creative tapas, such as steamed mussels and elk sausage for light snacks, and eight seafood mains for dinner. The main dishes include classics such as Hawaiian ahi with wasabi mashed potato, grilled ono with black sticky rice, and sea scallops served with white truffle and fava bean purée.

There's a great, albeit a tad preppy, happy-hour crowd in the summer. Not that there's anything wrong with that. Happy hour runs from 3:30pm to 5:30pm.

Jimmy's
STEAK $$$

(☏970-925-6020; www.jimmysaspen.com; 205 S Mill St; mains $13-64; ☺4pm-late, dining room to 10pm, 10:30am-2pm Sun brunch; ☻🖑) Jimmy's is a soulful tequila-, crab- and steakhouse with attitude that attracts a very A-list crowd. Settle into a booth and check out the writing on the wall in the main dining room. No, we're not being cryptic: Jimmy's idea of decorating is covering the walls with guest graffiti – bring a pen. You're paying a king's ransom to dine with the rich and famous, so you may as well leave your mark.

The perpetually packed bar serves a cheaper menu and 105 types of tequila and mescal. Thursday nights are devoted to the crab, with king crab legs going for a song. It hosts a salsa night on Saturdays.

🍷 Drinking

TOP CHOICE **Aspen Brewing Co** BREWPUB
(☑970-920-2739; www.aspenbrewing
company.com; 557 N Mill St; pints $2.75, flights $7;
☺noon-9pm Mon-Sat, noon-6pm Sun) Tibetan
prayer flags fly from the rafters, two flat-
screen TVs strobe ballgames, the shelves
are stuffed with board games, and reggae
sings from the hi-fi at this groovy streamside microbrewery.

Six flavors are brewed directly behind
the bar. Literally. You can get a pint for
just $2.75, and a flight for $7 if you want to
sample them all, from the flavorful blonde
to the peachy Independence Pass Ale (its
IPA signature), the mellower Conundrum
Red Ale and the chocolatey Pyramid Peak
Porter.

Woody Creek Tavern PUB
(☑970-923-4285; www.woodycreektavern.com;
2 Woody Creek Plaza, 2858 Upper River Rd; mains
$11-20; ☺11am-10pm, closed Thanksgiving and
Christmas; 🖫) Enjoying a 100% agave tequila
and fresh-lime margarita at the late, great
gonzo journalist Hunter S Thompson's
favorite watering hole is well worth the
8-mile trek from Aspen. Here since 1980,
the walls at this rustic funky tavern, a local
haunt for decades now, are plastered with
newspaper clippings and paraphernalia
(mostly dedicated to Thompson).

The menu features organic salads, low-
fat but still juicy burgers, popular Mexican
food including some quality guacamole,
and plenty of alcohol. Eleven gallons of
margaritas a day can't be wrong.

Victoria's Espresso & Wine Bar CAFE
(☑970-920-3001; www.aspenespressobar.com;
312 S Mill St; drinks from $2; ☺7am-8:30pm; 🖫)
It has baked goods and wine, full breakfasts (those ricotta pancakes look delish)
and espresso, but the must-try here is the
vanilla latte. Made with housemade syrup
crafted from real vanilla bark, it isn't too
overly sweet – just immediately and completely addictive.

Eric's Bar BAR
(☑970-920-6707; www.sucasaaspen.com; 315
E Hyman Ave; ☺7pm-2am) One of three bars
in the Su Casa complex, all of which are
owned by one savvy fellow. This one is by
far the coolest. It's a brick-walled lounge
with DJs on Thursday nights when the midnight freaks dance like mad. If the crowd
gets too tight, head over to the billiard hall
or upstairs to the cigar lounge.

J-Bar BAR
(☑970-920-1000; www.hoteljerome.com; 330 E
Main St; mains $12-20; ☺11:30am-1am; 🛜) Once
Aspen's premier saloon, back when the
word 'saloon' had its own unique meaning,
this bar was built into the Hotel Jerome in
1889 and remains full of historic charm and
packed with everyone from local shopkeep-
ers to Hollywood stars. Order the signature
cocktail, the Aspen Crud, if you're in the
mood for something sweet. It's a delicious
blend of bourbon and ice cream. The more
tart J-Rita is equally delicious. The menu
features gourmet American pub fare that's
nearly as tasty as the drinks.

☆ Entertainment

TOP CHOICE **Belly Up** LIVE MUSIC
(☑970-544-9800; www.bellyupaspen.
com; 450 S Galena St; cover varies; ☺hrs vary)
Long the top nightspot in Aspen, Belly Up
has built and maintained its street cred by
bringing in the best live acts to the Aspen
people. That means everything from local bluegrass bands to hip-hop globalist
K'NAAN, to Chrissy Hynde's brilliant new
band, to LCD Soundsystem DJ sets and intimate, up-close throwdowns with all-timers
such as Jane's Addiction (although, those
ain't cheap).

No matter who you see, the room will be
intimate and alive with great sound. Easily
the best venue this side of Denver.

Theatre Aspen THEATRE
(☑970-925-9313, box office 970-920-5770;
www.theatreaspen.org; 505 Rio Grande Pl; prices
vary; ☺hrs vary; 🖫) A nonprofit theater and
drama school that hosts classes, workshops
and periodic productions (mostly in the
summer and early autumn) from its gorgeous, tented complex in the heart of Rio
Grande Park. Matinees include bonus views
of the nearby mountains, evening productions play beneath a starry sky. Check website for details of upcoming shows and see
one if you can.

Expect to see productions such as Tony
award–winning romantic comedies and deliciously subversive musicals.

Wheeler Opera House ENTERTAINMENT VENUE
(☑970-920-5770; www.wheeleroperahouse.com;
320 E Hyman Ave; prices vary; ☺box office 9am-
7pm winter, to 5pm summer; 🖫) Built in 1887,
one of Aspen's oldest and finest examples
of Victorian architecture has been a working theater since it first opened – with the
exception of the 30 or so years things were

interrupted by fire, depression and reconstruction. The point is, this place is historic and was definitely part of Aspen's postwar revival. It still presents opera, films, concerts and musicals.

During summer the Aspen Music Festival holds concerts here.

Isis Theatre
CINEMA

(☑970-925-7584; www.metrotheatres.com; 406 E Hopkins Ave; adult/child, senior & matinees (before 6pm) $10/7, bargain Tue $7.50/5.50; ☺hrs vary; ⓘ) The only movie house in Aspen proper plays first-run Hollywood fare, but thankfully spices up the blockbusters with an ocassional pinch of art-house and foreign cinema. This is Aspen, after all. But eat and come early as there are no late shows.

🛍 Shopping

Aspen is for the professional shopper. Part Malibu, part Rodeo Dr, part Soho, this is Colorado's only professional shopper's strip. Everything from high-end hoodies to pro-grade outdoor gear to designer bling is available for a (high) price. There are also a couple of consignment shops worth sifting through, as well as more than a few art galleries, some of which are rather remarkable. For detailed information on local art galleries, pick up a free copy of Aspen Magazine's *Gallery Guide* from the Chamber Resort Association or log onto www.aspenmagazine.com/guide/gallery.

TOP CHOICE Explore Booksellers
BOOKS

(☑970-925-5336; www.explorebooksellers.com; 221 E Main St; ☺10am-7pm; ☜ⓘ) A sweet and intimate local bookshop, the kind that must survive if humanity is to preserve its literate soul. Little alcoves are stacked with biographies, history, adventure and nature tomes and, of course, new and classic literature. Note to readers: there is no gonzo section. We can't help but wonder why. Still, the staff tips are rock solid. By far the best excuse in Aspen to put down the iPad/Kindle and turn a page.

Radio Boardshop
SPORTING GOODS

(☑970-925-9373; www.radioboardshop.com; 400 E Hopkins Ave; skateboards incl helmets & pads per day $10-15; ☺10am-6pm; ⓘ) On the shortlist for the coolest shop in Aspen, this place does stylish top-shelf skateboards and snowboards, and sells the gear, shoes and boots to match. It's a mom-and-pop store with style to spare. Unfortunately,

it doesn't rent snowboards but does rent skateboards at great prices in the summer.

FREE Kemosabe
CLOTHING

(☑970-925-7878; www.kemosabe.com; 434 E Cooper Ave; ☺10am-5pm; ⓘ) The sister to Vail's cowboy apparel depot, it does the same handmade boots and Stetson hats – steam shaped to please. Expect friendly faces, a stuffed buffalo head, gleaming belt buckles and a bluegrass soundtrack.

Little Bird
CLOTHING

(☑970-920-3830; thelittlebirdaspen@gmail.com; 525 E Cooper Ave; ☺10am-6pm Mon-Sat, noon-5pm Sun) This gem of a consignment store has new and vintage luxury designer scarves, dresses, handbags, shoes and more. Gucci, Jimmy Choo, Blahnik – all the handsome boys are here. You can bargain too, and if staff have had the gear for more than 30 days you may strike a deal, but it still won't be cheap. You are in Aspen, after all.

Aspen Saturday Market
MARKET

(☑970-429-2687; S Hunter St, E Hopkins Ave & E Hyman Ave; ☺9am-3pm mid-Jun–Oct; ⓘ) This market blooms on Saturday mornings. It's more than just a farmers market, though self-caterers can grab their organic fruits and veggies, craftsmen cheese, and naturally and locally grown beef, bison and elk here. It also has tons of crafts, including handmade soap, silver jewelry and fixed-gear bikes built with vintage frames.

The market runs in a U-shape from Hyman to Hopkins on Hunter before turning down both Hyman and Hopkins to Galena.

ℹ Information

INTERNET ACCESS **Pitkin County Library** (☑970-429-1900; www.pitcolib.org; 120 N Mill St; ☺10am-9pm Mon-Thu, 10am-6pm Fri & Sat, noon-6pm Sun; @☜ⓘ) Another in a series of fantastic public libraries in the state of Colorado. It has books and films for the borrowing, free wi-fi and public terminals for surfing the web.

MEDIA **Aspen Magazine** (www.aspenmagazine.com/guide/gallery)

Aspen Times (www.aspentimes.com) The local paper has a decent website packed with relevant local and regional news and events.

MEDICAL SERVICES **Aspen Valley Hospital** (☑970-925-1120; www.avhaspen.org; 401 Castle Creek Rd; ☺24hr; ☜ⓘ) A small but up-to-the-minute community hospital with 24hr emergency services.

MONEY US Bank (☎970-925-3535; www.firstcoloradobank.com; 420 E Main St)

TOURIST INFORMATION Aspen Visitor Center (☎970-925-1940, 800-670-0792; www.aspenchamber.org; 425 Rio Grande Pl; ☺8am-5pm Mon-Fri; 🖤) Aspen Visitor Center has all the usual maps and information and is located in lovely Rio Grande Park.

Cooper St Kiosk (cnr E Cooper Ave & S Galena St; ☺10am-6pm)

USFS White River National Forest's Aspen Ranger District (☎970-925-3445; www.fs.fed.us; 806 W Hallam St; ☺8am-4:30pm Mon-Fri winter, 8am-4:30pm Mon-Sat summer; 🖤) The USFS White River National Forest's Aspen Ranger District operates nine campgrounds and is responsible for all the public land stretching from Independence Pass to Glenwood Springs, including the Maroon Bells Wilderness. This small office has knowledgeable staff and an assortment of useful topographic maps and literature, including the booklet *12 Short Hikes* ($4.95).

WEBSITES Ski.com (☎800-908-5000; www.ski.com; 233 W Airport Rd; ☺hrs vary; 🖤) An online travel agency offering cheap all-inclusive ski and snowboard packages that include everything from flights to lodging to rentals and lift tickets. You can find it online, and it also has a shingle at the airport.

ℹ Getting There & Away

Aspen is 41 miles south of Glenwood Springs. From Denver, Aspen is 208 miles via I-70 and Hwy 82. During winter months, Hwy 82 over 12,095ft Independence Pass to Leadville is closed.

Aspen-Pitkin County Airport (☎970-920-5380; www.aspenairport.com; 233 E Airport Rd; 🖤🖤) Four miles north of Aspen on Hwy 82, this surprisingly spry airport has commuter flights from Denver, and nonstops to Phoenix, Los Angeles, San Francisco, Minneapolis and Memphis. Colorado Mountain Express runs frequent shuttles to/from Denver International Airport ($99, three hours).

ℹ Getting Around; Away
To/From the Airport

Roaring Forks Transportation Authority runs a twice hourly, free bus to and from the Aspen-Pitkin County Airport. High Mountain Taxi makes the run from the airport to Aspen, Aspen Highlands and Snowmass Village.

Colorado Mountain Express (☎800-525-6363, 970-926-9800; www.cmex.com; Aspen-Pitkin County Airport; 🖤) Colorado Mountain Express runs frequent shuttles to/from the Denver International Airport ($99, three hours).

Bus

Roaring Fork Transportation Authority (RFTA; ☎970-925-8484; www.rfta.com; 430 E Durant Ave; ☺6:15am-2:15am; 🖤) Roaring Fork Transit Agency (RFTA) buses connect Aspen with Snowmass and Buttermilk via free ski shuttles, the Maroon Bells Wilderness ($6) – the only way to get to the trailhead after 9am – as well as the lower altitude towns of Basalt ($4, 30 minutes), Carbondale ($6, one hour) and Glenwood Springs ($7, 80 minutes). Drivers don't handle money so passengers must have exact change.

It also runs a free local bus to and from the Aspen-Pitkin County Airport, leaving the airport 15 and 45 minutes after the hour all day long. The Aspen depot is located at Durant Ave and Mill St at the Rubey Park Transit Center.

Car & Taxi

Although the bus service is reliable, given how spread out the Aspen area is, it does help to have a car if you're planning on hitting the summer trails. Rental agencies with counters at Pitkin-County Airport include Alamo, Avis, Budget, Dollar, Enterprise and Hertz. **High Mountain Taxi** (☎970-925-8294; www.hmtaxi.com; Aspen-Pitkin County Airport; to/from airport to Aspen $19-27, to Snowmass $27-38; ☺24hr) operates meter cabs 24 hours a day.

AROUND ASPEN

Independence GHOST TOWN (☎970-925-3721; www.aspenhistorysociety.com; Hwy 82; adult/child 12yr & under $3/free; ☺9am-5pm Jun 19-Labor Day; 🅿🖤) Just 16 miles from Aspen at the foot of Independence Pass, this gold-mining boom town turned ghost town started as a tented camp in the summer of 1879, when one lucky miner struck gold on the Fourth of July. Operated and preserved by the Aspen Historical Society, you can see the remains of the old livery, the general store and a miners cabin or three.

After its population had peaked at 1500 residents, the town fell away during the harsh winter storm of 1899 after supply routes were severed due to severe snowfall.

Maroon Bells

The road to Aspen's most iconic wilderness area branches from Hwy 82 at Aspen Highlands. It cuts through the wilderness and follows a gushing creek as it meanders between red-rock hills that crumble into boulders amid dramatic interplay between

ASHCROFT

The best access point to the 20 miles of groomed trails in the stunning Castle Creek Valley is the ghost town of Ashcroft (☎970-925-3721; www.aspenhistorysociety.com; Castle Creek Rd; adults $3, children 10yr & under free; ☺10am-4pm; ℗♿), a silver-mining town founded in 1880. What remains are mostly miners cottages (log cabins with tin roofs), a couple of broken-down wagons stranded in the waist-high grass, and a post office and saloon.

At its height 2500 people worked here, but in 1893 the silver market crashed and the town's population plummeted to 100 residents within two hours.

There's a fine picnic area down by the creek, and a series of displays profiling famous residents, and local transportation and communication of the day. Preserved by the Aspen Historical Society, it's well worth stopping for. Admission gets you a free tour if you show up during business hours. It's also easily explored out of hours.

lime-green aspen and deep-green conifers on the haunches of great mountains.

If you have but one day to enjoy a slice of the pristine, you'd be wise to spend your time here, whether it's aboard a horse and sleigh or bobsled in the winter, or on a long, grueling but supremely uplifting day hike during the summer. Or maybe you want to get really lost and spend days hiking, camping and contemplating some of the most stunning mountain scenery you'll find in Colorado.

The parking area spills onto the shores of Maroon Lake, an absolutely stunning picnic spot backed by those towering mountains. Here are nine passes over 12,000ft and six 14,000ft-plus. Some jut into jagged granite towers, others are a more generous slope and curve, nurturing a series of meadows that seem to gleam from the slopes.

🏃 Activities

Free guided naturalist hikes are led by ACES guides daily at 10:15am and 1:15pm leaving from the **Visitors Center** (☎970-925-3445; www.fs.usda.gov; Maroon Creek Rd; ☺9am-5pm Memorial Day-Oct; ♿). Assemble 10 minutes before each hike. Crater Lake is the most popular hike from the main trailhead. It's quick and dirty, just a bit over a mile each way, and while the setting – surrounded by gorgeous sculpted peaks and fed by a creek winding it's way down from the high county – is stunning, the lake itself is brown and shallow in the late season. Not all that special as far as mountain lakes go.

We suggest pressing onto Buckskin Pass (12,462ft). From the narrow granite ledge you can see mountains erupt from all directions. If you continue over the pass you'll

wind up at Snowmass Lake, a terrific campsite. Or you could diverge from the Buckskin Trail and head instead over Willow Pass (12,600ft) and either lunch or camp at Willow Lake (11,795ft). It takes about three hours to get there. Views are marvelous the entire way, especially at the top where you can see the Continental Divide.

As is the usual protocol in the Rockies, it's best to get off the pass before noon, as afternoon lightening is a real danger. Of course, a star like this has not gone unnoticed, and the Bells get some 200,000 visitors every summer.

❶ Getting There & Away

The road to the wilderness is closed to private vehicular traffic between 9am and 5pm, but you catch an RFTA bus from downtown Aspen or the Aspen Highlands (where you'll find ample free parking) throughout the day.

Basalt

Aspen's humble neighbor and down to earth little sister has plenty to flaunt. Set at the confluence of the Frying Pan and the Roaring Fork rivers, it is framed by gold-medal trout waters, making this cute but humble town something of a fly-fishing parades. Most Aspen outfitters will bring you down here to cast.

The town is tiny but blessed with a cute main street strip, plenty of tasty dining options, a couple of cheapish motels, and you're only 20 minutes from the Four Mountain slopes, and another 20 to the artsy range-land enclave that is up-and-coming Carbondale.

The people who live here are real working folks, and a breath of fresh air if the upper-crust atmosphere in Aspen has your head spinning.

☀ Activities

Taylor Creek Fly Shop   FISHING
(☏970-927-4374; www.taylorcreek.com; 183 Basalt Center Cir; rod rental per day $15, 1-/2-person half-day guided trips $255/325, full-day $395/325; ⏱8am-6pm; 🖶) This fly shop, with its prime location on the banks of the Frying Pan River, has gold-medal trout waters right in its backyard. It rents rods and waders, and offers casting clinics out back and more detailed instruction on its guided trips.

🛏 Sleeping & Eating

Aspenalt Lodge   MOTEL $$
(☏877-379-6476; www.aspenalt.com; 157 Basalt Center Cir; r $105-120; P😊❄🛜🖶) A roadside 1980s motel with saggy beds in super-clean, spacious rooms with wi-fi. It's set in a sweet location right on the Frying Pan River, but the rooms don't exactly do the lovely setting justice. Still, if you're looking for something cheap and doable, it's worth considering.

Green Drake   MOTEL $$
(☏800-905-6797, 970-927-4747; www.green-drake.com; 220 Midland Ave; r $89-119, incl kitchenettes $139; P😊❄🛜🖶) A cheapie on the main drag through town. It's your basic motel with clean, decent-sized rooms with industrial carpeting. Though it's now set in different digs, this was the original Basalt hotel when the town sprouted up circa 1920. The original was set in the brick building next door.

TOP CHOICE Cafe Bernard $$
(☏970-927-4292; 200 Midland Ave; mains $7.50-14; ⏱7:30am-2pm & from 6pm Tue-Sat; 😊🖶) Owned by a French chef, this is one of town's cutest, most beloved restaurants. Set on the main drag, this part diner, part bistro does creative comfort food such as tasty filet of trout, Caesar salad and grilled sandwiches.

Tempranillo   MEDITERRANEAN $$$
(☏970-927-3342; www.tempranillorestaurant.com; 165 Midland Ave; tapas $5-12, mains $17-35; ⏱11am-10pm; 😊🖶) If you're into tapas and wine you'll enjoy this Spanish-flavored joint set in an old, renovated Victorian. It offers a range of tapas, including Manilla clams in white-wine sauce, piquillo peppers stuffed with crab and lobster, and a sampling of Spanish sausages. During the summer there's lovely al fresco dining on the front porch, and the interior with its high, timber-beamed ceiling and fireplaces is always inviting.

Riverside Grill   CONTEMPORARY AMERICAN $$
(☏970-927-9301; www.riversidegrillbasalt.com; 181 Basalt Center Cir; mains $10.95-21.95; ⏱11:30am-8pm; 😊🖶) The most scenic and atmospheric place to eat in Basalt is this old timber warehouse that opens directly onto the Frying Pan River. The more laid-back sister restaurant to Syzygy (p204) in Aspen, flat-screens strobe sports on both sides of the double-sided bar, and the menu features interesting dishes such as buffalo tacos, beer-braised Texas brisket, smoked-trout chowder, truffle fries and tasty veggie burgers.

❶ Getting There & Away

Basalt is 18.5 miles northwest of Aspen and 23.1 miles southeast of Glenwood Springs on Hwy 82. If you're not driving, the entire region is served by the RFTA (p208).

ALONG HWYS 24 & 85

Minturn
POP 1200 / ELEV 7861FT

Squeezed between the burgeoning luxury condominium and resort developments of Vail and Beaver Creek, Minturn is a nice respite in the heart of Eagle County.

This small railroad town along the Eagle River was founded in 1887; its shops and homes retain the coziness and charm of a place that really has been around for a while. It's less a vacation destination and more an authentic and picturesque bedroom community for staff and business owners who work in and around the ski resorts. But there's charm and adventure to be found here too.

The townspeople have long been a bit anxious about Vail's rumored plans to one day connect Beaver Creek and Vail Mountain via Minturn. There is also a campaign to turn the rail line into a bike trail as part of the national 'Rails to Trails' program, though nothing was set at the time of writing.

If you're itching to head off the grid, consider the Minturn Mile. One of the most famous 'out-of-bounds' ski runs in the world, you can access it from the top of chairs 3 or 7 on Vail Mountain (p181).

At the top of the turn on the 'Lost Boy Trail' take the access gate and begin a descent of 3 miles to Minturn. Advanced skills are a must as you'll encounter a wide range of terrain – starting in a bowl and veering through the trees. At about the midway point you'll find the 'beaver ponds,' a terrific place to take a break and catch your breath before hitting the 'Luge,' an old fire road that gets narrow in spots and will lead you the rest of the way down.

Know that you'll be skiing into an area beyond the resort boundaries; it is not patrolled. If you get injured, you'll be on your own, and if you require rescue it will come at a considerable expense. It's best to ski along with someone who has prior knowledge of the terrain and route and be sure to have proper gear, equipment and an updated report on conditions. Of course, it is, by all accounts, a magnificent experience – one of the best in the Vail swirl – and requires a beverage at the Minturn Saloon upon arrival.

🏃 Activities

Minturn and Red Cliff (located about 10 miles farther south on US 24) are gateways to the **Holy Cross Wilderness Area**, where you'll find some of the most spectacular hiking and backcountry skiing in the area. Anyone heading up to the region should first check in with the USFS Holy Cross Ranger District (p180). It has free maps of all the area trails and campsites as well as complete information about degree of difficulty and trail conditions. Do not head up to the wilderness area without the proper information from the USFS and the appropriate equipment.

Fishing

Given that the Eagle River runs right through town, it should come as no surprise that the fishing in and around town is pretty damn special. Though the fish are bigger downstream, the higher altitude fishing is just tremendous and a terrific year-round activity. The fish are easier to find and the scenery absolutely stunning in winter.

Mountain Anglers   FISHING
(www.mountainanglers.com; 102 Eagle St; 🚻) Guides newbies along Gore Creek and the Upper Eagle River.

🍴 Eating

Minturn Saloon   MEXICAN/STEAKHOUSE **$$**
(🖋970-827-5954; www.minturnsaloon.com; 146 Main St; mains $6-17; 🚻) Always a restaurant and bar, she does have a tawdry past (but who doesn't?). Dynamite Mexican.

Nicky's Quickie   GREEK **$$**
(🖋970-376-7307; www.nickysquickie.com; 151 Main St; 🚻) The place to come if you're passing through and need something fast. It does a classic gyro pita (Nicky's Quickie) and a creative felafel that includes artichoke hearts and sundried tomatoes (Nicky's Veggie).

ℹ Getting There & Away

To get here, go 3 miles west of Vail on I-70 then 2 miles south on US 24.

Red Cliff

POP 350 / ELEV 8750FT

Both a working-class mountain holdout and a dream homestead for the paddling class, Red Cliff has a dual personality. It's set about 6 miles south of Minturn on US 24, on the way to the Holy Cross Wilderness Area, and the drive into town from the highway is spectacular. The road winds down along the Eagle River and passes beneath an old green bridge before easing into what looks like a well-to-do paddler's paradise.

When you get to Eagle St, the downtown area looks a bit more ragged, but still quite friendly, happy and tight knit. Which stands: only 350 people live here.

The town got it's launch during the 19th century gold mining boom. The last remaining mine, set between Red Cliff and Minturn, shifted to copper in the 20th century before getting shut down by the EPA in the 1980s. It's now a Superfund (toxic clean-up) site. Timber paid the bills for a chunk of the 20th century too, and now residents mostly commute to work in the Vail Valley.

Bikes and skates rule the streets in summer. Snowmobiles rule the winter. Red Cliff is a common take out on Eagle River trips from Vail. Early in the rafting season it's a put in for Class V kayakers.

In terms of sleeping and eating, your best bets are the **Green Bridge Inn** (✆970-827-5228; www.greenbridgeinn.com; 104 Water St; r $79-119; P ♿ ❀ 🏠 🛅) and **Mango's** (✆970-827-9109; www.mangosmountaingrill.com; 166 ½ Eagle St; mains $8-20; ⊙11:30am-late; 🛅).

If you're leaving Red Cliff and heading east, consider taking the Shrine Pass Rd. This 12.5-mile, graded but unpaved road cuts through some remarkable countryside before dropping down to the east side of Vail Pass. Be sure to stop at the top to check out the view of Mt of the Holy Cross behind you. 4WD vehicles are recommended. High clearance is a must.

Leadville

POP 2821 / ELEV 10,152FT

Nicknamed 'Cloud City' and 'Two Mile High City' for its altitude, Leadville was once the second biggest city in Colorado.

That was back in its boomtown heydey, and her glory days still attract visitors curious about the enormous mining operations and characters that put it on the map. But unlike other historic towns with mining roots, Leadville never made the switch to resort status, and with depressed mobile-home communities on either side of the charming historic district downtown, Leadville has a certain downmarket Appalachia vibe and more than a vague reminiscence to Napoleon Dynamite's hometown.

Still, those magnificent mountains that surround downtown are impossible to ignore and include Colorado's two highest peaks. They're ripe for adventure and the site of one of the largest mountain bike races in the world. And you can take heart that back in Leadville proper, the groovy Colorado Mountain College students certainly do their part to save this town's old soul. The principal route through town, US 24, follows a dogleg course from Harrison Ave in the south to E 9th St before continuing north on Poplar St.

☉ Sights

History looms large in Leadville. From the scenic historic district where you can tour three museums to the mines on the outskirts, it's hard not to notice that this place had a lot to do with the state's early success.

FREE **Camp Hale** MEMORIAL
(www.camphale.org; Camp Hale 1; P 🛅) North of Leadville, about halfway to Red Cliff, you'll pass a turnout that looks over a wide meadow backed by gentle, rolling peaks. Peer into the meadow carefully and you can still see the markings of old foundations and roads that made Camp Hale the home base of the famed 10th Mountain Division.

There's plenty of signage detailing the history of the 10th Mountain Division, but there are some stories about Camp Hale that aren't displayed – like the one about the 259 Tibetan guerrillas trained here by the CIA between 1959 and 1964.

TOP CHOICE **Healy House Museum & Dexter Cabin** MUSEUM
(✆719-486-0487; www.coloradohistory.org; 912 Harrison Ave; adult/senior/child 6-16yr/5yr & under $6/5.50/4.50/free; ⊙10am-5pm May-Sep; P 🛅) Two of Leadville's oldest surviving homes are decked out with the owners' original gear and period pieces resembling what they may have enjoyed. The Dexter Cabin was the original mining digs of wealthy gold mining investor, James V Dexter. The much grander 1878 Greek Revival home now known as Healy House was built by August R Meyer.

Healy House features lavish Victorian furnishings collected in Leadville, including objects belonging to silver tycoon Horace Tabor and his wife Augusta, among other Leadville pioneers. This is easily the best museum in town.

FREE **Matchless Mine** HISTORICAL MINE
(www.matchlessmine.com; E 7th Rd; P 🛅) One of three historic mining areas east of Leadville that make easy excursions. Take E 7th St to the Fryer Hill mining district, site of the Matchless Mine where Horace Tabor struck it rich, launching the silver boom of the 1870s and '80s. This route continues east over 13,186ft Mosquito Pass, but you'll need a 4WD to get there.

🏃 Activities

Leadville may not look like much at first, but there's adventure to be had in this

There's a reason that one of the largest mountain bike races in the world – the Leadville 100 (p214) – happens here. There are simply so many trails that you could bike for weeks and never retrace your strokes. **Mosquito Pass** presents a unique opportunity to ride above 13,000ft in treeless alpine scenery. This extremely challenging 7-mile ascent follows E 7th St from Leadville.

Another good destination where you can enjoy panoramic vistas is **Hagerman Pass** (11,925ft), west of Leadville. Riders follow a relatively easy railroad grade on USFS Rd 105 for 7 miles to Hagerman Pass from the junction on the south bank of Turquoise Lake Reservoir. On the way you pass **Skinner Hut** (☑970-925-5775; www.huts.org; per person $25; ☺Jul-Oct), maintained by the 10th Mountain Division Hut Association. The 10th Mountain's system of 12 huts is ideally suited to mountain-bike tours, as they are all accessible by USFS roads and trails outside the wilderness areas (where mountain biking is prohibited).

An easy ride follows the shoreline trail on the north side of **Turquoise Lake Reservoir** (Turquoise Lake Rd) for 6 miles between Sugar Loaf Dam and May Queen Campground. Another follows the Colorado Trail north from Tennessee Pass for 2½ miles to Mitchell Creek. For other suggestions, pick up a map from the USFS Leadville Ranger Station.

downbeat town. Here you can run a 100-mile race, mountain bike for 24 hours straight, or simply pedal at a more moderate pace above the treeline. You can hike the two tallest peaks in Colorado, cast into the headwaters of the second oldest fish hatchery in the US, or simply hop historic train to glimpse wildflowers. Your call.

The 10th Mountain Division Hut Association (p199) manages backcountry huts in the area.

FREE **Mt Massive Wilderness Area**
HIKING

(☑719-486-0749; www.coloradowilderness.com; ⛰) This 44-sq-mile wilderness area encompasses Colorado's two highest peaks, **Mt Massive** (14,421ft) and **Mt Elbert** (14,433ft). In addition to climbing the two peaks (some do them both in one very long day), consider visiting the many high lakes along Rock Creek on USFS Trail 1382, which intersects the Colorado Trail about 10 miles north of Elbert Creek Campground.

Another trailhead for the Rock Creek Lakes begins at Willow Creek near the fish hatchery west of town. More extended backpacking trips cross the Continental Divide into the adjacent Hunter-Fryingpan Wilderness Area to the west.

Tennessee Pass Nordic Center
CROSS-COUNTRY SKIING

(☑719-486-1750; www.tennesseepass.com; Ski Cooper; trail pass half-/full day $10/14, equipment $8-20, lessons per person $35; ☺Nov-Apr; ⛰)

Snowshoers and cross-country skiers come here to get their Leadville fix. There are over 15 miles of groomed trails, but the highlight is the 1-mile haul to the gourmet yurt that is the Tennessee Pass Cookhouse.

Leadville, Colorado & Southern Railroad
NARROW-GAUGE RAILWAY

(☑719-486-3936, 866-386-3936; www.leadville-train.com; 326 E 7th St; adult/child 4-12yr $32.50/19.50, under 4yr free, engine seating $35, caboose $25; ☺Memorial Day-1st weekend Oct; ⛴) Originating in Leadville, the LC&S follows the old Denver, South Park and Pacific, and Colorado and Southern lines to the Continental Divide. Time it right and you'll see fields of wildflowers give way to panoramas across the Arkansas River valley. Your tour guide will fill you in on Leadville's bawdy past along the way.

Ski Cooper
SKIING

(☑719-486-2277; www.skicooper.com; Camp Hale 1; rental per adult $15-25, child $12-25, adult/child lift ticket per day $42/23; ☺9am-4pm Nov-Apr; ⛰) Ski Cooper, at Tennessee Pass, 9 miles north of Leadville, offers about 500 acres of skiable terrain, a dedicated snowboard terrain park, as well as 24km of machine-set tracks for backcountry and cross-country skiing. A favorite cross-country outing is to ski about a mile to the Tennessee Pass Cookhouse for a gourmet five-course meal.

✹ Festivals & Events

Leadville Trail 100 — CYCLING

(☏719-486-3502; www.leadvilletrail100.com; 🐾)
The Leadville 100, held in June/July, is one
of the most famous and longest mountain-
bike races in the world. Think: 100 miles
of lung-crushing, adrenaline-feuled riding
on the old silver-mining roads that go from
9200ft to 12,424ft and back again. But the
Leadville Trail races are not just about the
mountain bikers.

The whole thing started as a 100-mile
foot race (45 racers started, only 10 finished), and they still offer that run every
year, along with a half-marathon, a 50-mile
bike race and a 24-hour mountain bike
race. If you're interested in the run, you
should also think about attending the annual training camp.

🛏 Sleeping

Facts are facts, and with far more appealing towns, settings and inns within a short
drive, there's no real need to bed down in
Leadville. But if you're here to explore the
mining days of yore, or better yet, to hike,
climb, bike or fish in the Leadville outback,
you'll probably need to spend the night. In
addition to the two places suggested here,
there are a couple of chain motels on Poplar
St in the north end of town.

Ice Palace Inn — B&B $$
TOP CHOICE
(☏719-486-8272; www.icepalaceinn.
com; 813 Spruce St; r $105-194; P🐾❄🤖🐾)
A cute, if more than slightly frilly, family-
run inn set in a restored Victorian in the
heart of historic Leadville. It's named for
an actual 90ft-high palace made of ice that
was built for the 1896 social season, when
Leadville was a silver-tongued boomtown.
There are five rooms to choose from, all
decorated with antiques, handmade quilts
and attached to private bathrooms (three
have bath tubs).

Delaware Hotel — HOTEL $

(☏719-486-1418, 800-748-2004; www.delaware
hotel.com; 700 Harrison Ave; r $60-199;
P🐾❄🤖🐾) If you are going to sleep in
Leadville, you may as well make it historic, which means you should consider this
historic mining-era hotel. The innkeeper
enjoys her burlesque hat and gloves, and
rooms have high ceilings and lace curtains.
They are also carpeted and clean and hall-
ways are lined with antiques. It's nothing
fancy but certainly solid value.

🍴 Eating

Tennessee Pass Cookhouse
TOP CHOICE
CONTEMPORARY AMERICAN $$$
(☏719-486-8114; www.tennesseepass.com; Ten-
nessee Pass Rd; dinner per person $75; ⊙dinner
5:30pm daily, lunch noon Sat & Sun Dec-Feb;
🐾🐾) Part cross-country ski or snowshoe
tour, part gourmet dining experience.
You'll be eating in a yurt heated by a wood-
burning stove. And you'll be eating very
well. This is an elegant four-course meal
featuring mains such as elk tenderloin,
local rack of lamb and grilled wild boar
sausage. Groups meet at the Nordic Center
(p213).

Burrito Bus — MEXICAN $

(☏970-376-1358; 2016 N Poplar St; tacos $1.55,
burritos $4.25; ⊙6:30-11:30am Tue-Sat, 11:30am-
8pm Wed-Sun; 🐾) You'll find one of two bur-
rito buses parked in the lot adjacent to Stop
'n Save, and across from Safeway, on the
north side of town. In the mornings it's the
breakfast bus. But you must come back for
lunch.

These savory tacos and burritos are filled
with pollo and carne asada, carnitas or bu-
che (pork stomach). It does ceviche tosta-
das and excellent green and red chile tama-
les (both with pork), and it serves Mexican
Coke and Fanta too. Is it any wonder this is
the go-to stop for Mexican locals?

Golden Burro — DINER $$

(☏719-486-1239; www.goldenburro.com; 710
Harrison Ave; mains $7.50-18.95; ⊙6:30am-9pm;
🐾🐾) The Golden Burro is an authentic
1938 diner with a Formica lunch counter,
huge breakfasts and historic Leadville
black and whites in the main dining room.
It's diner fare so don't expect Bobby Flay,
but older locals love that pie and linger for
hours over coffee.

ℹ Information

Leadville Ranger District (☏719-486-0749;
www.fs.usda.gov; 2015 N Poplar St; ⊙7:30am-
4:30pm Mon-Fri, 8am-4:30pm Sat; 🐾) Has
information, books and topo maps on the Mt
Massive Wilderness Area and other forest sites
like the Turquoise Lake Reservoir.

Leadville Visitor Center (☏888-532-3845;
www.leadvilleusa.com; 809 Harrison Ave; 🐾)
Connected to the Lake County Area Chamber of
Commerce; you can grab maps and brochures
here.

St Vincent General Hospital (☏719-486-
0230; www.svghd.org; 822 W 4th St; 🐾)

❶ Getting There & Away

At the northernmost headwaters of the Arkansas River, Leadville is 24 miles south of Summit County and I-70 via Hwy 91 over Fremont Pass. From Vail, Leadville is 38 miles south via I-70 and US 24 over Tennessee Pass. The Summit Stage serves Leadville via its Lake County Link.

❶ Getting Around

Dee Hive Tours & Transportation (☎719-486-2339; www.leadville.com/deetours; tours $10-20; ⊙by appointment; 🖷) Welcomes hikers, skiers and cyclists in need of local shuttle transportation. Rides to trailheads or ski areas cost $10 to $20 per person for groups of four to six. Dee Hive also offers 4WD tours on the backroads to old mines and mountain passes.

Summit Stage (☎970-668-0999; www.summitstage.com; per ride $5; ⊙from Leadville 6-8:45am, to Leadville 3:40-6:35pm; 🖷) Summit Stage's Lake County Link connects Frisco with Leadville, stopping at East Village in Copper Mountain along the way. At the time of research the bus was leaving from Leadville, heading to Frisco 12 times each morning, and returning 10 times each evening. Transfers to Breckenridge and Vail are available at the Frisco Transfer Station.

Fairplay

POP 550 / ELEV 8500FT

Just 23 miles from Breckenridge on Haighway 9, flanked by the Mosquito Range to the west and the Tarryall Mountains to the east, Fairplay represents the beautiful South Park area's only 'urban' center. The human inhabitants are probably outnumbered by the bison at Hartsel to the south ,and they were also supposedly the inspiration the cartoon *South Park*. It's a gorgeous prairie town that's a little but not completely down on its luck. But nobody can feel too unlucky when the pink-washed sunsets are this magnificent.

In the **Courthouse Sq** (cnr 5th & Main Sts; 🅿🖷) you'll find a small monument to 'Shorty, age 45, 1951'; on Front St there's a memorial to 'Prunes, A Burro 1867–1930.' These revered beasts of burden carried supplies to the mines and returned down the slopes loaded with ore. Since 1949, Fairplay has celebrated Burro Days (last weekend of July), featuring Colorado's indigenous sport: pack-burro racing. Racers run beside a loaded burro over a 30-mile course up Mosquito Pass (13,186ft) and back.

Fairplay has couple of other historical sites of note. The **Park County Public Library** (☎719-836-4297; http://parkcounty.colibraries.org; 418 Main St; ⊙11am-5pm Tue-Fri, 10am-2pm Sat; @🖷🛜🖷) is set in an authentic 19th century stone structure, and the restored South Park City has nothing to do with Cartman, Kyle and the boys. It's a collection of 35 original buildings, built in the 1870s and 1880s in places like Fairplay, Alma, Como and the surrounding South Park area. All were restored and moved to this site in the late 1950s to better preserve the structures and publicize the region's history. Among other buildings, there's a morgue, a barbershop and a bathhouse. It's all very *Deadwood*.

The best place to stay is the historic, green shingled **Fairplay-Valiton Inn** (☎719-836-4699; www.stayfairplay.com; 500 Main St; r from $77; 🛜). Front St has most of the dining options. You can go with grilled steaks, buffalo short ribs or grilled quail at the **South Park Steakhouse** (456 Front St; mains $7-16; ⊙11:30am-3pm, 4:30-9pm; 🖷 🖷), but the best and most popular option is the gourmet pizza and pasta at **Millonzi's** (☎719-836-9501; 501 Front St; mains $9-20; ⊙4-9pm daily, 9am-2pm Sun; 🖷🖷). Given the prices in Breck for a good meal, this would make a wise trek over the pass for dinner.

Fairplay is 23 miles south of Breckenridge on Hwy 9 but is most often approached from Denver 90 miles east on US 285, or else from Colorado Springs on US 24 over scenic Wilkerson Pass, then north on Hwy 9.

Twin Lakes

An alternative to staying in Leadville, Twin Lakes is a gorgeous historic mining camp set on the shores of the Twin Lakes and at the very base of the sinuous climb to Independence Pass. Fed by steady stage-coach lines, this was log cabin mining country in the late 19th century, and a convenient rest stop between Aspen and Leadville. First called Dayton during the 1860s gold rush, it was renamed Twin Lakes in 1879 when the silver rush revived the village.

❂ Sights & Activities

The Red Rooster Saloon – the rowdy base of night ops back in the day – is long gone but several historic structures still stand on the lake shore. The nearby **Interlaken Trail**

DON'T MISS

INDEPENDENCE PASS

Looming at 12,095ft, Independence Pass is one of the more high-profile mountain passes along the Continental Divide. Perhaps it's the proximity to Aspen (just 20 miles away on Hwy 82), or maybe it's the celeb quotient. (Kevin Costner lives on its western slope...) But we think it's the drive itself.

A narrow ribbon of road swerves above the timberline with gentle then hairpin turns. Views range from pretty to stunning to downright cinematic, by the time you glimpse swatches of glacier visible along the ridges just below the knife edge of peaks you'll be living in your own IMAX film. Late season you'll see everyone from bow hunters dressed in camo geat and last-gasp family vacationers (or a cocktail of the two), to two kinds of bikers: unshaven Harley riders with frayed bedrolls on the tailgate, and leg-shaven millionaire road bikers with iPhones in their saddle bag.

A paved nature trail wanders off the parking area at the top of the pass. It's tundra country up here so stay on trails lest you cause decades of unknowable damage in a single step.

If you do want to hike off-pavement, consider climbing 14,336ft **La Plata Peak** (www.14ers.org; South Fork Lake Trailhead; ⊙Jun-Sep). The trail leaves from South Fork Lake Trailhead on the eastern slope of Independence Pass. From the parking area, walk over the bridge and continue on the fire road for about a quarter of a mile to find a trailhead sign on the left. There's a trail fork about 100m after crossing the bridge over La Plata Gulch. Stay right on the main trail and follow it up to the top. It starts out mellow, but soon intensifies. It's a 9.5-mile round-trip. Start early and leave the peak before noon to avoid lightening.

There are some fantastic eastern slope campgrounds to base out of if you're here to climb the peak. Both **Parry Peak Campground** (www.forestcamping.com; Hwy 82; sites $14; ⊙Jun-Sep; P🐾), set 2.5 miles west of Twin Lakes, and the stunning **Twin Peaks Campground** (www.forestcamping.com; Hwy 82; sites $15; P🐾), nestled at the base of twin peaks, will do just fine.

(Trail Rd) takes you to a once-famous and now long-abandoned resort hotel, the Interlaken, considered very fashionable in the 1890s. The 5- to 6-mile out-and-back hike to the hotel begins from Lower Lake Dam. Ruins have good signage so you can even walk inside and explore the abandoned buildings. Plus, this high alpine country is absolutely glorious.

The cross country skiing and snow shoeing in the area is magnificent too (though you'll have to source your own gear), and you can ice skate on the vast Twin Lakes throughout the winter. It's all part of the San Isabel National Forest.

But no matter where you go or what you do (and sitting, reading, contemplating, vista marveling, frivolous breeze shooting, and napping are all worthy pursuits here) expect soaring mountain views, knee-high grasses and wildflowers in early summer, fall color in early September, and night sky vistas all season.

🛏 Sleeping

Olsen's Cabins   CABINS $$
(☎719-486-0228; 6563 Hwy 82; cabins from $89, 1-week minimum high season, 2-night minimum low season; ⊙Jun-Sep; P⊝❄🐾) Catherine Olsen's cabins are romantically rickety, located at the western-most end of town. The quilts on the beds are lovely, there are full kitchens in all but one of the cabins, and she is the elder on the mountain, with the stories, mounted animal heads, and Rocky Mountain know-how to prove it.

Jake Gyllenhaal is among the Hollywood stars who have bedded down here recently. Twin Lakes' original 19th-century school house is tucked behind her property.

Twin Lakes Roadhouse Lodge   LODGE $$
(☎719-486-9345; www.twinlakescolorado.com; 6411 Hwy 82; r $95-125; ⊙May-Oct 1; P⊝❄🛜🐾) This is the first inn you'll see if you're driving up Hwy 82 from the southeast. More refined, this sweet log cabin has been added onto tastefully and crafted into a white-

washed wooden house overlooking the upper lake. Views from the front porch are immobilizing, and that gurgling fountain only adds to the ambiance.

It does Italian dinners by reservation, offers homemade pastries at breakfast and has wi-fi too. It's easily the most comfortable option in town for sure.

ℹ Getting There & Away

Twin Lakes is just over Independence Pass and 36.9 miles from Aspen, on Hwy 82, which intersects Hwy 24 just over halfway from Buena Vista to Leadville. It's 22 miles southwest of Leadville and 26 miles northwest of Buena Vista.

Buena Vista

Buena Vista is a lot of things: a paddler's paradise, a rock rat's dream destination, an aging ranching community, and, oh yes, a prison town (facts are facts; but it's certainly the cutest prison town we've ever seen). It's also quickly emerging as the next hip Colorado adventureland.

◎ Sights

Like most of Colorado's mountain towns there's more to do than see here, but there are a few scenic drives that yield the most spectacular of sights.

🏃 Activities

Among the many wild diversions available to the thrill-seeking wanderer in Buena Vista, the top attraction has always been and will always be the Arkansas River – with 99 miles of white water accessible from Main St. The river season lasts from May to late August. The best rafting months are June and July. BV is also a terrific place to learn how to kayak, and July is the ideal month to learn the trade. The water is just a touch too wild for newbies in June. If you're looking for some fun on land, there's plenty of rock climbing, mountain biking, hiking, and hot spring soaking to do.

TOP CHOICE / FREE | **Collegiate Peaks Wilderness** HIKING

(☎719-539-3591; www.fs.usda.gov; Collegiate Peaks Wilderness; 🚶) Designated in 1980 and encompassing 166,938 acres laced with 105 miles of trails, Collegiate Peaks is one of the 10 largest wilderness areas in the state.

There are more 14ers within its lines than anywhere else in Colorado. In all, eight peaks exceed 14,000ft, including the state's 3rd- and 5th-highest summits, Mt Harvard and La Plata Peak.

Another half-dozen thrust above 13,800ft and it's home to more than 40 miles of the Continental Divide. Overall elevation ranges from 8500ft to 14,420ft. Buena Vista is one of 12 towns abutting this wilderness area. Others include Twin Lakes, Crested Butte and Aspen. Naturally, there are countless hiking options here. Your best bet is to consult the ranger district office in Salida.

Mt Princeton Hot Springs Resort
HOT SPRINGS

(☎719-395-2447, 888-395-7799; www.thespa mtprincetonhotspringsresort.com; 15870 Co Rd 162; adult/child Mon-Fri $10/7, Sat & Sun $15/10, spa treatments $40-110; ⊗9am-7pm; @🛜🚶) Straddling the Arkansas River as it thunders down the valley is this recently redone hot springs resort, abutting a looming rock face. While the Cottonwood is groovier, this sprawling 4-star resort property in a singular setting is terrific for families.

If you stay here – and only if you do – you can have access to the relaxation pool. There are some smaller pools, and the larger ones are perfect for kids, with lots of room to move and frolic, including an expansive swimming pool and a 300ft water slide. All told there are 30 natural pools on the property.

If you come for the day and want a more intimate experience then slip into the river just off the sundeck. That's where the hot water bubbles up from below and with a little ingenuity and a few stones you can make a nice natural hot spring of your own...direct from the source. Being a 4-star resort it has a full-service spa onsite, offering body wraps, exfoliations and five types of massage.

FREE | **Buena Vista Whitewater Park**
KAYAKING

(www.coloradokayak.com; E Main St; ⊗Jun-Sep; 🚶) Buena Vista's Whitewater Park – part of the Buena Vista River Park – reaches from the end of E Main St downstream into the South Main District. There are four main whitewater structures and numerous eddy and trail improvements, which make this one of the premier whitewater parks

BUENA VISTA SCENIC DRIVES

Cottonwood Pass (☑719-539-3591; www.fs.usda.gov; Co Rd 306; ☺Jun-Oct; P ⛟) Ever wonder what it's like to drive to the moon? Wind your way past the Collegiate Peaks Campground to Cottonwood Pass (12,126ft). This is the Continental Divide and the border between the San Isabel National Forest on the eastern slope and the Gunnison National Forest to the west.

On the eastern side of the road as you head uphill is a turnoff to the Avalanche Trailhead, which is a spur of the Colorado Trail with access to the Collegiate Peaks Wilderness. Further uphill you'll come to Denny Creek Trail, then Ptamargian Lake trailhead. Yes, there's no shortage of hiking options here. The drive to the pass goes from moderately sinuous to downright jagged as you approach the edge of the timberline, and to the east the Collegiate Peaks spread out against the big blue sky. It's spectacular country and a great place for a picnic, and just a 30-minute drive from town.

Tunnels Rd (Co Rd 371; ⛟) Take Colorado Ave north from Main St in Buena Vista and follow it a couple of miles. Keep driving after it becomes dirt, continuing on through a series of blasted-out tunnels in the rock, and a bit further on you'll come to Elephant Rock – you can't miss it.

in Colorado. All of the features were fine-tuned in the spring of 2008 to optimize hydraulic performance.

The Midtown Feature is a great beginner spot for aspiring surfers and spinners. The Town Feature is ideal for stroke and skills development with large eddies and in-stream boulders. The Downtown Feature is for advanced paddlers, so if you make it here you'd better know when to throw down and when to hold on.

FREE **Fourmile Travel Management Area** OUTDOORS ACTIVITIES
(☑719-395-3396; www.garna.org; Co Rd 304; ⛟) This large region is a stitched-together recreation area comprising BLM, Forest Service and state lands, catering to all manner of visitors, such as four-wheelers, mountain bikers and horseback riders. It can get a bit overrun, but it's so big you can often find yourself a secluded area of your own, perfect for camping, contemplating and wildlife watching. It's especially good during the low season.

It makes sense to have a 4WD to explore the area in its entirety though. The western part, just east of Johnson Village near the Collegiate Peaks Overlook, has the best pinyon-juniper habitat in the county and is a classic spot for birding; drive the graded Co Rd 304 past the overlook. The best time of year to visit is June to October.

Cottonwood Hot Springs Inn & Spa
HOT SPRINGS
(☑719-395-6434; www.cottonwood-hot-springs. com; 18999 Co Rd 306; adult/child 16yr & under Mon-Fri $15/12, Sat & Sun $20/17, towel rental $1; ☺8am-midnight; ⛟) Take W Main St across Hwy 24 and keep going up the mountain toward Cottonwood Pass, and you'll soon come to the hippiest of the hot springs in Buena Vista. These renovated springs are quite kitsch in style, set on leafy grounds with gushing fountains of hot water, dangling vines and wind chimes. The five pools range in temperature from 94°F to 110°F.

For those staying here, rooms (from $102 a night) are more kitsch than class, with slanted cottage-cheese ceilings, floral bed spreads and cheap wood furnishings, but they're super clean and if you stay here you can use the natural springs all night.

Buffalo Joe's Whitewater Rafting RAFTING
(☑866-283-3563; www.buffalojoe.com; 113 N Railroad St; day trip adult $64-105, child $45-69, 2-day trip adult/child $179/139; ☺8am-7pm; ⛟) One of the top river outfitters in the Buena Vista–Salida swirl, offering a range of trips that run every bit of the 99 miles of the Arkansas River. Also rents mountain bikes, and offers snowmobile tours in winter.

🛏 Sleeping

From free riverside campsites to sweet off the grid B&Bs to hot spring resorts big and small, you'll find a nest that feels right.

Las Manos B&B
B&B $$

(☑719-395-4567; www.lasmanosbandb. com; 32889 Co Rd 371; ste $125-185; P ⊜ ❄ ☎ ⛓) A simple and sweet B&B in an award winning green home, set off the grid outside of Buena Vista. Each of the two suites has blonde wood floors and features a large deck for taking in sweeping mountain views. Rates vary depending upon the time of year.

Linens are lush and that soaking tub in the private bath doesn't suck. The inn is set off of the Tunnels Rd, less than a mile past Elephant Rock. Look for the sign on the left.

TOP CHOICE | Liars' Lodge B&B
B&B $$

(☑719-395-3444; www.liarslodge. com; 30000 Co Rd 371; r $94-124, cabins $234; P ⊜ ☎ ⛓) An airy, spectacularly set log cabin perched on a finger of the Arkansas River, so close that the river will sing you to sleep. It has five rooms and a cabin, which sleeps up to four people. Breakfast is served on an outstanding riverside terrace, weather permitting. This place represents outstanding value and is easily the best in Buena Vista, so you'd best reserve ahead.

It's set just off Co Rd 371, which is the same road that leads you through the Tunnels, with great rock climbing, bouldering and paddling just a short drive away.

FREE | Elephant Rock
CAMPING $

(Co Rd 371; P ⛓) Just after passing through the series of blasted tunnels that give this stretch of graded earth it's name – Tunnels Rd – you'll find Elephant Rock looming over the Arkansas River with a wide, flat, sheltered patch that makes an exquisite free campsite. There are no bathroom facilities, but dig those massive mountain views. There are more, similar campsites further up the road.

✗ Eating

TOP CHOICE | Mothers
CAFE FOOD $

(☑719-395-4443; www.mothersbistrobv. com; 414 E Main St; mains $5-9; ☺7:45am-5pm Mon-Sat, 9am-5pm Sun; ⊜ ☎ ⛓) An uber-groovy neighborhood cafe where the staff bakes goodness such as peach scones, serves organic eggs and does great coffee and smoothies for breakfast. Lunch offerings include meatloaf sandwiches, Jerk chicken salads and pulled pork quesadillas. The sunny back patio leads to Daughters, its martini bar and tapas hangout.

Evergreen Cafe
DINER $

(☑719-395-8984; www.evergreencafebv.com; 418 US Hwy 24; mains $4.75-8.75; ⊜ ☎ ⛓) Fun and funky, this canary yellow traincar of a diner on Hwy 24 north of Main St is where you'll find some seriously tasty offerings, such as zucchini fries, milkshakes and sinful bread pudding, not to mention killer omelettes, melts, burgers and salads.

Asian Palate
PAN-ASIAN $$

(☑719-395-6679; www.theasianpalate.com; 328 E Main St; mains $11.95-21.95; ☺11:30am-10pm Mon-Fri, 5-10pm Sat & Sun; ⊜ ⛓) Eclectic

---

HIKING MT PRINCETON

One of the more accessible of the Collegiate Peaks, this 14er makes a terrific, if long, day trip from Buena Vista.

The road itself is often harder to find than the trail. From the center of town, drive west on the Co Rd 306 for 0.7 miles. Turn left on Co Rd 321 and continue south for 7.2 miles. Turn right onto Co Rd 322 at a large sign. On Co Rd 322, drive 0.8 miles to a fork in the road. Bear right and you'll be on Mt Princeton Rd.

If you have a two-wheel drive vehicle you'll be leaving it here at the large parking area (8900ft), and starting your walk up the road. If you begin here the total distance will be 13 miles. If you have a high-clearance 4WD, you can continue up the narrow road. Bear right at the fork, and drive 3 miles to the radio towers (10,800ft). There is parking here for a couple of vehicles or turn left and continue on the 322A Rd. Between 3.2 and 3.4 miles up the Princeton Rd, there are some small camping spots near 11,000ft, with some parking. If you start from here (and at this point everyone is on foot) the total distance will be about 6.25 miles.

After hiking about a half-mile, the road curves up to the left and heads south to the Lucky Mine. The Mt Princeton Trail will be on the right; follow it all the way to the summit.

An old gold mining ghost town tucked into the base of the Collegiate Peaks, St Elmo makes for a fun excursion. The drive is the best part. The road to St Elmo narrows as it runs further up the canyon with the river flowing by and towering mountains laid out on both sides, you can see why folks put a town here.

Of course, it wasn't all about the setting. There was gold in this here creek! And with so many retrofitted and restored buildings in mining country it's nice to see buildings as they have become. The remaining buildings were built in and around 1881, and the school house, an old mercantile and a miners exchange are among the best kept of the bunch.

Strangely St Elmo is now something of a staging ground for ATV and off road enthusiasts who take to these forest service roads and trails. If you want to join them, stop by the **St Elmo General Store** (☏719-395-2117; www.st-elmo.com; 25865 CR 162). It also rents a few cabins (per night $65). The **Cascade Campground** (☏719-395-3156; www. reserveamerica.com; Chalk Creek Rd; per night $15) is the closest (and best) campsite to St Elmo. It's mostly wooded, with sites set on a river and blessed with fire pits, restrooms, and nearby hiking and fishing.

St Elmo is set on County Road 162, about 24 miles from Buena Vista and 11.5 miles from Mt Princeton Hot Springs (p217). It's a straight shot from the hot springs resort until the road dead ends at St Elmo.

Asian fare is what passes for haute cuisine in Buena Vista. Dishes such as massaman curry, pork larb and beef with udon noodles are typical kitchen fare, while raw morsels appear from the sushi bar. All are served in minimalist environs – think high-beamed ceilings and burgundy walls strategically cracked to reveal swatches of original brick.

Eddyline Restaurant & Brewery
CONTEMPORARY AMERICAN **$$**

(☏719-966-6000; www.eddylinepub.com; 926 S Main St; mains $7.99-23.99; ☺10am-11pm; ☀) Soaring ceilings, a loft-style interior with a cozy bar area and sunny streetside patio seating, no wonder this South Main District brewpub is many a locals' choice for best restaurant in town. It serves woodfired pizzas, grassfed local beef, calzones with your choice of regular, wholewheat or gluten-free dough, along with faves such as green chile enchiladas and grilled fajitas.

Its brewery was brewing five flavors at research time, ranging from lager to stout.

Loback's Bakery
BAKERY **$**

(☏719-530-1077; 326 Main St; ☺6am-5pm Mon-Fri, to 4pm Sat; ☺☀) Set in an authentic 1879 building, here's a cute hangout for the octogenarian set. This place has been chugging along since 1936 on the strength of its sugary donuts, cookies and fresh bread. It doesn't serve much else, but, hey, a small-town bakery like this is a fun

place to poke your head into for a glimpse of times (and, truth be told, opinions) long since past.

Buena Vista Farmers Market

(http://ccfa.coop; 829 W Main St; ☺10am-2pm Sun late Jun-early Oct; ☀) A small gathering of local, organic farmers come together with storytellers, musicians and hungry people to form a fun and tasty summer market, held among the apple trees on an old homestead property off Main St.

☺ Getting There & Away

Buena Vista is 35 miles south of Leadville on Hwy 24, and about 27 miles north of Salida on the 285.

Bailey

This is the first (or last, depending upon which way you're headed) in a series of authentic mountain towns set just outside of suburban Denver's shadow on Hwy 285. Unlike nearby Conifer, it's got tumbledown charm blooming on the banks of the north fork of the South Platte River.

Signed as 'Town Park' from the highway, the **McGraw Memorial Park** (Hwy 285) is somewhat hidden behind the feedstore on the west side of the road. It's a monument to the pioneers Edward and Blanche McGraw, who were among the first settlers and opened the first grocery, now the Bailey country store on Main St. Among the somewhat ignored ruins, which include an old Colorado & Southern caboose and a schoolhouse, you'll see an old 19th-century wagon, and the Entriken Log Cabin built by Elizabeth Entriken, who came here in 1864 with her sister and brother-in-law William and Ann Bailey. She entertained many a prospector, millionaire and broke-ass dreamer alike, as well as writers such as William Byers and John Chivingto, and the great Ute leader, Chief Colorow.

The nearby footbridge over the river leads to a trail that makes for a fun hike through the forest. There are a couple of cafes here serving basic mountain grub, and back across the highway from the park, the **Knotty Pine** (☎303-838-5679; 60641 US Hwy 285; ⊙9am-5pm Mon-Tue & Thu-Sun; @) is notable for its diversity of services: coffee, espresso, cinnamon rolls, ammunition, hot dogs, trail maps, buck knives, internet. It's all here.

There is one nice place to stay in Bailey, as well. The **Lynwood Park Bed & Breakfast** (☎303-838-4243; www.lynwoodparkbailey. com; 59786 US Hwy 285; r $100-350; P ⊝ ❋ ⋒) is a rustic sprawling wood cabin right on the river, with a stocked trout pond out front, and lovely wooded grounds.

Northwest Colorado

Includes »

STEAMBOAT
SPRINGS 223

HOT SULPHUR
SPRINGS 233

CRAIG 234

DINOSAUR NATIONAL
MONUMENT. 234

MEEKER 237

GLENWOOD
SPRINGS 237

COLORADO NATIONAL
MONUMENT. 243

GRAND JUNCTION . . . 244

FRUITA 248

Best Places to Eat

» Six89 (p242)

» Hot Tomato Cafe (p248)

» Sweet Pea Market (p229)

» 626 On Rood (p246)

Best Places to Stay

» Strawberry Park Hot Springs (p227)

» Eagle Ridge Lodge (p229)

» Wine Country Inn (p243)

» Glenwood Hot Springs & Spa of the Rockies (p239)

Why Go?

Wild, wind-blown, picturesque solitude, and evidence of the distant past – dinosaur tracks, petroglyphs and ancient geological scars – await visitors down long and lonely stretches of road.

Leaving the I-70 corridor and heading north, you enter a corner of Colorado littered with clues to the region's ancient, mysterious past. Dinosaur National Monument straddles the rugged border with Utah. It's a long haul to get here but well worth it for history and archaeology; it's not only home to the most impressive dinosaur site in the state, but hiking trails allow you to walk in the footsteps of the region's ancients – literally. Within a few dusty square miles, a Camarasaurus skull grins mischievously, frozen in the rock of the Douglass Quarry and the figures of 'Big Foot' and 'Three Kings,' scratched into the rock by ancient Pueblo ancestors, beckon us with inscrutable messages from the past.

When to Go?

Dinosaur

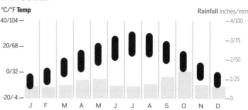

May–August	September & October	November–April
Canyon camping and mountain biking plus wineries, fruit stands and rodeos.	Cottonwoods turn gold, tourists roll through and temperatures drop.	Winter is a blustery affair, but there's plenty of action down the slopes.

STEAMBOAT SPRINGS

POP 10,115 / ELEV 6695FT

Forget about the posturing snow bunnies in Aspen and Vail. 'Steamboat,' as it's frequently truncated, is Colorado's down-to-earth ski town, a place where hitting the slopes isn't an attitude-packed dog-and-pony show.

The town itself, situated in the shadow of Mt Werner, might be less of a rancher's hub than a resort destination, but locals still regard flashy developments and instant-rise condos with disdain – before tipping their hat, hopping into their pick-up and rumbling away. Despite the sprawling Steamboat Village, built to service skiers, the core of the town retains some of its original low-rise charm and the natural setting is lovely. Summer is almost as popular as winter, with hiking, backpacking, whitewater rafting, mountain biking and a host of other outdoor activities.

Steamboat Springs consists of two major areas: the relatively regular grid of central Old Town which straddles US 40, and the newer warren of winding streets at Steamboat Village, centered around the Mt Werner ski area southeast of town. Only the former of these is worth wandering around by foot. US 40 is known as Lincoln Ave through Old Town.

◎ Sights

Tread of Pioneers Museum   MUSEUM
(⌨970-879-2214; 800 Oak St; adult/child/senior $5/1/4; ⊙11am-5pm Tue-Thu; ⍾) A favorite among the area's community history museums, these restored Victorian homes host an even-handed display about the history of the Native Americans in the area and a fascinating collection on the evolution of skiing. Visitors can also take guided tours and there are regular kids activities.

⛷ Activities

Mineral Springs

Most of Steamboat's numerous springs are warm rather than hot, and some have been damaged by highway construction. Probably the nicest spring is 3 miles from Old Town at Strawberry Park. It's open until midnight and you can actually bathe in it. Most of the other spas are in the area around 13th St on both sides of the river; look for the map and brochure *A Walking Tour of the Springs of Steamboat* for more information.

Mountain Biking

The *Steamboat Trails Map* shows mountain-bike routes around town, in Stagecoach (p231) and Pearl Lake State Parks (p232) and in the Mt Zirkel Wilderness. It's available at the visitors information center. Steamboat Mountain Resort promotes biking on Mt Werner, allows bikes on the Silver Bullet Gondola and rents them at the Thunderhead lift.

Orange Peel Bikes   BIKE RENTAL
(⌨970-879-2957; www.orangepeelbikes.com; 1136 Yampa St; bike rentals per day $30; ⊙10am-6pm Mon-Fri, to 5pm Sat; ⍾) In a funky old building at the end of Yampa, this is perfectly situated for renting a bike to ride the trails criss-crossing Howelsen Hill. A staff of serious riders and mechanics can offer tons of information about local trails. Coolest bike shop in town, hands down.

Snow Sports

The stats of the Steamboat Ski Area speak volumes to the town's claim as 'Ski Town, USA' – 165 trails, 3668ft vertical and nearly 3000 acres. There are runs at every level, a snowshoe area in the middle and race areas near the base. The area is particularly renowned for tree skiing, and the removal of saplings and fallen trees from the glades allows high-level intermediate skiers to weave through trees without the typical hazards of tree skiing. Serious skiers will also dig a number of mogul runs on the hill, and although these runs are a virtual factory of Olympic skiers and snowboarders, you don't have to be world-class to enjoy them. Compared with its foils in the Central Mountains, the sunny north-facing slopes are generally less aggressive. Wide, well-groomed runs are ideal cruising for intermediate skiers who might be a little rusty, making this hill among Colorado's best all-rounders.

The other hill in town, the Howelsen Hill Ski Area (p226), is among the country's oldest ski areas in continuous use and on the Colorado State Register of Historic Places. It's a relatively modest hill – only 14 runs and four lifts – even if there's some winter appeal for snowboarders and ski history buffs. There's an indoor ice-skating facility too, the Howelsen Ice Arena (p228), which operates from October until April.

Steamboat Mountain Resort   SNOW SPORTS
(Steamboat Mountain Resort; ⌨ticket office 970-871-5252; www.steamboat.com; lift ticket adult/child $94/59; ⊙ticket office 8am-5pm) Known

Northwest Colorado Highlights

1 Cruise the smooth, flat roads of Colorado's Wine Country, stopping for a basket of fresh peaches at **High Country Orchards** (p243)

2 Hike in the shadow of bizarre red-rock formations at **Rattlesnake Arches** (p244) near the Colorado National Monument

3 Spend the day on the slopes and the evening soaking – suit optional – at **Strawberry Park Hot Springs** (p227)

4 Navigate some of the country's best single-track mountain bike trails near Fruita, before slices and beer at **Hot Tomato Cafe** (p248)

5 Gape in wonder at skeletons and petroglyphs in **Dinosaur National Monument** (p234)

6 Hand over the keys and imbibe hand-crafted liqour at the **Peach Street Distillers** (p243)

7 Holler 'Get along, doggies!' and find your home on the range at **Vista Verde Guest Ranch** (p228)

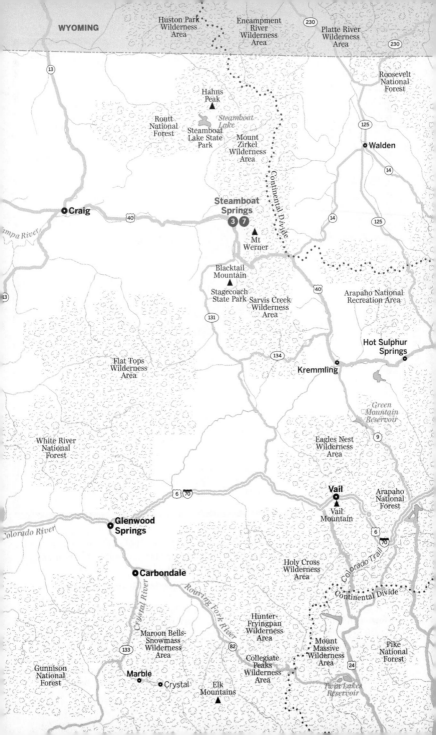

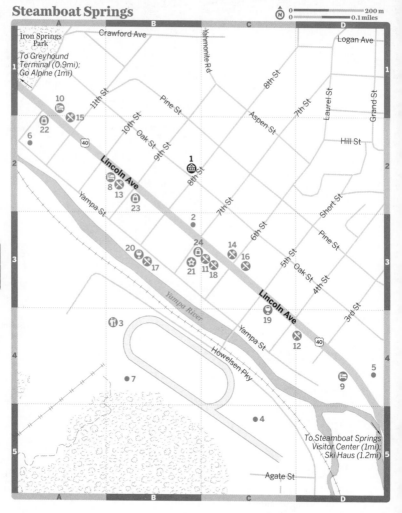

for a 3600ft vertical drop, excellent powder and trails for all levels, this is the main draw for winter visitors and some of the best skiing in the US. In the ski area there are (overpriced) food and equipment vendors galore.

Howelsen Hill Ski Area   SNOW SPORTS
(☏970-879-8499; Howelsen Parkway; lift tickets adult/child $17/12; ☺1-8pm Tue-Fri, 10am-4pm Sat & Sun; ⊕) Among the country's oldest ski areas in continuous use and on the Colorado State Register of Historic Places, this is a relatively modest hill by current

standards – only 14 runs and four lifts. It's the place to go if you're minding your budget.

Steamboat Ski Touring Center
                                  SNOW SPORTS
(☏970-879-8180; www.nordicski.net; Steamboat Bvd; day pass $18) Near the base of Mt Werner, this Nordic ski center has excellent cross-country trails, some on a golf course, others through the forest. The facility also has good food – home-cooked soups and chili served with homemade bread and baked goods.

Steamboat Springs

⊙ **Sights**
1 Tread of Pioneers Museum B2

Activities, Courses & Tours
2 Bucking Rainbow Outfitters B3
   Hosted Tours Adventures &
   Lodging Center .... (see 11)
3 Howelsen Hill Ski Area B4
4 Howelsen Ice Arena C5
5 Old Town Hot Springs D4
6 Orange Peel Bikes A2
7 Steamboat Springs Winter
   Sports Club B4

⊜ **Sleeping**
8 Hotel Bristol B2
9 Rabbit Ears Motel D4
10 Western Lodge A1

⊗ **Eating**
11 Backcountry Provisions C3

12 Bistro CV D4
13 Harwigs / L'Apogee B2
14 Old Town Pub & Restaurant C3
15 Riggio's A2
16 Steamboat Springs Farmers
   Market C3
17 Sweet Pea Market B3
18 Winona's C3

⊖ **Drinking**
19 Mahogany Ridge Brewery &
   Grill C4
20 Sunpies Bistro B3

⊛ **Entertainment**
21 Ghost Ranch Saloon B3

⊜ **Shopping**
22 Boomerang Sports Exchange A2
23 Off The Beaten Path B2
24 Urbane B3

Steamboat Central Reservations

SNOW SPORTS

(☎970-879-0740, toll-free 877-783-2628; www.steamboat.com; Mt Werner Circle, off Gondola Sq) This central booking office is the nerve center of the Steamboat Ski and Resort Corporation and can arrange ski packages, accommodation and all sorts of rentals. It's a corporate monolith, but it occasionally has good off-season specials.

Steamboat Springs Winter Sports Club

WINTER SPORTS

(☎970-879-0695; www.sswsc.org; 845 Howelsen Parkway; ⊙10am-7pm Mon-Sat, noon-6pm Sun with seasonal variations) This century-old winter sports club has scores of former and current Olympians as members. In winter they have programs and classes for all ages and ability levels.

Steamboat Ski & Snowboard School

SNOW SPORTS

(☎877-783-2628; www.steamboat.com; Mt Werner Circle; 3-day beginner adult course $299) There are a variety of classes for learning or sharpening skills at the Steamboat Ski Area. The beginner package lasts three days and is for absolute novices, including several hours of daily instruction and lift tickets. Serious skiers can take classes from Olympic champion Billy Kidd here too.

Water Sports

The Yampa River might roll lazily past parts of downtown, but the dynamic stretch of water is an ideal venue for water sports. It's particularly good for kayaks, with a 4-mile grade II to III white-water run which ends in two surfable holes.

Bucking Rainbow Outfitters

RAFTING, FLY-FISHING

(☎970-879-8747; www.buckingrainbow.com; 730 Lincoln Ave; ⊙daily) This excellent outfitter has fly-fishing, rafting, outdoor apparel and the area's best fly shop, but it's most renowned for its rafting trips on the Yampa and beyond. Rafting half-days start at $71. Two-hour in-town fly-fishing trips start at $155 per person.

Other Activities

TOP CHOICE / **Strawberry Park Hot Springs**

HOT SPRINGS

(☎970-879-0342; www.strawberryhotsprings.com; 44200 County Rd; per day adult/child $10/5, tent sites/cabins/covered wagons/cabooses $50/55/65/110; ⊙10am-10:30pm Sun-Thu, to midnight Fri & Sat; ⊞) Steamboat's favorite hot springs are actually outside the city limits, but offer great back-to-basics relaxation. Choose from covered wagons with a double mattress on the floor (quite unique) or rustic cabins. There's no electricity (you get gas lanterns) and you'll need your own linens.

Be sure to reserve. Weekend reservations require a two-night stay. Note that the thermal pools are clothing optional after dark.

Wild West Balloon Adventures

HOT-AIR BALLOONING

(☎800-748-2487; www.wildwestballooning.com; 42415 Deerfoot Lane; adult/child $200/125) Floating silently over the mountains is a breathtaking experience, and this 45-minute ride includes a snack and a champagne toast. The scenery is perhaps most stunning on clear winter mornings.

Old Town Hot Springs

HOT SPRINGS

(☎970-879-1828; www.steamboathotsprings. org; 136 Lincoln Ave; adult/student & senior/child $15/10/7; ⊙5:30am-9:45pm Mon-Fri, 7am-8:45pm Sat, 8am-8:45pm Sun; ⊞) Smack dab in the center of town, the water here is warmer than most in the area. Known by the Utes (a Native American tribe) as the 'medicine springs,' the mineral waters here are said to have special healing powers.

The springs recently underwent a $5-million renovation and now there's a new pool, a pair of 230ft-long waterslides and, perhaps coolest of all, an aquatic climbing wall!

Hosted Tours Adventures & Lodging Center

OUTDOORS ACTIVITIES

(☎970-870-7901; www.hostedtours.com; 635 Lincoln Ave; ⊙10am-7pm) This small shack sits right on the main drag and is operated by its ultra-friendly owner, Brad. His information about accommodation, activities and the local scene is excellent.

Howelsen Ice Arena

ICE SKATING

(☎970-879-0341, 970-879-8499-; Howelsen Parkway; adult/child $10/9; ⊙noon-6:15pm Mon-Wed, Fri & Sat; ⊞) Call for drop-in skate hours at this covered, seasonal facility at the base of the Howelsen Ski Area.

⚲ Festivals & Events

First Friday Art Walk

ARTS

(www.steamboatspringsartwalk.com; Lincoln Ave; ⊙5-9pm 1st Fri of each month; ⊞) Steamboat Springs' monthly Art Walk transforms local shops into galleries and sends wine-sipping visitors along the Lincoln Ave promenade between 4th and 12th Sts.

Yampa River Festival

WATER SPORTS

(www.friendsoftheyampa.com; Yampa St at 7th St; all-event ticket $30; ⊙1st weekend in Jun; ⊞) Held every year on the first weekend of June, with a kayak rodeo, which attracts national and international world class play-boaters, an upstream slalom race, and the Crazy River Dog Contest, in which dogs retrieve sticks from the river.

Strings Music Festival

MUSIC

(☎970-879-5056; www.stringsmusicfestival. com; 900 Strings Rd; ⊙Jun-Sep; ⊞) This long-running summer music festival hosts some 70 performances through the summer (June to September) with a range of genres, including rock, blues, bluegrass, jazz and chamber music. When the weather is nice you can snag cheap seats on the lawn.

Steamboat Springs Pro Rodeo Series

RODEO

(☎970-879-1818; www.steamboatprorodeo.com; 401 River Rd; adult/child $15/8; ⊙7:30-9:30pm Fri & Sat mid-Jun–Labor Day; ⊞) Every Friday and Saturday night from mid-June to Labor Day, this historic rodeo sees some of the best riding and roping in the West. It also has a helluva BBQ stand.

Hot Air Balloon Festival & Art In The Park

ARTS, BALLOONING

(☎877-754-2269; West Lincoln Park; ⊙mid-Jul; ⊞) Held in mid-July, this festival sends over 40 colorful balloons into the clear skies above town, while a large arts and crafts show unfolds in West Lincoln Park. Call Steamboat's Chamber of Commerce for more information.

🛏 Sleeping

🔺 Vista Verde Guest Ranch

RANCH $$$

(☎970-879-3858; www.vistaverde.com; 31100 Seedhouse Rd; per week per person from $2700; ❄🎏⊞) Simply put, this is the most luxurious of Colorado's top-end guest ranches. Here, you spend the day riding with expert staff, the evening around the fire in an elegantly appointed lodge, and the night in high-thread count sheets. If you have the means, this is it.

The staff takes the 'all-inclusive' concept to a satisfying endgame. There are cooking and photography classes, rock climbing and rafting in the summer and four-star meals that arrive with well-paired wines. If you're looking for a true-grit cowboy adventure, it's best to look elsewhere, but if luxury is a requisite, this is the best dude-ranch experience money can buy.

Sheraton Steamboat Resort

HOTEL $$$

(☎970-879-2220; www.starwoodhotels.com; 2200 Village Inn Court; d $129-179, suites $289-

310; P🚭❄️📶🏊🚗) If skiing is paramount to your adventures here, this is the only hotel in town with direct mountain access. The remodeled amenities are standard four-star plushness: thick sheets, flat-screen TVs and, if you're willing to pay a bit extra, great views of the mountain.

Rabbit Ears Motel
MOTEL $$

(☎800-828-7702; www.rabbitearsmotel.com; 201 Lincoln Ave; d $109-179; P❄️🚗) A diabolically chipper, pink-neon bunny welcomes guests at this simple roadside motel. The place is smart enough to exploit the kitsch appeal that makes so many other mid-century low-ride motels so drab, by keeping the rooms bright and spotless.

Eagle Ridge Lodge
RESORT $$$

(http://eagleridgesteamboat.com; Eagle Ridge Dr; d from $250; P🚭❄️📶🏊🚗) The style of this 40-room four-star hotel is clean, classic and elegant – white walls, heavy thread-counts, fluffy robes and stone fireplaces. In the summer, the huge outdoor swimming pool is delightful and when the snow flies the location makes it simple to get on the slopes.

The lodge also has a number of two- and three-bedroom options, all of high quality, for larger groups.

Hotel Bristol
HOTEL $$

(☎970-879-3083; www.steamboathotelbristol. com; 917 Lincoln Ave; r $109-249; 🚭📶) The elegant Hotel Bristol has small, but sophisticated, Western digs, with dark-wood and brass furnishings and Pendleton wool blankets on the beds. There's a ski shuttle, a six-person indoor Jacuzzi and a cozy restaurant.

Western Lodge
MOTEL $

(☎970-879-1050; 1122 Lincoln Ave; d $55; P❄️📶🚗) The rooms could benefit from a good airing, the coffee makers don't work and the decor might be what's considered 'Avuncular '70s Cowboyist,' but the beds are clean and comfortable and if you stay here midweek, it's the cheapest deal downtown. Peter, the Swiss-born owner, may talk your ear off if you let him.

✗ Eating

TOP CHOICE 🍴 **Bistro CV**
CONTEMPORARY AMERICAN $$$

(☎970-879-4197; www.bistrocv.com; 345 Lincoln Ave; mains $21-34; ⏱5-10pm; 🚭) Hands down the best fine dining in Steamboat, Bistro CV excels with its carefully prepared, creative New American dishes. The regularly

changing menu uses fresh, sustainable ingredients. The chicken-chorizo pot pie with a savory cornmeal crust is an excellent way to start. For mains, try the white truffle gnocchi or the $21 burger, topped with foie-gras and worth every penny.

🍴 Sweet Pea Market
SELF-CATERING, CONTEMPORARY AMERICAN $$

(☎970-879-1221; www.sweetpeamarket.com; 729 Yampa St; mains $12-20; ⏱9am-7pm Mon-Fri, 10am-5pm Sat & Sun; 🚭) With a mission dedicated to local farmers and organic food, Sweet Pea is a welcome newcomer to Steamboat's meaty scene. It stocks tons of fresh veggeis and bread and to-go items for picnics. In the summer chefs also serve local, organic contemporary American mains in a makeshift dining room.

Winona's
BREAKFAST $$

(☎970-879-2483; 617 Lincoln Ave; breakfast $10-15; ⏱7am-3pm Mon-Sat; 🚭🚗) Arriving here during the peak breakfast hours is a mistake: Winona's creative breakfast dishes have made it the most popular breakfast joint in town. And for good reason: gooey, monstrous cinnamon rolls and plump French toast is balanced by savory treats, such as crab eggs Benedict.

Cafe Diva
FUSION $$$

(☎970-871-0508; www.cafediva.com; 1855 Ski Time Square Dr; mains $21-40; ⏱5-10pm; 🚭) Asian flavors with French preparation combine for the most exciting dinner in the Mountain Area. 'Colorado Never Ever Beef Tenderloin' comes sided with mushroom bread pudding – the best of their cold-weather menu – but in summer, fresh salads and a crab-and-tomato bisque is equally as winning.

Backcountry Provisions
DELI $

(☎970-879-3617; www.backcountryprovisions. com; 635 Lincoln Ave; sandwiches $7-8; ⏱7am-5pm; 🚭) This Colorado sandwich chain is magic: the bread and ingredients are fresh, it opens early to sell hikers and outdoorsy types box lunches and it's staffed by a friendly crew of guys. The Timberline is a favorite around here: peanut butter, local honey and bananas.

Old Town Pub & Restaurant
PUB FOOD $$

(☎970-879-2101; http://oldtownpub.jimdo.com; 600 Lincoln Ave; mains $9-16; ⏱11am-late; 🚗) Perhaps this Wild West pub isn't as rowdy as days of yore (check out the bullet holes in the phone booth by the bar) but locals flock here for dinner and dancing. It hosts live bands most weekends, pours great margaritas and serves gourmet pub fare.

Harwigs / L'Apogee
FUSION $$$

(☎970-879-1919; www.lapogee.com; 911 Lincoln Ave; mains from $25; ⊙5-10pm; ☻) This fine-dining option serves Asian-influenced French fare in elegant, candlelit environs. The mains won't blow minds – rack of lamb, duck breast with black-eyed pea hash – but on Thai Night the prices drop and the flavors get more adventuresome. Occasionally a string quartet huddles in the corner.

Riggio's
ITALIAN $$$

(☎970-879-9010; www.riggiosfineitalian.com; 1106 Lincoln Ave; mains $13-28; ⊙5-10pm; ☻🖐) An older crowd patronizes Riggio's for the classic, elegant Italian 'restaurante' atmosphere. The fresh ravioli with mixed wild mushrooms is the worthy house special.

 ### Steamboat Springs Farmers Market
SELF-CATERING

(☎970-846-1800; www.mainstreetsteamboatsprings.com; cnr 6th St & Lincoln Ave; ⊙9am-2pm Sat Jun-Sep; 🖐) This market, held every Saturday, brings in local farmers from across northern Colorado. There are over 50 vendors selling veggies, baked goods and bread.

🍷 Drinking & Entertainment

Sunpies Bistro
BAR

(☎970-870-3360; www.sunpies.com; 735 Yampa Ave; ⊙noon-2am Tue-Sun; 🖐🖐) There's a big backyard that overlooks the creek, where locals pack in to drink and swap tales. They can be loud and rowdy, but it's a slice of the real Steamboat. The Texas Toothpicks (deep-fried jalapenos and onions) are a great snack at this bar and grill.

Mahogany Ridge Brewery & Grill
BREWPUB

(☎970-879-3773; 435 Lincoln Ave; ⊙4-11pm) Soft lighting, fresh beer and a cheap happy-hour tapas menu keep this place packed. As the only brewery in town, it has a corner on the market, even if the spread of mediocre beers isn't likely to change your world.

Ghost Ranch Saloon
LIVE MUSIC

(☎970-879-9898; www.ghostranchsaloon.com; 56 7th St; ⊙11am-2am Tue-Sat) The Ghost Ranch is a sure bet. Regardless of what's on stage, the crowd here is a mix of locals and visitors, and everyone seems determined to knock a few back and cut loose. The live music ranges from middling cover bands to national touring acts.

Emerald City Opera
OPERA

(☎970-879-1996; www.steamboatopera.com; adult/student $20/15; ⊙10am-8pm Mon-Sat, to 6pm Sun) This small company stages the classics: Bizet, Puccini etc. Performances are often held at the Perry Mansfield Julie Harris Theater between the fall and spring. Tickets are available through the website or **All That Jazz** (601 Lincoln Ave).

Shopping

Boomerang Sports Exchange
SPORTING GOODS

(☎970-870-3050; www.brangxchange.com; 1a, 1125 Lincoln Ave; ⊙10am-6pm Mon-Sat, noon-5pm Sun) If you are minding your budget, the deals at this used sporting goods shop can be *amazing*. It's a very mixed bag and quality of gear depends a lot on luck, but it's certainly worth a look if you plan on skiing, camping or getting outdoors in the area.

Off The Beaten Path
BOOKS

(☎970-879-6830; www.steamboatbooks.com; 68 9th St; ⊙8am-7pm Mon-Sat, 9am-6pm Sun; 📶) Among the crowded stacks and sharp fragrance of brewing coffee beans, patrons browse for books on local history and light vacation reads. The staff picks are good, and there is a tiny cafe on hand for cozy chats.

Urbane
CLOTHING

(☎970-879-9169; www.urbanesteamboat.com; B101, 703 Lincoln Ave; ⊙10am-8pm Mon-Sat, to 6pm Sun) No doubt the hippest clothing store on the Western Slope, Urbane stocks hip urban threads for men and women. It's a great little store and the perfect place to upgrade your mountain-biking dudes for a night on the town.

Ski Haus
OUTDOORS RENTAL

(☎970-879-0385; www.skihaussteamboat.com; 1457 Pine Grove Rd; ski & snowboard rental packages per day from $30; ⊙9am-6pm Mon-Sat, to 5pm Sun) After fitting skis for four decades, this place is the first and last stop for many snow-bound visitors. You can rent top quality gear here, or buy used rentals or demo skis. In the summer, it also rents bikes and camping gear. It also operate's a free pick-up shuttle.

ⓘ Information

Steamboat Springs Visitor Center (☎877-754-2269, 970-879-0880; www.steamboat-chamber.com; 125 Anglers Dr; ⊙8am-5pm Mon-Fri, 10am-3pm Sat) This visitors center, facing Sundance Plaza, has a wealth of local information, and its website is also excellent for planning.

USFS Hahns Peak Ranger Office (☑970-879-1870; www.fs.usda.gov; 925 Weiss Dr; ⊙8am-5pm Mon-Sat) Rangers staff this office offering permits and information about surrounding national forests including Mt Zirkel Wilderness, as well as information on hiking, mountain biking, fishing and other activities in the area.

❶ Getting There & Away

Greyhound Terminal (☑970-870-0504; 1505 Lincoln Ave) Greyhound's US 40 service between Denver and Salt Lake City stops here, about half a mile west of town.

Storm Mountain Express (☑877-844-8787; www.stormmountainexpress.com) This shuttle service runs to Yampa Valley Regional Airport ($33 one-way) and beyond, though trips to DIA and Vail get very pricey.

Go Alpine (☑970-879-2800, 800-343-7433; www.goalpine.com; 1755 Lincoln Ave) This taxi and shuttle service makes several daily runs between Steamboat and Denver International Airport ($85, four hours one-way). It also makes trips to the Yampa Valley Regional Airport and operates an in-town taxi.

❶ Getting Around

Steamboat Springs Transit (☑970-879-3717, for pick-up in Mountain Area 970-846-1279; http://steamboatsprings.net/) Steamboat Springs Transit runs a free bus service along Lincoln Ave from 12th St in the west to Walton Creek Rd in the east. It also goes up Mt Werner Rd to the gondola.

Though infrequent, it will also take you to a handful of towns to the west; the cost is $6.00 each way to Craig, $5.00 to Hayden, $3.50 each way from Milner. Check with the visitor center for seasonal schedules.

AROUND STEAMBOAT SPRINGS

Stagecoach State Park

Sixteen miles south of Steamboat Springs via US 40, Hwy 131 and Routt County Rd 14, **Stagecoach State Park** (☑reservation office 303-470-1144; 25500 County Road 14; sites $10-20; ⌂) is the nearest inexpensive camping to Steamboat Springs. The park is on the edge of a large reservoir in a good location for trips into the Flattops Wilderness, Sarvis Creek Wilderness and Blacktail Mountain.

In summer campers entertain themselves with fishing and a modest, 8-mile network of hiking trails while speed boats zoom along the water. In winter, camping is limited (rangers clear snow from four sites) and activities in the park include snowmobiling, Nordic skiing and ice fishing.

Mt Zirkel Wilderness

One of the five original wilderness areas in Colorado, Mt Zirkel Wilderness is an untamed, roadless expanse dotted with icy glacial lakes, granite faces and rife with opportunities for isolated backcountry hiking and camping. It's intersected by the Continental Divide and two major rivers, the Elk and the Encampment, both of which are being considered for protection under the Wild & Scenic Rivers Act.

Boldly rising from the center of the area is the 12,180ft **Mt Zirkel**, named by famed mountaineer Clarence King to honor the German petrologist with whom he reconnoitered the country in 1874. The area is *huge*, and this can provide a place to get off the grid, even during Colorado's busiest seasons.

The most popular entry points are in the vicinity of Steamboat Springs, though it's also approachable from Walden or Clark. Detailed maps and information on hiking, mountain biking, fishing and other activities in this beautiful area are available at the USFS Hahn's Peak Ranger Office.

Trails Illustrated publishes Hahn's Peak/Steamboat Lake and Clark/Buffalo Pass maps, while Jay and Therese Thompson describe the walks in *The Hiker's Guide to the Mt Zirkel Wilderness*.

Hahns Peak

On the wind-swept plain at the base of a picturesque peak lies this quasi–ghost town, 27 miles north of Steamboat Springs via Elk River Rd (Routt County Rd 129). It was once the terminus of the railroad from Wyoming, and has a rich history as a secluded harbor for outlaws. (Rumor has it that Butch Cassidy was jailed here in a bear cage.) It's an unfrequented destination that still has a handful of residents and a couple of interesting junk and crafts shops.

Nearby **Steamboat Lake State Park** (☑970-879-3922; www.parks.state.co.us; off County Road 129; campsites $16-20, camper

ARAPAHO NATIONAL WILDLIFE REGUGE

For birdwatchers, this is one of the best destinations in Colorado: nearly 200 species of birds frequent the summer sagebrush and wetlands of the USFWS' Arapaho National Wildlife Refuge, 105 (long, if lovely) miles west of Fort Collins by the Cache la Poudre–North Park Scenic Byway (Hwy 14). The star of the show is the sage grouse–its spring-mating ritual, the lek, an elaborate, territorial display of spiked tail feathers, puffy chests and nearly comic *braggadocio*. To find the **Refuge Headquarters** (☑970-723-8202; http://arapaho.fws.gov; 953 Jackson County Rd 32; ⊙7am-3:30pm Mon-Fri) head 8 miles south of Hwy 14 via Hwy 125, then 1 mile east on Jackson County Rd 32.

If you are visiting the refuge or its surrounding backcountry, the dusty hamlet of Walden is the nearest place for a hot shower and decent shelter.

cabins $80; 🐾) and **Pearl Lake State Park** (☑970-879-3922; www.parks.state.co.us; off County Rd 209; sites $16, yurts $60; P🐾) are both developed state parks on the side of reservoirs with shoreline camping, some short hiking trails and opportunities for fishing and boating.

WALDEN

POP 734 / ELEV 8099FT

Little Walden lies under the shadow of the rough Medicine Bow, Summer, Rabbit Ears and Park Ranges, at the center of the 1600-square-mile expansive valley of a region locals refer to as North Park. There isn't much to the self-proclaimed 'moose-watching capital of Colorado,' but the north–south Main St is scattered with motels, restaurants and a creaky old movie theater. The only incorporated town in Jackson County, Walden is a modest supply point for outdoor enthusiasts and hunters looking to grab a burger and get out of the elements for the night. And, yes, by the way, we did see moose.

KREMMLING

It's too bad that little Kremmling doesn't get much more than a cursory glance from the rushing traffic between Steamboat Springs and the Front Range; this wide spot in the road is a great place to get out and kick the tires a bit, and the locals are friendly. There are a couple of decent lunch spots and some antique shopping in the tiny downtown area. There are certain rewards to staying a bit longer too as well; it's long been known as a popular base for

hunters and snowmobilers and a lot of effort has recently been made to encourage mountain bikers and rafting expeditions.

🏃 Activities

Breckenridge Whitewater Rafting Kremmling Outpost   RAFTING
(☑800-370-0581; www.coloradorafting.net; 400 Park Ave; 🐾) Making runs in Upper Colorado and the Class IV and V stretch of Gore Canyon, this is the most reputable operator in Kremmling.

🛏 Sleeping & Eating

Allington Inn & Suites   HOTEL $$
(☑970-724-9800; www.allingtoninn.com; 215 W Central Ave; d $99-109; P🖥🕸🍽🐾) The nicest place to stay in Kremmling happens to be one of the best-value places around. The rooms are modern and comfortable, there's an indoor swimming pool and breakfast is included. Book a room on the north side of the building for cliff views.

Hotel Eastin   HOTEL, HOSTEL $
(☑866-546-0815; www.hoteleastin.net; 104 2nd St; d $35-59; ⊝🕸🐾) Jozef and Danka, the Slovakian couple who recently purchased this historic hotel, are excellent hosts, and their lower-level rooms with shared bathrooms are terrific value. Midrange rooms are clean but simply furnished, and top-end 'Western Rooms' have a bit more style and more: a television, microwave and coffee-maker.

Quarter Circle Saloon   GRILL $$
(☑970-724-9765; 106 W Park Ave; mains $7-15; ⊙11am-2am) This bar and grill serves up thick slabs of steak and pints and is about the best you'll do in Kremmling. The crowd gets rowdy, especially during pool tournaments on Tuesday night. If you go during

off-peak hours, the plate might well come straight from the microwave.

ℹ️ Information

BLM Kremmling Field Office (📞970-724-9004; 210 S 6th St; ⏰8:30am-4pm Mon-Fri) This office has information about multi-use federal land, issues permits and has maps of the area.

Kremmling Chamber & Visitor Center (📞970-724-3472, toll free 877-573-6654; 203 Park Ave; ⏰8:30am-5pm Mon-Fri, to 3pm Sat) The ladies at this centrally located visitor center could hardly be nicer; after chatting with them for 10 minutes you'll consider moving here. You can get information about local activities and suggestions about where to eat and sleep.

HOT SULPHUR SPRINGS

When you roll through the sleepy little village of Hot Sulphur Springs, it's hard to imagine its glory days as a happening tourist destination. In the late 1860s William Byers, founder of the Rocky Mountain News, acquired most of the land in the area from itinerant Utes with a combination of legal manoeuvring and the aid of the US Army, and he immediately began promoting it to tourists. At one time its rivalry with Grand Lake was so serious that a struggle over which town would be the Grand County seat led to a fatal shoot-out between elected officials. Hot Sulphur Springs prevailed politically, but never suffered the tourist invasion that has made Grand Lake so ticky-tacky – a blessing and curse, as these days it seems to be wilting in slow economic decline.

At the foot of 12,804ft Byers Peak, Hot Sulphur Springs is midway between Granby and Kremmling on US 40. It has no formal tourist office, but Grand County Museum is a good source of information.

⊙ Sights & Activities

Hot Sulphur Springs Resort & Spa

HOT SPRINGS, SPA

(📞970-725-3306; www.hotsulphursprings.com; 5609 County Rd 20) Unlike the hot pools in Glenwood Springs, this spa doesn't chlorinate the water, allowing the heady mix of sulfates, chloride, magnesium and other minerals to soothe bathers just as it has done for generations. The 21 pools have been enclosed by cement and tile and are separated by temperature, ranging from 95°F to a deeply satisfying, if challenging, 112°F.

Like most modern facilities of this kind, there's an added menu of spa options: body wraps, facials, massages and the like. If you want to spend the night, there is a lodge on hand with clean, comfortable facilities (double rooms start at \$108) that are on par with a better-than-average, wood-panelled airport hotel. It also has an 1840s cabin for rent (two people \$225).

Comparing this facility to the one in Glenwood Springs, you'll find Hot Sulphur Springs to be a bit simpler, less posh and less crowded – for better or for worse.

Pioneer Village Museum MUSEUM

(Grand County Historical Museum; 📞970-725-3939; www.grandcountymuseum.com; 110 E Byers Ave; adult/senior/child \$5/4/3; ⏰10am-5pm Wed-Sat; 👶) This small community museum has exhibits on early settlers (both native and white), skiing and artifacts from the nearby Windy Gap archaeology area.

Dave Perri's Guide Service

FISHING, HUNTING

(📞970-725-3531; www.traditionalelkhunt.com; 8 hours of guided fishing for 2 adults \$375) A local guide operating on the Colorado River, Perri is one of the few around licensed to work excellent waters in the area. Early spring and summer are the busiest time for wading trips. In winter, he leads week-long hunting trips in the Troublesome Basin Area for elk and mule deer, reached via a 7 to 10 mile horseback ride.

🛏️ Sleeping & Eating

There's no official campground but tent campers and RVs can take advantage of the shade and good fishing at Pioneer Park on the north bank of the river, where there's not even anyone to pester you for money. Get drinking and cooking water from the standpipe across from the Riverside Hotel near the bridge; there are portable toilets, but to clean up try the pools at Hot Sulphur Springs Resort & Spa.

Canyon Motel MOTEL **\$**

(📞888-489-3719; www.canyonmotelcolorado.com; 221 Byers Ave; d \$64-99; 🅿️👶) If you aren't staying at the hot springs, this roadside motel makes a clean stopover. The rooms are simple, paneled with pine and extremely clean. Some have kitchens and there's a grill for guests to use.

Glory Hole Cafe
BREAKFAST $

(☏970-725-3237; 512 W Byers Ave; breakfast $5-10; ☺6am-2pm Wed-Mon; 🖐) Most of the menu is standard diner fare in lumberjack portions, but the French toast – fluffy, expertly golden slices smothered in homemade blueberry syrup – is worth a stop. It gets absolutely slammed for breakfast on the weekends, so come off-hours or be prepared to wait.

❶ Getting There & Away

Greyhound (p241) will make a flag stop in Hot Sulphur Springs if it's arranged in advance.

CRAIG

Lying on the north bank on the Yampa River between the towns of Meeker and Steamboat Springs, Craig is little more that a pit stop on the way to or from Colorado's northwest corner. The downtown stands at a junction of roads leading elsewhere: US 40 goes east–west between Steamboat Springs and Dinosaur National Monument; Hwy 789/13 runs north through desolate, rolling hills near the Wyoming Border; and 394 follows the Yampa River south to Meeker.

The main drag is Yampa Ave, but its taxidermy shops, automotive suppliers and liquor stores offer a fairly grim stroll. At least there are big box stores and several grocers if you're stocking up for a trip out west.

◉ Sights & Activities

FREE Museum of Northwest Colorado
MUSEUM

(☏970-824-6360; www.museumnwco.org; 590 Yampa Ave; ☺9am-5pm Mon-Fri, 10am-4pm Sat; 🖐) The hats, chaps and saddles in the cowboy collection are the highlight of this community museum. But it's the handcrafted and etched spurs and hand-tooled boots that are the most cherished artifacts. It also has a small bookshop on hand with volumes on local history.

FREE Marcia Car
MUSEUM

(cnr E Victory Way & Washington St; ☺8am-5pm Mon-Fri Jun-Aug; 🖐) This private rail car was commissioned in 1906 by David Moffat, a prominent Denver banker who owned a number of gold mines. He was also instrumental in connecting Colorado to the national rail system. You can arrange tours at the Moffat County Visitors Center.

🛏 Sleeping & Eating

There is a cluster of hotel chains in the west part of town off the intersection where Hwy 13 splits south from US 40. Just west of downtown, on US 40, there is a string of mid-century motels, but they're fairly hit or miss. Accommodations are usually priced but prices typically rise during hunting season, mid-September to late November. For eats, fast food chains are overwhelmingly common, but the best bet for something local is downtown.

❶ Getting There & Away

Yampa Valley Regional Airport (County Rd 51A) is midway between Craig and Steamboat Springs. Buses from the **Craig Greyhound Depot** (☏970-824-5161; 470 Russell St) serves Denver (six hours, $52) and Salt Lake City (6½ hours, $69).

DINOSAUR NATIONAL MONUMENT

At the end of desolate stretches of black top in the sparsely populated northwest corner of the state, Dinosaur National Monument is Colorado's most remote destination, but for travelers fascinated by prehistoric life on earth, it is worth every lonely mile. It's one of the few places on earth that you can reach out and touch a dinosaur skeleton, snarling in its final pose, *in situ*.

Although dinosaurs once inhabited much of the earth, only a few places have the proper geological and climatic conditions to preserve their skeletons as fossils. Paleontologist Earl Douglass of Pittsburgh's Carnegie Museum discovered this dinosaur fossil bed, one of the largest in North America, in 1909. Six years later, President Woodrow Wilson acknowledged the scientific importance of the area, which straddles the Utah–Colorado border, by declaring it a national monument. It's been a rough few years for the monument. Major structural damage to the main visitor center has prevented anyone from accessing the stunning main attraction, the Dinosaur Quarry. Rangers assured us that a new visitor center would be ready for operation in the fall of 2011. Aside from the quarry, there's lots to see here. The monument's starkly eroded canyons provide the visitor with scenic drives, hiking, camping and river running.

⊙ Sights

Dinosaur Quarry

The Jurassic strata containing the fossils give a glimpse of how paleontologists transform solid rock into the beautiful skeletons seen in museums, and how they develop scientifically reliable interpretations of life in the remote past. Ranger-led walks, talks and tours explain the site; information can also be gleaned from brochures, audio-visual programs and exhibits. There is also a gift and bookshop. Dinosaur Quarry is open 8am to 7pm daily from Memorial Day to Labor Day; the rest of the year 8am to 4:30pm. The Quarry is completely enclosed to protect the fossils from weathering.

Fossil Discovery Trail

This short interpretive trial is excellent for families as its only 0.75 miles long and you can reach out and touch the bones of dinosaurs. Regardless of you knowledge or understanding of palaeontology, this is a stunning walk through some 65 million years of history. Walking along the hillside, visitors enter a small canyon, eventually arriving at the Morrison Formation, one of the most spectacular open-air collections of dinosaur bones in the world, Morrison Formation. The bones in these walls represent 10 species that range in size from about 7in to 76ft.

🏃 Activities

Both the Yampa River and Green River offer excellent river-running opportunities, with plenty of exciting rapids and choppy whitewater amid splendid scenery. From mid-May to early September trips range from one to five days. Adventure Bound (p245), in Grand Junction, is a popular rafting outfitter for the area. Fishing is permitted only with the appropriate state permits, available from sports stores or tackle shops in Dinosaur or Vernal, Utah. Check with park rangers about limits and the best places.

🍴 Sleeping & Eating

There are no lodges in the monument but Vernal has a good selection of motels and restaurants, and the town of Dinosaur also has a couple of motels and eateries. There are designated backcountry campsites only on the Jones Hole Trail; otherwise wilderness camping is allowed anywhere at least one-quarter mile from an established road

or trail. But lots of restrictions about backcountry camping apply, so backpackers should register at one of the visitors centers or ranger stations. Backcountry permits are free.

Camping

Dinosaur National Monument's main campground is **Green River Campground** (☑435-781-7700; Blue Mountain Rd; sites $12; ☺mid-April–early Oct), 5 miles east of Dinosaur Quarry along Blue Mountain Rd, with 88 sites. It has bathrooms and drinking water but no showers or hookups. A park host will sell firewood.

For camping during winter when Green River is closed, try nearby **Split Mountain Campground** (☑435-781-7700; Blue Mountain Rd; group sites $25 summer, free winter), which is a place for group camp sites in the summer, but is open to anyone in winter, when there's no fee.

ⓘ Information

Dinosaur National Monument is a 210,000-acre plot that straddles the Utah-Colorado state line. Monument headquarters and most of the land is within Colorado, but the quarry (the only place to see fossils protruding from the earth) is in Utah. There are several drives with scenic overlooks and interpretive signs, leading to a number of trailheads for short nature walks or access to the backcountry.

At the town of Dinosaur, a Colorado Welcome Center (p236) offers maps and brochures for the entire state. Information is available from **Dinosaur National Monument Headquarters Visitor Center** (☑970-374-3000; 4545 E Hwy 40; ☺8am-4:30pm Jun-Aug, Mon-Fri only Dec-Feb) (sometimes called the Cayon Visitor Center). It has an audio-visual program, exhibits and a bookstore. There's also a visitors center at Dinosaur Quarry, which, at the time of research was closed for major structural renovation. Entrance to the monument headquarters' visitors center is free, but entrance to other parts of the monument (including Dinosaur Quarry) is $10 per private vehicle, $5 for cyclists or bus passengers.

ⓘ Getting There & Away

The monument is 88 miles west of Craig via US 40 and 120 miles east of Salt Lake City, Utah, by I-80 and US 40. Dinosaur Quarry is 7 miles north of Jensen, UT, on Cub Creek Rd (Utah Hwy 149). Monument headquarters is just off US 40 on Harpers Corner Dr, about 4 miles east of the town of Dinosaur.

SOUTH OF DINOSAUR NATIONAL MONUMENT

Dinosaur

POP 350

Just a few miles east of the Utah border, on the doorstep of Dinosaur National Monument, it's easy to blow right by Dinosaur. In an effort to capitalize on its location by the monument, the town changed its name from Artesia in the mid-1960s and gave the streets dinosaur-themed monikers (Brachiosaurus Bypass, Triceratops Tce...). Junk car lots and forlorn homesteads dot the rolling hills of this windswept landscape.

Only a few things things entice travelers to hit the brakes on the way through town. The well-stocked **Colorado Welcome Center** (✆970-374-2205; 101 E Stegosaurus St; ⊙8am-6pm Memorial Day-Labor Day, 9am-5pm Labor Day-Memorial Day, closed Jan & Feb; ☏⚿) has maps to scenic drives, information on area rafting and camping. They're distributed by a pair of doting ladies who'll help you plan your travels in Colorado's west and know every little town between here and Denver.

If you're hungry, the best best is a greasy bite at **BedRock Depot** (✆970-374-2336; 214 W Brontosaurus Blvd; mains $3-9; ⊙11am-5:30pm Mon & Thu-Sat, 1-5pm Sun; ⚿), a nostalgic ice cream and espresso shop that serves a coy menu of dino-themed sandwiches like the 'Allosaurus Delight,' a savory chicken apple sausage on a roll. The potato roll of Leona, one of the owners, is famous around here, as is the homemade ice cream. The only other place to eat is 20 miles east of town, the **Massadona Tavern and Steakhouse** (✆970-374-2324; 22927 US Hwy 40; mains $8-18; ⊙4-8pm Tue-Fri, 11am-8pm Sat & Sun; ⚿). Way out on a lonely stretch of Hwy 40, it has the feel of a mid-century roadhouse and serves up passable chops, battered fish and chips, burgers and pints of beer. There are a few spare motels on Hwy 40, but none of them are recommended.

Rangely

POP 2000 / ELEV 5274FT

An isolated coal and oil town on Hwy 64, Rangely is about 56 miles west of Meeker and about 90 miles north of Fruita and Grand Junction via Hwy 139. Visitors to nearby Dinosaur National Monument may wish to detour through Rangely to access the very fine rock art sites along Hwy 139 just south of town, but Rangely itself is not much of a destination. The **Rangely Chamber of Commerce** (✆970-675-5290; www.rangely.com; 209 E Main St; ⊙1-5pm Mon-Fri) can provide information on local businesses.

The **Rangely Museum** (✆970-675-2612; 150 Kennedy Dr; ⊙10am-4pm summer, shorter hours winter; ⚿) is a good diversion with exhibits on energy production, Native Americans and ranching. There are several notable pre-Columbian rock art sites on nearby BLM lands; look for self-guided tour brochures along Hwy 64 East and West, the Dragon Trail south of Rangely and Cañon Pintado.

🛏 Sleeping & Eating

TOP CHOICE **Blue Mountain Inn & Suites**

HOTEL $$

(✆970-675-8888; www.bluemountaininnrangely.com; 37 Park St; r $100-150, suites $200; ⚿⚿⚿⚿) Certainly the nicest hotel within 100 miles of Dinosaur National Monument, this new roadside hotel would be slightly bland if it weren't for stone fireplaces and the timber-framed entranceway and a nice little indoor pool. The best value comes when you book directly through the website.

Budget Host Inn MOTEL $

(✆970-675-8461; www.budgethostrangely.com; 117 S Grand Ave; d $79-99; ⚿⚿) For something a bit cheaper than the Blue Mountain Inn, there's the no-frills Budget Host, which was also recently remodeled and has fast wi-fi and a grill for guests.

Rangely Camper Park CAMPGROUND $

(940 E Rangely Ave; sites $10-15; ⚿⚿) Located beneath a stand of cottonwoods, this city park has RV hook-ups and spacious sites. It's an excellent base for rock hounding.

Cañon Pintado National Historic District

To spend a few moments communing with these spectral, mysterious images – ghostly birds and life-size flutists – is well worth adding a few hours to the trip between Grand Junction and Dinosaur National Monument. The paintings, left as inscrutable messages from the region's early settlers, create Colorado's most desolate, haunting gallery.

The images are attributed to two of Douglass Canyon's first communities: the Fremont Culture, who lived here from about 0–1300AD, and the Ute, who lived here from around 1300–1881. It was the journal of Silvestre Vélez de Escalante, a Franciscan missionary who came through on the famed Dominguez-Escalante expedition of 1776, that first named this corridor Cañyon Pintado (Painted Canyon).

It's a unforgivably arid, dusty stretch, but over the past several years the BLM has made the self-guided drive much easier to access, with educational signs and maintained turn-offs and trails. Look for green and white BLM rods that indicate the sites along Hwy 139.

MEEKER

POP 2400 / ELEV 6239FT

The picturesque seat of Rio Blanco County, Meeker takes its name from infamous government agent Nathan Meeker, whose arbitrary destruction of a Ute racetrack precipitated a fatal confrontation in 1879. Contemporary Meeker is a small oil town, surrounded by sagebrush country where Greek American sheepherders graze huge flocks for their wool and silent pumpjacks rust on the hillsides.

⊙ Sights & Activities

FREE White River Museum
MUSEUM
(✆970-878-9982; www.meekercolorado.com; 565 Park St; ☺9am-5pm summer, 10am-4pm winter; ⦿) There's a rambling collection of eclectic Western memorabilia here: bear skin coats, a couple peace pipes and Nathan Meeker's printing press.

Sable Mountain Outfitters OUTDOORS
(✆970-878-4765; www.sablemountainoutfitters. com; 4-day pack trips $1200) This outfitter has been running hunting, fishing and wilderness trips for three decades. The trips into the Flat Top Wilderness come highly recommended from locals.

JML Outfitters FISHING, HORSEBACK RIDING
(✆970-878-4749; www.jmloutfitters.com; 300 County Rd 75; half-day trail rides from $55, day pack-trips from $300; ⦿) It hosts multiday adventures into the Flat Top Wilderness on horseback, allowing guests to ride between a string of camps and get far into the brush. The excursions are rustic, but with horses,

guides and a camp cook, it's a luxurious way to feel like you've worked for it.

The riders here also have lots of programs for kids.

🛏 Sleeping & Eating

Meeker gets booked up with hunters from late September to mid-November. Rates are a bit higher on weekends and during hunting season. Note that JML Outfitters also has cabins for rent ($70), even if you don't do an expedition with them. There are several independent restaurants in the small downtown, and lots of fast food options on the periphery.

Blue Spruce Inn HOTEL $
(✆970-878-0777; www.blueprucemeeker.com; 488 Market St; d $89; P✽☎) Sure, it's newly built, but what it lacks in out-of-the-box blandness is made up for by Michelle, who dispenses local advice and checks guests in to impeccably clean, spacious rooms. There's a little hot tub to soak in after a day of fishing and free breakfast.

White River Inn MOTEL $
(✆970-878-5031; www.whiteriverinn.com; 219 E Market St; d $70; P⊖☎) A simple, quiet option just a bit east of downtown, the updated rooms at the White River are a bargain. They all have refrigerators and microwaves.

❶ Getting There & Away

On the north bank of the White River near the junction of Hwy 13 and Hwy 64, Meeker is 45 miles south of Craig and 42 miles north of Rifle. The Flat Tops Scenic Byway is a stunning 82-mile drive through the wilderness to Yampa.

ALONG I-70

Glenwood Springs

POP 9053 / ELEV 5763FT

Let's start with the fun stuff. Doc Holliday – gun fighter, gambler, archetype of Wild West gentility – died here. Why he died *here* is the first clue to Glenwood Springs' long-standing appeal to travelers: thermal hot springs. In Holliday's day they were thought to have restorative powers – he hoped they'd ease chronic respiratory ailments.

Perched at the confluence of the Colorado and Roaring Fork Rivers at the end of Glenwood Canyon, these hot springs have been a travel destination for centuries. Ute

Indians meditated in steamy thermal caves. A mild climate and a range of summer and winter activities have rounded out the city's appeal, but the springs and large outdoor pool remain one of Colorado's more popular vacation destinations. Glenwood Springs also represents an inexpensive 'down-valley' winter alternative to Aspen areas. Only about 45 minutes west along I-70 from Vail and Beaver Creek, it's a thrifty base for skiing some of Colorado's best mountains.

Since 1896, Grand Ave has crossed the Colorado River and formed the main business street extending due south from the river. The resort spa and pool are north of the river, reached by a highway and pedestrian/bicycle bridge. West Glenwood Springs evolved north of the river along US 6, a route now followed by I-70.

◉ Sights

Glenwood Caverns Adventure Park
AMUSEMENT PARK
(Fairy Caves & Glenwood Caverns; ☎970-945-4228; www.glendwoodcaverns.com; 51000 Two Rivers Plaza Rd; adult/child $39/35; ⊗10am-9pm with seasonal variations; ⊕) This amusement park's Fairy Caves are a historic draw, and were once touted as the eighth wonder of the world. Today, there are cave tours and thrill rides, and the park enjoys a spectacular mountainside location.

The 'Wild Tour' of the caves is a heart-racing experience for would-be spelunkers, allowing guests to crawl through narrow passages, but our favorite ride is the canyon swing, which sends folks squealing 1300 feet in the air above the Colorado River at 50 miles an hour.

Glenwood Springs Center for the Arts
GALLERY
(☎970-945-2414; www.glenwoodarts.org; 601 E 6th St; ⊗9am-5pm Mon-Fri, noon-4pm Sat & Sun; ℗) For a town the size of Glenwood Springs, this is a surprisingly vibrant arts center, hosting dance and music performances, gallery shows of local artists and lots of classes. In the summer, it also stages an outdoor music series.

Linwood Cemetery
CEMETERY
(Pioneer Cemetery; cnr 12th St & Bennett Ave) Established in 1886, this is where John Henry 'Doc' Holliday was allegedly laid to rest in November 1887 (debate about this persists, since some scholars claim the ground would have been frozen). Harvey 'Kid Curry' Logan, a member of Butch Cassidy and Sundance Kid's gang, is also here.

Every year in October there's a guided cemetery ghost walk, which can be arranged through the Frontier Historical Museum.

🏃 Activities

The USFS White River National Forest Ranger Office (p241) has maps and information for all outdoor activities in the area.

Cycling

Rolling over the smoothly paved Glenwood Canyon Trail, under the vertical canyon walls, makes an excellent afternoon for riders of all abilities. The path follows the Colorado River upstream below the cantilevered I-70 and on the old highway. It's an easy 16.2 miles between the Yampah Vapor Caves and Dotsero.

Other local rides are shown on the free topographic Glenwood Springs Hiking & Mountain Bicycle Trail Map from the Chamber Resort Association and USFS headquarters.

Sunlight Ski & Bike Shop
BIKE RENTAL, SKI RENTAL
(☎970-945-9425; www.sunlightmtn.com; 309 9th St; adult bikes per hr/day $5/20; ⊕) In summer, this downtown shop rents comfort bikes, tandems and a selection of children's bikes, and runs a shuttle to Bair Ranch and Hanging Lake to let you pedal back. In winter, it has snow gear and free trips to the mountain. It's our favorite all-around shop in town.

Canyon Bikes
BIKE RENTAL
(☎970-945-8904, toll-free 800-439-3043; www.canyonbikes.com; 319 6th St; half-day rental per adult/child $19/15; ⊗8am-8pm Memorial Day-Labor Day, 9am-5pm Dec-Feb; ⊕) The paved 16-mile biking, hiking and in-line skating trail though Glenwood Canyon starts one block from this downtown bike shop. It's a great option for families too, as it operates a shuttle you can take one way.

Rafting

The snow-capped hills that make this area so attractive to skiers melt to into roaring rivers in the spring, when the Colorado offers tons of Class III-IV white water. Many of the trips depart from east of town, on the stretch below the Shoshone Dam. Families with young children can take shorter float trips at the Grizzly Creek turnoff from I-70,

'DOWN-VALLEY' SKIING

Serious skiers head 'up-valley' to Aspen, Aspen Highlands and Snowmass, or east on I-70 to Vail. But **Sunlight Mountain Resort** (☎970-945-7491, toll-free 800-445-7931; www.sunlightmtn. com; 10901 County Road 117; adult/child lift pass $50/40; ☉9am-4pm; ♿), 12 miles south of Glenwood Springs on Garfield County Rd 117, survives by offering good deals to families and intermediate skiers. The cross-country ski area features 18 miles of groomed track and snow-skating trails, plus snowshoeing and ice-skating areas. Call for the latest ski, swim and stay packages. There's free transportation to the hill from the corner of 11th and Grand Sts. Equipment and rentals are available at the mountain or in town at Sunlight Mountain Ski & Bike Shop (opposite)..

or travel the Colorado River later in the summer, during low flow. Two Rivers Park, north of the confluence of the Colorado and Roaring Fork Rivers, is a good take-out point.

Rock Gardens Rafting RAFTING
(☎970-957-6737, toll-free 800-958-6737; www. rockgardens.com; 1308 County Rd 129; half-day from $47; ☉8am-9pm, reduced hrs winter; ♿) Another reputable company in Glenwood Springs, these guys do the standard range of trips on the Roaring Fork and Colorado Rivers, and offers package combo deals with their partner company, Glenwood Canyon Zipline Adventures.

The best value for money and the friendliest guides in town.

Blue Sky Adventures RAFTING
(☎970-945-6605, toll-free 877-945-6605; www. blueskyadventure.com; 319 6th St; half-day from $47; ☉7:30am-8pm; ♿) One of the most established rafting companies in town, Blue Sky operates a spectrum of half- and full-day packages. For those who don't have the thirst for white water, it has mild trips offering a scenic float and views of Glenwood Canyon.

Colorado Whitewater Rafting RAFTING
(☎970-945-8477, toll-free 800-993-7238; www. coloradowhitewaterrafting.com; 2000 Devereux

Rd; half-day from $47; ♿) Just off the highway, this company does a variety of trips and has some family friendly packages, combining rafting with other local attractions.

Hiking

The relatively low elevations around Glenwood Springs means that there are no alpine trails above treeline but many are very scenic and easily accessible. Numerous trails head north from the Glenwood Canyon Trail, including the 1.2-mile-long Hanging Lake Trail, which leads to a breathtaking waterfall-fed pond perched in a rock bowl on the canyon wall. It's a strenuous 1½- to 3-hour round-trip with a 1020ft elevation gain, but well worth the huffing and puffing. Keep a sharp lookout for bighorn sheep in Glenwood Canyon. Take the Hanging Lake exit 8 miles east of town on I-70, or make a morning or afternoon of it and bike the Canyon Trail 10.5 miles to the Hanging Lake trailhead.

A short half-mile hike to the Linwood Cemetery, where gambling gunfighter John Henry 'Doc' Holliday was laid to rest, begins at the corner of 12th St and Bennett Ave.

Other Activities

TOP CHOICE Glenwood Hot Springs & Spa of the Rockies HOT SPRINGS
(☎970-945-6571, 800-537-7946; www.hotsprings pool.com; 401 N River St; admission $18.25; ☉7:30am-10pm Mar-Nove, from 9am Dec-Feb; ☎♿) The water here is only a fraction of the draw: there's a spa, a fancy lodge, a couple of water slides, even a miniature golf course.

A mess? Maybe a little, but if Glenwood Hot Springs is trying to be every kind of tourist attraction at once, it can also be a worthy and varied family attraction. While kids hit the slides or play golf (both for additional fees, of course), mom and dad can get pampered in the adjoining Spa of the Rockies. The full service spa is one of the nicest in the state, with a suite of offerings – massage tables, tubs to soak in (the guys' tub comes with a flat-screen ESPN overhead) and exercise equipment. When the 'rents rejoin the kiddies at the manic and crowded scene outside, the tranquil pan-flute filled interior will seem a million miles away.

Roaring Fork Anglers FLY-FISHING
(☎970-945-0180; www.roaringforkanglers.com; 2022 Grand Ave; half-day float trips from $360,

NORTHWEST COLORADO GLENWOOD SPRINGS

wait trips from $31; ⊙8:30am-5:30pm) This full-service fly shop has been operating on the rivers of the area for 30 years and offers a great guide service. It has half- and full-day trips on the river, starting at around $300.

Yampah Spa   THERMAL CAVES
(✆970-945-0667; www.yampahspa.com; 709 E 6th St; admission incl towel rental $12; ⊙9am-9pm; 🏵) Entering these caves feels like descending into one of Dante's layers of hell – at least in terms of temperature. It's *damn hot*. The steamy natural caves where Utes once soaked still draw bathers. The air is heavy with boron, lithium, arsenic and a score of other minerals.

The natural caves have been a commercial facility for 116 years and though they've been widened and slightly remodeled in the years since, they still have a primitive feel. (If you want something plush, visit Spa of the Rockies.) Towel-clad patrons pad around the cement floors in the slightly sulfuric air, heated by a constant flow of thermal water at 115°F. Current owners have added a full menu of spa treatments in the rooms upstairs.

★ Festivals & Events

Strawberry Days   FOOD
(✆970-945-6589; www.strawberrydaysfestival.com; Grand Ave & Hyland Park; ⊙mid-Jun; 🏵) This city carnival happens annually in mid-June, and is one of the longest-running civic festivals in Colorado.

🛏 Sleeping

It's easy to spot hotels on both sides of the freeway, but there are a number of quieter options away from the main drag.

TOP CHOICE **Sunlight Mountain Inn**   LODGE $$
(✆970-945-5225; www.sunlightinn.com; 10252 County Rd 117; d $79-129; ⊙❄🏵) A stone's throw from Sunlight Mountain Resort's ski area, this adorable mountain lodge has 20 Western-style rooms with quilted beds and fireplaces, and guests who congregate by the inviting fire.

Somehow, the hustle of the outside world doesn't make it through the door – there are no TVs and no cell-phone reception, and when it's blanketed by snow, it achieves a languid coziness. The comfortable dining room is open for dinner only in winter but serves breakfast all year-round and there's a bar to warm up with corrected coffee after a day on the slopes. For a romantic getaway place near skiing, this choice is excellent value and feels like a well-kept secret.

Glenwood Springs Hostel   HOSTEL $
(✆970-945-8545, toll-free 800-946-7835; www.hostelcolorado.com; 1021 Grand Ave; dm $16, r $25; 🛜🏵) In Western Colorado, this is one of the backpacker haunts. Even though rooms are smallish and a bit ragged, it has character galore in the common spaces. Some 3000 vinyl records, a pair of congas and couple of guitars litter the living room for guests to play.

There are family rooms, a couple of big kitchens and the staff has loads of great advice. It's a good place to meet travelers from abroad – many of whom are riding the Amtrak – and the hostel can help hook up ski or bike adventures at a discount.

Cedar Lodge Motel   MOTEL $$
(✆970-945-6579; www.cedarlodgemotel.net; 2102 Grand Ave; d $79, ste $130; 🅿️⊙🏊🏵) This mid-price motel is nothing too fancy, but

---

DOC HOLLIDAY'S LAST LABORED BREATH

It's slightly inappropriate that the hike to the purple headstone at Linwood Cemetery (p238) might leave you breathless: the life of the legendary man underfoot was shaped by labored breathing. Seeking relief for tuberculosis (then known as consumption) Holliday moved west from his native Georgia. He set up a dental practice in Texas, but the wheezing scared away patients, turning Holliday to gambling. While gambling in the saloons of the West, Holliday met Wyatt Earp, with whom he participated in the most famous shoot-out of Western lore at OK Corral.

Biographers paint Holliday as a hot tempered vagabond with a rapacious, caustic wit evident even in his last moments. Lying infirm in a hotel on the site of the current Hotel Colorado he gazed bemusedly at his bare feet and said, 'Well I'll be damned. This is funny.' No legendary gunfighter expects to die with his boots off. Holliday's exact place of burial is unknown; the records were lost when the cemetery was moved from an earlier location down the hill.

it hits the sweet spot for value. The tidy rooms are laid with green carpet and outfitted with microwaves, the views of the cliff across the street are winning, and the owners are sweet. The small pool on hand is sparkling.

Hotel Colorado HOTEL $$$
(☎800-544-3998; www.hotelcolorado.com; 526 Pine St; d $164-199; P☺☎📶📶) Understandably nicknamed the 'Grand Dame,' this imposing 19th-century hotel has rooms that have seen better days, but the ghosts of its past residents (presidents and gangsters, heiresses and gunmen) make for a remarkably unique stay.

Both Howard Taft and Teddy Roosevelt were guests, though the most lore surrounds Doc Holliday, who died in a former hotel on this site. The rooms, though updated several times, are fine but can't match its former glory – or, frankly, an average Holiday Inn. Ask to see a couple rooms before dropping the suitcase, because they vary in size.

✖ Eating & Drinking
If you're exploring on foot and get hungry, make for the neighborhood north of the highway on Grand Ave – it has the highest concentration and greatest range of restaurants.

TOP CHOICE Italian Underground ITALIAN $$
(☎970-945-6422; 715 Grand Ave; mains $8-18; ☺5-10pm; ☺📶) The smell of garlic packs a wallop as you descend the stairs to this family-run Italian joint. You may have to wait for a table, but plates of classic fare – lasagna, spaghetti and meatballs, pizza, cannoli – are worth it. Best, each meal finishes with a little bowl of spumoni.

Bluebird Cafe CAFE FOOD $
(☎970-384-2024; 730 Grand Ave; sandwiches $6-8; ☺6:30am-7pm Mon-Thu, to 10pm Fri, 7am-7pm Sat, 7am-5pm Sun; ☎📶) The vegetarian breakfast burrito is a yummy portable breakfast at this organic coffee shop and the lunch menu consists of simple sandwiches and homemade soup. Folk bands occasionally pop up outside the front window and in the summer there's breezy outdoor seating.

Juicy Lucy's Steakhouse STEAK $$
(☎970-945-4619; www.juicylucyssteakhouse. com; 308 7th St; mains $12-30; ☺11am-9:30pm Mon-Thu, to 10pm Fri-Sat; ☺📶) Despite the cornball name, people love Lucy's because

staff cook the meat perfectly and eschew the mannish brass-fitted steakhouse posture for a small town cafe feel. It serves game dishes, and has a good wine list, but the side of cheesy au gratin potatoes can nearly steal the show.

Glenwood Canyon Brewing Company
BREWPUB
(☎970-945-1276; www.glenwoodcanyon.com; 402 7th St; ☺11am-11pm Mon-Thu, to midnight Fri & Sat) You'll do better to eat elsewhere, but the beers here are fresh and the night scene is lively. The lighter beers on the spectrum – particularly the Hanging Creek Honey Ale and Red Mountain ESB – are the best, though the fresh root beer is truly outstanding.

Doc Holliday's Tavern DIVE BAR
(☎970-384-2379; 724 Grand Ave; ☺11am-2am) This is a dive bar par excellence, complete with creaking floors and surly, droop-eyed bartenders. It's a good place for a pint and some local color, and it would be a missed opportunity not to pose by the big neon six-shooter out front.

ℹ Information
Chamber Resort Association (☎970-945-6589, 888-445-3696; www.glenwoodsprings. net; 1102 Grand Ave; ☺8:30am-5pm Mon-Fri, 9am-3pm Sat & Sun) This information center can assist with booking rooms and activities.

USFS White River National Forest Ranger Office (☎970-945-2521; 900 Grand Ave; ☺8am-4:30pm Mon-Fri; 📶) This office has information about hunting, riding area trails and camping in the White River National Forest.

ℹ Getting There & Away
Glenwood Springs is 159 miles west of Denver and 90 miles east of Grand Junction along I-70.

Glenwood Springs Amtrak Station (☎970-945-9563; www.amtrak.com; 413 7th St; ☺9am-5pm) Amtrak's *California Zephyr* stops daily at the Glenwood Springs Amtrak Station. Trips to and from Denver happen once daily. The trip takes 5½ hours and costs $39.

Greyhound (☎970-945-2500; www.grey hound.com; 124 W 6th St) The Ramada serves as the unmanned Greyhound station in Glenwood Springs.

ℹ Getting Around
Colorado Mountain Express (☎970-949-4227, 800-525-6363; www.cmex.com) This door-to-door service makes runs to Denver International Airport (DIA), Summit County, Breckenridge and

other major ski areas. Make bookings online. A trip between Glenwood Springs and DIA costs $87 and takes four hours.

Ride Glenwood Springs (☑970-384-6437; www.ci.glenwood-springs.co.us) Buses operate on the half-hour between the Glenwood Springs Mall and the Roaring Forks Marketplace at the south end of town. Check the city website for routes and schedules.

Roaring Forks Transit Authority (☑970-925-8484; www.rfta.com) With several lines, this network of public transportation serves Glenwood Springs and Aspen. It operates several shuttles to the ski areas in the winter.

Carbondale

If you're driving between Colorado's central corridor, I-70, and Aspen or Black Canyon of the Gunnison National Park, Carbondale is far and away the most charming place to cool the engine. It has managed to retain lots of local flavor while hosting the stuff visitors go gaga for: galleries, interesting boutique shopping and excellent food. The postcard-perfect downtown has an offbeat, artsy sensibility and a mix of crunchy post-hippies, mountain men and tourists.

The **Carbondale Chamber of Commerce** (☑970-963-1890; www.carbondale.com; 981 Cowen Dr, Suite C; ☺8:30am-4:30pm Mon-Fri) has tourist information and it maintains an excellent website with local events and information. Be sure to eat at **Six89** (www.six89.com; 5:30-10pm Tue-Sun; mains $17-25), with one of the most exciting menus in the state.

Marble

At the headwaters of the Crystal River, Marble stands in the shadow of the impressive Elk Mountains, providing a detour into a genuine mountain town. The town is tiny, with only 105 full-time residents, and was founded to harvest nearby deposits of uniformly white, pure Yule Marble at the end of the 19th century. Marble's quarry, which is still in operation, supplied stone to some of the most famous statuary in the US, including the Lincoln Memorial and Tomb of the Unknown Soldier. The main reason to pass through is a side trip further up into the hills to visit the ghost town at Crystal.

◎ Sights & Activities

Marble is a good base for fishing and hunting trips, but most visitors pass through

on the way to explore Crystal. If you don't think your car is up to the task of the rough road (high clearance vehicles are recommended), contact **Crystal River Jeep Tours** (☑970-963-1991; www.crystalriverjeeptour.smith familycolorado.com; 575 W Park St; tours per 2 people $60), a reliable company that knows the route well. From their Jeep, the sweeping panoramas of the Maroon Bells-Snowmass Wilderness Area in the White River National Forest are breathtaking – even if you get jostled about like a rag doll.

If you want to get into the wilderness on horse back, contact **Out West Guides** (☑970-963-5525; www.outwestguides.com; 7500 County Rd 3; horseback rides per hr from $50), which operates horseback rides and half-day fly-fishing expeditions ($285 for two people).

❶ Getting There & Away

Marble is 40 miles south of Glenwood Springs via Hwy 82 and Hwy 133. The turnoff to Marble is about 22 miles south of Carbondale and clearly marked.

Crystal

One of Colorado's more easily accessible ghost towns, Crystal has iconic buildings that are photographic highlights if you're willing to make the detour. To get here from Marble requires a slow, rocky ride over unimproved roads and some hiking. Budget three or four hours for a visit.

The first mining in the Crystal area took place in the 1860s, but the roads were so poor it wasn't until the 1880s that it really picked up. There were a half-dozen mines by 1893 producing silver, lead and zinc. The average population in Crystal was 500. There was a hotel, a post office, two newspapers (one called the *Crystal River Current*, the other *The Silver Lance*), general stores, a pool hall, the Crystal Club and more. As the mines played out, so did the town, although the area has never really been deserted. The area is still a sportsman's paradise today and there are several cabins in the area. The road to Crystal goes through Marble and eventually winds through Schofield Pass and Gothic on its way to Crested Butte. The road is very rough and, unless you don't care about trashing the rental car, it should be approached using 4WD. Most people take the road from Marble to get to Crystal, which is significantly better.

PALISADE WINE REGION

Lush, leafy rows of vines and peach trees have a backdrop of red-rock canyons and wide, blue skies in Colorado's most inviting wine region. The plucky up-and-coming producers of the Grand Valley may not have the lore of valleys in Napa and Loire, but the long, arrow-straight blacktop surrounding Palisade connects many of Colorado's best vineyards. Here, family farms, hot summers and volcanic soil produce wines that are as bold and adventurous as the surroundings.

Pull off the highway in Palisade and hand over your keys: this town loves to get tight. According to tipsy locals, Palisade is the smallest town in the USA with an all-of-the-above approach to producing booze: a winery, a meadery, distillery and brewery within the city borders. Since it could be a long night, book a room in the **Wine Country Inn** (970-464-5777; www.coloradowinecountryinn.com; 777 Grande River Dr; d $139, ste $249; P✆❄@🛜🏊🚲), a swish, newly opened B&B which helps guests arrange bike or horse tours of the local wineries. Nearby **Canyon Wind Cellars** (www.canyonwind cellars.com; 3907 North River Rd; ⊙10am-5pm Mon-Sun; 🚲) is the most-established, but our favorite, an unpretentious family outfit called **Carlson Vineyards** (970-464-5554; www.carlsonvineyards.com; 461 35 Rd; ⊙10am-6pm Mon-Sun; 🚲), is just up the road. Carlson does a range of standard varietals, but the fruit-based wine is the most interesting, including some made entirely from aged Palisade peaches.

Further along is one of the area's top peach farms, **High Country Orchards** (970-464-1150; www.highcountryorchards.com; 3548 E 1/2 Rd; ⊙10am-5pm; P🚲), a favorite stop of the Obama family during the 2008 campaign. Families who don't have Air Force One waiting should take the short drive to the **Suncrest Orchards** (970-464-4862; www.suncrestorchardalpacas.net; 3608 E 1/4 Rd; ⊙9am-5pm Tue, Thu & Sat; P🚲), where Scott and Cindy can offer tours of their Alpaca farm and kids can pet the inquisitive beasts.

After sending the kids to bed, start with a sampling of the exquisite homemade cocktails at **Peach Street Distillers** (970-464-1128; www.peachstreetdistillers.com; 144 Kluge Ave; ⊙noon-10pm) (it produces a spectrum of spirits, but the gin is a delicate, aromatic and well-balanced favorite) and then make for Palisade's finest dining room, **Inari's A Palisade Bistro** (970-464-4911; www.inarisbistro.com; 336 Main St; mains $11-25; ⊙5-9pm Tue-Sat, 10am-2pm Sun), where – you guessed it – there's a killer wine list. If the siren call of Palisade's nightlife persists, take in a nightcap at the **Palisade Brewing Company** (970-464-1462; 200 Peach Ave; ⊙noon-10pm).

Colorado National Monument

The Colorado National Monument is the crown jewel of the Western Slope, a place where the setting sun seems to set fire to otherworldly red-rock formations, hikers test themselves against a starkly beautiful environment and campers are treated to a frequent display of lightening storms rolling across the distant planes.

These canyons rise from the Uncompahgre Uplift of the Colorado Plateau, 2000ft above the Grand Valley of the Colorado River to reveal a stunning view. The twinkling lights of Grand Juction, the green strip of the Colorado River, the black ribbon of I-70, the tree-lined farm fields of the Grand Valley – these are all far below, together a

memorable contrast of Colorado's ancient geological past and modern present.

Once dinosaur country, this 32-sq-mile scenic wonder is one of the most rewarding side trips possible from an interstate highway, well worth a detour by car but even better for backcountry exploration. Open all year, the Colorado National Monument is an exceptional area for hiking, camping and road biking.

🏃 Activities
Colorado National Monument contains a variety of hiking trails starting on Rim Rock Drive, most of them relatively short, such as the half-mile hike starting from the **Coke Ovens Trailhead** or a quarter-mile stroll starting at the **Devils Kitchen Trailhead**. The numerous canyons are

more interesting, but the rugged terrain makes loop hikes difficult or impossible; a steep descent from the canyon rim means an equally steep ascent on the return. One alternative is to use either a car or bicycle shuttle, since some trailheads outside the park are reached most easily from Hwy 340, the Broadway/Redlands Rd between Fruita and Grand Junction.

Perhaps the most rewarding trail is the 6-mile **Monument Canyon Trail**, leading from Rim Rock Dr down to Hwy 340, past many of the park's most interesting natural features, including the Coke Ovens, the Kissing Couple and Independence Monument. Another possibility is the less precipitous Liberty Cap Trail, which links up with the much steeper Ute Canyon Trail to form a lengthy 14-mile loop.

If you have half a day and lots of ambition, it's interesting to make for **Rattlesnake Arches**, the largest collection of natural arches anywhere outside Arches National Park. Getting here is a bit tricky, since the arches can be accessed by trailheads in the BLM Black Ridge Wilderness Area or within the national monument. If you make it, the scenery is worth it. Inquire about directions at the BLM office in Grand Junction or the Saddlehorn Visitor Center.

🛏 Sleeping

Saddlehorn Campground　　　CAMPGROUND $
(☑970-858-3617; Rim Rock Dr; sites $10; ⌖) The only organized camp in the monument is a fantastic value for car camping, and there are expansive views. It's easy for RVs and near the visitor center.

ℹ Information

Saddlehorn Visitor Center (☑970-858-3617; www.nps.gov/colm/; Rim Rock Dr; ⊙8am-6pm Mon-Sun Jun-Oct, low season hrs vary) The Saddlehorn Visitors Center is the only place in the Colorado National Monument to get backcountry permits for camping and the best place for information about climbing. The rangers are happy to suggest hikes and outings. There's also a small on-site bookstore.

Grand Junction

POP 35,000 / ELEV 4586FT

In truth, Grand Junction has long been about as utilitarian as its name might suggest. The town lies near two major rivers, and the intersection of highways today are built over trading routes centuries old. It ain't much to see on its own, if you're headed anywhere in the western part of this state, you're bound to pass through.

Amid one of Colorado's most fertile agricultural zones, Grand Junction is a cow town at heart – despite being western Colorado's main urban hub. Planners have partially turned downtown Main St into a pleasant pedestrian mall by reducing roads, planting trees, providing benches and littering it with sculptures. The effort has helped the city retain something of a small-town atmosphere, and it's a nice enough base for exploring the nearby scenic wonders of the region.

👁 Sights

Most of the banner sights of the area are actually outside city limits. Grand Junction's sightseeing action is concentrated in the pleasant downtown. The self-explanatory Art On The Corner program makes for a pleasant stroll along Main St.

Museum of Western Colorado　　MUSEUM
(☑970-242-0971; www.museumofwesternco.com; 462 Ute Ave; adult/senior/child $5.50/4.50/3; ⊙9am-5pm Mon-Sat, noon-4pm Sun May-Sep, 10am-3pm Tue-Sat Oct-Apr; ⌖) The most impressive of Grand Junction's sites, this well-arranged museum is the largest in the region, featuring impressive multidisciplinary displays on regional history (such as the awesome Thrailkill Collection of firearms) and special exhibits. Look for the modern bell tower downtown, the most central of the museum's three facilities.

Western Colorado Botanic Gardens
　　　　　　　　　　　　　　　　　GARDENS
(☑970-248-3288; www.wcbotanic.org; 655 Struthers Ave; adult/student & senior/child $5/4/3; ⊙noon-5:30pm Tue-Fri, from 10am Sat & Sun; P🐾) The Orchid Display is the jewel in the crown of this small community botanic gardens, and makes a steamy reprieve from the elements in the blustery winter. A leisurely visit should take about an hour.

🏃 Activities
Mountain Biking

Some of Colorado's finest mountain biking is to be had around Grand Junction, and travelers with even a cursory interest in it would be remiss not to spend a couple hours exploring. Major trails include the 142-mile Grand Junction to Montrose Tabegauche Trail (pronounced 'tab-a-watch'), and the 128-mile Kokopelli Trail, which stretches from nearby Fruita to Moab, Utah. The latter is an epic, requiring multiday planning, and traversing miles of ruggedly beautiful terrain. While doing the full length of any these trails requires extensive preparation, both offer plenty of loops and other shorter ride possibilities.

If you only have a short time to rent a bike and get on a trail, you're better served to go up the road to Fruita (p248), where you can easily pedal north of the village to reach numerous sights.

Other Activities

There's some fine climbing to be had nearby, notably in Unaweep Canyon and Monument Canyon in the Colorado National Monument. Climbers can stop by Summit Canyon Mountaineering (p247) for climbing equipment, books, topographic maps and tips on where to go.

Mt Garfield Stables HORSEBACK RIDING
(970-242-4008; 4331 Blair Rd; ⊙per hr from $17) is located north of town near its namesake mountain, which towers over the airport and I-70. Rides in the scenic areas around Mt Garfield and the Bookcliffs start at $17 per hour. The friendly staff offer free pick-up from your hotel with a minimum two-hour ride.

Adventure Bound WATER SPORTS
(970-245-5428,800-423-4668;www.adventure boundusa.com; 2392 H Rd; 1-day trip from $90; ⊕) This excellent operator is fully licenced on all BLM and NPS land and runs extended excursions on isolated, pristine sections of western Colorado's rivers. Shorter runs – such as a day trip down the Ruby and Horsethief Canyons – are quality, but Adventure Bound's trip to the Yampa River is the one most packed with great rapids and excellent scenery.

Over four or five days, the trip passes through extremely remote wilderness with opportunities to hike in Dinosaur National Monument and follow the route of mid-19th–century explorer John Wesley Powell.

🛏 Sleeping

Grand Junction has abundant accommodations. If you're blowing through town on the highway, the I-70 exit for Horizon Dve is downright silly with hotels from just about every major chain. Downtown is a bit more pleasant – you can walk to restaurants and bars – though there are fewer options.

Grand Junction Bookcliffs Bed & Breakfast B&B $$
(970-261-3938; www.grandjunctionbnb.com; 3153 F Rd; d $99-150; P⊕❄☞⊕) Amid farms and fields north of town, this family-operated B&B looks out to the Book Cliffs and is an excellent alternative to Grand Junction's mostly bleak hotels. The rooms are simply decorated and cozy, and there's a backyard and nearby park for the kids to run around.

Castle Creek B&B B&B $$
(970-241-9105; www.castlecreekbandb.com; 638 Horizon Dr; d from $95; P⊕❄☞⊕) From the driveway, Castle Creek looks like little more than an enormous suburban mansion, but the details are spot on – chocolates on the pillow, a big selection of movies, popcorn by the microwave, and a hot tub from which to take in the fresh night air. The spacious grounds allow for a quiet stay.

Hotel Melrose HOSTEL $
(970-242-9636; www.historicmelrosehouse. com; 337 Colorado Ave; dm/s/d $25/50/55; P⊕☞) The sole survivor of Grand Junction's 12 original hotels is tough to read. Is it a hostel? A hotel? A halfway house? Either way, it's clean, the staff is friendly and two-bed dorms are the cheapest in town. Just don't be shocked when people start swapping stories about their shady pasts.

Camping

Skip Grand Junction's RV-loaded private camping for some of the excellent state and national land in the area. Visit the BLM Grand Junction Field Office (p247) for information about wilderness camping on BLM land in the area or head into the Colorado National Monument to camp at Saddlehorn Campground. For information about camping or renting a cabin in Grand Mesa, Uncompahgre and Gunnison National Forests, visit the USFS Grand Junction Ranger District Office (p247).

James M Robb Colorado River State Park CAMPING $
(970-434-3388; www.parks.state.co.us; sites $10-20; P⊕) This is a unique state park, conceived by its namesake as a 'string of pearls' along the Colorado. It consists of five small parks in one and is an excellent option for those who want to camp but not necessarily rough it. The Fruita Section of the park is within walking distance to

Dinosaur Journey and has over 60 sites, including a nice loop for tents along the a small lake and some with RV hook ups.

There's also a swimming beach.

✖ Eating

Dream Café
BREAKFAST $

(☎970-424-5353; 314 Main St; breakfast $6.50-10; ⏱6:45am-2:30pm Mon-Sun; 🖘🐾) Before hitting the trails or heading to work, families and young professionals gather at this bright, sleekly designed cafe for Grand Junction's best breakfast. Our favorite of the five eggs Benedict dishes is the California Dreamin' Bene, topped with red peppers, avocado, asparagus and hollandaise sauce. If you're into sweet stuff instead, opt for the pineapple upside-down pancakes.

Il Bistro Italiano
ITALIAN $$

(☎970-243-8622; www.ilbistroitaliano.com; 400 Main St; mains $10-20; ⏱11:30am-2pm & 4:30-9pm; 🖘) Stuffed mushrooms, stone oven-fired pizzas and rustic mains are excellent, but the seasonal homemade pasta, lovingly made by Brunella Gualerzi, is what puts this rustic provincial Italian place on top. The dining area – exposed brick and white tablecloths – manages to be upscale without getting stuffy.

626 On Rood
CONTEMPORARY AMERICAN $$$

(☎970-257-7663; www.626onrood.com; 626 Rood Ave; mains $19-34; ⏱11am-11pm Mon-Sat, 4-10pm Sun; 🖘) The most elegant dining room in western Colorado serves inventive New American fusion, such as 'crispy' house-made mozzarella balls in Asian pumpkin breading or pancetta-and-pistachio-stuffed quail. Artful mains change with the seasons and are paired with an excellent wine list.

If you're interested in a taste without going all out for dinner, try a few small plates from the sharing menu or stop by for lunch, when uptown versions of classic sandwiches dominate the menu for around $10.

Main Street Bagels
BAGELS, DELI $

(☎970-241-2740; www.mainstreetbagels.net; 559 Main St; sandwiches $7-9; ⏱6:30am-6:30pm Mon-Sat, 7am-2:30pm Sun; 🖘🛜🐾) A big open space with communal guitars hung up on the wall, this is where the town comes to gossip, clack away at their laptops and and sip coffee. The sandwiches and bagels make tasty, quick carb-loading lunches before hitting the trails outside town.

Pablo's Pizza
PIZZA $

(☎970-255-8879; www.pablospizza.com; 319 Main St; mains $6-10; ⏱11am-8:30pm Sun-Thu, to 9pm Fri & Sat; 🐾) This is the best pizza in town because of the small-town vibe, sidewalk seating and creative pies. Inspired by Picasso, this place serves steaming thin-crust pizzas with names like Dracula's Nemesis, The Cowboy, and Naked Truth. The white wine and salmon variety? *That's* abstract!

Nepal Restaurant
INDIAN, NEPALESE $$

(☎970-242-2233; 356 Main St; mains $6-12; ⏱11am-2:30pm & 5-9pm Mon-Sat; 🖘) In a town without much ethnic food, the Nepalese lunch buffet fills a niche. The meat curries are better-than-average Indian, but vegetarian dumplings, dipped in a spicy oil, make for a tasty, easy snack. There are plenty of vegan dishes as well.

Zen Garden Asian Grill & Sushi Bar
PAN-ASIAN $$

(☎970-254-8898; 2886 North Ave; mains $10-14; ⏱11am-9:30pm; 🖘) The owner, Max, keeps a close watch over Grand Junction's best sushi joint as the waitstaff zips around delivering plates of sushi with oddball attitude. The boxed lunches are good value, and the warmly lit, intimate atmosphere is great when the weather is nasty.

🍸 Drinking & Entertainment

TOP CHOICE Kannah Creek Brewing Company
BREWPUB

(☎970-263-0111; www.kannahcreekbrewingco.com; 1960 N 12th St; mains $8-12; ⏱11am-10pm Sun-Thu, to 11pm Fri-Sat) Kannah's Broken Oar is probably the best IPA on the Western Slope, and the Black Bridge Stout – an Irish-style dry stout with lots of depth – isn't fooling around either. Students from Mesa State, beer lovers and mountain bikers pack this place to drink and eat off the menu of calzone and brick-oven pizza in creative combos.

Tenacious Brothers Pub
BAR

(☎970-424-5354; www.myspace.com/tenaciousbrospub; 118 S 7th St; ⏱6pm-2am) This place has an anything-goes spirit, a photo booth, stiff pours and the most happening gay scene in Grand Junction. The bartenders are chipper, the crowd gets wild and it's a great place to party. Also hosts occasional live music.

Rockslide Brewery
BREWPUB

(☎970-245-2111; www.rockslidebrewpub.com; 401 Main St; ⏱11am-midnight Mon-Sat, 8am-11pm Sun) Though locals like it more for the beer, the open kitchen at the Rockslide turns out fine enough fare. It's probably best not to push it with the culinary offerings – stick with the fish and chips, which come piping hot and crisply battered. The huge patio is an amiable gathering place on summer weekends.

Avalon Theatre CINEMA, LIVE MUSIC

(☎970-263-5700; www.tworiversconvention.com/ avalon; 645 Main St; prices vary; ⊙hrs vary; ⊕) This enormous historic theater hosts arthouse films, live comedy shows and live music. It might be the only stage in the world that can boast hosting both composer John Philip Sousa and pop songstress Pat Benatar. During movies, it serves beer and wine.

Mesa Theater & Club LIVE MUSIC, NIGHTCLUB

(☎970-241-1717; www.mesatheater.com; 538 Main St; prices vary; ⊙hrs vary) Though it sometimes hosts live music from national touring acts and multiple-band bills that are big with the college set, this small theater serves more as a nightclub, popular with students from the local university who come to dance to hip-hop and drink away the weekend. The website details upcoming events and evenings.

🛍 Shopping

Grand Valley Books BOOKS

(☎970-242-3911; 350 Main St; ⊙10am-7pm Mon-Sat, to 4pm Sun) By exchanging store credit for used books, this downtown shop is a godsend for avid readers. It has a big selection of titles about regional history, Native American culture and the West. For those who want something a bit lighter, it also has scores of westerns, genre fiction and lots of smutty paperbacks too.

Summit Canyon Mountaineering

SPORTING GOODS

(☎800-360-6994, 970-243-2847; www.summit canyon.com; 461 Main St; ⊙10am-8pm Mon-Sat, to 5pm Sun) You're in good hands here: the bearded dude behind the desk greets you as 'bro,' breaks down the region's climbs with back-of-hand familiarity and, a moment later, reminds his female counterpart (an avid mountain-biker herself) that it's Jerry Garcia's birthday.

REI SPORTING GOODS

(☎970-254-8970; www.rei.com/stores/70; 644 North Ave; ⊙10am-8pm Mon-Fri, 10am-6pm Sat, 11am-5pm Sun) It's not as mammoth as some of the other sporting-good outlets in town, but for camping and climbing, REI sells the best gear and the enthusiastic staff gives the best advice.

ℹ Information

BLM Grand Junction Field Office (BLM; ☎970-244-3000; 2815 H Rd; ⊙7:30am-4:30pm Mon-Fri) The Grand Junction branch of the Bureau of Land Management, located opposite Walker Field Airport, has helpful staff and a good selection of books.

Two Rivers Convention Center (☎970-263-5700; www.tworiversconvention.com; 159 Main St; 🛜) This is the largest convention center in the western part of Colorado, and hosts frequent conferences.

USFS Grand Junction Ranger District Office (☎970-242-8211; 764 Horizon Dr; ⊙8am-5pm Mon-Fri) This office has permits, maps and information about the Grand Mesa, Uncompahgre and Gunnison National Forests.

Visitors Center (☎970-256-4060, toll-free 800-962-2547; www.visitgrandjunction.com; 740 Horizon Dr; ⊙8:30am-6pm Mon-Sat, from 9am Sun; 🛜) This volunteer-staffed information center is a quick minute from the highway, and offers information about accommodations, attractions and local events.

ℹ Getting There & Away

Walker Field (Grand Junction Regional Airport; ☎970-244-9100; www.gjairport.com; 2828 Walker Field Dr), Grand Junction's commercial airport, is 6 miles northeast of downtown. It connects to six cities in the western US, including Las Vegas, Phoenix and Los Angeles, but most flights go to and from Denver.

From the **Greyhound station** (☎970-242-6012; www.greyhound.com; 230 S 5th St) there are buses to Denver; Las Vegas, Nevada; and Salt Lake City, Utah. Amtrak's daily *California Zephyr* between Chicago, Illinois, and Oakland, California, stops at the passenger depot; there's a small information booth here. There is one train to and from Denver via the *California Zephyr* (8 hours, $46 one-way).

Hertz, Avis, National and Budget have locations at the airport. Grand Junction is on I-70, 248 miles west of Denver via and 30 miles east of the Utah state line.

Grand Junction Amtrak (www.amtrak.com; 339 S 1st St; ⊙ticket office 9am-6pm)

ℹ Getting Around

The city core is easily seen on foot (it's only one street after all). Getting around the city or out to the monument is much easier with a car. Those without wheels should look for the **Grand Valley Transit** (GVT; ☎970-256-7433; http://gvt.mesacounty.us; ⊙5:45am-

6:15pm Mon-Sat), which operates 11 fixed routes serving Grand Junction, Palisade, Clifton, Orchard Mesa and Fruita. A ride costs $1 and all the buses accept bikes. You can also rent a bike from numerous shops in town, and those with legs for the climb will be rewarded by the slow view of the area scenery.

Fruita

Fruita wouldn't be much more than a village that's slowly being swallowed by the Grand Junction suburbs if it weren't for one small exception: it's home to some of the best single-track mountain biking in the US. As such, the services for travelers cater to cyclists. Fruita is also the gateway to the 550-mile Dinosaur Diamond Prehistoric Hwy, a recent addition to the Scenic & Historic Byways network, which leads north to Dinosaur National Monument and into Utah.

⊙ Sights & Activities

Mountain Biking

Aside from those in Moab, Utah, the single-track rides around Fruita are the best in the West – some argue the best in the world – and worth the long drive to western Colorado for any serious enthusiast. The rides here are set in a dry, mild high-desert climate that allows for a long riding season between late April and mid-November. You can ride 142 miles of dirt to Moab on the Kokopelli Trail, but those with less ambition have tons of options in the two areas near town: the 18 Road area, which is more suited toward beginners, and the Kokopelli area trails, which are best for those of a high-intermediate and expert level. Maps are available at Fruita's bike shops.

There are two bike shops in town that sell, service and rent bikes: **Over the Edge Sports** (www.otefruita.com; 202 E Aspen Ave; bike rental $50-80; ⊙9am-6pm) and **Single Tracks** (☑970-858-3917, 800-878-3917; www.single-tracks.com; 150 South Park Sq; ⊙9am-6pm Mon-Sat, to 3pm Sun, shorter hrs winter). Of these two, Over the Edge, which has been advocating for responsible use of the trails for years, has the slight edge. It's the folks at this shop that put Fruita on the map. Rental bikes from either shop will cost between $50 and $80, depending on the quality of bike.

Dinosaur Sites

Dinosaur lovers will find Fruita to be a requisite stop as well. In 1900 paleontologist Elmer Riggs discovered the enormous and previously unknown *Brachiosaurus altithorax* near Grand Junction at a site called Dinosaur Hill. He soon followed up with a nearly intact *Apatosaurus excelsus* (known commonly, if non-scientifically, as the brontosaurus) at this site south of the Colorado River near Fruita. The site, which includes Riggs's original quarry and several fossil remnants in place, is now commemorated with a small reserve and interpretive trail. To get there, take Hwy 340 (I-70 exit 19) south from Fruita; the road continues south to Colorado National Monument.

Also situated between Grand Junction and Fruita is **Dinosaur Journey** (☑970-858-7282; www.museumofwesternco.com; 550 Jurassic Ct; adult/senior/child $7/6/4; ⊙10am-4pm Mon-Sat, from noon Sun; ⚐), a small museum with a fantastic collection of grizzly animatronic dinos that snort steam and jerk around, bestial skeletons and interesting multimedia demonstrations. It's a little bit corny at times, but thrilling for the younger members of the family.

🛏 Sleeping

If you're looking for an overnight in town, there are some national chain hotels on the south side of I-70, off the Fruita exit.

✗ Eating & Drinking

TOP CHOICE 🌱 **Hot Tomato Cafe** PIZZA $$ (☑970-858-1117; www.hottomatocafe.com; 124 N Mulberry St; large pizzas $16-25; ⊙11am-9pm Tue-Sat) This pizza joint and cyclist hangout is run by Jen and Anne, a pair of bike enthusiasts who espouse a sustainable business ethos. The pizza here comes in thick slices and it has a row of Colorado beer on tap. When it gets late, there's a fun scene on the small outdoor patio.

Apsen Street Coffee SANDWICHES $ (☑970-858-8888; 136 E Aspen Ave; sandwiches $7; ⊙6:30am-5pm; 🖥) With simple wraps, strong coffee and homemade granola, this is a great spot to stock up before the ride.

Colorado Wine Room WINE BAR (☑970-858-6330; www.coloradowineroom.com; 455 Kokopelli Blvd; ⊙10:30am-5:30pm) To skip the wine tours and do it in one shot, visit this tasting room, where there's a small display on the history of wine-making in the region and over 20 carefully selected bottles from Colorado producers.

ℹ️ Information
Fruita Chamber of Commerce (✆970-858-3894; www.fruita.org) Call for more info on local attractions, lodgings and events.

Grand Mesa
Towering above the Grand Valley, this 'island in the sky' is a lava-capped plateau rising more than 11,000ft at its highest point. Its broad summit offers a delightful respite from the Grand Valley's summer heat, alpine scenery and a fairly interesting four-hour loop drive from Grand Junction via I-70, Hwy 65 and US 50 (with plenty of opportunities for side trips and stopovers). The highway passes through a number of distinct environments as it climbs the 6000ft mesa, ranging from canyons of sage, piñons (a species of pine) and junipers through areas of scrub oak and montane forests of Engelmann spruce and Douglas fir to subalpine forests and meadows.

🏃 Activities
Hiking
There's descent hiking here, but the nearby ATVs and omnipresent power lines aren't pretty, and overall there's better hiking elsewhere in the state. The best way to stretch the legs on the mesa is on Crag Crest National Recreation Trail. Starting about half a mile west of Carp Lake on Hwy 65, this 10-mile loop follows the crest of the mesa before returning via a lower section past a series of attractive lakes; there's also an eastern trailhead from USFS Rd 121, a lateral off Hwy 65 just south of Carp Lake. The trail offers views of the Grand Valley and Uncompahgre Plateau to the west, Battlement Mesa to the north, the Elk Mountains to the east and the San Juan Mountains to the south.

Skiing
Powderhorn Resort   SNOW SPORTS
(✆970-268-5700; www.powderhorn.com; 48338 Powderhorn Rd) Barely half an hour east of Grand Junction, this resort is on the northern slopes of Grand Mesa. Though it's hardly the most challenging terrain in the state, it often has excellent quality powder.

🛏️ Sleeping
There are 12 USFS campgrounds in the Grand Mesa National Forest, most of which levy fees of between $7 and $10. Many of these campgrounds are on the Mesa's 300 lakes, which is ideal for fishing, and also ideal for mosquitoes. There are cabins to rent at **Alexander Lake Lodge** (✆970-856-2539; www.alexanderlakelodge.com; 21211 Baron Lake Dr; cabins $130-350; 🐾) and Powderhorn Resort. Some lodges close for the winter, so call ahead to check.

ℹ️ Information
There are several visitors centers on and around the mesa, including the **Grand Mesa Byway Welcome Center** (✆970-856-3100; www.grandmesabyway.org; 400 SW 2nd St) in Cedaredge, on the southern side. The best source of information and permits is atop the Mesa near Cobbet Lake, the **Grand Mesa Visitor Center** (✆970-856-4153, 970-242-8211; www.grandmesabyway.org; 20090 Baron Lake Dr; ⊙9am-5pm daily, Sat & Sun only Sep-Feb). This sharply remodeled ranger office is at the intersection of Hwy 65 and USFS Rd 121 and has a small store on hand. All the centers generally operate from late May to mid-October.

Maps of trails and campsites and information on accommodations are also available from the visitors center in Grand Junction. *The Grand Mesa Scenic Byway* is an annual publication that includes maps, important phone numbers, lodging, restaurant and historical information for the area.

Southwest Colorado

Includes »

BLACK CANYON
OF THE GUNNISON
NATIONAL PARK....252

GUNNISON.........257

CRESTED BUTTE ...259

TELLURIDE.........264

SAN JUAN
MOUNTAINS 269

OURAY.............270

SILVERTON 273

DURANGO 275

MESA VERDE & THE
FOUR CORNERS 289

Best Places to Eat

» Timberline Restaurant (p261)

» Brown Dog Pizza (p268)

» The Butcher & The Baker (p267)

» Secret Stash (p261)

Best Places to Stay

» Hotel Columbia (p266)

» Jersey Jim Lookout Tower (p295)

» Ruby of Crested Butte (p260)

Why Go?

A landscape of shocking diversity, this corner of Colorado is interrupted by jagged canyons and mountain peaks, lush pine forests and barren desert terrain.

Jump in the car for a few hours and you'll feel as if you've traveled across an entire continent – this is a place where you can eat a breakfast burrito at the base of snowy slopes and have a plate of enchiladas for lunch in the bone-dry desert. The furthest regions of Colorado's southwest feel *wild* – wrinkled by arid canyons, punctuated by 14,000ft peaks and capped by gusty high-desert plateaus.

The geological and environmental drama of the area may have also contributed to some of the greatest archaeological sites in the US, with the mysteriously abandoned cliff dwellings of early Native Americans in Mesa Verde National Park.

When to Go?

Durango

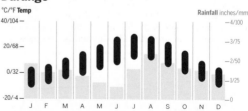

May–August Ideal camping and hiking in the San Juans brings the people.	**September–November** Cool high-desert air allows uncrowded visits to two national parks.	**December–April** Snow bunnies from near and far make for the hills of Telluride.

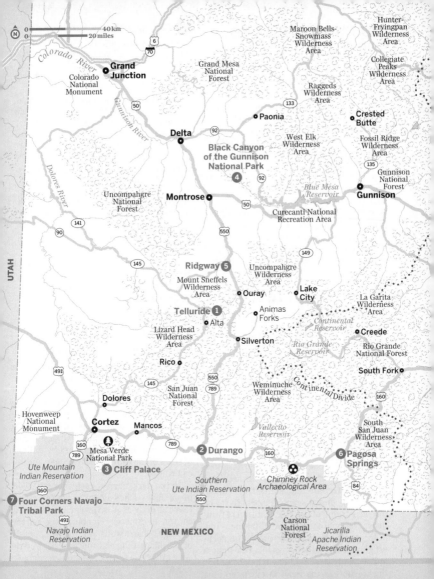

Southwest Colorado Highlights

1 Spend the day riding world-class slopes on Colorado's most pristine mountain at the **Telluride Ski Resort** (p264)

2 Board the **Durango & Silverton Narrow Gauge Railroad** (p277) and cruise through jaw-dropping scenery

3 Retrace the steps of Ancestral Puebloans at **Cliff Palace** (p292)

4 Climb down to the floor of the dizzying **Black Canyon of the Gunnison National Park** (p252)

5 Saunter up to the bar at the **True Grit Cafe** (p270) where John Wayne drank

6 Soak sore muscles after a day of hiking at Pagosa's swish **Springs Resort & Spa** (p281)

7 Drive to the point where four states (almost) meet: **Four Corners Navajo Tribal Park** (p300)

GRAND JUNCTION TO CORTEZ

Gas up and grab a sandwich: the drive from Grand Junction to Cortez is a long and lonely haul, with few services for motorists. But it's also a driving enthusiast's delight. Hugging the winding turns of Hwy 141 brings you into the Unaweep Canyon after Gateway, Colorado, where the curving road becomes closed in by the steep walls of a red-rock canyon.

Minus the pavement, it's just like the backdrop of an old cowboy movie. With the right tunes on the radio and the right frame of mind, this can be a truly enchanting drive, but don't expect to look at much more than western Colorado's rugged nature – the only city along the route with a post office is Naturita, which has basic services.

CRESTED BUTTE & GUNNISON

This region of Colorado's southwest is a playground for outdoorsy types, with skiing dominating in the winter and hiking, river-rafting and mountain-biking popular in summer. Fly-fishing is another activity that draws both locals and domestic tourists in waders to the icy waters of the great Gunnison River. Others come to hunt, and antlers and trophy mounts are a popular decorative feature in homes and ranch houses.

The Gunnison River, whose headwaters gather near Crested Butte, 8867ft above sea level, has carved its way through this incredible terrain that shifts from alpine forests to desert-scape tablelands. The physical drama of the Black Canyon of Gunnison National Park is breathtaking – one of the world's longest, narrowest and deepest gorges. The park brings hikers, campers and a steady stream of day-trippers all trying to squeeze the magnificent panorama into a photo frame.

Hwy 50 and the roads around the Gunnison region carry lots of RVs, many bigger than school buses, with Jeeps, boats or trailers of all-terrain quad bikes in tow behind. There are also monster SUVs towing enormous caravans, and the region is a popular touring route for thundering gangs of Harley-Davidson riders. This, after all, is recreation country – some of the greatest of the great outdoors.

ⓘ Getting There & Around

Gunnison County Airport (☎970-641-2304; W Rio Grande Ave) Gunnison Airport is serviced by American Airlines, Delta and United. Avis, Budget and Hertz rental cars are represented at the airport.

BUS & SHUTTLE Dolly's Mountain Shuttle (☎970-349-2620, mobile 970-209-9757; www.dollysmountainshuttle.vpweb.com; Crested Butte one-way van $225) Dolly's runs private groups of up to 10 around the Gunnison Valley, to the ski fields and mountain-bike trail heads.

Mountain Express (Gunnison Valley RTA; ☎970-349-5616; www.gunnisonvalleyrta.org; ☉6:30am-8pm) The Gunnison Valley RTA runs the free Mountain Express between Gunnison and the Crested Butte mountain top between 6.30am and 8pm.

CAR RENTAL Budget (☎970-641-4403; www.budget.com; 711 W Rio Grande Ave)

Hertz (☎970-641-2881; www.hertz.com; 711 W Rio Grande Ave)

Avis (☎970-641-0263; www.avis.com; 711 W Rio Grande Ave)

Black Canyon of the Gunnison National Park

The Colorado Rockies are most famous for their mountains, but the **Black Canyon of the Gunnison National Park** (☎970-249-1915, 800-873-0244; www.nps.gov/blca; 7-day admission per vehicle $15; ☉8am-6pm summer, 8:30am-4pm fall, winter & spring; P ♿) is the inverse of this geographic feature – a massive yawning chasm etched out by millions of years of the Gunnison River flow and volcanic uplift.

Here a dark, narrow gash above the Gunnison River leads down a 2000ft chasm that's as eerie as it is spectacular. No other canyon in America combines the narrow openings, sheer walls and dizzying depths of the Black Canyon, and a peek over the edge evokes a sense of awe (and vertigo) for most.

The 32,950-acre park takes its name from the fact that it's so sheer, deep and narrow, sunlight only touches the canyon floor when the sun is directly overhead. In just 48 miles of traveling through the canyon, the Gunnison River loses more elevation than the entire 1500-mile Mississippi. This fast-moving water, carrying rock and debris, is powerfully erosive. In fact, if it weren't for the upstream dams, the river would carry five times its current volume of water.

Head to the 6 mile-long South Rim Rd, which takes you to 11 overlooks at the edge of the canyon, some reached via short trails up to 1.5 miles long (round-trip). At the narrowest part of Black Canyon, Chasm View is 1100ft across yet 1800ft deep. Rock climbers are frequently seen on the opposing North Wall. Colorado's highest cliff face is the 2300ft Painted Wall. To challenge your senses, cycle along the smooth pavement running parallel to the rim's 2000ft drop-off. You definitely get a better feel for the place than you do trapped in a car.

In summer the East Portal Rd is open. This steep, winding hairpin route takes you into the canyon and down to the river level where there are picnic shelters and superb views up the gorge and the craggy cliff faces. This area is popular with fly-fishers.

For a surreal experience, visit Black Canyon's South Rim in winter. The stillness of the snow-drenched plateau is broken only by the icy roar of the river at the bottom of the canyon, far, far below.

The park is 12 miles east of the US Hwy 550 junction with US Hwy 50. Exit at Hwy 347 – well marked with a big brown sign for the national park – and head north for 7 miles.

History

This massive canyon has presented an impassable barrier to human beings since they first trod these lands. Utes had settlements along Black Canyon's rim, but there's no evidence of human habitation within the chasm itself. Early Spanish records of sojourns through this part of the country make no mention of the gorge. John W Gunnison, who was commissioned to survey the Rockies for a future Pacific railroad, sought a crossing over the river that would later bear his name. He bypassed the canyon in 1853 and continued west until he and his party were massacred near Lake Sevier, Utah, by Utes (though there are some who believe they were killed in a Mormon conspiracy).

The 1871 Hayden geological survey – again seeking a route for a Pacific railroad – was the first to document the canyon. By 1900 settlers seeking water for irrigating crops in the nearby Uncompahgre Valley looked to the river as a source. In 1901, Abraham Fellows and William Torrence floated through the canyon on rubber mattresses, traveling 33 miles in nine days. By 1905 construction of the 5.8-mile Gunnison Diversion Tunnel had begun and it still provides water to farms today.

Though moves were afoot to protect the canyon as a national park as early as the 1930s, it took until 1999 for its park status to be declared, protecting 14 of the canyon's 48 miles.

🏃 Activities

Hiking

The South Rim Visitor Center (p254) has maps and information on the park's hiking trails.

The Rim Rock Trail connects Tomichi Point with the visitors center only a quarter-mile away. From the visitors center, the easy 1.5-mile Oak Flat Trail passes through Gambel oak, Douglas fir and aspen, and offers good views of Black Canyon. Take the Warner Point Nature Trail, a 1.5-mile round-trip beginning at the end of South Rim Rd, before watching the sunset from either High Point or Sunset View overlooks. From the remote North Rim, the SOB Draw trail heads to the river.

Rangers at the visitor center can issue a backcountry permit, if you want to descend one of the South Rim's three unmarked routes to the infrequently visited riverside campsites.

Fishing

The Gunnison River, designated as Gold Medal Water and Wild Trout Water, offers some of the best fishing in Colorado. (Of the 9000 miles of trout rivers in Colorado, less than 2% qualify as Gold Medal Water.) However, strict regulations are enforced to maintain this status. A Colorado fishing license is required and bait fishing is not allowed – only lures and flies. If caught, all rainbow trout must be released, and a limit of four brown trout per person per day (with a bag limit of eight) applies. Fishing within 200 yards of the Crystal Dam is prohibited.

The best access to the river is down the summer-only East Portal Rd. Anglers can also access the river from one of the many tracks leading into the canyon, however, they are extremely steep and difficult, and anyone attempting this should be very fit. A free backcountry permit must be obtained from the South Rim Visitor Center or the North Rim Ranger Station.

Rock Climbing

Mountain climbers who know what they are doing and have their own equipment can get their kicks in Black Canyon – this is not a place for beginners. Routes are not well charted and even the easier climbs are multi-pitch traditional routes in remote areas of the canyon.

If you are an experienced climber, this is a wonderful site. Most of the climbing in the park occurs on the North and South Chasms, which measure 1820ft. Black Canyon is also home to Colorado's tallest vertical cliff, Painted Wall, measuring 2300ft from the bottom of the canyon and named for its fabulous marble stripes. There are a number of different climbing routes to the top of Painted Wall. Check the website for updates – when we visited, some routes were closed due to nesting raptors (it's a national park after all).

For information on specific routes and difficulty levels, visit the park's excellent website. Also check out *Black Canyon Rock Climbs* by Robbie Williams.

🛏 Sleeping

The park has three campgrounds although only one is open all year round. Water is trucked into the park and only the **East Portal Campground** (☑970-249-1915; www. nps.gov/blca; sites $12; ☀spring to fall; 🐾) has river-water access. Firewood is not provided and may not be collected in the national park – campers must bring their own firewood into the campgrounds.

ℹ Information

South Rim Visitor Center (☑970-249-1915, 800-873-0244; www.nps.gov/blca; ☀8:30am-4pm fall, winter & spring, 8am-6pm summer) Two miles past the park entrance on South Rim Dve, the visitor center is well stocked with books and maps, and enthusiastic National Parks Service staff offer a wealth of information on hiking, fishing and rock climbing. There's also a mini-theater which shows interesting orientation and historical films.

Montrose

15,700 / 5974FT

Montrose, an agricultural center and wholesale supply point for Telluride, 65 miles to the south, is blessed with an enviable location with the lofty San Juan Mountains to the south, the Black Canyon National Park to the east, the Grand Mesa to the north and the Uncompahgre Plateau to the west. The town has some excellent historic buildings in the old center, but the huge chain stores, motels and fast-food restaurants that flank US 550 running north–south through Montrose offset much of the town's character.

For all that it's a rather perfunctory place with some good museums, antique stores and a clutch of decent restaurants. But perhaps the best reason to stay in Montrose is to daytrip to the awesome Black Canyon of the Gunnison National Park and to try your hand at mountain-biking on the Uncompahgre Plateau. And then drive south through Ouray and the stunning Million Dollar Hwy.

◉ Sights

The vestiges of the old town can be found along Main St and near the old Denver & Rio Grande Railroad Depot on N Rio Grande Ave. Some of the buildings date from the early 1880s, although the grander edifices were constructed around the turn of the 20th century as Montrose moved from frontier railroad town to significant financial center. A set of 12 interpretive signs is installed in the historic five-block central area around Main St.

Montrose is also a good base from which to explore the **Cimarron Railroad Exhibit** (www.nps.gov/cure/; P 🐾), about 20 miles east of town.

TOP CHOICE / 🎦 **Ute Indian Museum** MUSEUM
(☑970-249-3098; 17253 Chipeta Dve; adult/child $3/1.50; ☀9am-4:30pm Fri & Sat, from 11am Sun mid-May–mid-Oct; P 🐾) One of the few museums in the country dedicated to one tribe. The Ute are the traditional people of western Colorado. The museum is situated on a homestead that belonged to legendary Uncompahgre Ute chief Ouray and his wife Chipeta. The museum has reduced hours in winter – call ahead for exact times. There's a visitor information center attached to the museum.

Museum of the Mountain West MUSEUM
(☑970-249-4162; www.mountainwestmuseum. com; 68169 E Miami Rd; adult/child $10/5; ☀8:30am-4:30pm Mon-Fri; P 🐾) The Museum of the Mountain West has a staggering number of pieces on display from the 1880s to the 1930s. There's a recreated Old West town replete with storefonts, a saloon, drugstore and doctor's surgery. The original Diehl Carriage Works building is where

1919–26 world heavyweight boxing champion Jack Dempsey trained.

🏃 Activities

BMX

Gear can be purchased or hired from local bike shops including Cascade Bicycles (p256) and Jeans Westerner (p256).

FREE **BMX Complex** BIKE PARK
(☎970-433-7159; www.montrosebmx.org; 1001 N 2nd St; 🚼) This excellent BMX complex is located at the Montrose County Fairgrounds. The local BMX community is very welcoming to new and visiting riders.

Fishing

This area offers some of the best trout fishing in the whole US. The Gunnison River has been designated Gold Medal Waters and the Uncompahgre River, which flows through Montrose, offers outstanding year-round angling. Fishers must have a license and comply to local regulations and bag limits. (Rainbow trout are strictly catch-and-release.) There are several companies that can get you kitted out and onto the water.

🎣 **Cimarron Creek** FISHING TOURS
(☎970-249-0408; www.cimarroncreek. com; 317 E Main St; tours from $250; 🚼) This angler's shop provides customized guided fly-fishing tours to the Gunnison and Uncompahgre Rivers and beyond.

Hiking

The area around Montrose offers lots of opportunities for hikers, from simple strolls to more challenging overnight hikes and mountaineering expeditions. Contact the Montrose Chamber of Commerce & Tourism (p256) for maps and more information.

Mountain Biking

Surrounded by wonderful and varied landscapes, and with a network of cycling trails in and around town, mountain-bikers are spoilt for choice. For more challenging mountain-biking head out on Hwys 50 and 347 for the Black Canyon and ride along the paved edge of the Southern Rim. *Bicycling the Uncompahgre Plateau*, by Bill Harris, is a comprehensive guide to cycling the plateau, including the famous Tabeguache Trail. For bike rentals, gear and advice, go to Jeans Westerner (p256) or Cascade Cycles (p256).

Rafting

Like much of southwest Colorado, Montrose makes a great base for river rafting. The Gunnison Gorge, downstream from the Black Canyon, is a popular spot with rapids ranging from Class II to IV. Several companies can get you out on the water, including Rigs Fly Shop & Guide Service (p269) in Ridgway, Gunnison River Expeditions (p263), based in Delta, and Buena Vista–based **Wilderness Aware Rafting** (☎800-462-7238; www.inaraft.com; 12600 Hwy 24 & 285; 1-/2-day rafting trips $225/489; ⊘summer 7:30am-8pm, winter 8am-5pm Mon-Fri; 🚼).

Skateboarding

TOP CHOICE **FREE** **Montrose Skate Park**
SKATING
(540 S Rio Grande Ave; 🚼) If you've got your deck or rollerbades, head for Montrose Skate Park, 15,000 sq ft of concrete action judged one of the best in the USA by *Thrasher Magazine*.

🛏 Sleeping

For the most part Montrose's sleeping options are dominated by the big motel chains, but there are a couple of terrific B&Bs and a few places to pitch a tent or hook up an RV. There are several camping areas around Montrose run by the Bureau of Land Management and the National Park Service; ask at the Montrose Chamber of Commerce & Tourism (p256) for more information.

Canyon Creek Bed & Breakfast B&B $$
(☎970-249-2886, toll-free 877-262-8202; www. canyoncreekbedandbreakfast.com; 820 E Main St; d $135; ᴘ❄✳🛜🚼) This beautiful 1909 house on the town's main street has been carefully refurbished into an immaculate B&B – the only one of it's type in Montrose. Just three suites comprise the facility: each is unique and individually decorated. Flat-screen TVs, wireless internet and full cooked breakfasts are some of the perks on offer.

Black Canyon Motel MOTEL $
(☎970-249-3495, toll-free 800-348-3495; www. blackcanyonmotel.com; 1605 E Main St; d $70-100; ᴘ❄✳🛜🚼) East Main St heading into Montrose is lined with chain motels. The Black Canyon is one of the few independents, offering good lodgings at a reasonable price. There are family rooms and complimentary breakfast.

Uncompahgre Lodge Bed & Breakfast

B&B $$

(☎970-240-4000, toll-free 800-318-8127; www.
uncbb.com; 21049 Uncompahgre Rd; d $110-
150; P ⊖ ❋ ☞) This refitted former school
house is about 10 minutes' drive south of
Montrose. It's large, with eight rooms each
decorated with a slightly oddball sense of
pioneer-American kitsch. The rooms are all
different, some with king beds, some with
singles and some with Jacuzzis. The cooked
breakfast is great.

Cedar Creek RV Park

CAMPSITE, RV SITE $

(☎877-425-3884, toll-free 970-249-3884; www.
cedarcreekrv.com; 126 Rose Ln; RV hook-up/tent
site $33/20, cabins from $38; P ☞ ☞) One of
several RV parks in Montrose, this facility
is well equipped, including a coin-laundry.

✖ Eating

TOP CHOICE / **Cazwellas** FRENCH, ITALIAN $$$
(☎970-252-9200; 320 E Main St;
mains $15-25; ☺6-11pm Tue-Sat; ⊖☞) This is
one of Montrose's best restaurants. Servings are small, with an eye for quality over
quantity and locally sourced organic and
seasonal produce. The eclectic list of start-
ers alone is mouth-watering: try the beef
carpaccio or the New Orleans–style crab
cakes, or dig into the blue-cheese stuffed
filet mignon. The desserts and cocktails are
excellent.

Camp Robber

SOUTHWESTERN $$

(☎970-240-1590; www.camprobber.com; 1515
Ogden Rd; mains $10-17; ☺11am-9pm Mon-Sat,
9am-2pm Sun; ⊖☞) Camp Robber is a terrific
place: a smart fine-dining restaurant that's
not too stuffy or pretentious. The eclectic
menu offers tricked-up Americana fused
with contemporary Mexican and Italian fla-
vors. The signature dish is the green-chile
pistachio-crusted pork medallions served
in a rich cream sauce. 'Camp Robber' is a
reference to the gray jaybird that helps itself
to campers' provisions.

Stone House

PASTA, SEAFOOD, STEAK $$$

(☎970-240-8899; www.stonehousemontrose.
com; 1415 Hawk Pkwy; mains $11-25; ☺11am-
10pm; ⊖☞) With prompt, affable service
and a menu as long as your arm, the Stone
House offers an eclectic mix of Modern
American, Italian and Caribbean-style
dishes. Fresh fish and seafood are specialties, and prime beef comes in 8oz, 12oz or
14oz cuts. The baked lobster is a steal at...
market price.

Red Barn Steakhouse

STEAK $$$

(☎970-249-9202; 1413 E Main St; mains $15-30;
☺11am-10:30pm Mon-Sat, from 9am Sun; ⊖☞)
Serving only selected cuts of Sterling Sil-
ver Premium Beef, aged for at least 21 days,
the Red Barn is serious about its steaks –
and it charges accordingly. All the steaks
are hand-cut on the premises. A selection
of salads, soups and desserts is available
as well.

Pahgre's

ITALIAN $

(☎970-249-6442; www.pahgres.com; 1541 Ox-
bow Dve; mains $8-13; ☺11am-10pm Tue-Sun;
⊖☞) Serving pizzas, paninis, salads and
pasta, Pahgre's is a favorite among Mon-
trose locals. Try the pizzas (our picks are
the Motherlode or the Blue Mesa), which
are said to be the best in town. A healthy
rage of inventive salads offers vegetarians
some genuine choices come dinnertime.

🔒 Shopping

Montrose is renowned for its antique stores;
pick up the detailed *Montrose Antique Trail*
brochure from the Montrose Chamber of
Commerce & Tourism.

Outdoor Supplies

Jeans Westerner

SPORTING GOODS

(☎800-426-6756; www.jeanswesterner.com; 147
N Townsend Ave; ☞) This mixed business has
a great range of quality cycling and sports
gear, camping and fishing equipment, ski-
ing and snowsports stuff, and western
wear including chaps, Stetson hats, cowboy
boots and jeans.

Cascade Bicycles

BICYCLES

(☎970-249-7375; 21 N Cascade Ave; ☞) This
local bike shop has been outfitting cy-
clists and supporting local cycling events
for years. For great local advice on moun-
tain-biking, touring and BMX, talk to the
friendly owners.

ℹ Information

**Montrose Chamber of Commerce & Tour-
ism** (☎970-249-5000; www.visitmontrose.
com; 1519 E Main St; ☺9am-5pm) Right near
the outskirts of town as you approach from
the east, this tourist office is well stocked with
brochures, maps and travel information on
Montrose and its environs. The friendly folks
can help you out with itineraries, information
on mountain-biking, skiing and river-rafting,
as well as cultural information on Montrose's
museums and historic buildings.

ℹ️ Getting There & Away

Montrose Airport (☎970-249-3203; www.montroseairport.com; 2100 Airport Rd; ♿) is serviced several times each day from Denver Airport (p94) by United Express (one-way from $394), **United Airlines'** (☎800-864-8331; www.united.com) regional flier. **Continental Airlines** (☎800-523-3273; www.continental.com) flies to Montrose daily from Houston (one-way from $405) year-round, as well as twice-weekly direct from Newark (one-way from $466) in winter. Delta Airlines flies in from Salt Lake City daily year-round (one-way from $440) and daily direct from Atlanta (one-way from $243) in winter. American Airlines flies to Montrose on weekends from Dallas and Chicago during winter.

ℹ️ Getting Around

Montrose Airport has rental car agencies represented on site, including **Avis** (☎970-240-4802; www.avis.com; Denver Airport, 2100 Airport Rd; 🕐9am-7:15pm & 10:15pm-10:45pm Wed-Mon, 9am-5pm & 10:15pm-10:45pm Tue), **Budget** (☎970-249-6083; www.budget.com; Denver Airport, 2100 Airport Rd; 🕐8am-11pm Sun-Fri, 8am-9pm Sat) and **Hertz** (☎970-240-8464; www.hertz.com; Denver Airport, 2100 Airport Rd; 🕐9am-5pm & 10-11pm). **Enterprise** (☎970-240-3835; www.enterprise.com; 437 N Townsend Ave; 🕐8am-5pm Mon-Fri, 8am-noon Sat) has a rental yard in town.

Curecanti National Recreation Area

The Gunnison River, which once flowed freely through the canyons, is now plugged by three dams creating the Curecanti National Recreation Area. A more apt, and its official title, is the Wayne N Aspinall Storage Unit, named for a US representative, in office between 1948 and 1973, who never met a water project he did not like. Many RVs are strangely attracted to the bleak and windy shores of chilly Blue Mesa Reservoir, which Curecanti surrounds. The calm waters of the Blue Mesa are popular with windsurfers, as well as boating and fishing families. Stunning landforms that survived immersion are the unsinkable Curecanti Needle and Dillon Pinnacles, a volcanic breccia capped by welded tuff.

There are no entrance fees for Curecanti, unless entering through the main entrance of the Black Canyon of the Gunnison National Park.

🏃 Activities

Morrow Point Boat Tour
BOAT TOUR

(☎970-641-2337 ext-205; adult/child $16/8; ♿) The popular Morrow Point boat tour is run by the National Park Ranger Service, and takes visitors on a gentle 1½-hour tour through the upper Black Canyon on a 42-seat pontoon. Access to the Pine Creek boat dock is via a 1½-mile round-trip trail that includes 232 steps. The trailhead is just off Hwy 50, between Montrose and Gunnison, at the 130-mile marker. Bookings are essential.

The views from the boat are superb and the ranger delivers a commentary on the stunning scenery and wildlife. Allow an hour to walk from the trailhead to the boat dock.

🛏️ Sleeping

Curecanti has 10 campgrounds, and some, such as **Elk Creek** (☎970-641-2337; www.nps.gov/cure; US Hwy 50; per night Loops B & C $12, Loop A $12 plus $3 booking fee, Loop D $18 plus $3 booking fee; 🕐year-round; 🅿️♿) and **Lake Fork** (☎970-641-2337; www.nps.gov/cure; US Hwy 50; per night $12 plus $3 booking fee; 🕐year-round; ♿), are developed, with showers and flush toilets, while others are more basic. For hikers there are also small campgrounds at the end of the Curecanti Creek Trail (2 miles) and Hermit's Rest Trail (3 miles). The latter descends 1800ft, so be prepared for a steep climb back out.

ℹ️ Information

There are information centers at Cimarron and Lake Fork, which only operate from late May to late September.

Elk Creek visitor center (☎970-641-2337 ext 205; www.nps.gov/cure; 102 Elk Creek; Blue Mesa boating fees annual/14-day/2-day passes $30/20/4; 🕐8am-6pm summer, 8am-4:30pm rest of year) Part of the Black Canyon of Gunnison National Park, the Elk Creek visitor center is the main office serving the Curecanti National Recreation Area and offers topographic maps and exhibits describing the area's cultural and natural history. It's on US 50, 6 miles west of the junction with Hwy 149 to Lake City.

Gunnison

POP 5600 / ELEV 7703FT

In summer, the Utes tribe hunted on the plains surrounding the present-day town of Gunnison, where the Gunnison River and Tomichi Creek meet. The first white settlers established Richardson's Colony in 1874, but soon abandoned it. Captain John W Gunnison and a party of 60 men had surveyed much of the area in search of a Pacific railroad route in 1853, and when, in 1879, the site was resettled it was named after him.

The town – nondescript and functional for the most part – is home to the handsome campus of Western State College of Colorado, which opened in 1911. The giant W on the hill southeast of town is a reference to the college. However, a walk through the older residential neighborhoods will reveal numerous Victorians and masonry homes, their lawns and trees watered by the unique Gunnison ditch system.

Few people stop in Gunnison, other than to restock and refuel. Most are in a hurry to get up to Crested Butte to the skiing and mountain-biking opportunities it affords. But there are some good lodgings and restaurants in town, and it can be a good base for the outdoors activities - hiking, camping and fly-fishing – that are a feature of the region. In winter, a free shuttle bus plies between Gunnison and Crested Butte continuously each day, and staying off the mountain can make skiing vacations a little less expensive.

◉ Sights

Gunnison doesn't have a lot of sights to excite the jaded traveler, but a few old buildings are worth looking at if you've got the time.

🛏 Sleeping

Water Wheel Inn HOTEL **$$**
(☑970-641-1650, toll-free 800-642-1650; www. waterwheelinnatgunnison.com; 37478 W Hwy 50; d $70-155; P ⊖ ❋ 🛜 🐾) This is the pick of Gunnison's lodgings. It's in a quiet spot a little west of town, and is surrounded by trees and ponds (but no water wheel!). The well-appointed rooms with free cable TV and wi-fi, and a few larger rooms have kitchenette. Free breakfasts and in-room fridges and tea- and coffee-making facilities are standard. Pets welcome in designated rooms.

Wanderlust Hostel HOSTEL **$**
(☑970-901-1599; www.thewanderlusthostel .com; 221 N Boulevard; dorm/d $23/45; P ⊖ ❋ 🛜 🐾) This is a bit of a find in downtown Gunnison – a bright, cheap and cheerful backpackers with a progressive worldly outlook. There's a large and well-equipped communal kitchen and living area, and a

nice back yard. There are bikes for guests to use and an emphasis on sustainability. The owners have heaps of good advice about touring the area and outdoor activities.

Tall Texan Campground CAMPGROUND **$**
(☑970-641-2927; www.talltexancampgroundof gunnison.com; 194 County Rd 11; tent sites $18.50, RV hook-ups $27-32, d cabin $70-90; P 🛜 🐾) In 10 acres off the Crested Butte road north of Gunnison, this places has RV hook-ups, cabins and site for campers with tents.

Alpine Inn HOTEL **$**
(☑970-641-2804, toll-free 866-299-66; www. gunnisonalpineinn.com; 1011 W Rio Grande; d $59-129; P ⊖ ❋ 🛜 🏊 🐾) This is a good inexpensive choice. Recently remodeled, the Alpine Inn has a range of room types – including family rooms – all with cable TV and wireless internet, and free continental breakfast. There's an indoor pool and pets are welcome.

🍴 Eating & Drinking

Garlic Mike's ITALIAN **$$**
TOP CHOICE (☑970-641-2493; www.garlicmikes.com; 2674 State Hwy 135; mains $13-19; ⊙5pm-late; ⊖ 🚗 🐾) This place, just north of Gunnison on the road to Crested Butte, is generally regarded as the town's best place to eat. And for rural Colorado, it's a pretty darn authentic taste of Italy. Mike Busse, chef and restaurateur, regularly appears on Colorado talk radio, and his restaurant has won many awards.

Try Mike's special shrimp scampi, a classic Italian dish of garlic and shrimps tossed through fresh linguine.

Firebrand Deli SANDWICHES **$**
(☑970-641-6266; 108 N Main St; mains $4-8; ⊙7am-3pm Tue-Sun; ⊖ 🚗 🐾) If you're after healthy breakfast and lunchtime eating in Gunnison, it's hard to go past the Firebrand Deli. The freshly made sandwiches are always terrific with a great selection of breads and fillings. Vegetarians (who have it hard in Gunnison) can come to Firebrand and expect more than lip service.

Sugah's Cafe CAJUN, SOUTHERN AMERICAN **$$**
(☑970-641-4990; www.sugahscafe.com; 206 N Main St; mains $14-27; ⊙11am-9pm Mon-Fri, 10am-9pm Sat & Sun; ⊖ 🚗 🐾) A favorite place with locals, Sugah's is a vaguely Cajun place dishing up shrimp and grits, osso bucco, and pork loin served stuffed with boudin. All ingredients are locally sourced (organic where possible) and all the sauces are handmade. There's a kids menu too.

Gunnisack BURGERS, STEAK $
(☑970-641-5445; 142 N Main St; mains $8-11; ⊙11am-9pm Tue-Sat, to 4pm Sun; ☺🍴🚼) This 'cowboy bar and bistro' is energetic and friendly. Everything is freshly handmade from scratch. Burgers, fried chicken and steaks are the staples. It's a family-friendly place, with a kids' menu and some wicked deserts.

Gunnison Brewery BREWPUB
(☑970-641-2739; www.gunnisonbrewery.com; 138 N Main St; ⊙11am-midnight Mon, Wed & Thu, 11am-2am Tue, Fri & Sat, 4pm-midnight Sun; 🚼) Gunnison's only brewery operates out of a Main St shopfront. Its local brews are on tap: a dark lager, pale ale, wheat beer and the Hopalicious IPA. The Gunnison Pale Ale is excellent, sold by the pint glass, and when combined with a pub meal or bar snacks, it gets easy to settle in and order another.

ℹ️ Information

Gunnison Bank & Trust (☑970-641-0320; www.gunnisonbank.com; 232 W Tomichi Ave) This bank on the main drag has an ATM.

Gunnison Chamber of Commerce (☑970-641-1501, toll-free 800-323-2453; www.gunnisonchamber.com; 500 E Tomichi Ave; ⊙9am-5pm Mon-Sat; 🚼) Pick up a self-guided historic walking tour booklet, maps of area mountain-bike trails, as well as lists of accommodations and activities.

Gunnison Post Office (☑toll-free 800-275-8777; www.usps.com; 200 N Wisconsin St; ⊙7:30am-5:15pm Mon-Fri, 9am-noon Sat)

Gunnison Valley Hospital (☑970-641-1456; www.gvh-colorado.org; 711 N Taylor St)

ℹ️ Getting There & Away

Denver is about 3½ hours' drive away, while Colorado Springs is about three hours. Gunnison lies on US Hwy 50, 65 miles east of Montrose and 34 miles west of Monarch Pass. The highway to the Divide is a scenic trip following Tomichi Creek.

Crested Butte

POP 1500 / ELEV 8885FT

In a valley ringed by three wilderness areas, remote and beautiful Crested Butte is void of pretension. Despite being one of Colorado's best ski resorts (some say *the* best), it doesn't put on airs. There's nothing haughty, or even glossy, about the town – just lovely fresh mountain air, a laid-back attitude and friendly folk. The old town center is a beautifully preserved Victorian-era mining town with many old buildings refitted with shops and businesses.

During winter, it's all about the skiing on Mt Crested Butte, the conical mountain strangely positioned in the centre of the valley floor. But during summer the wildflowers rule the grasslands around this charming hamlet – so much so that the Colorado State Senate officially recognized the town as the state's wildflower capital. Summer also brings the mountain-bikers, who take to the trails and slopes with reckless abandon.

◉ Sights

TOP CHOICE Crested Butte Mountain Heritage Museum MUSEUM
(☑970-349-1880; www.crestedbuttemuseum.com; 331 Elk Ave; adult/child $3/free; ⊙10am-8pm summer, noon-6pm winter; 🅿️🚼) This fascinating museum is really worth a visit. It's installed in one of the oldest buildings in Crested Butte. Exhibits range from geology and mining to early home life, tools and hardware as well as a terrific scale model railway celebrating the history of the Denver Rio Grande Railroad. The Mountain Bike Hall of Fame is also located in the museum.

The picturesque old town center is a delight to walk around, surrounded by forested hills and wilderness areas of aspens and pines, and the giant brooding form of Mt Crested Butte overseeing all. The old buildings live and breathe as working businesses, their ancient chimneys issuing smoke from wood heaters and fires. Elk Ave is the heart of Crested Butte, but a walk through some of the backstreet and residential areas is rewarding too with all sorts of old homes that have been lovingly refurbished.

Crested Butte Center for the Arts
GALLERY, PERFORMANCE SPACE
(☑970-349-7487; www.crestedbuttearts.org; 606 6th St; prices vary; ⊙10am-6pm; 🅿️🚼) This art gallery and performance space looms large in the cultural life of Crested Butte. With shifting exhibitions of local artists and a stellar schedule of live music and performance pieces, there's always something lively and interesting happening.

FREE Crested Butte Cemetery CEMETERY
(Gothic Rd) Many of the town's pioneers are buried in the cemetery, about 0.25 miles north of town towards Mt Crested Butte. Also interred here are 59 miners who

died in the Jokerville Mine explosion of 1884, many of them boys and adolescents.

Mountain Bike Hall of Fame   MUSEUM
(970-349-1880; www.mtnbikehalloffame.com; 331 Elk Ave; adult/child $3/free; ⊙10am-8pm summer, noon-6pm winter; P⚐) Inside the Crested Butte Mountain Heritage Museum is the Mountain Bike Hall of Fame. There's a great collection of historic photos and some very cool old bikes to see.

🏃 Activities

TOP CHOICE Crested Butte Mountain Resort
SKIING

(970-349-2222; www.skicb.com; 12 Snowmass Rd; lift ticket adult/child $87/44; ⚐) Crested Butte Mountain Resort sits 2 miles north of the town at the base of the impressive mountain of the same name. Surrounded by forests, rugged mountain peaks, and the West Elk, Raggeds and Maroon Bells-Snowmass Wilderness Areas, the scenery is breathtaking. The resort caters mostly to intermediate and expert riders. It's comprised of several hotels and apartment buildings, with variable accommodation rates.

Crested Butte Nordic Center
CROSS-COUNTRY SKIING

(970-349-1707; www.cbnordic.org; 620 2nd St; day passes adult/child $15/10; ⊙8:30am-5pm; ⚐) This center manages and grooms the 50km of cross-country ski trails around Crested Butte. It issues day and season passes, manages hut rental and organizes events and races. You can hire skis and equipment, and arrange lessons. The center also offers ice-skating, snowshoeing and guided tours of the alpine region.

Adaptive Sports Center
OUTDOORS ACTIVITIES

(970-349-2296; www.adaptivesports.org; 10 Crested Butte Way; ⚐) This nonprofit group is dedicated to providing opportunities for people with disabilities to participate in outdoors activities and adventure sports.

Fantasy Ranch   HORSEBACK RIDING
(970-349-5425, toll-free 888-OUTFIT; www.fantasyranchoutfitters.com; 935 Gothic Rd; 1½-hr/3-hr/day rides $55/85/120; ⚐) Offering trail rides for everybody over seven years and under 240lbs, Fantasy Ranch does pony rides and short trips, as well as wilderness day rides and multiday pack trips. A stunning ride from Crested Butte to Aspen and back is a feature.

Alpineer   MOUNTAIN BIKING
(970-349-5210; www.alpineer.com; 419 6th St; bike rental per day $20-65; ⚐) Crested Butte is a famous mountain-biking mecca, full of excellent high-altitude single-track trails; this store offers maps, information and rentals. It also hires out skis and hiking and camping equipment.

Crested Butte Guides   OUTDOORS ACTIVITIES
(970-349-5430; www.crestedbutteguides.com; off Elk Ave) If you're keen on doing some hardcore backcountry skiing, ice-climbing, mountaineering or you want to learn how to survive an avalanche, talk to these guys. They've been guiding in the area for more than a decade and can get you into (and out of) some seriously remote wilderness. They're full outfitters, too, so you can leave the equipment to them.

Black Tie Ski Rentals   SNOW SPORTS
(970-349-0722, toll-free 888-349-0722; www.blacktieskis.com; Unit A/719 4th St; ⊙7:30am-10pm winter; ⚐) Black Tie hires skis, skiing equipment and snowboards.

Christy Sports   SNOW SPORTS
(970-349-6601, toll-free 877-754-76278; www.christysports.com; 10 Crested Butte Way; ⚐) Ski and ski equipment hire. Rental snowboards, snowshoes and sales too, and clothing.

🛏 Sleeping

Visitors to Crested Butte can stay either in the main town, which is better for restaurants and nightlife, or in one of the many options at the mountain resort. Some of the Mt Crested Butte hotels and apartment buildings close over the shoulder seasons in spring and fall, but others offer great discounts and longer-stay incentives – check the websites, compare prices and bargain. If you've come for the hiking, mountain-biking or to enjoy the wildflowers, you can do very well at these times.

TOP CHOICE Ruby of Crested Butte   B&B $$
(800-390-1338; www.therubyofcrestedbutte.com; 624 Gothic Ave; d $129-249, suite $199-349; P⊝❄🖥⚐) Stylish and understated, this is the pick of the town's accommodation options. It's been thoughtfully fitted out with a terrific communal lounge and dining areas, Jacuzzi, library, ski-gear drying room, free wi-fi and complimentary use of some super-cool retro townie bikes. The rooms are brilliant, with heated floors, high-definition flat-screen TVs with DVD players (and a library), iPod docks and deluxe linens.

Inn at Crested Butte

BOUTIQUE HOTEL $$

(970-349-2111, toll-free 877-343-211; www.inn atcrestedbutte.net; 510 Whiterock Ave; d $130-200; P✳🛜🐾) This recently refurbished boutique hotel offers intimate lodgings in stylish and luxurious surrounds. With just a handful of rooms, some opening onto a balcony with views over Mt Crested Butte, and all decked out with antiques, flat-screen TVs, coffee-makers and minibars, this is one of Crested Butte's nicest vacation addresses.

Crested Butte International Hostel

HOSTEL $

(970-349-0588, toll-free 888-389-0588; www. crestedbuttehostel.com; 615 Teocalli Ave; dm $25-31, r $65-110; 🛜🐾) If you're looking for the privacy of a hotel with the lively ambience of a hostel, grab a room here, one of Colorado's nicest hostels. The best private rooms have their own baths. Dorm bunks come with reading lamps and lockable drawers, and the communal area has a stone fireplace and comfortable couches. Rates vary with the season, with winter being high-season.

Extended stays attract discounts.

Elevation Hotel & Spa

HOTEL $$$

(970-349-2222; www.skicb.com; 500 Gothic Rd; r from $200; P🐾) If you're more swank than budget, try this hotel at the base of Crested Butte Ski Resort. Just steps from a major chairlift, this classy place has over-sized rooms right by one of the main lifts, so you can ski straight back to your modern country-western abode. Check online for specials, particularly at the beginning and end of the season.

The Atmosphere Restaurant is a trendy place to grab a meal, while the hotel's slope-side deck is the spot to drink a beer by the fire pit and watch the snowboarders whiz by. Elevation is one of a number of hotels run by the ski resort.

Crested Butte Mountain Resort Properties

RENTAL AGENCY

(CBMR Properties; 888-223-2631; www.skicb. com) This property-management group, part of the Crested Butte Mountain Resort, handles reservations for dozens of the lodges, hotels and apartment buildings at Mt Crested Butte.

🍴 Eating & Drinking

Timberline Restaurant

CONTEMPORARY $$$

(970-349-9831; www.timberlinerestaurant. com; 201 Elk Ave; mains $17-32; 5:30-10:30pm; 🐾) The Timberline Restaurant was popular in the Butte before Heidi Montag and MTV's cameras made it famous. Owned and run by Montag's mother and stepfather, the family bistro serves a seasonal mostly American and Italian menu – think double-cut pork chops and BBQ *frites* or shrimp, basil pesto and tomato linguini.

Secret Stash

PIZZA $$

(970-349-6245; www.thesecretstash.com; 21 Elk Ave; mains $8-20; 5-10pm; 🚗🐾) Certainly not a secret, the Secret Stash is by far the most happening restaurant in Crested Butte. This enticing pizza and calzone joint has a hip interior where you can sit on the floor upstairs or park yourself in a velvety chair on the lower level and catch up on the gossip. The cocktail list is impressive.

Avalanche Bar & Grill

AMERICAN $

(970-349-7195; www.avalanchebarandgrill. com; off Gothic Rd; mains $7-19; 7:30am-9pm winter, from 11:30am summer; 🚗🐾) One of the favorite *après ski* venues, Avalanche is right on the slopes and has a big menu of American comfort foods (tuna melts, burgers, club sandwiches, pizzas) as well as an impressive lineup of desserts and beverages. There's a kids menu too.

Bacchanale

ITALIAN $$

(970-349-5257; www.bacchanale.net; 209 Elk Ave; mains $9-20; 5-10pm; 🍽🐾) This is the original fine-dining restaurant in Crested Butte. For 35 years it has been serving great Italian staples and seafood specialties, as well as homemade tiramisu and espresso coffee. There's a terrific kids menu too.

Princess Wine Bar

WINE BAR

(970-349-0210; 218 Elk St; 8am-midnight; 🐾) An intimate joint, perfect for sitting and chatting, and sampling the select regional wine list. Regular live music features acoustic and easy-listening tunes and local singer-songwriters. A popular *après ski* spot.

☆ Entertainment

Eldo Brewpub

LIVE MUSIC

(970-349-6125; www.eldobrewpub.com; 215 Elk Ave; cover charge varies; 3pm-late, music from 10:30pm; 🐾) Crested Butte has an interesting music scene year-round. This lively joint, one of the town's most popular micro-breweries, doubles as the club where most out-of-town bands play. Check out the great outdoor deck. The food is mostly burgers, steaks and sandwiches, but the riffs are sweet and the beats deadly.

Lobar
NIGHTCLUB, SUSHI BAR

(970-349-0480; www.thelobar.com; 303 Elk Ave; occasional cover charge;) Starting life in 2005 as nightclub, Lobar evolved into a nightclub-cum-sushi-bar (mains $8 to $12). The room is warmly lit with Japanese lanterns and candles. Then the disco lights and the mirror balls transform the place into an upbeat dance room with DJs and sometimes live music. Lobar is the only nightclub in Crested Butte.

Crested Butte Mountain Theatre
THEATRE

(970-349-0366; www.cbmountaintheatre.org; 403 2nd St; prices vary; varies;) Since 1972 the Crested Butte Mountain Theatre has been showcasing the best local and community theatre. It's a registered charity and survives solely on ticket sales and subscriptions. There's always shows on or in development – tickets for dress rehearsal shows are cheap.

Information

Crested Butte Visitor Center (970-349-6438; www.cbchamber.com; 601 Elk Ave; 9am-3pm) Crested Butte's visitor center is packed with information and staffed by helpful people.

Post Office (970-349-5568; www.usps.com; 217 Elk Ave; 7:30am-4:30pm Mon-Fri, 10am-1pm Sat)

Getting There & Away

Crested Butte is about four hours' drive from Denver, while Colorado Springs is about 3½ hours. Head for Gunnison on US Hwy 50 and from there head north to Crested Butte on Hwy 135, about a 30-minute drive from Gunnison.

Paonia

POP 1660 / ELEV 5674FT

As you descend into the valley of the North Fork River – the Grand Mesa flanking one side and Mt Lamborn towering on the other, Hwy 133 runs right through charming little Paonia. It doesn't have many attractions of its own but it's an excellent stop over between Carbondale and Montrose. The city's founder wanted to name the town 'Paeonia,' the Latin name for the peony flower, but according to local legend an austere postmaster wouldn't allow the city moniker to have so many vowels.

For its size, Paonia offers a surprising combination of natural beauty, working-class society and liberal culture. Surround-ed by the North Fork Valley's charming countryside of farms and wildlands, it also has a bundle of late-19th-century buildings in superb condition, and is the home of *High Country News*, one of the country's most outspoken environmental publications. The casual visitor hardly notices that coal mining is still a significant local industry. Today, most of its residents are a mix of coal miners and boomers who found a place mostly off the grid. The historic downtown – all 10 blocks of it or so – is just south of the highway.

Sleeping

Fresh & Wyld Farmhouse Inn
B&B $$

(970-527-4374; www.freshandwyld.com; 1978 Harding Rd; d from $95;) Guests at this 1908 bedroom farmhouse, with seven bright bedrooms, are fed organic breakfasts grown out back. Owner Dava Parr also hosts cooking classes ('Cooking in a Crockpot' and the like) so even if you don't get a bed, there's a chance to soak in the homespun warmth of the place.

A series of magazine articles about the place have raised its profile considerably, so try to book in advance.

Information

Paonia Chamber of Commerce (970-527-3886; www.paoniachamber.com; 302 2nd St; 9am-3pm Mon-Fri) A good source of local information.

USFS Paonia Ranger Station (970-527-4131; 403 N Rio Grande; 8am-4pm)

Delta

POP 4500 / ELEV 4890FT

Once known as Uncompahgre, Delta is the gateway to the north rim of Black Canyon of the Gunnison National Park. It's a small crossroads town that travelers to southwest Colorado can hardly miss.

Its downtown district is graced by a series of interesting murals along Main St and cross streets depict Delta's history, society and environment. The murals are a good reason to stop here for lunch and an afternoon stroll along the shopping district. The favorite shop is the **Davis Clothing Co** (970-874-4370; 401 Main St; 9:30am-5:30pm Tue-Fri, 9am-5pm Sat;), a dry goods store from a different era. The manly outfitter stocks Woolrich shirts, Stetsons and lots of denim and has a big selection of top-quality hats, which, like everything else here, are made to last.

⊙ Sights & Activities

TOP CHOICE FREE **Dry Mesa Dinosaur Quarry**
DINOSAUR SITE

(📞970-874-6638; Uncompahgre National Forest; P 📶) Within the borders of the Uncompahgre National Forest, this bone-rich area yielded one of the most diverse Jurassic vertebrate collections in the world. Over a dozen different dinosaurs have been unearthed here since the first dig in 1971, including the terrifying Torvosaurus and various birds, crocodiles and mammals.

The quarry is southeast of town, along Escalante Creek. The location of the quarry will vary because the dig remains ongoing. For more information about the visit, inquire at the USFS forest station. A short hike will also bring you to a Utes rock-art site.

Fort Uncompahgre HISTORIC BUILDING

(📞970-874-1718; 205 Gunnison River Dr; admission $3; ⊙9am-3pm Apr-Sep; 📶) Delta's history as a fur-trading center and frontier outpost comes alive with a self-guided tour behind the rough timber walls of this 1828 fort. Plan on about an hour for a visit of the site.

Gunnison River Expeditions
FISHING, RAFTING

(📞970-874-8184; www.gunnisonriverexpeditions. com; 14494 F Rd; full-day river rafting from $255; 📶) This adventure-tour company offers fly-fishing, river-rafting and hunting trips. It has a hunting lodge bedecked in trophy mounts near Hotchkiss.

🛏 Sleeping

Frankly, Delta isn't so pretty, but it's location makes it a likely stop-over. You won't have trouble spotting any number of mid-century roadside motels along the central corridor. It's not an easy choice, since none of them are too nice.

✗ Eating & Drinking

El Tapatio MEXICAN $$

(📞970-874-4100; 353 Main St; mains $10-21; ⊙10am-10pm Mon-Sat, to 8pm Sun; 📶) The bright booths are ornately carved, and the plates of Mexican food are moderately priced and delicious. The lunch deals are great; our favorite is the plate of Enchiladas Suizas, smothered in green chili and white cheese.

Daveto's ITALIAN $$

(📞970-874-8277; 520 Main St; mains $8-15; ⊙10am-9pm; 📶) This place has generous plates of pasta, big pizzas and inexpensive lunches. It also goes boldly where few Italian restaurants dare tread: into the Mexican-Italian fusion. Mexican calzone anyone?

Moca Joe's CAFE FOOD

(📞970-874-1133; 352 Main St; ⊙6am-7pm Mon-Fri; 🛜) Good coffee, a warm atmosphere and free wi-fi make this the best pit stop in town.

☆ Entertainment

Tru Vu Drive-In DRIVE-IN THEATER

(📞970-874-9556; www.deltaegyptiantheatre. com; 1001 Hwy 92; tickets $7; ⊙summer only; 📶) When the evening air is warm and dusk falls on Delta, this historic drive-in has a magical atmosphere. It is one of the few remaining such facilities in Colorado, and there are only a handful in the entire USA. There's nothing quite like taking in a summer blockbuster on the big outdoor screen. Always a treat for the family.

The theater is owned by the same people behind the historic Egyptian theater in the heart of town.

ℹ Information

Delta Chamber of Commerce (📞970-874-8616; www.deltacolorado.org; 301 Main St; ⊙9am-5pm Mon-Fri) The volunteer staff doesn't have encyclopedic information about the area, but this place is wall-to-wall with brochures and maps.

USFS Grand Mesa, Uncompahgre & Gunnison National Forest Headquarters (📞970-874-6600; 2250 US Hwy 50; ⊙9am-4:30pm Mon-Fri)

ℹ Getting There & Away

The **Delta TNM&O/Greyhound Station** (📞970-874-9455; 270 E Hwy 92) sends buses to Montrose, Durango, and Albuquerque, New Mexico, and Montrose, Salida and Pueblo. There are also daily buses to Grand Junction, where you can connect with buses and trains to Denver, Salt Lake City, Utah, and points beyond.

Delta lies 40 miles southeast of Grand Junction and 21 miles northwest of Montrose via US 50.

TELLURIDE

POP 2500 / ELEV 8750FT

At the base of a box canyon, surrounded on three sides by towering 13,000ft peaks, Telluride feels protected from the noise of the outside world. Strong coffee, historic buildings and endless days of perfect skiing define a particular vision of paradise.

No one makes it here by accident; the nearest major airport, Colorado Springs, is four hours away by car. Denver is 6½ hours. But it's *so* worth the commute. With 300in of snow annually, a 3000ft vertical drop to the ski lifts in town, a dramatic setting and a rich mining history, Telluride is one of Colorado's most pristine ski towns. Ever since Telluride was designated a National Historic Landmark in 1964 – well before skiing arrived – conscientious citizens have strictly protected the place with a preservationist spirit. Many newer buildings follow Victorian designs so closely that it is sometimes difficult to tell modern constructions from historic ones.

Orientation

Colorado Ave, also known as Main St, is where you'll find most of the restaurants, bars and shops. The town's small size means you can get everywhere on foot, so you can leave your car at the intercept parking lot at the south end of Mahoney Dr, near the visitors center (p269), or wherever you're staying. From town you can reach the ski mountain via two lifts and the gondola. The latter also links Telluride with Mountain Village, the true base for the Telluride Ski Area. Located 7 miles from town along Hwy 145, Mountain Village is a 20-minute drive east on Hwy 145, but only 12 minutes away by gondola, which is free for foot passengers. Ajax Peak, a glacial headwall, rises behind the town to form the end of the U-shaped valley that contains Telluride.

To the right (south) of Ajax Peak, Colorado's highest waterfall, Bridal Veil Falls, cascades 365ft; a switchback trail leads to a restored Victorian powerhouse atop the falls. To the south, Mt Wilson reaches 14,246ft among a group of rugged peaks that form the Lizard Head Wilderness Area.

🏃 Activities

Telluride Ski Resort
SNOW SPORTS

(☑970-728-7533, 888-288-7360; www.tellurideskiresort.com; 565 Mountain Village Blvd; lift tickets $98) Covering three distinct areas, Telluride Ski Resort is served by 16 lifts. Much of the terrain is for advanced and intermediate skiers, but there's still ample choice for beginners.

Telluride Ski & Snowboarding School
SNOW SPORTS

(☑970-728-7507; www.tellurideskiresort.com; 565 Mountain Village Blvd; full-day adult group lessons $170) If you'd like to sharpen your skills while in Telluride, the resort offers private and group lessons with good teachers through this school, which offers classes for children and sessions specific to women, with women instructors.

San Juan Hut System
SNOW SPORTS, MOUNTAIN BIKING

(☑970-626-3033; www.sanjuanhuts.com; huts $30) Experienced cross-country skiers will appreciate the strong series of crude huts along a 206-mile route stretching from Telluride west to Moab, Utah. In summer these huts, equipped with bunks and cooking facilities, are popular with mountain bikers. Book well in advance, as huts fill quickly.

Telluride Flyfishers
FISHING

(☑800-294-9269; www.tellurideflyfishers.com; ½-day for 2 $280) Housed in Telluride Sports (p268), this outfit offers fishing guides and instruction.

Ride with Roudy
HORSEBACK RIDING

(☑970-728-9611; www.ridewithroudy.com; County Rd 43Zs; 2hr trips $45; 🐎) Offers all-season trail rides through the surrounding hills. Roudy moved here as 'one of the old hippies' in the 1970s and has been leading trips for 30 years. His pleasant 'awe shucks' hospitality recalls Telluride's yesteryear. Call for an appointment and pricing details.

Telluride Nordic Center
SNOW SPORTS

(☑970-728-1144; www.telluridetrails.org; 500 E Colorado Ave) There are public cross-country trails in Town Park, as well as along the San Miguel River and the Telluride Valley floor west of town. Instruction and rentals are available from the Telluride Nordic Center.

Paragon Ski & Sport
BIKE RENTAL

(☑970-728-4525; www.paragontelluride.com; 213 W Colorado Ave) Has branches at three locations in town and a huge selection of rental bikes. It's a one-stop shop for outdoor activities in Telluride.

Telluride

To Telluride Central Reservations (0.2mi); Telluride Visitor Center (0.2mi); Clark's Market (0.4mi)

To Telluride Nordic Center (0.2mi); Telluride Town Park Campground (0.2mi)

Telluride

Activities, Courses & Tours

1	Easy Rider Bike & Sport	C2
2	Paragon Ski & Sport	B2

Sleeping

3	Aspen Street Inn	A2
4	Camel's Garden	A4
5	Hotel Columbia	A3
6	New Sheridan Hotel	B2
7	Telluride Alpine Lodging	A2
8	Victorian Inn	A2

Eating

9	221 South Oak	A3
10	Brown Dog Pizza	C2
	Cosmopolitan	(see 5)
11	Excelsior Cafe	B2
12	Fat Alley	A2
13	Honga's Lotus Petal	C2
14	La Marmotte	B4
15	The Butcher & The Baker	D2

Drinking

16	Last Dollar Saloon	C2
17	New Sheridan Bar	B2
18	Smugglers Brewpub & Grille	C3

Entertainment

19	Fly Me to the Moon Saloon	C2
20	Sheridan Opera House	B1

Shopping

21	Between The Covers	B2
22	Scrape	D3
23	Telluride Sports	C2

Easy Rider Bike & Sport   BIKE RENTAL
(☎970-728-4734; 101 W Colorado Ave) This full-service shop rents bikes. It has a variety to choose from, as well as maps and information.

✨ Festivals & Events

Mountainfilm   FILM
(www.mountainfilm.org; ⊘Memorial Day weekend) A four-day screening of outdoor adventure and environmental films.

Telluride Bluegrass Festival   MUSIC FESTIVAL
(☎800-624-2422; www.planetbluegrass.com; 4-day pass $175; ⊘late Jun) Held in late June, this festival attracts thousands for a weekend of top-notch rollicking alfresco bluegrass. Stalls sell all sorts of food and local microbrews to keep you happy, and acts continue well into the night. Camping out for the four-day festival is very popular. Check out the website for info on sites, shuttle services and combo ticket-and-camping packages – it's all very organized!

Telluride Mushroom Festival   FOOD
(www.tellurideinstitute.org) Fungiphiles sprout up at this festival in late August.

Telluride Film Festival   FILM
(☎603-433-9202; www.telluridefilmfestival.com; tickets $20-650; ⊘early Sep) Held in early September, national and international films are premiered throughout town, and the event attracts big-name stars. For more information on the relatively complicated pricing scheme, visit the film festival website.

Brews & Blues Festival   BEER, MUSIC
(www.tellurideblues.com; ⊘mid-Sep) Telluride's festival season comes to a raucous end at this mid-September event, where blues musicians take to the stage and microbrews fill the bellies of fans.

🛏 Sleeping

Aside from camping, there's no cheap places to stay in Telluride. If you arrive during the summer or winter peak seasons, or during one of the city's festivals, you'll pay dearly for a room. Rates drop quite a bit during the off season, sometimes up to 30%.

Some of the huge properties in Mountain Village can offer a descent rate if you book online, but none have the character of the smaller hotels at the foot of the mountain. Most people who come into town during the ski season stay in vacation rentals – there are scores of them. If you're interested in booking a room in one, the most repu-table agency is **Telluride Alpine Lodging** (☎888-893-0158; www.telluridelodging.com; 324 W Colorado Ave).

[TOP CHOICE] **Hotel Columbia**   HOTEL $$$
(☎970-728-0660, toll-free 800-201-9505; www.columbiatelluride.com; 300 W San Juan Ave; d $425; [P][⊖][❄][🖥][🛜][🏊]) Since shelling out big cash is a given in Telluride, skiers might as well stay right across the street from the gondola. There's more than just location through – each of the hotel's 21 rooms has a balcony, a fireplace and a mountain view.

Baths are larger than average, and breakfast is included. Other highlights include a rooftop hot tub and fitness room. The food at the connected Cosmopolitan is also excellent – many say its the best dining room in Telluride.

Lumière   HOTEL $$$
(☎907-369-0400, 866-530-9466; www.lumiere hotels.com; 118 Lost Creek Lane; d from $289, ste from $379; [P][⊖][❄][@][🛜][🏊]) This is the best of the best on the Mountain Village side of town, a luxury lodge and suites that look over the mountains. In the morning, guests enjoy an elegant breakfast reception, and the staff is always on hand to grant your every wish.

Even with the luxurious amenities, amazing views, comfortable beds, excellent spa menu and cozy suites, the property's greatest appeal might be the ski-in, ski-out location, which allows you to go from the slopes to a bubble bath in minutes.

Aspen Street Inn   BOUTIQUE HOTEL $$$
(☎970-728-3001, toll-free 800-537-4781; www. telluridehotels.com; 330 W Pacific Ave; d from $195; [♿]) The favorite high-end option, an elegant small hotel with individually decorated rooms, is near the chairlift. Its prices are a bit high for the dog-eared B&B vibe, but loyal visitors rave about the hospitality. Snacks are served in the stone- and wood-lined common room.

Inn at Lost Creek   BOUTIQUE HOTEL $$$
(☎970-728-5678; www.innatlostcreek.com; 119 Lost Creek Lane; r from $189; [⊖][🛜]) A boutique luxury hotel that manages to feel unpretentious and as comfortable as your own home, the inn is poised at the bottom of Telluride's main lift. Service is personalized but not overbearing, and the rooms are impeccably decorated. Be sure to visit the two rooftop spas. Rates are reasonable value; check the website for packages.

CAMPING

Right in Telluride Town Park, **Telluride Town Park Campground** (2970-728-2173; 500 E Colorado Ave; campsites $20; ⊙mid-May–mid-Sep; 🏕) offers 42 campsites, showers and swimming and tennis from mid-May to October. Developed campsites cost $20 and are all on a first-come, first-served basis.

Two campgrounds in the Uncompahgre National Forest are within 15 miles of Telluride on Hwy 145 and cost $20. **Sunshine Campground** (2970-327-4261; off County Rd 145; sites $20) is the nearest and the best, with offers 15 first-come, first-served campsites; facilities at **Matterhorn Campground** (2970-327-4261; Hwy 145; sites $20; ⊙May-Sep; 🏕), a bit further up the hill, include showers and electrical hookups for some of the 27 campsites.

Camel's Garden   HOTEL **$$$**
(2970-728-9300; www.camelsgarden.com; 250 W San Juan Ave; r from $275; P ⊕ ❄ ﹫ 🏊) This modern and luxurious choice is located at the base of the gondola. The lobby is filled with local artwork and the large rooms feature custom-crafted furniture and Italian marble bathrooms with oversized tubs. Don't miss the giant 25ft hot tub on the top level.

The complex also features restaurants, bars and spa treatments. The Chair 8 Bar is a favorite with the *après-ski* crowd.

Victorian Inn   LODGE **$$**
(2970-728-6601; www.tellurideinn.com; 401 W Pacific Ave; r from $99; ⊕ ❄ ﹫ 🏕) The smell of fresh cinnamon rolls greets visitors at one of Telluride's better deals, offering comfortable rooms (some with kitchenettes) and a hot tub and dry sauna. Best off all, there are fantastic lift-ticket deals for guests. Kids aged 12 years and under stay free, and you can't beat the downtown location.

New Sheridan Hotel   HOTEL **$$**
(2970-728-4351, 800-200-1891; www.newsheridan.com; 231 W Colorado Ave; d from $129; ⊕ ﹫) Centrally located, this brick hotel was erected in 1895 and it has been updated to provide upscale lodging. The location, right in the center of the main drag, is perfect, but some of the rooms are quite small for the large price.

✗ Eating & Drinking

[TOP CHOICE] 🍴 **The Butcher & The Baker**   CAFE FOOD **$$**
(2970-728-3334; 217 E Colorado Ave; mains $8-14; ⊙7am-7pm Mon-Sat, 8am-2pm Sun; ⊕ 🏕) Two veterans of upscale local catering started this heartbreakingly cute cafe, and no one beats it for breakfast. The to-go sandwiches – a daily rotation that includes turkey and cranberry on crunchy multigrain bread – are the best bet for a gourmet meal on the trail.

It's the kind of place that represents the new, smart trends in simple, quality food: the ethos here is local, organic and perfect. We're simply head over heels.

221 South Oak   FUSION **$$$**
(2970-728-9505; www.221southoak.com; 221 S Oak St; mains $19-25; ⊙5-10pm; ⊕) This is an intimate restaurant in a historic home, with a small but innovative menu mixing world flavors and yielding excellent results. Dishes are meat-, fish- and seafood-based with lots of fresh vegetables. A vegetarian menu is available upon request.

La Marmotte   FRENCH **$$$**
(2970-728-6232; www.lamarmotte.com; 150 W San Juan Ave; mains from $20) Seasonal plates of French cuisine and candlelit warmth make an excellent juxtaposition with the building's former use as a 19th-century ice-house. Start to finish it's a dizzyingly romantic affair.

Excelsior Cafe   EUROPEAN **$$$**
(2970-728-4250; 200 W Colorado Ave; mains from $20; ⊙5-10pm; ⊕) One of Telluride's hottest restaurants, Excelsior gets rave reviews for its Euro wine-bar vibe. The menu features a little bit of everything, from Moroccan lamb chops to Montana buffalo short ribs. If you are short on cash, order from the less expensive, but equally tantalizing, bar menu.

Fat Alley   BBQ **$$**
(2970-728-3985; 122 S Oak St; mains $10-15; ⊙11am-10pm; 🏕) You can pick something off the chalkboard our just take what the other guy has his face in – a cheap and messy delight. Go for the pulled pork sandwich with coleslaw on top. Do it right by siding it with a bowl of crispy sweet-potato fries. The can beer specials are outrageous.

Cosmopolitan   CONTEMPORARY AMERICAN **$$$**
(2970-728-0660; www.columbiatelluride.com; 300 W San Juan Ave; mains from $20; ⊙dinner)

The on-site restaurant at the Hotel Columbia is one of Telluride's most respected for fine modern dining with a twist – can you resist Himalayan yak ribeye or lobster corn dogs? The food is certainly inventive, which makes up for the snooty service.

Brown Dog Pizza
PIZZA $$

(✆970-728-8046; www.browndogpizza.net; 10 E Colorado Ave; pizzas $10-22) The pizza? It's thin crust and fair enough, but the crowd makes the place interesting. Ten minutes after you belly up to the bar for a slice and a cheap pint of Pabst, you'll be privy to all the local dirt. It's one of the most affordable meals on the strip.

Honga's Lotus Petal
PAN-ASIAN $$$

(✆970-728-5134; www.hongaslotuspetal.com; 135 E Colorado Ave; mains $17-33) Upscale and elegant, Honga's offers a pricey fix for pan-Asian cuisine in a large, two-story dining space. The dishes are elegantly presented – the Korean short ribs just about fall off the bone – and the nightly specials range from Thai to Japanese flavored. We'll forgive the pan flutes.

Clark's Market
SELF-CATERING

(www.clarksmarket.com; 700 W Colorado Ave; ◔7am-9pm) Put the condo kitchenette to good use after picking up supplies at Clark's, the nicest market in town. It stocks specialty goods and scores of treats, with fresh fruit and deli meats.

Smugglers Brewpub & Grille
PUB

(✆970-728-0919; www.smugglersbrew.com; 225 S Pine St; ◔11am-2am; ▥) Beer-lovers will feel right at home at casual Smugglers, a great place to hang out, sample local brew and eat fried stuff. With at least seven beers on tap, it's a smorgasbord, but go for the chocolatey Two Plank Porter or the Smugglers' Scottish Strong Ale.

The American pub fare (mains $7 to $12) features burgers, fries, salads and sandwiches and snacks. The Smuggler's Nuggets – a mass of fried, sweet dough – will do no wonders for your waistline, but they are a gooey ending.

New Sheridan Bar
BAR

(✆970-728-3911; www.newsheridan.com; 231 W Colorado Ave; ◔5pm-2am) Most of this historic bar survived the waning mining fortunes even as the adjoining hotel sold off chandeliers and fine furnishings to pay the heating bills. These days, overdressed visitors chat about upcoming film releases next to the occasional old-timer who hasn't been driven out by escalating property values.

In season, it can get obnoxiously loud and crowded, but locals take over at other times of the year, when it's a cool place to kick off the evening.

Last Dollar Saloon
BAR

(✆970-728-4800; www.lastdollarsaloon.com; 100 E Colorado Ave; ◔3pm-2am) For a splash of local color, forget about cocktails and grab a cold can of beer at this long-time favorite. With the best selection of imported beers in town, as well as pool tables and darts, it's no wonder this creaky wooden bar is so popular.

☆ Entertainment

Fly Me to the Moon Saloon
LIVE MUSIC

(✆970-728-6666; 132 E Colorado Ave; ◔3pm-2am) Let your hair down and kick up your heels to the tunes of live bands at this saloon, the best place in Telluride to party hard.

Sheridan Opera House
THEATER

(✆970-728-4539; www.sheridanoperahouse.com; 110 N Oak St) This historic venue has a burlesque charm and is always the center of Telluride's cultural life. It hosts the Telluride Repertory Theater, and frequently has special performances for children.

🔒 Shopping

Telluride Sports
SPORTING GOODS

(✆970-728-4477; www.telluridesports.com; 150 W Colorado Ave; ◔8am-8pm) There are branches and associated shops in Mountain Villiage, making this the biggest network of outdoor suppliers in town. It covers everything outdoors, has topographical and USFS maps, sporting supplies and loads of local information.

Between The Covers
BOOKS

(✆970-728-4504; www.between-the-covers.com; 224 W Colorado Ave) This is the town's reliable source for books, with a big selection of local interest, creaking floors and a doting staff. It's a terrific place to browse for paperback vacation reads too, and the coffee counter in back turns out a mean espresso milk shake.

Scrape
CLOTHING

(✆970-728-1513; ww.shopscarpe.com; 250 E Pacific Ave; ◔10am-7pm) The hand-picked selection of women's shoes, skirts and accessories makes Scrape the best clothing boutique in town. Things here feel timeless, designed by a fleet of names which include a good number of locals.

ℹ️ Information

Telluride Central Reservations (☎888-355-8743; 630 W Colorado Ave) Handles accommodations and festival tickets. Located in the same building as the visitor center.

Telluride Medical Center (☎970-728-3848; 500 W Pacific Ave) Handles skiing accidents, medical problems and emergencies.

Telluride Visitor Center (☎888-353-5473, 970-728-3041; www.telluride.com; 630 W Colorado Ave; ⏰9am-5pm winter, to 7pm summer) This well-stocked visitor center has local info in all seasons. Restrooms and an ATM make it an all-round useful spot.

ℹ️ Getting There & Around

Commuter aircraft serve the mesa-top **Telluride Airport** (☎970-778-5051; www.tellurideairport.com; Last Dollar Rd), 5 miles east of town on Hwy 145. If weather is poor flights may be diverted to Montrose, 65 miles north. For car rental, National and Budget both have airport locations.

In ski season Montrose Regional Airport (p257) has direct flights to and from Denver (on United), Houston, Phoenix and limited cities on the east coast.

Shuttles from the Telluride Airport to town or Mountain Village cost $15. Shuttles between the Montrose Airport and Telluride cost $48. Contact **Telluride Express** (☎970-728-6000; www.tellurideexpress.com).

SAN JUAN MOUNTAINS

Ridgway

POP 806 / ELEV 6985FT

The drive through southwestern Colorado is enchanting because of little towns like Ridgway, where quirky locals, walkable commercial districts and a zesty history make it hard to just blow through. On top of that, Ridgway has another proud feather in its cap: it was the backdrop for John Wayne's 1969 cowboy classic, *True Grit*.

The town is situated at the crossroads of US 550, which goes south to Durango, and Hwy 62, which leads to Telluride, but the downtown area is tucked away a bit west of this junction, on the west side of the Uncompahgre River. Through town Hwy 62 is called Sherman and all the perpendicular streets are named for his daughters. Ridgway Area Chamber of Commerce (p270) has a lot of information about local activities in the area.

👁️ Sights & Activities

FREE **Ridgway Railroad Museum** MUSEUM (☎970-626-5181; www.ridgwayrailroadmuseum.org; 150 Racecourse Rd; ⏰10am-6pm May-Sep, reduced hrs Oct-Apr; 🚻) Ridgway was the birthplace of the Rio Grande Southern Railroad, a narrow-gauge rail line that connected to Durango with the 'Galloping Goose', a kind of hybrid train and truck that saved the struggling Rio Grand Southern for a number of years. This museum is dedicated to the plucky rail line.

The volunteers who staff the museum are true railroad zealots – one even reconstructed a Galloping Goose engine outside from photos and sketches. The permanent collection has maps, historical photos and a really cool diorama of the Pleasant Valley Trestle and Motor #2. It's also the de facto historical museum for the town, and it has good brochures for a short self-guided tour.

Riggs Fly Shop & Guide Service

FLY-FISHING

(☎970-626-4460, toll-free 888-626-4460; www.fishrigs.com; Suite 2, 565 Sherman St; half-day fishing tours per person from $225; 🚻) Riggs Fly Shop offers guided fly-fishing tours out of Ridgway from half-day beginners' trips to multiday camp outs for more experienced fisherfolk. Riggs also does white-water rafting and other soft-adventure itineraries in and around southwest Colorado.

Chicks with Picks

ROCK, ICE CLIMBING

(☎cell 970-316-1403, office 970-626-4424; www.chickswithpicks.net; 163 County Rd 12; prices vary) This group is dedicated to getting women onto the rocks and ice, giving instruction for all-comers (beginners included) about typical sausage parties such as rock-climbing, bouldering and ice-climbing. The programs change frequently and often involve multi-day excursions or town-based courses. Men are included on some activities, but most are women-only.

FREE **Ridgway State Park & Recreation Area**

FISHING

(☎970-626-5822; www.parks.state.co.us/parks/ridgway; 28555 US Hwy 550; admission free; ⏰dawn-dusk) Fishing aficionados should head to Ridgway State Park and Recreation Area, 12 miles north of town. The reservoir here is stocked with loads of rainbow trout, as well as German brown, kokanee, yellow perch and the occasional large-mouth bass. There are also hiking trails and campsites.

🛌 Sleeping & Eating

Chipeta Sun Lodge & Spa LODGE **$$$**
(📞970-626-3737; www.chipeta.com; 304 S Lena
St; r from $160; 🅿) The southwestern adobe-
style lodge is a swank, upscale sleeping op-
tion. Rooms feature hand-painted Mexican
tiles, rough-hewn log beds and decks with
a view. It's very classy and upmarket, and
there are wonderful public areas on the
property.

Have a read in the Great Room or a chat
in the solarium, or head out to the hot tubs
on the property for a quiet soak. The on-site
spa features treatments developed by the
Utes and daily yoga classes. Check Chipeta's
website for ski, soak and stay deals, where
you can ride the slopes at Telluride, soak in
the hot springs pools in Ouray and spend
the night in Ridgeway.

TOP **Kate's Place** AMERICAN **$$**
CHOICE (📞970-626-9800; 615 W Clinton St;
mains $9-13; ⏰7am-2pm; 🅿🚼) Consider
yourself lucky if the morning starts with
a chorizo-stuffed breakfast burrito and
white cheddar grits from Kate's: it's the
best breakfast joint for miles. But the restaurant's dedication to local farmers, cute
and colorful interior and bubbly wait staff
seal the deal.

True Grit Cafe AMERICAN **$$**
(📞970-626-5739; 123 N Lena Ave; mains $8-15;
⏰lunch & dinner) Scenes from the original
True Grit were filmed at this appropriately
named cafe, also Ridgway's best watering
hole. It's a kind of shrine to John Wayne,
with pictures and memorabilia hung on
the walls. Burgers, tasty chicken and fried
steaks are served, and a crackling fire
warms patrons in the winter.

ℹ Information

Ridgway Area Chamber of Commerce
(📞970-626-5181, 800-220-4959; www.ridgway
colorado.com; 150 Racecourse Rd; ⏰9am-5pm
Mon-Fri)

Ouray & the Million Dollar Hwy

POP 850 / ELEV 7760FT

Experiencing tiny Ouray (*you*-ray) is some-
thing that stays with you forever. No matter
how many times you visit, Ouray's setting
and the vistas that surround it knock your
socks off every time. Sandwiched between
imposing peaks, tiny Ouray is beautiful,
surreal and other-worldly, like an elabo-
rate set erected for a fantasy film. Here the
mountains don't just tower over you, they
stand and confront you rising as dizzying
walls that leave barely a quarter-mile of val-
ley floor for the town.

Between Silverton and Ouray, US 550 is
known as the Million Dollar Hwy. Why?
Well, some say it's because the fill for the
roadbed is rich in valuable gold ore. Oth-
ers say it's because the road cost $1 million
per mile to build. The whole of US 550 has
been called the Million Dollar Hwy, but
more properly it's the amazing stretch of
road south of Ouray through the Uncom-
pahgre Gorge up to Red Mountain Pass at
11,018ft, passing abandoned mine head-
frames and slag piles from the former Ida-
rado Mine.

The alpine scenery is truly awesome and
driving south towards Silverton positions
drivers on the outside edge of the skinny,
winding road, a heartbeat away from free-
fall. Vehicles traveling the other way sit
more snugly on the inside edge. Much of
the road is cut into the mountainsides and
gains elevation by switching back on itself
in tight hairpins and S-bends. The brood-
ing mountains loom large and close, their
bulk and flanks intimidating, with snow
clinging to their lofty misty peaks even in
high summer.

In good weather the road is formidable.
In drizzle or rain, fog or snow, the Million
Dollar Hwy south of Ouray is downright
scary, so take care.

Ouray is named after the legendary Ute
chief who maintained peace between the
white settlers and the crush of miners who
descended on the San Juan Mountains in
the early 1870s. Ouray relinquished the Ute
tribal lands, preventing the slaughter of his
people.

👁 Sights

Little Ouray, 'the Switzerland of America,'
is very picturesque and littered with old
houses and buildings. The visitors center
(p273) and **museum** (📞970-325-4576; www.
ouraycountyhistoricalsociety.org; 420 6th Ave;
adult/child $5/1; ⏰1-4:30pm Thu-Sat April 14-
May 14, 10am-4:30pm Mon-Sat & noon-4:30pm
Sun May 15-Sep 30, 10am-4:30pm Thu-Sat Oct
1-30, closed Dec 1-Apr 14; 🚼) issue a free leaf-
let with details of an excellent walking
tour that takes in two-dozen buildings and
houses constructed between 1880 and 1904.

Birdwatchers come to Ouray to to sight rare birds. The Box Canyon Falls have the USA's most accessible colony of protected black swifts. There are surprising numbers of unusual birds in town, including warblers, sparrows and grosbeaks. The visitor center has resources for bird-watchers, and the excellent **Buckskin Booksellers** (970-325-4071; www.buckskinbooksellers.com; 505 Main St; 9am-5pm Mon-Sat;) has books and guides.

Activities

There are stacks of things to do in and around Ouray. Remember that Ouray falls within the purview of tour and activities providers in nearby Ridgway, Montrose and Silverton, and even Durango and Gunnison; check the Activities sections in those towns too.

Ouray Ice Park ICE CLIMBING
TOP CHOICE FREE (970-325-4061; www.ouray icepark.com; Hwy 361; 7am-5pm mid-Dec–March;) Climbing the face of a frozen waterfall can be a sublime experience. Head to the Ouray Ice Park to try it yourself. This park spans a 2-mile stretch of the Uncompagre Gorge that has been dedicated to public ice-climbing. The park is the world's first, and draws enthusiasts from around the globe to try their hand at climbs for all skill levels.

Ouray Hot Springs HOT SPRINGS
(970-325-7073; 1220 Main St; adult/child $10/8; 10am-10pm Jun-Aug, noon-9pm Mon-Fri & 11am-9pm Sat & Sun Dec-Feb;) Ouray's stunning scenery isn't the only ace up the town's sleeve. For a healing soak, try the historic Ouray Hot Springs. The crystal-clear natural springwater is free of the sulphur smells plaguing other hot springs around here, and the giant pool features a variety of soaking areas at temperatures from 96°F to 106°F.

The Ouray Hot Springs complex also offers a gym and massage service.

Ouray Mule Carriage Co CARRIAGE TOURS
(970-708-4946; www.ouraymule.com; 834 Main St; adult/child $15/5; hourly departures 1-6pm Jun-Aug;) The mule-drawn coach you see clip-clopping along Ouray's main streets is the nine-person dray that takes visitors (and locals) around on interpretive tours of the old town. The old Ouray Livery has been in the same family since 1944. Charters are available for larger groups.

Ouray Livery HORSEBACK RIDING
(970-708-7051, 970-325-4340; www.ouray livery.com; 834 Main St; 1-/2-hr rides $40/60, half-/full-day rides $80/120;) The Ouray Livery offers short and day-long guided horseback riding in the mountains surrounding the town. This group has special-use permits to tour the Grand Mesa, Uncompaghre and Gunnison National Forests.

San Juan Scenic Jeep Tours 4WD, FISHING
(970-325-0090, 888-624-8403; www.historic westernhotel.com; 210 7th Ave; adult/child half-day $54/27, full day $108/54;) The friendly folks at the Historic Western Hotel operate a Jeep-touring service that is customized to clients' needs. Abandoned ghost towns of the old mining days are always popular, as are off-road tours of the nearby peaks and valleys. Hiking, hunting and fishing drop-offs and pick-ups can be arranged.

If you're staying at the Historic Western Hotel you can get some good package deals for these tours.

San Juan Mountain Guides CLIMBING, SKIING
(970-325-4925, 866-525-4925; www.ouray climbing.com; 474 Main St;) Ouray's own professional guiding and climbing group is certified with the International Federation of Mountain Guides Association (IFMGA). It specializes in ice- and rock-climbing and wilderness back-country skiing.

Festivals & Events

Ouray Ice Festival ICE CLIMBING
(970-325-4288; www.ourayicefestival.com; donation for evening events $15; Jan;) The Ouray Ice Festival features four days of climbing competitions, dinners, slide shows and clinics in January. You can watch the competitions for free, but to check out the various evening events you will need to make a $15 donation to the ice park. Once inside you'll get free brews from popular Colorado microbrewer New Belgium.

Sleeping

Beaumont Hotel HOTEL $$$
TOP CHOICE (970-325-7000; www.beaumonthotel. com; 505 Main St; r $145-280;) Ouray's classiest lodging option, this small hotel offers 12 rooms elegantly appointed with period furnishings. Established in 1886, the hotel was closed for more than 30 years before undergoing extensive renovations and reopening five years ago. It also boasts a spa and three unique boutiques.

Wiesbaden
HOTEL $$

(☎970-325-4347; www.wiesbadenhotsprings. com; 625 5th St; r from $130; ☯🔊🖥) The best bit about slumbering at this posh hotel is that guests can use the fantastic natural indoor vapor cave for free. Rooms are cozy and romantic in a European ski-lodge style. Outside you'll find a selection of hot-spring pools. Couples should rent the private, clothing-optional soaking tub with a waterfall that can be reserved for $35 per hour.

The on-site Aveda salon provides relaxing massages and soothing facials to make your mountain detox complete.

Box Canyon Lodge & Hot Springs
LODGE $$$

(☎800-327-5080, 970-325-4981; www.boxcan yonouray.com; 45 3rd Ave; r $115-350; 🔊🖤) It's not every hotel that offers geothermal heated rooms, and these are spacious and accommodating. The real treat here is four wooden spring-fed hot tubs for guests, perfect for a romantic stargazing soak. This place is very popular with returning visitors, so book well ahead.

Amphitheater Forest Service Campground
CAMPING $

(☎877-444-6777; www.ouraycolorado.com/ amphitheater; US Hwy 550; tent sites $16; ☺Jun-Aug; 🖤) A drive south of town on Hwy 550 takes you to a signposted left-hand turn. This takes you to this USFS campground at 8400ft east of town with great tent sites under the trees. It's not really suitable for longer vehicles. On holiday weekends a three-night minimum applies.

Historic Western Hotel, Restaurant & Saloon
HOTEL $

(☎970-325-4645; www.historicwesternhotel. com; 210 7th Ave; r $35-105; 🅿🖤) Old Wild West meets Victorian charm at this place, one of the largest remaining wooden structures on Colorado's western slope. It offers rooms for all budgets; the cheapest have shared bathrooms. The open-air 2nd-floor veranda commands stunning views of the Uncompahgre Gorge, while the Old West Saloon serves affordable meals and all sorts of drinks in a timeless setting.

Ouray Victoria Inn
HOTEL $$

(☎970-325-7222, toll-free 800-846-8729; www. victorianinnouray.com; 50 3rd Ave; d $75-160; 🅿☯🔊🖤) Refurbished in 2009, 'The Vic' has a terrific setting next to Box Canyon Park on the Uncompahgre riverfront near the Ouray Ice Park. All the rooms have cable TV, fridges and coffee-makers, and there's free wi-fi throughout. There are also designated pet-friendly rooms, some opening onto wonderful balcony spaces with splendid views.

Rates vary widely by season, but the low-season rates are a steal.

St Elmo Hotel
HOTEL $$

(☎970-325-4951, toll-free 866-243-1502; www.stelmohotel.com; 426 Main St; d $75-190; ☯❄🖤) Circa-1897 St Elmo is a renovated gem, one of the showpieces of the Ouray museum's historic walking tour. There are nine unique rooms decorated with period furnishings. Some of the busy 1900s floral-print wallpaper might be a bit too authentic for modern minimalist tastes, but the rooms and the amenities are a delight.

All rooms have private bathroom facilities. Downstairs, Bon Ton Restaurant is one of Ouray's best.

🍴 Eating & Drinking

TOP CHOICE **Tundra Restaurant at the Beaumont** CONTEMPORARY AMERICAN $$$

(☎970-325-7040; www.beaumonthotel.com/ Tundra+Restaurant; 505 Main St; mains from $20; ☺5-10pm; 🖤) The pick of places to eat in Ouray, this elegant restaurant has won several awards. It has a legendary wine cellar and does Thursday-evening tastings. Billing itself as serving 'High Altitude' cuisine, it focuses on regional specialties with great results.

Buen Tiempo Mexican Restaurant & Cantina
MEXICAN $$

(☎970-325-4544; 515 Main St; mains $7-19; ☺6-10pm; ☯🍴) Buen Tiempo is one of Ouray's most popular restaurants – an unfussy casual place serving Mexican favorites and Tex-Mex spin-offs. The blue corn-chips and enchiladas are novel and fried ice-cream is another house specialty. It claims to have Colorado's 10 best margaritas. We only tried the one and it was pretty good.

Silver Nugget Café
CONTEMPORARY AMERICAN $$

(☎970-325-4100; 746 Main St; mains $7-20; ☺8am-9pm; 🍴🖤) A busy, contemporary eatery in a historic building, Silver Nugget features a very large breakfast menu as well as deli-style sandwiches at lunch. Dinner offerings include deep-fried Rocky Mountain rainbow trout, and liver and onions.

Bon Ton Restaurant
FRENCH, ITALIAN $$$

(☎970-325-4951; www.stelmohotel.com; 426 Main St; mains $12-22; ☺6-11pm; ☯🍴) Bon Ton has been trading in a beautiful room under the historic St Elmo Hotel for as long as anyone can remember. In fact, the basement room of the old hotel has been serving supper for around 100 years. Bon Ton does a few house specialties on its French-Italian menu, including escargot and crawfish tails, and veal piccata.

Some say its standards have slipped over recent years, but it's still worth a visit.

Outlaw Restaurant AMERICAN $$
(☏970-325-4366; www.outlawrestaurant.com; 610 Main St; mains $9-23; 🖶) This convivial bar-restaurant specializes in door-stopper steaks cut and cooked to your liking. There's a select wine list and menu of cocktails as well as ubiquitous Colorado micro-brewed beers. The decor is fun – a shingle wall is covered with sports memorabilia, antiques and, allegedly, John Wayne's hat.

Ouray Brewery BREWPUB
(☏970-325-7388; http://ouraybrewery.com; 607 Main St; ⊙4-9pm) Ouray Brewery is the newest thing in Ouray. So new, it hadn't even opened for trade when we came through, so we couldn't list any prices. There's a food menu on the website and a list of tasty-sounding beers – maybe it's all free?

ℹ Information

Ouray Chamber Resort Association (☏970-325-4746, 800-228-1876; www.ouraycolorado.com; 1230 Main St; ⊙10am-5pm Mon-Sat, 10am-3pm Sun; 🖶) The visitor center is at the Ouray hot-springs pool.

Post Office (☏970-325-4302; 620 Main St; ⊙9am-4:30pm Mon-Sat)

ℹ Getting There & Away

Ouray is on Hwy 550, 70 miles north of Durango, 24 miles north of Silverton and 37 miles south of Montrose. There are no bus services in the area and private motorcar is the only way to get to and around the town.

Silverton

POP 550 / ELEV 9318FT

Silverton, surrounded by mountains covered in blankets of aspens, is Colorado's best rediscovered vintage gem and definitely worth visiting. Whether you're into snowmobiling, biking, fly-fishing or just basking in the sunshine, Silverton delivers.

It's a two-street town, but only one is paved. The main drag, Greene St, is where you'll find most businesses. Blair St, still unpaved, runs parallel to Greene and is a blast from the past. During the silver rush, Blair St was a notorious home to thriving brothels and boozing establishments.

Although Silverton is a tourist town by day in summer, once the final Durango-bound steam train departs it turns back to local turf. Visit in the middle of the winter for a real treat – only the most hard-core residents stick around, and you'll find many of the tourist shops, and even hotels and restaurants, board up come first snowfall. Snowmobiles become a main means of transportation, and Silverton turns into a winter adventure playground for intrepid travelers.

One of Silverton's highlights is just getting here from Ouray on the Million Dollar Hwy – an awe-inspiring stretch of road that's one of Colorado's best road trips.

◉ Sights & Activities

Silverton Railroad Depot

TOP CHOICE NARROW-GAUGE RAILWAY
(☏970-387-5416, toll-free 877-872-4607; www.durangotrain.com; 12th St; adult/child return from $81/49; ⊙departures 2pm, 2.45pm & 3.30pm; 🖶) You can buy one-way and return tickets for the brilliant Durango & Silverton Narrow Gauge Railroad (p277) at the Silverton terminus. The Silverton Freight Yard Museum is located at the Silverton depot. The train ticket provides admission two days prior to, and two days following, your ride on the train.

The train service offers combination train-bus return trips (the bus route is much quicker). Tickets are also available for the website. Hikers use the train to access the Durango and Weminuche Wilderness trailheads.

Mining Heritage Center MUSEUM
(☏970-387-5838; www.silvertonhistoricalsociety.ca; 1559 Greene St; adult/child $5/free; ⊙9am-5pm Jun-Oct; 🅿🖶) This specialist museum is dedicated to Silverton's mining history. Old mining equipment is displayed and there's a re-created machine shop and blacksmith shop.

Silverton Museum MUSEUM
(☏970-387-5838; www.silvertonhistoricsociety.org; 1557 Greene St; adult/child $5/free; ⊙10am-4pm Jun-Oct; 🅿🖶) Installed in the original 1902 San Juan County Jail, the Silverton Museum is interesting with a collection of local artifacts and ephemera.

Mayflower Gold Mill   HISTORIC BUILDING
(970-387-0294; www.silvertonhistoricsociety.
org; County Rd 2; adult/child $8/free; 10am-
4pm May 25-Sep 30; P) This mill was once
a major employer in Silverton. The Aerial
Tram House is a highlight of the self-guided
tour.

Silverton Mountain Ski Area   SKIING
(970-387-5706; www.silvertonmountain.com;
State Hwy 110; daily lift ticket $49, all-day guide &
lift ticket $99) This is one of the most inter-
esting and innovative ski mountains in the
US – a single lift takes advanced and expert
backcountry skiers up to the summit of an
area of ungroomed ski runs. The numbers
are limited to 475 skiers on unguided days
and just 80 on guided days.

The lift rises from the 10,400ft base to
12,300ft. Imagine heli-skiing *sans* helicop-
ter. You really need to know your stuff – the
easiest terrain here is comparable to skiing
double blacks at other resorts.

Old Hunded Gold Mine Tour   TOURS
(970-387-5444, toll-free 800-872-3009; www.
minetour.com; County Rd 4a; adult/child $17/8;
hourly 10am-4pm May 15-Oct 15;) Fifteen
minutes east of town, the hour-long Old
Hundred Mine Gold Tour is hugely popular.
A tram travels a third of a mile into a tunnel where passengers alight and are guided
around the old gold-mine workings. There
are demonstrations of drilling equipment
and 1930s-era mining machinery.

Panning for gold is included in the tour
price – an area is regularly 'salted' with gold
dust. Significantly, the tour is totally wheelchair accessible.

Kendall Mountain Recreation Area   SKIING
(970-387-5522; www.skikendall.com; Kendall
Pl; daily lift tickets adult/child $15/10; 11am-
4pm Fri & Sat Dec-Feb;) The Kendall Mountain Recreation Area is managed by the
town itself. There's just one double 1050ft
chairlift and four runs, all of them suitable
for beginners. It's a great place to learn skiing and popular for people goofing around
on sleds and tubes, and is super cheap and
family-friendly. Skis, tubes, sleds and snowboards can be rented from the Kendall
Mountain Community Center.

San Juan Backcountry   TOURS
(970-387-5565, toll-free 800-494-8687;
www.sanjuanbackcountry.com; 1119 Greene St;
2hr tours adult/child $55/40, half/full-day tours
adult $75/150 child $50/90; May-Oct;) Offering both 4WD tours and rentals, the

folks at San Juan Backcountry can get you
out and into the brilliant San Juan Mountain wilderness areas around Silverton.
The tours take visitors around in modified
open-top Chevy Suburbans.

Sleeping

Wyman Hotel & Inn   B&B $$$
(970-387-5372; www.thewyman.com; 1371
Greene St; d $145-280;) In a handsome
red-sandstone building, this hotel is on the
National Register of Historic Places. Rooms
are uniquely decorated with late-19th-
century antiques and feature Victorian-era
wallpaper and top-quality beds and linens.
High ceilings and arched windows are the
norm throughout the place. The price in-
cludes a full breakfast plus afternoon wine
and cheese tasting.

Bent Elbow   HOTEL $$
(970-387-5775, toll-free 877-387-5775; www.
thebent.com; 1114 Blair St; d $60-105; P)
Smack in the middle of town, this place
stays open year-round. Each of the quaint,
good-sized guest rooms is decorated
slightly differently, but all have a Western
flavor. In winter, the Bent Elbow arranges
snowmobiling, guided ice-climbing and
dog-sledding trips on nearby Molas Pass, a
pristine wilderness area.

Locals say the restaurant (mains $6 to
$12) has the best chef in town. It's a cheerful
dining room with a gorgeous old wood shot-
gun bar that serves Western American fare.

**Inn of the Rockies at the Historic Alma
House**   B&B $$
(970-387-5336, toll-free 800-267-5336; www.
innoftherockies.com; 220 E 10th St; r from $110;
P) Opened by a local named Alma
in 1898, this inn has nine unique rooms fur-
nished with Victorian antiques. The hospi-
tality is first-rate and its New Orleans–in-
spired breakfasts, served in a chandelier-lit
dining room, merit special mention. There's
also a hot tub in the garden for soaking af-
ter a long day. Breakfast is included.

Silver Summit RV Park   CAMPING $
(970-387-0240, toll-free 800-352-1637; www.
silversummitrvpark.com; 640 Mineral St; RV sites
$36 plus electricity $3; May 15-Oct 15; P)
Like so much else in Silverton, Silver Sum-
mit is a mixed business running rental
Jeeps out of the RV park headquarters
(two-/four-door Jeep Wranglers $155/185).
The park has good facilities including a
laundry, hot tub, fire pit and free wi-fi.

Red Mountain Motel & RV Park

MOTEL, CAMPING $

([☎]970-382-5512, toll-free 800-970-5512; www.redmtmotelrvpk.com; 664 Greene St; motel r from $78, cabins from $70, RV/tent sites $38/20; [P][♿][🌐][🐾]) This operation covers everything from tent camping and RV facilities, cabins and motel rooms to Jeep and ATV hire and guided tours, snowmobiling, fishing and hunting. The managers are friendly and keen to make sure guests and customers have a good time. It's a pet-friendly place that stays open year-round.

The tiny log cabins stay warm and make good use of their limited space – ours came with a double bed, a bunk, a tiny TV with HBO and a fully outfitted little kitchenette. The river, with good fishing, is just a few minutes' walk away.

✖ Eating & Drinking

Stellar Bakery & Pizzeria
PIZZA, CAFE FOOD $$

([☎]970-387-9940; 1260 Blair St; mains $8-15; [🕙]11am-10pm; [♿][🐾]) This friendly place is a good choice for lunch or dinner. Locals come here for the stellar pizzas, friendly service and easy atmosphere. Beers by the bottle are available and the baked quiches, pastas and freshly made salads are always good.

Handlebars
AMERICAN $$

([☎]970-387-5395; www.handlebarssilverton.com; 117 13th St; mains $10-20; [🕙]May-Oct; [🐾]) Yes, it's a bit touristy, but you can't argue about the goodness of the baby-back ribs basted in this eclectic-looking restaurant's famous secret BBQ sauce. The decor, a mishmash of old mining artifacts, mounted animal heads and cowboy memorabilia, gives this place a ramshackle museum-meets-garage-sale feel.

After dinner, kick it up on the dance floor to the sounds of live rock and country music.

Grumpy's at the Grand Imperial
AMERICAN $$

([☎]970-387-5527; 1219 Greene St; mains $8-15; [🕙]7:30am-9pm daily Jun-Aug, Thu-Sun Dec-Feb; [♿][🐾]) Serving three meals daily, Grumpy's does American fare pretty well – burgers, fries, soups and salads. The summertime Mexican buffet brings in the mums and dads with kids in tow. Trophy mounts and Americana decorate the walls, and there's sometimes live piano music. The full bar is well serviced by locals and visitors alike.

Pride of the West
BAR

([☎]970-387-5150; 1323 Greene St; mains $8-20; [🐾]) Pride of the West is Silverton's best bar. A gigantic creaking no-frills place, this is the kind of bar where locals gather late into the night, talking at the long bar, or playing a game of pool upstairs.

Silverton Brewery & Restaurant
BREWPUB

([☎]970-387-5033; www.silvertonbrewing.com; 1333 Greene St; [🐾]) This hugely popular brewpub consistently wins a thumbs-up for its brews, food and atmosphere. The food (mains $7 to $19) is a clever mix of comfort favorites. The bratwurst cooked in beer, with its wicked homemade sauerkraut, is kind of a house specialty.

ℹ Information

Silverton Chamber of Commerce & Visitor Center ([☎]970-387-5654, toll-free 800-752-4494; www.silvertoncolorado.com; 414 Greene St; [🕙]9am-5pm; [🐾]) The Silverton Chamber of Commerce & Visitor Center provides information about the town and surrounds. It's staffed by friendly volunteers and you can buy tickets for the Durango & Silverton Narrow Gauge Railroad here.

Radio KSJC 92.5 FM, a nonprofit community radio station, broadcasts out of an adjoining room in the same building – think about that when you're stomping down the hallway to the public restrooms.

ℹ Getting There & Away

Silverton is on Hwy 550 midway between Montrose, about 60 miles to the north, and Durango, some 48 miles to the south. Other than private car, the only way to get to and from Silverton is by using the Durango & Silverton Narrow Gauge Railroad (p277), or the private buses that run its return journeys.

Durango

POP 14,800 / ELEV 6580FT

The darling of this region, Durango is nothing short of delightful. It's an archetypal old Colorado mining town filled with graceful hotels, Victorian-era saloons, with mountains dominating the periphery as far as the eye can see. It's a place seemingly frozen in time; the waitress slinging drinks at the scarred wooden bar is dressed straight out of the early 19th century. The antique-laden inn and the musician pounding ragtime on worn ivory keys add to the surrealism.

Yet Durango has effortlessly and gracefully modernized, with its old buildings

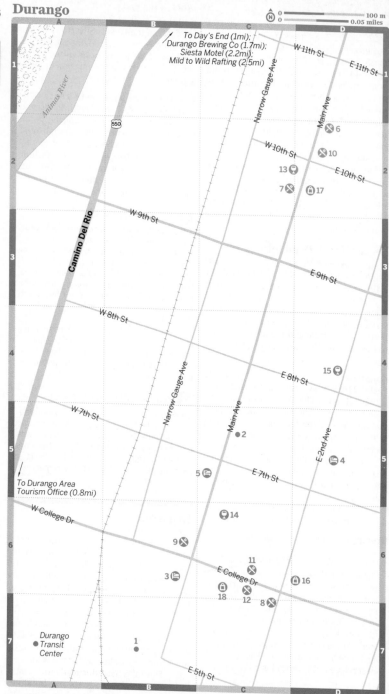

SOUTHWEST COLORADO SAN JUAN MOUNTAINS

0   100 m
0   0.05 miles

To Day's End (1mi);
Durango Brewing Co (1.7mi);
Siesta Motel (2.2mi);
Mild to Wild Rafting (2.5mi)

W 11th St
E 11th St

Narrow Gauge Ave

Main Ave

W 10th St
E 10th St

550

Camino Del Rio

W 9th St

E 9th St

W 8th St

Narrow Gauge Ave

E 8th St

W 7th St

Main Ave

E 2nd Ave

E 7th St

To Durango Area
Tourism Office (0.8mi)

W College Dr

E College Dr

Durango
Transit
Center

E 5th St

Aminas River

Activities, Courses & Tours
1 Durango & Silverton Narrow
   Gauge Railroad B7
2 Durango Rivertrippers C5

Sleeping
3 General Palmer Hotel........................... B6
4 Rochester House D5
5 Strater Hotel C5

Eating
6 Carver Brewing Co D2
7 Durango Diner.. C2
8 East by Southwest................................ C7
9 Jean Pierre Bakery B6
10 Olde Tymers Café................................. D2

11 Ore House C6
12 Randy's C6

Drinking
   Diamond Belle Saloon.................... (see 5)
13 El Rancho Tavern C2
14 Lady Falconburgh's............................... C6
15 Steamworks Brewing............................ D4

Entertainment
   Henry Strater Theatre .... (see 5)

Shopping
16 2nd Avenue Sports D6
17 Maria's Bookshop D2
18 Pedal the Peaks..................................... C6

refitted as galleries of Navajo art and hand-made silver jewelry. The town's historic central precinct is home to boutiques, bars, restaurants and theater halls. These classy sales spaces and restaurants combined with the relaxed well-groomed locals and the art and live-music scene make Durango the cultural center of Southwest Colorado and a great base for the many excursions and activities nearby.

Durango is also a great base for exploring the enigmatic ruins at Mesa Verde National Park, 35 miles to the west.

Sights

Wander through Durango's historic district and admire its great stock of early buildings. Listen for the train driver riding the steam whistle of the famous 1882 Durango & Silverton Narrow Gauge Railroad as it issues plumes of steam, pulling into the town's historic railyards. Most visitor facilities are along Main Ave, including the Narrow Gauge Railroad Depot at the south end of town. The historic downtown area is compact and easy to walk in a few hours.

Activities

This town is a hub for travel and soft adventure in Colorado's southwest and as such all sorts of outdoor activities can be arranged here. There are several river-rafting outfitters and prices are competitive.

TOP CHOICE **Durango & Silverton Narrow Gauge Railroad** NARROW-GAUGE RAILWAY
(970-247-2733, toll-free 877-872-4607; www.durangotrain.com; 479 Main Ave; adult/child re-turn from $81/49; ⏱departures at 8:15am, 9am, 9:45am; 👶) Riding the Durango & Silverton Narrow Gauge Railroad is a Durango must. These vintage steam locomotives have been making the scenic 45-mile trip north to Silverton (3½ hours each way) for more than 125 years. The dazzling journey allows two hours for exploring Silverton. This trip operates only from May through October. Check online for different winter options.

Durango Mountain Resort SNOW SPORTS
(☎970-247-9000; www.durangomountainresort.com; 1 Skier Pl; lift tickets adult/child from $65/36; ⏱mid-Nov–Mar; @🛜👶) Durango Mountain Resort, 25 miles north on US 550, is Durango's winter highlight. The resort, also known as Purgatory, offers 1200 skiable acres of varying difficulty and boasts 260in of snow per year. Two terrain parks offer plenty of opportunities for snowboarders to catch big air.

Check local grocery stores and newspapers for promotions and 2-for-1 lift tickets and other promotional ski season specials before purchasing directly from the ticket window.

Trimble Spa & Natural Hot Springs
HOT SPRINGS, MASSAGE
(☎970-247-0111, toll-free 877-811-7111; www.trimblehotsprings.com; 6475 County Rd 203; day pass adult/child $14.50/9.50; ⏱10am-9pm Sun-Thu, 10am-10pm Fri & Sat; 👶) If you need a pampering massage or just a soak in some natural hot springs after hitting the ski runs or mountain bike trails, then this is the place. Qualified massage therapists can work out

BIKING IN DURANGO

Biking goes hand in hand with imbibing alcohol in Colorado, so it's little surprise a town supporting such a lively microbrew community would also be considered paradise to mountain bikers. Bike geeks take note: Durango is home to some of the world's best cyclists, like Ned Overend and Travis Brown. From steep single-tracks to scenic road rides, Durango has hundreds of trails to choose from. Some are well marked; others the locals like to keep secret (much in the manner of surf spots) and you'll have to do a bit of snooping if you want to hit pay dirt. For an easy ride, try the Old Railroad Grade Trail, a 12.2-mile loop that uses both US Hwy 160 and a dirt road following the old rail tracks. From Durango, take Hwy 160 west through the town of Hesperus. Turn right into the Cherry Creek Picnic Area, where the trail starts.

For something a bit more technical, try Dry Fork Loop, accessible from Lightner Creek just west of town. It has some great drops, blind corners and copious vegetation.

There are quite a few sports shops on Main Ave that rent mountain bikes.

those knotted muscles and tired limbs with treatment ranging from acupressure to trigger-point myotherapy. Five miles north of Durango.

Phone or check the website for last-minute specials, which sometimes include two-for-one deals and other discounts.

Durango Soaring Club GLIDING
(Val-Air Gliderport; ☏970-247-9037; www.soardurango.com; 27290 US Hwy 550 North; 15min per person from $85; ☉9am-6pm mid-May–mid-Oct; ☝) One- and two-person gliding flights are a memorable way to see the spectacular scenery around the San Juan Mountains and Animas River. In the summer afternoons, when the earth is warmed, the chance of catching rising thermal air currents is best.

Mild to Wild Rafting RAFTING
(☏970-247-4789, toll-free 800-567-6745; www.mild2wildrafting.com; 50 Animas View Dr; trips from $55; ☝) In spring and summer whitewater rafting is one of the most popular sports in Durango. Mild to Wild Rafting is one of numerous companies around town offering rafting trips on the Animas River. Beginners should check out the one-hour introduction to rafting, while the more adventurous (and experienced) run the upper Animas, which boasts Class III to V rapids.

Durango Rivertrippers RAFTING
(☏970-259-0289, toll-free 800-292-2885; www.durangorivertrippers.com; 720 Main Ave; 2hr trip adult/child $25/17, half-day $40/30; ☝) This family-operated outfit is the oldest accredited rafting operator in Durango and highly reputed. It offers various river-rafting trips on the Delores and Animas Rivers,

from two-hour family runs to six-day wilderness adventures.

★ Festivals & Events

San Juan Brewfest BEER
(www.cookmanfood.com/brewfest; Main Ave, between 12th & 13th Sts; ☉early Sep; ☝) Showcasing 30-odd specialist brewers from Durango, around Colorado and interstate, this annual festival is a highlight held in early September. Official judging takes place late in the afternoon but all attendees ($20; must be aged 21 and over to taste) get to vote for the San Juan Brewfest's People's Choice award. There are bands and food and a carnival atmosphere.

🛏 Sleeping

TOP
CHOICE **Strater Hotel** HOTEL $$
(☏970-247-4431; www.strater.com; 699 Main Ave; d $130-210; ☕✳@☎☝) The interior of this lovely, old-world hotel is museum worthy – check out the Stradivarius violin or the gold-plated commemorative Winchester in the lobby. Romantic rooms feature antiques, crystal and lace. Beds are heavenly and comfortable, with impeccable linens.

The hot tub is a major romantic plus (it can be reserved by the hour) as is the summertime melodrama (theater) the hotel runs. In winter, rates drop by more than 50%, making it a virtual steal. Look online.

Rochester House HOTEL $$
(☏970-385-1920, toll-free 800-664-1920; www.rochesterhotel.com; 721 E 2nd Ave; r $120-260; ☕✳☎☝) Influenced by old Westerns (movie posters and marquee lights adorn the hallways), the Rochester is a little bit of old

Hollywood in the new West. Rooms are spacious, with high ceilings. Two formal sitting rooms, where you're served cookies, and a breakfast room in an old train car, are other perks at this pet-friendly establishment.

Hometown Hostel HOSTEL $
(970-385-4115; www.durangohometownhostel.com; 736 Goeglein Gulch Rd; dm $30; reception 3:30-8pm; P@🛜) This is a brand-new place – a better class of backpackers. It's all-inclusive, with linen, towels, lockers, wi-fi and even sales and lodging tax in the quoted price. There are two single-sex dorms and a larger mixed dorm, and a great common kitchen and lounge area. This is the bee's knees of hostels. Room rates fall with extended stays.

Siesta Motel MOTEL $
(970-247-0741; www.durangosiestamotel.com; 3475 N Main Ave; d $50-170; P) This family-owned motel is one of the town's cheaper options. It's a welcoming place offering spacious and comfortable rooms. There's a little courtyard with a BBQ grill, plus a grassy area with a slide for the kiddies to play on.

Day's End MOTEL $
(970-259-3311; www.daysenddurango.com; 2202 N Main Ave; r from $42; P) The best budget motel bet is on a small creek just north of town. Rooms are well maintained and many have king-size beds. In winter, it offers discounts for skiing at Purgatory. There's an indoor hot tub and BBQ grill by the creek. Pets are welcome.

General Palmer Hotel HOTEL $$
(970-247-4747, toll-free 800-523-3358; www.generalpalmer.com; 567 Main Ave; d $120-225;) A Victorian landmark from 1898, the hotel features pewter four-poster beds, quality linens and even a teddy bear for snuggling. Rooms are small but elegant, and if you tire of TV, there's a collection of board games at the front desk. Check out the cozy library and the relaxing solarium.

✗ Eating

TOP CHOICE **Randy's** STEAK, SEAFOOD, PASTA $$
(970-247-9083; www.randysrestaurant.com; 152 E College Dr; mains $20-25; 5-10pm;) Randy's is a fine-dining establishment serving an eclectic menu of mainly seafood and steak. It's an intimate place that's popular for romantic coupling. Eat between 5pm and 6pm and get the same menu for $12 to $14. Happy hour runs from 5pm to 7pm. Locals

say this is the finest restaurant in town for top-end dining.

Durango Diner DINER FOOD $
(970-247-9889; www.durangodiner.com; 957 Main Ave; mains $7-18; 6am-2pm Mon-Sat, 6am-1pm Sun;) To watch Gary work the grill in this lovable greasy spoon is to be in the presence of greatness. Backed by a staff of button-cute waitresses, Gary's fluid, graceful wielding of a Samurai spatula turns out downright monstrous plates of eggs, smothered potatoes and plate-sized French toast. The best diner in the state? No doubt.

Carver Brewing Co BURGERS, SANDWICHES $$
(970-259-2545; www.carverbrewing.com; 1022 Main Ave; lunch $5-7, dinner $12-18; 6:30am-10pm;) A local institution and longtime favorite among beer drinkers, this relaxed brewery churns out 1000 barrels of brew annually; enjoy a pint with burgers and sandwiches in the outdoor beer garden.

Ore House STEAKHOUSE $$$
(970-247-5707; www.orehouserestaurant.com; 147 E College Dr; mains $20-30; 5-10pm;) The best steakhouse in town, with food served in casual and rustic environs. Order a hand-cut aged steak, or try the steak, crab leg and lobster combo known as the Ore House Grubsteak. It's easily big enough for two people. There's also a large wine cellar.

East by Southwest PAN-ASIAN $$
(970-247-5533; http://eastbysouthwest.com; 160 E College Dr; sushi $4-13, mains $12-24; 11:30am-3pm Mon-Sat, 5-10pm;) Thai, Vietnamese, Indonesian and Japanese cuisine, including a full sushi bar, is served in a congenial low-key setting. The food is delicious and can be washed down with a creative martini or sake cocktail. Locals rave about this establishment.

Olde Tymers Café BURGERS $
(970-259-2990; www.otcdgo.com; 1000 Main Ave; mains $4-10; 11am-10pm;) Voted as having the best burger in Durango by the local paper, the Olde Tymers is popular with the college crowd, especially during $5-burger nights. Well-priced American classics are served at cozy booths under pressed-tin ceilings in a big open dining room or on the patio outside. Ask about the cheap daily specials.

Jean Pierre Bakery SANDWICHES, PASTRIES $
(970-247-7700; www.jeanpierrebakery.com; 601 Main Ave; mains $5-16; 7am-9pm;)

Visit this charming patisserie for a taste of France in Colorado. The mouthwatering delicacies are made from scratch. Don't miss the soup-and-sandwich lunch special ($12), which includes a sumptuous French pastry chosen from the large counter display. Well worth at least one meal.

Drinking & Entertainment

Ska Brewing Company BREWPUB
(970-247-5792; www.skabrewing.com; 225 Girard St; 11am-3pm Mon-Wed, 11am-3pm & 5-8pm Thu, 11am-8pm Fri) Big on flavor and variety, these are the best beers in town. Although the small, friendly tasting-room bar was once mainly a production facility, over the years it's steadily climbed in the popularity charts. Today it is usually jam-packed with friends meeting for an after-work beer.

Despite the hype, the place remains surprisingly laid-back and relaxed. Ska does weekly BBQs with live music and free food. Call for dates – they are never fixed.

Steamworks Brewing BREWPUB
(970-259-9200; www.steamworksbrewing. com; 801 E 2nd Ave; mains $10-15; 1pm-midnight Mon-Fri, 11am-2am Sat & Sun) Industrial meets ski lodge at this popular microbrewery, with high sloping rafters and metal pipes. There's a large bar area, as well as a separate dining room with a Cajun-influenced menu. At night there are DJs and live music.

El Rancho Tavern BAR
(970-259-8111; www.elranchotavern.com; 975 Main Ave) A bar with a long history, this place attracts loads of loyal locals who come to drink their whiskey well into the night. A dive with attitude, its long bar is made for serious boozing. Don't miss the mural on the outside, and there are pool tables in the back. El Rancho gets progressively rowdier as the night progresses.

Lady Falconburgh's PUB
(970-582-9664; www.ladyfalconburgh.biz; 640 Main Ave; 11am-10pm) It's no secret that this place, which has the largest selection of microbrews and imports in the Four Corners region, is popular. There's a brick-and-brass theme with original murals on the walls and more than a hundred beers on offer – 38 of which are on tap.

Durango Brewing Co BREWERY
(970-247-3396; www.durangobrewing.com; 3000 Main Ave; tap room 9am-5pm) These guys concentrate on the brews with taproom tastings and sales open seven days a week.

Diamond Belle Saloon BAR
(970-376-7150; www.strater.com; 699 Main Ave; 11am-late) Ensconced in the imposing 1887 Strater Hotel, this is an elegant and cozy period place right down to the waitress dressed in Victorian-era fishnets and garter, and with a feather in her hair. The piano player pumps out ragtime tunes and takes requests. There are half-price appetizers and drink specials from 4pm to 6pm.

Henry Strater Theatre LIVE MUSIC, COMEDY
(970-375-7160; www.henrystratertheatre. com; 699 Main Ave; adult/child from $20/18) An eclectic program at the famous Henry Strater Theatre sees old-world music-hall shows, live bands, comedy, community theatre and more. The theatre has been operating continuously for nearly 50 years.

Shopping

Pedal the Peaks SPORTING GOODS
(970-259-6880; www.pedalthepeaks. biz; 598b Main Ave; full-suspension rentals $80; 9am-5pm Mon-Sat, 10am-5pm Sun) This specialist bike store offers the works from mountain- and road-bike sales and rentals, custom-worked cycles, trail maps and accessories. The staff are all hardcore riders, and their friendly advice and local knowledge are second to none.

2nd Avenue Sports SPORTING GOODS
(970-247-4511; www.2ndavesports.com; 600 E 2nd Ave; 9am-6pm Mon-Sat, 10am-5pm Sun) This sports store offers skiing and mountain-biking gear for sale and hire.

Maria's Bookshop BOOKS
(970-247-1438; www.mariasbookshop.com; 960 Main Ave; 9am-9pm) Maria's is a good general bookstore – independently owned and well stocked.

Information

Durango Area Tourism Office (970-247-3500, toll-free 800-525-8855; www.durango. org; 111 S Camino del Rio; 8am-5pm Mon-Fri) The visitor center is south of town, at the Santa Rita exit from US 550.

Durango Public Library (970-375-3380; www.durangopubliclibrary.org; 1900 E 3rd Ave; 9am-8pm Mon-Wed, 10am-5:30pm Thu, 9am-5:30pm Fri & Sat) Free internet access.

Mercy Regional Medical Center (☏970-247-4311; www.mercydurango.org; 1010 Three Springs Ave) Outpatient and 24-hour emergency care.

San Juan-Rio Grande National Forest Headquarters (☏970-247-4874; www.fs.fed.us/r2/sanjuan; 15 Burnett Ct; ⊙8am-5pm Mon-Sat) Offers camping and hiking information and maps. It's about a half-mile west on US Hwy 160.

ⓘ Getting There & Away

Durango lies at the junction of US Hwy 160 and US Hwy 550, 42 miles east of Cortez, 49 miles west of Pagosa Springs and 190 miles north of Albuquerque in New Mexico.

AIR Durango-La Plata County Airport (DRO; ☏970-247-8143; www.flydurango.com; 1000 Airport Rd) Durango-La Plata County Airport is 18 miles southwest of Durango via US Hwy 160 and Hwy 172. Both United and Frontier Airlines have direct flights to Denver; US Airways flies to Pheonix.

BUS Greyhound (p376) buses run daily from the Durango Bus Center north to Grand Junction and south to Albuquerque, NM.

ⓘ Getting Around

Check the website of **Durango Transit** (☏970-259-5438; www.getarounddurango.com) for local travel information. All Durango buses are fitted with bicycle racks. The bright-red T shuttle bus trundles up and down Main St. It's free to ride.

Chimney Rock Archaeological Area

Like the architects of the elaborate structures in Chaco Canyon – with which this community was connected – the people of the Chimney Rock Archaeological Area (☏off-season 970-264-2287, visitor cabin 970-883-5359; www.chimneyrockco.org; Hwy 151; per vehicle $10, guided tours adult/child $10/5; ⊙9am-4:30pm mid-May–late Sep, additional evening hours for special events, tours at 9:30am, 10:30am, 1pm & 2pm; ❀) were dedicated astronomers and this was a place of spiritual significance. Remains of 100 permanent structures are at their base of two large red-rock buttes.

Today, the rock monuments remain, though the thriving religious and commercial center has been reduced to sketches in stone – hearths and shafts for ventilation, holes for roof beams and storage areas. The largest pair of buildings here, the Great Kiva and Great House, are both impressive examples of Chacoan architecture. Designated an Archaeological Area and National Historic Site in 1970, the entire area covers more than 4000 acres of the **San Juan National Forest** land. If the local politicos get their way, Chimney Rock Archaeological Area will soon be designated a National Monument.

Pagosa Springs

POP 1815 / ELEV 7126FT

West of Durango, on US 160 at the junction with US 84 south to New Mexico, the open ponderosa pine forests give way to the tourist billboards of Pagosa Springs. Pagosa is a Ute term for 'boiling water' and refers to the town's main draw: hot springs that provide heat for some of the town's 1900 residents. The steam rises from many spots along the San Juan River as it flows past volcanic rock formations in the center of town.

Pagosa Springs is a bit confusing to navigate. There's a historic downtown centered at the intersection of Hot Springs Blvd and US 160. The other developed area of town is filled with condos and vacation rentals along a winding series of roads two miles to the west, over a small rise. For most visitor services, make for the historic downtown.

◎ Sights & Activities

TOP CHOICE **Fred Hartman Art Museum & The Red Ryder Roundup** MUSEUM
(☏970-731-5785; www.harmanartmuseum.com; 85 Harman Park Dr; adult/child under 6yr $4/0.50; ⊙10:30am-5pm Mon-Sat; P❀) The Red Ryder's image might be lost on today's whippersnappers, but Fred Hartman's comic book hero was born in Pagosa Springs, and today Harman's home is a small museum. It's a kitschy and off-beat roadside attraction, but Hartman himself is often on hand to show you around his studio.

The Red Ryder is also the hero of Pagosa Springs' biggest annual event, the Red Ryder Roundup, held on a weekend near July 4. The event includes a large rodeo, an art show and carnival atmosphere, and ends with a fireworks display. It's held across the highway from Hartman's studio.

Springs Resort & Spa SPA
(☏970-264-4168; www.pagosahotsprings.com; 165 Hot Springs Blvd; adult/child from $20/12; ⊙7am-1am Jun-Aug, to 11am Sun-Thu & to 1am Fri & Sat Sep-May) Soaking in the glorious riverside pools here is a must for visitors to the

area. The pool area is impressively decorated; some pools have tumbling waterfalls, others resemble Yellowstone's geysers. The pools front a tangerine Spanish-style mansion (now the changing area) on one side and the San Juan River on the other.

Craggy peaks surround and the air is scented with pine. The healing, mineral-rich waters are drawn from the Great Pagosa Aquifer, which is the largest and deepest hot mineral spring in the world. Each pool is a different size and shape, but all are designed to look as natural as possible, and the views are beyond stupendous. Temperatures vary from 83°F to 111°F. The hottest pool is appropriately named 'the lobster pot.'

Guests here (rooms from $150) enjoy all-you-can-hot-tub privileges, along with commendable rooms. The cheapest are nothing special, but you're paying for the healing waters. The deluxe rooms feature thicker mattresses, higher thread-count sheets, more floor space and kitchenettes.

The terraced pink adobe hotel overlooking the banks of the San Juan also features a spa, offers ski packages and welcomes pets.

Pagosa Outside
RAFTING

(☑970-264-4202; www.pagosaoutside.com; 350 Pagosa St; trips from $34; ⊙10am-6pm, reduced hrs winter; ⊛) In the spring this outfitter loads up its rainbow-colored vans for whitewater trips on the San Juan and Piedra Rivers. Though the rapids only ever reach Class III, the most exciting trip on offer is through Mesa Canyon, which is also a good chance to spot eagles and other wildlife.

Later in the summer, when the flows decrease, the company turns its attention to mountain-biking trips and mountain-bike rentals ($35 per day). The biggest thrill for a guided tour comes with the single-track route at Turkey Creek.

⌯ Sleeping

Since the springs are a year-round draw, hotels in the area hold their rates fairly steady. A number of motels and new hotels sprawl out from the city center on US 160. Usually there's a fairly straightforward equation: the further away from the hot springs, the better the deal.

TOP CHOICE Fireside Inn Cabins
CABINS $$

(☑888-264-9204; www.firesidecabins.com; 1600 E Hwy 160; cabins from $105, 2-bedroom cabins from $174; P⊛⊛⊛⊛) Hands down our favorite place in town – each log cabin comes with the Webber and planters

of wild flowers. And if they're cute from outside, the interiors are even better, with immaculate kitchenettes, wood floors and rustic appointments.

Equestrians love the place because of its corral, and the games for lend at the central office are great for families. For the price, this is head-and-shoulders better than other options in the upmarket category.

Pagosa Huts
CABINS $

(www.pagosa-huts.com; San Juan National Forest; cabins $60; ⊛) These remote, basic huts are perfect for people trying to get out into the national forest, and they are available to both hikers and recreational motorists. Getting here is a little rough – the roads can be a mess in the spring – but they offer excellent solitude. Inquire about availability and exact location through the website.

Alpine Inn Motel
MOTEL $

(☑970-731-4005; www.alpineinnofpagosasprings.com; 8 Solomon Dr; d $59; P⊛@⊛) A converted chain motel, this is an excellent value option near town. The rooms, each with dark carpet and balconies, are a standard size, but the owners are great guides to the local area and there's a continental breakfast on site.

✗ Eating

Pagosa Brewing Company
BREWPUB $$

(☑970-731-2739; www.pagosabrewing.com; 118 N Pagosa Blvd; mains $8-12; ⊙11am-10pm Mon-Sat; ⊛) Brewmaster Tony Simmons is a professional beer judge, and the Poor Richard's Ale is structured with astute standards – the corn and molasses mix is inspired by the tipple of Ben Franklin. After a few, move on to a menu of made-from-scratch pub food, at this, Pagosa's fun dinner spot.

JJ's Riverwalk Restaurant Pub
CONTEMPORARY AMERICAN $$$

(☑970-264-9100; 356 E Hwy 160; mains $15-40; ⊝) Overlooking the San Juan River, JJ's has a great vibe, tasty food, a decent wine list and pleasant service. It can be very spendy, but the menu includes early-bird cheap meals and a nightly happy hour. In summer sit outside on the patio overlooking the river and watch the kayakers float by.

ⓘ Information

Pagosa Springs Area Chamber of Commerce
(☑970-264-2360; www.visitpagosasprings.com; 402 San Juan St; ⊙9am-5pm Mon-Fri)

WOLF CREEK SKI AREA

Riding on a powder day at the **Wolf Creek Ski Area** (☎970-264-5629; www.wolfcreekski. com; Wolf Creek Pass, Hwy 160 E; lift ticket adult/child $52/28, child ski school per half-day $50, beginner $40; ☺Nov–mid-Apr; 🖶), which gets more than 450in of snow per year, feels like being on a tidal wave of snow. Located 25 miles north of Pagosa Springs on US 160, this family-owned ski area is one of Colorado's last and best-kept secrets – at least for now. In recent years major development of the area has been proposed by Red McCombs, a founding father of Clear Channel Communications whose name often pops up on *Forbes* magazine's list of the richest Americans. McCombs' current plan is to create Colorado's newest mega-resort atop Wolf Creek Pass. Environmental groups have dug in their heels to protest the development, which they argue would have an adverse effect on the area's wildlife. At least for now, it's still mostly a locals' place that isn't overrun with the out-of-state crowd and covered in high-end boutiques.

Regardless of the dust-up about its development, Wolf Creek can be an awesome place to ride. The powder can be waist-high after a big storm blows through. The seven lifts service 70 trails, from wide-open bowls to steep tree glades. The on-site ski school has lessons for beginners and children.

For cross-country skiing, many backcountry and groomed trails that lead into quiet, pristine forest are available. It's some of the most remote Nordic skiing in the state. Contact the USFS Pagosa Ranger Station for details.

Those who want to ski the hill more than one day should lodge in Pagosa Springs, on the west side of the pass, or South Fork, on the east.

The Pagosa Springs Area Chamber of Commerce operates a large visitor center located across the bridge from US Hwy 160.

USFS Pagosa Ranger Station (☎970-264-2268; 180 Pagosa St; ☺8am-4:30pm Mon-Fri)

South Fork

POP 400 / ELEV 8300FT

The appeal of visiting South Fork is hardly evident in the low-slung stretch of buildings along US 160, 31 miles west of Monte Vista. But look beyond the borders of town and it's easy to see the draw: situated at the confluence of the South Fork and Rio Grande Rivers, it's an excellent base from which to fish the Gold Medal waters of the Rio Grande.

In ski season, South Fork is a more affordable lodging alternative than Pagosa Springs for skiers at Wolf Creek. Exceptional backcountry hiking in the Weminuche Wilderness of the Rio Grande National Forest, Colorado's largest pristine area, is readily accessible from trailheads near South Fork. An abundance of nearby campgrounds also attracts vacationers who want to enjoy a forested mountain setting.

At South Fork, US 160 turns south from the Rio Grande toward Wolf Creek Pass 18 miles away, and Hwy 149 continues upstream 21 miles to Creede before crossing the Continental Divide to Lake City.

🛏 Sleeping

Ute Bluff Lodge MOTEL $
TOP CHOICE (☎719-873-5595, 800-473-0595; www. uteblufflodge.com; 27680 US Hwy 160; d $74-84, cabins from $94; 🅿☺❄🖶) This impeccably clean hotel is the best option in town. Run by a South Carolina transplant named Debbie, the rooms have new carpet, wood paneling and a great location on the border of USFS land where there are hiking trails. There are also a couple moderately priced cabins here, which are a good option for families.

Blue Creek Lodge LODGE, CABINS $
(☎719-658-2479; 11682 Hwy 149; d $50, cabins $77-120; 🖶) This lodge, 7 miles up the road, is another faux-rustic bed-and-breakfast, restaurant and beauty salon. It's housed in a former saloon with lots of deer heads on the wall and a juicy chicken fried-steak breakfast.

Chinook Lodge & Smokehouse MOTEL $$
(☎719-873-9993, 888-890-9110; www.chinook lodge.net; 29666 US Hwy 160; cabins $75-130; 🅿🖶) Carnivorous folk will appreciate this lodge and smokehouse, where copious meats are smoked on the premises (sample its amazing beef jerky). Guests stay in rustic, century-old cabins, most with handsome rock fireplaces and kitchens.

Spruce Lodge B&B $

(☑719-873-5605, 800-228-5605; 29431 US Hwy 160; d $69, ste $159; 🛜🐾) Bed and breakfast with shared bath are on offer at this woodsy lodge, which is about 1 mile east of the visitors center, and has a relatively plush Jacuzzi room.

🍴 Eating

Chalet Swiss EUROPEAN $$

(☑719-873-1100; 31519 US Hwy 160; mains $15-25) This restaurant, serving continental fare in an elegant, airy dining room, is a bit out of place among the town's roughshod lumberjack joints. Menu highlights are the amazing cheese fondue and whiskey schnitzel.

Rockaway Cafe CAFE FOOD $

(☑719-873-5581; 30333 US Hwy 160; mains $5-12; ⏰7am-6pm; 🛜🐾) This humble, friendly diner sends out a good breakfast of big pancakes and enormous cups of coffee. If you are headed into the wilderness and need to do a little planning, it also has complementary wi-fi and a little book exchange.

ℹ️ Information

Silver Thread Interpretive Center (☑719-873-5512, toll-free 800-571-0881; www.southfork.org; 28 Silver Thread Lane; ⏰9am-5pm Mon-Fri, 10am-4pm Sat-Sun Jun-Aug) The name of South Fork's visitor cente is a reference to the Silver Thread Byway leading to Creede. It has information on outdoor activities and lodging and sells biking and hiking trail maps.

Around South Fork

COLLER STATE WILDLIFE AREA

The grassy riverbanks in the **Coller State Wildlife Area** (Hwy 149) attract elks, deer and moose in winter. From South Fork, follow Hwy 149 toward Creede for about 7 miles, and there's a sign on the left; turn there and you enter the area after a couple hundred yards. You can see bighorn sheep throughout the year on the south-facing Palisade cliffs extending from the Coller State Wildlife Area to Wagon Wheel Gap. At the gap, golden eagles soar above the cliff faces and fish the Rio Grande.

WEMINUCHE WILDERNESS AREA

Named for a band of the Ute tribe, the **Weminuche Wilderness Area** is the most extensive wilderness in Colorado, with an area of more than 700 sq miles. The Weminuche extends west along the Continental Divide from Wolf Creek Pass to the Animas River near Silverton. By early July you can reach Archuleta Lake (11,800ft) near the Divide by following USFS Trail 839 for about 7 miles from the Big Meadows Reservoir (9200ft) along Archuleta Creek into the wilderness area.

Along the Continental Divide National Scenic Trail (USFS Trail 813) you will find many secluded hiking opportunities as the trail passes through 80 miles of the Weminuche Wilderness between Wolf Creek Pass and Stony Pass. One trail of particular interest leads to an undeveloped natural hot spring west of the Divide. To reach **Wolf Creek Pass Hot Spring** take USFS Trail 560 west from the Divide, descending more than 6 miles through the Beaver Creek drainage to the West Fork headwaters of the San Juan River. The spring, with more than 100°F water, is to the right on USFS Trail 561, about half a mile above the trail junction.

To get to the trailhead at Big Meadows Reservoir, travel south on US 160 for 11 miles to the turnoff on the right (to the west). Proceed to the boat-ramp parking area on the north side of the reservoir. You will need maps of both the Rio Grande and San Juan National Forests. Ranger stations for the Rio Grande National Forest are in either Del Norte or Creede; the nearest San Juan National Forest ranger station (p283) is in Pagosa Springs.

Creede & Around

Welcome to the middle of the mountains and the middle of nowhere. Creede is the only incorporated city in Mineral County, which joins neighboring Hinsdale Counties as one of Colorado's least-populated counties: each has less than 900 people.

If you couldn't tell by the name, Mineral County dug its wealth from the ground: underfoot are huge reserves of silver, lead and zinc. Since 1988 all the silver mines of Mineral County have ceased operation and become tourist attractions. Today you can tour the rugged mining landscape north of town, where tremendous mills cling to spectacular cliffs. Below the vertical-walled mouth of Willow Creek Canyon, narrow Creede Ave is a mix of galleries and shops in historic buildings.

For scenic beauty, the country surrounding Creede is difficult to beat. Relatively untrampled-upon trails into the immense surrounding wilderness areas provide appreciative hikers and backpackers with beauty and solitude, as well as access to unique sights like the bizarre volcanic spires and pinnacles of the Wheeler Geologic Area.

⊙ Sights & Activities

Creede Historic Museum
MUSEUM

(☎719-658-2374; 17 Main St; adult $2; ⊙10am-4pm Mon-Sat Memorial Day-Labor Day) Mineral treasures attracted miners by the trainload, but this museum chronicles the more intriguing opportunists and scoundrels who arrived to take advantage of Creede's short-lived prosperity. It's housed in the former railroad depot, behind City Park.

Creede Underground Mining Museum
MUSEUM

(☎719-658-0811; 407 N Loma Ave; adult/child $5/3; ⊙10am-4pm Jun-Aug, 10am-3pm Sep-May, closed weekends Dec-Feb; ⛢) Opened in 1992, this fascinating museum was hewn from the ground by mine workers, and the tours, which really bring home the grim reality of life in the mines, are also led by miners. It's a chilling exhibit in more ways than one: with the temperature a steady 51°F year-round, visitors are advised to bring jackets.

Hiking & Backpacking

The hike through the upland meadow called Phoenix Park is especially appealing, as it begins at the King Solomon Mill at the top of East Willow Creek Canyon and proceeds past waterfalls and beaver ponds. You can pick up maps at the **Amethyst Emporium** (☎719-658-2430; 129 N Main St; ⊙9am-6pm Mon-Sat Jun-Aug).

Hiking options are nearly limitless within the extensive Weminuche and La Garita Wilderness Areas on either side of the Rio Grande Valley. Colorado's largest wilderness naturally presents many additional options beyond the scope of this book. A good source of information if you wish to explore the Continental Divide east of Stony Pass is Dennis Gebhardt's *A Backpacking Guide to the Weminuche Wilderness*. You can rent hiking packs and tents at San Juan Sports.

Rafting

On the Rio Grande below Wagon Wheel Gap, scenic float trips with a few rapids and quality fishing are the primary attractions of the 20-mile run to South Fork. A good place to put in along Hwy 149 is the Goose Creek Rd Bridge immediately west of the gap. During high water, rafters should beware the closely spaced railroad bridge abutments at Wagon Wheel Gap. Rafting tours and equipment rental are available from **Mountain Man Rafting & Tours** (☎719-658-2663; www.mountainmantours.com; 702 S Main St).

Fishing

Above the Wagon Wheel Gap on the Rio Grande, anglers have two choice sections of the river with special regulations for catch-and-release of rainbow trout using either artificial fly or lure. There's a two-bag limit on brown trout more than 12in long. One section between Creede's Willow Creek and Wagon Wheel Gap is mostly private and boat access is necessary. Further upstream, however, you can fish from public lands on both sides of the Rio Grande at USFS Marshall Park and Rio Grande campgrounds.

The fishing is good at Ruby Lakes (11,000ft), accessible by USFS Trail 815, a 4-mile hike or horseback ride along Fern Creek. The trailhead is about 1¼ miles along USFS Rd 522, 16 miles southwest of Craig off Hwy 149. The Brown Lakes State Wildlife Area (9840ft) is stocked by the Division of Wildlife (DOW) with rainbow and brook trout, but the large browns and native cutthroat are the real attraction. The lakes are surrounded by spruce and fir forests and are located 2 miles west of Hwy 149 and the USFS Silver Thread Campground, 25 miles west of Creede.

Fishing supplies, information and guide services are available at the **Rio Grande Angler** (☎719-658-2955; www.southforkanglers.com; 13 S Main St; ⊙10am-6pm Mon-Sat Jun-Aug). Guided river fishing is offered by Mountain Man Rafting & Tours.

Bachelor Loop

While in Creede, bouncing along the 17 mile–loop tour of the abandoned mines and town sites immediately north of town is a fun, DIY adventure and a good way to punish the rental car. The loop is well signposted and is easy to follow with a 25-page booklet ($1) from the Chamber of Commerce. It offers outstanding views of La Garita Mountains (San Luis Peak is 14,014ft) and Rio Grande Valley. Sections of the road are very narrow and steep, but not difficult, so long as the road is dry and you drive slowly enough to avoid destroying your car.

MOUNTAIN BIKING

Creede is a serious base for mountain biking, and free from the crowds which jam up more easily accessed trails in other parts of the mountains. It's also a great area to hike and bike, if you're interested in seeing the dilapidated mining equipment that is slowly being overtaken by nature. The main area to bike is about 9 miles north of town, starting from the West Willow Creek trailhead. Although it's a rough road, you won't need a 4WD most of the year. Even so, it's a tough start when you get on the bike: the 2000ft rise in elevation during the initial 2 miles along West Willow Creek was called the 'Black Pitch' by miners. Below the Black Pitch, failed brakes on loaded teamster wagons often pulled unfortunate animals to their end at Dead Horse Flats. Continue up this treacherous section to arrive at the Amethyst, one of Colorado's richest silver mines. You can still see part of the high-rotary tram system that sent ore down the steep canyon. You can see remnants of the tall towers up the steep slope to the east of the Black Pitch.

Some cyclists may prefer to tour mines along the gentler grades of East Willow Creek, which are accessed via the same trailhead.

An excellent illustrated tour booklet ($1) prepared by local historians is available from the Creede Chamber of Commerce, the USFS, the Creede Museum or from a dispenser at the first interpretive stop: the West Willow–East Willow Creek junction, immediately north of the rock spires that mark the gateway to Willow Creek Canyon.

You can rent a mountain bike for $19 per day at **San Juan Sports** (☎719-658-2359, 888-658-0851; 102 Main St; bike rental per day $19; ⊙10am-5pm). The shop also carries a thorough collection of USGS topographic maps. Guided mountain-bike tours and bike rentals are offered by Mountain Man Rafting & Tours (p285).

Wheeler Geologic Area

Visiting the dramatic stone forms of the Wheeler Geologic Area – resembling rows of sharp animal teeth, and bearing names like City of Gnomes, White-Shrouded Ghosts, Dante's Lost Souls – makes a specular and fairly strenuous full-day hike. Carved by wind and rain into volcanic tuff framed by evergreen forest, the bizarre area was declared a national monument 1908. But the remote 11,000ft setting near the Continental Divide kept all but the hardiest visitors away and by 1950 its monument status was removed. In 1993, the Wheeler Geologic Area was again granted wilderness protection when federal lawmakers approved the area's addition to La Garita Wilderness.

The USFS East Bellows Trail (Trail 790) is a 17-mile roundtrip hike that climbs nearly 2000ft from the Hanson's Mill campground to the base of the geologic formations. To get to the trailhead, drive southeast along Hwy 149 for slightly more than 7 miles and turn left on USFS Rd 600 (Pool Table Rd). Continue along this road for 9½ miles to Hanson's Mill campground. The trail affords some great views and there are lots of places to camp along the way. From Hanson's Mill there is also a 14-mile 4WD road that leads to the area.

North Clear Creek Falls

Twenty-five miles west of Creede and only half a mile from signs on Hwy 149, the impressive falls are visible from an overlook on the fenced edge of a deep gorge. From the parking area a short walk over the ridge away from the falls takes you to another viewpoint above the sheer-walled canyon with Bristol Head in the distance. Far below your feet a metal aqueduct carries Clear Creek away from its natural course to the Santa Maria Reservoir as part of a massive effort to regulate the flow of the Rio Grande headwaters.

🛏 Sleeping

Wason Ranch   RANCH $$$
(☎719-658-2413; www.wasonranch.com; 19082 Hwy 149; d $350, cabins $325, 3-night minimum; 🛗) Two miles southeast of Creede, this ranch has two-bedroom cabins equipped with kitchenettes (available May through October). Riverside cottages with three bedrooms and two baths are available year-round with a minimum stay of three days. The ranch also offers fly-fishing lessons, fishing guides and a dory.

Creede Hotel B&B   HOTEL $$
(☎719-658-2608; www.creedehotel.com; 120 N Main St; d $105-115) This hotel has four rooms with private bathrooms. Both the hotel and

its excellent restaurant are closed October to May.

Bruce's Snowshoe Lodge
MOTEL $

(☎719-658-2315; www.snowshoelodge.net; cnr 202 East 8th & Hwy 149; d $65-139; ☐) Rates at this clean, friendly place, on the southeast edge of town, include a continental breakfast and, unlike a lot of places around, it's open all year.

Antlers Rio Grande Lodge
RANCH $$

(☎719-658-2423; www.antlerslodge.com; 26222 Hwy 149; d from $129, cabins per week from $930; ⊕) Families are welcome at Antlers Ranch, which is 5 miles southwest of Creede, and offers motel-style rooms and cabins on both banks of the Rio Grande.

Soward Ranch
RANCH $$

(☎719-658-2295; 4698 Middle Creek Rd; cabins $90-110; ⊕) About 8 miles southwest of Creede is this beautiful ranch, which opens May to October. It's the only 'centennial' ranch in the area – meaning it's been operated by the same family for more than 100 years. Guests can enjoy fishing from four lakes as well as 4 miles of trout creek on the 1500-acre property.

Twelve cabins range in price depending on size and amenities. To get there, take Hwy 149 southwest for 7 miles, turn left on Middle Creek Rd, continue for a mile and when you get to the fork in the road, bear right, following the signs to the ranch.

ℹ Information

Creede/Mineral County Chamber of Commerce (☎719-658-2374, 800-327-2102; www.creede.com; 904 S Main St; ⊕8am-5pm Mon-Sat Jun-Aug, from 9am Mon-Fri Dec-Feb) Pick up a copy of an excellent illustrated tour booklet ($1) prepared by local historians.

USFS Divide District Ranger Station (☎719-658-2556; cnr 3rd St & Creede Ave; ⊕8:30am-4pm Mon-Fri)

ℹ Getting There & Away

Creede is 23 miles northwest of South Fork on the Silver Thread National Scenic Byway, which follows Hwy 149 for 75 miles between South Fork and Lake City.

Lake City & Around

POP 380 / ELEV 8671FT

It's hard to believe that this tiny town, lovingly referred to by residents as the 'flyspeck' seat of Hinsdale County, was once

known as the Metropolis of the Mines. But back in the 1870s, while so many other mining towns would swell and dwindle with the prosperity of the lodes, Lake City boasted a population of 5000 people who seemed here to stay. Settlers built Greek and Gothic Revival buildings and tree-lined streets that reflected a nostalgia for their homes back east. Today, less than a fifth of that population remains, but Lake City is a quiet, remote base for exploring the mountains.

Lake City is on Hwy 149 (Gunnison Ave in town), 47 miles south of the intersection with US 50, which in turn leads west to Gunnison and east to Montrose. It lies west of the Continental Divide at Spring Creek Pass and the giant Slumgullion landslide, which dammed the Lake Fork of the Gunnison River and formed Lake San Cristobal south of town. To the west rises Uncompahgre Peak and four others peaks over 14,000ft, creating a barrier between Lake City and Ouray. This wall of mountains is crossed only by the USFS Alpine Byway, which requires 4WD vehicles or a mountain bike and a strong pair of legs. From Lake City it's 50 miles south on Hwy 149 to Creede.

🏃 Activities

Sportsman Outdoors & Fly Shop
BIKE RENTALS

(☎970-944-2526; www.lakecitysportsman.com; 238 S Gunnison Ave; bike rental per day $25, tent rental 1st/subsequent night $15/10, car camping kit $125/100; ⊕7am-7pm Jun-Aug, 9am-6pm Tue-Sat Sep-Dec, 10am-4pm Jan-April) This full-service outfitter is a godsend in Lake City. It rents camping and fishing gear, bikes and has tons of local information, plus leads trips into the area.

Alpine Loop Byway

After 16 miles up Hensen Creek, this unpaved byway becomes a rugged route over Engineer Pass suited only for Jeeps and mountain bikes headed to Ouray. Another part of the 4WD loop heads south along the Lake Fork of the Gunnison River and crosses Cinnamon Pass to Silverton. Fat-tire fans are for rent at the Sportsman Outdoors & Fly Shop. You can rent from a fleet of cute red Jeeps at the **Pleasant View Resort** (☎970-944-2262; www.pleasantviewresort.net; 549 S Gunnison Ave; cabins from $125-175, Jeep rentals from $165; ☐). The resort is at the south end of Lake City, on Hwy 149 near mile marker 72. There's a lot of great information about driving, biking and hiking on the byway's website.

Hiking & Backpacking

Alpine wildflowers are a prime attraction on the many summer trails in the area. West of Lake City and north of Hensen Creek is the Big Blue Wilderness Area, featuring many stunning peaks that are more than 13,000ft, including two 14ers: Uncompahgre Peak and Wetterhorne Peak.

Northeast of Lake City, the Powderhorn Wilderness Area features the 4-mile Bureau of Land Management (BLM) Trail 3030 to Powderhorn Lakes, crossing a huge alpine meadow loaded with wildflowers.

South of Lake San Cristobal, day hikes in the BLM's Alpine Loop Byway offer high altitude scenery and peak ascents, but the lower parts of most trails are shared with 4WD vehicles that disperse wildlife and disrupt the solitude.

You can rent tents and other gear in Lake City, at Sportsman Outdoors & Fly Shop (p287), which packages together a 'car camping' kit. The shop also has complete information and leads trips into the area.

Rafting

Local white-water enthusiasts enjoy the uncrowded Lake Fork of the Gunnison River stretching from High Bridge Creek, 8 miles north of Lake City, for 30 miles to the BLM Redbridge Campground, where the river is stilled as it enters Blue Mesa Reservoir. On the way, the river passes through the spectacular volcanic columns breached by the river to form the Gate, a giant notch visible for miles. There are two companies that raft in the area, Scenic River Tours (☑970-641-3131; www.scenicrivertours.com; 703 W Tomichi Ave; 2-/5-hr tour $35/96; ⊛), out of Gunni-

son, and Three Rivers Resort (☑970-641-1303, toll-free 888-761-3474; www.3riversresort.com; 130 County Rd 742; rafting trips $35-100; ⊛), from Almont.

Nordic Skiing

For cross-country skiing there's an excellent opportunity in the area thanks to the Hinsdale Haute Route (☑970-944-2269; www.hinsdalehauteroute.org; yurts 1st night $100, subsequent nights $75), a nonprofit organization that maintains four yurts on the Divide between Lake City and Creede. Among the niche of hut-to-hut backcountry skiers, this system has a flawless reputation for the scenery and the quality of the huts. Even novice skiers can enjoy the 2 miles of backcountry travel from Hwy 149 to an overnight stay at the first yurt. The yurts sleep up to eight people, and have cooking facilities.

🛏 Sleeping

TOP CHOICE Matterhorn Motel   MOTEL $
(☑970-944-2210; www.matterhornmotel.com; 409 Bluff St; d with/without$89/99; ⟦⊛⟧) Our favorite motel in the downtown area is the Matterhorn, a smartly remodeled 1940s motel with red trim and scalloped siding, where some rooms have kitchenettes

Inn At The Lake   MOTEL $$
(☑936-499-1323; www.innatthelake.org; 600 Country Rd 33; d from $90; ⟦P⊛⟧) On the shores of Lake San Cristobal, this is a log-fitted motel where potted flowers sway in the breeze. It has 10 rooms, all of which enjoy a view of the water.

Camping & Cabins

There are a couple of private campgrounds in town, but the state and federal land nearby is a better option. For RVs, try the Elkhorn RV Resort & Cabins (☑970-944-

---

SLUMGULLION SLIDE

In AD 1270 a catastrophic earth flow moved almost 5 miles down the mountainside and dammed the Gunnison River to form Lake San Cristobal, creating Colorado's second-largest lake. The land is still moving, but it has slowed down; today the persistent flow that began about 350 years ago and continues to advance between 2ft and 20ft per year. This active section of the slide, whose name comes from the yellowish mud's resemblance to the watery miner's stew, is mostly barren, and spotted in patches with forests of crooked trees. It's best viewed in the morning from Windy Point Overlook, south of town off Hwy 149, at 10,600ft. Another good view is from the top of Cannibal Plateau Trail (USFS Trail 464), the site where prospector Alfred Packer is said to have had his companions for dinner. The trailhead is below Slumgullion Campground, off Cebolla Creek Rd.

When the wind whips through the greying wood frames at Animas Forks, and clear, cold air whistles through the former bedrooms and parlors of long-dead 19th-century prospectors, there's something truly ghostly about this abandoned mining town.

It's one of the most photogenic stops on the Alpine Loop. If you're coming up the road from Lake City in the middle of the summer, inquire with locals before you attempt the trip here in a 2WD vehicle, but you'll probably make it. In spring or fall, you'll probably need a 4WD. In winter? Your best bet is a dogsled.

This high mountain mining outpost suffered an unfortunately timed founding in 1883, the year the bottom fell out of the silver market. The community of 300 residents limped along for a few years; many survived by spending the brutal winters further down the mountain and returning in the warmer months. But the last mill closed in 1910 and the last resident moved away in 1920. Today, the 10 remaining buildings are a playground for yellow-tailed marmots and the alpine plain is punctuated with shells of a couple cars, wildflowers and rusting mining equipment. The biggest home is the grand, Gothic Duncan residence, which you can enter safely thanks to the efforts of the BLM, which has stabilized many of the dilapidated structures.

2920; www.elkhornrvresort.com; 713 N Bluff St; cabins $44-59, sites $20-33; P 🛜 🐕), where there are RV hookups, some utilitarian tent camping and simple 'camping cabins,' which come without linens. Dispersed camping is available on USFS lands along Hensen Creek immediately east of town. Free BLM riverside campsites are available at the Gate, 20 miles north next to Hwy 149, and at Gateview and Redbridge along Lake County Rd 25, which continues beside the river where Hwy 149 turns east from the river course.

Nine miles southwest of town, immediately below Slumgullion Pass (elevation 11,361ft), the USFS Slumgullion Campground offers 21 campsites for $10 per site. The **Wupperman Campground** (📞970-944-2225; County Rd 33; sites $15; 🐕) on Lake San Cristobal is a good option for those who want to be near the water. Sites are $15.

Additional primitive sites are available by continuing east on Cebolla Creek Rd, where rarely used trails enter La Garita Wilderness Area in the Gunnison National Forest's Cebolla Ranger District.

🍴 Eating

Alpine Moose Lodge   AMERICAN $$
(📞970-944-2415; www.alpinemooselodge.com; 1221 N Hwy 149; mains $12-19; ⏰8am-8pm Jun-Aug, reduced hrs Sep-May) If you want to eat something with a fork, and not just your hands, try this lodge. It's hearty, as you might expect for a mountain lodge, but plates are flavorful and presented with style.

Lake City Bakery   PASTRIES $
(📞970-944-2613; 922 Hwy 149) The best snacks in town come from this to-go bakery just north of town. It is only open in the summer, but the pies and doughnuts are delicious and always very fresh.

ℹ️ Information

Lake City/Hinsdale County Chamber of Commerce (📞970-944-2527, 800-569-1874; www.lakecity.com; 800 Gunnison Ave; ⏰1-4pm Mon, Tue, Thu & Fri) The chamber also acts as the USFS and BLM visitors center, selling topo maps and offering free trail information. Booklets with maps of local fishing spots area available for $1.

MESA VERDE & THE FOUR CORNERS

Mesa Verde National Park
ELEV 7000–8000FT

More than 700 years after its inhabitants disappeared, the mystery of Mesa Verde (📞970-529-4465; www.nps.gov/meve; 7-day pass private cars/motorcycles $15/8 Apr-Aug 6, $10/5 Sep-May 31; P 🐕) remains unsolved. It is here that a civilization of Ancestral Puebloans appears to have vanished into thin air in the 1300s. Today their last known home is preserved as Mesa Verde, a fascinating, if slightly eerie, national park. Anthropologists will love it here; Mesa Verde is unique among American national parks in its focus on maintaining this civilization's cultural relics rather than its natural treasures.

Ancestral Puebloan sites are found throughout the canyons and mesas of the park, perched on a high plateau south of Cortez and Mancos. If you only have time for a short visit, check out the Chapin Mesa Museum (p292) and try a walk through the Spruce Tree House (p292), where you can climb down a wooden ladder into the cool chamber of a kiva.

Mesa Verde rewards travelers who set aside a day or more to take the ranger-led tours of Cliff Palace (p292) and Balcony House (p292), explore Wetherill Mesa (the quieter side of canyon), linger around the museum or participate in one of the campfire programs run at Morefield Campground (p293).

Preserving the Ancestral Puebloan sites while accommodating ever-increasing numbers of visitors continues to challenge the National Park Service (NPS). The NPS strictly enforces the Antiquities Act, which prohibits the removal or destruction of any antiquities and prohibits public access to many of the approximately 4000 known Ancestral Puebloan sites.

The North Rim summit at Park Point (8571ft) towers more than 2000ft above the Montezuma Valley. From Park Point the mesa gently slopes southward to a 6000ft elevation above the Mancos River in the Ute Mountain Tribal Park. Parallel canyons, typically 500ft below the rim, dissect the mesa-top and carry the drainage southward. Mesa Verde National Park occupies 81 sq miles of the northernmost portion of the mesa and contains the largest and most frequented cliff dwellings and surface sites.

Orientation

The park entrance is off US 160, midway between Cortez and Mancos. From the entrance, it's about 21 miles to park headquarters, Chapin Mesa Museum and Spruce Tree House. Along the way are Morefield Campground (4 miles), the panoramic viewpoint at Park Point (8 miles) and the Far View Visitor Center (p294) opposite the Far View Lodge (p294) – about 11 miles. Towed vehicles are not allowed beyond Morefield Campground.

South from park headquarters, Mesa Top Rd consists of two one-way circuits. Turn left about a quarter mile from the start of Mesa Top Rd to visit Cliff Palace and Balcony House on the east loop. From the junction with the main road at Far View Visitor Center, the 12-mile mountainous Wetherill Mesa Rd snakes along the North Rim, acting as a natural barrier to tour buses and indifferent travelers. The road is open only from Memorial Day in late May to Labor Day in early September.

History

A US army lieutenant recorded the spectacular cliff dwellings in the canyons of Mesa Verde in 1849–50. The large number of sites on Ute tribal land, and their relative inaccessibility, protected the majority of these antiquities from pothunters.

The first scientific investigation of the sites in 1874 failed to identify Cliff Palace, the largest cliff dwelling in North America. Discovery of the 'magnificent city' occurred only when local cowboys Richard Wetherill and Charlie Mason were searching for stray cattle in 1888. The cowboys exploited their 'discovery' for the next 18 years by guiding both amateur and trained archaeologists to the site, particularly to collect the distinctive black-on-white pottery.

When artifacts started being shipped overseas, Virginia McClurg of Colorado Springs was motivated to embark on a long campaign to preserve the site and its contents. McClurg's efforts led Congress to protect artifacts on federal land, with the passage of the Antiquities Act establishing Mesa Verde National Park in 1906.

◉ Sights

PARK POINT

The fire lookout at Park Point (8571ft) is the highest elevation in the park and offers panoramic views. To the north are the 14,000ft peaks of the San Juan Mountains; in the northeast are the 12,000ft crests of the La Plata Mountains; to the southwest, beyond the southward sloping Mesa Verde plateau, is the distant volcanic plug of Shiprock; and to the west is the prone, humanlike profile of Sleeping Ute Mountain.

CHAPIN MESA

There is no other place in Mesa Verde where so many remnants of Ancestral Puebloan settlements are clustered so closely together, providing an opportunity to see and compare examples of all phases of construction – from pothouses to Pueblo villages to the elaborate multiroom cities tucked into cliff recesses. Pamphlets describing the

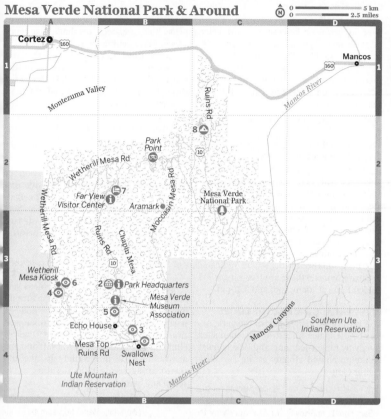

SOUTHWEST COLORADO MESA VERDE NATIONAL PARK

Mesa Verde National Park & Around

◎ Sights
1 Balcony House	B4
2 Chapin Mesa Museum	B3
3 Cliff Palace	B4
4 Long House	A3
5 Spruce Tree House	B4
6 Step House	A3

🛏 Sleeping
7 Far View Lodge	B2
8 Morefield Campground	C2

Eating
Far View Terrace Café	(see 7)
Metate Room	(see 7)

most excavated sites are available at either the visitor center or Chapin Mesa Museum.

On the upper portion of Chapin Mesa are the Far View Sites, which make up perhaps the most densely settled area in Mesa Verde after 1100. The large-walled Pueblo sites at Far View House enclose a central kiva and planned room layout that was originally two stories high. To the north is a small row of rooms and an attached circular tower that likely used to extend just above the ad-

jacent 'pygmy forest' of piñon pine and juniper trees. This tower is one of 57 in Mesa Verde that may once have served as watchtowers, religious structures or astronomical observatories for agricultural schedules.

South from park headquarters, the 6-mile Mesa Top Rd circuit connects 10 excavated mesa-top sites, three accessible cliff dwellings and many vantages of inaccessible cliff dwellings from the mesa rim. It's open 8am to sunset.

Chapin Mesa Museum
MUSEUM

(970-529-4475; www.nps.gov/meve; Chapin Mesa Rd; admission included with park entry; 8am-6:30pm Apr–mid-Oct, 8am-5pm mid-Oct–Apr; P) The Chapin Mesa Museum has exhibits pertaining to the park. It's a good first stop. Staff at the museum provide information on weekends when the park headquarters are closed.

FREE Spruce Tree House
ARCHEOLOGICAL SITE

(Chapin Mesa Rd; admission included with park entry; 8:30am-6:30pm Apr-Sep 6, 9am-6:30pm Sep 7-Oct 16, 9am-5pm daily Oct 17-May 30; P) This Ancestral Puebloan ruin is the most accessible of the archaeological sites although the half-mile round trip access track is still a moderately steep climb. Spruce Tree House was once home to 60 or 80 people and its construction began around AD 1210. Like other sites, the old walls and houses have been stabilized.

During winter, there are free ranger-led guided tours at 10am, 1pm and 3:30pm.

CLIFF PALACE & MESA TOP LOOPS

This is the most visited part of the park. Access to the major Ancestral Puebloan sites is only by ranger-led tour, and tickets must be pre-purchased already at the Far View Visitor Center.

Cliff Palace
ARCHEOLOGICAL SITE

(Cliff Palace Loop; one-hour guided tour $3; 9am-5pm 11 Apr-Nov 6;) The only way to see the superb Cliff Palace is to take the hour-long ranger-led tour. The tour retraces the steps taken by the Ancestral Puebloans – visitors must climb down a stone stairway and four 10 ft ladders. This grand representative of engineering achievement, with 217 rooms and 23 kivas, provided shelter for 250 or 300 people.

Its inhabitants were without running water. However, springs across the canyon, below Sun Temple, were most likely their primary water sources. The use of small 'chinking' stones between the large blocks is strikingly similar to Ancestral Puebloan construction at distant Chaco Canyon.

Balcony House
ARCHEOLOGICAL SITE

(Cliff Palace Loop; one-hour guided tour $3; 9am-5pm Apr11-Nov 6; P) Tickets are required for the one-hour guided tours of Balcony House, on the east side of the Cliff Palace Loop. A visit is quite an adventure and will challenge anyone's fear of heights

or small places. You'll be rewarded with outstanding views of Soda Canyon, 600ft below the sandstone overhang that once served as the ceiling for 35 to 40 rooms.

The Balcony House tour requires you to descend a 100 ft-long staircase into the canyon, then climb a 32 ft-tall ladder, crawl through a 12 ft-long tunnel and climb an additional 60 ft of ladders and stone steps to get out. It's the most challenging tour in the park but might just be the most rewarding, not to mention fun!

WETHERILL MESA

The less-frequented western portion of Mesa Verde offers a comprehensive display of Ancestral Pueblo relics. The Badger House Community consists of a short trail connecting four excavated surface sites depicting various phases of Ancestral Puebloan development.

Long House
ARCHEOLOGICAL SITE

(Wetherill Mesa Rd; one-hour guided tour $3; Apr-Sep 6;) On the Wetherill Mesa side of the canyon is Long House. It's a strenuous place to visit and can only be done as part of a ranger-led guided tour (organised from the visitor center). Access involves climbing three ladders – two at 15ft and one at 4ft – and a 0.75-mile round-trip hike, and there's an aggregate 130ft elevation to descend and ascend.

FREE Step House
ARCHEOLOGICAL SITE

(Wetherill Mesa Rd; admission included with park entry; Apr-Sep 6) Step House was initially occupied by Modified Basketmaker peoples residing in pithouses, and later became the site of a Classic Pueblo–period masonry complex with rooms and kivas. The 0.75-mile trail to Step House involves a 100 ft descent and ascent.

Activities

Hiking

Hiking is a great way to explore the park, but remember to follow the rules. Backcountry access is specifically forbidden and fines are imposed on anyone caught wandering off designated trails or entering cliff dwellings without a ranger. Please respect these necessary regulations so that the fragile and irreplaceable archaeological sights and artifacts remain protected for centuries to come.

When hiking in Mesa Verde always carry water and avoid cliff edges. Trails can be muddy and slippery after summer rains and winter snows, so wear appropri ate footwear. Most park trails, except the Soda Canyon Trail, are strenuous and involve steep elevation changes. Hikers must register at the respective trailheads before venturing out.

The 2.8-mile Petroglyph Loop Trail is accessed from Spruce Tree House. It follows a path beneath the edge of a plateau before making a short climb to the top of the mesa, where you'll have good views of the Spruce and Navajo Canyons. This is the only trail in the park where you can view petroglyphs.

The 2.1-mile Spruce Canyon Loop Trail also begins at Spruce Tree House and descends to the bottom of Spruce Tree Canyon. It's a great way to see the canyon bottoms of Mesa Verde.

Mountain Biking

Finding convenient parking at the many stops along Mesa Top Rd is no problem for those with bikes. Only the hardy will want to enter the park by bike and immediately face the grueling 4-mile ascent to Morefield Campground, quickly followed by a narrow tunnel ride to reach the North Rim. An easier option is to unlimber your muscles and mount up at Morefield, Far View Visitor Center or park headquarters.

Skiing & Snowshoeing

Winter is a special time in Mesa Verde. The crowds disperse and the cliff dwellings sparkle in the snow. The skies are often blue and sunny and you may be the only person around. In recent years there has been enough snow to ski or snowshoe on most winter days after a snowstorm (although Colorado's dry climate and sunshine cause the snow to melt quickly). Before setting out, check the current snow conditions by calling the park headquarters (p294).

Two park roads have been designated for cross-country skiing and snowshoeing when weather permits. The Cliff Palace Loop Rd is a 6-mile, relatively flat, loop located off the Mesa Top Loop Rd. The road is closed to vehicles after the first snowfall, so you won't have to worry about vehicular traffic. Park at the closed gate and glide 1 mile to the Cliff Palace overlook, continuing on past numerous other scenic stopping points. The Morefield Campground Loop Rds offer multiple miles of relatively flat terrain. The campground is closed in winter, but skiers and snowshoers can park at the gate and explore to their heart's content.

☞ Tours

The NPS and the park concessioner Aramark (☎602-331-5210; www.visitmesaverde.com) run various organized tours for walkers as well as small-group bus tours.

Wetherill Mesa Experience HIKING (per person $35; ⊙departs 9:45am late May-early Sep;) Limited to 14 people, this five-hour ranger-led walking tour departs from the Wetherill Mesa Kiosk (Wetherill Mesa Rd;). Binoculars are recommended for walkers as the trail has superb views across the canyon to multiple cliff dwellings.

Spring House Hiking Tour HIKING (per person $35; ⊙8am, May 4–Sep 30) If you're really fit and well decked out with hiking boots, sun protection and adequate water, you'll really enjoy this premium experience. Rangers lead these 6-mile interpretive hiking tours that take eight hours and involve strenuous climbs and descents, and rough trails. Remote sites such as Buzzard House and Teakettle House are part of the itinerary.

⚑ Festivals & Events

12 Hours of Mesa Verde MOUNTAIN BIKE RACE (www.12hoursofmesaverde.com; per rider early-bird/regular $65/80; ⊙May) This annual 12-hour relay-endurance bike event is popular. Teams race against each other over an incredible network of trails across the national park. All proceeds raised go to the Montezuma County Partners – a mentoring program for youth at risk.

🛏 Sleeping

There are plenty of accommodation options in nearby Cortez and Mancos, and Mesa Verde can be easily visited as a day trip from Durango (36 miles to the east). Within the national park, visitors can stay in luxury at the lodge, or rough it camping. For something in between, rent one of the canvas tents with cots at Morefield Campground. An overnight stay in the park allows convenient access to the many sites during the best viewing hours, participation in evening programs and the sheer pleasure of watching the sun set over Sleeping Ute Mountain from the tranquility of the mesa top.

Morefield Campground CAMPING $ (☎970-529-4465; www.nps.gov/meve; N Rim Rd; campsite $20, canvas tents from $40; ⊙May–mid-Oct;) Gourmet campers will dig the big canvas tents kitted out with two cots and a lantern. The park's camping option, located 4 miles from the entrance gate, also has 445 regular tent sites on grassy grounds conveniently located near Morefield Village. The village has a general store, gas station, restaurant, showers and laundry.

Free evening campfire programs take place nightly from Memorial Day (May) to Labor Day (September) at the Morefield Campground Amphitheater.

Far View Lodge LODGE **$$**
(☑970-529-4421, toll-free 800-449-2288; www.visitmesaverde.com; N Rim Rd; r from $100; ☺mid-Apr-Oct; 🅿🐕❄👶) Perched on a mesa top 15 miles inside the park entrance, this tasteful Pueblo-style lodge has 150 Southwestern-style rooms, some with kiva fireplaces. Don't miss sunset over the mesa from your private balcony. Standard rooms don't have air con (or TV) and summer daytimes can be hot. You can even bring your dog for an extra $10 per night.

🍴 Eating

Metate Room CONTEMPORARY AMERICAN **$$**
(☑800-449-2288; www.visitmesaverde.com; N Rim Rd; mains $15-25; ☺5-7:30pm year-round, & 7-10am Apr–mid-Oct; 🐕🍴👶) This restaurant, located in the Far View Lodge, has an innovative menu inspired by Native American food and flavors. Try the oven-roasted chicken breast with green chili stuffing, and buffalo fajitas.

Far View Terrace Café CAFE FOOD **$**
(☑970-529-4421, toll-free 800-449-2288; www.visitmesaverde.com; N Rim Rd; dishes from $5; ☺7-10am, 11am-3pm & 5-8pm May–mid-Oct; 🐕🍴👶) Housed in Far View Lodge immediately south of the visitor center, this self-service place offers reasonably priced meals. Don't miss the house special – the Navajo Taco.

ℹ Information

MAPS Good maps are issued to visitors at the national park gate on entry. Quality topographical maps can be bought at the visitor center and the museum as well as in stores in Durango and Cortez.

TOURIST INFORMATION Far View Visitor Center (☑800-305-6053, 970-529-5034; www.nps.gov/meve; N Rim Rd; ☺8am-7pm daily Jun-early Sep, 8am-5pm early Sep–mid-Oct, closed mid-Oct–May; 👶) The Far View Visitor Center, 15 miles from the entrance, where visitors must buy the $3 tickets for tours

of the magnificent Cliff Palace, Balcony House or Long House. The (far) views across the red-desert tablelands are superb and provide excellent geographical context to the story of the Ancestral Puebloan people.

Mesa Verde Museum Association (☑970-529-4445, toll-free 800-305-6053; www.mesaverde.org; Chapin Mesa Rd; ☺8am-6:30pm Apr–mid-Oct, 8am-5pm mid-Oct–Apr; 👶) Attached to the Chapin Mesa Museum, this nonprofit organization sponsors research activities and exhibits. It has an excellent selection of materials on the Ancestral Puebloans and modern tribes in the American Southwest, and has books, posters and glossy calendars for sale.

Park Headquarters (☑970-529-4465; www.nps.gov/meve; Chapin Mesa Rd; 7-day park entry per vehicle $10, cyclists, hikers & motorcyclists $5; ☺8am-5pm Mon-Fri; 👶) The Mesa Verde National Park entrance is off US 160, midway between Cortez and Mancos. From the entrance it is 21 miles to the park headquarters. You can get road information and the word on park closures (many areas are closed in winter).

ℹ Getting There & Around

Although there are some operators running tours to and around Mesa Verde National Park from Durango (contact the Durango tourist office, p280), most people visit with a private car or motorcycle. Vehicular transport is necessary to get to the sites from the front park gate as well as to get between them.

Mancos
POP 1260 / ELEV 7028FT

A quick sprint through tiny Mancos and you'll think you've stumbled upon yet another Colorado ghost town. But slow down for a minute and wander amid the historic homes and landmark buildings and you'll be in for a great surprise. Sleeping and eating options are limited, but the ones that do exist are charming and eclectic. Mesa Verde National Park is just 7 miles to the west, so if visiting the park is on your itinerary, staying in Mancos makes an appealing alternative to the rather nondescript motels in Cortez.

🛏 Sleeping

Flagstone Meadows Ranch Bed & Breakfast B&B
(☑970-533-9838; www.flagstonemeadows.com; 38080 Rd K-4; 🐕) This elegant ranch is a decidedly more romantic option than any of

the motels in town. Guests sit on the deck to enjoy the stars at night, or warm themselves by the field stone fireplace. During the day it's dead quiet; you can take in big views across the plain to Mesa Verde or walk on nearby trails.

Willowtail Springs
LODGE, CABINS $$$

(☎800-698-0603; www.willowtailsprings.com; 10451 County Rd 39; cabins $249-279; ☑☎☀) As plush as Flagstone, but more secluded, are the three small residences at Willowtail. This place is a true retreat with shake shingles and elegant interiors, and art and photography workshops. You can glide across the small on-site lake in a canoe, spend the evening dining by starlight and practice tai chi in the morning. This place is out of budget for many, but it's also a little slice of heaven. For families, the lake house sleeps six.

Echo Basin Ranch
RANCH $$

(☎970-533-7000; www.echobasin.com; County Rd M; cabins per night/week from $119/600; ☀) Traveling with horse? Stop for the night at Echo Basin Ranch, an affordable unnstructured dude ranch. The A-frame cabin accommodation is very cool (as long as you don't mind rustic, and by that we mean basic). We love the pitched roof and big windows – very Rocky Mountain high.

The deluxe cabins are not posh, but plenty comfortable, with multiple rooms and more artistic decor. There is a two-night minimum to stay here, and it is much cheaper (and in scale with what you pay for, amenities-wise) if you stay at least four nights. Dogs are welcome, and horses stay for $10 per night. The ranch offers a host of activities, from guided horseback riding to a putting green. The on-site restaurant and saloon mean you don't have to drive to eat. Echo Basin is about 7 miles from Mancos.

Jersey Jim Lookout Tower
LOOKOUT TOWER $

(☎970-533-7060; r $40; ☉mid-May–mid-Oct) How about spending the night in a former fire-lookout tower? Standing 55ft above a meadow 14 miles north of Mancos at an elevation of 9800ft, this place is on the National Historic Lookout Register and comes with an Osborne Fire Finder and topographic map.

The tower accommodates up to four adults (bring your own bedding) and must be reserved long in advance; there's also a two-night minimum stay. The reservation office opens on the first workday of March

(1pm to 5pm) and the entire season is typically booked within days.

Enchanted Mesa Motel
MOTEL $

(☎970-533-7729; www.enchantedmesamotel.com; 862 W Grand Ave; r from $45; ☑☎) Hipper than most independent motels, this place has shiny lamps and solid wooden furniture, along with king- and queen-size beds. There's a big playground out front for the kids. Best of all, you can play a game of pool while waiting for your whites to dry – there's a billiards table in the laundry room!

✖ Eating & Drinking

Absolute Baking & Cafe
SANDWICHES $

(☎970-533-1200; 110 S Main St; mains $6-8; ☉7am-2pm; ☎☀) The most happening spot in town, this cafe serves healthy and delicious homemade meals including wraps, salads, pastas and sandwiches. The amiable owners are rightly justified in advertising 'sublime breads and food with integrity.' Only organic flours and grains go into the fresh-baked breads and pastries.

If you're in the market for a new read, the cafe has a decent collection of used books for sale; so grab a cup of coffee and just chill out.

Millwood Junction
SEAFOOD $$

(☎970-533-7338; www.millwoodjunction.com; cnr Main St & Railroad Ave; mains $10-20; ☉11am-2pm daily, 5:30-10:30pm Mon-Fri; ☀) This is a popular steak and seafood dinner joint. Folks from miles around come to Mancos on Friday night for the seafood buffet ($14). The restaurant often doubles as a club, showcasing live music.

Columbine Bar
PUB

(☎970-533-7397; 123 W Grand Ave; ☉10am-2am) More than a century after Columbine Bar first opened its doors, the saloon, established in 1903 and one of Colorado's oldest continuously operating bars, is still going strong.

Locals come for pints of ice-cold local brews and good pub food (mains $5), but visitors will love the Old West feel this smoky old saloon oozes. The mounted animal heads keep watch as you shoot pool.

Mancos Valley Distillery
DISTILLERY

(www.mancosvalleydistillery.com; 116 N Main St; ☉hours vary) If you're interested in tasting something *really* local, make your way to this distilery, where artisan distiller Ian James crafts delicate rum. He opens up his distillery to live blues and bluegrass, but generally only for special occasions. Check the website for more information.

❶ Information

Mancos Valley Visitors Center (☑702-533-7434; www.mancosvalley.com; 101 E Bauer St; ⊙9am-5pm Mon-Fri) Historic displays and a walking-tour map are available at the visitor center. It also has information on outdoor activities and local ranches that offer horseback rides and Western-style overnight trips.

Cortez

POP 8630 / ELEV 6201FT

Cortez probably won't beguile you, but its location, 10 miles west of Mesa Verde National Park, makes it the best base for exploring the park. Plus Cortez is a hot spot for mountain biking, with hundreds of great single-track rides in its vicinity.

Typical of small-town Colorado, downtown Cortez is lined with squat buildings housing shops that sell hunting rifles, trinkets and surprisingly eclectic, clothing; family-style restaurants dishing up homemade meat-and-potatoes fare; and the requisite microbrewery. The outer edges of the town are jam-packed with independent motels and fast-food outlets. Far-off mountain vistas complete the picture. There's not really much by way of action in Cortez, but those seeking a more relaxed environment can try Mancos, 17 miles east, or Dolores, 11 miles north.

◉ Sights & Activities

Cultural Park   MUSEUM
(⊙10am-9pm Mon-Sat summer, to 5pm winter) The Cultural Park is an outdoor space at the Cortez Cultural Center where Ute, Navajo and Hopi tribe members share their cultures with visitors through dance and crafts demonstrations. Weaving demonstrations and Ute mountain art also are displayed and visitors can check out a Navajo hogan.

Summer evening programs feature Native American dances six nights a week at 7:30pm, followed at 8:30pm by cultural programs such as Native American storytellers.

FREE **Cortez Cultural Center**   MUSEUM
(☑702-565-1151; www.cortezculturalcenter.org; 25 N Market St; ⊙10am-9pm Mon-Sat May-Oct, to 5pm Nov-Apr; ⚑) Exhibits on the Ancestral Puebloans, as well as visiting art displays, make this museum worthy of a visit if you have a few hours to spare.

Summer evening programs feature Native American dances six nights a week at 7:30pm, followed at 8:30pm by cultural programs that often feature Native American storytellers.

Crow Canyon Archaeology Center
ARCHAEOLOGICAL SITE
(☑970-565-8975, 800-422-8975; www.crowcanyon.org; 23390 Rd K; adult/child $55/30; ⊙9am-5pm Wed & Thu Jun–mid-Sept; ⚑) This cultural center, about 3 miles north of Cortez, offers a day-long educational program that visits an excavation site west of town. Programs teach the significance of regional artifacts and are an excellent way to learn about Ancestral Puebloan culture first-hand.

Travelers who want to stay longer can partake in week-long sessions, where guests share in traditional Pueblo hogans and also study excavation field and lab techniques.

Kokopelli Bike & Board   BIKE RENTALS
(☑970-565-4408; www.kokopellibike.com; 30 W Main St; per day $20; ⊙9am-6pm Mon-Fri, to 5pm Sat) The friendly staff at this local bike shop are happy to talk trail with riders, and also rent and repair mountain bikes. The rental price includes helmet, air pump, water bottle and tools. For some pre-trip planning, visit the shop's website. It has great trail descriptions.

Come Dance Tonight   BALLROOM DANCING
(www.comedancetonight.com; 30 W Main St; drop-in dance lessons $8; ⊙evenings, hrs vary) Behind the trophy-cluttered windows, this nondescript storefront opens to a surreal world, where Friday nights finds couples cha-cha-ing across the wide wooden floor along to the buoyant clapping of Denise. A ballroom studio and social club that seems from another era, this is a truly weird and awesome scene.

🛏 Sleeping

Cortez has heaps of budget motels along its main drag, and rates and rooms are much the same at most. In winter, prices drop by almost 50%. Sadly, the only campground in town not right next to a highway or dedicated to RVs is the **Cortez-Mesa Verde KOA** (☑970-565-9301; 27432 E Hwy 160; sites $25-32, cabins $50; ⊙Apr-Oct; 🛜🏊⚑) at the east end of town. It's open mid-May to mid-September.

MOUNTAIN BIKING IN THE FOUR CORNERS AREA

The Four Corners area around Cortez offers some epic mountain-bike trails among piñon-juniper woodland and over the otherworldly 'slickrock' mesa. The dispersed sites at Hovenweep National Monument are ideal riding destinations. In fact, the roads are slightly better suited for biking than driving.

A good ride begins at the Sand Canyon archaeological site west of Cortez and follows a downhill trail west for 18 miles to Cannonball Mesa near the state line. If you're looking for a shorter ride, at the 8-mile mark the Burro Point overlook of Yellow Jacket and Burro Canyons is a good place to turn back. Test your skills riding the 27-mile Stoner Mesa Loop, a challenging intermediate to expert ride beginning with 8 miles of paved road along the west fork of the Dolores River. The tough part comes during the 7-mile dirt-road climb (you'll gain nearly 2000ft in elevation) to the top of Stoner Mesa. When (or maybe if) you reach the top, the views are splendid, and you'll be rewarded with a long, mellow downhill through amazing forests of aspens and open meadows. The last 2 miles are the most technical, consisting of an endless number of tight switchbacks and rock and root steps that take you down to the trailhead in a steep descent. Stoner Mesa is most beautiful in fall, when the aspens add a golden glow to the ride.

Pick up a copy of *Mountain and Road Bike Routes for the Cortez-Dolores-Mancos Area*, available at the Colorado Welcome Center (p298) and at local chambers of commerce. It provides maps and profiles for several road and mountain-bike routes. The friendly staff at Kokopelli Bike & Board (p296) are happy to talk trail with riders, and also rent and repair mountain bikes. The rental price includes helmet, air pump, water bottle and tools. For some pre-trip planning, visit the shop's website. It has great trail descriptions.

Kelly Place B&B $$
(☎970-565-3125; www.kellyplace.com; 14663 Montezuma County Rd G; r & cabins $80-175; ⊖ 🛜 📶) This unique adobe-style guest lodge is situated on 40 acres of red-rock canyon and Indian ruins 15 miles west of Cortez. Founded by a well-respected local botanist, the late George Kelly, the place still has fabulous orchards. Rooms are tasteful and rates include a full hot buffet breakfast.

We like the adobe cabins, especially the one with a private flagstone patio and whirlpool tub. Kelly Place also offers horseback riding, cultural tours and archaeological programs. At night put a DVD on the big-screen TV in the communal lounge and chill with a glass of wine or a tasty microbrew; the lodge serves both.

Best Western Turquoise Inn & Suites
HOTEL $$
(☎970-565-3778; www.bestwestern.com; 535 E Main St; r from $89; 🅿 ⊖ ❄ 🛜 🌊) With two swimming pools to keep the young ones entertained, this is a good choice for families (kids stay free, and the restaurant has a kiddy menu). Rooms here are spacious, and bigger families can grab a two-room suite.

If you're exploring Mesa Verde all day and just want an affordable and clean, if slightly bland, hotel to crash at night this comfortably laid out Best Western will do the trick.

Tomahawk Lodge LODGE $
(☎970-565-8521, 800-643-7705; www.angelfire.com/co2/tomahawk; 728 S Broadway; r from $75; ❄ 📶) Friendly hosts welcome you at this clean, good-value place. It feels more personable than the average motel with unique Native American art on the walls. A few rooms allow pets and there's a pool out front.

🍴 Eating

Main Street Brewery & Restaurant
MEXICAN, ITALIAN $$
(☎970-544-9112; 21 E Main St; mains $8-15; ⊙lunch & dinner; 📶) The excellent German-style house-brewed beers are listed on the wall, right next to the cheery hand-painted murals at this cozy place. The large menu features everything from southwestern cuisine to Mexican and Italian, and includes the requisite burgers and pizzas.

After dinner kick it up a notch in the downstairs game room, where you can enjoy a beer and some billiards.

Stonefish Sushi & More JAPANESE $$
(☑970-565-9244; 16 W Main; mains $10-16;
☺4:30-9pm Mon-Thu, to 10pm Sat) With blues
on the box and a high tin ceiling, this is a
sushi place for the southwest. The rolls are
standard fare, but specialties, like the Colo-
rado rancher seared beef and wasabi, liven
things up. Cool light fixtures, black tiles
and globe-shaped fish tanks behind the bar
complete the scene.

Burger Boy BURGERS $
(☑970-565-7921; 400 East Main St; mains $5-10;
☺11am-8pm Jun-Aug; ⚐) From gum-chomp-
ing high-school girls, to cheapie trays of
burgers and fries, this drive-in is no throw-
back; it's the real deal. The service is so
sweet and the experience is so classically
mid-century American that it matters none
if most of the food goes from deep freezer to
the deep fryer.

Blondie's PUB FOOD $
(☑970-565-4015; www.blondiespubandgrub.
net; 45 East Main St; mains $8-12; ☺11am-2am)
If you're lucky, there's a bike rally that's
pulled in here for some cold ones and a few
shots of Jager, and a local band that goes
by the name Gods of Thunder are about to
take the stage. If these rough-cut pine walls
could speak, they'd probably have a dirty
mouth.

But for all the rowdies at the bar and all
the bikini girls on the wall, this place is also
the most fun in town and the pub food –
burgers, fries, big ol' salads – is pretty good.
Factoid: the elk above the bar used to be-
long to a local homesteader.

Tequila's Mexican Restaurant MEXICAN $
(☑970-565-6868; 1740 E Main St; mains $4-10;
☺lunch & dinner; ⚐) Good-tasting food at
bargain prices draws the crowds on any giv-
en night. The restaurant serves the usual
Americanized Mexican staples, but does a
great job with them. The chicken *mole*, sea-
food tacos and *carne asada* all win raves as
do margaritas with fresh lime juice. Expect
a wait on weekends.

Mr Happy CAFE FOOD $
(☑970-565-9869; 332 E Main St; breakfast $5-
10; ☺6am-2pm; ⚐) Dave, man behind the
bright yellow smiley face, isn't reinventing
the wheel with his scones, muffins and deli-
cious egg dishes, but one called the Huevos
Festival – a layered mess of eggs, fresh sal-
sa, cheese, sausage and cheese – is the best
breakfast in town.

No frills here: just a cement floor and
vinyl chairs, but the food keeps the place
full. His wedding cakes, though probably of
little interest to travelers, are a work of art.
Oddly, it also serves cocktails.

ℹ Information
Colorado Welcome Center (☑970-565-4048;
928 E Main St; ☺9am-5pm Sep-May, to 6pm
Jun-Aug) Maps, brochures and some excellent
pamphlets on local activities like fishing and
mountain biking.

Southwest Memorial Hospital (☑970-565-
6666; 1311 N Mildred Rd) Provides emergency
services.

ℹ Getting There & Away
In the extreme southwest corner of the state,
Cortez is easier to reach from either Phoenix,
Arizona or Albuquerque, New Mexico, than from
Denver, 379 miles away by the shortest route.
East of Cortez, US 160 passes Mesa Verde Na-
tional Park on the way to Durango, the largest
city in the region, 45 miles away. To the north-
west, Hwy 145 follows the beautiful Dolores
River through the San Juan Mountains on an old
Rio Grande Southern narrow-gauge route over
Lizard Head Pass to Telluride, 77 miles distant.

Cortez Municipal Airport (☑970-565-7458;
22874 County Rd F) is served by United Express,
which offers daily turboprop flights to Denver.
The airport is 2 miles south of town off US
160/666.

Dolores
POP 915 / ELEV 6936FT
Sandwiched between the walls of a nar-
row canyon of the same name, Dolores of-
fers history buffs a hearty meal of Native
American artifacts, fishers the best angling
in the southwest and romantic couples a
charming place to rest their heads. Typical
of other small towns in the area, there are
no buildings that stand more than a couple
of stories high and the nights are fairly
quiet, but it's an excellent, slow-paced es-
cape. The **Dolores Visitor Center** (☑702-
882-4018, 800-807-4712; 421 Railroad Ave;
☺9am-5pm Mon-Fri) is housed in a replica
of the town's old railroad depot, it has re-
gional information on lodging and outdoor
activities.

◉ Sights & Activities
The Bureau of Land Management man-
ages the **Anasazi Heritage Center** (☑970-
882-5600; 27501 Hwy 184; admission $3, free

Dec-Feb; ☺9am-5pm Mar-Nov, 10am-4pm Dec-Feb; P⛖), a good stop for anyone touring the area's archaeological sites. It's three miles west of town, with hands-on exhibits including weaving, corn grinding, tree-ring analysis and an introduction to the way in which archaeologists examine potsherds. You can walk through the Dominguez Pueblo, a roofless site from the 1100s that sits in front of the museum and compare its relative simplicity to the Escalante Pueblo, a Chacoan structure on a nearby hillside.

Dolores is home to McPhee Lake, the second-largest body of water in Colorado. Covering 4470 surface acres and 50 miles of shoreline stretching north and west of town, McPhee Lake is one of the top fishing spots in the San Juan basin. Located in a canyon of the Dolores River, McPhee offers many angling spots accessible only by boat. In the lake's skinny, tree-lined side canyons, wakeless boating zones have been established to allow for awesome still-water fishing without the buzz and disturbance of motor craft. Talk about getting away from it all. With the best catch ratio in all of southwest Colorado – according to the state division of wildlife – it's a great place to teach younger anglers. Plus the surrounding mountain scenery is easy on the eye. Make sure you have a valid Colorado fishing license.

🛏 Sleeping

If you want to camp, you can find out about nearby sites in the San Juan National Forest from the **USFS Dolores Ranger Station** (☑970-882-7296; 29211 Hwy 184; ☺8am-5pm Mon-Fri), which has the best camping options. Otherwise, the **Dolores River RV Park** (☑970-882-7761; www.doloresriverrvpar-kandcabins.com; 16680 Hwy 145; tent/RV sites $24/35, cabins $45; ⛖) is fine enough if you're just looking for a place for the night, and especially easy for RVs. It is located about 1.5 miles east of town, has pleasant enough (if overpriced) sites. The small cabins are the best deal going.

Rio Grande Southern Hotel   HOTEL **$$**

(☑866-882-3026; www.rgshotel.com; 101 S 5th St; r $85-110; 🛜⛖) By far the best sleeping option in town is this National Historic Landmark, where Norman Rockwell prints and an old-world front desk beckon guests. A cozy library and antique-filled guest rooms add to the charm. Bedrooms

are small, but all four units are multiroom suites, so there's enough leg room.

Try for Room 4, where Zane Gray is rumored to have stayed while writing *Riders of the Purple Sage*. A full breakfast is included.

Outpost Motel   MOTEL **$**

(☑800-382-4892, 970-882-7271; www.dolores lodgings.com; 1800 Central Ave; d with/without kitchen $70/65, cabins $125; ⛖) At the east end of town, it has small but clean rooms, as well as cabins. Some rooms have kitchenettes and the courtyard features a pleasant little wooden deck overlooking the Dolores River. The motel also takes RVs.

🍴 Eating & Drinking

Rio Grande Southern Restaurant

CONTEMPORARY AMERICAN **$$**

(☑866-882-3026; www.rgshotel.com; 101 S 5th St; mains $5-15; ☺7am-8pm Wed-Sat; ⛖) Downstairs from the historic hotel, this is a welcoming dining room and good for dinner, regardless of whether you are here to sleep. Under the domain of Dolores' former mayor turned chef, Tommy Lux, it offers a solid á la carte American menu and does weekly specials including a fish fry and Chicago pizza night.

Old Germany Restaurant, Lounge & Beer Garden   GERMAN **$$**

(☑702-882-7549; 200 S 8th St; mains $9-15; ☺4-8pm Tue-Sat; ⛖⛖) For something other than the typical American pub grub a lot of restaurants serve, head to Old Germany, which has been dishing up platters of bratwurst and Wiener schnitzel for more than 20 years. Repeat customers swear it's the best German food in the region, and portions are large and fairly priced.

In the summer, tipping back a few Paulaners in the beer garden is a great way to unwind with the locals.

ℹ Getting There & Away

Dolores is 11 miles north of Cortez on Hwy 145, also known as Railroad Ave.

Rico

POP 250 / ELEV 8825FT

At the base of a steep climb to Telluride, it's probably no surprise that Rico (meaning 'rich') was founded when prospectors sought silver in the hills, and local wags will claim that is Colorado's last boom

SOUTHWEST COLORADO MESA VERDE & THE FOUR CORNERS

town. Stiff Ute resistance thwarted the first several efforts at mining here, but the Utes signed the Brunot Agreement to effectively surrendered the entirety of land in San Juan Mountains in 1878, and the miners came rushing back. A boom from the Enterprise Lode brought some 5000 residents at the town's peak in 1892, but the timing was too late. Things went bust with the Silver Panic of 1893, and the town all but folded up. There's little history left, aside from a few historic buildings and the Van Winkle Headframe and Hoist Structure, a towering piece of mining equipment alongside the road which makes a quick photo op.

☉ Sights & Activities

Visit in summer for fabulous fishing along the Dolores River (which conveniently runs through town). Anglers score big with cutthroat, rainbow and brown trout. You can also hike the 9-mile loop from the top of Lizard Head Pass to the base of Lizard Head Peak, a crumbling 13,113ft tower of rock. Aside from that, it's mostly a place to gas up and move on.

Hovenweep National Monument

Hovenweep, meaning 'deserted valley' in the Ute language, is a remote area of former Ancestral Puebloan settlements straddling the Colorado–Utah border, 42 miles west of Cortez via McElmo Canyon Rd from US 160. This was once home to a large population before drought forced people out in the late 1200s. Six sets of unique tower ruins are found here, but only the impressive ruins in the Square Tower area are readily accessible. For people who love ticking off a checklist of America's national parks and monuments, this is only a half-day diversion from the sites at Mesa Verde National Park.

🕴 Activities

Three easy-to-moderate loop hiking trails (none longer than 2 miles) leave from near the ranger station and pass a number of buildings in the Square Tower area. The trails give both distant and close-up views of the ancient sites whose fragile unstable walls are easily damaged – please stay on the trail and don't climb on the sites. Visitors are reminded that all wildlife is

protected – including rattlesnakes – but you are more likely to see the iridescent collared lizard scampering near the trail. Brochures are available for the self-guided tours and also describe plant life along the trails.

🛌 Sleeping

Hovenweep NPS Campground   CAMPING $
(sites $10) This campground is about a mile from the ranger station and is open year-round on a first-come, first-served basis. The 31 sites rarely fill, but are busiest in summer. There are toilets and picnic facilities. Spring water is available when weather permits, usually from April to October only.

ℹ Information

Hovenweep National Park Service Ranger Station (☎970-562-4282; McElmo Route; ☉8am-6pm Apr-Sep, to 5pm Oct-Mar; ♿)

ℹ Getting There & Away

From US 160/US 666 south of Cortez, turn at the sign for the Cortez Airport onto Montezuma County Rd G, which follows McElmo Canyon east through red-rock country north of Sleeping Ute Mountain and Ute tribal lands. At the Utah border you cross onto the Navajo Reservation and can expect sheep, goats or even cattle on the road. A signed road to the monument turns right (north) from McElmo Creek.

Four Corners Navajo Tribal Park

Don't be shy: do a spread eagle for the folks on top of the **Four Corners Navajo Tribal Park** (☎928-871-6647; www.navajonationparks. org; off US 160; adult $3; ☉7am-5pm Oct-May, 7am-8pm Jun-Sep) corners marker that signifies you're in four states at once. It makes a good photograph, even if it's not 100% accurate – an April 2009 news story had government surveyors admitting that the marker is almost 2000ft east of where it should be, but that the marker is a legally recognized border point, regardless. Put a foot into Arizona and plant the other in New Mexico. Slap a hand in Utah and place the other in Colorado.

The monument is really in the middle of nowhere: there's a small visitors center, picnic tables and portable toilets. The nearest gas station is 6 miles south in Teec Nos Pos. Vendors have set up around its edge selling food, Native American crafts and jewelry and knickknacks. The best snack to nosh on is a flat piece of fried dough from a **Navajo Fry Bread Cart** (Four Corners Navajo Tribal Park; fry bread $3; ⊘11am-5pm), to your right as you exit the parking area.

Ute Mountain Indian Reservation

Ute people once inhabited this entire region – from the San Luis Valley west into Utah – and, after a series of forced relocations and treaties from the 1860s to 1930s, control only this small strip of land in the dry high plains of the Colorado Plateau. The relationship between Utes and the federal government is one of conflict and ongoing tension; the Ute tribe won their first rights for potable water on this arid reservation in 1988. The tribal land includes a number of archaeological sites, including petroglyphs and cliff dwellings, but can only be accessed through guided tour. The **Ute Mountain Tribal Park** (⌨970-749-1452; www.utemountainute.com; Morning Star Lane; half-day tours per person from $28; ⊘by appointment) can set up half- and full-day tours, which include lots of rough and dusty driving over back roads.

The tribe operates the **Ute Mountain Casino, Hotel & Resort** (⌨hotel reservations 800-258-8007; 3 Weeminuche Dr; d $75-95, sites $30), near Sleeping Ute Mountain.

San Luis Valley

Includes »

WESTCLIFFE &
SILVER CLIFF 304

CRESTONE 306

GREAT SAND DUNES
NATIONAL PARK 307

SAN LUIS STATE
PARK 310

ALAMOSA &
AROUND 311

SAN LUIS 313

ANTONITO 314

CONEJOS RIVER 315

MONTE VISTA. 316

LA GARITA. 317

DEL NORTE. 318

Best Places to Eat

» Pachelli's Deli & Bakery (p317)

» Cel Dor Asado (p305)

» San Luis Valley Brewing Company (p312)

Best Places to Stay

» Mansion B&B (p317)

» Historic Windsor Hotel (p319)

» USFS Mogote Campground (p316)

Why Go?

Couched between jagged mountains, the wide plains of San Luis Valley are home to farm towns, wetland wildlife sanctuaries and the stark beauty of the Great Sand Dunes.

Look to the east: the 14,000ft crags of the Sangre de Cristo Mountains are as arresting as their name suggests. Here lies Colorado's least trampled wilderness – Crestone Peak was the last of Colorado's 14ers to be climbed and huge herds of bighorn sheep, Colorado's state animal, scramble up the rough slopes. Now look west: across the broad plain there's another view of the volcanic San Juan Mountains, where the Rio Grande's headwaters flow by the historic mining camps. In the south of this immense valley the landscape is dotted with adobe churches and historic Hispanic villages to evoke images of the old southwest, while the Great Sand Dunes National Park looks like a misplaced patch of the Sahara.

When to Go?

Salida

May–September	October & November	December–April
Hike under blue skies in the volcanic ranges of the region.	Changing aspens make rail rides a spectacular display of color.	Wild winds and snow see visitors huddle in fire-warmed cabins.

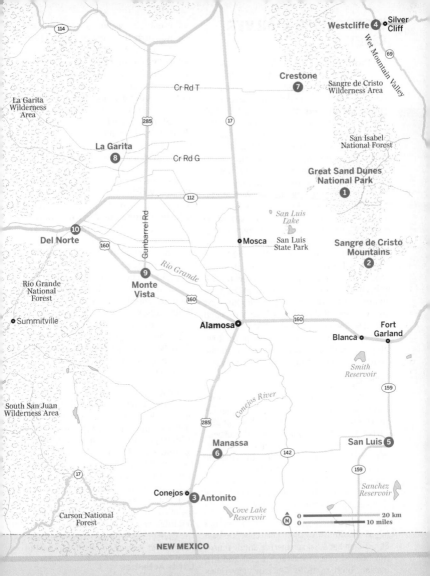

San Luis Valley Highlights

① Board down the towering sand dunes at **Great Sand Dunes National Park** (p307)

② Follow a herd of bighorn sheep on the hills of **Music Pass** (p304), in the Sangre de Cristo Mountains

③ Chug across the mountains on the **Cumbres & Toltec Scenic Railroad** (p315)

④ Catch Colorado's best bluegrass pickers at the **High Mountain Hay Fever Bluegrass Festival** (p305)

⑤ Follow the Penitente Brotherhood at San Luis' **Stations of the Cross** (p313)

⑥ Throw a punch at the tiny **Jack Dempsey Museum** (p314)

⑦ Get zen at **Crestone** (p306), a new-age spiritual hub

⑧ Climb the ragged ash formations of **La Garita** (p317)

⑨ Watch a drive-in movie from your room at the **Best Western Movie Manor Motor Inn** (p317)

⑩ Have a pint at Del Norte's **Three Barrel Brewery** (p319)

WESTCLIFFE & SILVER CLIFF

For travelers headed west from the I-25 corridor, these two connected historical towns serve as the introduction to Colorado's outer regions. South of the Arkansas River Canyon in the Wet Mountain Valley, Westcliffe and Silver Cliff (combined population 700) are only a mile apart, surrounded by alpine valley scenery, and within striking distance of the beautiful Sangre de Cristo Mountains. Within the towns there are a number of well-preserved historical buildings.

Mountain grassland in the Wet Mountain Valley extends for about 35 miles between the jagged peaks of the Sangre de Cristo Mountains to the west and the Wet Mountains to the east, capped by the granitic summit of Greenhorn Peak (12,347ft). Access to US Forest Service lands on either side of the valley is limited to a few routes; otherwise, dire signs threaten trespassers on cattle-grazing lands with Old West justice. Nevertheless it's fairly easy to reach the magnificent Sangre de Cristo mountain range, which includes five 14ers in the Crestone Peak group. Other 14ers rise to the south around the prominent Blanca Peak.

⊙ Sights

If you're interested in taking in historic buildings from the 19th century, make for downtown Westcliffe's 'Dutch Row' on 2nd Street. Once home to saloons and brothels, these historic facades include the 19th-century feed-supply store (now the Historic Feed Store Pub & Grill (p305) and an old state bank where scenes from *Comes a Horseman*, the 1978 flick starring James Caan and Jane Fonda, were shot.

Silver Cliff Museum   MUSEUM
(☑719-783-2615; www.silvercliffco.com; 606 Main St; ◔1-4pm Sat & Sat summer) A small museum housed in a former town hall and fire station, built in 1879. You can view relics and photographs of the valley's history.

🏃 Activities

Hiking & Backpacking

Climbers use **South Colony Lakes** as a base camp, yet even if you don't wish to scale peaks, the 12,000ft tarns beneath the rugged Crestone Needle are worthy of a visit. To reach the South Colony Lakes Trailhead, drive 4 miles south of town on Hwy 69. Turn right onto Colfax Lane, which

will eventually become a T junction at Colony Rd. Turn right and continue along the rough road to the trailhead. You can hike out to the lake under the needle and back in under three hours. Another hiking option in this area traverses the ridge at **Music Pass** (11,400ft) leading to Sand Creek Lakes on the west side of the range. The area was named by hikers who claimed to hear music made by the wind whistling through the trees. It is accessed from Colfax Lane as well, and well marked with signs for Music Pass.

For outstanding views from Comanche and Venable Passes on the crest of the Sangre de Cristo Mountains, plus a waterfall, the **Comanche-Venable Loop Trail** (USFS Trail 1345) is hard to beat. This is a spectacular hike – lots of granite faces, dark-blue alpine lakes and huge horizons – but you really have to earn it. The 13-mile loop gains some 3600ft in elevation.

For information about the San Isabel National Forest and the Sangre de Cristo Wilderness, check with the Bureau of Land Management (p335) in Cañon City or **La Veta District Office** (☑719-742-3588; cnr Moore Ave & Poplar Sts; ◔8am-4pm Mon-Fri). For USGS maps, try Valley Ace Hardware, south of Westcliffe on US 69 (toward Walsenburg).

Fishing

Close to Westcliffe is Middle Taylor Creek State Wilderness Area, where restrooms, open camping and picnic tables are close to fishing spots along the stream. A 4WD road continues to Hermit Lake and Horseshoe Lake in USFS lands near the 13,000ft summits of the Sangre de Cristo Mountains.

The regularly stocked DeWeese Reservoir and Grape Creek, which flows from it, are included in the DeWeese Reservoir State Wildlife Area; for more information contact the **Division of Wildlife** (☑719-561-5300; 600 Reservoir Rd; ◔8am-5pm Mon-Fri) in Pueblo.

Other Activities

Mountain bikers will find plenty of opportunities in San Isabel National Forest lands on either side of the Wet Mountain Valley. The most popular rides use portions of the Rainbow Trail (USFS Trail 1336), a 100-mile route along the Sangre de Cristo foothills between Salida and Music Pass, about 15 miles south of Westcliffe.

Bear Basin Ranch (☑719-783-2519; www.bearbasinranch.com; 473 County Rd 271; half-day rides from $60, full-day incl lunch from $110; ⊛),

11 miles east of Westcliffe, offers horseback rides on its extensive ranch property in the Wet Mountains. All-day trips into the mountains are also available.

Among the five jagged 14,000ft peaks in the Crestone group (Crestone Peak, Crestone Needle, Kit Carson Mountain, Challenger Point and Humboldt Peak), only Humboldt Peak is a nontechnical climb. Gary Ziegler, who owns Bear Basin Ranch, is a local authority on the peaks and can guide climbing trips.

✺ Festivals & Events

High Mountain Hay Fever Bluegrass Festival MUSIC
(www.highmountainhayfever.org) This town loves bluegrass, and this festival is a chance to see some of the best 'grass heads' in Colorado. It happens on the first weekend in July.

Custer County Fair & Stampede Weekend RODEO
(☑877-793-3170; www.custercountytourism. com; 59000 N Hwy 69; ⊙last week of Jul; ⊞) A rodeo and dance are the featured events at the Custer County Fair, held the last weekend in July.

Jazz in the Sangres MUSIC
(☑877-793-3170; Downtown Westcliffe; ⊙2nd weekend Aug) Over the second weekend of August, young jazz artists perform both day and night at this jazz festival, the culmination of a week-long jazz performance camp that draws students from around Colorado. Contact the chamber of commerce for details.

🛏 Sleeping

If you're in search of rock-bottom prices, there are several midcentury motels off the highway, though none are too pleasant. Budget travelers are much better off camping.

Abundant open campsites can be found at nearby Middle Taylor Creek SWA and DeWeese SWA, and on local USFS lands. Middle Taylor Creek is about 8 miles northeast of Westcliffe; DeWeese is about 4 miles northeast of Westcliffe. The USFS Alvarado Campground has 47 sites available for $8. Head south from Westcliffe on Hwy 69 for 3 miles and turn right (west) on Custer County Rd 302 (Schoolfield Rd); it's 7 miles to the trailhead. A bit further out is Lake Creek Campground, which has 11 sites for $17 each. Go 15 miles north on Hwy 69 to Hillside (store and post office),

turn left on Custer County Rd 198; it's 4 miles to campsites and USFS Trail 300 to Rainbow Lake.

Main Street Inn B&B B&B $$
(☑719-783-4000, 877-783-4006; www.main streetbnb.com; 501 Main St; d $105-140; ❷❋🐾📶⊞) This charming inn makes a pleasant choice for couples seeking a quiet weekend as it is not a family-oriented place. The five double rooms, some with whirlpool baths, are tastefully decorated, with lots of Persian rugs and a comfortable common area. The owners can also help arrange a stay at the associated Barn Loft, which is a better option for families who need lots of space to run around.

Courtyard Country Inn Bed & Breakfast B&B $$
(☑719-783-9616; www.courtyardcountryinn.com; 410 Main St; d $90-100; ❷📶⊞) This place features featherbeds and down comforters (but no room phones). The owners, Mo and John, make a great continental breakfast with homemade breads and Starbucks coffee, and the grounds are ornately landscaped with waterfalls, outdoor fire pits and leafy patios.

🍴 Eating

Of the two small towns, there are better options by far in downtown Westcliffe, though nothing that's a likely highlight.

⬛**TOP CHOICE** **Cel Dor Asado** MEXICAN $$
(☑719-783-2650; www.celdorasado.com; 213 Main St; mains $8-15; ⊙11am-9pm Wed-Sat) The best place to eat in town is this relative newcomer, a Uruaguayan meat house, in an inviting space where platters of chicken, sausage and steak are cooked over a wood fire behind the bar. There's also homemade ice cream to finish things off.

Historic Feed Store Pub & Grill AMERICAN $$
(☑719-783-3333; wwwwestcliffefeedstore.com; 116 N 2nd St; mains $7-12; ⊙10am-10pm Mon-Thu, to midnight Fri & Sat, to 8pm Sun; ❷⊞) This pub is certainly more upscale than other places in Westcliffe. It serves classic American dishes – blackened ahi, savory pork tenderloin and, naturally, burgers – in a big, red historic feed-storage barn.

Oak Creek Grade General Store & Steakhouse STEAKHOUSE $
(☑719-783-2245; www.oakcreekgradegeneral store.com; County Rd 255/Oak Creek Grade Rd;

breakfast $5-9; ⊘6am-2pm, plus 4-10pm Sat Jun-Aug; ⊞) Midway between Cañon City and Westcliffe, this historic general store and steakhouse, which was formerly a general store, pours the Old West atmosphere on thick. In the summer it hosts bluegrass sessions for a Saturday night dinner show, which brings together the area's best pickers, including members of Sons & Brothers, former National Bluegrass Champions.

ℹ Information

Custer County Chamber of Commerce

(☑719-783-9163, toll free 877-793-3170; www.custercountytourism.com; 101 N 3rd St; ⊘9am-6pm Mon-Fri) Pick up a copy of the Custer County Visitors Guide here. Its website has extensive listings of local government agencies, restaurants, activities and small festivals.

ℹ Getting There & Away

Westcliffe and Silver Cliff lie on Hwy 96, which continues east through the Wet Mountains to Pueblo, 54 miles away. An alternate route from Cañon City, 52 miles away, turns south onto Hwy 69 at the Texas Creek junction with US 50 on the Arkansas River. Hwy 69 offers little traffic through pastoral scenery from the north end of the Wet Mountain Valley to the Huerfano River in the south and on to I-25 at Walsenburg.

CRESTONE

POP 85 / ELEV 7923FT

Despite a population of less than 100 souls, Crestone is world-famous in spiritual circles. A former mining town in the heart of the Sangre de Christo Mountains, it has become a center of retreat and meditation.

Look around the small grid of streets and you can choose from a buffet of spirituality – there's a Hindu temple and a pair of ashrams, a clutch of Buddhist Zen retreats, a crunchy Carmelite hermitage, a Baptist church, several Tibetan meditation centers and seekers of every stripe. Though there are several theories explaining Crestone's status as a powerful spiritual magnet – that it has to do with the energy flow that follows waters off the Continental Divide, or that the mountains themselves call spiritual travelers – but some of the draw likely has to do with Maurice Strong, a former UN undersecretary-general and entrepreneur. Strong planned a large housing development here in the late 1970s, but when it didn't take off he donated plots to various spiritual organizations. Regardless, there's no question about Crestone's setting: the backdrop of the 14,000ft peaks of the Sangre de Cristo Mountains is truly stunning.

🏃 Activities

Hiking & Backpacking

Two outstanding trails into the high Sangre de Cristo Wilderness Area begin in Crestone's backyard. Hikers on the South Crestone Creek Trail travel about 5 miles to South Crestone Lake, a cirque beneath Mt Adams (13,931ft). This prime bighorn sheep habitat harbors more than 500 sheep that range between Hermit and Music Passes. Begin from the top of Galena St above the post office; within a mile you reach USFS Trail 949, following the north side of South Crestone Creek for 1.5 miles to a junction. On the right, across the creek, is USFS Trail 865 to Willow Creek Lakes (and waterfall); to the left USFS Trail 860 continues to South Colony Lake.

Another option is to go up North Crestone Creek Trail to either North Crestone Lake below Fluted Peak (13,554ft) or to cross the ridge to the east side over either Comanche or Venable Passes. From the North Crestone Creek Campground reached by USFS Rd 950, USFS Trail 744 follows the north side of North Crestone Creek for 1.5 miles to a three-way junction: on your right the southernmost trail continues for 3 miles to North Crestone Lake; the middle trail, USFS Trail 746, passes north of Comanche Peak before dropping into the Wet Mountain Valley on USFS Trail 1345; and the northern choice, USFS Trail 747, heads toward Venable Pass.

For information about hiking on the west side of the Sangre de Cristo Wilderness Area contact the **USFS Saguache Ranger District** (☑719-655-2547; 46525 Hwy 114; ⊘8am-4:30pm Mon-Fri).

Spiritual Retreats & Classes

For the most part, it takes extensive advance planning to make a spiritual retreat or stay at an ashram in Crestone, but there are facilities of a wide spectrum of faiths that have dormitory accommodations and seminars for visitors. The best resource to see them all at a glance is through the Crestone Area Visitors Agency (p307) website. Many of the spiritual centers also have drop-in classes, and prayer and meditation services.

Sleeping & Eating

Sangre De Christo Inn   HOTEL $
(☎719-256-4975; www.sangredecristoinn.com; 116 S Alder St; d $74-84; 🅿) The best option in town is this hotel, where simple motel rooms come with quilted bedspreads.

Rainbow Bed & Breakfast   B&B $
(☎719-256-4110; www.rainbowbb.com; 223 Rainbow Overlook; s $55, d $65; ⊜🛜) In the Baca Grande area, Rainbow Bed & Breakfast is a modern home near the mountains. Rooms have tasteful decor and shared bathrooms. To get here from Sagauche County Rd T, take the turnoff into the Baca Grande estates for 1 mile, then turn left up a dirt road: it's up 350 yards on the left.

USFS North Crestone Creek
Campground   CAMPING $
(☎719-852-5941; Alder Terrace Rd; sites $9) Camping is available about 2 miles north of Crestone, past the historical community center on Alder Terrace Rd.

Desert Sage   BHUTANESE $
(☎719-256-4402; 242 Baca Townhouse; mains $6-13; ⊙10am-7pm with seasonal variations; ⊜) In the Baca Grande area, just south of town, this place is open daily and features outstanding breads and other baked goods.

ℹ Information
Crestone Area Visitors Agency (☎866-351-2282, 719-256-5210; www.crestonevisit.com; 116 S Alder St; ⊙10am-3pm Mon-Sat, with variations)

ℹ Getting There & Away
Crestone is on the east side of the San Luis Valley, north of Great Sand Dunes National Monument. From Alamosa, Hwy 17 follows a straight course for 40 miles to Saguache County Rd T, which then heads 13 miles east to Crestone.

GREAT SAND DUNES NATIONAL PARK

ELEV 7500–13,000FT

For all of Colorado's striking natural sights, this sea of sand – the country's youngest national park – is a place where nature's magic is on full display.

At the center of the park is a 55-sq-mile dune of sand, surrounded by rigid mountain peaks on one side and glassy wetlands on the other. After long drives on the straight highways of high plains or twist-

ing byways through the Rocky Mountains, it's a bit unnerving to find yourself so suddenly standing amid the landscape of the Sahara.

This is a place of stirring optical illusions. From the approach up CO 150, watch as the angles of sunlight make shifting shadows on the dunes; the most dramatic time is the day's end, when the hills come into high contrast as the sun drops low on the horizon. Hike past the edge of the dune field to see the shifting sand up close; the ceaseless wind works like a disconsolate sculptor, constantly creating and revising elegant ripples underfoot. Lose all perspective in the shadow of the dunes – the largest of which rise almost 700ft. In this monochromatic, uninterrupted landscape, the only tool by which to judge distance is the sight of other hikers, trudging along like ants on the faraway dunes in this surreal, misplaced desert.

🏃 Activities
Most visitors limit their activities to a narrow juncture where the curious Medano Creek divides the main dune mass from the towering Sangre de Cristo Mountains. The remaining 85% of the park's area is designated wilderness.

From the visitor center (p310), a short trail leads to the Mosca Picnic Area next to Medano Creek, which you must ford to reach the dunes. Across the road from the visitors center, the Mosca Pass Trail enters the Sangre de Cristo Wilderness, and the short Wellington Ditch Trail heads north to campsites and the Little Medano Trail.

Hiking
There are no trails through this expansive field of sand, but it's the star attraction for hikers. Two informal hikes afford excellent panoramic views of the dunes. The first is a hike to High Dune (strangely, not the highest dune in the park), which departs from a parking area just beyond the visitor center. It's about 2.5 miles out to the peak and back, but be warned: it's not easy. As you trudge along up the hills of sand it feels like you're taking a half-step back for every one forward. If you're up for it, try pushing on to the second worthy goal. Just west of High Dune is Star Dune, the tallest in the park.

In the middle of the summer, hikers should hit the hills during the morning, as the sand can reach 140°F during the heat

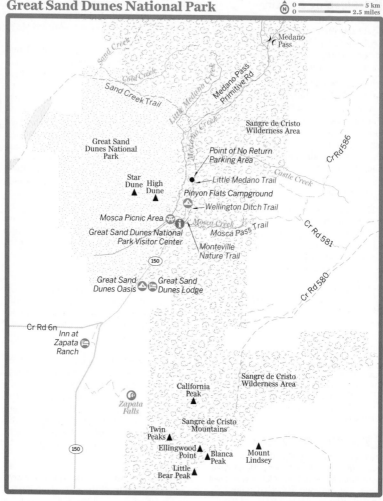

SAN LUIS VALLEY GREAT SAND DUNES NATIONAL PARK

of the day. Those with limited mobility can borrow a dunes-accessible wheelchair from the visitor center.

Mountain Biking

Off-road cyclists should plan for a real slog. The unimproved roads of the park get washed over in sand and are very difficult until the road climbs the beautiful narrow valley to Medano Pass. The pass is 11 miles from the Point of No Return parking area at the north end of the paved road. A detailed mileage log for the Medano Pass Primitive Rd is available at the visitor center (p310).

For a shorter fat-tire ride, visit the spectacular area around Zapata Falls, south of the park, which also offers outstanding views of the valley. A consortium of 13 agencies has opened 4 miles of trail in the Zapata Falls Special Recreation Area on the west flank of Blanca Peak.

BIKE HIRE

Bicycle rentals, repairs and riding information are available at Kristi Mountain Sports (p312) in Alamosa.

Dune Sledding & Sandboarding

The heavy wooden sled may seem like a bad idea when you're trudging out to the dunes, but the gleeful rush down the slopes is worth every footstep. There's a bit of a trick to making this work. Sand conditions are best after a recent precipitation; when it's too dry you'll simply sink. Also, the best rides are had by those who are relatively light, so if you've bulked up on microbrew and steaks, don't expect to zip down the hill.

During the winter days when snow covers the dunes, the sledding is excellent. To rent or buy a board, visit Kristi Mountain Sports (p312) in Alamosa or the Great Sand Dunes Oasis at the edge of the park.

☞ Tours

Throughout summer NPS rangers lead interpretive nature walks from the visitors center. Inquire at the visitors center (p310) about specific programs and times.

Great Sand Dunes Tours   4WD
(tours adult/child $14/8) Tours carry passengers past the dunes and partway up the primitive road to Medano Pass in open-air 4WD vehicles from May to November. The trips take about two hours and leave from the Great Sand Dunes Oasis at 10am and 2pm. Contact the Oasis for details.

🛏 Sleeping
Camping

Adventurous souls will want to inquire about free backcountry camping in the dunes. You have to hike in your water – no easy feat – but it's worth it when you get a glimpse of the star-filled skies. There are other free backcountry campsites accessible from trails near the so-called 'Point of No Return.' Take Little Medano Trail and the Medano Pass Primitive Rd for wilderness camping. These don't require permits, but the road closes when the snow flies.

Pinyon Flats Campground   CAMPING $
(www.recreation.gov; Great Sand Dunes National Park; sites $14; ☉year-round; ⊡) In the peak months of July and August, visitors often fill the 88 sites here. Most sites are available on a first-come, first-served basis; some can be reserved via the website. Water is available here year-round.

Great Sand Dunes Oasis CAMPGROUND, CABIN $
(☎719-378-2222; www.greatdunes.com; 5400 Hwy 150; camp/RV sites $18/28, cabins $40; ⊡) There are facilities to shower and do laundry but the sites are fairly bleak. The cabins on hand are also very spartan, and usually require advance reservation. A reasonable option if camping sites are full.

RECOMMENDED HIKES

Monteville Nature Trail

The Montville Store once stood at the foot of Mosca Pass Trail. It was built in the 1830s by fur trader Antoine Robidoux, who used the pass to transport supplies to his posts in western Colorado and eastern Utah. Many miners passed here on their way west to the San Juan Mountains. Today, a half-mile trail next to Mosca Creek provides a self-guided tour through a variety of ecosystems, leading to a grand view of the San Luis Valley and the dunes. The Montville Nature Trail starts opposite the visitors center (p310), and is a good option for those visiting the area with children.

Mosca Pass Trail

This is a moderate hike, a there-and-back 3.5-mile trail that climbs through meadows and stands of aspen along Mosca Creek. Near the start of the trail is a bronze plaque etched with the impression of Zebulon Pike, who described the dunes as 'appearing exactly as a sea in storm except as to color.' It begins at the Monteville Nature Trail trailhead.

Zapata Falls

After a long day of sweating in the dunes, the short hike to Zapata Falls, south of the park, is a refreshing diversion. A rush of water cuts through a glacier rock wall, which freezes in the winter. The hike is short and, though moderately uphill from the trailhead, is easy for families. The turnoff to the trailhead is between the visitors center (p310) and US 160, and affords an excellent view of the dunes.

Other Options

Inn at Zapata Ranch   INN $$
(☎719-378-2356; www.zranch.org; 5303 Hwy
150; d $159-175; ❄🖨) Owned and operated
by the Nature Conservancy, this delightful
nature preserve is set amid groves of cot-
tonwood trees, and is a working cattle and
bison ranch. The peaceful property con-
tains several historic buildings and offers
up distant views of the sand dunes.

There are several facilities that accom-
modate large and small parties including
the Main Inn, a refurbished 19th-century
log structure.

Horseback riding, mountain-bike rentals
and massage therapy are also on offer.

Great Sand Dunes Lodge   MOTEL $$
(☎719-378-2900; www.gsdlodge.com; 7900
Hwy 150; d $89-95; ☺mid-Mar–Nov; P🐕) Has
rooms with balconies offering fine views of
the dunes. There's also a restaurant and an
indoor pool, but in general, this isn't a great
option.

ℹ Information

**Great Sand Dunes National Park Visitor
Center** (☎719-378-6399; www.nps.gov/grsa;
11999 Hwy 150; ☺8:30am-6:30pm summer,
9am-4:30pm winter, to 5pm spring & fall) An
attractive and modern facility. Stop by here before venturing out to chat with a ranger about
hiking or backcountry camping options, or to
purchase books and maps. Be sure to ask about
scheduled nature walks and nightly programs
held at the amphitheater near Pinyon Flats.

ℹ Getting There & Away

Great Sand Dunes National Park is northeast of
Alamosa. To get here, travel east on US 160 for
14 miles toward prominent Blanca Peak, turn left
(north) on Hwy 150 and follow the road for 19
miles to the visitors center, 3 miles north of the
park entrance; access to the dunes is another
mile along the road.

SAN LUIS STATE PARK

This state park is a patch of bleak terrain
on the edge of the Great Sand Dunes National Park, where dunes covered with salt-
bush and rabbitbrush stand in contrast to
the grassy wetlands – the secondary ben-
eficiary of this governmental largesse. Waterfowl, shorebirds and birdwatchers enjoy
the newly created wetlands and reservoir,
which is open to boating and water sports
when the water level is high enough.

The **Mosca Campground** (☎719-378-
2020; Lane 6 N; sites $20, daily vehicle fee $7;
☺May-Sep) has a bathhouse, laundry and
drinking fountains and is a convenient
alternative to camping in the Great Sand
Dunes National Park, though the park is
only open for camping between May and
the end of September. The park is 8 miles
west of Hwy 150 on Alamosa County Rd
6N. To get from Alamosa to the park, drive
13 miles north on Hwy 17, then turn right
(east) on County Rd 6N for 8 miles.

BLANCA

POP 300 / ELEV 7700FT

Blanca seems to cower in the shadow of
the massive 14,345ft form of the Blanca
Massif, a set of peaks so imposing that
it's easy to see why native Ute consider
them sacred. This scrappy ranching town
straddles US 160, 5 miles east of Hwy 150.
There's nothing of note here for travelers,
really – just a couple churches and some
boarded-up businesses on a small grid of
streets – but visitors to Great Sand Dunes
National Park and nearby wildlife areas
will most certainly pass through. The
only place to stay in town is the **Blanca
RV Park** (☎719-379-3201; 521 Main St; tent/
RV sites $12/20), where shaded tent sites in-
clude hot showers.

The **Mt Blanca Game Bird & Trout
Lodge** (☎719-379-3825; Rd 12) is an oasis
near the small noncommercial airport 3
miles south of Blanca. Visitors can fish at
several stocked ponds on the 9-sq-mile
property or shoot clay pigeons. It's located
2.5 miles down a small dirt road off US 160
just east of Blanca.

The closest that Denver–Albuquerque
buses come to Great Sand Dunes National
Monument is Blanca, though you have to
ask the driver to make the roadside stop
and you'll most certainly have to pay for
a ticket all the way to Alamosa. Call Greyhound for the latest schedule.

FORT GARLAND

POP 430 / ELEV 7936FT

Fort Garland was established to protect
white settlers in the San Luis Valley from
Ute raids, and Union troops stationed
here marched in a campaign against confederates in Texas during the Civil War.

For a short time the outpost was under the direction of famed frontier scout Kit Carson. Though Carson successfully negotiated a period of peace with Utes, all hell broke loose with tribal–federal relations after the so-called Meeker Massacre in 1879. After that, Fort Garland became a major base of operations in the effort that would fully remove Utes from the area. All told, Fort Garland was occupied from 1858 to 1883.

Today Fort Garland – all five square blocks of it – is the first town encountered by westbound travelers after making the big climb up and over La Veta. Visitor information can be found at the **Fort Garland Museum** (☎719-379-3512; Hwy 159; adult/child $4/2.50; ⏱9am-5pm winter, 10am-4pm Thu-Mon summer; ♿), where a restoration of the fort's buildings and exhibits are maintained by the Colorado Historical Society.

🛏 Sleeping

Lodge Motel MOTEL $
(☎719-379-2880; www.thelodgemotelcolorado.com; 825 Hwy 160; d $55; P❤) Overnight accommodations are available at this motel, an extremely friendly and comfortable place that is open year-round. Rooms here are basic, but they're clean and some of them have wi-fi. There are also microwaves and refrigerators.

Fort Garland Motor Inn MOTEL $
(☎719-379-2993; www.garlandmotorinn.com; 411 Hwy 160/4th Ave; d $79-105; ❄) This motel is located right on the highway. It's also very clean, but doesn't have much by way of personality.

ℹ Getting There & Away

From Fort Garland it's 10 miles east to the Hwy 150 turnoff to Great Sand Dunes National Monument, 26 miles east to Alamosa or 17 miles south to San Luis via Hwy 159.

ALAMOSA & AROUND

POP 7960 / ELEV 7543FT

In the heart of the San Luis Valley, Alamosa is the largest city in the valley, thanks mostly to a small university, Adams State College. From the highway, its car garages and Mexican joints aren't so different to other towns in the valley, but the college students bring some life to its restaurants and bars. Its greatest appeal for travelers

Those who love driving can embark on the so-called Fort Garland Loop from here; it's an easy cruise down 100 miles of back roads that go through Manassa and San Luis. The drive offers a scenic glimpse into the high plains wilderness and takes about three hours.

are its convenience as an overnight stop for visiting nearby Great Sand Dunes National Park or riding the excellent Cumbres & Toltec Scenic Railroad steam train (p315) from Antonito to the south.

Main St, with its small walking district, runs parallel to US 160, one block north of the highway. It's far more enjoyable to approach downtown on foot by walking along the river. The river walk starts at the information depot in Cole Park and offers views of Blanca Peak and a stroll through tree-lined neighborhood streets to the downtown area. Paths follow the Rio Grande on both banks from the information depot, but most walkers and joggers will prefer the wide, well-drained levee on the east side.

⊙ Sights & Activities

San Luis Valley Museum MUSEUM
(☎719-589-4624; www.sanluisvalleymuseum.org; 401 Hunt Ave; adult/student $2/1; ⏱10am-4pm Tue-Sat) Located behind the Chamber Depot, this museum has a small but well-arranged collection of 'then and now' photographs and artifacts from early farm life in the valley. Knowledgeable volunteers answer questions and can help plan excursions to historical sites.

For a regional museum, there's some off-beat stuff here, including an interesting exhibit about the nearby La Jara Buddhist Church, the story of the Japanese in the valley and a Nazi uniform worn by a prisoner of war stationed near here during WWII.

FREE **Alamosa National Wildlife Refuge Visitors Center** WILDLIFE SANCTUARY
(☎719-589-4021; 9383 El Rancho Lane; ⏱7:30am-4pm Mon-Fri) Outside Alamosa, a 2.5-mile trail along the Rio Grande and a panoramic overlook on the east side of the refuge give visitors views of the wetland

marshes, ponds and river corridor. In the spring and fall look for sandhill cranes and whooping cranes (a rare sight – only about 400 of the endangered species exist in the wild).

In the early spring look for large concentrations of bald eagles. The USFS operates the Alamosa National Wildlife Refuge Visitors Center. To get here from Alamosa, go 3 miles east on US 160 (to just past the Outhouse restaurant), then south on El Rancho Lane.

Blanca Wetlands

The Bureau of Land Management (BLM) recently restored the wildlife habitat at Blanca Wetlands, east of Alamosa. Activities include fishing for bass or trout in newly created ponds and viewing waterfowl, shorebirds and other species. Hiking trails lead throughout the many marshes and ponds but are closed in the nesting season from February 15 to July 15. Nevertheless, one 'watchable wildlife area' is open all year.To get here from Alamosa, travel 6 miles east on US 160, then 5 miles north on Alamosa County Rd 116S.

Kristi Mountain Sports　　OUTDOORS RENTAL
(☎719-589-9759; www.slvoutdoor.com; 3323 Main St; ☺10am-6pm Mon-Sat) Offers bicycle rentals, repairs and riding information. Also rents and sells sand boards.

🛏 Sleeping

For chains, you have you're pick – just head out along US 160/US 285 at the western edge of town

Comfort Inn Alamosa　　MOTEL $
(☎719-587-9000; 6301 US Hwy 160; d $75-95; P☺🛜🀄) Of the corporate hotels, the best value for your buck comes here, thanks to a good breakfast, plasma TVs, and a pool and hot tub. There's also a coin laundry.

Alamosa Lamplighter Motel　　MOTEL $
(☎719-589-6636, 800-359-2138; www.alamosa lamplightermotel.com; 425 Main St; d $59-69; P❄🛜🀄) This central motel is the best independent motel in town, but that's not saying much. It also has an annex five blocks away with a pool, hot tub and sauna and offers guests a big breakfast.

Camping

Campgrounds are found on the east and west sides of Alamosa, and the information center can provide details for camping op-

tions around Great Sand Dunes National Park, the Rio Grande National Forest and San Luis Lakes State Park.

Alamosa KOA　　CAMPING $
(☎719-589-9757, 800-562-9157; 6900 Juniper Lane; tent/RV sites from $18/25; ☺May-Oct; 🛜🀄) Although the local state and federal camping areas are more spacious, this campground does have a pool and wi-fi, and it rents bikes. It's 3 miles east of town on US 160 then north on Juniper Lane.

🍴 Eating

Milagro's Coffee House　　CAFE FOOD $
(☎719-589-6175; 529 Main St; ☺7am-6pm Mon-Sat, 8am-4pm Sun; ☺@🛜🀄) Breakfasts are good here – it has bagel and egg sandwiches, which are pretty tasty – and it also offers some healthy lunch choices. But the best stuff here is the gooey cherry cobbler bars. This is a great little stop-off for travelers; there's wi-fi, computer terminals to use for a small fee, and a shelf of used books for sale.

Mrs Rivera's Kitchen　　MEXICAN $
(☎719-589-0277; 1019 6th St; mains $5-12; ☺11am-8pm Mon-Thu, to 9pm Fri & Sat; ☺🀄) This favorite has kind service and dimly lit tables, even if the leather-backed chairs and low light lend it a medieval feel. The carnitas tacos are serious.

San Luis Valley Brewing Company
　　GRILL $
(☎719-587-2337; www.slvbrewco.com; 631 Main St; mains $7-16; ☺11am-2am; ☺🀄) You can select from Colorado microbrews with a burger or sandwich at this brewery, which is both classy and casual. Housed in an old bank, it has dark-wood, high-top tables and a brightly polished vault door.

The food (such as a chicken-and-chive chili, or a thick Ruben) is better-than-average pub grub, but it excels with the stuff on tap. Try the green chili–infused ale or homemade black-cherry creme soda.

ℹ Information

Alamosa County Chamber of Commerce
(☎719-589-4840, 800-258-7597; www.ala mosa.org; 610 State St; ☺8am-6pm summer, to 5pm winter; 🛜) This chamber of commerce offers tourist information and also operates an information center at the Narrow-Gauge Engine, Car & Depot History Center in Cole Park at 3rd St and the west bank of the Rio Grande.

ⓘ Getting There & Away

The **Alamosa San Luis Valley Regional Airport** (☎719-589-9446; 2500 State Ave), south of the central district, has daily flights to Denver via Pueblo on Great Lakes Airline, an independent partner of United Airlines.

Greyhound stops in Alamosa on the daily Denver–Albuquerque service at the **bus depot** (☎719-589-4948; 1924 Stockton St) on the west side of town, south of the railroad tracks.

Alamosa is 73 miles west of Walsenburg on US 160 and 23 miles north of Antonito, near the New Mexico border, on US 285, which turns at Alamosa toward Monte Vista, 31 miles west.

SAN LUIS

POP 800 / ELEVATION 7965FT

Tucked into the far southeast margin of the San Luis Valley, the town of San Luis, which happens to be Colorado's oldest settlement is a wide spot in the road lined with chamisa shrubs. It largely escaped the 'progress' that revoked Hispanic tenure in other parts of the valley following the arrival of the railroad; today the town remains almost 90% Hispanic, a harbor of cultural diversity among Colorado's largely white population. It's an appealing, friendly place, worth a detour for those who want to experience the scenic, slow pace of the deep San Luis Valley.

The character of San Luis – today and throughout history – is largely the result of its isolation. To Spain, the upper Rio Grande was a lost province best left to the mounted nomadic Native American tribes that Spain was unable to dominate. Mexico encouraged civilian settlement and agriculture with the Sangre de Cristo Land Grant in 1843, yet did not establish a plaza at San Luis until 1851. Under the threat of Ute raids, and being far from the mercantile and spiritual centers at Taos and Santa Fe, San Luis developed as a self-sufficient outpost.

⊙ Sights

TOP CHOICE **Stations of the Cross** SCULPTURES
(cnr Hwys 142 & 159) Following a path up a small hill, local sculptor Huberto Maestas' 15 dramatic life-sizes statues of Christs' crucifixion are a powerful testament to the Catholic heritage of communities near the

---

LONESOME SONG OF THE PENITENTE

Of the characters who populate the pre-American history of Colorado's deep south – native Utes, Franciscan missionaries, Spanish prospectors – none are more mysterious than Los Hermanos Penitente, a secretive religious sect of men that thrived in the early 19th century. Some say the Penitente's membership drew from the furthest outcasts of 19th-century southwestern society, a servant class of Native Americans who worked as housekeepers and shepherds, called *genízaros*. Because of their remote location and cast-off social status, Los Hermanos had limited access to the sacred traditions of Spanish Catholicism, which had taken root in the region – some communities were visited by a priest as little as once a year. So they took matters into their own hands. Meeting in humble meeting houses called *moradas*, their ceremonies evolved into a fairly grizzly brand of mystical Catholicism that sought spiritual awakening through the suffering of the Passion of Christ. *Penitente* rituals involved lashing each other with amole weed or binding themselves to a heavy wooden cross. Some sects ended their Good Friday ceremonies with an actual crucifixion, the last fatal instance of which was recorded in the 1890s. If you visit San Luis near Easter, the echoes of this tradition are evident in the town's elaborate Holy Week celebrations.

The mournful songs of Los Hermanos Penitente are called *alabados*, haunting, unaccompanied hymns that blend Hispanic *folclórica* with elements of droning Native American song. Often sung at death rituals, funeral processions and burials, *alabados* have themes that are, like the group itself, fixated on the suffering and torture of Christ. New World Records has compiled an excellent compilation of salvaged historical recordings of Penitente chapters singing *alabados* – *Dark & Light in Spanish New Mexico: Alabados y Bailes*, the only released recording of the music and the perfect soundtrack to the long, dry scenery of a drive through the region. For more information about Los Hermanos Penitente, look to Dr Marta Weigle's definitive study, *Brothers of Light, Brothers of Blood*, published by the University of New Mexico Press.

'Blood of Christ' Mountains. They are stationed along a 1-mile pathway, an excellent chance to stretch the legs.

Beginning with Jesus being condemned to death, the bronze statues continue through the Resurrection. From the crucifixion on the mesa summit during late afternoon sunsets you can observe the reddish light cast on the Sangre de Cristo mountain range, including Culebra Peak (14,069ft), giving the mountains their 'Blood of Christ' name. You can also look out over San Luis and its surrounding fields and pasture. For many years, San Luis residents re-enacted the capture, trial and crucifixion of Christ during Holy Week (Easter) and also made pilgrimages to the Stations of the Cross every Friday during Lent. During the Centennial Jubilee of the Sangre de Cristo Parish in 1986, parish members conceived the Stations of the Cross Shrine to formalize this re-enactment.

San Luis Museum & Cultural Center
MUSEUM
(☑719-672-3611; 401 Church Pl; adult $2; ☺10am-4pm summer, 9am-4pm Mon-Fri winter; ♠) This handsome museum and gallery chronicles Hispanic culture in southern Colorado, in a modern building that blends sustainable concepts with traditional regional architecture. Exhibits on the Penitente Brotherhood are especially intriguing for their insight into this formerly secretive local sect of Catholicism. The theater in the Cultural Center is open weekends.

Viejo San Acacio
CHURCH
(Costilla County Rd 15) The beautiful Viejo (old) San Acacio is a historic Catholic church where mass is still occasionally held. To get here, go 4 miles east of San Luis on Hwy 142, then turn left (south) on Costilla County Rd 15. The church is near Culebra Creek.

🛏 Sleeping

El Convento B&B
B&B $
(☑719-672-3685; 512 Church Pl; d $70) This unique property, owned by the Sangre de Cristo Parish, was originally built as a school in 1905, and the substantial adobe

---

JACK DEMPSEY MUSEUM

Manassa is the home of the **Jack Dempsey Museum** (☑719-843-5207; 412 Main St; ☺9am-5pm Tue-Sat summer), dedicated to the rugged heavyweight champ who was born there.

---

building later served as a convent. Five upstairs rooms, each with private bathroom, are decorated with antiques and handcrafted furniture. Downstairs you can purchase local handmade crafts in the Centro Artesano gallery. Opposite the church.

San Luis Inn Motel
MOTEL $
(☑877-672-3331; 138 Main St; d $69) This may be the only lodging choice available in winter. It has an indoor hot tub.

ℹ Information
San Luis Visitors Center (☑719-672-3002; 408 Main St; ☺9am-1pm Thu-Sun)

ℹ Getting There & Away
San Luis is 42 miles from Alamosa. By car, first head 26 miles east on US 160 to Fort Garland, then south on Hwy 159 for 16 miles. From Romeo on US 285 between Antonito and Alamosa, Hwy 142 heads east through Manassa.

ANTONITO

POP 870 / ELEV 7890FT
Pick up trucks with fishing tackle in back rumble through the dusty, run-down little berg of Antonito. It's sadly fitting that the only two real attractions here are methods of transportation to get somewhere *else*: there's the northern terminus of the Cumbres & Toltec Scenic Railroad (C&TS); a narrow-gauge railway that goes over the mountains to Chama, New Mexico; and scenic Hwy 17, which follows the Conejos River into the Rio Grande National Forest.

The Cumbres & Toltec Scenic Railroad Depot is a mile south of Antonito at the junction of US 285 (Main St) and Hwy 17. The **Antonito Visitors Center** (☑719-376-2049, 800-835-1098; www.conejosvacation.com; 200 Main St; ☺9am-5pm Mon-Fri Jun-Aug) is opposite the railroad depot and only open in summer. For visitor information call the **Antonito Chamber of Commerce** (☑719-376-2277, 800-323-9469; 220 Main St; ☺9am-5pm Mon-Fri).

With lodging or campsites available nearby in the beautiful Conejos River Canyon to the west on Hwy 17 – some camps and cabins are only 5 miles away – there's no reason to stay in glum Antonito. If you do get stuck, a short walk from the C&TS depot is the **Narrow Gauge Railroad Inn** (☑800-323-9469; www.narrowgaugerailroadinn.info; 5200 State Hwy 285; d $59, RV parking $17; ☏♠) a standard motel with free wi-

CUMBRES & TOLTEC SCENIC RAILROAD

One of several historic narrow-gauge trains in the state, this impressive ride is a chance to mount the Cumbres Pass by power of steam.

In 1880 the Denver & Rio Grande Western Rail (D&RG) completed a track over Cumbres Pass, linking Chama, New Mexico, with Denver by way of Alamosa. The twisting, mountainous terrain was suited to narrow-gauge track, which is only 3ft wide instead of the standard gauge of 4ft 8in. Within a few years the line was extended to Durango, Farmington and the Silverton mining camp, 152 miles away. Railroad buffs encouraged Colorado and New Mexico to buy the scenic Cumbres Pass segment when the Antonito–Farmington line came up for abandonment in 1967. Their efforts led to a compact between Colorado and New Mexico to save the railway as a National Register site, and churning along its track, past hills of pine and aspen and expansive views of the high plains and mountains, makes an excellent way to spend a day.

Today, chugging steam engines pull passenger cars up the 10,022ft Cumbres Pass between Antonito and Chama – the longest and highest narrow-gauge steam line in North America. Along the way, the train follows a precipitous rock ledge 600ft above the Rio Los Pinos in the Toltec Gorge. At a plodding 12mph to 15mph, the 64-mile ride takes slightly more than six hours, including water stops and a lunch stop midway at Osier. You can take a round-trip to Osier, or a trip to the beautiful Cumbres Pass. The through trip to Chama returns by van in slightly more than an hour. All trips require a full day.

The C&TS can also provide access to the backcountry and prime fishing streams in the USFS lands along the border between Colorado and New Mexico. Backpackers can make reservations for drop-off and a later pickup at the water stops. If you wish to camp in Chama, Rio Chama RV Campground offers tent sites only two blocks north of the depot.

Trains run daily, roughly from Memorial Day to mid-October, from the **Cumbres & Toltec Scenic Railroad Depot** (☎719-376-5483; www.cumbrestoltec.com; 5250 Hwy 285; adult coach class $75-91, parlor class $150-182, child 11yr & under half-fare). Dress warmly as the unheated cars, both enclosed and semi-enclosed, can get extremely cold. There are currently eight day-trip options to choose from. Call ahead or check the website for current schedules and reservations.

fi and RV parking. For a stay with a more personal touch, try the **River's Inn and Swiss Cottage Bed & Breakfast** (☎719-376-6029; www.antonitobedandbreakfast.net; 317 River St; d $98-148; ⊖🛜🅿). Situated in an old brick home with a wraparound porch, the antique-loaded bedrooms feel like they were decorated by a fussy aunt.

Cheesy Mexican food and standard US dishes are available at the **Dutch Mill** (☎719-376-2373; 407 Main St; mains $6-12; ⊙6:30am-9pm), a place that's the best in town mostly because of lack of competition.

CONEJOS RIVER

Although a few travelers explore historical sites along the lower Conejos River near Antonito, the upstream portions of the river to the west of Antonito along Hwy 17 draw fisherman, hikers and game hunters.

The Conejos is a top fishery, and numerous tributaries and nearby high-elevation lakes, accessible by well-maintained forest roads, also provide gold-medal fishing. Bighorn sheep, elk and deer can be spotted near the river or on canyon cliffs. On the steep Hwy 17 ascent toward the Cumbres Pass you can catch superb vistas of the Conejos River and sheer face of Black Mountain across the valley. The winding route passes the picturesque upland meadow, created by fire in 1879, and an historic wooden water tank at Los Pinos. The volcanic character of the San Juan Range from this angle is vivid, with ragged rock outcrops that rise before drivers who make it over Cumbres Pass.

To reach the Conejos River from Antonito, travel directly west on Hwy 17. Or take a short detour to the north along the river, passing the scrawny county seat at Conejos and Colorado's oldest church, the **Nuestra Señora de Guadalupe**, before rejoining

Hwy 17. Another example of early Spanish architecture is the adobe **San Pedro y San Rafael Church** at Paisaje. This handsome building, topped by an octagonal wooden bell tower, can also be reached by Hwy 17; turn right on Conejos County Rd 1075, 3 miles west of Antonito.

🏃 Activities
Hiking & Backpacking
There is a lot of good hiking and camping in the remote South San Juan Wilderness Area, a part of the Rio Grande National Forest. Don't expect a crowded trail; this area is probably the least used wilderness in southern Colorado. It straddles the Continental Divide and is traversed by the Continental Divide National Scenic Trail, which emerges from the backcountry at the Cumbres Pass depot.

Trailheads and campsites are located along the river on USFS Rd 250, northwest of Elk Creek. Near Cumbres Pass USFS Rd 118 leads to Trujillo Meadows Wilderness Area and a USFS campground before reaching a trailhead on the southern boundary of the wilderness. You can also camp along the edge of the Platoro Reservoir, from which there are hikes to the region's tallest point, Summit Peak.

For maps and information about these hikes, contact the **USFS Conejos Peak Ranger District** (📞719-274-8971; 15571 County Rd T5; 🕐8am-4pm Mon-Fri), 11 miles north of Antonito (3 miles south of La Jara) on US 285.

Fishing
Specially managed Wild Trout Waters are designated by the Colorado Division of Wildlife on the uppermost Lake Fork, plus sections of the Conejos River next to the South San Juan Wilderness and below the Menkhaven Lodge for 4 miles. These streams support self-sustaining native cutthroat trout populations. The Division of Wildlife manager in Antonito prepares a map and handout on fishing the Conejos River for each season; it's available at the Antonito Visitors Center (p314) and tackle shops. On your way in stop at Cottonwood Cabins & Fly Fishing Service, 5 miles west of Antonito, for information on fishing conditions and specific regulations for the season. The shop also offers fishing guides for your choice of wading, hiking or horseback-riding trips on the Conejos River and its tributaries from May to November.

🛏 Sleeping
If you have the time to explore a little, there's no problem finding a nice place to camp or a basic cabin along the river. There's a string of private and public campgrounds and cabins along Hwy 17. A few lodges provide very comfortable accommodations. Most places close from late October to April. The following selection is organized by distance from Antonito along Hwy 17.

Only 5 miles from Antonito, Hwy 17 crosses the Conejos River where large cottonwood groves shade nice tent sites with showers at **Mogote Meadow Cabins & RV Park** (📞719-376-5774; 34127 Hwy 17; sites $18-28, cabins $76-90; 🚿). Further down, **Cottonwood Cabins & Fly Fishing Service** (📞719-376-5660; 34591 Hwy 17; 🚿) also has cabins and a riverside setting.

The **USFS Mogote Campground** (📞ranger district office 877-444-6777; Hwy 17; sites $16), 13 miles west of Antonito, has popular sites for $16 next to the river or in an upper area shaded by ponderosa pines. A laundry and showers are available 1 mile downstream at **Conejos River Campground** (📞719-376-5943; 26714 Hwy 17; sites $28-33), but the tent sites are not very appealing. Several more USFS campgrounds lie upstream on the river, including at Aspen (16 miles) and Elk Creek (23 miles), where Hwy 17 leaves the river. Fees at both are $16.

Top-end cabins and B&B accommodations, all with private bathroom, are available at **Conejos River Ranch** (📞719-376-2464; www.conejosranch.com; 25390 Hwy 17; cabins $140-235, lodges d $98-125; 🛜🚿), 16 miles west of Antonito. Six fully equipped riverside cabins are on hand – our favorite is the bright and airy La Cassita – and there are eight comfortably furnished lodge rooms. All of them include breakfast. There are even facilities for horses.

MONTE VISTA
POP 5100 / ELEV 7666FT

Monte Vista, a small farming village of only a few square blocks that's fairly typical of the region, is on the west side of the San Luis Valley floor. Heading east and following the Rio Grande, it is at the intersection of US 160 and US 285 (Gunbarrel Rd). The local economy relies on potatoes, barley for the Coors Brewing Company and tourists. Nearby wildlife areas should appeal to birdwatchers, and a few notable lodgings may entice you to spend the night, but most of the tourist flock continues west to roost in the forests along the Rio Grande.

Visitor information is available from a kindly staff at the Monte Vista Chamber of Commerce (☑719-852-2731, 800-562-7085; www.monte-vista.org; 1035 Park Ave). There are also some taxidermy heads to pet. The Rio Grande National Forest Headquarters (☑719-852-5941; 1803 W US Hwy 160; ☉8am-4:30pm Mon-Fri) is west of town and the place to get maps and information on public lands in the Rio Grande headwaters. Bird-watchers and anglers should stop by the Monte Vista Colorado Department of Wildlife Office (☑719-587-6900; http://wildlife.state.co.us; 722 South Rd 1 E; ☉8am-5pm Mon-Fri) on the east side of town, south of US 160/US 285. Turn right near Haefeli's Honey Farms onto Rio Grande County Rd 1E.

◉ Sights

Monte Vista National Wildlife Refuge
WILDLIFE SANCTUARY
(☑Colorado DOW 719-587-6900; off County Rd 15) Six miles south of town on Hwy 15, the Monte Vista National Wildlife Refuge features a 2.5-mile self-guided driving loop, the Avocet Trail, that provides views of waterfowl. In fall a few endangered whooping cranes may be spotted among the thousands of migrating sandhill cranes.

🛏 Sleeping & Eating

Rio Grande Motel
MOTEL $
(☑800-998-7129; www.riograndemotel.net; 25 N Broadway; d $68; ⓟ⊖❋☎) What the place lacks in charming location (it's right off the road, overlooking a gas station) is made up for by the menagerie decorating the rooms. Owned by an avid (and apparently well-armed) outdoor enthusiast, the Rio Grande is a clean and serviceable midcentury motel loaded with local spirit.

Best Western Movie Manor Motor Inn
HOTEL $$
(☑719-852-5921; 2830 US Hwy 160; r $79-109; ⓟ⊖❋🖤) Two miles west of Monte Vista, you can watch movies on a drive-in screen from the picture window of your motel room (sound is piped into the room). All rooms have screen views. Movies are only screened from April to September.

Mansion Bed & Breakfast
B&B $$
(☑719-852-5151; www.themansionbandb.com; 1030 Park Ave; d $100-125; ⊖☎) The upscale option in Monte Vista is decorated and themed out of regional history (all the rooms are named for great women in Colorado's history) but restraint and good taste help it succeed where so many frilly B&Bs fail.

The Susan Anderson Room in back has a balcony view of the distant hills. Perfect for soaking up the setting sun after the evening serving of sherry and chocolates.

TOP CHOICE Pachelli's Deli & Bakery
ITALIAN $
(☑719-852-2466; 1042 Park Ave; mains $5-11; ☉10am-3pm Mon-Fri; 🖤) If you're hungry, you'll fall in love with Pachelli's. It's nothing fancy – just an open room with a checkered floor – but the smell of garlic and warm bread as you walk through the door is a prelude to the excellent food to come.

Fred, the charismatic owner, makes his own crusty loaves and piles them with fresh meatballs. His homemade lasagna is so good it drives him to the point of swearing. 'It's friggin' awesome!' he yells...and he's right.

Baldo's Mexican Restaurant
MEXICAN $
(☑719-852-0222; 1100 Park Ave; mains $7-13; ☉10am-7pm Mon-Sat, to 6pm Sun; 🖤) The messy buffet lunch at this passable, brightly painted Mexican joint is perfect for starving outdoorsmen.

Nino's
MEXICAN $
(118 Adams St; mains $6-10; 🖤) This is a busy lunch spot where locals huddle around vinyl tablecloths and shovel down cheesy, saucy platters of enchiladas, washing them back with margaritas in big glass mugs. Right on Main St downtown.

Johnny B Good's
DINER $
(☑719-852-2344; 138 Adams St; mains $6-8; ☉7am-3pm; ⊖🖤) The simplest choice for families is this throw-back diner. It serves diner food with nostalgic trimmings, and patrons line up at the long counter for thick milkshakes.

LA GARITA

ELEV 7831
Climbing the rim surrounding La Garita (*garita* is Spanish for 'overlook') yields an expansive view: the wide green valley cut through by the Rio Grande, snowcapped 14,000ft peak of San Luis Mountain and

the dramatic spine of the Continental Divide. Down inside this caldera (a geologic depression formed in the aftermath of a volcanic explosion), the ash formations rise like alien spires, creating one of Colorado's most varied climbing destinations. This is one of Colorado's original five wilderness areas, where outstanding climbing and hikes through volcanic terrain take place among historical Hispanic landmarks. The volcano that shaped this place happened 28 million years ago and scientists have discerned that it was one of the most violent eruptions in the history of the planet.

◉ Sights & Activities

Historical Sites

For those more interested in history than heights, you can also find low adobe root cellars; a former Hispanic workers union hall, identified by the abbreviation 'SPMDTU'; and an offshoot of the Penitente Brotherhood (see p313). A chapel, known as La Capilla de San Juan Bautista, listed on the National Register of Historic Places, and a cemetery stand in stark splendor on a prominent site above the village. The chapel was originally built in 1861 but was rebuilt in 1924 following a fire. Though it was remodelled extensively by Artes de Valle, a nonprofit collective of women artists, the building was reclaimed by the Catholic church, who open the building only occasionally.

Rock Climbing

Experienced climbers are attracted to the bolted face climbs on the rhyolite rock walls in Penitente Canyon and Rock Canyon. But with more than 400 routes in the area, there are opportunities for all levels of experience – some of which are even bolted. Some consider these among the best short climbing routes in Colorado. You can get more information about the area at the USFS Divide District Ranger Station (opposie), which is in Del Norte and has several developed campgrounds in the area.

Supplies

Getting supplies for this area requires a bit of advance arrangements, as several small climbing shops nearby have recently closed. The best bet is to get supplies in Colorado Springs, if you're coming from the east, or Pagosa Springs, if you're coming from the west.

ℹ Getting There & Away

To get to La Garita from Monte Vista, travel north 20 miles on US 285, turn left (west) at the sign on Saguache County Rd G for 8 miles. Penitente Canyon is southwest from the chapel on County Rd 38.

DEL NORTE

POP 1590 / ELEV 7879FT

Sun-bleached and lazy, Del Norte (pronounce it like a local and rhyme 'Norte' with 'port') is a place most travelers blast through on the way to or from sites in Colorado's southwest. The town is seated next to the Rio Grande del Norte, for which it was named, in the foothills west of the San Luis Valley on US 160. One of Colorado's oldest towns, it was founded in 1860 and by 1873 it was a thriving supply point for mining in the San Juan Mountains. Now Del Norte marks the beginning of Gold Medal fishing on the Rio Grande and is a popular jumping-off point for rock climbers (pardon the pun) and mountain bikers on their way to La Garita.

◉ Sights & Activities

FREE Rio Grande County Museum & Cultural Center

MUSEUM, CULTURAL CENTER

(☏719-657-2847; 580 Oak St; ◷10am-5pm Tue-Sat Jun-Aug, noon-5pm Tue-Sat Dec-Feb; ⊕) This museum and cultural center features Pueblo and Ute rock art, Hispanic history and early photographs of Monte Vista's 'potato row' wagons loaded high with valley spuds at the turn of the 20th century. Special programs include talks and outdoor excursions led by local historians and naturalists. The museum has information for people who want to visit local rock-art sites.

Mountain Biking

Fat-tire bikes are permitted on all public trails with the exception of designated wilderness areas. A relatively easy ride heads north about 10 miles to La Ventana, a natural arch 'window' in a volcanic dike. To get there from Del Norte, cross the river and follow Rio Grande County Rd 22 for 8 miles, passing the small airport; turn right on USFS Rd 660 for a quarter of a mile; then turn left and follow the road for about 2 miles to the short trail to the volcanic wall.

Another ride recommended by the USFS follows an old stock driveway along an alpine ridge on USFS Trail 700 from Grayback Mountain (12,616ft) east 7 miles to Blowout Pass (12,000ft). To reach the Grayback Mountain trailhead, you have to travel about 20 miles south of Del Norte on USFS Rd 14, then continue another 5 miles on USFS Rd 330.

Fishing
Gold-medal fishing on the Rio Grande begins a mile upstream at the Farmer's Union Canal. From here to the Hwy 149 bridge at South Fork is one of Colorado's most productive fisheries, producing 16in to 20in trout. You access the river and signed public property via the bridges on Rio Grande County Rds 17, 18 and 19, plus the Hwy 149 bridge above South Fork.

🛏 Sleeping
On the east side of Grande Ave (US 160) there are a pair of motels that offer comparably drab rooms, but they're a cheap option that's right on the road. At the time of research, there were much better eating and sleeping options just up the road in Monte Vista, but the lovingly restored **Historic Windsor Hotel** (www.windsorhotel.org; cnr Grand & Columbia Aves) might well change all that. When we stopped in, this centrally located landmark had yet to fully emerge from the scaffolding, but when it does it could well be the nicest place to stay in the region. A community organiza-tion has put years of work into the project and the renovations underway were meticulous, right down to the original paint colors and custom reproductions of the tin ceiling panels. The 1st floor hosts a dining room.

🍴 Eating & Drinking
Boogie's Restaurant AMERICAN, MEXICAN **$$**
(☎719-657-2905; 410 Grand Ave; mains $8-14) This joint makes for a family-friendly lunch stop. The menu is all over the place (Tex Mex, burgers, big salads) but the portions are big and the service is attentive.

Three Barrel Brewery BREWPUB
(☎719-852-3314; www.threebarrelbrew.com; 586 Columbia Ave; ⊗9am-5pm) Welcome to Colorado's smallest brewery. It produces only 350 barrels of beer from the nondescript brick building just a block off the main drag. But its damn good beer. The 'just one more' inclination inspired by the Threedom Ale – a rich, aromatic, spicy blonde ale – might be the best reason to spend the night in town.

❶ Information
Del Norte Chamber of Commerce (☎719-657-2845, 888-616-4836; 505 Grande Ave; ⊗8:30am-5pm Mon-Fri)
USFS Divide District Ranger Station (☎719-657-3321; 1308 Grand Ave; ⊗8:30am-5pm Mon-Fri)

Eastern Colorado

Includes »

COLORADO
SPRINGS 321

FLORISSANT FOSSIL
BEDS NATIONAL
MONUMENT 331

PUEBLO 332

CAÑON CITY &
ROYAL GORGE 334

TRINIDAD 339

SANTA FE TRAIL 341

BENT'S OLD FORT
NATIONAL HISTORIC
SITE 341

NORTHEAST
COLORADO 342

Why Go?

Although it is tempting to dismiss eastern Colorado on your way to better known destinations, this is a region steeped in Old West history and stocked with gorgeous secrets. Here are dinosaur footprints and old wagon ruts that speak to millions of years of migration.

In addition to brontosaurus families, the Pony Express, Overland Trail and the Santa Fe Trail all blazed through these plains and over nearby mountain passes, as did a half-dozen Native American tribes. Their history is palpable here. The stand-alone Spanish Peaks, with their spectacular dikes erupting from below, are nothing short of spectacular, and if you have the days to spare, shoot the Royal Gorge, go antiquing in Florence, and check into the old-world luxury of one of the Broadmoor, one of America's finest hotels.

Best Places to Eat

» Blue Star (p328)

» Cliff House at Pikes Peak (p327)

» Hopscotch Bakery (p333)

» Nana & Nano's (p340)

Best Places to Stay

» Broadmoor (p327)

» Cliff House at Pikes Peak (p327)

» Tarabino Inn (p340)

When to Go?

Colorado Springs

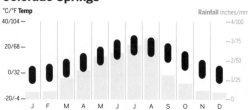

June–August	September–November	December–February
Hike into the stunning, untrammeled and oft-ignored Spanish Peaks Wilderness.	Hike through hip-high grass in the Pawnee National Grassland.	Ski, snowshoe or take the railway to Pikes Peak summit.

COLORADO SPRINGS

POP 369,815 / ELEV 6035–7200FT

As beautiful as any city in Colorado, and in many ways the perfect urban allegory for contemporary America, Colorado Springs certainly leaves an impression.

Cradled sweetly below stunning Pikes Peak (visible from all points of town) and erupting with a craggy, striking red-rock vein that juts and runs for more than 10 miles, Colorado Springs does look damn good.

Pinned down with four military bases, it's also a strange and sprawling quilt of neighborhoods that bounce between old (and new) money in Broadmoor to the evangelized planned community that is Briargate, to the hippie stronghold of Manitou Springs, to the progressive old pioneer capitol of Old Colorado City, and finally to a downtown district that offers a mix of fine art, Olympic dreams and, yes, a touch of downbeat desperation.

This is a town that spawned one of the country's first destination resorts. It gave us flame-throwing Hall of Fame relief pitcher Goose Gossage, and nurtured Apollo Ohno to Olympic Stardom. Colorado Springs is where evangelical megachurch pastor Ted Haggard's headline-making sex and drugs scandal played out (and where his comeback was sparked), and where this century's most notorious band of outlaws, the Texas 7, were captured.

Clean and safe, it's a city of athletes and health nuts, adventurers, sober soldiers and flamboyant ice dancers. For better or worse (and it's mostly for the better), here is America in a nutshell, and one of the few places in Colorado where dramatic natural beauty doesn't come with an inflated-for-the-tourist price tag.

⊙ Sights

TOP CHOICE **Pikes Peak** MOUNTAIN SUMMIT
(☎719-385-7325; www.springsgov.com; Pikes Peak; per adult/child/car (5 people) $12/5/40, cog railway round-trip adult/child $33/18; ⊙9am-3pm winter, 7:30am-8pm Memorial Day-Labor Day, 9am-5pm 1 Oct-Memorial Day; P⛟; ⓇCog Railway) At 14,110ft, Pikes Peak may not be one of the tallest of Colorado's 54 14-ers, but it's certainly the most famous. Maybe because it's the only one with a road and a train to the top? That's where you'll find an observation platform and a kitschy gift shop in the Summit House selling Pikes Peak sweaters and hackeysacks, and homemade fudge is for sale in the cafeteria.

Down slope are seven reservoirs – Pikes Peak is the water source for this entire region, and from the summit you can see Kansas, the Oklahoma panhandle, the Wyoming Continental Divide and the Spanish Peaks in New Mexico.

Colorado Springs Fine Arts Center
MUSEUM
(FAC; ☎719-634-5583; www.csfineartscenter.org; 30 W Dale St; adult/senior & student $10/8.50; ⊙10am-5pm Tue-Sun; P⛟; 🖰9) This recently re-done $28-million art museum and 400-seat theatre, opened in 1936. The museum's collection is surprisingly sophisticated, with some terrific Latin American art and photography, and a great series, in the original, pebbled marble wing, by local artist Eric Bransby on the history of navigation. But these are just some of the 23,000 pieces in its permanent collection

There are Mexican clay figures, Native American basketry and quilts, wood-cut prints from social justice artist Leopoldo Mendez, terrific abstract work from local artists such as Vance Kirkland and Floyd Tunson. Its biggest and most famous work is Richard Diebenkorn's *Urbana No. 4*, an abstract that's exhibited around the world.

The sculpture garden and vast lawn out back are great for lounging and occasional concerts, and the Bemis School of Art is attached to the museum. That's the school that gave us Sushe Felix.

The founder of the center was Alice Bemis Taylor, who leaned on her vast connections in the New York art world. And her influence has stuck.

FREE **Garden of the Gods** PARK
(☎719-634-6666; www.gardenofgods.com; 1805 N 30th St; ⊙8am-8pm Memorial Day-Labor Day, 9am-5pm Labor Day-Memorial Day; P⛟) A compound of 13 bouldered peaks and soaring red-rock pinnacles accessed by a network of concrete paths and trails. From the main parking area you'll see the Kissing Camels, White Rock and Tower of Babel right away. The Cathedral Towers and Sleeping Giant are further on.

It's a great place for families, as little ones love rambling the paths, while lovers snuggle or quarrel in shadows, and resident deer prance among the brush. This land was originally purchased in 1879 by Charles Elliot Perkins. He'd always wanted to make it an official public park and his kids carried out his wishes after his death. It became a park in 1909.

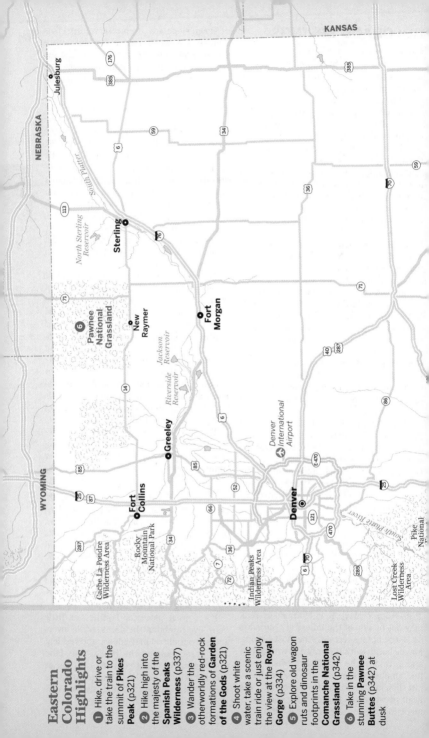

Eastern Colorado Highlights

1 Hike, drive or take the train to the summit of **Pikes Peak** (p321)

2 Hike high into the majesty of the **Spanish Peaks Wilderness** (p337)

3 Wander the otherworldly red-rock formations of **Garden of the Gods** (p321)

4 Shoot white water, take a scenic train ride or just enjoy the view at the **Royal Gorge** (p334)

5 Explore old wagon ruts and dinosaur footprints in the **Comanche National Grassland** (p342)

6 Take in the stunning **Pawnee Buttes** (p342) at dusk

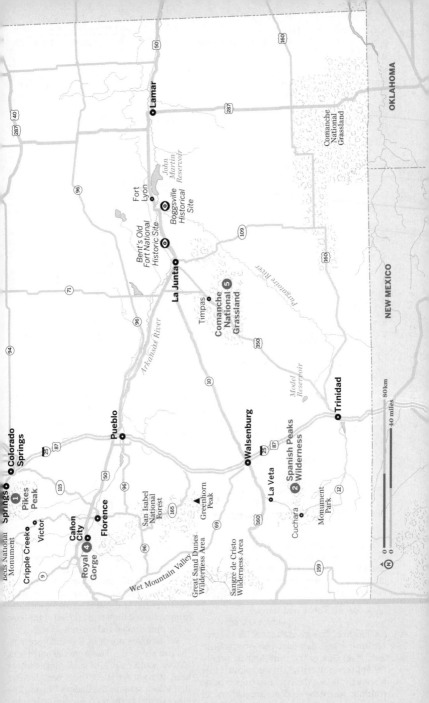

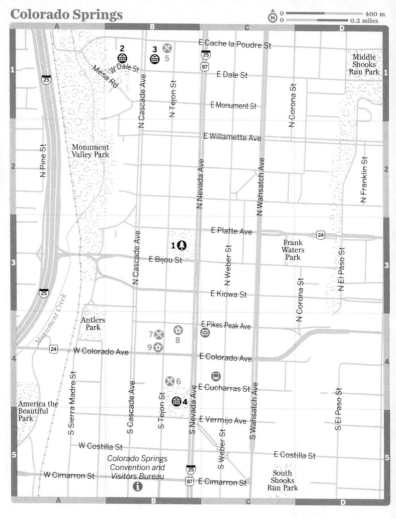

To be clear, this is not a wilderness experience, but it is beautiful. Rock climbing is heavily restricted and you must have a permit to rope in. You can apply for one at the visitors center.

FREE US Air Force Academy

MILITARY BASE, UNIVERSITY

(☎719-333-2025; www.usafa.af.mil; US Air Force Academy; ☺base 8am-6pm, visitor center 9am-5pm; P🚼) One of the third-highest profile US military universities in the country, this is something like the Ivy Leage meets basic training, where the students are soldiers, all have killer academic and extra-curricular

backgrounds and work full-time while going to school. It can be a surreal place, but it's well worth visiting, especially if fighters are rocketing into the sky from the airfield.

Did we mention they have a decent football team and are nestled on their own base-campus tucked high on a plateau at the base of the pine draped red earth Rockies?

Set 14 miles north of Colorado Springs, you can access the base from the north (exit 156) or south (exit 150) gate. Most visitors head straight for the visitors center. After that take a walk to the Cadet's Chapel. The lower chapel is always open; the upper cha-

Colorado Springs

◎ **Sights**
1 Acacia Park	B3
2 Colorado Springs Fine Arts Center	B1
3 Cornerstone Arts Center	B1
4 Pioneers Museum	B4

◎ **Eating**
Amuzé	(see 2)
5 La'au's	B1
6 Nosh	B4
7 Pikes Perk Coffee & Teahouse	B4

◎ **Entertainment**
| 8 Kimball's Twin Peak Theatre | B4 |
| 9 Thirsty Parrot | B4 |

pel is more stunning but can be closed for special events. Right outside the lower chapel doors you'll find the Honor Court with plaques memorializing those who died in uniform.

The terrazzo below the chapel enclosed by minimalist glass rectangular buildings is where the cadets form up and march. There's a cool B52 bomber staged at North gate, and a vintage Thundercat installed at the entrance to the airfield. If you're looking to take a hike, hit the Stanley Canyon trail. It's 2.1 miles long and will provide some beautiful bird's-eye views of the base and all of Colorado Springs.

Cave of the Winds CAVERNS
(☑719-685-5444; www.caveofthewinds.com; 100 Cave of the Winds Rd; Lantern Tour adult/child $22/12, Discovery Tour $18/9, child under 5yr free; ⊘9am-9pm Mar-Nov 10am-5pm Dec-Feb, closed Christmas Day; ℙ⬆) Set on the rim of a craggy canyon is this developed cavern concession. You'll forgive the cheesy entry and elevator music because here are the stalactites and stalagmites of your dreams. Most opt for the 45-minute Discovery Tour, but the Lantern Tour goes twice as deep, gets twice as dark and lasts twice as long.

Manitou Cliff Dwellings ARCHAEOLOGICAL SITE
(☑719-685-5242; www.cliffdwellingsmuseum. com; 10 Cliff Dwellings Rd; adult/child/senior $9.50/7.50/8.50; ⊘9am-6pm; ℙ⬆) A set of stunning Ancestral Puebloan cliff dwellings grooved into the red-rock hills at 6530ft just east of Manitou Springs off Hwy 24. You'll see the adobe facades, and get a feel for the cool cave interiors with their

grain-storage turrets and beamed ceilings in what is a string of half-a-dozen multiple family homes. Talk about an efficient use of space!

There's also a museum gift shop and snacks on site in a groovy Pueblo-style structure that looms from the hills. The museum has a terrific pottery display downstairs and interesting video displays throughout, including inside the bathroom! It's not exactly Mesa Verde, but it'll do if you can't make it to the Four Corners.

Cheyenne Mountain Zoo ZOO
(☑719-633-9925; www.cmzoo.org; 4250 Cheyenne Mountain Zoo Rd; adult/child 3-11yr /senior $14.25/7.25/12.25, Mountain Sky Ride adult/child $5/4, pony/carousel rides $5/3; ⊘9am-6pm, last admission 4pm; ℙ⬆) Layered high up on Cheyenne Mountain, the largest private zoo in the country was launched with holdovers from Penrose's private animal collection. These days it takes conservation more seriously and is proud of its giraffe breeding program. The habitats are decent with instructional elements built in. There are some nice play areas for kids.

And the cast of characters (gorillas, Komodo dragons, orangutans, tigers, Siberian snow leopard, hippos and elephants) will keep you interested. The Mountaineer Sky Ride, a brief chairlift experience, will give you a bird's-eye view of the whole zoo.

FREE **Acacia Park** PARK
(www.springsgov.com; 115 E Platte Ave; ⊘fountain noon-6pm Wed-Sun May-Aug, farmers markets Mon 10am-3pm Jun-Oct; ⬆; ☐5) The home of the Monday farmers market and the much loved Uncle Wilbur's Fountain, a lifeguard-monitored pop jet fountain with over 200 water jets, 52 of which are part of a play area where kids run and try to stem the unstoppable streams with their pitter patter. It's a good time, but remember this is also something of a downbeat gathering place for the road weary and lost among us.

FREE **Pioneers Museum** MUSEUM
(☑719-385-5990; www.springsgov.com; 215 S Tejon St; ⊘10am-4pm Tue-Sat; ℙ⬆; ☐10, 11) Colorado Springs' municipal museum is set in the old El Paso County Courthouse, built in 1903. The collection and exhibition of some 60,000 pieces sums up the region's history. Particularly good is the Native American collection, which features hundreds of items from the Ute, Cheyenne and Arapaho nations.

FREE **Cornerstone Arts Center**   GALLERY
(☏719-389-6607; www.coloradocollege.edu; 825 N Cascade Ave; ⊘hrs vary; P⛨; ☐9) Colorado College's striking, $30 million LEED (Leadership in Energy & Environmental Design)-certified arts complex across the street from the Fine Arts Center. You'll see sculpture on the front lawn, and there's a free gallery inside and frequent guest lecturers and film screenings. Past guests have incuded filmmakers, prominent feminists, Buddhist masters and big-time video-game producers.

🏃 Activities

It's all about big nature and stunning vistas when it comes to Colorado Springs. Hike the trail with your bike or boots, then take the scenic Pikes Peak drive to the sky.

TOP CHOICE **Manitou & Pikes Peak Cog Railway**   HIKING, RAILWAY
(☏719-685-5401; www.cograilway.com; 515 Ruxton Ave; round-trip adult/child $33/18; ⊘Apr-Jan; ⛨) Travelers have been making the trip to the summit of Pikes Peak (14,110ft) on the Pikes Peak Cog Railway since 1891, when Spencer Penrose built it. Katherine Lee Bates was so impressed by her 1893 trip to the summit that she was inspired to write 'America the Beautiful.' Diesel-powered, Swiss-built trains smoothly make the round-trip in three hours and 10 minutes, which includes 40 minutes at the top.

The train makes no official stops, but engineers will drop hikers at Mountain View for Barr Trail. It's the best way to day hike Pikes Peak, and you may as well take the train back down – you've paid for it (it only sells round-trip tickets). Trains depart from the Manitou Springs Depot, 6 miles west of Colorado Springs on US Hwy 24 in groovy little Manitou Springs.

FREE **Barr Trail**   HIKING
(www.fotp.com/BarrTrailMap.htm; 515 Ruxton Ave; cog railway adult/child $33/18; ⛨) The main trail to Pikes Peak is a popular 12.8-mile trudge from the trailhead near the Manitou Springs Depot at an elevation of 6600ft. That makes for an elevation gain of 7510ft to the summit at 14,110ft. Many hikers split the trip into two days, stopping to overnight at Barr Camp at the halfway point (10,200ft).

The alternate option is to but a return ticket (no one-way options) on the Manitou & Pike Peak Cog Railway. As noted above, engineers will drop off hikers despite the lack of official stops. You'll be let out onto a spur trail 1.5 miles from Barr Camp where you can join the main trail to the summit. Then you can take the train down. That makes the trip a fun 7.5-mile day hike.

Many hikers leave the main trail once the peak is in sight after Barr Camp. Just take the path of least resistance to the top of the world. The best time to hike is between June and October.

FREE **Red Rock Canyon Park**
OUTDOORS ACTIVITIES
(www.redrockcanyonopenspace.org; 2002 Creek Crossing St; ⛨) Red Rock Canyon is one of the region's newest and best slices of open space. A former quarry, and part of a red-rock vein that runs through Colorado Springs to the Garden of the Gods, this 787-acre park was nearly developed into a golf course and townhouses.

Thanks to committed residents who fought the good fight, Red Rock Canyon is, and will remain, open to all, including hikers, runners, cyclists and equestrians. Trails from Red Rock connect to Bear Creek Regional Park and North Cheyenne Canyon Park. Rock climbers have access to over 80 bolted climbing routes, but they must register at the Garden of the Gods Visitors Center first or risk a $500 fine. Some trails are for hikers only. Dogs must be leashed except on designated off-leash trails.

Challenge Unlimited   CYCLING
(☏800-798-5954, 719-633-6399; www.bikithikit.com; 204 S 24th St; per person $115; ⊘twice daily May-Oct; ⛨; ☐3, 16) An Old Colorado City–based outfitter who for 20 years has lead cyclists on the lovely, fully supported downhill ride from the Pikes Peak summit into Manitou Springs. There are rides twice a day – in the morning and afternoon. Advance reservations are a must. It has a handful of other Colorado cycling itineraries too.

CS West Bikes   CYCLING
(☏719-633-5565; www.cswestbikes.com; 2403 W Colorado Ave; mountain bike rental per 4hr $20, per 24hr $40, per week $100; ⊘10am-6pm Mon-Fri, 9am-5pm Sat, 10am-4pm Sun; ⛨; ☐3) Based in Old Colorado City, it rents high-quality mountain bikes, does repairs and will suggest the best mountain bike trails in the area. A terrific resource.

🎪 Festivals & Events

Emma Crawford Coffin Races COFFIN RACE
(www.manitousprings.org; Manitou Ave; ⊙Sat before Halloween; 🚗; 🚌3) In 1929 the coffin of Emma Crawford was unearthed by erosion and slid down Red Mountain. Today, coffins are decked out with wheels and run down Manitou Ave for three hours on the Saturday before Halloween.

Pikes Peak International Hill Climb
CAR RACE
(📞719-685-4400; www.usacracing.com/ppihc; tickets $40-45, VIP $80; ⊙last weekend in June; 🚗) A legendary car race first launched by Spencer Penrose after he first built the road to Pikes Peak. These days the cars are faster and the drivers more skilled. The course along Pikes Peak Toll Road is 12.42 miles in total, beginning at 9390ft just uphill from the tollgate. There are 156 turns and the finish line is at the 14,110ft summit.

It's an interesting race as the thin air usually saps up to 30% off an engine's horsepower. The race has around 10 classes, including super stock car, pro truck and motorcycle classes in a combined field approaching 200 competitors.

Colorado Balloon Classic BALLOONING
(📞719-471-4833; www.balloonclassic.com; 1605 E Pikes Peak Ave; ⊙Labor Day weekend; 🚗) Once a year, for 35 years running, hot-air ballooners, both amateur and pro, have been launching technicolor balloons into the sky just after sunrise for three straight days. Most colors of the rainbow are represented along with various corporate logos and novelties, like, say, the Energizer bunny. You'll have to wake with the roosters to see it all, but it's definitely worth your while.

FREE **Great Fruitcake Toss** CATAPULT
(📞719-685-5089; www.manitousprings. org; ⊙1st Sat in Jan; 🚗) Don't miss this famous post-Christmas fruitcake toss, when locals make homemade slingshots to catapult the suckers. One rule: you must have fruitcake. The cake that flies furthest wins. Held on the Manitou Springs High School Track.

🛌 Sleeping

TOP **Broadmoor** RESORT $$$
CHOICE (📞719-634-7711; www.broadmoor.com; 1 Lake Ave; r from $300; P🚗❄@🛜🏊🚗; 🚌4) One of the top five-star resorts in the US, the 744-room Broadmoor sits in a picture-perfect location against the blue-green slopes of Cheyenne Mountain. Everything here is exquisite: acres of lush grounds and a shimmering lake, a glimmering pool, world-class golf, ornately decorated public spaces, myriad bars and restaurants, an incredible spa and ubercomfortable European-style guest rooms. Service is spectacular.

Oh, and your fluffy friends are welcome too. Hell, they even have their own house dog (he goes by Ruger). There's a reason that literally hundreds of Hollywood stars, A-list pro athletes, and every president since FDR (with the exception of Truman and LBJ) have made it a point to visit (and that includes Obama). Of course, W may not be back. This was the site of his infamous birthday blowout that put him on the wagon for good.

Seasonal online deals start from $190.

Cliff House at Pikes Peak HOTEL $$
(📞719-685-3000; www.thecliffhouse.com; 306 Canon Ave; r $84-169; P🚗❄@🛜🏊🚗; 🚌3) Nestled at the foot of Pike's Peak, the Cliff House offers the discriminating traveller a Victorian boutique experience in charming Manitou Springs. It started as a 20-room boarding house and stagecoach stop in 1844. Today it's a luxurious country inn with an old-fashioned vibe and fabulous mountain views.

Complete with turrets and amazing views of Pikes Peak and the surrounding mountains, rooms are styled in late-1800s decor. Warm yellow wallpaper, soothing white duvets and thick gilded drapes set an old fashioned tone, while 21st-century conveniences such as towel warmers, steam showers, gas fireplaces and spa tubs built for two bring this four-diamond hotel up to modern standards.

The dining room is first-class.

Hyatt Place HOTEL $
(📞719-265-9385; www.coloradosprings.place. hyatt.com; 503 West Garden of the Gods Rd; r $71-99; P🚗❄@🛜🏊🚗) Even with its unabashed corporate sheen and Ikea-chic decor, we dig this place. Okay, it's a chain and a bit close to Hwy 25, but rooms are sizable and super clean with cushy linens, new beds, massive flat-screens and a comfy sitting area. Factor in the helpful staff and free continental breakfast, and you have yourself a steal.

Two Sisters Inn　　　　　　　B&B $$
(☎719-685-9684; www.twosisinn.com; 10 Otoe Pl; r with shared bath $79, with private bath $135-155; P ☟ ✳ ☜; ☐3) A longtime favorite among B&B afficionados, this place has five rooms (including the honeymoon cottage out back) set in a rose-colored Victorian home, built in 1919 by two sisters. It was originally a boarding house for school teachers, and has been an inn since 1990. There's a magnificent stained-glass front door, a 1896 piano in the parlor and it has won awards for its breakfast recipes.

Avenue Hotel　　　　　　　B&B $$
(☎719-685-1277; www.avenuehotelbandb.com; 711 Manitou Ave; r incl breakfast $79-129; P ☟ ✳ ☜; ☐3) This Victorian mansion, on a hill in downtown Manitou Springs, began as a boarding house in 1886. One hundred years later, it reopened as the city's first B&B. Decorated in warm colors, the seven rooms, reached via a fantastic three-floor, open turned staircase, have claw-foot tubs, lush fabrics and canopied wrought-iron beds.

Families should ask about the bigger Carriage House, which has a private kitchen.

Barr Camp　　　　　　　CAMPING $
(www.barrcamp.com; Barr Trail; tents $12, lean-tos $17, cabins $28; ☺year-round; ☝; ☒Cog Railway) Located at the halfway point on the Barr Trail, about 6.5 miles from the Pikes Peak summit, you can pitch a tent, shelter in a lean-to or reserve a bare-bones cabin. There's drinking water and showers; dinner ($8) is available Wednesday to Sunday. Reservations are essential and must be made on-line in advance. The camp books up even in the winter.

✖️ Eating

TOP CHOICE Amuzé　　CONTEMPORARY AMERICAN $$$
(Amuzé at the FAC; ☎719-477-4377; www.amuzebistro.com; 30 W Dale St; lunch mains $9.75-19, dinner $26-48; ☺11am-2pm & 5-10pm Tue-Sat, 9am-1:30pm Sun; ☟; ☐9) Set in the spectacular 1936 Fine Arts Center (Colorado Springs' excellent art museum), where you'll see two Andy Warhols on the wall, inlaid murals, parquet floors and exquisite Rocky Mountain views (including Pikes Peak) through the floor-to-ceiling windows.

That's a lot of atmosphere for food to live up to, but chef Bill Sherman works magic in that kitchen. There's tempura-fried tarragon goat's cheese; beef carpaccio with fried capers and avocado Parmesan crisp; and red and yellow beet salad with mixed

greens, feta, maple-glazed bacon dressed in sherry vinaigrette. And that bone in the ribeye is massive, with a wild mushroom demilglaze sweetened with Palisade peaches. The all-natural hormone-free beef comes from right down the road, it gets some produce and all its herbs from right across the street at Dayle Street Urban Gardens, and its catering trucks run on Amuzé fryer oil. The menu usually changes monthly and sometimes weekly. The point is, the food is fresh and seasonal. Oh, and save room for homemade ice cream.

Blue Star　　　CONTEMPORARY AMERICAN $$
(☎719-632-1086; www.thebluestar.net; 1645 S Tejon St; mains $10-25; ☺5:30-9pm Sun-Thu, to noon Fri & Sat; ☐10, 11) One of Colorado Springs' most popular gourmet eateries, the Blue Star is in the quiet Broadmoor neighborhood just south of downtown. The menu at this landmark spot changes regularly, but always involves fresh fish, top-cut steak and inventive chicken dishes, flavored with Mediterranean and Pacific Rim rubs and spices.

The colorful bar area, with metal and sleek wood decor and booth or high-top tables, is more social than the open-kitchen dining room in the back. There's occassional live jazz here, and the menu is slightly less expensive. Blue Star also has an impressive 8500-bottle wine cellar that includes organic varietals.

House of Jerusalem　　MIDDLE EASTERN $
(☎719-685-1325; www.heartofjerusalemcafe.com; 718 Manitou Ave; mains $4.99-11.99; ☺11am-9pm Mon-Sat, to 8pm Sun; ☟ ☝; ☐3) A fabulous Middle Eastern greasy-spoon haunt, and exactly the kind of place you wouldn't expect to find in Colorado Springs. It does cheap and savory shawarma, felafel and 'chickofel' or 'beefofel' (a mix of meat and falafel) sandwiches as well as tasty kebab plates. Veggies will appreciate the veggie plate, with hummus, tabbouleh, falafel, dolmas dripping in olive oil and lemon juice and served warm, and warm pita seasoned with za'atar spice mix. It has sage iced-tea, ice cream, smoothies and Turkish coffee too!

Nosh　　　　　CONTEMPORARY AMERICAN $$
(☎719-635-6674; www.nosh121.com; 121 S Tejon St; small plates $9-21; ☺11am-10pm; ☝; ☐3) Everyone's favorite downtown dining room. There's color and art everywhere you look. It's in the entry way with those giant red paper clips, across the street in the nearby

sculpture garden, on the wide patio with dangling lights and firepits, on the tables and walls, and especially in the kitchen where stunning and tasty small plates are created.

Think: bison dumplings, lentil dumplings, scallop crudo, chili-glazed burgers and all manner of roasted veggies. The best downtown eats by far.

Adam's Mountain Cafe

CONTEMPORARY AMERICAN **$$**

(☎719-685-1430; www.adamsmountain.com; 934 Manitou Ave; mains $7-16; ☺8am- 3pm & 5-9pm Tue-Sat, to 3pm Sun; ♿; ☐MM Transit, 3) A groovy new age Colorado cafe with a slow food ethos. It does veggie burgers and burritos at lunch, orange-almond French toast and huevos rancheros at breakfast, and an eclectic dinner menu that ranges from udon noodles to Senegalese veggies to Brazilian spiced barramundi. The interior is airy and attractive with marble floors and exposed rafters, and there's patio dining too.

La'au's

TACOS **$**

(☎719-578-9158; www.laaustacoshop.com; 830 N Tejon St; dishes $6-9; ☺11am-9pm; ♿♿; ☐9) Tucked into Spencer Center, near Colorado College, and the Fine Arts Center, this creative minimalist, Hawaiian taco shack offers tasty, fast and healthy fare in the form of taco, bowl, (massive, brain-sized) burrito or salad. Choose your protein (shrimp, steak, mahi, chicken or pork), and your salsa and toppings style (Baja, Kona, Hilo or Maui) and grab some coconut flan for dessert.

Pikes Perk Coffee & Teahouse CAFE FOOD **$**

(☎719-635-1600; http://pikesperkcoffee.com/; 14 S Tejon St; espresso & snacks from $2; ☺6am-10pm Mon-Thu, to 11pm Fri, 7am-11pm Sat, to 8pm Sun) With a fantastic rooftop boasting unobstructed views of Colorado Springs' signature mountain, Pikes Perk is our all-time-favorite regional coffee shop. Read a magazine, write a novel or just a chat with friends in the cozy 2nd-floor lounge or on the rooftop deck when the weather's nice.

Pike's Perk serves the usual range of espresso drinks, all excellent quality, as well as a range of pastries, bagels, breakfast burritos and other light meals.

Jake & Telly's

GREEK **$$**

(☎719-633-0406; www.greekdining.com; 2616 W Colorado Ave; mains $9-23; ☺11:30am-9pm Sun-Thu, to 10pm Fri & Sat; ♿; ☐MM Transit, 3) One of the best choices in Old Colorado City is set on the 2nd-story terrace of a mini-mall. Inside it looks like a Greek mountain lodge

with standard-issue Greek monument murals, blue tablecloths and dark-wood beamed ceilings. It does a nice Greek-dip sandwich as well as traditional dishes such as souvlaki, dolmadas and spanakopita.

🍷 Drinking

The downtown Tejon Strip, between Platte and Colorado Sts, is where most of the after-dark action happens, although don't expect too much. Colorado Springs is nobody's party town.

TOP CHOICE **Swirl**

WINE BAR

(☎719-685-2294; www.swirlwineempor ium.com; 717 Manitou Ave; ☺4-10pm Sun-Thu, to midnight Fri & Sat; ☐3) At first it just looks like a stylish, inviting bottle shop with all regions represented and local art on the walls, but as you venture in you'll see a deep blue-walled wine lounge filled with arm chairs and love seats. Next comes the intimate, fun-loving wine bar and behind that is a garden patio dangling with lights and vines. This is the place to meet for a drink, to celebrate life and beauty and love.

Trinity Brewing Co

BREWPUB

(☎719-634-0029; www.trinitybrew.com; 1466 Garden of the Gods Rd; ☺11am-midnight Thu-Sat, 11am-10pm Sun-Wed) Inspired by Belgium's beer cafes, the ecofriendly Trinity Brewing Co is an extremely cool addition to the Colorado Springs pub scene. Owned by two self-admitted beer geeks, it serves 'artisanal beers' (made from rare ingredients and potent amounts of alcohol) and has a menu focused on creating a 'Slow Food dining experience based on...environmental sustainability.'

The vegan BBQ sandwiches, spicy Thai curry soup, vegetarian 'chicken wings' and other healthy, organic choices are definitely a departure from usual pub fare (mains $5 to $8). But don't fret, carnivores: there is some meat on offer. If you're still hungry after dinner, wash your tofu down with a beer float. A 10% discount is given if you arrive on foot or by bike. Look for the brewery in a strip mall one block west of Centennial Blvd. It's about a 15-minute bike ride northwest of downtown.

Hotel Bar

BAR

(☎719-577-5733; Broadmoor, 1 Lake Ave) On a warm summer afternoon there's no better spot for a drink with a view than this bar overlooking a private lake. Order a chilled glass of wine and a cigar, and sit back and watch the ducks pass by. When the weather turns cool, the outdoor stone fireplaces are lit.

Jives Coffee Lounge COFFEE HOUSE
(☎719-357-7285; www.jivescoffeelounge.com; 16 Colbrunn Ct; ⊙8am-midnight Mon-Thu, to 1am Fri & Sat; 🛜♿; 🚌3) Easily the hippest hand on the Old Colorado City stretch, this large brick-wall coffee lounge has ample sofas, wi-fi and a bandstand featuring regular live music and a Wednesday open-mic night. It does all the coffee drinks and a selection of all-fruit, no-sugar smoothies.

Maté Factor CAFE
(☎719-685-3235; http://thematefactorcafe.com; 966 Manitou Ave; ⊙24hr except from 6pm Sat to 2pm Fri; 🛜♿; 🚌3) This groovy treehouse of a cafe specializes in that Amazonian pick-me-up, coffee-substitute, Paraguayan petrol known as yerba maté. Technically a tea, it's fair trade, organic and highly caffeinated, and is made into lattes, mixed with vanilla and hazelnut or raspberry, and served by the cup and shot. Pick a cozy nook lit by stylish peach basket lamps and stay a while.

☆ **Entertainment**

Loft LIVE MUSIC
(www.loftmusicvenue.com; 2502 W Colorado Ave; cover $15; ⊙hrs vary; 🚌3) One of the most interesting venues in Colorado Springs, this Old Colorado City spot features indie artists in an underground performance space sans liquor license. It's all about the performance, not the party, here. But that doesn't mean you won't have a great time. Check the website for details about upcoming shows.

Kimball's Twin Peak Theatre CINEMA
(☎719-447-1945; www.kimballstwinpeak.com; 113 E Pikes Peak Ave; adult $8.50; ⊙screenings 2:30-8:30pm; ♿; 🚌3) A beer-drinking, wine-swilling downtown indie cinema. It's staffed by artsy movie geeks who present first-run foreign and indie films. Quite simply one of the best downtown diversions we experienced.

Thirsty Parrot LIVE MUSIC
(☎719-884-1094; www.thirstyparrot.net; 32 S Tejon St; ⊙from 4pm Tue-Sat; 🚌3, 4, 60) However cheeseball this place looks – and it certainly looks it – it does provide a blast of much-needed nightlife on Tejon St, with big band jazz playing live on Wednesday nights and rock bands doing their thing on Thursdays. Crowds pack the boozy joint as DJs spin on Fridays.

Manitou Penny Arcade ARCADE
(☎719-685-9815; 900 Manitou Ave; ⊙10am-10pm; ♿; 🚌3) If you or someone you love is the type that loves a vintage arcade (you know the kind: they miss games like Pole Position and Ski Ball, Galaga and Out Run, Supershot and air hockey) this sprawling complex, stretched between Canon and Manitou Avenues, is for you. And it might even help ween the kids off modern video games. Or not.

🛍 **Shopping**

Most, if not all, of the best shopping can be found in Old Colorado City – where there's a surprising abundance of groovy galleries and boutiques – and Manitou Springs.

ℹ️ **Information**

Colorado Springs Convention and Visitors Bureau (☎719-635-7506; www.visitcos.com; 515 S Cascade Ave; ⊙8:30am-5pm; 🛜♿; 🚌MM Transit 4, 16, 65) The Colorado Springs Visitor Center has all the usual tourist information.

Penrose Library (☎719-531-6333; www.ppld.org; 30 N Cascade Ave; ⊙10am-9pm Mon-Thu, 10am-6pm Fri & Sat, 1-5pm Sun; @🛜♿; 🚌MM Transit 60) The central branch of the Pikes Peak Library District is located in the heart of downtown.

St Francis Health Center (☎719-776-5000; www.penrosestfrancis.org; 825 E Pikes Peak Ave; ⊙24hr; 🛜♿; 🚌MM Transit 7) Centrally located hospital with emergency services.

US Postal Service (☎800-275-8777; www.usps.com; 201 E Pikes Peak Ave; ⊙7:30am-5:30pm Mon-Fri, 8am-1pm Sat; ♿; 🚌MM Transit 3, 10 & 11) This is the main downtown branch.

ℹ️ **Getting There & Away**

Colorado Springs Municipal Airport (☎719-550-1972; www.springsgov.com/airportindex.aspx; 7770 Milton E Proby Parkway; ♿) A smart alternative to Denver. At the time of research six airlines had regular routes to Colorado Springs, inluding American, Continental and Delta.

Greyhound (☎719-635-1505; www.greyhound.com; 120 S Weber St; ♿; 🚌MM Transit 1, 10, 11) Greyhound buses between Cheyenne, WY, and Pueblo, CO, roll through town daily.

ℹ️ **Getting Around**

Mountain Metropolitan Transit (☎719-385-7433; www.springsgov.com; adult $1.75; ♿) A reliable bus line that serves the entire Pikes Peak area, from Garden of the Gods in the north to Manitou Springs in the west, and as far south as Fountain. Maps and schedule information is available online.

Yellow Cab (☎719-777-7777; 🚖) The Yellow Cab fare from the airport to the city center is about $30. It's about $49 to Manitou Springs.

SOUTHERN FRONT RANGE

Florissant Fossil Beds National Monument

In 1873, Dr AC Peale, as part of the USGS Hayden expedition, was on his way to survey and map the South Park area, when he reputedly discovered these ancient lake deposits, which were buried by the dust and ash from a series of volcanic eruptions.

The monument is located about 35 miles west of Colorado Springs via US Hwy 24. The place to start is the visitor center, in the middle of the monument on Teller County Rd 1, some 2 miles south of Hwy 24. Museum-quality fossil exhibits are on display, and rangers provide guides to nearby trails and conduct daily interpretive programs. Special presentations and guided walks are scheduled each summer – call ahead for a calendar of events.

⊙ Sights & Activities

The highlight of the site is the ancient, enormous petrified tree stumps. Subsequent excavations revealed some 1200 insect species and 150 plant species, plus several fish, birds and small mammal species, including the tapir-like Oreodont and the Mesohippo.

The park has 14 miles of trails through open meadows and rolling hills – all can be reached on foot from the **visitor center** (☎719-748-3253; www.nps.gov/flfo; County Rd 1; admission $3; ⊙8am-7pm Memorial Day-Labor Day, to 4:30pm Labor Day-Memorial Day; 🚻). No one should miss the **Walk Through Time Nature Trail**, a 0.5-mile loop. The 1-mile **Petrified Forest Loop** leads to several petrified stumps, including the remains of a giant sequoia measuring 38ft in circumference. Interpretive brochures are available for both trails.

Signs of deer and elk often are seen along the southeastern segment of the **Hornbeck Wildlife Loop**, which crosses the highway in front of the visitors center. After a mile it intersects Shootin' Star Trail, which leads to the Barksdale Picnic area, near Lower Twin Rock Rd. Between late June and mid-August, visitors make special trips to Florissant (French for 'blooming') for ranger-guided walks held at 10:30am on Friday. Admire, but don't pick.

Of course, the location itself is both historically beautiful and intriguing in its evolution. Here's a gorgeous swatch of high country with dozens of wildflower-freckled meadows, boulder-crusted hills and views of spectacular Pikes Peak, but there are some additional sights to consider. Adeline Hornbeck settled the first 160-acre homestead, the nearby **Hornbeck House**, in the valley in 1878 with her four children. The outbuildings include a bunkhouse, carriage shed, barn and root cellar. All have been restored or rebuilt by the NPS.

Around the Monument

Colorado Wolf & Wildlife Center

WILDLIFE SANCTUARY

(☎719-687-9742; www.wolfeducation.org; County Rd 42; adult/child 12yr & under $10/7; ⊙tours 10am, noon, 2pm & 4pm May 1-Sep 30; 🅿🚻) Further northeast along Hwy 24 this private, nonprofit wildlife sanctuary shelters a pair of Mexican gray wolves and four swift foxes, and offers tours to educate the public about the importance of these creatures to the ecosystem of the Rocky Mountains.

Rocky Mountain Dinosaur Center

MUSEUM

(☎719-686-1820; www.rmdrc.com; 201 S Fairview St; adult/child $11.50/7.50; ⊙9am-6pm Mon-Sat, 10am-6pm Sun; 🅿🚻) In Woodland Park, the kids won't want to miss this private museum owned by working paleontologists, where you can watch lab techs assemble casts and clean fossils from digs across the Western states, from Montana to Texas.

Most of the 35 pieces on display are casts based on the fossils they've found. There's a massive Toxochelys and Protostega gigas, a giant turtle, in the atrium, but, as always, the T-Rex is the coup de grace. We also liked many of the video exhibits and the marine wing. There are occasional events here too, including local Native American powwows. Check the website for details. As you drive up Hwy 24 into Woodland Park, look for the cheesy fake palms in the rock garden. But don't snicker too much. When the dinosaurs roamed these were native palms in Colorado.

🛏 Sleeping

No overnight stays are allowed in the monument. The nearest accommodations are in Lake George (4 miles west) and Woodland Park (15 miles east). Both towns are located on US Hwy 24. Florissant Fossil Beds National Monument is also an easy day trip from Colorado Springs, Cripple Creek and Cañon City.

Pueblo

POP 157,244 / ELEV 4695FT

When America first expanded west, one pioneer at a time along the Santa Fe Trail, the Arkansas River was the border between the United States and Old Mexico. Eventually the Mexican–American war was fought and won, and American developers began turning this Eastern Colorado market town, which is divided by the river, into a railroad hub and steel manufacturing center, eventually earning the title, Pittsburgh of the West thanks to the success of Colorado Fuel & Iron.

Business flagged after WWII, the company crumbled following the steel market crash in 1982. Once Colorado's second-largest city, it has now dropped to sixth largest. But all that history makes for an interesting downtown wander. Seventy buildings and places are listed in the national historic registry, and plaques have been installed detailing local history along Grand and Union Aves, between 1st and B Sts

Historic downtown is in the midst of a murmuring rennaissance with a few groovy cafes and galleries, and a monthly art walk during Pueblo's long summer. In the middle of it all, of course, is the Arkansas River and the relatively new River Walk, a fine place to stretch your road weary legs. Unless it's State Fair season, outside of downtown there's not a lot to see, and you don't need to stay the night. But Pueblo remains a fine place to stop for a meal, a stroll, and you may as well duck into a museum or two.

👁 Sights & Activities

TOP CHOICE El Pueblo History Museum MUSEUM
(☑719-583-0453; www.coloradohistory.org/hist_sites/pueblo/pueblo.htm; 301 N Union Ave; adult/senior, student & child $5/4, child under 6yr free, under 12yr free on Sat; ⊙10am-4pm Tue-Sat; P 👪) Set on central plaza, the original site of Fort Pueblo (an American fort established in 1842 and held until 1854, seven years after a raid by Ute on Christmas Day in 1847 that portended the end of days), this airy, modern museum with a stunning interior houses treasures from the Pueblo past.

Exhibits include an old canon, a family teepee and a cut from a massive old tree that once stood over present-day Union Ave and was ominously called the hanging tree. Saturday is family day, and kids are granted free admission.

FREE Riverwalk WATERFRONT
(☑719-595-0242; www.puebloharp.com; 101 S Union Ave; pedal boats per 30min $10, gondola tours $5; ⊙boat rental & tours weekends May-Aug; 👪) A pedestrian-friendly and peacefully lazy, channeled slice of the Arkansas – the rest of it is running more fiercely underground – this is the center of historic Pueblo. There are sidewalks on both sides of the river and plenty of shady seating too. It runs for about four blocks and during the summer months you can book pedal boats or take a gondola tour.

The city hosts occasional concerts and events here too.

Rosemount Museum MUSEUM
(☑719-545-5290; www.rosemount.org; 419 West 14th St; adult/child under 6yr/child 6-18yr/senior $6/free/4/5; ⊙10am-4pm Tue-Sat, last tour at 3:30pm; P 👪; ☐Pueblo Transit) Pueblo's premier historic attraction is this three-story, 37-room Victorian mansion, constructed in 1893 of pink rhyolite stone. It contains elaborate stained glass and elegant, original furnishings. The top floor features an Egyptian mummy and other assorted booty from Andrew McClelland's global travels during the early 20th century.

FREE Nature & Raptor Center of Pueblo WILDLIFE SANCTUARY
(☑719-549-2414; www.natureandraptor.org; 5200 Nature Center Rd; ⊙dawn-dusk Tue-Sat, Sun Memorial Day-Labor Day only, Raptor Rehabilitation Center 11am-4pm Tue-Sun; P 👪) Riverside trails, reptile displays, picnic and playground areas and a raptor center brings the people beneath the cottonwoods on the Arkansas River. The raptor program began in 1981 to assist the Department of Wildlife in rehabilitating injured birds of prey. The turnoff for Nature Center Rd is 3 miles west of downtown, north of the Pueblo Ave Bridge.

Sangre de Cristo Art Center　MUSEUM

(☑719-295-7200; www.sdc-arts.org; 210 N Santa Fe Ave; adult/child $4/3; ⊗11am-4pm Tue-Sat; ℗🚻) Set in three brick buildings, housing six galleries that feature both fine and regional historical arts and crafts, this is more than just Pueblo's art museum. It's also an arts center with more than 100 music, dance and fine arts classes each quarter. This is also the home of the Buell Children's Museum.

Buell Children's Museum　MUSEUM

(☑719-295-7200; www.sdc-arts.org/bcm.html; 210 N Santa Fe Ave; per person $2; ⊗9:30am-4pm Tue-Sat; ℗🚻) This is the place to climb into classic cars, jam to old rock-and-roll, build bridges, swim with jellyfish, create magical fairy lands and discover the power of numbers while exploring exhibits that help kids think (and – gasp! – learn) with a smile on their face.

🛌 Sleeping

You'll need to make a room reservation during the state fair in late August and early September, when rates can soar above those we quote. If you'd rather not nest downtown, Eagleridge Rd in north Pueblo has more than a half-dozen chain options.

Hampton Inn (☑719-543-6500; http://hamptoninn.hilton.com; 4790 Eagleridge Cir; r $99-109; ℗🅿🏃❄@🛜🏊🚻) is the newest and the best of the bunch.

TOP CHOICE **Cambria Suites**　HOTEL $$

(☑719-546-1234; www.cambriasuites.com; 150 S Santa Fe Ave; ste from $109; ℗🏃❄🛜🏊🚻) This two-year-old Choice Hotels branch is of the all-suites variety and offers very modern Ikea-chic rooms with high ceilings and sofa-nook flat-screen TVs. Clearly the best downtown option, there's an indoor pool and a terrific fitness room too, but not everyone will love the space-age columns in the lobby. Just saying.

Just off the First St exit, and adjoining the I-25 South on-ramp.

Abriendo Inn　B&B $$

(☑719-544-2703; www.abriendoinn.com; 300 W Abriendo Ave; s $69-130, d $75-155; ⊗check in 4-8pm; ℗🏃❄🛜🚻) The only indie, historic option in all of Pueblo and a short walk from the historic district. This old brick B&B gets rave reviews for its gourmet breakfasts and antique furnishings. The wide old verandah out front, with rattan rocking chairs, oozes warm Americana.

ℹ DANGERS & ANNOYANCES

Downtown Pueblo, though on the comeback, is still a somewhat depressed place and there are more than a few vagrants and unbalanced characters around. Keep your wits about you, even in the daylight.

🍴 Eating

Nana's B Sreet Bistro　CAFE FOOD $

(121 West B St; mains $3.99-8.95; ⊗8am-3pm; 🍴🚻) A delightful cafe right across from historic Union Station. It is not a stretch to call it the best breakfast spot in town with delicious French toast and waffles. It does breakfast burritos too, and burgers and sandwiches at lunch time, all served on the sunny streetside or in the cute, checkered-tile wood-paneled interior.

Hopscotch Bakery　BAKERY, ICE CREAM $

(☑719-542-4467; www.hopscotchbakery.net; 333 S Union Ave; sandwiches $7.95-9.95; ⊗7am-4pm Mon-Sat, 8am-4pm Sun; 🍴🚻) If you are just passing through long enough to see a few sights and grab a bite to eat, make that bite happen here. It does fresh pastries, scones and quiche of the day, cookies and tarts, and some terrific gourmet sandwiches with capicola ham, chicken breast and balsamic vinegar–soaked portobello, and it makes its own ice cream with traditional and nontraditional flavors such as basil and lavender.

Papa Jose's　MEXICAN $

(☑719-545-7476; 320 S Union Ave; mains $4.69-9.89; ⊗11am-8pm Mon-Sat; 🍴🚻; 🚌Pueblo Transit) Here's a dirty little Colorado secret: the Mexican food is almost always underwhelming. But this town, called Pueblo and down south of the Arkansas River, was part of Mexico until relatively recently. Translation: feel free to get your hopes up, because Papa Jose's will oblige.

It does tacos and burritos, enchiladas and tostadas, tamales and green chili by the pint. The savory aroma wafts from this Mexican greasy spoon all the way out to the street. There's a reason it's popular at lunch hour.

Bingo Burger　BURGERS $

(☑719-225-8363; www.bingoburger.com; 101 Central Plaza; burgers $3.45-6.75; ⊗11am-9pm

Mon-Sat; ☻🅟) A locally owned downtown burger joint, it uses only locally produced grass-fed lamb and beef, and it does chicken and portobello burgers too. Cheese options include bleu and goat's cheese, shakes and malts are made with Hopscotch Ice Cream, and it has both sweet potato and traditional fries.

❶ Information

Parkview Episcopal Medical Center (☎719-584-4000; www.parkviewmc.com; 400 W 16th St; ☺24hr; 🅢🅟; 🚌Pueblo Transit) Just north of the central area, Parkview Episcopal Medical Center provides 24-hour emergency services.

Pueblo Chamber of Commerce (☎800-233-3446; www.pueblochamber.org; 302 North Santa Fe Ave; ☺8am-5pm Mon-Fri; 🅟; 🚌Pueblo Transit) Provides maps, lodging information and walking-tour directions and has a useful website too.

❶ Getting There & Around

Pueblo is 112 miles south of Denver at the crossroads of I-25 and US 50.

Greyhound (☎719-543-2775; www.greyhound.com; 1080 Chinook Lane; 🅟) Pueblo's main Greyhound bus depot offers service north to Colorado Springs and Denver, and south into New Mexico. Buses also stop at the downtown station on the corner of First and Court Sts.

Pueblo Memorial Airport (☎719-553-2760; www.pueblo.us; 31201 Bryan Circle; ☺vary; 🅟; Pueblo Transit) A small airport 8 miles east of central Pueblo on US 50/Hwy 96. At the time of research Allegiant Air was offering regular direct service to Las Vegas, and Great Lakes Airlines was flying to Denver twice daily.

Pueblo Transit (☎719-553-2727; www.pueblo.us; Transit Center, 123 Court St; adult/student $1/0.75; ☺6am-6:30pm; 🅟; 🚌Pueblo Transit) It doesn't run late into the evening, but this system has 12 routes covering most of the city, with buses arriving at each stop approximately every 30 minutes.

Cañon City & Royal Gorge

POP 15,889 / ELEV 5332FT

There's no getting around it. This here's a prison town. In fact, if you drive into town from Royal Gorge on Hwy 50 the first thing you'll see is the prison. Gleaming, rambling and tucked up against the Rocky Mountains, it's almost beautiful.

But before you start judging, consider the fact that there's something honest about a small town with a prison on Main St. And because it's an honest place, locals will soon inform you that there are actually seven prisons in the immediate area. A factoid which, we concur, takes a second to digest.

◉ Sights

TOP CHOICE Royal Gorge Bridge & Park

BRIDGE, AMUSEMENT PARK

(☎719-275-7507; www.royalgorgebridge.com; 4218 County Rd 3A; adult/child/senior $25/21/19; ☺10am-7pm mid-Jun–mid-Aug, hrs vary rest of year; 🅟🅟) The main attraction in this region is the bridge (and attached park) spanning the massive Royal Gorge above the Arkansas River. The 1260-ft long bridge was built in 1929, further promoting the already popular gorge as a tourist attraction. Since then, plenty more attractions, such as a petting zoo and the Skycoaster, have been added.

If you want a good view without the adrenaline fix, there's a fantastic viewpoint just east of Skycoaster. From here you can see the entire high plains shelf, backed by muscular mountains, come to an end abruptly at the edge of the gorge. If you've driven through those plains it hits you especially hard.

Admitedly, there is a fair bit of tourist-trap chic going on here, but the sheer human ingenuity and engineering of both the bridge and the incline railway, as well as the spectacular natural majesty of the gorge itself make it both a worthy trip and the area's top attraction.

Of course, you don't have to come to the park to see the gorge. The savvy traveler can walk to the edge from the parking lot just outside the North Gate entrance on Royal Gorge Rd, 8 miles west of Cañon City, then get a from-the-river view by rafting down the Arkansas River.

FREE Garden Park Fossil Area

PALEONTOLOGICAL SITE

(☎719-269-8500; Garden Park Shelf Rd; 🅟🅟) The second largest Jurassic graveyards in Colorado, but still one of the largest in North America, these are the quarries that spawned the Great Bone Wars and produced five entirely unknown species of the dinosaur back in the late 1800s. They're still standing in the Smithsonian today.

Set on Bureau of Land Management (BLM) land, it's helpful to stop by Dinosaur

Depot to buy a brochure with a terrific self-guided tour of the site.

FREE **Prospect Heights** HISTORICAL SITE
(4th St; P🕭) When United Artists were making John Wayne Westerns in Cañon City, this is where they lived and worked. A turn-of-the-20th-century Colorado Fuel & Iron company town before Hollywood came and went, Cañon City was legally dry, so the drinkers, like Wayne and cowboy actor Tom Mix, came down to this area to drink and fight. You'll see remnants of the old stone jail and brick storefronts. To get here follow 4th street from Main over the river and across the tracks.

FREE **Cañon City Municipal Museum**
MUSEUM
(☎719-269-9036; 612 Royal Gorge Blvd; ☉10am-4pm Tue-Sat; P🕭) Cañon City's municipal museum is attached to the public library and set in an old railyard warehouse. Behind it is the Rudd Cabin, built by the town's original homesteaders in 1860.

Dinosaur Depot MUSEUM
(☎719-269-715; www.dinosaurdepot.com; 330 Royal Gorge Blvd; adult/child 4-12yr $4/2; ☉10am-4pm Wed-Sun; P🕭) A smallish museum run by the Garden Park Paleontology Society in Cañon City proper with a working paleontological laboratory in-house. This private, non-profit museum prepares

and sells a terrific self-guided brochure to the Garden Park site outside of town and has some fossilized skeletons and replicas on display. A terrific resource.

🏃 Activities

Skycoaster CABLE SWING
(www.royalgorgebridge.com; Royal Gorge Bridge; per person $25) Think of a playground swing on steroids. First you're harnessed in, then you're hiked up on a cable 98ft above the platform before swinging out 65ft over the edge of Royal Gorge and 1600ft above the Arkansas River. Most folks get between three to 10 swings in a single shot.

There's never been any tragedies, though operators have seen 'every type of body fluid imaginable.'

Royal Gorge Route Railroad RAILROAD TRIP
(☎888-724-5748, 719-276-4000; www.royalgorgeroute.com; 401 Water St; tickets from $33; ☉8am-5pm; 🕭) In 1999, following a 32-year hiatus, passenger service on the Royal Gorge Route, a 12-mile segment of the old D & RG train line, was restored. Visitors can make the two-hour ride in carriages or open-air observation cars from Cañon City to Parkdale and back through the majestic gorge. Riding these rails along the Arkansas River is unforgettable.

Trips range from the basic to more eventful journeys with lunch, dinner, wine, and

---

SHOOTING THE GORGE

The best way to see the Royal Gorge is on a raft, but the 7 miles of Class IV and V Arkansas River white water are not for the timid. Half-day trips start a few miles upriver from the gorge and are 10 to 12 miles in length. Full-day trips are approximately 20 to 22 miles. Tour operators typically require rafters to be over 18 years of age in the early season or over 12 years when the flow diminishes by midsummer.

There's a large gathering of rafting guides near the Royal Gorge turnoff, 8 miles west of Cañon City, and a few others who operate out of Salida and Buena Vista run this trip too. Most years the trip runs from May to September. Thrills are at their highest in the early season. Do-it-yourself river rats should contact the **BLM office** (☎719-269-8500; www.blm.gov; 3028 E Main St; 🕭) in Cañon City or the **Arkansas Headwaters State Recreation Area** (☎719-539-7289; www.parks.state.co.us; 307 West Sackett Ave; ☉8am-5pm Mon-Fri; 🕭) office in Salida for maps and information about river access points.

» **Buffalo Joe's** (☎719-395-8757; www.buffalojoe.com; half-/full day $71/124; 🕭)

» **Raft Masters** (☎800-568-7238; www.raftmasters.com; 2315 E Main St; half-/full day $64/99; 🕭)

» **Echo Canyon River Expeditions** (☎800-755-3246; www.raftecho.com; 45000 Hwy 50; half-day $66-71; 🕭)

» **River Runners** (☎877-723-8938; www.riverrunnersltd.com; 24070 Co Rd 301; adult $55-110, child $43-74; ☉reservations 7:30am-9pm; 🕭)

even a murder. Make that a staged murder, which you can help solve. Then there's the Santa Express, a popular family trip during the Christmas season. Trips begin and end at the old Santa Fe Depot in Cañon City.

Fort Royal Stables HORSEBACK RIDING
(☎866-678-8880; www.fortroyalstables.com; 44899 Hwy 50; per person per hr $25; ☉9am-5pm; ⊞) Cañon City's top horseback outfitter, just east of the Royal Gorge turnoff, offers some tremendous rides through high plains country with massive mountain and Royal Gorge views. It accepts walk-ins, but the three-hour rides require a reservation and a four-person minimum.

🛏 Sleeping & Eating

TOP CHOICE **Hampton Inn** HOTEL $$
(☎719-269-1112; www.canoncity.hamptoninn.com; 102 McCormick Parkway; r from $85; ▣⊕✻@☎☎⊞) Stark and standing alone at the eastern end of town, past Walmart, it's the newest, and by far the best, choice in the area. It's a chain, yes, but rooms are large with wood furnishings, flat screens, granite washbasins, indoor pool and hot tub too. You get a hot breakfast in the morning, and service is excellent.

American Inn MOTEL $
(☎719-269-1158; 1231 Royal Gorge Blvd; r $34; ▣⊕✻☎⊞) No frills, and clean and as cheap as rooms get in Cañon City. Sure, you get more than a touch of the prison visitor traffic, but that's all part of the adventure.

Arkansas River Inn & Suites MOTEL $$
(☎719-275-3377; 1925 Hwy 50; d $79, family units $98; ▣⊕✻☎☎⊞) The biggest, and in many ways the splashiest, place in downtown Cañon City, it has a tiny mini-golf course, a pool and a hot tub, and rooms are decent value and three-star quality with fresh paint, a rather nice showerhead, and crown moldings.

Family units are huge with two queen beds, and a sofa, but you do get Hwy 50 traffic noise here.

El Caporal MEXICAN $$
(☎719-276-2001; 1028 Main St; mains $8.15-14.95; ☉11am-10pm Mon-Sat, 11am-9pm Sun; ⊕⊞) Authentic Mexican food is surprisingly hard to find in Colorado. But you can find it at this funky, family-owned and -operated diner. Tuck into *carne asada,* grilled chicken dinners with refried beans, rice and guacamole, tasty chicken *tacos al carbon,* enchiladas, burritos, chimichangas and a fine *arroz con*

pollo (chicken with rice). The tortilla and green chile soups get raves too.

Merlino's Belvedere Restaurant ITALIAN $$
(☎719-275-5558; www.belvedererestaurant.com; 1330 Elm Ave; mains $8-12; ☉lunch & dinner Mon-Fri, noon-9pm Sat, noon-7:30pm Sun; ⊕⊞) Back when Cañon City was less enlightened the Italian immigrants – who came here to work the land and grow food – were confined to these south of the river plains. A generation later, Merlino's opened up in 1945 and it's still running.

Think: handmade pasta and aged steaks cut and crafted in-house. Tasty, hearty, Americanized Italian meals are served in a basement dining room that resembles something from the *Love Boat.* There are lavender booths, kitschy fountains and silk plants, but you aren't here for the decor. If you don't get a steak, order the handmade cavatelli (potato pasta), spaghetti, manicotti or fettucini and top it with chicken, meatball or house-made sausage.

❶ Getting There & Away

Cañon City is on US 50, 35 miles west of Pueblo and 48 miles east of Salida.

Florence

Lying in the southeastern Colorado lowlands, amidst the old pasturelands and, relatively speaking, devoid of the sort of mountain views that define much of the state (including nearby Cañon City), is the flowering of something funky and beautiful. Here's a town in transition from depressed farming community to regional magnet for the antique-collector set. People come from across Colorado to sift through bins and hunt for gems almost every weekend, while the area's shop owners work together to promote their goods. It's a nice cooperative movement, with more than a dozen galleries lined up on historic Main St.

There are couple of cafes of note, the terrific **Main Street Grille** (☎719-784-3224; mainstreetgrille@live.com; 132 W Main St; mains from $9.95; ⊕⊞) and the award-winning **Florence Rose** (☎719-784-4734; www.florencerose.net; 1305 W 3rd St; r $119-149; ▣⊕✻☎), if you just can't bear to leave. It's one of Colorado's secretly special spots.

Florence is about 8 miles southeast of Cañon City. To get here take 9th St south across the river and you'll be on Colorado Hwy 115, which takes a rather sinuous route on its way to Florence. You'll need to look out for the signs to make sure you stay on 115.

La Veta & Around

POP 857 / ELEV 7013FT

Beautifully set in high country rangeland and at the base of the stunning Spanish Peaks, La Veta, a small historic town, is undiscovered Colorado at its finest.

It comes with all the magnificent beauty of the best of the Rockies with none of the crowds, and a touch of small-town charm too. Here's a place where paved streets are outnumbered by churches, and it would take a serious effort to get lost in La Veta – its compass-oriented grid is divided by north–south Main St (Hwy 12). Most businesses are at the north end near the old narrow-gauge railroad. The Cucharas River flows along the western edge of town just a block west of Main St.

⊙ Sights & Activities

TOP CHOICE **FREE** **Spanish Peaks Wilderness**

HIKING, TREKKING

(⊘Cañon City 719-260-8500, La Veta 719-742-3681; www.spanishpeakscountry.com; ⊘best Jun-Oct; ♿) Long before you make it into town the twin Spanish Peaks, named for their past life as part of Old Mexico, loom majestic over this valley. The East Peak is 12,683ft, while West Spanish peak is nearly 1000ft higher at 13,625ft.

With incredible vertical stone dikes erupting from the earth and down their shoulders like some kind of primordial fenceline and wide meadows carved by countless creeks, these are mountains begging to be explored. Add in the lack of tourism and you can see the appeal.

The **La Veta Work Center** on Main St is a branch office of the forest service. It doesn't always have staff in the office, but you'll find a kiosk with a map labeled with nearby trailheads. Of course, you'll need your own map, so stop at the forest service office in Pueblo or Cañon City.

All told there are 65 miles of trails and three campgrounds, one each at Blue Lake, Bear Lake and Purgatoire. If you drive up to Cuchara, you'll pass the trailhead to West Spanish Peak. This steep trail will take you up for a tough 2.5 miles to the timberline. From there you'll be able to pick your way through the scree and stones

to the peak. Just make sure to keep track of your progress so you can find your way back. And start early to avoid afternoon lightning.

Walsenberg Mining Museum   MUSEUM

(⊘719-738-1992; www.spanishpeakscountry.com/WalsenburgMiningMuseum.aspx; 112 W 5th St; adult/child $2/free; ⊘10am-4pm Mon-Fri, 10am-1pm Sat, 1-4pm Sun; ♿♿) This is really the only reason to stop in Walsenberg on the way to La Veta. Set in the old jailhouse (built in 1896), it's a monument to the struggle for labor laws in the Colorado mining industry, in the days leading up to the 1913 Ludlow Massacre.

That's when Mother Jones was held for civil disobedience in the basement of the county courthouse next door. She was held there for 20 days when she was 82 years old! There's a great picture of her leading a march through Trinidad. There is also an interesting display on the 1927 strike by the Industrial Workers of the World (IWW; also known as Wobblies), and it has old mining equipment like bellows and trip hammers and old lanterns. The docent will lead you through the museum.

SPACe Gallery   GALLERY

(Gallery in the Park; ⊘719-742-3074; www.spanishpeaksarts.org; 132 W Ryus St; ⊘hrs vary; ♿♿) More than two-dozen artists display paintings, pottery, glasswork and weavings at this cooperative gallery built in 1983 by the origins of what has become the Spanish Peaks Arts Council. It's a two-minute walk east of La Veta Inn in Railroad Park. It presents special shows too.

FREE **Francisco Fort Museum**   MUSEUM

(⊘719-742-5501; www.lavetacucharachamber.com; 306 S Main St; ⊘11am-3pm Thu-Sat, noon-3pm Sun; ♿♿) Next to the library, it's set on the site of the original 1862 fort, with a couple of the real deal buildings still left. It was built by 12 men as a base of operations for settlement, trade and Indian protection – meaning protection from Native Americans, which consisted of attacks on the Ute and surrounding tribes.

There's a gift shop housed in a saloon, and tours are available if you call ahead.

Cuchara

A stunning stretch of Hwy 12 connects La Veta with Cuchara, a small ranch town in the Spanish Peaks Wilderness. Here are lush green hills crowned with the Spanish

GREAT DIKES OF THE SPANISH PEAKS

Some of the Kapota band of the Ute tribe aptly expressed their infatuation with the striking volcanic Spanish Peaks (p337) southeast of La Veta by regarding them as 'breasts of the earth.' Spanish and American travelers relied on these twin sentinels to guide their approach to the Front Range across the eastern Great Plains.

On closer inspection, you'll find hundreds of magnificent rock walls radiating like fins from the peaks. Called 'dikes,' they were formed from fissures surrounding the volcanic core, where molten rock was injected into the earth's crust and cast into solid rock as it cooled. Subsequent erosion has exposed the dikes, leaving a peculiar landscape of abrupt perpendicular rock formations protruding from the earth.

For an opportunity to see wildlife and wildflowers, instead of cattle, you can explore the Great Dikes of the Spanish Peaks on foot by following the **Wahatoya Trail** (USFS Trail 1304; www.fs.usda.go; Huerfano County Rd 360; ☺best Jun-Sep; 🚶) along the saddle between the East and West Spanish Peaks, or from the road over scenic Cordova Pass (11,743ft). Cordova Pass is on USFS Rd 415, 6 miles east of Cucharas Pass on Hwy 12, 17 miles south of La Veta. Trail information, maps and a wildflower brochure are available at the La Veta Work Center (p337) in La Veta.

Peaks' Great Dikes: stark vertical granite walls jutting like an archaic boundary up from somewhere deep. They rise and recede through meadows and on mesas, and always looming behind them are those Spanish Peaks, which happen to be two million years older than the Continental Divide.

The town of Cuchara is even smaller than La Veta, with just one dirt road (Cuchara Ave). That's where you'll find its only restaurant and a couple of inns. All around here are unbelievable snowshoeing and cross-country skiing trails in winter, and hiking and climbing routes in summer. If you attempt to bag the peaks, know that because they stand alone lightning is a real hazard. Get off the high ground before noon and you'll be fine.

There is a downhill slope here too and one defunct lift. It's been dormant for more than a decade, but rumor has it that winter 2012 may see its re-birth.

Walsenberg

On your way up to La Veta, on Hwy 160 from I-25, you'll find Walsenberg in that last gasp of plains before the Spanish Peaks rise to the west. The city is simply another in a string of seemingly depressed east Colorado mining and ranching towns, but there is some rather progressive political history here that's worth stopping for.

Monument Park

Evergreen forests surround Monument Park, 29 miles south of La Veta and 36 miles west of Trinidad on Hwy 12. The park is named for a rock formation rising from the waters of an attractive mountain reservoir. Numerous summer activities are offered, including fishing on the trout-stocked lake, horseback riding and mountain biking.

The popular **Monument Park Lake Resort** (☎719-868-2226; www.monumentlakeresort.com; 4789 Hwy 12; sites $14, RVs $18-28, cabins & lodges $80-100; ☺mid-May–mid-Sep; 🅿☺🏊🚶) has camping and RV sites, as well as showers and coin-op laundry. There's also lodge rooms and cabins decorated Southwestern style. The resort's restaurant serves decent home-style American food. The resort is only open in the summer. West of the resort, the **San Isabel National Forest** offers primitive campgrounds on the flanks of the Sangre de Cristo range.

Trinidad

POP 9125 / ELEV 6025FT

Tucked into a chimney top Mesa, quiet, lazy Trinidad sits on the Purgatoire River which flows down from the heights of the Sangre de Cristo Mountains and the Spanish Peaks in the west. The town's past – from its origins as a Spanish outpost, to it's Santa Fe Trail heyday, to it's coal mining period when it played a central role in a groundbreaking labor dispute – is documented in its museums and on the brick-paved streets in Corazon de Trinidad, the 'heart' of downtown, which has been designated a National Historic District. Look out for the 'Canary in the Coal Mine' sculpture on Main St.

While the history buffs may want to take their time here, before exploring the rutted history of the Santa Fe Trail further east, outdoorsy types will smell adventure on the pine-tinged winds streaming down from Cucharas Pass in the San Isabel National Forest.

⊙ Sights & Activities

TOP CHOICE **Trinidad History Museum** MUSEUM
(☎719-846-7217; www.coloradohistory. org; 312 E Main St; adult/6-12yr/senior $8/3/6; ⊙10am-4pm Mon-Sat May-Sep, limited hrs Oct-Apr; ⊛) This is a lot of museum, a full city block in fact, set smack dab on Main St, which fittingly was on the Santa Fe Trail. Your admission buys you a free tour, which gathers and leaves from the *placita* outside the Santa Fe Trail Museum.

First you'll visit the Baca Housem, a two-story home made from adobe brick in 1870. There's a wood burning stove and worn wood floors in the kitchen, an original bed upstairs, and a tin Jesus made from an oyster bucket.

Next door is the stunning Second Empire Bloom mansion, a symmetrical brick building with French eaves and moldings on the exterior and wrought iron on the roof and terraces.

The Santa Fe Trail museum set in the Baca's adobe workers cottage built in 1874 is the real prize here. Displays wander over early days Trinidad when it was a town with Mexican and Spanish roots, to the birth of the Santa Fe Trail.

Arthur Roy Mitchell Memorial Museum of Western Art GALLERY, MUSEUM
(The Mitch; ☎719-846-4224; www.armitchell. org; 150 E Main St; adult/child $3/free, Sun free; ⊙10am-4pm Tue-Sat, noon-4pm Sun; ⊛) Also known as 'The Mitch,' this pleasant gallery was built in honor of local cowboy artist, and the original, if unofficial, town historian, AR Mitchell. Set in an old late-19th-century department store (those tiled ceilings are original), the groud floor is the permanent collection of Mitchell's work: cowboys, horses, western landscapes, more horses and more cowboys.

Upstairs, there's a rotating exhibition space and the basement has a terrific collection of historic Trinidad photos. There are Mitchell pieces for sale along with turquoise jewelry and quirky cowboy gifts in the adjacent gift shop.

FREE **Ludlow Massacre Memorial**
MONUMENT
(Colorado County Rd 44; P ⊛) In 1914 striking migrant workers were living in a large tent city in Ludlow. After a series of conflicts, the Colorado National Guard were called in. An ensuing clash saw the tent city raised and three strikers – two women – killed. This well-executed stone monument, just north of Trinidad, was dedicated by the United Mine Workers to tell the story.

Displays include testimonials of those involved with the strike and tent camp, and a timeline of the mine workers struggle. There's also a display about company towns and a practice used by management to create a climate of indentured servitude.

FREE **Southside Park**
SKATEBOARDING, DISC GOLF
(Trinidad Community Center; ☎719-846-4454; www.historictrinidad.com; 1309 Beshore Dr; ⊙8am-10pm; ⊛) This viable community center at the south end of Trinidad has acres of athletic fields, a public pool, and, according to the legendary Tony Hawk, one of the top skate parks in the US. The sport's longest grind is possible on the 120ft flat wall.

The skatepark provides challenging and fast full-arena runs, but also accommodates young beginners. Next to the skate park is Trinidad's new disc golf course.

Trinidad Lake State Park HIKING
(☎800-678-2267, 719-846-6951; www.parks. state.co.us; Hwy 12; vehicle pass per day $4; ⊛) Three miles west of the city off Hwy 12, this park sits on a bluff above the Purgatoire River, downstream from the reservoir dam. Hiking, wildlife viewing, an interpretive nature trail, fishing and boating on the reservoir are available. Additional campsites are available at **Carpios Ridge Campground** (☎800-678-2267; www.parks.state. co.us; tent sites $16, RV sites $20-24).

James M John State Wildlife Area
HIKING, MOUNTAIN BIKING
(☎719-680-1412; www.wildlife.state.co.us; Hwy 526; admission $10.25, free with purchase of hunting or fishing license; ⊛) Trails for hikes and mountain bikes provide the only access to this habitat for birds, elk, mule deer and black bear. The area is open to hunting and fishing in season, but you must be licensed. It's a good idea for nonhunters to know their seasons too.

CH...CH...CH...CHANGES

Before arriving here you'll probably hear that Trinidad is unofficially credited with being the sex-change capital of the USA. However, you won't find much evidence among the local population. Dr Stanley Biber, who was chiefly responsible for this reputation via his supposedly cash-only practice that changed the genders of 4500 people, passed away in 2006.

🛏 Sleeping

TOP CHOICE **Tarabino Inn** B&B $$
(☎719-846-2115; www.tarabinoinn.com; 310 E 2nd St; r $84-129; 🛜🅿) There are four guest rooms in this beautifully restored Italianate villa, by far the classiest sleep in Trinidad, with antique and antique-style furnishings. The cheaper rooms on the 3rd floor share a bath (though they do have prime access to the top-floor widow's walk), while the two suites have private bathrooms with huge claw-foot tubs.

This place is listed among ghost hunters as a possessor of benevolent spirits. Guests have felt a presence. Even the skeptical host admits to the possibility.

Holiday Inn & Suites HOTEL $$
(☎719-845-8400; www.holidayinn.com; 3130 Santa Fe Trail; r $107-124; 🅿🚭❄🛜🖥🅰) The newest option in town, this is the best of the chains that are scattered a couple of miles south of downtown. Rooms are large with a king or two queen beds, huge Samsung flat-screens, free wi-fi throughout and excellent service. It's exactly what you want from a chain: clean, new and up to date.

Trail's End MOTEL $
(☎719-846-4425; 616 E Main St; s/d $44/49; 🅿🚭❄🛜🅰) Blessed with a classic vintage neon sign and a nice flowery sundeck, this hole-in-the-wall motel isn't fancy but it is great value and very friendly. Family-owned and operated, it has small rooms with fresh paint, satellite TV and wi-fi, and will do for a one-night pit stop.

It's set at the end of the mythic Santa Fe Trail, and the owners are avid bikers who get their fair share of enduro riders navigating the US on dirt roads.

🍴 Eating

Although there are a handful of tasty restaurants in this sleepy town, it's worth noting that most are closed Sundays, Mondays and Tuesdays.

TOP CHOICE **Danielson Dry Goods** CAFE FOOD $
(☎719-846-7119; 135 E Main St; dishes $6.50-8.95; ⏰7:30am-3pm Tue-Fri, 9am-3pm Sun & Mon; 🚭🛜🅰) This cafe, adjacent to a cute housewares boutique, is a terrific find. In the morning, it does gourmet egg wraps, such as the Santa Fe (eggs, bacon, spicy corn salsa, Anaheim chile, cheese and crème fresh, or the Farmers Market (eggs, artichoke hearts, oven-roasted tomatoes, Parmesan and creamy basil spread).

And it does some pretty marvelous sandwiches and salads at lunch too. Vegetarians will like the Mediterranean open-face sandwich; the rest of us can add chicken to it. Divine.

Nana & Nano's ITALIAN $
(☎719-846-2696; 418 E Main St; mains $5.95-11.50; ⏰10:30am-7:30pm Wed-Sat; 🚭🅰) Given the historical connection of Italian miners to the area it shouldn't be a surprise that this Italian deli and pasta house is a Trinidad institution with fine meats, specialty cheese and homemade sandwiches. It does excellent meatball and sausage heroes as well as a 'heavenly combo' with a roasted green chili. The pasta dinners are likewise popular, and come with salad and bread.

Black Jack's Saloon STEAKHOUSE $$
(☎719-846-9501; www.blackjackssaloon.com; 225 W Main St; burgers from $11.95, mains $13.95-24.95; ⏰4-8pm Mon-Thu, to 9pm Fri & Sat; 🚭🅰) Named for the legendary train robber nabbed in Trinidad, this saloon and steakhouse is known for its steaks: filets, NY strip, flatirons and ribeyes. Dinner comes with baked or mashed potatoes, salad, baked beans and Texas toast.

It mostly serves the local cowboys and cowgirls (yes, they wear the hats), and though the salad bar isn't award winning, the grill is out in the open and it does ring a dinner bell when it's all ready for you.

Bella Luna PIZZA $$
(☎719-846-2750; 121 W Main St; mains $10-15; ⏰11am-3pm Mon & Wed-Sat 5-9pm Mon & Wed-Sat, noon-6pm Sun; 🚭🅰) Wood-fired pizza in an antiquated dark-wood historic Main St dining room with exposed brick walls, high ceilings and twirling fans. Locals rave.

Information

Carnegie Public Library (☎719-846-6841; www.carnegiepubliclibrary.org; 202 N Animas St; ⊘9am-7pm Mon, to 5pm Tue-Fri, to 3pm Sat; @🛜♿) Free internet access.

Colorado Welcome Center (☎719-846-9512; www.colorado.com; 309 Nevada Ave; ⊘8am-6pm Memorial Day-Labor Day, to 5pm Labor Day-Memorial Day; ♿) One of 10 state-run welcome centers in the state, this one serves travelers coming north from New Mexico and offers an array of maps and brochures detailing tourism options in southeast Colorado. Trinidad-Las Animas County Chamber of Commerce shares the space, offers local information and can recommend guides to the Corazon de Trinidad National Historic District.

Mt San Rafael Hospital (☎719-846-9213; www.msrhc.org; 410 Benedicta Ave; ⊘24hr; 🛜♿)

Post Office (www.usps.com; 301 E Main St; ⊘9am-5pm Mon-Fri, 9am-noon Sat)

Getting There & Around

Greyhound buses stop at **JR's Travel Shoppe** (☎719-846-6390; www.greyhound.com; 639 W Main St; ♿), a Conoco gas station near I-25 exit 13B. **Amtrak's** (☎800-872-7245; www.amtrak.com; 110 West Pine St; ♿) Southwest Chief passes through Trinidad on its daily Chicago–Los Angeles route.

SANTA FE TRAIL

For those who like to walk along the old wagon ruts of history, time travel in their mind's eye from now back to a more rugged day when 'cowboys and Indians' wasn't a game, but a way of life, driving the Santa Fe Trail will offer a fun day of diversion. For others, well, it's just a series of informational plaques along the highway – but no one will be able to miss the real beauty of the journey

That wild sunny prairie unfurling on both sides of the open two-lane highway where horses and cattle graze lazily and deer and antelope patrol the savanna. Eighty miles northeast of Trinidad along Hwy 350 is La Junta, and although you're still very much in Colorado, this is where you can feel the Midwestern wheat-field vibe begin to take over. It's all grasslands and wheat fields, farms and railroad yards. One of the best parts of driving the Santa Fe Trail is the glimpses of true small-town America.

Bent's Old Fort National Historic Site

Seven miles east of town is La Junta's claim to fame and easily the best sight on the Santa Fe Trail. **Bent's Old Fort National Historic Site** (35110 Hwy 194; adult/child under 5yr/child 5-12yr $3/free/2; ⊘9am-4pm Sep 1-May 31, to 6pm Jun-Aug; P♿), set just north of the Arkansas River, the natural and official border between the US and Old Mexico until 1846, was once a cultural crossroads. Between 1833 and 1849 trappers, explorers and profiteers, Native Americans and Hispanics came into this borderland. Business blossomed. Peace was the way. An adobe outpost, it was built by 150 Mexican laborers brought over from Taos (then part of Mexico) and hired by the Bent brothers, Charles and William.

The old fort has been restored beautifully. There's a blacksmith's shop and a wood shop, and the general store is stocked with rifles, sacks of grain, barrels of sugar, cases of wine, whiskey, ammo and buffalo pelts, and furnished with 19th-century antiques.

It's staffed by knowledgeable guides in period clothing. A paved trail leading from the parking lot to the fort skirts a natural wetland, and a very flat, easy hiking trail (about 1 mile) runs around the fort to the edge of the Arkansas River and back to the parking lot. Staff offer two tours per day most of the year (10:30am and 1pm), four during summer.

Boggsville Historic Site

You can continue in Kit Carson's footsteps to the **Boggsville Historic Site** (☎719-456-0453; www.santafetrailscenicandhistoricbyway.org; Hwy 101; ⊘10am-4pm Fri-Sun May, 10am-5pm Memorial Day-Labor Day, 10am-4pm Wed-Sun Sep-Nov; P♿), about 16 miles east of the fort and 2 miles south on Colorado Hwy 101. Nestled on the Purgatoire River, this was Carson's homestead and trading center, which he built in the 1860s after the demise of Bent's Fort. Eventually it became the first county seat for Bent County when the railroad arrived in 1873.

You'll see an old wagon under the cottonwoods, a cabin and a decrepit old barn and newer, yet still historic, homes. It's a pleasant enough wander but not even close to being as captivating as the fort.

Fort Lyon

The Bents did build another fort east of their old fort in 1853 and it was a profitable trading post – most of the folks they traded with were Native Americans – until 1857, when a Colorado gold strike spurred unrest among the Colorado Native Americans, largely because they were being pushed off their land. As a result, the US cavalry built Fort Fauntleroy to protect settlers.

Later renamed Fort Lyon, it was from here that on November 29, 1864, John Chivington led the Colorado Volunteers in a dawn attack on Chief Black Kettle and his band, who had been told they would be safe if they moved to this desolate reservation. Over 100 Cheyenne and Arapahoe men, women and children were slaughtered, and their corpses grotesquely mutilated, bringing a new wave of conflict to Colorado's high plains along the Santa Fe Trail. This event is commemorated at the **Sand Creek Massacre National Historic Site** (☑719-438-5916; www.nps.gov/sand; cnr County Rd 54 & County Rd W; ☺9am-4pm; P ⛾).

A year later the fort was moved to present-day Las Animas, where it eventually became a military hospital and tuberculosis sanitarium. More recently Fort Lyon was turned into a state prison.

Timpas & the Comanche National Grassland

Heading west from La Junta, back in the direction of Trinidad, you'll pass another of the Santa Fe Trail's signature sites in Timpas, Colorado – the gateway to the **Comanche National Grassland**, an unforgiving wilderness of hip-high grasses and wild grains, rising into small hills and diving into shallow canyons. This was prime buffalo-hunting ground and wagon trains could be easily ambushed here too. Which is why wagons would take staggered formations rather than follow one another in a single file. Still, after several thousand crossings, this clay soil got worn into ruts and at **Iron Spring** (www.santafetrailscenicandhistoricbyway.org/istsv.html; cnr County Rd 9 & Hwy 350; P ⛾), just a mile down a well-graded dirt road off Hwy 350, you can actually still see the wagon ruts, so deep was the impression they left in the

clay. Walking along the ruts, with the dry wind in your hair, it's easy to imagine the challenges they faced.

Iron Spring is a 1-mile drive down County Rd 9. It intersects Hwy 350 about 11 miles west of Timpas, Colorado, 27 miles from La Junta and 42 miles from Trinidad.

PICKETWIRE DINOSAUR TRACKSITE
Also in the Comanche National Grasslands, but only accessible by organized tour, or on foot, is a whole different kind of tracksite. This one is all about the migration of dinosaurs.

The 0.25-mile **Picketwire Dinosaur Tracksite** (☑719-384-2181; www.fs.usda. gov; Ranger District Office, 1420 E 3rd St; ☺by reservation, office 8am-5pm Mon-Fri; P ⛾) is the largest documented site of its kind in North America, with as many as 1300 visible tracks. Some 150 million years ago, two types of dinosaurs, allosaurs and apatosaurs (brontosaurs), migrated along the muddy shoreline of a large prehistoric lake. Massive brontosaur families, including some of their young, left 40% of the tracks. Allosaurs were two-footed, ferocious, carnivorous scavengers. They're thought to have hunted in packs. Perhaps the two species met on more than one occasion

There are no fees to see this site, but you must arrange in advance for a guided auto tour through La Junta Ranger District if you intend to drive. You can also hike from the Withers Canyon trailhead off Forest Service Rd 500A for 3 miles; follow the signs. From here it is a 5.25-mile hike along Picket Wire Canyon Trail to the dinosaur prints.

NORTHEAST COLORADO

Pawnee National Grassland

If, like some of us, you happen to be fishtailing at high speeds along the graded dirt roads that thread through the private-public checkerboard quilt that is the 193,060-acre **Pawnee National Grassland** (☑Camping Reservations 877-444-6777, Crow Valley Recreation Area, Briggsdale 970-353-5004, Greeley Ranger District office 970-346-5000; www.fs.usda.gov; Pawnee National Grasslands; ⛾) as dusk descends on another summer day, you'll notice a few things. As the sun slants down it enlightens all the many shades of greens and golds in this savanna that seems to roll unending in all directions. Without all that harsh light and interminable heat to distract you, you'll begin to notice textures. The folds and grooves and water cuts, the undulating rhythm of hip-high grasses dancing in the winds.All of a sudden those fine dust clouds rising from your tires and those of the trucks that pass at equally high speeds with a hearty wave, are no longer brown, but pink, as the sky morphs from a faded baby blue to lavender. Then it's as if the sun is descending into a spectacular pool of hot pink light.

If you've managed to negotiate these peculiar roads just so, next you'll come upon the two towering blond, sandstone towers that are the historic and majestic **Pawnee Buttes**. You'll stop among the herds of cattle that wander free, and listen to the rusted water mill spin and bang its tail, and if you're lucky glimpse a white-tailed antelope bounding through the fields as the wind pours free and fast. This is the glory of the Pawnee National Grasslands, the saving grace of the entire northeastern plains.

It doesn't take a whole lot of imagination to turn these cattle into bison in your mind's eye, and to envision the glint of a wolf's eye in the midnight savanna and the rolling exhale of a prairie fire somewhere in the war-dancing, earth medicine American past.

🛏 Sleeping

If you wish to camp in the grasslands, head to the **Crow Valley Recreation Area** (✍www.fs.usda.gov; Weld County Rd 77; sites $10-14; ℗🚻) off Hwy 14 near Briggsdale. It's not the most stunning campsite of your life, but it is elm and cottonwood shaded with potable water, restrooms and fire pits. There's even a volleyball court and baseball diamond.

Fort Morgan

Another former prairie trading post on the Overland Trail that has become an interstate city, Fort Morgan has a cute though dated center that could use an economic upturn, although it's not as depressed as the prairie towns further east, thanks to constant Interstate traffic that has brought mostly corporate franchise fast food and motels.

◉ Sights & Activities

The best thing about Fort Morgan is its proximity to the surprisingly transporting Pawnee National Grasslands and Pawnee Buttes. In town there are two sights (kind of) worth seeing. The **Fort Morgan Museum** (✍970-542-4010; www.cityoffort morgan.com; 414 Main St; ⊙8am-5pm Mon & Wed, 10am-8pm Tue & Thu, 10am-5pm Fri, 11am-5pm Sat; ℗🚻) tells the tale of the town of Fort Morgan through antiques that have trickled down from the founders. The arrowhead collection is particularly cool. It was in the midst of a redesign at research time, but should be worth a once over when it reopens.

The **I-76 Speedway** (✍970-867-2101; www.i-76speedway.com; 16359 County Rd S; adult/senior/child 6-12yr/child under 6yr $10/8/4/free; ⊙varies Jun-Aug, Sat evenings Apr-Oct; 🚻) offers a summer racing season with four- to six-car divisions competing on Saturday evenings. There are usually sprint cars, street stock cars, late models, dwarfs, mod-lites and hornets revving up most nights. Don't turn your nose up at minor league racing. It's an experience, if nothing else.

🛏 Sleeping

Day's Inn   MOTEL $
(✍970-542-0844; www.daysinn.com; 1150 N Main St; r from $72; ℗🚻❄🌐🚻) Your best bet if you plan to stay the night. You may not like the Christmas carpeting, but rooms are large, very clean and far enough from the interstate roar to get a decent night's sleep.

Sterling

When the sweet old ladies at the **Visitors Information Center** (✍970-522-8962; www.sterlingcolo.com; 12510 County Rd 370; ⊙9am-5pm Mon-Sat; 🚻) in the rest area are asked what there is to see around here, and they reply with a shrug and 'Not much,' you get the feeling that this once major stop on the Overland Trail, a covered wagon superhighway that brought settlers west to gold country, has seen its best and most historic days.

Across the road from the visitors center is the **Overland Trail Recreation Area** (✍970-522-9700; www.sterlingcolo.com; Overland Trail; ⊙4:30am-11pm; 🚻). Once part of the Overland Trail, this now-concrete path follows the river for just over half a mile and according to signs you can fish small and large mouth bass here. Of course, the river had a major algae problem when we visited, but there are picnic benches and if you want to stretch your legs and walk beneath the trees, it isn't a bad diversion.

And you should definitely visit the Sterling Overland Trail Museum (☎970-522-3895; www.sterlingcolo.com; 21053 County Rd 370; adult/child $3/1.50; ◎9am-5pm Apr-Oct, 10am-4pm Mon-Sat, 1-5pm Sun Nov-Mar; ⓟⓐ), which sports a great collection gleaned from the town's founding families. Out front in the gravel beds are vintage plows and tractors, and inside are five rooms packed with exhibits ranging from minerals to an insane collection of authentic arrowheads, as well as 19th-century firearms, bear- and buffalo-skin coats, and vintage pianos, dolls and radios. It even has dinosaur fossils.

Out back there's a 13-building replica of old Main St from the 1930s along with a covered wagon. Together it all paints a picture of Sterling's human and natural history. Further north of the interstate, Old Sterling sits in a cozy six-square block grid. Edged by an active railyard, it still has dated brick-house charm, but it's a pretty depressed place with a few pawn shops and payday loan joints beckoning on the new Main St strip. Clearly, there's no reason to stay the night in Sterling, but there is a fun place to eat.

✖ Eating

J & L Cafe DINER **$**
(☎970-522-3625; 423 N 3rd St; mains $6.25-9.99; ◎5:15am-8pm; ⊝ⓐ) A local joint steeped in country music where the men wear cowboy hats and the women talk with a hint of western twang. It serves breakfast all day, burgers, chili and chicken fried steak. And pie. Always pie. And strong coffee. Diner coffee. This is real Americana as you live and breathe.

❶ Getting There & Away

Sterling is 125 miles northeast of Denver off Interstate 76.

Julesberg

If you're heading into Colorado from the northeast on I-76, one of the first spots you'll see is the Colorado Welcome Center (☎970-474-2054; www.colorado.com/Julesburg WelcomeCenter.aspx; 20934 County Rd 28; ◎8am-6pm Memorial Day-Labor Day, to 5pm Labor Day-Memorial Day; ⓐ). Part rest area, part information center, it's bordered by corral fencing around waist-high grass dotted with teepee-like shade structure and buffalo sculpture.

There's also a rather cool cast-iron monument to the Pony Express here too. On the first Pony Express expedition in 1860–61, the riders travelled 1943 miles between St Joseph and San Francisco, stopping in present-day Julesburg, then known as Overland City because it was also a major stop on the Overland Trail (over 350,000 people came through here in the mid-19th century).

Launched as a trading post in 1850 and known as the 'Wickedest City in the West' by the 1860s, the town of Julesburg moved three times before settling in its present location. First it was moved because of a raid by Native Americans, then to be closer to the railroad. In 1880 it became a rail junction for Union Pacific. These days, though, Julesburg is another dying prairie town that makes Sterling feel like a metropolis. But if you are curious about Overland Trail history, take the South Platte River Scenic Byway (www.byways.org; 20934 County Rd 28; ⓐ), a 19-mile loop that circuits Ovid, the original Julesburg site, and Fort Sedgewick, with pull-outs and interpretive panels installed throughout.

Julesburg is set just over the Colorado border from Nebraska on I-76, 180 miles northeast of Denver.

Understand Colorado

COLORADO TODAY **346**
Colorado's boom industries have weathered the financial storm well enough. Politically, it's a bit harder to predict.

HISTORY **348**
From Wild West frontier to outdoor haven and ski central: Colorado has a whole lot of history.

WAY OF LIFE **353**
'Rugged individualism' is a cliché but that doesn't mean it's an inaccurate description.

THE ARTS **356**
Art doesn't figure in many people's concept of Colorado – let's see if we can change that.

COLORADO CUISINE **359**
Steak and Rocky Mountain oysters? Sure. But there's plenty more on the menu.

WILDLIFE & THE LAND **362**
If you're coming here, you're likely heading outdoors. Here's a taste of what's waiting for you.

DINOSAURS **365**
Colorado is one of the world's top stops for dinosaur fossils and tracks.

population per sq mile

DENVER   COLORADO   USA

♟ ≈ 40 people

Colorado Today

Growing Young

Once a mining, ranching and farming stronghold, today's Colorado is a young state getting younger, with 25% of the five million residents under the age of 18.

Most these residents are living in and around Denver. Development in Denver suburbs on what was farmland fueled a real estate boom in the 1990s. And it was in those suburbs that tragedy struck on April 20, 1999, in the form of the deadliest school shooting in American history at Columbine High School.

That event overshadowed what was otherwise a pivotal and positive decade for the state in terms of economic growth as Denver and Boulder cashed in on the technology boom. Some of those jobs were lost in the late '90s tech bust, but the area weathered the storm. This growth not only sparked suburban sprawl but also urban gentrification. Denver's once blighted LoDo neighborhood came back strong with residential loft construction and the opening of dozens of bars and restaurants. Young college grads flocked in from across the US, with an eye toward pairing an outdoor, weekend-warrior lifestyle with a high-paying tech gig. Which is why Boulder and Denver were fixtures on the Forbes list of Best Cities for Singles throughout the mid-2000s.

Another stumble in the tech industry between 2000–04 cost the area some jobs, and there were other signs of a sustained slump. But it wasn't all bad news. In 2006, another industry gripped northern Colorado, and we aren't talking about the marijuana industry, although that's growing, too. Known as the Colorado Clean Energy Cluster, there are now 32 clean-energy companies working together to promote and produce green energy in the Denver–Boulder area.

No, you're not hallucinating: Colorado really is extremely Caucasian. More than 70% of the population is white.

Dos

» Dress in full Tour de France gear on casual training rides about town.

» Drink lots of water, or the high altitude and the high-gravity beers will do you in.

» Tip generously – 15 to 20% is the norm.

Don'ts

» Look John Elway directly in the eye.

» Pee in communal hot springs.

Books

On The Road (Jack Kerouac) – The Denver doldrums and the origins of road-tripper culture

Whiteout: Lost in Aspen (Ted Conover) – Aspens in the 1980s

Plainsong (Kent Haruf) – Examines a Colorado farming community

belief systems
(% of population)

67 — Christian

2 — Jewish

1 — Muslim

25 — Unaffiliated

5 — Other

if Colorado were 100 people

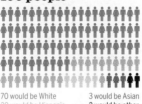

70 would be White
20 would be Hispanic
4 would be African American
1 would be Native American

3 would be Asian
2 would be other

Red State, Blue State

Politically, Colorado is a mixed bag. It definitely has a strong and deep conservative streak, with an Evangelical base in Colorado Springs and ranching and mining interests throughout the state, but there are plenty of progressives here too, particularly in Denver, Boulder and throughout the Front Range.

Still, Colorado has voted Republican in all but three of the last 12 presidential elections (they voted for Obama in 2008), which is why it was something of a surprise when Democrats won both a Senate seat and the governor's mansion during the 2010 midterm election, which was dominated by the Republicans nationally. The gubernatorial race was won by rising political star John Hickenlooper, a Democrat and former geologist turned entrepreneur who started a microbrewery, owned several restaurants and helped transform Denver's LoDo. A Quaker, he is beloved by Colorado progressives.

The Senate race was more contentious. Tea Party candidate, and relative unknown, Ken Buck defeated establishment Republican Jane Norton – the sitting lieutenant governor – in the primary before taking on Democrat Michael Bennett, the incumbent senator. Buck's meteoric rise was part of a national movement of anti-establishment right-wing politicians competing for congressional and senatorial seats. Bennett, on the other hand, couldn't have been more tied into the Democratic power structure. Bennett won by 15,400 votes out of a possible 1.4 million. That's about 1% of the vote.

> Since 2000, Colorado's population has increased by 16.5% to 5,024,748.

Movies

Butch Cassidy & The Sundance Kid (1969) – The seminal cliff-jumping scene was shot on the Durango & Silverton Narrow-Gauge Railroad
True Grit (1969) – Set in Arkansas but filmed in the San Juan Mountains

The Shining (1980) – Inspired by the Stanley Hotel in Estes Park
Things to Do in Denver When You're Dead (1995) – An off-beat noir flick

Downloads

NowHere – A killer new snowboard film; the trailer's on Vimeo and the film can be bought at the iTunes store
Beatport (www.beatport.com) – Denver-based download site attracts big-name DJs to Denver and Boulder

History

Colorado's history is written in petroglyphs, gold dust and ski tracks. It's a story about the making of today's United States, and a parable for the European domination of the New World. Here were ambitious adventurers and salespeople, colonizing politicians and warriors blending and spreading slowly across Colorado, once the domain of Native Americans who had formed complex cultures that at the time of first contact had survived countless generations.

On November 7, 1893, Colorado became the first US state – and one of the first places in the world – to grant women the right to vote.

The Santa Fe Trail led west through hostile country from Missouri through Kansas and Colorado. The trail was launched in the early 1830s and by 1833 the brothers William and George Bent had built a fort that was an oasis for pioneers traveling on the trail. In 1839, journalist John L O'Sullivan suggested in his essay 'Manifest destiny' that it was white America's destiny to own the American continent from coast to coast and tip to tip. Inevitably his philosophy did become US policy under then president James Polk. This in turn spiked westward settlement and caused inevitable violent clashes with both Mexico – which owned southern Colorado – and native people. The Mexican–American War raged in the mid-1840s, and by its end Charles Bent, appointed first governor of New Mexico, had been assassinated by Pueblo Indians in Taos, and his brother William was married to a Cheyenne woman in Colorado.

Discovery of gold in 1859 brought more miners and pioneers, among them Barney Ford, an escaped slave and would-be millionaire. Not long after the Pony Express blazed the Overland Trail through the Pawnee Grassland to deliver the US mail, and after the Civil War had burned out, Confederate families from Tennessee used it to pick up the pieces and plant sugar beets in northeast Colorado. The less-publicized Indian Wars were the euphemism for the violent subjugation of Colorado's native people by the Colorado Volunteers. The exclamation point was the Sand Creek Massacre.

TIMELINE

AD 100	1300s	1775–6
The region's dominant indigenous cultures emerge. The Hohokam settle in the desert, the Mogollon in the mountains and valleys and Ancestral Puebloans build cliff dwellings around the Four Corners.	One of history's most enduring unsolved mysteries occurs when the entire civilization of Ancestral Puebloans living in Mesa Verde abandons this sophisticated city of cliff dwellings.	Spanish missionaries Francisco Atanasio Domínguez and Silvestre Vélez de Escalante lead an expedition through the Colorado Plateau in the search for overland routes to California.

Railroads brought first gold, then silver, then copper and iron, and finally coal to American manufacturing centers. Villages turned into towns, and towns turned into cities as Colorado grew on the strength of its natural resources. With the post-WWII economic boom in full swing and an expanding middle class, veterans of the 10th Mountain Division arrived home from war and dreamed up a whole new industry. They built the state's first ski lift out of spare parts and went on to help open ski resorts in Loveland, Arapahoe Basin and eventually Vail and Aspen.

Pre-America

Late Paleo-Indian artifacts of the Cody Cultural Complex indicate reliance on the modern bison, while around 7500 years ago some peoples switched to hunting smaller game – a likely indicator of human population pressure on the declining bison. Petroglyphs along the canyon walls of central Idaho's mighty rivers testify to more than 8000 years of human habitation. The most complex societies in North American antiquity, however, were the agricultural pueblos of the Colorado Plateau, where cliff dwellers left behind impressive ruins in areas like Mesa Verde.

Many Native American groups occupied the Rocky Mountain region at the time of European contact. The Utes consisted of six eastern bands in Colorado and five western bands in Utah; their Colorado territory stretched from the Uinta Mountains and the Yampa River in the north to the San Juan River in the south, and as far east as the Front Range.

Exploration & Settlement

The first Europeans explorers were Spaniards moving north from Mexico. They founded Santa Fe at the end of the 16th century, and established land grants as far north as the Arkansas River in present-day Colorado. In the search for overland routes to California, the Domínguez-Escalante Expedition of 1775–76 explored the Colorado Plateau.

Early 18th-century French explorers and fur traders converged on the northern plains from eastern Canada, but by the early 19th century the Spanish had moved throughout the western half of present-day Colorado, the southwestern corner of Wyoming and even shared, at least formally, occupation of parts of Montana with the British. Virtually all of New Mexico, Arizona, California, Utah and Nevada were under Spanish authority.

In 1803 the USA, under Thomas Jefferson's presidency, acquired a huge parcel of land from the French territorial claim to Louisiana. Known as the Louisiana Purchase, the ill-defined area included the coveted port of New Orleans, virtually all of present-day Montana, three-quarters of Wyoming and the eastern half of Colorado. Shortly after

Museums & Stately Buildings

» Black American West Museum, Denver

» Brown Palace Hotel, Denver

» Colorado State Capitol, Denver

» Byers-Evans House Museum, Denver

» Colorado History Museum, Denver

» Stanley Hotel, Estes Park

» Colorado Springs Fine Arts Center, Colorado Springs

» Wheeler Opera House, Aspen

» Trinidad History Museum, Trinidad

» Barney Ford Museum, Breckenridge

» Broadmoor Hotel, Colorado Springs

» Strater Hotel, Durango

1803	1821	1849	1858
US President Thomas Jefferson commissions Lewis and Clark to explore the western interior – the first US overland expedition to the Pacific Coast and back.	After 11 years of war, Mexico gains independence from Spain. The US acknowledges Mexico's hegemony over most of the West, including three-quarters of Colorado.	Regular stagecoach service starts along the Santa Fe Trail. The 900-mile trail will serve as the country's main shipping route for the next 60 years, until the railway finally makes it to town.	General William H Larimer pegs out a square-mile plot of land, establishing the settlement that will grow into present-day Denver after gold is discovered nearby.

the purchase, which would guarantee conflict with Spain, Jefferson invited army captain Meriwether Lewis to command an exploratory expedition; Lewis invited his colleague William Clark to serve as co-commander.

The official rationale for Lewis and Clark's Corps of Discovery was to benefit American commerce by seeking a 'Northwest Passage' to the Pacific Ocean, but the expedition was also to make serious scientific observations on flora, fauna, climate and the inhabitants of the region.

Lewis and Clark's was the most successful of early US expeditions to the west; others ended in disaster. After a foray into Colorado in 1806–07, Zebulon Pike was arrested in New Mexico by Spanish police. Pike never climbed the famous peak that bears his name.

Fur Trade & Emigrant Trails

The first European to explore the Idaho Panhandle was David Thompson, a fur trader and cartographer who crossed the Rocky Mountains and in 1809 established Kullyspell House on Lake Pend Oreille, where he traded with friendly tribes.

Spaniard Manuel Lisa built a fort at the mouth of the Bighorn River and recruited John Colter from the Lewis and Clark expedition to explore Yellowstone. Colter and others such as Kit Carson, Jim Bridger, Jim Beckwourth (a free African American) and Thomas Fitzpatrick knew the Rockies backcountry better than any European.

The Denver Mint struck and minted its first gold and silver coins on February 1, 1906. It is the largest producer of coins in the world. The mint was robbed of $200,000 in broad daylight on 18 December, 1922.

Even into the 20th century, hundreds of thousands of emigrants followed the Oregon Trail across the Continental Divide to South Pass, where they split up to reach various destinations. The Mormons came fleeing persecution in New York and the Midwest. In the late 1860s, completion of the Transcontinental Railroad across southern Wyoming slowed the inexorable march of wagon trains.

Water & Western Development

Americans began to think of occupying the area between the coasts. The lingering image of the Great American Desert, a myth propagated by explorers such as Pike and Long, had deterred agricultural settlers and urban development.

Water was a limiting factor as cities such as Denver began to spring up at the base of the Front Range. Utopians such as Horace Greeley, who saw the Homestead Act of 1862 as the key to agrarian prosperity, planned agricultural experiments on the nearby plains. This act envisioned the creation of 160-acre family farms to create a rural democracy on the Western frontier.

Government agents encouraged settlement and development in their assessments of the region, but differed on how to bring these

1864
Colonel John Chivington leads 700 troops and militia in the infamous Sand Creek Massacre. The heads of Arapaho victims are paraded through today's LoDo district in grizzly celebration.

1870
Two railroads reach Denver: the Denver Pacific Railroad connects with the Union Pacific's Transcontinental line, and the Kansas Pacific arrives from Kansas City.

» Durango & Silverton Narrow Gauge Railroad

The US governments signed treaties to defuse Native American objections to expanding settlement, and established huge reservations and issued rations to compensate Native Americans for the loss of hunting territory. Under pressure from miners and other emigrants, the federal government continually reduced the reservations' size and shifted some to less desirable areas.

Ute territorial sovereignty survived a bit longer than that of other Native Americans in the region but ,with the influx of silver miners west of the Divide in the 1870s, Chief Ouray had little option but to sign treaties relinquishing traditional lands. In 1879, the White River Band of Utes attacked federal troops and White River Indian Agent Nathan Meeker and his family near the present-day town of Meeker. All Utes suffered vicious American reprisals. By 1881, Utes not removed to forsaken lands in Utah were left with a narrow 15-mile-wide strip of plateau land in southwestern Colorado.

HISTORY

changes about. Two of the major figures were Frederick V Hayden of the United States Geological Survey (USGS) and John Wesley Powell, first of the Smithsonian Institute and later of the USGS. Hayden, who had surveyed the Yellowstone River area and played a major role in having it declared a national park, was so eager to promote economic development in the West that he exaggerated the region's agricultural potential.

Powell, a great figure in American history, made a more perceptive assessment of the potential and limitations of the region. Famous as the first man to descend the Colorado River through the Grand Canyon, Powell knew the region's salient feature was aridity and that its limited water supply depended on the snowpack that fell in the Rockies. The 160-acre ideal of the Homestead Act was inappropriate for the West. His masterful *Report on the Lands of the Arid Regions of the United States* challenged the tendency toward exploitation of the region's minerals, pastures and forests, and proposed distributing land according to its suitability for irrigation.

Powell recommended dams and canals to create an integrated, federally sponsored irrigation system administered by democratically elected cooperatives. Unfortunately, his vision collided with the interests of influential cattle barons. Nor did it appeal to real estate speculators. These interests united to undermine Powell's blueprint; what survived was the idea that water development was essential to the West.

Twentieth-century development took the form of megaprojects, such as the Glen Canyon Dam on the Colorado River, and water transfers from Colorado's Western Slope to the Front Range and the plains via

Colorado has around 500 ghost towns, a legacy of the boom-bust cycle of the gold- and silver-mining days.

1876	1879	1917	1962–70s
Colorado is granted statehood, becoming the 38th state of the Union. This takes place 28 days after the US Centennial, earning Colorado its 'Centennial State' moniker.	Thornburg and his officers are killed in a Ute ambush, as are Indian Agent Nathan Meeker and his 10 staff. The women and children are taken hostage. This becomes known as the Meeker Massacre.	William F 'Buffalo Bill' Cody dies and is buried at Mt Lookout, overlooking Denver. Today you can visit the Buffalo Bill Museum & Grave from Golden.	A series of industrial and environmental accidents combined with urbanization pressures lead to green activism that causes state and federal authorities to clean up military facilities and waste sites.

a tunnel under the Continental Divide. These, in turn, provided subsidized water for large-scale irrigators and electrical power for users far from their source.

Statehood

American expansion in the West spread to Colorado with the discovery of gold in the mountains west of Denver in 1859. In 1861, the boundaries of Colorado Territory were defined, and President Lincoln appointed William Gilpin the first governor.

In 1870 two sets of railroad tracks reached Denver, ending Colorado's isolation. The Denver Pacific Railroad connected Denver with the Union Pacific's transcontinental line at Cheyenne, WY, and the Kansas Pacific arrived from Kansas City, MO. That same year, General William Palmer began planning the Denver & Rio Grande's narrow-gauge tracks into the mountain mining camps. The mining emphasis shifted from gold to silver during the 1870s as mountain smelter sites, like Leadville and Aspen, developed into thriving population centers almost overnight.

National political expedience led to Colorado statehood in 1876, the centennial of US independence.

Post-WWII

From its earliest days the West was, and still is, the country's most urbanized region; when Colorado became a state in 1876, more than a third of its residents lived in Denver. In part this urbanization was a function of the tourist economy, as Americans, who had flocked to the national parks during the economic boom after WWII, began to appreciate the Rockies as a place to live rather than just to visit. The federal government played a role by providing employment, thanks in large part to investment in Cold War military installations such as Norad, a facility near Colorado Springs. People relocated to remote towns such as Telluride as communications decentralized some sectors of the economy.

Increasingly well-educated locals and emigrants in the late 1960s and early '70s expressed environmental concerns. Military facilities, such as the Rocky Mountain National Arsenal near Colorado Springs and the Rocky Flats nuclear weapons facility near Denver, came under attack by activists concerned with environmental contamination, and were declared priority cleanup sites under the federal Environmental Protection Agency's Superfund program.

Tourism is now an economic mainstay in the Rockies. While the region's natural attractions have drawn visitors since the 1870s, mostly only wealthy travelers could see the backcountry. But after WWII, general prosperity and the improvement of roads brought larger numbers of middle-class tourists.

Historic Sites

» William F 'Buffalo Bill' Cody's Grave, Golden

» Overland Trail, Sterling

» Santa Fe Trail, Timpas

» Cliff Palace, Mesa Verde National Park

» Durango & Silverton Narrow-Gauge Railroad, Durango and Silverton

» Pikes Peak Highway, near Colorado Springs

» Cripple Creek & Victor Narrow-Gauge Railroad, Cripple Creek

» Ouray Mule Carriage Co, Ouray

1998–9	1999	2000	2010
The Denver Broncos beat the Green Bay Packers and then Atlanta Falcons to win back-to-back Super Bowls XXXII and XXXIII. Denver, and the rest of Colorado, is ecstatic.	Students Eric Harris and Dylan Klebold kill 12 students and one teacher before committing suicide at Columbine High School, near Denver.	Coloradans vote for Amendment 20 in the state election, which provides for the dispensing of cannabis to registered patients. A proliferation of medical marijuana clinics ensues over the next decade.	Fires burn for 11 days near Boulder causing mass evacuations and property damage. Over 1000 firefighters are deployed, and 7000 acres and 169 houses are burnt.

Way of Life

The Colorado personality is as random as a straw poll, as dense and impenetrable as Colorado hero John Elway's hair. This is a place where people as disparate as Hunter S Thompson and Ken Buck can make a run for public office; where escaped slaves and beat-down Confederates picked up the pieces after the Civil War; where stone-faced right-wing militias gather and just plain stoned ecoterrorists plot. Here there's a market for competitive ice sculpting, fruitcake tossing and coffin racing. Some have come to seek wealth and fortune, others arrived to stick it to the man. A place with this many folks pulling in so many directions is bound to have some quirks.

It's no myth. Colorado really does average 300 days of sun annually, and 300,000 people float down Colorado rivers every year.

Quite the Pioneers

In a state littered with characters deep and crusty from its tawdry pioneering past, a handful stand out and paint a picture of the varying influences still at play in Colorado.

It would be difficult to be more hardcore pioneer than Charles and William Bent. The Missouri brothers were as integral to America's westward expansion as anyone. For 16 years, beginning in 1830, Charles led the Santa Fe Trail trade caravans across what was then an extremely hostile and unsettled prairie. William managed their famous Old Fort (p341) and some field operations. He forged harmonious relations with neighboring tribes, married a Cheyenne woman and once hid two Cheyenne from a band of armed Comanche. The fort was like a multicultural oasis, with Spanish, Mexican, American and Native Americans bartering and mixing, drinking and dancing. The brothers mingled with John C Fremont, escorted the prospectors on their way to California and hired frontier scout Kit Carson.

Eventually Charles became New Mexico's first American governor, but was assassinated at his Taos home by an angry mob composed mostly of Pueblos before he could take the post. William's son, George, saw a massacre of a different kind. Half Cheyenne, he also married within the tribe and was present at Sand Creek in 1864 when the Colorado Volunteers attacked a village Cheyenne and Arapaho, a grisly event that would end the 'Indian Wars' and clear the way for further expansion and gold mining on Native American land.

When Leadville was fat on silver, local bigwigs built a 90ft-high Ice Palace from blocks of ice. It was party central for the 1896 social season.

Barney Ford was born a Virginian slave in 1822. When he was 17 he and his mother escaped via the underground railroad. His mother, who had instilled within him the value of an education and taught him to read, died along the way, and he was recaptured and forced to work the Georgia gold fields. Eventually he escaped to Chicago, where he continued his education. He dreamt of the California gold rush but was waylaid in Nicaragua before finally pursuing his dreams in Breckenridge, right after the first Colorado gold strike. The man who made his living in Chicago as a barber eventually opened restaurants and hotels, funded gold explorations and sold equipment to miners in Denver and

As strange and disparate as all the many strands of Colorado may seem, everyone here has one thing in common. A palpable, and some might say blind, passion for all things sport. Here are some facts worth knowing.

» If you're in a bar playing a local ball club on the TV, everyone – and we do mean everyone – will be rooting for the home team. This isn't one of those places where you can move here and maintain past allegiances. Even newbies love their Broncos, Nuggets, Rockies and Avs.

» John Elway is the greatest quarterback of all time. He looms from billboards in the airport, peers down upon the interstate, smiles and winks from the morning paper. You might wonder, 'who the hell is this guy?' Fair point. He is one of America's great quarterbacks and the only one to lead the Broncos to a Superbowl title. He did it twice, in 1998 and '99.

» If you get ensnared in a debate with a local sports freak, said sports freak will likely try to assert that his or her best player is the greatest player in the league, regardless of how absurd that may seem to the non-Coloradan.

» Even many noncompetitive cyclists shave their legs. And most claim to have ridden with Lance Armstrong or Ironman Dave Scott.

» Everyone in Colorado is always in training for...something. It could be a big 10km where they're gunning for their PB (personal best), getting 'their body right' for ski season, tackling a grueling and highly technical 100-mile mountain.

Breckenridge. He became the wealthiest man in Breckenridge and was eventually elected to the state legislature.

Spencer Penrose, in some ways, was Ford's polar opposite. He was born rich, educated at Harvard and spurned a cushy bank gig to go adventuring in the mountains in 1892. He made a killing in gold and copper. His weakness for Colorado girls may be why he didn't marry until he was well into his 40s. He was the sort who would ride horses into the lobby of his business rival's hotel to make an offer on the land, then when he was spurned built the best hotel in America, the Broadmoor (p327). He also built the Pikes Peak Highway (p43) and christened it by staging a car race with his buddies. The Pikes Peak Hill Climb (p327) is still in operation. He gave Colorado Springs a zoo and access to Pikes Peak, and he helped build and promote Colorado tourism as nobody ever had.

Industry was Mary Harris 'Mother' Jones' foil when she came to Trinidad to join a particularly contentious miners' strike. She was 82 years old and taking on the Rockefeller family's Colorado Fuel & Iron. The miners, mostly European immigrants, were evicted from their company homes and set up a tented camp in Ludlow. Jones bonded with the workers and led marches through downtown, bringing the national spotlight on Colorado. Eventually she was arrested and forced into 20 days of solitary confinement while the state militia stormed and torched the tented camp, killing three miners, two women and 11 children. The tragedy humiliated the Rockefellers and led to labor law reformation.

Today Colorado remains a state full of top-shelf outdoor folk and adventurers, political warriors, and visionary leaders of all backgrounds.

Don't knock a prison town. Buena Vista and Cañon City both have a groovy, up and coming edge. In the mountains, Buena Vista runs cooler and deeper, but historic Cañon City has the Royal Gorge and fabulous dinosaur sites in the area.

Extremism in the Rockies

With so much environmentalism and so many progressives in towns such as Boulder, Denver, Aspen, Crested Butte and Telluride, it's easy to forget that Colorado has a bold right-wing streak. This state birthed the militia movement of the 1990s.

Fringe preacher Peter J Peters sparked the flame in a 1992 meeting in Estes Park. Among those in attendance were Aryan Nations leader Richard Butler, Texas Ku Klux Klan leader Louis Beam and controversial attorney Kirk Lyons. Held in response to a botched federal raid at Ruby Ridge, the attendees came up with a solution to stem such overreaches by government forces: form militias. Soon there were militias in Montana, Michigan, Indiana and Colorado, where three men were arrested in connection with a pipe bomb in 1997. Of course, militias really made news when Timothy McVeigh detonated a truck bomb outside the Oklahoma City Federal Building on April 19, 1995, killing 168 people. According to militia watchdogs, the movement waned after the bombing and subsequent Colorado arrests, although activity has resurfaced in the years since President Barack Obama took office.

But it's the radical left wing that has caused actual physical damage in Colorado. Members of the Earth Liberation Front set fire to Vail chair lifts and a restaurant to protest the expansion of Blue Sky Basin into endangered Canadian lynx habitat. Damages came to $12 million but there were no casualties. Arrests were made, and William Rodgers, the man accused of setting the fires, killed himself on the eve of his trial.

Smoke Up

If you've spent any time in Boulder, Aspen, Fort Collins, Telluride, Manitou Springs and other liberal strongholds, you've no doubt noticed the preponderance of medical marijuana dispensaries. In a state that's no stranger to boom economies, this one seemed to crop up over night. Not true. Colorado's medical marijuana ballot measure was passed way back in 2000. It took a few years, and some pioneering minds in California and Vermont to show them how it was done, before the law impacted the streets. But the floodgates finally opened for the sticky, green herb. If only Hunter S Thompson were alive to see this. Then again, he'd be appalled to learn that new regulations have been passed to rein in the herbal revolution.

WAY OF LIFE

Bizarre & Haunted

» Stanley Hotel, Estes Park

» Great Fruitcake Toss, Colorado Springs

» Emma Crawford Coffin Races, Colorado Springs

» Ullr Fest, Breckenridge

» Delaware Hotel, Leadville

» Tarabino Inn, Trinidad

» Frozen Dead Guy Days, Nederland

The Arts

More jock than painter, more adventurer than poet, Colorado isn't the first place most folks think of when contemplating the arts. But whenever and wherever there is a convergence of certain key ingredients – transcendent natural beauty, extreme conditions and hard bodies – there are sure to be inspired souls painting, singing, sculpting and otherwise distilling life experience into cathartic work worthy of their muse.

In the Beginning

The Ancestral Puebloan people lived in sandstone cliff dwellings in the Four Corners region of Colorado. And while their architecture, including their signature cylindrical ceremonial kivas is striking, and the decorated pottery and basketry pretty special, these were born from utilitarian need. But their rock and cave paintings are something else entirely. Sure, some may have been bored classroom doodles that somehow withstood the test of time, but the kind of effort that must have been required just to create them, and the interpretations offered by Native American elders, indicate that most have deeper meanings. If you come to places like Mesa Verde National Park's (p289) Petroglyph Point, you'll see spirals and palm prints, human and animal figures. Some help mark time, others hold more spiritual and ritualistic meaning, or display social rank. A petroglyph at Hovenweep National Monument on the Utah border has a well-known solstice marker. Shafts of sunlight strike the spiral differently at the winter and summer solstices.

Pottery, basketry and rock art played a central role in Native American life for hundreds of years. Evidence of Arapahoe, Cheyenne, Apache and Ute artifacts can be viewed in museums across the state. Ute pieces are especially visible. You'll likely see their buffalo hide paintings, beaded horse bags, rattles and drums made from buffalo rawhide, but if you want to experience ceremonial drumming, chanting and dancing in traditional dress you'll need to find your way to a powwow. The Southern Ute hold an annual powwow in Ignacio in early September.

Aesthetically Speaking

Folk art was the way from the days of indigenous freedom into the pioneering period. While there was certainly live music, song and dance in saloons that doubled as brothels, there wasn't much of what we would now consider fine art in nascent Colorado. In fact, even as the state grew into a ranching, mining and railroad force in the first half of the 20th century, sophisticated art wasn't part of the equation.

Enter Alice Bemis Taylor, the wife of a powerful mining tycoon. She leaned on her vast connections in the New York art world and, with the help of other wealthy philanthropists, founded the Colorado Springs

Top Public Art

» *Dancers*, Denver

» *I See What You Mean*, Denver

» *Stations of the Cross*, Alamosa

» *Swetsville Zoo*, Fort Collins

» *Blue Mustang*, Denver

Fine Arts Center (p321), where Martha Graham danced on stage in its 400-seat theatre on opening night. Today the center is still arguably the best museum in Colorado.

But what about iconic Western imagery? The Denver Art Museum (p59), which also has a vast collection of contemporary and global art, as well as the largest Native American art collection in the US, is perhaps most famous for its gallery of cowboy art, including the iconic *Long Jakes, the Rocky Mountain Man* by Charles Deas. The Arthur Roy Mitchell Memorial Museum of Western Art (p339) is a decidedly smaller but earnest Western art gallery in Trinidad. Also known as 'the Mitch', it was built in honor of this local cowboy artist in a late 19th-century department store.

THE ARTS

Willie Nelson's seminal album, *Red Headed Stranger* (ranked as country music's greatest album of all time in 2006 by Country Music Television), is a concept album about a fugitive Montana cowboy on the run from the law after killing his wife and her lover. Inspired by Colorado's Rocky Mountains, Nelson purportedly wrote the tracks while driving back from a ski weekend.

Gallery Hopping

Iconic Western art certainly has its place in Colorado, but we prefer the same with a twist of quirk and faded Americana. The best examples that we saw in the state were in Old Colorado City photographer Kathleen McFadden's Range Gallery. You'll see shots of old rusted gas pumps, lonely roadside diners and fish-eyed horses, and curved-frame prints of cascading rivers and gnarled trees. Another pro photographer, Curtis Ritchie of *Rolling Stone* fame, curates Michael's on Main in Cañon City, which is otherwise hardly an art mecca. Antique and some vintage art galleries are also cropping up in nearby Florence, and even Pueblo's fledgling art scene is coming together to sponsor First Friday art walks in the summer. Of course, the most-established and best-connected art scene in Colorado is in Aspen.

The sheer number of galleries in Aspen is mind-boggling. They're tucked between fashion boutiques, perched over courtyard restaurants and occupy entire mini-malls in the historic downtown. Of course, some of it is gawdy and less than stellar, but there is one spot that stands out. One of Aspen's most forward-thinking galleries is 212 Gallery (p195) – the attitude here is very New York.

Festivals

For the past 60-odd years, the Aspen Music Festival (p201) has given this town its artistic gravitas. This is when some of the best classical musicians from around the world come to perform and learn from the masters of their craft. Students form orchestras led by world-famous conductors and perform at the Wheeler Opera House or the Benedict Music Tent, or in smaller duets, trios, quartets and quintets on Aspen street corners. All told there are more than 350 classical music events taking place over eight weeks. You can't escape – nor would you want to.

FEAR & LOATHING

If Colorado has a rebellious literary soul – and it does – then its leader is the late, great Hunter S Thompson. Here's a man who ran for sheriff on the Freak Power Ticket, made his name by hanging with the Hells Angels, heckling Nixon, downing experimental drug cocktails and having his ashes blasted out of a canon. Actually, his name was well made by the time of that last one.

If you want to walk in his footsteps, head to the tavern in Woody Creek (p206). One of Thompson's inspirations was Jack Kerouac, who also did some time on freight trains and downbeat street corners in Colorado. Another Beat poet (and Pulitzer Prize winner) who's had a lasting impact on Colorado is Allen Ginsberg. The author of *Howl* was a founding poet of Jack Kerouac's School of Disembodied Poetics at Naropa University (p107), where he taught for more than two decades.

Jack Kerouac's *On The Road* has more than one scene on Larimer St in Denver. The author's favorite bar was Paul's Place at 2219 Larimer St. There's still a bar, My Brother's Bar, at that address.

If you're hungry to hear the best music in the sweetest venue, the Benedict is a must. And you don't even have to pay – just unfurl a blanket on the Listening Lawn.

And that's not even the only music festival worth mentioning in Aspen. Jazz Aspen Snowmass (p200) is a twice-annual event held at the beginning and end of the summer featuring jazz masters such as Christian McBride, Nicholas Payton and Natalie Cole in June, and major pop and rock acts such as Wilco around Labor Day. Theatre Aspen (p206) is another annual tradition, where Tony-winning romantic comedies and deliciously subversive musicals are staged (mostly in the summer and early autumn) in a gorgeous, tented complex in the heart of Rio Grande Park.

Of course, summer music festivals aren't exclusive to Aspen. Breckenridge hosts a similar summer-long classical music festival with free concerts along the Blue River, and Telluride hosts a bluegrass festival (p266) in June that attracts a mix of straight-up bluegrass players, up-and-coming rockers and global icons. It's worth planning your life around. And bluegrass isn't even what put Telluride on the map. That would be the Telluride Film Festival (p266). It's now considered on par with Sundance, featuring indie and edgy domestic and international fare, and attended by Hollywood stars and career-makers.

Colorado Cuisine

For many decades, Colorado was a meat and potatoes kind of place. With ranches on both sides of the Rockies, sprawling in those spectacular high-country plateaus, this was a place of cattle drives and slaughter houses, where culinary diversity was restricted to various cuts of beef. Some cowboys got, um, adventurous, and developed mainstays such as Rocky Mountain Oysters. Beer is another staple in the Colorado diet, where Coors has long been a household name.

Recently, innovation has hit Colorado kitchens in the form of ethnic and artisan farm-to-table twists and top-shelf chefs. Even the beer – especially the beer – is getting fancy, with microbreweries springing up almost as quickly as medical marijuana dispensaries. Wine and whiskey have stormed the scene, too.

But that doesn't make the food great across the board. On the whole, prices can be high and you don't always get what you pay for. Still, recent trends are positive, and there are definitely reasons to get excited at dinnertime.

Locals Only

The most interesting, tasty – and perhaps longest overdue – movement in Colorado dining is the general drift toward high-end farm-to-table cuisine. It's been a grass-roots movement inspired by a widening interest and dependency on farmers markets as a whole. From May (at the latest) until early October there are terrific weekly farmers markets in towns such as Denver, Boulder, Aspen, Telluride, Vail and tiny Minturn – and that doesn't even scratch the surface. It was only a matter of time before restaurants embraced the local breadbasket too.

The 'eat local' ethos is grounded in the philosophy made famous in Michael Pollan's *The Omnivore's Dilemma*: that food loses both nutrients and flavor the further it has to travel. In other words, food is always healthiest and most delicious when mileage is limited. Plus, without huge distances to cover, it's (theoretically) cheaper, and untold pollution linked to freight is mitigated.

The problem for food-producing states such as Colorado has long been that out-of-state demand has trumped local dollars. For years much of the best-quality beef, lamb, pork and vegetables left town. No more. Denver's Root Down (p79), in the chic Highlands area, is a terrific example of a New American farm-to-table restaurant, and the Squeaky Bean (p80) is the city's second-best option. In Boulder you can dine at Salt (p120), a tremendous newcomer; Vail's Kelly Liken (p188) leans heavily on local suppliers; and the best in the state can be found in small, sweet, and up-and-coming Carbondale, located in farm country just 25 minutes from Aspen. That's where you'll find Six89 (p242), a destination restaurant with sustainability on the brain, beaucoup flavor on the tongue, and widely considered the best restaurant in the entire Aspen swirl.

Top Steak-houses

» Syzygy, Aspen

» Jimmy's, Aspen

» Elway's, Denver

» Farley's, Frisco

» Sweet Basil, Vail

» Black Jack's Saloon, Trinidad

» Craftwood Inn, Colorado Springs

» Red Barn Steakhouse, Montrose

» Randy's, Durango

From the Four Corners to the Front Range, there are scores of new wineries in Colorado, crushing and aging major varietals. However, most do not grow their own grapes; they purchase Californian grapes and make the wine in the Rocky Mountain State.

Sushi is Love

Sushi, unfortunately, does not fall into the 'produce locally' category. You need an ocean for that. And a good chef, well-connected to fishers on both coasts, with a keen eye for freshness, a sharp knife and, for land-locked locations such as Colorado, a nearby airport. These four ingredients aren't as easy to find as you might think, and just because there's an abundance of sushi houses in the state does not mean you should grind blindly. However, there are a few flawless diamonds that should not be missed.

Our favorite is Osaki's (p187) in Vail. A tiny hole-in-the-wall, Chef Osaki was a disciple of the great Nobu Matsuhisa in Los Angeles, back when Nobu only had the one restaurant. Given that there would be no Osaki's without Nobu, we should note that his fifth restaurant, and only the second-named Matsuhisa (p205), can be found in Aspen. The sushi is good. Very good. But the cooked food is phenomenal. A lesser-known and still delicious Aspen spot, Takah Sushi (p205) is where you go for the raw. Denver's Sushi Sasa has been garnering incredible buzz since its 2010 opening. And one Breckenridge haunt has truly delicious raw tuna and albacore with a budget price tag: Wasabi (p176) is tucked away in a mini-mall and worth finding. Order the Volcano Bowl.

A dish endemic to New Mexico and southern Colorado, green chile is a sauce made from roasted and stewed green and red chiles, cumin, oregano, cilantro and chunks of pork. It's served hot, often poured over burritos, enchiladas and tamales.

You Call This Mexican?

Strange as it may seem for a state that borders New Mexico, with a portion of it once belonging to Old Mexico, Colorado's Mexican food is mostly underwhelming. Time and again you'll wander into appetizing-looking restaurants optimistically, but, if you truly love Mexican food, you'll probably leave disappointed. However, if you stick around long enough and look hard enough, you can get your fix.

Pueblo is the Hispanic heartland of the state, with half the city on the south side of the Arkansas River, once the official Mexican–American border. Papa Jose's (p333), a cheap, tasty greasy spoon, is a Pueblo institution in historic downtown that you must find if you're hungry for some authentic green chile (sold by the pint). It does damn good burritos, enchiladas, tostadas, tacos and tamales, too.

In the Aspen area, the best Mexican food (and the best margaritas) is found at the Woody Creek Tavern (p206), Hunter S Thompson's old haunt. Leadville's Burrito Bus (p214) is authentic and beloved by local Latinos, but we think the tastiest of the Mexican menus is handed out at the Minturn Saloon (p211). Less Southwestern greasy spoon and more Jalisco-styled Mexican cuisine, here the barbecued duck and quail come with frijoles and buttered tortillas.

BREAKFAST BURRITOS

There is one Mexican-inspired food group mastered far and wide in Colorado: the breakfast burrito. It's served in diners and Jewish delis in Denver, in ski-punk coffee shops in Snowmass, straight from a bus in Leadville, and in cafés and bakeries from Telluride to Trinidad. In many ways, it is the perfect breakfast – packed with protein (eggs, cheese, beans), fresh veggies (or is avocado a fruit?), hot salsa (is that a vegetable?), and rolled to go in paper and foil. Peel it open like a banana and let the savory steam rise into your olfactories. Smuggle it onto the gondola, grind it in the car, hell, store it in your purse (but not for too long).

When paired with strong coffee it can kick-start a morning better than a Red Bull and ease a hangover better than a Bloody Mary. Heat your system for cold mornings on the slopes better than a bandit hat. (Side note: nobody eats breakfast burritos in Mexico.)

Happy Hour Happiness

Perhaps a side effect of a booming tourist industry, Colorado meals don't come cheap. You can often get better value per plate in cities such as New York, Los Angeles – hell, even London. As a result, budget travellers are often faced with the unenviable choice between fast food (again) and self-catering. But with a little strategy you can find tasty night bites with ample atmosphere for a small dent in the pocket. The solution is, of course, happy hour.

A Colorado staple, most restaurants and pubs offer limited, discounted happy-hour menus between around 3:30pm and 6pm (sometimes until 7pm). A few spots offer late-night happy hours from 10pm until close during the week. In Denver we love happy hour at Stueben's (p77). Old Boulder stand-bys the Med (p120) and Jax (p117) are still rocking, and every ski town, pub and brewhouse in the state will have at least one gem that brings down the price of a decent dinner.

On a Vegan Note

With such a strong green current running through Colorado, you might be surprised at the lack of exclusively vegetarian restaurants. You'll find them here and there, but usually vegetarians and vegans will have to eat with the carnivores. Still, many restaurants (even some steakhouses) will have at least one or two vegetarian dishes. As always, Indian, Italian and Thai restaurants have the most selections.

In all the glory of Colorado microbrews, don't overlook the whiskey. Based in Denver, Stranahan's is a small batch distiller that makes its whiskey from only 12 barrels per week out of locally grown barley.

COLORADO CUISINE

Wildlife & the Land

Colorado is an interdependent quilt: arid canyons and extraordinary geologic formations to the south and west, vast unbroken plains to the east and a burly Rocky Mountain backbone. Much of Colorado enjoys some level of protection and management by local, state and federal agencies, but industry has had its say, too. In the early years mining took its backcountry toll; today the biggest threat to land and wildlife is both residential and ski resort development.

Geology

Tectonic shifts and volcanic activity known as the Laramide Revolution shook, folded and molded the Colorado landscape, where granite peaks rise nearly 10,000ft above adjacent plains. The highest point is Colorado's 14,433ft Mt Elbert. Behind the Front Range lie several scattered mountain ranges and broad plateaus; their most notable geologic feature is the spectacular Rocky Mountain Trench, a fault valley 1100 miles long.

The Spanish Peaks, in southern Colorado near La Veta are not part of the Rocky Mountains, but rather extinct volcanoes.

Glaciers also shaped the land. The Laurentide Ice Sheet left deep sediments as it receded into the Arctic during the warming of the Quaternary period. A cordilleran glacier system formed at higher altitudes in the Rockies, leaving moraines, lakes, cirques and jagged alpine landforms as they melted. Their melting also formed massive rivers that eroded and shaped the state's spectacular canyons on the Colorado Plateau to the southwest.

Flora

Colorado's vegetation is closely linked to climate, which in turn depends on both elevation and rainfall. Vegetation at altitude can still vary depending upon exposure and the availability of water. That's why the San Juans and Spanish Peaks can look so different in places from the Maroon Bells and Rocky Mountain National Park.

Sparse piñon-juniper forests cover the Rockies' lower slopes from about 4000ft to 6000ft, while ponderosa pines indicate the montane zone between 6000ft and 9000ft, where deciduous alders, luscious white-barked aspens (their lime-green foliage turns gold in autumn), willows and the distinctive blue spruce flourish in damper areas. In the subalpine zone, above 9000ft, Engelmann spruce largely replace pine (though some stands of lodgepoles grow higher), while colorful wildflowers such as columbine, marsh marigold and primrose colonize open spaces. In the alpine zone above 11,500ft, alpine meadows and tundra supplant stunted trees, which can grow only in sheltered, southern exposures.

East of the Rockies, the Great Plains are an immense grassland of short and tall grasses, interrupted by dense gallery forests of willows and cottonwoods along the major rivers. The best example of intact savanna are found in the Pawnee National Grassland, where the Pawnee Buttes loom. A good example of eastern Colorado's riparian (riverbank) foliage is found along the Arkansas River near Bent's Old Fort on the Santa Fe Trail. Those arid zones closest to the Rockies consist of shorter species such as wheatgrass, grama and buffalo grass, which grow no higher than about 3ft.

Wildlife

Colorado wildlife correlates in part (but not completely) to elevation and climate, and the number of animals, especially that of the more mobile ones, varies seasonally. In the alpine zones, for instance, small rodents such as pikas inhabit rockfalls throughout the year, but larger mammals such as Rocky Mountain elk and bighorn sheep are present only in summer.

The Great Plains have their own singular fauna, such as the swift pronghorn antelope and prairie dogs. The swift pronghorn grazes short-grass plains nearest the mountains, while the prairie dog neither inhabits the prairies nor is a dog: related to the squirrel, it lives in sprawling burrows known as prairie dog 'towns.' Species such as mule deer and coyotes range over a variety of zones from the plains to the peaks. The solitary, lumbering moose prefers riparian zones. If luck is on your side, you'll see them wading in lakes and trudging through wetlands in the Kawuneeche Valley in Rocky Mountain National Park.

The most famous animal of the Colorado plains was, of course, the magnificent buffalo or bison that grazed the prairies in enormous herds until its near extinction. The bison survives in limited numbers in Wyoming, but the last-known wild Colorado resident was killed in the South Park area in 1897. There are still bison in Colorado, but they're not wild. They're livestock raised for beef.

Bears

The black bear is probably the most notorious animal in the Rockies. Despite the name the bears' fur can have a honey or cinnamon tint, their muzzle can be tan, and some even have white spots on their chest. Adult males weigh from 275lb to 450lb; females weigh about 175lb to 250lb. They measure 3ft high on all fours and can be over 5ft when standing on their hind legs. The largest populations of black bears live in areas where aspen trees propagate, and near open areas of chokecherry and serviceberry bushes. Their range can stretch to 250 square miles.

The grizzly bear, America's largest meat eater, is classified as an endangered species in Colorado, but it is almost certainly gone from the state. The last documented grizzly in Colorado was killed in 1979.

Bighorn Sheep

Rocky Mountain National Park is a special place: 'Bighorn Crossing Zone' is a sign you're unlikely to encounter anywhere else. From late spring through summer, three or four volunteers and an equal number of rangers provide traffic control on US 34 at Sheep Lakes Information Station, 2 miles west of the Fall River Entrance Station. Groups of up to 60 sheep – typically only ewes and lambs – move from the moraine ridge north of the highway across the road to Sheep Lakes in Horseshoe Park. Unlike the big under-curving horns on mature rams, ewes grow swept-back crescent-shaped horns that reach only about 10in in length. The Sheep Lakes are evaporative ponds ringed with tasty salt deposits that attract the ewes in the morning and early afternoon after lambing in May and June. In August they rejoin the rams in the Mummy Range.

Four species of fox are native to Colorado. Red foxes live in mountain riparian zones, gray foxes like canyons, swift foxes live in the eastern plains and kit foxes live in the western deserts.

To see bighorn sheep on rocky ledges you'll need to hike or backpack. The estimated 200 animals in the Horseshoe Park herd live permanently in the Mummy Range. On the west side, an equally large herd inhabits the volcanic cliffs of the Never Summer Mountains. A smaller herd can be seen along the Continental Divide at a distance from the rim of the crater near Milner Pass. Three miles west of the Alpine Visitors Center on Trail Ridge Rd, Crater Trail follows a steep course for 1 mile to the observation point.

Elk

Seeing a herd of North American elk, or *wapiti* (a Native American term meaning white, a reference to the animal's white tail and rump), grazing in their natural setting is unforgettable. According to NPS surveys, about 2000 elk winter in the Rocky Mountain National Park's lower elevations, while more than 3000 inhabit the park's lofty terrain during summer months. The summer visitor equipped with binoculars or a telephoto lens is almost always rewarded by patiently scanning the hillsides and meadows near the Alpine Visitors Center. Traffic jams up as motorists stop to observe these magnificent creatures near the uppermost Fall River Rd or Trail Ridge Rd. Visitors are repeatedly warned by signs and park rangers not to harass, call to or come in contact with the animals.

Mature elk bulls may reach 1100lb, cows weigh up to 600lb. Both have dark necks with light tan bodies. Like bighorn sheep, elk were virtually extinct around Estes Park by 1890, wiped out by hunters. In 1913 and '14, before the establishment of the park, people from Estes Park brought in 49 elk from Yellowstone. The elk's natural population increase since the establishment of Rocky Mountain National Park is one of the NPS's great successes, directly attributable to the removal of their principal predator: men with guns.

Other Mammals

You are likely to encounter mule deer, named for their large mule-like ears, somewhere along your journey as they browse on leaves and twigs from shrubs at sunny lower elevations. Howling coyotes commonly serenade winter campfires – lucky visitors may spy a coyote stalking small rodents. Other large carnivores such as the bobcat and mountain lion are very rarely seen. Small but ferocious long-tailed weasel hunt near their streamside dens at night.

Best Birding

» Rocky Mountain National Park
» Pawnee National Grassland
» Alamosa National Wildlife Refuge
» Arapahoe National Wildlife Refuge
» Chautauqua Park

Birds

An astounding 465 bird species have been identified in the state of Colorado. Among them are flycatchers, burrowing (federally listed as threatened) and great horned owls, crows, mourning doves, mountain plovers, chickadees, Canadian geese, bluebirds and cranes. The newly classified and unique Gunnison sage grouse, found in the southwest, is listed as a Species of Special Concern and a candidate to be placed on the federal endangered species list. There are two types of eagle. The more prevalent golden eagle has a wingspan of 7ft and ranges throughout North America. The bald eagle only relatively recently bounced back from near extinction and remains on the endangered species list. At its low point only two or three nesting pairs nested in Colorado, but that number has increased by eight or nine each year, and at last count there were 51 breeding pairs and a stable population of over 800 eagles in the state.

Dinosaurs

Although dinosaurs once flew, swam, strutted, grazed, marauded, hunted and migrated voraciously (sound familiar?) for over 100 million years, only a few places have the proper geological and climatic conditions to preserve their skeletons as fossils and their tracks as permanent evolutionary place holders. Colorado is near the top of that list. If you or your loved ones are dinophiles, you've come to the right state.

Fossils, You Say?

Back in the *really* olden days – like during the Jurassic (144 to 208 million years ago) and Cretaceous (144 to 65 million years ago) periods – Colorado was a decidedly different place. The Rockies hadn't yet risen and Pangea had only recently split (what's a million years?), meaning present-day Colorado was close to the equator.

Most, if not all, of the sites where fossilized dinosaur bones were found en masse are thought to have been in or near a floodplain, meaning the area was under water (and an important water source) during the wet season, but could be bone dry in the dry season. Often times dinosaurs would migrate for miles and days and weeks in search of water. If they arrived at the flood plain at the wrong time of year, many simply died. Winds would rise and cover their bodies in layer after layer of dust, and when the rains did come floods would further coat their bones in mud. It takes many thousands of layers of dust and mud and approximately 12,000 years for these bones to become fossils. It also takes a pressurized environment, which is why layers of water over the earth is a key (but not vital) ingredient to fossilization.

With time and pressure the porous bones begin to absorb the minerals from the dust and stone which replace the bones' original cell structure, turning them into fossils.

The Bone Wars

In 1877 two great palaeontologists, Edward Drinker Cope of the Academy of Natural Sciences in Philadelphia and Othniel Charles Marsh of Yale University, set up two rival quarries in what is known as the Garden Park Fossil Area, just outside Cañon City. The first find in the area occurred in 1869, and another was discovered by Henry Felch in 1876. Felch brought the fossils to a Dr FJ Lewis, who recognized them as dinosaur bones. Meanwhile, the local school superintendent Oramel Lucas started digging in Garden Park, found more bones in 1877 and reached out to both Cope and Marsh.

Cope responded immediately, and began excavations in the area, while Marsh was busy with less productive projects in Morrison (what is now known as Dinosaur Ridge). Eventually both men arrived on the Garden Park scene, competing desperately for the biggest and best finds, and occasionally raiding one another's camps. Politics aside, these digs yielded some incredible finds, including five types of species (the first recorded

Best Dinosaur Sites

» Denver Museum of Nature & Science, Denver

» Dinosaur Ridge, near Morrison

» Dinosaur National Monument, near Dinosaur

» Garden Park Fossil Area, near Cañon City

» Dinosaur Depot, Cañon City

» Picketwire Dinosaur Track Site, near La Junta

DINOSAURS

Before embarking on your dino-tracking tour, make sure to stop by the Denver Museum of Nature & Science (p62). After the initial wave of excavations was complete, dinosaur bones stopped being shipped for display in East Coast museums and instead migrated here. A good primer for what you'll see in the field, the prehistoric wing has the most complete Stegosaurus skeleton discovered, as well as an Allosaurus skeleton and an egg nest.

discoveries) of dinosaur, including stegosaurus, allosaurus, diplodocus and ceratosaurus, all of which are still standing at the Smithsonian. Garden Park, meanwhile, is on Bureau of Land Management (BLM) land, free and open to the public. Dinosaur Depot (p335) in Cañon City sells a helpful brochure that offers a self-guided tour.

A Monument Born

Earl Douglass, a palaeontologist at the Carnegie Museum in Pittsburgh, decided to spend a summer fossil prospecting in the Utah high desert in 1909. He was originally directed to the town of Vernal, where he'd found a Diplodocus femur the summer before. But after a week's dig he found most of the best bones gone, the rest broken and the soil churned up. He moved camp to a gulch with a hard sandstone bed. At the top of the ledge near a saddle, he made the discovery of his life. Here were eight tail bones of an apatosauras. What was supposed to be a summer gig became a 13-year excavation.

Most of the bones were shipped back east to the Carnegie Museum, and President Woodrow Wilson was sufficiently impressed to declare Douglass Quarry (also known as the Carnegie Quarry) Dinosaur National Monument. Today, the visitors center opens up onto a quarry wall where more than 1400 dinosaur bones (all from the Jurassic period) are clearly visible, labeled, yet still embedded into the sandstone wall.

Marsh and Cope's desire to beat each other to the punch meant they often had to rush their findings. Those who listed the brontosaurus as their favorite as a child will be saddened to learn it technically never existed: the skeleton Marsh named has been confirmed as an apatosaurus.

Tracking the Giants

Fossils are sexier, but if you have a (rather large) foot fetish, you'll enjoy Colorado's tracksites. Footprints work a bit differently to fossils. On Skyline Drive in Cañon City, the ankylosaurs tracks were made in sand that crystalized into sandstone, which wrenched with the upheaval of the Rockies and became invisible to the eye. But as that sandstone eroded, the tracks began to reveal themselves, at times in the oddest way: jutting out from an otherwise sheer sandstone cliff above a residential neighborhood.

Meanwhile, the Picketwire Track Site, in the eastern plains, was made in mud. These animals (thought to be apatosaurs and allosaurs) were tromping through swampy sludge; when that swamp water receded as climates shifted it dried into clay, preserving those tracks. Another intriguing track site much closer to Denver can be found on Dinosaur Ridge in Morrison. Accidentally discovered during the construction of the West Alameda Parkway 1937, there are now 300 identified tracks (including what are thought to be tyrannosaurus rex, edmontosaurus, and triceratops tracks) on the 1.5-mile-long ridge.

Survival Guide

DIRECTORY A-Z 368

Accommodations....... 368

Business Hours 370

Discount Cards......... 370

Electricity 371

Gay & Lesbian
Travelers 371

Health...................371

Insurance...............372

Internet Access.........372

Legal Matters 372

Public Holidays..........374

Tourist Information 374

Travelers with
Disabilities..............374

Volunteering 374

Work 374

TRANSPORTATION...375

Air 375

Land 376

Air 376

Bicycle 376

Bus 377

Car & Motorcycle........377

Hitchhiking 378

Train 378

Directory A-Z

Accommodations

Colorado provides a vast array of accommodation options: from pitching a tent under a starlit sky and budget motels to midrange B&Bs, adobe inns and historical hotels to four-star lodgings, luxurious spas and dude ranches. The most comfortable accommodations for the lowest price are usually found in that great American invention, the roadside motel.

For last-minute deals, check the following options:

Triporati (www.triporati.com)

Sidestep (www.sidestep.com)

Expedia (www.expedia.com)

Travelocity (www.travelo city.com)

Orbitz (www.orbitz.com)

Priceline (www.priceline.com)

Hotels.com (www.hotels. com)

B&Bs

Many B&Bs are high-end romantic retreats in restored historic homes run by personable, independent innkeepers who serve gourmet breakfasts. These B&Bs often take pains to evoke a theme – Victorian, rustic and

so on – and amenities range from merely comfortable to hopelessly indulgent. Rates normally top $150, and the best run to more than $300. Many B&Bs have minimum-stay requirements, and some exclude young children.

European-style B&Bs can be found in Colorado: these may be rooms in someone's home, with plainer furnishings, simpler breakfasts, shared baths and cheaper rates. They often welcome families.

B&Bs can close out of season and reservations are essential, especially for high-end places. To avoid surprises, always ask whether bathrooms are shared or private.

There are plenty of B&B listings online.

Bed & Breakfast Inns Online (www.bbonline.com)

BedandBreakfast.com (www.bedandbreakfast.com)

BnB Finder (www.bnbfinder. com)

Pamela Lanier's Bed & Breakfast Inns (www. lanierbb.com)

Select Registry (www. selectregistry.com)

Camping

Camping is the cheapest, and in many ways the most enjoyable, approach to a vacation. Visitors with a car and a tent can take advantage of hundreds of private and public campgrounds and RV parks at prices of $10 to $25 per night.

Some of the best camping areas are on public lands (national forests, state and national parks...) and Bureau of Land Management (BLM; ☑303-239-3600; www. co.blm.gov) lands. Free dispersed camping (meaning you can camp almost anywhere) is permitted in many public backcountry areas. Sometimes you can camp along a dirt road, especially in BLM and national forest areas. In other places, you can backpack your gear into a cleared campsite.

Information and maps are available from ranger stations or BLM offices, and may be posted along the road. Sometimes, a free camping permit is required, particularly in national parks.

WASTE & FACILITIES

When camping in an undeveloped area choose a site at least 200 yards from water and wash up at camp, not in the stream, using biodegradable soap. Dig a 6in-deep hole to use as a latrine and cover and camouflage it well when leaving the site. Burn toilet paper, unless fires are prohibited. Carry out all trash.

BOOK YOUR STAY ONLINE

For more accomodation reviews by Lonely Planet authors, check out hotels.lonelyplanet.com/colorado. You'll find independent reviews, as well as recommendations on the best places to stay. Best of all, you can book online.

Use a portable charcoal grill or camping stove; don't build new fires. If there already is a fire ring, use only dead and downed wood or wood you have carried in yourself. Make sure to leave the campsite as you found it.

Developed areas usually have toilets, drinking water, fire pits (or charcoal grills) and picnic benches. Some don't have drinking water, and some turn the water off out of season. It's always a good idea to have a few gallons of water when camping. These basic campgrounds usually cost about $10 to $15 a night. Some areas have showers or RV hookups and often cost $15 to $25.

RESERVATIONS

National forest and BLM campgrounds are usually less developed, while national park and state park campgrounds are more likely to have more amenities. The less-developed sites are often on a 'first-come, first-served' basis, so arrive early, preferably during the week, as sites fill up fast on Friday and weekends. More developed areas may accept or require reservations.

PRIVATE CAMPGROUNDS

Private campgrounds are usually close to towns or nearby. Most are designed for RVs but tents can be erected at most. Camp fees are higher than for public campgrounds. Fees are usually quoted for two people per site, with additional fees for extra people (about $5 per person). Some places charge just per vehicle. Facilities can include hot showers, coin laundry, swimming pool, full RV hookups, a games area, a playground and a convenience store.

ONLINE RESOURCES

» **Camping USA** (www.camping-usa.com) A great resource with more than 12,000 campgrounds in its database, including RV parks, private campgrounds, BLM areas and state and national parks

» **Kampgrounds of America** (KOA; ☑888-562-0000; www.koa.com; $20-35 depending on hookups) A vast national network of private campgrounds with sites usually ranging from $20 to $35, depending on hookups. You can purchase the annual directory of KOA campgrounds at any KOA, or by calling.

» **Recreation.gov** (☑877-444-6777, toll-free 518-885-3639; www.recreation.gov). Organizes reservations for campsites on federal land

Dude Ranches

Most visitors to dude ranches today are city-slickers looking for an escape from a fast-paced, high-tech world.

Dude ranches dates back to the late 19th century, when two brothers saw the potential earnings from their home and lifestyle. These days you can find anything from a working-ranch experience (smelly chores and 5am wake-up calls included) to a Western Club Med. Typical week-long visits start at over $100 per person per day, including accommodations, meals, activities and equipment.

While the centerpiece of dude-ranch vacations is horseback riding, many ranches feature swimming pools and have expanded their activity lists to include fly-fishing, hiking, mountain biking, tennis, golf, skeet-shooting and cross-country skiing. Accommodations range from rustic log cabins to cushy suites with whirlpools and cable TV. Meals range from family-style spaghetti dinners to four-course gourmet feasts.

» **Colorado Dude & Guest Ranch Association** (☑866-942-3472; www.coloradoranch.com)

» **Dude Ranchers' Association** (☑307-587-2339, toll-free 866-399-2339; www.duderanch.org; 1122 12th St)

Hostels

Staying in a private double at a hostel can be a great way to save money and still have privacy (although you'll usually have to share a bathroom). Dorm beds allow those in search of the ultimate bargain to sleep cheap under a roof. Dorms cost between $18 and $28, depending on the city and time of year. A private room in a Colorado hostel costs between $35 and $50.

US citizens and residents can join **Hostelling International-USA** (HI-USA; ☑301-495-1240; www.hiusa.org; 8401 Colesville Rd; annual membership adult/child $28/free) by calling and requesting a membership form or by downloading a form from the website. However, HI-USA doesn't have any hostels in

Colorado. The HI card may be used for discounts at some local merchants and for local services, including some intercity bus companies.

Hostels.com (www.hostels.com) Lists hostels throughout the world.

Hostelworld (www.hostelworld.com)

Hotels

Colorado's hotels are mostly found in cities, and they're generally large and luxurious, except for a few boutique hotels, which tend to be small, understated and lavish. Prices start at around $200 and shoot straight up; ask about discounts and special packages when making reservations. Always check online first when booking a hotel.

Long-Term Rentals

Houses or condominiums can be rented for anywhere from two days to two months. This type of lodging is most often found in resort areas and almost always includes kitchens and living rooms.

Several people can lodge for the same price, so long-term can be more economical than motels or hotels on a per person basis, especially if you can cook your own food. The chambers of commerce in resort towns have information on condominium listings and can give advice on renting.

Also consider some of the corporate housing agencies such as **Avenue West** (☑303-825-7625, toll-free 877-944-8283; www.avewest.com; 1440 Market St) or **Oakwood** (☑877-902-0832; www.oakwood.com; 2222 Corinth Ave; ☺6:30am-9pm Mon-Fri, 7am-6:30pm Sat & Sun).

Motels

Budget chain motels are prevalent throughout Colorado; in smaller towns they're often the only option. Many motels have at-the-door parking, with exterior room doors. These are convenient, though some folks, especially single women, may prefer the more

expensive places with more secure interior corridors.

Advertised prices are referred to as 'rack rates' and are not written in stone. Asking about specials can often save quite a bit of money. Children are often allowed to stay free with their parents.

Business Hours

In some parts of the country, all businesses except a few restaurants may close on Sunday.

» **Businesses** 9am to 5pm Monday to Friday

» **Banks** 8:30am to 4:30pm Monday to Thursday, to 5:30pm Friday; some open 9am to noon or 1pm on Saturday

» **Stores** 10am to 6pm Monday to Saturday, noon to 5pm Sunday; in malls and downtown shopping areas hours may extend to 8pm or 9pm

» **Supermarkets** 8am to 8pm; most cities have 24-hour supermarkets

» **Restaurants** Hours can fluctuate with seasonal demand; generally, breakfast is from 7am to 10:30am Monday to Friday, with weekend brunch from 9am to 2pm; lunch runs from 11:30am to 2:30pm Monday to Friday; and dinner is served between 5pm and 9:30pm, often later on Friday and Saturday

» **Bars & Pubs** 5pm to midnight, to 2am on Friday and Saturday; nightclubs tend to open after 9pm and close around 2am Wednesday to Saturday; hours can be longer in major cities

Discount Cards

Visitors to Colorado should look into all the standard national and international discount cards. Travelers can find all sorts of ways to shave costs off hotel rooms, meals, rental cars, museum admissions and just about

anything else that can be had for a price. Persistence and ingenuity go a long way when it comes to finding deals in Colorado.

Students

» Benefit from many kinds of savings

» Should ask for a discount whenever booking a room, reserving a car or paying an entrance fee

» Generally receive discounts of 10% or so, but sometimes as much as 50%

» Should consider investing in a **Student Advantage Card** (www.studentadvantage.com) or an **International Student Identity Card** (ISIC; www.isiccard.com)

» Should always carry proof of student status

Youths

» Should look into the **International Youth Travel Card** (IYTC; www.isic.org)

Seniors (Over 62)

» Benefit from many kinds of savings

» Should ask for a discount whenever booking a room, reserving a car or paying an entrance fee

» Generally receive discounts of 10% or so, but sometimes as much as 50%

» Should consider an **America the Beautiful Senior Pass** (http://store.usgs.gov/pass/senior.html; $10 valid for the lifetime of the pass owner) for 50% discounts on fees such as camping on federal recreational lands

» Should always carry proof of age

Over 50s

» Should contact the **American Association of Retired Persons** (☑888-687-2277; www.aarp.org; 601 E St NW) for travel discounts, typically 10% to 25% off hotels, car rentals, entertainment etc.

Motorists

Card-carrying members of automobile associations

are entitled to similar travel discounts. **AAA** (AAA; ☑866-625-3601; www.colorado.aaa. com) has reciprocal agreements with several international auto associations, so bring your membership card from home.

Other Discounts

Other people whose status might lead to discounts are. US military personnel and veterans, travelers with disabilities, children, business travelers and foreign visitors. These discounts may not always be advertised – it pays to ask.

Discount Coupons

Discount coupons can be found at every tourist locale. They always have restrictions and conditions, so read the fine print. Some are hardly worth the effort, but scour tourist information offices and highway welcome centers for brochures and fliers, and you'll find a few gems. For online hotel coupons, browse **Roomsaver.com** (www. roomsaver.com).

Electricity

120V/60Hz

120V/60Hz

Gay & Lesbian Travelers

Colorado is very much a mixed bag for gay and lesbian travelers. Denver is a progressive place with a thriving gay and lesbian scene, but Boulder doesn't have a single gay or lesbian venue (though there is a strong and growing gay scene).

Some other areas in the state are characterized by conservative attitudes and old-school ideas of machismo. The more affluent ski areas and artsy communities seem to be less uptight about same-sex relationships, but there's no mistaking the region for San Francisco.

According to www.epo dunk.com, here's how some of Colorado's cities fare on a 'gay index', a comparative score based on the percentage of same-sex households in a state. A score of 100 is the national norm; the higher the number, the more gays and lesbians there are.

» Denver 216
» Boulder 138
» Fort Collins 85
» Colorado Springs 78
» Grand Junction 78

Resources

Good national guidebooks include *Damron Women's Traveller*, *Damron Men's Travel Guide* and *Damron Accommodations*, with listings of gay-owned or gay-friendly accommodations nationwide. All three are published by the **Damron Company** (☑415-255-0404, toll-free 800-462-6654; www.damron.com).

Another good resource is the **Gay & Lesbian Yellow Pages** (☑toll-free 800-697-2812; www.glyp.com), with 33 national and regional directories.

National resources include the **National Gay & Lesbian Task Force** (☑202-393-5177; www.thetaskforce.org) in Washington, DC, and the **Lambda Legal Defense Fund** (☑Los Angeles 213-382-7600, New York City 212-809-8585; www.lamb dalegal.org).

Health

Colorado has an extraordinary range of climates and terrains, from the freezing heights of the Rockies to the searing midsummer heat of the desert tablelands. Because of the high level of hygiene, infectious diseases will not be a significant concern for most travelers, who are unlikely to experience anything worse than a little diarrhea, sunburn or a mild respiratory infection.

Insurance

» The USA offers possibly the finest health care in the world, but it can be prohibitively expensive.

» International travelers should check if their regular policy covers them in the US; if it doesn't, travel insurance is essential.

Vaccinations

No special vaccines are required or recommended for travel to or around the USA. All travelers should be up-to-date on routine immunizations.

In general, if you have a medical emergency, the best bet is for you to find the nearest hospital and go to its emergency room. If the problem isn't urgent, you can call a nearby hospital and ask for a referral to a local physician, which is usually cheaper than a trip to the emergency room. Standalone, for-profit urgent-care centers can be convenient, but may perform large numbers of expensive tests, even for minor illnesses.

If you're heading to more remote areas of the state, it pays to be aware of the closest emergency medical services. If heading into backcountry areas, stop by the local ranger station or visitors center for information.

International visitors may find that some medications that are available over-the-counter in their home country require a prescription. If you don't have insurance to cover the cost of prescriptions, they can be very expensive.

Wildlife

Common sense approaches to animal bites and stings are the most effective.

» Wear boots when hiking to protect from snakes.

» Wear long sleeves and pants to protect from ticks and mosquitoes.

» If you're bitten, don't overreact. Stay calm and seek the relevant treatment.

ANIMAL BITES

» Do not attempt to pet, handle or feed any nondomestic animal. Most animal-related injuries are directly related to a person's attempt to touch or feed the animal.

» Any bite or scratch by a mammal, including bats, should be promptly and thoroughly cleansed with large amounts of soap and water, followed by application of an antiseptic, such as iodine or alcohol.

» Local health authorities should be contacted immediately for possible rabies treatment, regardless of immunization.

» It may also be advisable to start an antibiotic; wounds caused by animal bites and scratches frequently become infected.

SNAKE BITES

» There are several varieties of venomous snakes in Colorado; unlike in other countries, these snakes do not cause instantaneous death, and antivenins are available.

» Place a light constricting bandage over the bite, keep the wounded part below the level of the heart and move it as little as possible.

» Stay calm and get to a medical facility as soon as possible.

» Bring the dead snake for identification if you can, but don't risk being bitten again.

» Do not use the mythic 'cut an X and suck out the venom' trick.

Insurance

No matter how long or short your trip, make sure you purchase adequate travel insurance before departure. At a minimum, you need coverage for medical emergencies and treatment, including hospital stays and an emergency flight home if necessary.

Aso consider coverage for luggage theft or loss and trip cancellation. If you already have a home-owner's or renter's policy, see what it will cover and consider getting supplemental insurance to cover the rest. If you've prepaid a large portion of your trip, cancellation insurance is a worthwhile expense. A comprehensive travel insurance policy that covers all these things can cost up to 10% of the total cost of your trip.

If you will be driving, it's essential that you have liability insurance. Car-rental agencies offer insurance that covers damage to the rental vehicle and separate liability insurance, which covers damage to people and other vehicles.

Worldwide travel insurance is available at www.lonely planet.com/ travel_services. You can buy, extend and claim online anytime – even if you're already on the road.

Internet Access

» Internet cafés typically charge $3 to $12 per hour for online access.

» Accommodations, cafés, restaurants, bars etc that provide guest computer terminals for going online are identified by the internet icon @; the wi-fi icon 🛜 indicates that wireless access is available. There may be a fee for either service.

» Free or fee-based wi-fi hot spots can be found at major airports; many hotels, motels and cafés; and some tourist information centers, museums, bars and restaurants.

» Free public wi-fi is proliferating and even some state parks are now wi-fi–enabled.

» To find more public wi-fi hot spots, search www. wififreespot.com or www. jiwire.com.

» Public libraries have internet terminals (online time may be limited, advance sign-up required and a nominal fee charged for out-of-network visitors) and, increasingly, free wi-fi access.

Legal Matters
Rights

» People arrested for a serious offence in the US have the right to remain silent, to an attorney and to make one phone call. They

Entering the Region

» Every foreign visitor entering the USA needs a passport.

» Passports must be valid for at least six months longer than the intended stay.

» Apart from most Canadian citizens and those under the Visa Waiver Program, all visitors need to obtain a visa from a US consulate or embassy abroad.

» For a complete list of US customs regulations, visit the official portal for US Customs & Border Protection (www.cbp.gov).

Embassies & Consulates

There are no foreign embassies or diplomatic representatives in Colorado.

International travelers who want to contact their home country's embassy while in the US should visit Embassy.org (www.embassy.org), which lists contact information for all foreign embassies in Washington, DC. Most countries have an embassy for the UN in New York City.

Money

ATMs are widely available in stores and businesses. Most businesses accept credit cards.

Post

No matter how much people like to complain, the US Postal Service (USPS; www.usps.com) provides great service for the price.

Private shippers such as United Parcel Service (UPS; ☎800-742-5877; www.ups.com) and Federal Express (FedEx; ☎800-463-3339; www.fedex.com) are useful for sending more important or larger items.

Telephone

CALLING CODES

» Country code: 1

» Area codes: 303, 719, 720, 970

» International access code: 011

CELL (MOBILE) PHONES

» You'll need a multiband GSM phone in order to make calls in the USA.

» A prepaid SIM card is usually cheaper than using your home network.

» There are plenty of holes in the coverage; don't assume you'll have reception.

Time

Colorado is on Mountain Standard Time (MST), seven hours behind GMT/UTC. Colorado switches to Mountain Daylight Time (or Pacific Daylight Time), one hour later, from the first Sunday of April to the last Saturday of October.

are presumed innocent until proven guilty.

» International visitors who are arrested and don't have a lawyer or family member to help should call their embassy or consulate.

Age Restrictions

These are the minimum age requirements for the following activties.

» **Drink alcohol** 21

» **Drive a car** 16

» **Own a gun** 18

» **Smoke tobacco** 18

» **Vote** 18

Travelers should be aware that they can be prosecuted under the law of their home country regarding age of consent, even when they're abroad.

Smoking

» Smoking is banned all workplaces, including bars and restaurants.

» Private residences and automobiles are exempt unless used for child day care.

» Some hotels/motels and other businesses may have designated smoking rooms or areas.

» Local governments may have stricter smoking regulations than the state government.

Drugs

» Despite state-approved use of marijuana for medicinal purposes, recreational use of marijuana remains illegal. Access to medicinal marijuana is restricted to prescribing physicians.

» Possession of any kind of illicit drug, including cocaine, ecstasy, LSD, heroin, hashish or more than one ounce of cannabis, is a felony potentially punishable by lengthy jail sentences. For foreigners, conviction of any drug offence is grounds for deportation.

Public Holidays

» **New Year's Day** January 1

» **Martin Luther King Jr Day** 3rd Monday of January

» **Presidents Day** 3rd Monday of February

» **Easter** March or April

» **Memorial Day** Last Monday of May

» **Independence Day** July 4

» **Labor Day** 1st Monday of September

» **Columbus Day** 2nd Monday of October

» **Veterans Day** November 11

» **Thanksgiving** 4th Thursday of November

» **Christmas Day** December 25

Tourist Information

Colorado Travel & Tourism Authority (☏800-265-6723; www.colorado.com; PO Box 3524)

Travelers with Disabilities

Travel within Colorado is getting easier for people with disabilities, but it's still not easy. Public buildings are required by law to be wheelchair accessible and to have appropriate restroom facilities. Public transportation services must be made accessible to all, and telephone companies have to provide relay operators for the hearing impaired. Many banks provide ATM instructions in braille, curb ramps are common, many busy intersections have audible crossing signals, and most chain hotels have suites for guests with disabilities. Still, it's best to call ahead to check.

A number of organizations specialize in the needs of travelers with disabilities:

» **Mobility International USA** (☏541-343-1284; www.miusa.org; 132 E Broadway, Eugene, OR 97440)

» **Society for the Advancement of Travel for the Handicapped** (SATH; ☏212-447-7284; www.sath.org; 347 Fifth Ave, Suite 610) Travelers with disabilities seeking outdoor adventures should check out the **Adaptive Sports Center** (☏970-349-2296; www.adaptivesports.org; 10 Crested Butte Way; ♿) in Crested Butte.

Volunteering

Opportunities for volunteering in Colorado are plenty and various, and it can be a great way to break up a long trip. Volunteering can also provide truly memorable experiences: you'll get to interact with people, society and the land in ways you never would by just passing through.

There are numerous casual, drop-in volunteering opportunities in the big cities,

and you can socialize with locals and help out nonprofit organizations. Check weekly alternative newspapers for calendar listings, or browse the free classified ads online at Craigslist. The public website Serve.gov and private websites Idealist.org and VolunteerMatch offer free searchable databases of short- and long-term volunteer opportunities nationwide.

More formal volunteer programs, especially those designed for international travelers, typically charge a hefty fee of $250 to $1000, depending on the length of the program and what amenities are included (eg housing, meals). None cover travel to the USA.

Resources

Habitat for Humanity (☏800-422-4828; www.habitat.org; 121 Habitat St)

Sierra Club (☏415-977-5500; www.sierraclub.org; 2nd Floor, 85 2nd St)

Volunteers for Peace (☏802-259-2759; www.vfp.org; 1034 Tiffany Rd; ♿)

Wilderness Volunteers (☏928-556-0038; www.wildernessvolunteers.org)

World Wide Opportunities on Organic Farms-USA (WWOOF-USA; ☏949-715-9500; www.wwoofusa.org; 430 Forest Ave; ♿)

Work

Seasonal work is possible in national parks and other tourist sites, especially ski areas; for information, contact park concessions or local chambers of commerce. These are usually low-paying service jobs filled by young people (often college students) who are happy to work part of the day so they can play the rest. You can't depend on finding a job just by arriving in May or June and looking around.

Transportation

GETTING THERE & AWAY

Most travelers arrive in Colorado by air or car, with arrivals by bus a distant third. There is also a daily Amtrak train service that pulls into Denver's Union Station.

Flights, tours and rail tickets can be booked online at lonelyplanet.com/bookings.

Air

Airports & Airlines

Denver is the region's main air hub, although there are various alternatives if you are coming on a domestic flight. You might want to consider landing in a neighboring state and driving into Colorado through the Rocky Mountains. Colorado has dozens of smaller airports throughout the state.

Denver International Airport (DIA; ☑information 303-342-2000; www.flydenver. com; 8500 Peña Blvd; ☺24hrs; @☏)

Aspen-Pitkin County Airport (☑970-920-5380; www.aspenairport.com; 233 E Airport Rd; ☏☷)

Colorado Springs Airport (☑719-550-1972; www.springs gov.com; 7770 Milton E Proby Parkway; ☷)

Durango-La Plata County Airport (DRO; ☑970-247-8143; www.flydurango.com; 1000 Airport Rd)

Eagle County Regional Airport (☑970-524-9490;

www.eaglecounty.us/airport; 219 Eldon Wilson Drive; ☺Dec-early April)

Grand Junction Regional Airport (Walker Field Airport; ☑970-244-9100; www.gjairport.com; 2828 Walker Field Dr)

Gunnison-Crested Butte Regional Airport (☑970-641-2304; W Rio Grande Ave)

Yampa Valley Airport (County Road 51A)

Montrose Regional Airport (☑970-249-3203; www.montroseairport.com; 2100 Airport Rd; ☷)

Telluride Regional Airport (☑970-778-5051; www.tellurideairport.com; Last Dollar Rd)

Airlines handling the main routes in and out of Colorado:

Allegiant Airlines (☑702-505-8888; www.allegiantair.com)

Alaskan Airlines (☑800-252-7522; www.alaskaair.com)

AirTran Airways (☑800-247-8726; www.airtran.com)

American Airlines (☑800-433-7300; www.aa.com)

Continental (☑800-523-3273; www.continental.com)

Delta (☑800-221-1212; www.delta.com)

Frontier (☑800-432-1359; www.frontierairlines.com)

Jet Blue (☑800-538-2583; www.jetblue.com)

Southwest (☑800-435-9792; www.southwest.com; 2702 Love Field Dve, Texas)

United Airlines (☑800-864-8331; www.united.com)

CLIMATE CHANGE & TRAVEL

Every form of transport that relies on carbon-based fuel generates CO_2, the main cause of human-induced climate change. Modern travel is dependent on airplanes, which might use less fuel per person than most cars but travel much greater distances. The altitude at which aircraft emit gases (including CO_2) and particles also contributes to their climate change impact. Many websites offer 'carbon calculators' that allow people to estimate the carbon emissions generated by their journey and, for those who wish to do so, to offset the impact of the greenhouse gases emitted with contributions to portfolios of climate-friendly initiatives throughout the world. Lonely Planet offsets the carbon footprint of all staff and author travel.

US Airways (☎800-428-4322; www.usairways.com)

Tickets

» Airfares to the US and Colorado range from incredibly low to obscenely high.

» The best deals are almost always found on the internet.

» STA Travel (☎toll-free 800-781-4040; www.statravel.com), which offers online booking, also has offices (with real, live people!) in major cities in the USA and across the world.

» Fares into Colorado can be higher during the December to March ski season, when thousands flock to the slopes in these states.

Land

Bus

» Greyhound (☎800-231-2222, 312-408-5800; www.greyhound.com; 630 W Harrison St) runs cross-country buses between San Francisco and New York via Wyoming, Denver and Chicago; and between Los Angeles and New York via Las Vegas, Denver and Chicago.

» There are also bus services from other eastern seaboard cities such as Philadelphia and Washington, DC, and southern cities such as Atlanta and Miami.

» Fares are relatively high and bargain air fares can undercut buses on long-distance routes. On shorter routes it can be cheaper to rent a car than to ride the bus.

» Very long-distance bus trips are often available at bargain prices by 'web only fares' from the Greyhound website.

Car & Motorcycle

» I-70 runs nearly the entire length of the USA, passing through central Colorado.

» I-25 runs north–south from New Mexico through Colorado and ends at a junction with I-90 in northern Wyoming.

Train

» Amtrak (☎toll-free 800-872-7245; www.amtrak.com) provides cross-country passenger services between the West Coast and Chicago. Travelers to or from the East Coast must make connections in Chicago. Amtrak trains service only a few destinations in Colorado besides Denver.

» The daily *California Zephyr* from San Francisco (via Emeryville, California) passes through Colorado en route to Chicago. In Colorado the train stops at Fort Morgan, Denver's Union Station, Fraser-Winter Park, Granby, Glenwood Springs and Grand Junction.

» The *Southwest Chief* goes from Los Angeles via Albuquerque and the southern Colorado towns of Trinidad, La Junta and Lamar to Kansas City and Chicago.

TICKETS

Amtrak tickets may be purchased aboard the train without penalty if the station is not open 30 minutes prior to boarding. Rail travel is generally cheaper if you purchase tickets in advance. Roundtrips are the best value, but even these can be as expensive as air fares.

For further travel assistance, call Amtrak, surf its website or ask your travel agent. Note that most small train stations don't sell tickets. Instead you must book them with Amtrak over the phone or buy online. Some small stations have no porters or other facilities, and trains may stop there only if you have bought a ticket in advance.

» Amtrak offers some good value USA Rail Passes.

» Children aged between two and 15 years travel for 50% of the adult fare only when accompanied by an adult. Kids under two are free.

» Seniors 62 years and over are entitled to a 15% discount (with some limitations) on adult fares.

» AAA members get a 10% discount and students with a Student Advantage or ISIC card get 15%. Active military personnel, their spouses and dependents get a 10% discount and Veterans Advantage card holders get 15%.

GETTING AROUND

Colorado has fairly comprehensive coverage by commuter flights, although the cost may deter most travelers. On the ground, public transportation leaves much to be desired, and travelers without their own vehicles need to be patient and flexible to take advantage of the limited possibilities. The most enjoyable way to travel within the state is by car or motorbike.

Air

Colorado has many small commercial airports. All are served by flights out of Denver, and Grand Junction also has flights to and from Salt Lake City, UT. During ski season, resort airports offer direct flights to major cities around the US.

Bicycle

Cycling is a cheap, convenient, healthy, environmentally sound and, above all, fun way of traveling. In Colorado, because of altitude, distance and heat, it's also a good workout.

Cycling has increased in popularity so much in recent years that concerns have risen over damage to the environment, especially from unchecked mountain biking. Know your environment and regulations before you ride. Bikes are restricted from entering wilderness areas and some designated trails but may be used in National Park Service (NPS) sites, state parks, national and state forests and Bureau of Land Management single-track trails.

» Cyclists should carry at least a gallon of water and refill bottles at every opportunity since dehydration can be a major problem.

» Airlines accept bicycles as checked luggage; contact them for specific rules.

» City and long-haul buses and trains can carry bikes, and in the mountains shuttles are fitted with racks for skis in winter and mountain bikes in summer.

» Rental bicycles are widely available.

» In Colorado's legendary mountain-biking regions the range of rental options can be bewilderingly comprehensive. Hard-tail mountain bikes rent for around $30 a day while fancy full-suspension rentals go for more like $70.

» Bicycles are generally prohibited on interstate highways if there is a frontage road. However, where a suitable frontage road or other alternative is lacking, cyclists are permitted on some interstates.

» Cyclists are generally treated courteously by motorists.

» Colorado currently has no legal requirement for cyclists to wear helmets (but they do reduce the risk of head injury).

Bus

The main bus line for the region is **Greyhound** (☎800-231-2222, 312-408-5800; www. greyhound.com; 630 W Harrison St, Chicago), and has a network of fixed routes and its own terminal in most central cities. The company has an excellent safety record, and the buses are comfortable and usually on time.

Regional parts of Colorado are poorly serviced by buses.

» Greyhound tickets can be bought over the phone or online with a credit card and mailed if purchased 10 days

in advance, or picked up at the terminal with proper identification.

» Discounts apply to tickets purchased 14 or 21 days in advance.

» All buses are nonsmoking, and reservations are made with ticket purchases only.

Car & Motorcycle

One of the great ways to experience Colorado is to drive its roads and byways. The road conditions are generally very good and it's always rewarding when you point the car down an unknown backroad just to see where it goes. Good maps and road atlases are sold everywhere.

The penchant Coloradans have for monster SUVs and mega motorhomes can be a little intimidating when you're put-putting up a steep mountain road in your clapped-out Korean rental car. But fellow drivers are courteous and generous with their friendly conversation at roadside diners and gas stations. 'Where you headed?' is a common opener. Tuning into local radio stations is part of the immersive cultural experience.

Rental

The rental-car market is crowded and competitive, which means you can get some good deals, especially if you hire for a week or more.

With advance reservations for a small car, the daily rate with unlimited mileage is about $30 to $40; typical weekly rates are $150 to $200. Rates for midsize cars may be a tad higher. You can often snag great last-minute deals via the internet. Renting in conjunction with an airplane ticket often yields better rates too.

Bidding for cars on **Priceline** (www.priceline.com) is a cheap way to hire a vehicle. Or try some of the web consolidator engines, such as **Kayak** (www.kayak.com).

Ask about any extra surcharges, such as one-way rentals and additional drivers.

Some companies won't rent vehicles to people without a major credit card; others require things such as prepayment or cash deposits. Booking can be secured with a credit card and then paid by cash or debit card.

Car-rental companies always offer extra insurance, but if you're adequately covered under a travel-insurance policy or other then don't be suckered by the compelling sales pitch. Basic liability insurance is required by law and included in the basic rental price. Check with your insurance company regarding any extended coverage.

Many rental agencies stipulate that damage a car suffers while being driven on unpaved roads is not covered by the insurance they offer.

Companies operating in Colorado:

Alamo (☎toll-free 800-327-9633; www.alamo.com)

Avis (☎toll-free 800-831-2847; www.avis.com)

Budget (☎toll-free 800-527-0700; www.budget.com)

Dollar (☎toll-free 800-800-4000; www.dollar.com)

Enterprise (☎toll-free 800-325-8007; www.enterprise.com)

Hertz (☎toll-free 800-654-3131; www.hertz.com)

National (☎toll-free 800-227-7368; www.nationalcar.com)

Rent-A-Wreck (☎800-944-7501; www.rent-a-wreck.com)

Thrifty (☎toll-free 800-847-4389; www.thrifty.com)

Drive-aways

Drive-away agencies find people to take a car from one destination to another for the owner. If you have a valid license and a clean driving record, you can apply. Generally you'll pay the gas and a small refundable deposit. This can be a cheap way to

COLORADO ROAD DISTANCES (MILES)

	Alamosa	Aspen	Boulder	Colorado Springs	Denver	Dinosaur	Durango	Fort Collins	Grand Junction	Gunnison	La Junta	Steamboat Springs	Vail
Alamosa	-												
Aspen	153	-											
Boulder	230	219	-										
Colorado Springs	163	157	97	-									
Denver	212	162	30	70	-								
Dinosaur	361	180	297	353	286	-							
Durango	149	249	347	302	332	275	-						
Fort Collins	274	223	46	132	65	369	394	-					
Grand Junction	249	130	254	287	248	108	169	308	-				
Gunnison	122	146	212	166	196	233	173	245	126	-			
La Junta	147	247	203	105	175	457	296	237	350	224	-		
Steamboat Springs	254	155	167	209	166	130	345	160	194	238	303	-	
Vail	172	102	65	142	98	200	292	159	61	156	258	98	-

get around if you meet eligibility requirements.

Drive-away companies are listed in the yellow pages of telephone directories under 'Automobile Transporters & Drive-Away Companies.' You need to be flexible about dates and destinations when you call.

Legal Matters

» Speed limits on Colorado state highways range from 55mph to 65mph, and go as high as 75mph on I-70. Limits in city central business districts is 25mph and it's 35mph in residential areas. On open mountain highways the speed limit is 40mph.

» Texting from cell phones while driving is prohibited, and drivers under the age of 18 years are prohibited from using cell phones.

» Colorado's highway patrol is famously intolerant of speeding and if you're consistently flouting the speed limit you'll get booked.

» Seat belts are required for the driver and front seat passenger and for all passengers on highways and interstates. On motorcycles, helmets are required for anyone under 18.

» Driving while impaired (DWI) is defined as having a blood-alcohol level of 0.05% or above, and will probably land you in jail and definitely earn you heavy fines.

Safety

» Much of Colorado is open-range country in which cattle and, less frequently, sheep forage along the highway. Pay attention to the roadside, especially at night.

» During winter months, tire chains may be required. Roads may be closed to cars without chains or 4WD. It's a good idea to keep a set of chains in the trunk.

» Other cold-weather precautions include keeping a wool blanket, warm clothing, extra food, a windshield ice-scraper, a snow shovel, flares and an extra set of gloves and boots in the trunk for emergencies.

» While Colorado doesn't require motorcycle riders over 18 years to wear helmets, the use of a helmet is highly recommended.

» Weather is a serious factor throughout Colorado, especially in winter. For road

and travel information as well as state highway patrol information by telephone, dial ☎877-315-7623.

» Do not leave expensive items visibly lying about in the car. Don't leave valuables in the car overnight.

Hitchhiking

Hitchhiking is illegal in Colorado. Pedestrians on the highway must walk in the opposite direction of traffic.

Train

Rail service within Colorado is very limited beyond the interstate options.

Tourist trains include the **Durango & Silverton Narrow-Gauge Railroad** in southern Colorado, the **Georgetown Loop**, the **Cumbres & Toltec Scenic Railroad** from Antonito to Chama in New Mexico, and the **Pikes Peak Cog Railway** in Manitou Springs. Although they are tourist trains, the Durango and Cumbres lines allow hikers and anglers access to wilderness areas.

behind the scenes

SEND US YOUR FEEDBACK

We love to hear from travelers – your comments keep us on our toes and help make our books better. Our well-traveled team reads every word on what you loved or loathed about this book. Although we cannot reply individually to postal submissions, we always guarantee that your feedback goes straight to the appropriate authors, in time for the next edition. Each person who sends us information is thanked in the next edition – and the most useful submissions are rewarded with a free book.

Visit **lonelyplanet.com/contact** to submit your updates and suggestions or to ask for help. Our award-winning website also features inspirational travel stories, news and discussions.

Note: We may edit, reproduce and incorporate your comments in Lonely Planet products such as guidebooks, websites and digital products, so let us know if you don't want your comments reproduced or your name acknowledged. For a copy of our privacy policy visit lonelyplanet.com/privacy.

AUTHOR THANKS

Nate Cavalieri

As one of the most demanding projects I've ever taken on with Lonely Planet, it has also proved to be the most rewarding. It wouldn't have been so without my colleagues at Lonely Planet – Adam, Rowan, Gus, Dan, Suki – who I'm grateful to also count among my friends. The support of the Melbourne LPOS team was also incredible. Thanks to Charlie Philbrick for the sleeping bag, Charlie Koltak for the fashionable boots and all the other companions along the way, Swedish or otherwise.

Adam Skolnick

First and foremost I'd like to thank my extended Colorado family: Kelton and Tracy Reid in Denver, and Danny Ferry, Chrystal Nelthropp, and all my lovely Friedmans in Boulder-town. Thanks also to Amanda Boxtel in Basalt (you're my hero), Ariane Zurcher in Aspen, my wildlife guru and hostess Laurie Reid in Snowmass, Crystal Moriarty in Breckenridge, Jenna Pfingston in Buena Vista, Chelsy Murphy, Floy Kennedy and fabulous Alison Scott in Colorado Springs, and Mayor Tony Greer in Cañon City. I was lucky enough to be part of a team full of

wonderfully talented dreamers, writers, ninjas and editors at Lonely Planet. Thanks go to Suki, Gus, Dan, Lauren, Liz, Erin, Alan and the entire LPOS team. That includes my fellow wanderers/authors Nate and Rowan. And lots of love and eternal gratitude to the sweet and beautiful Georgiana Johnson.

Rowan McKinnon

I'd like to thank my esteemed fellow authors, Nate and Adam, for keeping the faith on this special project. I'd especially like to thank editor Dan Corbett and geo-analyst Erin McManus – gatekeepers and handlers – who've been on this journey with me since our first trials and tests in suburban Melbourne (Australia). Gus Balbontin fired us with the vision and cleared the path, Alan Castles was a project hero and Lauren Hunt reinvented the content wheel. Thanks too to the bevy of amazing technical brains for support in development and on the road; foremost among them were Justin Wark, Rob Hunter, Jani Patokallio, Alex Ikin, Ken Hoetmer, Daniel Heath and Ross Macaw. To Suki Gear, thanks for commissioning a great team and providing the blueprint for a wonderful guidebook. And thanks, as always, to my family: Jane, Wesley, Lauren, Eadie and Lewis.

ACKNOWLEDGMENTS

Climate map data adapted from Peel MC, Finlayson BL & McMahon TA (2007) 'Updated World Map of the Köppen-Geiger Climate Classification', *Hydrology and Earth System Sciences*, 11, 163344.

Cover photograph: The old mill at Marble, White River National Forest, Colorado, Greg Gawlowski/Lonely Planet Images. Many of the images in this guide are available for licensing from Lonely Planet Images: www.lonelyplanetimages.com.

THIS BOOK

This guidebook was commissioned in Lonely Planet's Oakland office, and produced by the following:

Commissioning Editor Suki Gear

Coordinating Editor Daniel Corbett, Lauren Hunt

Coordinating Cartographer Erin McManus

Coordinating Layout Designer Paul Iacono

Managing Editors Bruce Evans, Liz Heynes

Managing Cartographer Alison Lyall

Managing Layout Designers Indra Kilfoyle, Celia Wood

Assisting Editors Adrienne Costanzo, Peter Cruttenden, Carly Hall, Victoria Harrison, Shawn Low, Susan Paterson, Martine Power, Rose Press, Averil Robertson

Assisting Cartographers Anita Banh, Alex Leung

Cover Research Aude Vauconsant

Internal Image Research Sabrina Dalbesio

Thanks to Mark Adams, Dan Austin, Gus Balbontin, Imogen Bannister, Chris Boden, David Burnett, Alan Castles, Gordon Christie, David Connolly, Melanie Dankel, Stefanie Di Trocchio, Heather Dickson, Chelsea Eaw, Janine Eberle, Joshua Geoghegan, Mark Germanchis, Chris Girdler, Michelle Glynn, Daniel Heath, Ken Hoetmer, Rob Hunter, Alex Ikin, Laura Jane, David Kemp, Yvonne Kirk, Nic Lehman, Edmond Lew, Ross Macaw, John Mazzocchi, Rob Mitchell, Dan Moore, Wayne Murphy, Ben Nolan, Jani Patokallio, Adrian Persoglia, Piers Pickard, Ian Posthumus, Lynne Preston, Anthony Reinbach, Lachlan Ross, Michael Ruff, Julie Sheridan, Rebecca Skinner, Darryl Slabe, Laura Stansfeld, Navin Sushil, John Taufa, Nick Thorpe, Angela Tinson, Sam Trafford, Sue Visic, Justin Wark, Mike Williams, Juan Winata, Emily Wolman, Nick Wood.

The map data in this book was supplied by NAVTEQ

NAVTEQ is the world's leading provider of street level map data. We're passionate about keeping NAVTEQ® Maps reliable and up-to-date, allowing users to get to wherever they need to go in the world. By literally driving and walking the roads of the world and adhering to rigorous quality standards, NAVTEQ powers many of the world's leading mapping and cartographic publishers, like Lonely Planet. Our consistent investment in developing and using the latest mapping technology means that as a traveller you can rely on NAVTEQ® Maps, wherever your journey takes you. To learn more about NAVTEQ, visit www.navteq.com

NOTES

index

SYMBOLS
'14ers' 12, 31, see also mountains & peaks
internet resources 19

A
accommodations 368-70
activities 31-8, see also individual activities
air travel
to/from Colorado 375-6
within Colorado 376
Alamosa 311-13
amusement parks
Elitch Gardens 63
Glenwood Caverns Adventure Park 238
Peak 8 Fun Park 173-4
Royal Gorge Bridge & Amusement Park 334
Ancestral Puebloans 289-94, 296, 298-9
animals 23, 363-4
safety 372
Animas Forks 289
Antonito 314-15
aquariums, see zoos & aquariums
Arapahoe Basin Ski Area 36, 161-2
Arapaho National Wildlife Refuge 232
archaeological sites, see historic & archaeological sites
area codes 19, 373
art galleries, see galleries
arts 55, 356-8
festivals 67, 159, 168, 228, 357-8
folk art 356-7
Ashcroft 209
Aspen 7, 34, 194-208, **196**
accommodations 201-3
activities 195-200
drinking 206

entertainment 206-7
festivals & events 200-1
food 203-5
internet access 207
medical services 207
shopping 207
sights 194-5
tourist information 208
travel to/from 208
travel within 208
Aspen Music Festival 25, 201
ATMs 373

B
Bachelor Loop 285
backpacking, see hiking
Bailey 220-1
Basalt 209-10
bears 363
Beaver Creek 191-4
beer 6, 22, see also microbreweries
Coors Brewery 96
festivals 25-6, 67, 266, 278
Bennett, Michael 347
Bent, Charles 341, 353
Bent, William 341, 353
Bent's Old Fort National Historic Site 341
Biber, Stanley 340
bicycle travel, see cycling & mountain biking
Big Sweep 61
bighorn sheep 363-4
birds 364
birdwatching 218, 232, 271, 310, 364
Black Canyon of the Gunnison National Park 16, 252-4, **16**
Blanca 310
Boggsville Historic Site 341
books 346
Boulder 5, 49, 104-29, **105**, **108-9**, **115**, **5**
accommodations 104, 114-17
activities 111-14
children, travel with 121
climate 104
drinking 122-4
entertainment 124-5
festivals & events 114
food 104, 117-22
highlights 105
history 106
itineraries 118
shopping 125-8
sights 106-11
tourist offices 128
travel seasons 104
travel to/from 128

travel within 128-9
walking tours 112
Boulder Creek Festival 25, 114
Breckenridge 34, 169-79, **170**
accommodations 175-6
activities 172-4
courses 174-5
drinking 177-8
entertainment 178-9
festivals & events 175
food 176-7
history 169, 178
shopping 179
sights 169-72
tourist information 179
tours 174-5
travel to/from 179
travel within 179
Breckenridge Spring Massive 24
brewpubs, see microbreweries
Buck, Ken 347
budget 18
Buena Vista 217-20
Buffalo Bill 96
bus travel
to/from Colorado 376
within Colorado 377
business hours 370

C
Cache la Poudre River 151
camping 368-9
Cañon City 334-6
Cañon Pintado National Historic District 236-7
Carbondale 242
Carson, Kit 311, 341
Carter, Edwin 170
car travel 19, 376, 377-8, see also scenic drives
rental 377
road distance chart 378
road rules 378
cell phones 19, 373
central mountains 50, 155-221, **156-7**
accommodations 155
climate 155
food 155
highlights 156-7
travel seasons 155
children, travel with 47-8
Boulder 121
Denver 92
Chimney Rock Archaeological Area 281
Clark, William, see Lewis & Clark Expedition

climate 18, *see also* individual locations
Cody, William F 'Buffalo Bill' 96
colleges & universities
  Naropa University 107
  University of Colorado at Boulder 106-7
  US Air Force Academy 324-5
Collegiate Peaks Wilderness Area 217, 219
Coller State Wildlife Area 284
Colorado National Monument 8, 243-4, **8**
Colorado Springs 9, 321-31, **324**
  accommodations 327-8
  activities 326
  drinking 329-30
  entertainment 330
  festivals & events 327
  food 328-9
  medical services 330
  postal services 330
  shopping 330
  sights 321-6
  tourist information 330
  travel to/from 330
  travel within 330-1
Colorado Trail 32, 103
Colter, John 350
Comanche National Grassland 342
Conejos River 315-19
consulates 373
Coors Brewery 96
Coors Field 89
Cope, Edward Drinker 365-6
Copper Mountain Ski Resort 35, 167-9
Cortez 296-8
Cottonwood Pass 218
courses 66
Craig 234
credit cards 373
Creede 284-7
Crested Butte 36, 259-62
Crestone 306-7
cross-country skiing, *see* snow sports
Crystal 242
Cuchara 337-8
culture 346-7, 353-5
Cumbres & Toltec Scenic Railroad 315
Curecanti National Recreation Area 257
currency 18
customs regulations 373
cycling & mountain biking 37, 376-7, **10**
  Aspen 197-9

Boulder 111
Breckenridge 172
Buffalo Creek Mountain Bike Area 103
Colorado Springs 326
Creede 286
Crested Butte 260
Del Norte 318-19
Durango 278
festivals 159, 175, 293
Fort Collins 147
Four Corners area 297
Frisco 164
Fruita 10, 23, 248
Glenwood Springs 238
Golden 96
Grand Junction 244-5
Great Sand Dunes National Park 308
Lake City 287
Mesa Verde National Park 293
Montrose 255
Rocky Mountain National Park 134
Silver Cliff 304-5
Steamboat Springs 223
Telluride 264-6
Vail 181, 184
Westcliffe 304-5

D
day spas, *see* springs & spas
Del Norte 318-19
Delta 262-3
Denver 4, 49, 54-95, **58-9**, **68**, **78**, **82**, **4**
  accommodations 54, 67-72
  activities 55, 64
  art 55
  budgeting 80
  children, travel with 92
  climate 54
  courses 66
  day trips 55
  drinking 81-6
  entertainment 8, 86-9
  festivals & events 67
  food 8, 54, 72-81
  history 56
  internet access 93
  internet resources 55
  itineraries 57
  medical services 93
  postal services 93
  region highlights 57
  shopping 89-93
  sights 56-64
  tourist information 93-4
  tours 66

travel seasons 54
travel to/from 94
travel within 94-5
walking tours 65
Dillon 163-4
Dinosaur 236
Dinosaur National Monument 9, 234-5, **9**
dinosaurs 21, 365-6
  museums 62, 331, 335
dinosaur sites
  Dinosaur National Monument 9, 234-5, **9**
  Dinosaur Ridge 101
  Dry Mesa Dinosaur Quarry 263
  Fruita 248
  Garden Park Fossil Area 334-5
  Picketwire Dinosaur Tracksite 342
disabilities, travelers with 374
distilleries 22, 361
  Mancos Valley Distillery 295
  Peach Street Distillers 243
Dolores 298-9
drinks, *see also* beer, distilleries, microbreweries, whiskey, wine
  festivals 25-6, 67, 266, 278
drive-aways 377-8
driving, *see* car travel, road trips, scenic drives
dude ranches 369
Durango 13, 275-81, **276**, **13**
Durango & Silverton Narrow Gauge Railroad 273, 277, **11**, **350**

E
Earth Liberation Front 355
eastern Colorado 51, 320-44, **322-3**
  accommodations 320
  climate 320
  food 320
  highlights 322-3
  travel seasons 320
economy 346
Eldora Ski Area 144-5
Eldorado Canyon State Park 114
electricity 371
elk 364
embassies 373
emergencies 19
Empire 101
Estes Park 137-43, **138**
  accommodations 139-41
  activities 137-9
  drinking 141-2
  food 141-2
  sights 137-9
  travel to/from 142

Estes Park *continued*
 travel within 142-3
 visitors centers 142
European settlement 349-50
events, *see* festivals & events
exchange rates 19

F
Fairplay 215
festivals & events 24-6, *see also* film
 festivals, music festivals
 12 Hours of Mesa Verde 293
 Alpine Art Affair 159
 Bolder Boulder 114
 Boulder Creek Festival 25, 114
 Boulder Creek Hometown Fair 114
 Boulder Pride Fest 114
 Breck Bike Week 175
 Breckenridge Spring Massive 24
 Brews & Blues Festival 266
 CarniVail 185
 Cherry Creek Arts Festival 67
 Cinco de Mayo 67
 Colorado Balloon Classic 327
 Copper Country Arts Festival 168
 Custer County Fair & Stampede
  Weekend 305
 Emma Crawford Coffin
  Races 327
 Fat Tire Classic 159
 Frozen Dead Guy Days 144
 Great American Beer Festival
  25-6, 67
 Great Fruitcake Toss 327
 Hot Air Balloon Festival & Art
  in the Park 228
 International Snow Sculpture
  Championship 175
 King of the Mountains 159
 Kingdom Days 175
 Leadville Trail 100 214
 Lights of December 114
 Mardis Gras 175
 Ouray Ice Festival 271
 Pikes Peak International Hill
  Climb 327
 San Juan Brewfest 278
 Snow Daze 185
 Spring Massive 175
 Steamboat Springs Pro Rodeo
  Series 228
 Strawberry Days 240
 Taste of Colorado 67
 Taste of Vail 185
 Telluride Mushroom Festival 266

 Ullr Fest 175
 Yampa River Festival 228
film festivals
 Boulder Adventure Film Festival 114
 Mountainfilm 266
 Telluride Film Festival 26, 266
 Vail Film Festival 185
film locations 23
fishing
 central mountains 165, 173, 200,
  210, 211
 northwest Colorado 233, 237,
  239-40, 242
 San Luis Valley 304, 316, 319
 southwest Colorado 253, 255, 263,
  264, 269, 271, 285, 300
Flatirons 113-14
Florence 336-7
Florissant Fossil Beds National
 Monument 331-2
folk art 356-7
food 23, 359-61
 festivals 67, 185, 240, 266
 green chile 360
 Rocky Mountain oysters 13, **13**
Ford, Barney 169, 353-4
Fort Collins 13, 145-50, **146, 13**
Fort Garland 310-11
Fort Lyon 342
Fort Morgan 343
fossils, *see* dinosaur sites
Fourmile Fire 129
Fraser 158-60
Frisco 164-7
Fruita 10, 23, 248-9
fur trade 350

G
galleries, *see also* museums
 212 Gallery 195
 Arthur Roy Mitchell Memorial
  Museum of Western Art 339
 Cornerstone Arts Center 326
 Crested Butte Center for the
  Arts 259
 David B Smith Gallery 59
 Denver Art Museum 59
 Glenwood Springs Centre for the
  Arts 238
 Illiterate Media 63
 Museum of Contemporary Art 59
 Plus Gallery 62
 Quandary Antiques Cabin &
  Ceramics Studio 171
 Robischon Gallery 56
 Rule Gallery 63-4
 SPACe Gallery 337
 Tin Shop 171
Garden of the Gods 14, 321-4, **14**

Garden Park Fossil Area 334-5
gay travelers 125
 Boulder 125
 Denver 88
 festivals & events 114
geology 22, 362
Georgetown Loop Railroad 100
ghost towns
 Animas Forks 289
 Ashcroft 209
 Crystal 242
 Independence 208
 St Elmo 220
Ginsberg, Allen 357
 Naropa University 107
Glen Haven 143
Glenwood Springs 237-42
Golden 95-8, **97**
Granby 154
Grand Junction 244-8
Grand Lake 151-4
Grand Mesa 249
Great American Beer Festival
 25-6, 67
Great Sand Dunes National
 Park 14, 307-10, **308, 14**
green chile 360
Gunnison 257-9

H
Hahns Peak 231-2
Hayden, Frederick V 351
health 371-2
Hickenlooper, John 347
hiking 12, 20, 31-4, *see also*
 mountains & peaks
 Aspen 199
 Black Canyon of the Gunnison
  National Park 253
 Boulder 32, 111-14
 Breckenridge 172-3
 Collegiate Peaks Wilderness Area
  217, 219
 Colorado National Monument
  243-4
 Colorado Springs 326
 Conejos River 316
 Creede 285
 Crestone 306
 Grand Mesa 249
 Great Sand Dunes National Park
  307-8, 309
 Independence Pass 216
 James M John State Wildlife
  Area 339
 Lake City 288
 Leadville 213
 Maroon Bells 209
 Mesa Verde National Park 292-3

Montrose 255
Mt Massive 213
Pike National Forest 103
Rocky Mountain National Park 32, 133-4, 12
safety 32
Silver Cliff 304
Spanish Peaks Wilderness 337
sustainability 33
Trinidad Lake State Park 339
Twin Lakes 215-16
Vail 182, 183
Westcliffe 304
historic & archaeological sites 20, 352
Bent's Old Fort National Historic Site 341
Boggsville Historic Site 341
Cañon Pintado National Historic District 236-7
Chimney Rock Archaeological Area 281
Fort Lyon 342
Fort Uncompahgre 263
Holzwarth Historic Site 133
La Garita 318
Manitou Cliff Dwelling 325
Mesa Verde National Park 289-94
Prospect Heights 335
history 348-52
hitchhiking 378
Holliday, John Henry 'Doc' 237, 240
resting place 238
horseback riding
central mountains 181, 183, 199
Denver region 99
eastern Colorado 336
northern mountains 153
northwest Colorado 237, 242, 245
southwest Colorado 260, 264, 271
Hovenweep National Monument 300

I
Idaho Springs 99-100
Independence 208
Independence Pass 216
Indian Peaks Wilderness Area 145
insurance 372
health 371
internet access 372
internet resources 19
INVESCO Field at Mile High 89
itineraries 27-30
Boulder 118
Denver 62
road trips 39-46

J
James M John State Wildlife Area 339
Jones, Mary Harris 'Mother' 354
Julesberg 344

K
kayaking, see rafting
Kerouac, Jack 357, 358
Naropa University 107
Keystone Ski Resort 35-6, 162
Kremmling 232-3

L
La Garita 317-18
La Veta 337-8
Lake City 287-9
Leadville 212-15
Leadville, Colorado & Southern Railroad 213
legal matters 372-4
lesbian travelers 125
Boulder 125
Denver 88
Lewis & Clark Expedition 350-2
Lisa, Manuel 350
Longs Peak 133, 12
Los Hermanos Penitente 313
Louisiana Purchase 349
Loveland Ski Area 36, 161
Ludlow Massacre 339

M
Mancos 294-6
Manitou Cliff Dwelling 325
Manitou & Pikes Peak Cog Railway 326
Marble 242
marijuana 355, 374
Maroon Bells 208-9
Marsh, Othniel Charles 365-6
McVeigh, Timothy 355
medical services 372
Meeker 237
Mesa Verde National Park 7, 289-94, 291, 7
Mesteño 64
Mexican food 360
microbreweries 6, 21, see also beer
Aspen Brewing Co 206
Breckenridge Blake St Pub 84
Breckenridge Brewery 178
Carber Brewing Co 279
CooperSmith's Pub & Brewing 148
Del Norte Brewing Company 86
Denver Chophouse & Brewery 84
Dillon Dam Brewery 163-4
Draft House 123
Durango Brewing Co 280
Eddyline Restaurant & Brewery 220
Eldo Brewpub 261
Estes Park Brewery 142
Grand Lake Brewing Co 153
Glenwood Canyon Brewing Company 241
Great Divide Brewing Company 83
Gunnison Brewery 259
Kannah Creek Brewing Company 246
Mahogany Ridge Brewery & Grill 230
Mountain Sun Pub & Brewery 123
New Belgium Brewery 147, 6
Odell Brewing Company 149
Ouray Brewery 273
Pagos Brewing Company 282
Palisade Brewing Company 243
Rock Bottom Restaurant & Brewery 85
Rockslide Brewery 246-7
San Luis Valley Brewing Company 312
Silverton Brewery & Restaurant 275
Ska Brewing Company 280
Steamworks Brewing 280
Three Barrely Brewery 319
Tommyknockers Brewery & Pub 100
tours 66
Trinity Brewing Co 329
Uptown Brothers Brewery 85
Walnut Brewery 124
Wild Mountain Smokehouse & Brewery 144
Wynkoop Brewing Co 84
militias 355
Million Dollar Hwy 12, 270-3, 12
mineral springs, see springs & spas
Minturn 210-11
mobile phones, see cell phones
Moffat Rd 160-1
money 18, 19, 370-1, 373
Monte Vista 316-17
Montezuma 162-3
Montrose 254-7
Monument Park 338
Morrison 101-2
motorcycle travel 377-8
mountain biking, see cycling & mountain biking
mountaineering 37-8, see also hiking, rock & ice climbing
mountains & peaks 12, 31
Hahns Peak 231-2
Longs Peak 133, 12
Mt Elbert 213

mountains & peaks *continued*
Mt Evans 98-9
Mt Massive 213
Mt Princeton 219
Mt Zirkel 231
Quandary Peak 173
Twin Sisters Peak 133
movies 347
Mt Massive Wilderness Area 213
Mt Zirkel Wilderness Area 231
museums 349, *see also* galleries
American Mountaineering Museum 96
Argo Gold Mill & Museum 99
Arthur Roy Mitchell Memorial Museum of Western Art 339
Aspen Art Museum 195
Barney Ford Museum 169
Black American West Museum & Heritage Center 61-2
Boulder History Museum 110
Boulder Museum of Contemporary Art 107
Buell Children's Museum 333
Buffalo Bill Museum & Grave 96
Byers-Evans House Museum 61
Chapin Mesa Museum 292
Children's Museum 63
Colorado History Museum 56
Colorado Railroad Museum 96
Colorado Ski Museum 180
Colorado Sports Hall of Fame 63
Colorado Springs Fine Arts Center 321
Cortez Cultural Center 296
Creede Historic Museum 285
Creede Underground Mining Museum 285
Crested Butte Mountain Heritage Museum 259
Denver Firefighters Museum 56
Denver Museum of Nature & Science 62
Dinosaur Depot 335
Edwin Carter Museum 170
El Pueblo History Museum 332
Enos Mills Cabin Museum & Gallery 143
Estes Park Museum 137-9
Forney Transportation Museum 63
Fort Collins Museum & Discovery Center 146
Francisco Fort Museum 337
Fred Hartman Art Museum & the Red Ryder Roundup 281
Frisco Historic Park & Museum 164

MacGregor Ranch Museum 143
Marcia Car 234
Mining Heritage Center 273
Molly Brown House Museum 60
Museum of Northwest Colorado 234
Museum of the Mountain West 254-5
Museum of Western Colorado 244
Pioneers Museum 325
Ridgway Railroad Museum 269
Rio Grande County Museum & Cultural Center 318
Rocky Mountain Dinosaur Museum 331
Rosemount Museum 332
Sangre de Cristo Art Center 333
San Luis Museum & Cultural Center 314
San Luis Valley Museum 311
Silver Cliff Museum 304
Silverton Museum 273
Sterling Overland Trail Museum 344
Tread of Pioneers Museum 223
Trinidad History Museum 339
Ute Indian Museum 254
Walsenberg Mining Museum 337
music 42, 347
music festivals
29th Street Live 114
Aspen Music Festival 25, 201
Breckenridge Music Festival 175
Brews & Blues Festival 266
Copper Country Arts Festival 168
High Mountain Fever Bluegrass Festival 305
Jazz Aspen Snowmass 200-1
Jazz in the Sangres 305
NedFest 144
Strings Music Festival 228
Telluride Bluegrass Festival 266
Vail Jazz Festival 185
Winter Park Jazz Festival 159

N
Naropa University 107
national parks, *see* wilderness reserves
Native Americans 349, 351
Ancestral Puebloans 289-94, 296, 298-9
arts 356
Fremont Culture 237
Ute 237, 254, 301, 349, 351
Nederland 144
Nelson, Woody 357
northern mountains 50, 130-54, **131**
accommodations 130

climate 130
food 130
highlights 131
travel seasons 130
northwest Colorado 50, 222-49, **224-5**
accommodations 222
climate 222
food 222
highlights 224-5
travel seasons 222

O
opening hours 370
Ouray 270-3, **12**
Overland Trail 344, 348

P
paddling, *see* rafting
Pagosa Springs 281-3
Palisade 243
Paonia 262
parks & gardens, *see also* wilderness reserves
Central Park 107
Chautauqua Park 106
Civic Center Park 61
Commons Park 63
Confluence Park 62-3
Denver Botanic Gardens 61
Garden of the Gods 14, 321-4, **14**
Monument Park 338
Overland Trail Recreation Area 343-4
Red Rock Canyon Park 326
Red Rocks Park & Amphitheatre 102
Reynolds Park 102
Wheeler Geologic Area 286
passports 373
Pawnee National Grassland 342-3
Peak to Peak Hwy 44, 143
peaks, *see* mountains & peaks
Penitente Brotherhood 313
Penrose, Spencer 354
Picketwire Dinosaur Tracksite 342
Pike National Forest 102-3
Pike, Zebulon 350
Pikes Peak 321, 327
Pikes Peak Hwy 43
planning, *see also* individual locations
budgeting 18
calendar of events 24-6
children 47-8
Colorado basics 18-19
Colorado's regions 49-51
internet resources 19
itineraries 27-30

000 Map pages
000 Photo pages

outdoors 31-8
  road trips 39-46
  travel seasons 18, 24-6
plants 362-3
politics 347, 354-5
population 346
postal services 373
post-WWII 352
Powell, John Wesley 351
Pre-America 349
Pueblo 332-4

Q
Quandary Peak 173

R
rafting 11, 38, **11**
  central mountains 174, 181, 183-4,
    217-18
  northwest Colorado 227, 232, 235,
    238-9
  southwest Colorado 255, 263, 278,
    282, 285, 288
railways, see train travel, scenic
    railways
Rangely 236
Rattlesnake Arches 244
Red Cliff 211-12
Red Feather Lakes 150-1
Red Rock Canyon Park 326
Red Rocks Park & Amphitheatre
    102
religion 347
Rico 299-300
Ridgway 269-70
road trips 39-46, see also car travel,
    scenic drives
rock & ice climbing 37-8, 271
  Black Canyon of the Gunnison
    National Park 254
  Boulder 111-14
  festivals 271
  La Garita 318
  Ouray 271
  Ridgway 269
  Rocky Mountain National Park 134
Rocky Mountain National Park 6, 32,
    131-7, **132**, **6**, **12**
  accommodations 135-6
  activities 133-5
  fees 136
  maps 134
  medical services 136
  money 136
  permits 136
  ranger stations 136
  safety 135
  sights 132-3
  telephone services 136

  travel to/from 137
  travel within 137
  visitor centers 136-7
Rocky Mountain oysters 13, **13**
Rodgers, William 355
Rollins Pass 160-1
Royal Gorge 334-6, **10**

S
safety 32, 372
San Juan Skyway 41-2
San Luis 313-14
San Luis State Park 310
San Luis Valley 51, 302-19, **303**
  accommodations 302
  climate 302
  food 302
  highlights 303
  travel seasons 302
Sand Creek Massacre 342, 353
Santa Fe Trail 45-6, 341-2
scenic drives, see also road trips
  central mountains 216, 218
  Denver region 98-9
  eastern Colorado 344
  San Luis Valley 311
  southwest Colorado 285, 287-8
scenic railways 11, 22
  Cumbres & Toltec Scenic Railroad
    315
  Durango & Silverton Narrow Gauge
    Railroad 273, 277, **11**, **350**
  Georgetown Loop Railroad 100
  Leadville, Colorado & Southern
    Railroad 213
  Manitou & Pikes Peak Cog Railway
    326
  Royal Gorge Route Railroad 335-6
sculpture
  Bronco Buster 61
  Dancers 56, **4**
  I See What You Mean 56
  Mesteño 64
  Stations of the Cross 313-14
  Yearling, The 61
senior travelers 370
sheep, see bighorn sheep
Silver Cliff 304-6
Silverton 9, 273-5, **9**
skiing, see snow sports
Slumgullion Slide 288
snow sports 20, 34-6
  Arapahoe Basin 161-2
  Aspen 196-7, 198
  Beaver Creek 192-3
  Breckenridge 172
  Copper Mountain Ski Resort
    167-9

  Crested Butte 260
  Durango 277
  Eldora Mountain Resort 144-5
  Frisco 165
  Grand Mesa 249
  Keystone Ski Resort 162
  Lake City 288
  Leadville 213
  Loveland 161
  Mesa Verde National Park 293
  Minturn 211
  Ouray 271
  Rocky Mountain National Park
    134-5
  Silverton 274
  Steamboat Springs 223-7
  Telluride 264
  Twin Lakes 216
  Vail 180-5
  Winter Park Resort 158
  Wolf Creek Ski Area 283
South Fork 283-4
southwest Colorado 51, 250-301, **251**
  accommodations 250
  climate 250
  food 250
  highlights 251
  travel seasons 250
Spanish Peaks Wilderness 337, 338
springs & spas 21
  Active Healing 173
  Box Canyon Lode & Hot Springs
    272
  Cottonwood Hot Springs Inn &
    Spa 218
  Glenwood Hot Springs & Spa of the
    Rockies 239
  Hot Sulphur Springs 233-4
  Indian Springs Resort & Spa 99
  Mt Princeton Hot Springs Resort
    217
  Ouray Hot Springs 271
  Pure Vida Fitness & Spa 64
  Springs Resort & Spa 281-2
  Steamboat Springs 223
  Strawberry Park Hot Springs
    227-8, 228
  Trimble Spa & Natural Hot
    Springs 277-8
  Yampah Spa 240
sports 354
  Colorado Sports Hall of
    Fame 63
St Elmo 220
St Mary's Glacier 100
Stagecoach State Park 231
statehood 352
state parks, see wilderness
    reserves

Steamboat Springs 15, 223-31, **226**, 15
accommodations 228-9
drinking 230
entertainment 230
festivals & events 228
food 229-30
shopping 230
sights 223
tourist information 230-1
travel to/from 231
travel within 231
Sterling 343-4
sushi 360

T
Taylor, Alice Bemis 356-7
telephone services 19
Telluride 15, 36, 264-9, **256**, 15, 21
Telluride Film Festival 26
thermal springs, *see* springs & spas
Thompson, David 350
Thompson, Hunter S 357
time 373
Timpas 342
tourist information 374
train travel, *see also* scenic railways
to/from Colorado 376
within Colorado 378
travel seasons 18, 24-6
travel to/from Colorado 375-6
travel within Colorado 376-8
Trinidad 338-41
Trinidad Lake State Park 339
tubing 38
Boulder 111, 121
central mountains 162, 167, 181
Twin Lakes 215-17

U
Ute 237, 254, 301, 349, 351
University of Colorado at Boulder 106-7
US Air Force Academy 324-5

V
Vail 34, 180-91, **182**
accommodations 185-7
activities 180-5
drinking 189
entertainment 189
festivals & events 185
food 187-9
history 188
medical services 190
shopping 190
sights 180
tourist information 190-1
travel to/from 191
travel within 191
vegetarian travelers 361
visas 19, 373
volunteering 374

W
Walden 232
Walsenberg 338
weather 18, *see also* individual locations
Weminuche Wilderness Area 284
Westcliffe 304-6
Western development 350-2
Wheeler Geologic Area 286
whiskey 361
white-water rafting, *see* rafting
wilderness reserves 35, *see also* parks & gardens
Arapaho National Wildlife Refuge 232
Black Canyon of the Gunnison National Park 16, 252-4, **16**
Cañon Pintado National Historic District 236-7
Collegiate Peaks Wilderness Area 217, 219
Coller State Wildlife Area 284
Colorado National Monument 8, 243-4, **8**
Comanche National Grassland 342
Curecanti National Recreation Area 257
Dinosaur National Monument 9, 234-5, **9**
Eldorado Canyon State Park 114
Florissant Fossil Beds National Monument 331-2
Great Sand Dunes National Park 14, 307-10, **308**, 14
Indian Peaks Wilderness Area 145
Hovenweep National Monument 300
James M John State Wildlife Area 339
Mesa Verde National Park 7, 289-94, **291**, 7
Maroon Bells 208-9
Monte Vista National Wildlife Reguge 317
Mt Massive Wilderness Area 213
Mt Zirkel Wilderness 231
Pawnee National Grassland 342-3
Pike National Forest 102-3
Ridgway State Park & Recreation Area 269
Rocky Mountain National Park 6, 32, 131-7, **132**, 6, 12
San Luis State Park 310
Spanish Peaks Wilderness 337, 338
Stagecoach State Park 231
Trinidad Lake State Park 339
Weminuche Wilderness Area 284
wine 243, 359
Winter Park 36, 158-60
Wolf Creek 36
Wolf Creek Ski Area 283
work 374

Z
zoos & aquariums
Cheyenne Mountain Zoo 325
Colorado Wolf & Wildlife Center 331
Denver Zoo 61
Nature & Raptor Center of Puelbo 332
Swetsville Zoo 145

how to use this book

These symbols will help you find the listings you want:

◉ Sights	⁂ Festivals & Events	☆ Entertainment
🏃 Activities	🛏 Sleeping	🛍 Shopping
🍴 Courses	🍽 Eating	ℹ Information/Transport
🚩 Tours	🍷 Drinking	

Look out for these icons:

TOP CHOICE — Our author's recommendation

FREE — No payment required

🖉 — A green or sustainable option

Our authors have nominated these places as demonstrating a strong commitment to sustainability – for example by supporting local communities and producers, operating in an environmentally friendly way, or supporting conservation projects.

These symbols give you the vital information for each listing:

🕿 Telephone Numbers	🛜 Wi-Fi Access	🚌 Bus
⊙ Opening Hours	🏊 Swimming Pool	⛴ Ferry
P Parking	🥗 Vegetarian Selection	M Metro
⊖ Nonsmoking	📖 English-Language Menu	S Subway
❄ Air-Conditioning	👪 Family-Friendly	⊖ London Tube
@ Internet Access	🐾 Pet-Friendly	🚋 Tram
		🚆 Train

Reviews are organised by author preference.

Map Legend

Sights
- ◎ Beach
- ▲ Buddhist
- ◎ Castle
- ✛ Christian
- ⊕ Hindu
- ◉ Islamic
- ✡ Jewish
- ❶ Monument
- ▦ Museum/Gallery
- ◎ Ruin
- ◉ Winery/Vineyard
- ◎ Zoo
- ◎ Other Sight

Activities, Courses & Tours
- ⊝ Diving/Snorkelling
- ◎ Canoeing/Kayaking
- ◎ Skiing
- ◎ Surfing
- ◎ Swimming/Pool
- ◎ Walking
- ◎ Windsurfing
- • Other Activity/Course/Tour

Sleeping
- ◎ Sleeping
- ◎ Camping

Eating
- ◎ Eating

Drinking
- ◎ Drinking
- ◎ Cafe

Entertainment
- ◎ Entertainment

Shopping
- ◎ Shopping

Information
- ◎ Post Office
- ❶ Tourist Information

Transport
- ◎ Airport
- ◎ Border Crossing
- ◎ Bus
- ◎ Cable Car/Funicular
- ◎ Cycling
- ◎ Ferry
- M Metro
- ◎ Monorail
- ℗ Parking
- S S-Bahn
- ◎ Taxi
- ◎ Train/Railway
- ◎ Tram
- ◎ Tube Station
- ◎ U-Bahn
- • Other Transport

Routes
- Tollway
- Freeway
- Primary
- Secondary
- Tertiary
- Lane
- Unsealed Road
- Plaza/Mall
- Steps
- Tunnel
- Pedestrian Overpass
- Walking Tour
- Walking Tour Detour
- Path

Boundaries
- International
- State/Province
- Disputed
- Regional/Suburb
- Marine Park
- Cliff
- Wall

Population
- ◎ Capital (National)
- ◉ Capital (State/Province)
- ● City/Large Town
- • Town/Village

Geographic
- ◎ Hut/Shelter
- ◎ Lighthouse
- ◎ Lookout
- ▲ Mountain/Volcano
- ◎ Oasis
- ◎ Park
-)(Pass
- ◎ Picnic Area
- ◎ Waterfall

Hydrography
- River/Creek
- Intermittent River
- Swamp/Mangrove
- Reef
- Canal
- Water
- Dry/Salt/Intermittent Lake
- Glacier

Areas
- Beach/Desert
- +++ Cemetery (Christian)
- ××× Cemetery (Other)
- Park/Forest
- Sportsground
- Sight (Building)
- Top Sight (Building)

OUR STORY

A beat-up old car, a few dollars in the pocket and a sense of adventure. In 1972 that's all Tony and Maureen Wheeler needed for the trip of a lifetime – across Europe and Asia overland to Australia. It took several months, and at the end – broke but inspired – they sat at their kitchen table writing and stapling together their first travel guide, *Across Asia on the Cheap*. Within a week they'd sold 1500 copies. Lonely Planet was born.

Today, Lonely Planet has offices in Melbourne, London and Oakland, with more than 600 staff and writers. We share Tony's belief that 'a great guidebook should do three things: inform, educate and amuse'.

OUR WRITERS

Nate Cavalieri

Denver, Boulder, Northern Mountains, Northwest Colorado, Southwest Colorado, San Luis Valley Nate's first extended stay in Colorado was unexpected: his touring rock band couldn't afford the gas to get out of Fort Collins. His next several trips through the state were more intentional, hiking and camping in the Rockies and the parks in the southwest. He's authored a handful of titles for Lonely Planet on California, the western United States and Latin America. After a year-long trip around the world in 2010, he now lives with his better half in Brooklyn, New York.

Adam Skolnick

Boulder, Central Mountains, Eastern Colorado Adam is a third-generation Los Angeleno whose family moved from the old country to Boyle Heights, the Fairfax district and finally to Santa Monica. A freelance journalist, he writes about travel, culture, health, sports and the environment for Lonely Planet, *Men's Health, Outside, Travel & Leisure* and *Spa*. He worked on nine previous Lonely Planet guidebooks and has written a few unsold screenplays. He lives in Santa Monica and Bali, but has an increasing fondness for Downtown and Echo Park. Read more about Adam at www.adamskolnick.com. Adam also worked on the Plan, Understand and Survive sections of this book.

Rowan McKinnon

Denver, Southwest Colorado Rowan is an Australian freelance travel writer and lapsed rock musician. He lives in Melbourne with his partner and children. Rowan leapt at the chance of working in Colorado and casting his antipodean eye across its rarefied Rocky Mountains landscapes, its cities and its rural communities. Rowan's written about the US, the Caribbean and Australia, but his specialist area is the island states of the South Pacific. See www.rowanmckinnon.com for more information. Rowan also worked on the Understand and Survive sections of this book.

Published by Lonely Planet Publications Pty Ltd
ABN 36 005 607 983
1st edition – May 2011
ISBN 978 1 74179 417 5
© Lonely Planet 2011   Photographs © as indicated 2011
Map data © 2011 NAVTEQ North America, LLC. All rights reserved.
10 9 8 7 6 5 4 3 2
Printed in China